Survival Communications
in Arizona: Colorado Plateau Region

John E. Parnell, KK4HWX

13 ISBN 978- 1-62512-002-1

Cover design by:
Lynda Colón
FREELANCE GRAPHIC DESIGN &
MARKETING COMMUNICATIONS
www.hirelynda.webs.com

I do wish to acknowledge the hard work of **Angie Shirley** in putting together the database required for this book. Without her efforts, this book could not have been done.

Titles available in this series:

Survival Communications in Alabama
Survival Communications in Alaska
Survival Communications in Arizona
Survival Communications in Arkansas
Survival Communications in California
Survival Communications in Colorado
Survival Communications in Connecticut
Survival Communications in Delaware
Survival Communications in Florida
Survival Communications in Georgia
Survival Communications in Hawaii
Survival Communications in Idaho
Survival Communications in Illinois
Survival Communications in Indiana
Survival Communications in Iowa
Survival Communications in Kansas
Survival Communications in Kentucky
Survival Communications in Louisiana
Survival Communications in Maine
Survival Communications in Maryland
Survival Communications in Massachusetts
Survival Communications in Michigan
Survival Communications in Minnesota
Survival Communications in Mississippi
Survival Communications in Missouri

Survival Communications in Montana
Survival Communications in Nebraska
Survival Communications in Nevada
Survival Communications in New Hampshire
Survival Communications in New Jersey
Survival Communications in New Mexico
Survival Communications in New York
Survival Communications in North Carolina
Survival Communications in North Dakota
Survival Communications in Ohio
Survival Communications in Oklahoma
Survival Communications in Oregon
Survival Communications in Pennsylvania
Survival Communications in Rhode Island
Survival Communications in South Carolina
Survival Communications in South Dakota
Survival Communications in Tennessee
Survival Communications in Texas
Survival Communications in Utah
Survival Communications in Vermont
Survival Communications in Virginia
Survival Communications in Washington
Survival Communications in West Virginia
Survival Communications in Wisconsin
Survival Communications in Wyoming

The above titles are available from your favorite online or brick-and-mortar bookstore or directly from the publisher at Tutor Turtle Press LLC, 1027 S. Pendleton St. – Suite B-10, Easley, SC 29642.

TABLE OF CONTENTS

Appendix A – Arizona Ham Radio Clubs

ARRL Affiliated Amateur and Ham Radio Clubs – By City

Appendix B – Arizona: Colorado Plateau Region Amateur Radio Licensees by City

Survival Communications in Arizona

Perhaps you have prepared for WTSHTF or TEOTWAWKI with respect to food, water, self-defense and shelter. But what about communication?

Whenever there is a disaster (hurricane, earthquake, economic collapse, nuclear war, EMF, solar eruption, etc.), the normal means of communication that we're all reliant upon (cell phone, land line phone, the Internet, etc.) will probably be, at best, sporadic and at worst, non-existent.

As this author sees it, short of smoke signals and mirrors, there are three options for communication in "trying times": (1) GMRS or FRS radios; (2) CB radios; and (3) ham or amateur radio. Let's consider each of these options to come up with the most acceptable one.

GMRS (General Mobile Radio Service) / FRS (Family Radio Service)

GMRS (General Mobile Radio Service) / FRS (Family Radio Service) radios work optimally over short distances where there is minimal interference. Originally designed to be used as pagers, particularly inside a building or other such confined area, these radios are low-cost and convenient to carry. Unfortunately their small size and light weight comes with a trade-off – short range and short battery life. These radios are supposed to be able to communicate for up to 25-30 miles. Right. That's on level terrain, without buildings or trees getting in the way. While battery life technology is constantly improving, you will need spare batteries to keep communicating or someway of recharging the ones in the radio. In this author's opinion, GMRS/FRS radios are not first choice when concerned with medium or long range communication.

CB (Citizens Band)

CB (Citizens Band) radios operate in a frequency range originally reserved for ham or amateur radio operation. Because of the overwhelming number of people wishing quick, low-cost, regulation-free communication, the FCC (Federal Communication Commission) split off a portion of the frequency spectrum and allowed anyone to purchase a CB radio and start communicating. No test. No license. Just personal/business communication. Today, CB radios are readily available in such outlets as eBay and Craigslist. This author has seen them at yard/garage/tag sales and at flea markets.

CB radios come in a variety of "flavors." Fixed units, sometimes referred to as base units are intended for home use. For the most part, they derive their power from the utility company. In the event of loss of electricity, most base units can also be connected to a 12-volt battery, like that in your car/truck. If you choose to obtain a fixed unit, make sure you know how to connect the unit to the battery – ahead of time. Trying to figure this out when you're under extra stress is not a good situation.

A second type of CB radio is designed to be mobile, that is, installed in your car/truck. It gets its power from the vehicle's battery. You can either attach an antenna permanently to the vehicle or have a removable, magnetic type antenna.

The third type of CB radio is designed for handheld use. They are small and light. Most weigh less than a pound and operate on batteries. Yes, using batteries in a CB poses the same limitations as those by the GMRS/FRS radios, but have the added advantage that most handheld units come with a cigarette lighter adapter. Comes in handy when you are on the move and wish to be able to communicate both from a vehicle and also when you have to abandon it.

While they have a greater range than GMRS/FRS radios, CB radios are, legally, limited to operate on 40 channels, with a power rating of four (4) watts or less. Yes, it is possible to alter CB radios to get around these limitations, but not legally,

Ham/Amateur Radio

Ham/Amateur radio is very appealing. With a ham radio, you are not limited to less than 50 miles, but can communicate with anyone in the world (who also has access to a ham radio, of course).

Standardized Amateur Radio Prepper Communications Plan

In the event of a nationwide catastrophic disaster, the nationwide network of Amateur Radio licensed preppers will need a set of standardized meeting frequencies to share information and coordinate activities between various prepper groups. This Standardized Amateur Radio Communications Plan establishes a set of frequencies on the 80 meter, 40 meter, 20 meter, and 2 meter Amateur Radio bands for use during these types of catastrophic disasters.

Routine nets will not be held on all of these frequencies, but preppers are encouraged to use them when coordinating with other preppers on a routine basis. Routine nets may be conducted by The American Preparedness Radio Net (TAPRN) on these or other frequencies as they see fit. However, TAPRN will promote the use of these standardized frequencies by all Amateur Radio licensed preppers during times of catastrophic disaster. The promotion of this Standardized Amateur Radio Communications Plan is encouraged by all means within the prepper community, including via Amateur Radio, Twitter, Facebook, and various blogs.

Standardized Frequencies and Modes
80 Meters – 3.818 MHz LSB (TAPRN Net: Sundays at 9 PM ET) 40 Meters – 7.242 MHz LSB 40 Meters Morse Code / Digital – 7.073 MHz USB (TAPRN: Sundays at 7:30 PM ET on CONTESTIA 4/250) 20 Meters – 14.242 MHz USB 2 Meters – 146.420 MHz FM

Nets and Network Etiquette

In times of nationwide catastrophic disaster, the ability of any one prepper to initiate and sustain themselves as a net control may be limited by the availability of power and other resource shortages. However, all licensed preppers are encouraged to maintain a listening watch on these frequencies as often as possible during a catastrophic disaster. Preppers may routinely announce themselves in the following manner:

• This is [Your Callsign Phonetically] in [Your State], maintaining a listening watch on [Standard Frequency] for any preppers on frequency seeking information or looking to provide information. Please call [Your Callsign Phonetically]. Preppers exchanging information that may require follow up should agree upon a designated time to return to the frequency and provide further information. If other stations are utilizing the frequency at the designated time you return, maintain watch and proceed with your communications when those stations are finished. If your communications are urgent and the stations on frequency are not passing information of a critical nature, interrupt with the word "Break" and request use of the frequency.

For More Information

Catastrophe Network: http://www.catastrophenetwork.org or @CatastropheNet on Twitter The American Preparedness Radio Network: http://www.taprn.com or @TAPRN on Twitter

In order to use a ham radio, legally, one must be licensed to do so by the FCC (other countries have analogous governmental bodies to regulate ham radio). To obtain a license is quite easy – take a test and pay your license fee. There are currently three classes of license – Technician, General, and Amateur Extra. With each of these licenses come specific abilities.

Technician class is the beginning level. The exam consists of 35 multiple choice questions randomly drawn from a pool of 395 questions. The question pool is readily available online for free downloading (http://www.ncvec.org/downloads/Revised%20Element%202.Pdf) or in such publications at *Ham Radio License Manual Revised 2nd Edition* (ISBN 978-0-87259-097-7). The current Technician pool of questions is to be used from July 1, 2010 to June 30, 2014. Be sure the question pool you are studying from is current. You will need to score at least 26 correct to pass. (Do not worry, Morse Code is no longer on the test, although many ham operators use it anyway.) You do not need to take a formal class in order to qualify to take the exam. You can learn the material on your own. Most people spend 10-15 hours studying and then successfully take the exam. The cost of taking the exam is under $20. The exam is given in MANY locations throughout the US. Usually the exam is given by area ham clubs. You do not have to belong to the club to take the exam. Check Appendix A for a listing of clubs in Arizona.

Topics for the Technician License in Amateur Radio

The Technician license exam covers such topics as basic regulations, operating practices, and electronic theory, with a focus on VHF and UHF applications. Below is the syllabus for the Technician Class.

Subelement T1 – FCC Rules, descriptions and definitions for the amateur radio service, operator and station license responsibilities

[6 Exam Questions – 6 Groups]

T1A – Amateur Radio services; purpose of the amateur service, amateur-satellite service, operator/primary station license grant, where FCC rules are codified, basis and purpose of FCC rules, meanings of basic terms used in FCC rules

T1B – Authorized frequencies; frequency allocations, ITU regions, emission type, restricted sub-bands, spectrum sharing, transmissions near band edges

T1C – Operator classes and station call signs; operator classes, sequential, special event, and vanity call sign systems, international communications, reciprocal operation, station license licensee, places where the amateur service is regulated by the FCC, name and address on ULS, license term, renewal, grace period

T1D – Authorized and prohibited transmissions

T1E – Control operator and control types; control operator required, eligibility, designation of control operator, privileges and duties, control point, local, automatic and remote control, location of control operator

T1F – Station identification and operation standards; special operations for repeaters and auxiliary stations, third party communications, club stations, station security, FCC inspection

Subelement T2 – Operating Procedures

[3 Exam Questions – 3 Groups]

T2A – Station operation; choosing an operating frequency, calling another station, test transmissions, use of minimum power, frequency use, band plans

T2B – VHF/UHF operating practices; SSB phone, FM repeater, simplex, frequency offsets, splits and shifts, CTCSS, DTMF, tone squelch, carrier squelch, phonetics

T2C – Public service; emergency and non-emergency operations, message traffic handling

Subelement T3 – Radio wave characteristics, radio and electromagnetic properties, propagation modes

[3 Exam Questions – 3 Groups]

T3A – Radio wave characteristics; how a radio signal travels; distinctions of HF, VHF and UHF; fading, multipath; wavelength vs. penetration; antenna orientation

T3B – Radio and electromagnetic wave properties; the electromagnetic spectrum, wavelength vs. frequency, velocity of electromagnetic waves

T3C – Propagation modes; line of sight, sporadic E, meteor, aurora scatter, tropospheric ducting, F layer skip, radio horizon

Subelement T4 - Amateur radio practices and station setup

[2 Exam Questions – 2 Groups]

T4A – Station setup; microphone, speaker, headphones, filters, power source, connecting a computer, RF grounding

T4B – Operating controls; tuning, use of filters, squelch, AGC, repeater offset, memory channels

Subelement T5 – Electrical principles, math for electronics, electronic principles, Ohm's Law

[4 Exam Questions – 4 Groups]

T5A – Electrical principles; current and voltage, conductors and insulators, alternating and direct current

T5B – Math for electronics; decibels, electronic units and the metric system

T5C – Electronic principles; capacitance, inductance, current flow in circuits, alternating current, definition of RF, power calculations

T5D – Ohm's Law

Subelement T6 – Electrical components, semiconductors, circuit diagrams, component functions

[4 Exam Groups – 4 Questions]

T6A – Electrical components; fixed and variable resistors, capacitors, and inductors; fuses, switches, batteries

T6B – Semiconductors; basic principles of diodes and transistors

T6C – Circuit diagrams; schematic symbols

T6D – Component functions

Subelement T7 – Station equipment, common transmitter and receiver problems, antenna measurements and troubleshooting, basic repair and testing

[4 Exam Questions – 4 Groups]

T7A – Station radios; receivers, transmitters, transceivers

T7B – Common transmitter and receiver problems; symptoms of overload and overdrive, distortion, interference, over and under modulation, RF feedback, off frequency signals; fading and noise; problems with digital communications interfaces

T7C – Antenna measurements and troubleshooting; measuring SWR, dummy loads, feedline failure modes

T7D – Basic repair and testing; soldering, use of a voltmeter, ammeter, and ohmmeter

Subelement T8 – Modulation modes, amateur satellite operation, operating activities, non-voice communications

[4 Exam Questions – 4 Groups]

T8A – Modulation modes; bandwidth of various signals

T8B – Amateur satellite operation; Doppler shift, basic orbits, operating protocols

T8C – Operating activities; radio direction finding, radio control, contests, special event stations, basic linking over Internet

T8D – Non-voice communications; image data, digital modes, CW, packet, PSK31

Subelement T9 – Antennas, feedlines

[2 Exam Groups – 2 Questions]

T9A – Antennas; vertical and horizontal, concept of gain, common portable and mobile antennas, relationships between antenna length and frequency

T9B – Feedlines; types, losses vs. frequency, SWR concepts, matching, weather protection, connectors

Subelement T0 – AC power circuits, antenna installation, RF hazards

[3 Exam Questions – 3 Groups]

T0A – AC power circuits; hazardous voltages, fuses and circuit breakers, grounding, lightning protection, battery safety, electrical code compliance

T0B – Antenna installation; tower safety, overhead power lines

T0C – RF hazards; radiation exposure, proximity to antennas, recognized safe power levels, exposure to others

Once your name and call sign are available in the FCC database, you have the privilege of operating on all VHF (2 m) and UHF (70 cm) frequencies above 30 megahertz (MHz) and HF frequencies 80, 40, and 15 meter, and on the 10 meter band using Morse code (CW), voice, and digital mode. For a Technician license in Arizona, your call sign will consist of a two-letter prefix beginning with K or W, the number seven (7), and a three-letter suffix. The single digit number in the call sign is determined according to which area of the US you obtain your first license. Even though you may move to another state, you keep this number in your call sign. This is also true should you upgrade to a higher license and get a new call sign. The numeral portion of your call sign stays the same.

Call Sign Numbers

Below is a chart showing the various numbers and the state(s) in which you would obtain the number.

Call Sign Number	State(s)
0	CO, IA, KS, MN, MO, NE, ND, SD
1	CT, ME, MA, NH, RI, VT
2	NJ, NY
3	DE, DC, MD, PA
4	AL, FL, GA, KY, NC, SC, TN, VA
5	AR, LA, MS, NM, OK, TX
6	CA
7	AZ, ID, MT, NV, OR, WA, UT, WY
8	MI, OH, WV
9	IL, IN, WI

Residents of Alaska may have any of the following call sign prefixes assigned to them: AL0-7, KL0-7, NL0-7, or WL0-7. Likewise, residents of Hawaii may have the prefix AH6-7, KH6-7, NH6-7, or WH6-7 assigned.

Once you obtain your Technician license, do not stop there. Go and get your General license.

General is the second of three ham license classes. Like the Technician license, to get a General license, you merely have to take a 35-question multiple choice exam and pay your license fee. Passing is still at least 26 correct answers and the fee is the same (less than $20). Again the question pool is available for free online (http://www.ncvec.org/page.php?id=358). It is also available in such print publications as *The ARRL General Class License Manual 7th Edition* (ISBN 978-0-87259-811-9). The current General pool of questions is to be used from July 1, 2011 to June 30, 2015. Be sure the question pool you are using is current. Being a bit more comprehensive than the Technician license, the General license usually requires 15-20 hours of study to learn the material. Check Appendix A for a listing of clubs in Arizona where you might take your exam. Once your name and NEW call sign is listed in the FCC database, you're good to go. For a General license in Arizona, your call sign will consist of a one-letter prefix beginning with K, N or W, the number seven (7), and a three-letter suffix.

Topics for the General License in Amateur Radio

The General license exam covers regulations, operating practices and electronic theory. Below is the syllabus for the General Class.

Subelement G1 – Commission's Rules
(5 Exam Questions – 5 Groups) G1A – General Class control operator frequency privileges; primary and secondary allocations G1B – Antenna structure limitations; good engineering and good amateur practice, beacon operation; restricted operation; retransmitting radio signals G1C – Transmitter power regulations; data emission standards G1D – Volunteer Examiners and Volunteer Examiner Coordinators; temporary identification G1E – Control categories; repeater regulations; harmful interference; third party rules; ITU regions

Subelement G2 – Operating procedures
(5 Exam Questions – 5 Groups) G2A – Phone operating procedures; USB/LSB utilization conventions; procedural signals; breaking into a OSO in progress; VOX operation G2B – Operating courtesy; band plans, emergencies, including drills and emergency communications G2C – CW operating procedures and procedural signals; Q signals and common abbreviations; full break in G2D – Amateur Auxiliary; minimizing interference; HF operations

G2E – Digital operating; procedures, procedural signals and common abbreviations

Subelement G3 – Radio wave propagation

(3 Exam Questions – 3 Groups)

G3A – Sunspots and solar radiation; ionospheric disturbances; propagation forecasting and indices

G3B – Maximum Usable Frequency; Lowest Usable Frequency; propagation

G3C – Ionospheric layers; critical angle and frequency; HF scatter; Near Vertical Incidence Sky waves

Subelement G4 – Amateur radio practices

(5 Exam Questions – 5 Groups)

G4A – Station Operation and setup

G4B – Test and monitoring equipment; two-tone test

G4C – Interference with consumer electronics; grounding; DSP

G4D – Speech processors; S meters; sideband operation near band edges

G4E – HF mobile radio installations; emergency and battery powered operation

Subelement G5 – Electrical principles

(3 Exam Questions – 3 Groups)

G5A – Reactance; inductance; capacitance; impedance; impedance matching

G5B – The Decibel; current and voltage dividers; electrical power calculations; sine wave root-mean-square (RMS) values; PEP calculations

G5C – Resistors; capacitors and inductors in series and parallel; transformers

Subelement G6 – Circuit components

(3 Exam Questions – 3 Groups)

G6A – Resistors; capacitors; inductors

G6B – Rectifiers; solid state diodes and transistors; vacuum tubes; batteries

G6C – Analog and digital integrated circuits (ICs); microprocessors; memory; I/O devices; microwave ICs (MMICs); display devices

Subelement G7 – Practical circuits

(3 Exam Questions – 3 Groups)

G7A – Power supplies; schematic symbols

G7B – Digital circuits; amplifiers and oscillators

G7C – Receivers and transmitters; filters, oscillators

Subelement G8 – Signals and emissions

(2 Exam Questions – 2 Groups)

G8A – Carriers and modulation; AM; FM; single and double sideband; modulation envelope; overmodulation

G8B – Frequency mixing; multiplication; HF data communications; bandwidths of various modes; deviation

Subelement G9 – Antennas and feed lines

(4 Exam Questions – 4 Groups)

G9A – Antenna feed lines; characteristic impedance and attenuation; SWR calculation, measurement and effects; matching networks

G9B – Basic antennas

G9C – Directional antennas

G9D – Specialized antennas

Subelement G0 – Electrical and RF safety

(2 Exam Questions – 2 Groups)

G0A – RF safety principles, rules and guidelines; routine station elevation

G0B – Safety in the ham shack; electrical shock and treatment, safety grounding, fusing, interlocks, wiring, antenna and tower safety

With a General license, you can use all VHF and UHF frequencies and most of the HF frequencies. You would have access to the 160, 30, 17, 12, and 10 meter bands and access to major parts of the 80, 40, 20, and 15 meter bands. Of course, this is in addition to all bands available to Technician license holders.

Amateur Extra is the third of three ham license classes. Like the Technician and General classes, you merely have to pass a test and pay your fee to get your Amateur Extra license. This class of license is more comprehensive than the lower license classes. The exam is longer – 50 questions – and the minimum passing score is higher – 37. However, once you get your Amateur Extra license, all ham frequencies, VHF, UHF and HF are available for your enjoyment. The Extra exam covers regulations, specialized operating practices, advanced electronics theory, and radio equipment design.

Like for the other license classes, the question pool for the Amateur Extra license is available online for downloading (http://www.ncvec.org/downloads/REVISED%202012-2016%20Extra%20Class%20Pool.doc). It is also available in print form in such publications as *The ARRL Extra Class License Manual Revised 9th Edition* (ISBN 978-0-87259-887-4).

Topics for the Extra License in Amateur Radio

Below is the syllabus for the Amateur Extra Class for July 1, 2012 to June 30, 2016.

Subelement E1 – Commission's Rules

[6 Exam Questions – 6 Groups]

E1A – Operating Standards: frequency privileges; emission standards; automatic message forwarding; frequency sharing; stations aboard ships or aircraft

E1B – Station restrictions and special operations: restrictions on station location; general operating restrictions, spurious emissions, control operator reimbursement; antenna structure restrictions; RACES operations

E1C – Station control: definitions and restrictions pertaining to local, automatic and remote control operation; control operator responsibilities for remote and automatically controlled stations

E1D – Amateur Satellite service: definitions and purpose; license requirements for space stations; available frequencies and bands; telecommand and telemetry operations; restrictions, and special provisions; notification requirements

E1E – Volunteer examiner program: definitions, qualifications, preparation and administration of exams; accreditation; question pools; documentation requirements

E1F – Miscellaneous rules: external RF power amplifiers; national quiet zone; business communications; compensated communications; spread spectrum; auxiliary stations; reciprocal operating privileges; IARP and CEPT licenses; third party communications with foreign countries; special temporary authority

Subelement E2 – Operating procedures

[5 Exam Questions – 5 Groups]

E2A – Amateur radio in space: amateur satellites; orbital mechanics; frequencies and modes; satellite hardware; satellite operations

E2B – Television practices: fast scan television standards and techniques; slow scan television standards and techniques

E2C – Operating methods: contest and DX operating; spread-spectrum transmissions; selecting an operating frequency

E2D – Operating methods: VHF and UHF digital modes; APRS

E2E – Operating methods: operating HF digital modes; error correction

Subelement E3 – Radio wave propagation

[3 Exam Questions – 3 Groups]

E3A – Propagation and technique, Earth-Moon-Earth communications; meteor scatter

E3B – Propagation and technique, trans-equatorial; long path; gray-line; multi-path propagation

E3C – Propagation and technique, Aurora propagation; selective fading; radio-path horizon; take-off angle over flat or sloping terrain; effects of ground on propagation; less common propagation modes

Subelement E4 – Amateur practices

[5 Exam Questions – 5 Groups]

E4A – Test equipment: analog and digital instruments; spectrum and network analyzers, antenna analyzers; oscilloscopes; testing transistors; RF measurements

E4B – Measurement technique and limitations: instrument accuracy and performance limitations; probes; techniques to minimize errors; measurement of "Q"; instrument calibration

E4C – Receiver performance characteristics, phase noise, capture effect, noise floor, image rejection, MDS, signal-to-noise-ratio; selectivity

E4D – Receiver performance characteristics, blocking dynamic range, intermodulation and cross-modulation interference; 3rd order intercept; desensitization; preselection

E4E – Noise suppression: system noise; electrical appliance noise; line noise; locating noise sources; DSP noise reduction; noise blankers

Subelement E5 – Electrical principles

[4 Exam Questions – 4 Groups]

E5A – Resonance and Q: characteristics of resonant circuits: series and parallel resonance; Q; half-power bandwidth; phase relationships in reactive circuits

E5B – Time constants and phase relationships: RLC time constants: definition; time constants in RL and RC circuits; phase angle between voltage and current; phase angles of series and parallel circuits

E5C – Impedance plots and coordinate systems: plotting impedances in polar coordinates; rectangular coordinates

E5D – AC and RF energy in real circuits: skin effect; electrostatic and electromagnetic fields; reactive power; power factor; coordinate systems

Subelement E6 – Circuit components

[6 Exam Questions – 6 Groups]

E6A – Semiconductor materials and devices: semiconductor materials germanium, silicon, P-type, N-type; transistor types: NPN, PNP, junction, field-effect transistors: enhancement mode; depletion mode; MOS; CMOS; N-channel; P-channel

E6B – Semiconductor diodes

E6C – Integrated circuits: TTL digital integrated circuits; CMOS digital integrated circuits; gates

E6D – Optical devices and toroids: cathode-ray tube devices; charge-coupled devices (CCDs); liquid crystal displays (LCDs); toroids: permeability, core material, selecting, winding

E6E – Piezoelectric crystals and MMICs: quartz crystals; crystal oscillators and filters; monolithic amplifiers

E6F – Optical components and power systems: photoconductive principles and effects, photovoltaic systems, optical couplers, optical sensors, and optoisolators

Subelement E7 – Practical circuits

[8 Exam Questions – 8 Groups]

E7A – Digital circuits: digital circuit principles and logic circuits: classes of logic elements; positive and negative logic; frequency dividers; truth tables

E7B – Amplifiers: Class of operation; vacuum tube and solid-state circuits; distortion and intermodulation; spurious and parasitic suppression; microwave amplifiers

E7C – Filters and matching networks: filters and impedance matching networks: types of networks; types of filters; filter applications; filter characteristics; impedance matching; DSP filtering

E7D – Power supplies and voltage regulators

E7E – Modulation and demodulation: reactance, phase and balanced modulators; detectors; mixer stages; DSP modulation and demodulation; software defined radio systems

E7F – Frequency markers and counters: frequency divider circuits; frequency marker generators; frequency counters

E7G – Active filters and op-amps: active audio filters; characteristics; basic circuit design; operational amplifiers

E7H – Oscillators and signal sources: types of oscillators; synthesizers and phase-locked loops; direct digital synthesizers

Subelement E8 – Signals and emissions

[4 Exam Questions – 4 Groups]

E8A – AC waveforms: sine, square, sawtooth and irregular waveforms; AC measurements; average and PEP of RF signals; pulse and digital signal waveforms

E8B – Modulation and demodulation: modulation methods; modulation index and deviation ratio; pulse modulation; frequency and time division multiplexing

E8C – Digital signals: digital communications modes; CW; information rate vs. bandwidth; spread-spectrum communications; modulation methods

E8D – Waves, measurements, and RF grounding: peak-to-peak values, polarization; RF grounding

Subelement E9 – Antennas and transmission lines

[8 Exam Questions – 8 Groups]

E9A – Isotropic and gain antennas: definition; used as a standard for comparison; radiation pattern; basic antenna parameters: radiation resistance and reactance, gain, beamwidth, efficiency

E9B – Antenna patterns: E and H plane patterns; gain as a function of pattern; antenna design; Yagi antennas

E9C – Wire and phased vertical antennas: beverage antennas; terminated and resonant rhombic antennas; elevation above real ground; ground effects as related to polarization; take-off angles

E9D – Directional antennas: gain; satellite antennas; antenna beamwidth; losses; SWR bandwidth; antenna efficiency; shortened and mobile antennas; grounding

E9E – Matching: matching antennas to feed lines; power dividers

E9F – Transmission lines: characteristics of open and shorted feed lines: 1/8 wavelength; 1/4 wavelength; 1/2 wavelength; feed lines: coax versus open-wire; velocity factor; electrical length; transformation characteristics of line terminated in impedance not equal to characteristic impedance

E9G – The Smith chart

E9H – Effective radiated power; system gains and losses; radio direction finding antennas

Subelement E0 – Safety

[1 exam question – 1 group]

E0A – Safety: amateur radio safety practices; RF radiation hazards; hazardous materials

Once your new call sign is listed in the FCC database, you are good to go. For an Amateur Extra license in Arizona, your call sign will consist of a prefix of K, N or W, the number seven (7), and a two-letter suffix, or a two-letter prefix beginning with A, N, K or W, the number seven (7), and a one-letter suffix, or a two-letter prefix beginning with A, the number seven (7), and a two-letter suffix.

Ham radio equipment can be expensive or you can do it "on the cheap." The cost will run from a couple hundred dollars to well in the thousands, depending on what you have available. eBay, and Craigslist are good places to start looking. Most ham clubs do some sort of hamfest annually wherein club members or others are willing to part with older equipment. See Appendix A for a list of clubs in Arizona.

Another excellent source of equipment, as well as advice on setting the equipment up and how to use it properly, is current ham operators. In Appendix B, the author has listed all the FCC licensed ham operators in Arizona, listed by city, and then sorted by street and house number on the street. Who knows, maybe someone who lives close to you is a ham operator. Be a good neighbor, stop by and have a chat with him/her.

Like CB radios, ham radios come in three formats – base, mobile, and handheld. They can use the electric company for power, or operate off a car battery. In the opinion of this author, in spite of the slightly higher cost of the equipment and having to take a test to legally use the equipment, ham radio is the way to go when concerned about communication during times of crisis.

Canadian Call Sign Prefixes

Because of our proximity to Canada, many times ham contact is made with our northern neighbors. Below is a chart showing the origin of Canadian call sign prefixes.

Call Sign Prefix	Provence or Territory
CY0	Sable Island
CY9	St. Paul Island
VA1, VE1	New Brunswick, Nova Scotia
VA2, VE2	Quebec
VA3, VE3	Ontario
VA4, VE4	Manitoba
VA5, VE5	Saskatchewan
VA6, VE6	Alberta
VA7, VE7	British Columbia
VE8	North West Territories
VE9	New Brunswick
VO1	Newfoundland
VO2	Labrador
VY0	Nunavut
VY1	Yukon
VY2	Prince Edward Island

Common Radio Bands in the United States

Certain radio bands are more popular with ham radio enthusiasts than others. Below is a chart showing these bands and when they are most popular.

	Band (meter)	Frequency (MHz)	Use
HF	160	1.8 – 2.0	Night
	80	3.5 – 4.0	Night and Local Day
	40	7.0 – 7.3	Night and Local Day
	30	10.1 – 10.15	CW and Digital
	20	14.0 – 14.350	World Wide Day and Night
	17	18.068 – 18.168	World Wide Day and Night
	15	21.0 – 21.450	Primarily Daytime
	12	24.890 – 24.990	Primarily Daytime
	10	28.0 – 29.70	Daytime during Sunspot highs
VHF	6	50 – 54	Local to World Wide
	2	144 – 148	Local to Medium Distance
UHF	70 cm	430 – 440	Local

Common Amateur Radio Bands in Canada

160 Meter Band - Maximum bandwidth 6 kHz
1.800 - 1.820 MHz - CW
1.820 - 1.830 MHz - Digital Modes
1 830 - 1.840 MHz - DX Window
1.840 - 2.000 MHz - SSB and other wide band modes

80 Meter Band - Maximum bandwidth 6 kHz
3.500 - 3.580 MHz - CW
3.580 - 3.620 MHz - Digital Modes
3.620 - 3.635 MHz - Packet/Digital Secondary
3.635 - 3.725 MHz - CW
3.725 - 3.790 MHz - SSB and other side band modes*
3.790 - 3.800 MHz - SSB DX Window
3.800 - 4.000 MHz - SSB and other wide band modes

40 Meter Band - Maximum bandwidth 6 kHz
7.000 - 7.035 MHz - CW
7.035 - 7.050 MHz - Digital Modes
7.040 - 7.050 MHz - International packet
7.050 - 7.100 MHz - SSB
7.100 - 7.120 MHz - Packet within Region 2
7.120 - 7.150 MHz - CW
7.150 - 7.300 MHz - SSB and other wide band modes

30 Meter Band - Maximum bandwidth 1 kHz

10.100 - 10.130 MHz - CW only
10.130 - 10.140 MHz - Digital Modes
10.140 - 10.150 MHz - Packet

20 Meter Band - Maximum bandwidth 6 kHz

14.000 - 14.070 MHz - CW only
14.070 - 14.095 MHz - Digital Mode
14.095 - 14.099 MHz - Packet
14.100 MHz - Beacons
14.101 - 14.112 MHz - CW, SSB, packet shared
14.112 - 14.350 MHz - SSB
14.225 - 14.235 MHz - SSTV

17 Meter Band - Maximum bandwidth 6 kHz

18.068 - 18.100 MHz - CW
18.100 - 18.105 MHz - Digital Modes
18.105 - 18.110 MHz - Packet
18.110 - 18.168 MHz - SSB and other wide band modes

15 Meter Band - maximum bandwidth 6 kHz

21.000 - 21.070 MHz - CW
21.070 - 21.090 MHz - Digital Modes
21.090 - 21.125 MHz - Packet
21.100 - 21.150 MHz - CW and SSB
21.150 - 21.335 MHz - SSB and other wide band modes
21.335 - 21.345 MHz - SSTV
21.345 - 21.450 MHz - SSB and other wide band modes

12 Meter Band - Maximum bandwidth 6 kHz

24.890 - 24.930 MHz - CW
24.920 - 24.925 MHz - Digital Modes
24.925 - 24.930 MHz - Packet
24.930 - 24.990 MHz - SSB and other wide band modes

10 Meter Band - Maximum band width 20 kHz

28.000 - 28.200 MHz - CW
28.070 - 28.120 MHz - Digital Modes
28.120 - 28.190 MHz - Packet
28.190 - 28.200 MHz - Beacons
28.200 - 29.300 MHz - SSB and other wide band modes
29.300 - 29.510 MHz - Satellite
29.510 - 29.700 MHz - SSB, FM and repeaters

160 Meters (1.8-2.0 MHz)

1.800 - 2.000 CW
1.800 - 1.810 Digital Modes
1.810 CW QRP
1.843-2.000 SSB, SSTV and other wideband modes
1.910 SSB QRP
1.995 - 2.000 Experimental
1.999 - 2.000 Beacons

80 Meters (3.5-4.0 MHz)

3.590 RTTY/Data DX
3.570-3.600 RTTY/Data
3.790-3.800 DX window
3.845 SSTV
3.885 AM calling frequency

40 Meters (7.0-7.3 MHz)

7.040 RTTY/Data DX
7.080-7.125 RTTY/Data
7.171 SSTV
7.290 AM calling frequency

30 Meters (10.1-10.15 MHz)

10.130-10.140 RTTY
10.140-10.150 Packet

20 Meters (14.0-14.35 MHz)

14.070-14.095 RTTY
14.095-14.0995 Packet
14.100 NCDXF Beacons
14.1005-14.112 Packet
14.230 SSTV
14.286 AM calling frequency

17 Meters (18.068-18.168 MHz)

18.100-18.105 RTTY
18.105-18.110 Packet

15 Meters (21.0-21.45 MHz)

21.070-21.110 RTTY/Data
21.340 SSTV

12 Meters (24.89-24.99 MHz)

24.920-24.925 RTTY
24.925-24.930 Packet

10 Meters (28-29.7 MHz)

28.000-28.070 CW
28.070-28.150 RTTY
28.150-28.190 CW
28.200-28.300 Beacons
28.300-29.300 Phone
28.680 SSTV
29.000-29.200 AM
29.300-29.510 Satellite Downlinks
29.520-29.590 Repeater Inputs
29.600 FM Simplex
29.610-29.700 Repeater Outputs

6 Meters (50-54 MHz)

50.0-50.1 CW, beacons
50.060-50.080 beacon subband
50.1-50.3 SSB, CW
50.10-50.125 DX window
50.125 SSB calling
50.3-50.6 All modes
50.6-50.8 Nonvoice communications
50.62 Digital (packet) calling
50.8-51.0 Radio remote control (20-kHz channels)
51.0-51.1 Pacific DX window
51.12-51.48 Repeater inputs (19 channels)
51.12-51.18 Digital repeater inputs
51.5-51.6 Simplex (seven channels)
51.62-51.98 Repeater outputs (19 channels)
51.62-51.68 Digital repeater outputs
52.0-52.48 Repeater inputs (except as noted; 23 channels)
52.02, 52.04 FM simplex
52.2 TEST PAIR (input)
52.5-52.98 Repeater output (except as noted; 23 channels)
52.525 Primary FM simplex
52.54 Secondary FM simplex
52.7 TEST PAIR (output)
53.0-53.48 Repeater inputs (except as noted; 19 channels)
53.0 Remote base FM simplex
53.02 Simplex
53.1, 53.2, 53.3, 53.4 Radio remote control
53.5-53.98 Repeater outputs (except as noted; 19 channels)
53.5, 53.6, 53.7, 53.8 Radio remote control
53.52, 53.9 Simplex

2 Meters (144-148 MHz)

144.00-144.05 EME (CW)
144.05-144.10 General CW and weak signals
144.10-144.20 EME and weak-signal SSB
144.200 National calling frequency
144.200-144.275 General SSB operation
144.275-144.300 Propagation beacons
144.30-144.50 New OSCAR subband
144.50-144.60 Linear translator inputs
144.60-144.90 FM repeater inputs
144.90-145.10 Weak signal and FM simplex (145.01,03,05,07,09 are widely used for packet)
145.10-145.20 Linear translator outputs
145.20-145.50 FM repeater outputs
145.50-145.80 Miscellaneous and experimental modes
145.80-146.00 OSCAR subband
146.01-146.37 Repeater inputs
146.40-146.58 Simplex
146.52 National Simplex Calling Frequency
146.61-146.97 Repeater outputs
147.00-147.39 Repeater outputs
147.42-147.57 Simplex
147.60-147.99 Repeater inputs

1.25 Meters (222-225 MHz)

222.0-222.150 Weak-signal modes
222.0-222.025 EME
222.05-222.06 Propagation beacons
222.1 SSB & CW calling frequency
222.10-222.15 Weak-signal CW & SSB
222.15-222.25 Local coordinator's option; weak signal, ACSB, repeater inputs, control
222.25-223.38 FM repeater inputs only
223.40-223.52 FM simplex
223.52-223.64 Digital, packet
223.64-223.70 Links, control
223.71-223.85 Local coordinator's option; FM simplex, packet, repeater outputs
223.85-224.98 Repeater outputs only

70 Centimeters (420-450 MHz)

420.00-426.00 ATV repeater or simplex with 421.25 MHz video carrier control links and experimental
426.00-432.00 ATV simplex with 427.250-MHz video carrier frequency
432.00-432.07 EME (Earth-Moon-Earth)
432.07-432.10 Weak-signal CW
432.10 70-cm calling frequency

432.10-432.30 Mixed-mode and weak-signal work
432.30-432.40 Propagation beacons
432.40-433.00 Mixed-mode and weak-signal work
433.00-435.00 Auxiliary/repeater links
435.00-438.00 Satellite only (internationally)
438.00-444.00 ATV repeater input with 439.250-MHz video carrier frequency and repeater links
442.00-445.00 Repeater inputs and outputs (local option)
445.00-447.00 Shared by auxiliary and control links, repeaters and simplex (local option)
446.00 National simplex frequency
447.00-450.00 Repeater inputs and outputs (local option)

33 Centimeters (902-928 MHz)

902.0-903.0 Narrow-bandwidth, weak-signal communications
902.0-902.8 SSTV, FAX, ACSSB, experimental
902.1 Weak-signal calling frequency
902.8-903.0 Reserved for EME, CW expansion
903.1 Alternate calling frequency
903.0-906.0 Digital communications
906-909 FM repeater inputs
909-915 ATV
915-918 Digital communications
918-921 FM repeater outputs
921-927 ATV
927-928 FM simplex and links

23 Centimeters (1240-1300 MHz)

1240-1246 ATV #1
1246-1248 Narrow-bandwidth FM point-to-point links and digital, duplex with 1258-
  1260.
1248-1258 Digital Communications
1252-1258 ATV #2
1258-1260 Narrow-bandwidth FM point-to-point links digital, duplexed with 1246-1252
1260-1270 Satellite uplinks, reference WARC '79
1260-1270 Wide-bandwidth experimental, simplex ATV
1270-1276 Repeater inputs, FM and linear, paired with 1282-1288, 239 pairs every 25
  kHz, e.g. 1270.025, .050, etc.
1271-1283 Non-coordinated test pair
1276-1282 ATV #3
1282-1288 Repeater outputs, paired with 1270-1276
1288-1294 Wide-bandwidth experimental, simplex ATV
1294-1295 Narrow-bandwidth FM simplex services, 25-kHz channels
1294.5 National FM simplex calling frequency
1295-1297 Narrow bandwidth weak-signal communications (no FM)
1295.0-1295.8 SSTV, FAX, ACSSB, experimental
1295.8-1296.0 Reserved for EME, CW expansion

1296.00-1296.05 EME-exclusive
1296.07-1296.08 CW beacons
1296.1 CW, SSB calling frequency
1296.4-1296.6 Crossband linear translator input
1296.6-1296.8 Crossband linear translator output
1296.8-1297.0 Experimental beacons (exclusive)
1297-1300 Digital Communications

2300-2310 and 2390-2450 MHz

2300.0-2303.0 High-rate data
2303.0-2303.5 Packet
2303.5-2303.8 TTY packet
2303.9-2303.9 Packet, TTY, CW, EME
2303.9-2304.1 CW, EME
2304.1 Calling frequency
2304.1-2304.2 CW, EME, SSB
2304.2-2304.3 SSB, SSTV, FAX, Packet AM, Amtor
2304.30-2304.32 Propagation beacon network
2304.32-2304.40 General propagation beacons
2304.4-2304.5 SSB, SSTV, ACSSB, FAX, Packet AM, Amtor experimental
2304.5-2304.7 Crossband linear translator input
2304.7-2304.9 Crossband linear translator output
2304.9-2305.0 Experimental beacons
2305.0-2305.2 FM simplex (25 kHz spacing)
2305.20 FM simplex calling frequency
2305.2-2306.0 FM simplex (25 kHz spacing)
2306.0-2309.0 FM Repeaters (25 kHz) input
2309.0-2310.0 Control and auxiliary links
2390.0-2396.0 Fast-scan TV
2396.0-2399.0 High-rate data
2399.0-2399.5 Packet
2399.5-2400.0 Control and auxiliary links
2400.0-2403.0 Satellite
2403.0-2408.0 Satellite high-rate data
2408.0-2410.0 Satellite
2410.0-2413.0 FM repeaters (25 kHz) output
2413.0-2418.0 High-rate data
2418.0-2430.0 Fast-scan TV
2430.0-2433.0 Satellite
2433.0-2438.0 Satellite high-rate data
2438.0-2450.0 WB FM, FSTV, FMTV, SS experimental

3300-3500 MHz

3456.3-3456.4 Propagation beacons

5650-5925 MHz
5760.3-5760.4 Propagation beacons

10.00-10.50 GHz
10.368 Narrow band calling frequency 10.3683-10.3684 Propagation beacons
10.3640 Calling frequency

Now that you have your license (you do, don't you?), and your equipment, you are ready to go live. Below is a suggested start.

1) Assuming you have the HT set up to the appropriate frequency, and offset, press the mic button on the HT and say, "KK4HWX listening." Replace the KK4HWX with your own call sign, the one assigned to you by the FCC (it's the law). If no one responds to your call, you may wish to try again. Hopefully someone will respond to your call.

2) Once you get a response, it will be in the form of something like, "KK4HWX this is ??1??? in Eastport returning. My name is Florence. Back to you. ??1???" then a tone. Let us examine the response more closely. She first acknowledged your call sign (KK4HWX), then identified hers (??1???). From the 1 in her call sign, you know that she first got her license in Region 1, meaning she got it while a resident of CT, ME, MA, NH, RI, or VT. She then told you where she's transmitting from (Eastport). The term "returning" means that she is returning your call. Her name is Florence. The phrase, "Back to you" indicates that she is turning over the conversation to you. She then repeats her call sign. The tone indicates to you that it is okay to proceed with your response. BTW if she had used the term "Over" instead of "Back to you," it would mean the same thing, just fewer words.

3) At this point, press the mic button and continue with the conversation. You should restate your call sign often during the conversation (perhaps every 10 minutes or less and whenever you begin transmitting). Don't forget to say, "Over" or "Back to you" whenever you are giving Florence control of the conversation again.

4) When you are ready to stop the conversation, you should say goodbye or use the phrase "73", meaning "best wishes." Your conversation would end something like, "??1??? 73, this is KK4HWX clear and monitoring." The "clear and monitoring" indicates that you are going to continue to monitor the frequency. If you are not going to continue monitoring, you may wish to end the conversation with Florence with, "clear and QRT" instead. The QRT means that you are stopping transmissions.

Call Sign Phonics

Because of different accents of various people, sometimes it is difficult to understand call sign letters when spoken. For this reason, most ham operators verbalize their call sign using phonics. Below is a table listing the accepted phonics for letters and numbers.

A = ALFA	S = SIERRA
B = BRAVO	T = TANGO
C = CHARLIE	U = UNIFORM
D = DELTA	V = VICTOR
E = ECHO	W = WHISKEY
F = FOXTROT	X = X-RAY
G = GOLF	Y = YANKEE
H = HOTEL	Z = ZULU (ZED)
I = INDIA	1 = ONE
J = JULIETT	2 = TWO
K = KILO	3 = THREE (TREE)
L = LIMA	4 = FOUR
M = MIKE	5 = FIVE (FIFE)
N = NOVEMBER	6 = SEVEN
O = OSCAR	7 = SEVEN
P = PAPA (PA-PA')	8 = EIGHT
Q = QUEBEC (KAY-BEK')	9 = NINE (NINER)
R = ROMEO	0 = ZERO

The words in parentheses are the pronunciation or the alternate pronunciations for the words or numbers, but you will hear both used. With the letter Z, (ZED) is by far the most commonly used. With the number 9, NINER is the most common and easiest to understand ON THE AIR.

If you wish to use Morse code (CW) instead of voice communication, the "conversation" would follow the same steps, with a few modifications. To type out each word would require a lot of typing and translating. If you are like this author, more means more, i.e., more typing means more typos are likely. To help with this situation, CW enthusiasts have developed a language all their own – they use abbreviations for common phrases. Below is a chart showing some of these abbreviations.

Abbreviation	Use
AR	Over
de	From or "this is"
ES	And
GM	Good Morning
K	Go
KN	Go only
NM	Name
QTH	Location
RPT	Report
R	Roger
SK	Clear
tnx	Thanks
UR	Your, you are
73	Best Wishes

Morse Code and Amateur Radio

If you wish to use CW, but are concerned about accuracy, you might consider purchasing a Morse code translator. This is an electronic device that you place in front of your speakers. It takes the CW sounds and translates them into English and displays the transmission on an LCD display. For the reverse, you can pick up a CW keyboard. With the keyboard, you type in your message and it converts the text to Morse code. The translator does not need to be attached to your ham equipment, whereas the keyboard would.

For your convenience, below is a table showing the Morse code signals and their meaning.

Character	Code
A	· —
B	— · · ·
C	— · — ·
D	— · ·
E	·
F	· · — ·
G	— — ·
H	· · · ·
I	· ·
J	· — — —
K	— · —
L	· — · ·
M	— —
N	— ·
O	— — —
P	· — — ·
Q	— — · —
R	· — ·
S	· · ·
T	—
U	· · —
V	· · · —
W	· — —
X	— · · —
Y	— · — —
Z	— — · ·
0	— — — — —
1	· — — — —
2	· · — — —
3	· · · — —
4	· · · · —
5	· · · · ·

6	— · · · ·
7	— — · · ·
8	— — — · ·
9	— — — — ·
Ampersand [&], Wait	· — · · ·
Apostrophe [']	· — — — — ·
At sign [@]	· — — · — ·
Colon [:]	— — — · · ·
Comma [,]	— — · · — —
Dollar sign [$]	· · · — · · —
Double dash [=]	— · · · —
Exclamation mark [!]	— · — · — —
Hyphen, Minus [-]	— · · · · —
Parenthesis closed [)]	— · — — · —
Parenthesis open [(]	— · — — ·
Period [.]	· — · — · —
Plus [+]	· — · — ·
Question mark [?]	· · — — · ·
Quotation mark ["]	· — · · — ·
Semicolon [;]	— · — · — ·
Slash [/], Fraction bar	— · · — ·
Underscore [_]	· · — — · —

An advantage of using Morse Code is that when broadcasting CW, you are using reduced power, thereby saving your battery. Your battery is used only while actually transmitting or receiving.

International Call Sign Prefixes

As was stated earlier, all ham radio call signs begin with letters (or numbers) taken from blocks assigned to each country of the world by the *ITU - International Telecommunications Union,* a body controlled by the United Nations. The following chart indicates which call sign series are allocated to which countries.

Call Sign Series	Allocated to
AAA-ALZ	**United States of America**
AMA-AOZ	Spain
APA-ASZ	Pakistan (Islamic Republic of)
ATA-AWZ	India (Republic of)
AXA-AXZ	Australia
AYA-AZZ	Argentine Republic
A2A-A2Z	Botswana (Republic of)
A3A-A3Z	Tonga (Kingdom of)
A4A-A4Z	Oman (Sultanate of)
A5A-A5Z	Bhutan (Kingdom of)

A6A-A6Z	United Arab Emirates
A7A-A7Z	Qatar (State of)
A8A-A8Z	Liberia (Republic of)
A9A-A9Z	Bahrain (State of)
BAA-BZZ	China (People's Republic of)
CAA-CEZ	Chile
CFA-CKZ	Canada
CLA-CMZ	Cuba
CNA-CNZ	Morocco (Kingdom of)
COA-COZ	Cuba
CPA-CPZ	Bolivia (Republic of)
CQA-CUZ	Portugal
CVA-CXZ	Uruguay (Eastern Republic of)
CYA-CZZ	Canada
C2A-C2Z	Nauru (Republic of)
C3A-C3Z	Andorra (Principality of)
C4A-C4Z	Cyprus (Republic of)
C5A-C5Z	Gambia (Republic of the)
C6A-C6Z	Bahamas (Commonwealth of the)
C7A-C7Z	World Meteorological Organization
C8A-C9Z	Mozambique (Republic of)
DAA-DRZ	Germany (Federal Republic of)
DSA-DTZ	Korea (Republic of)
DUA-DZZ	Philippines (Republic of the)
D2A-D3Z	Angola (Republic of)
D4A-D4Z	Cape Verde (Republic of)
D5A-D5Z	Liberia (Republic of)
D6A-D6Z	Comoros (Islamic Federal Republic of the)
D7A-D9Z	Korea (Republic of)
EAA-EHZ	Spain
EIA-EJZ	Ireland
EKA-EKZ	Armenia (Republic of)
ELA-ELZ	Liberia (Republic of)
EMA-EOZ	Ukraine
EPA-EQZ	Iran (Islamic Republic of)
ERA-ERZ	Moldova (Republic of)
ESA-ESZ	Estonia (Republic of)
ETA-ETZ	Ethiopia (Federal Democratic Republic of)
EUA-EWZ	Belarus (Republic of)
EXA-EXZ	Kyrgyz Republic
EYA-EYZ	Tajikistan (Republic of)
EZA-EZZ	Turkmenistan
E2A-E2Z	Thailand
E3A-E3Z	Eritrea
E4A-E4Z	Palestinian Authority

E5A-E5Z	New Zealand - Cook Islands (WRC-07)
E7A-E7Z	Bosnia and Herzegovina (Republic of) (WRC-07)
FAA-FZZ	France
GAA-GZZ	United Kingdom of Great Britain and Northern Ireland
HAA-HAZ	Hungary (Republic of)
HBA-HBZ	Switzerland (Confederation of)
HCA-HDZ	Ecuador
HEA-HEZ	Switzerland (Confederation of)
HFA-HFZ	Poland (Republic of)
HGA-HGZ	Hungary (Republic of)
HHA-HHZ	Haiti (Republic of)
HIA-HIZ	Dominican Republic
HJA-HKZ	Colombia (Republic of)
HLA-HLZ	Korea (Republic of)
HMA-HMZ	Democratic People's Republic of Korea
HNA-HNZ	Iraq (Republic of)
HOA-HPZ	Panama (Republic of)
HQA-HRZ	Honduras (Republic of)
HSA-HSZ	Thailand
HTA-HTZ	Nicaragua
HUA-HUZ	El Salvador (Republic of)
HVA-HVZ	Vatican City State
HWA-HYZ	France
HZA-HZZ	Saudi Arabia (Kingdom of)
H2A-H2Z	Cyprus (Republic of)
H3A-H3Z	Panama (Republic of)
H4A-H4Z	Solomon Islands
H6A-H7Z	Nicaragua
H8A-H9Z	Panama (Republic of)
IAA-IZZ	Italy
JAA-JSZ	Japan
JTA-JVZ	Mongolia
JWA-JXZ	Norway
JYA-JYZ	Jordan (Hashemite Kingdom of)
JZA-JZZ	Indonesia (Republic of)
J2A-J2Z	Djibouti (Republic of)
J3A-J3Z	Grenada
J4A-J4Z	Greece
J5A-J5Z	Guinea-Bissau (Republic of)
J6A-J6Z	Saint Lucia
J7A-J7Z	Dominica (Commonwealth of)
J8A-J8Z	Saint Vincent and the Grenadines
KAA-KZZ	**United States of America**
LAA-LNZ	Norway
LOA-LWZ	Argentine Republic

LXA-LXZ	Luxembourg
LYA-LYZ	Lithuania (Republic of)
LZA-LZZ	Bulgaria (Republic of)
L2A-L9Z	Argentine Republic
MAA-MZZ	United Kingdom of Great Britain and Northern Ireland
NAA-NZZ	**United States of America**
OAA-OCZ	Peru
ODA-ODZ	Lebanon
OEA-OEZ	Austria
OFA-OJZ	Finland
OKA-OLZ	Czech Republic
OMA-OMZ	Slovak Republic
ONA-OTZ	Belgium
OUA-OZZ	Denmark
PAA-PIZ	Netherlands (Kingdom of the)
PJA-PJZ	Netherlands (Kingdom of the) - Netherlands Antilles
PKA-POZ	Indonesia (Republic of)
PPA-PYZ	Brazil (Federative Republic of)
PZA-PZZ	Suriname (Republic of)
P2A-P2Z	Papua New Guinea
P3A-P3Z	Cyprus (Republic of)
P4A-P4Z	Netherlands (Kingdom of the) - Aruba
P5A-P9Z	Democratic People's Republic of Korea
RAA-RZZ	Russian Federation
SAA-SMZ	Sweden
SNA-SRZ	Poland (Republic of)
SSA-SSM	Egypt (Arab Republic of)
SSN-STZ	Sudan (Republic of the)
SUA-SUZ	Egypt (Arab Republic of)
SVA-SZZ	Greece
S2A-S3Z	Bangladesh (People's Republic of)
S5A-S5Z	Slovenia (Republic of)
S6A-S6Z	Singapore (Republic of)
S7A-S7Z	Seychelles (Republic of)
S8A-S8Z	South Africa (Republic of)
S9A-S9Z	Sao Tome and Principe (Democratic Republic of)
TAA-TCZ	Turkey
TDA-TDZ	Guatemala (Republic of)
TEA-TEZ	Costa Rica
TFA-TFZ	Iceland
TGA-TGZ	Guatemala (Republic of)
THA-THZ	France
TIA-TIZ	Costa Rica
TJA-TJZ	Cameroon (Republic of)
TKA-TKZ	France

TLA-TLZ	Central African Republic
TMA-TMZ	France
TNA-TNZ	Congo (Republic of the)
TOA-TQZ	France
TRA-TRZ	Gabonese Republic
TSA-TSZ	Tunisia
TTA-TTZ	Chad (Republic of)
TUA-TUZ	Côte d'Ivoire (Republic of)
TVA-TXZ	France
TYA-TYZ	Benin (Republic of)
TZA-TZZ	Mali (Republic of)
T2A-T2Z	Tuvalu
T3A-T3Z	Kiribati (Republic of)
T4A-T4Z	Cuba
T5A-T5Z	Somali Democratic Republic
T6A-T6Z	Afghanistan (Islamic State of)
T7A-T7Z	San Marino (Republic of)
T8A-T8Z	Palau (Republic of)
UAA-UIZ	Russian Federation
UJA-UMZ	Uzbekistan (Republic of)
UNA-UQZ	Kazakhstan (Republic of)
URA-UZZ	Ukraine
VAA-VGZ	Canada
VHA-VNZ	Australia
VOA-VOZ	Canada
VPA-VQZ	United Kingdom of Great Britain and Northern Ireland
VRA-VRZ	China (People's Republic of) - Hong Kong
VSA-VSZ	United Kingdom of Great Britain and Northern Ireland
VTA-VWZ	India (Republic of)
VXA-VYZ	Canada
VZA-VZZ	Australia
V2A-V2Z	Antigua and Barbuda
V3A-V3Z	Belize
V4A-V4Z	Saint Kitts and Nevis
V5A-V5Z	Namibia (Republic of)
V6A-V6Z	Micronesia (Federated States of)
V7A-V7Z	Marshall Islands (Republic of the)
V8A-V8Z	Brunei Darussalam
WAA-WZZ	**United States of America**
XAA-XIZ	Mexico
XJA-XOZ	Canada
XPA-XPZ	Denmark
XQA-XRZ	Chile
XSA-XSZ	China (People's Republic of)
XTA-XTZ	Burkina Faso

XUA-XUZ	Cambodia (Kingdom of)
XVA-XVZ	Viet Nam (Socialist Republic of)
XWA-XWZ	Lao People's Democratic Republic
XXA-XXZ	China (People's Republic of) - Macao (WRC-07)
XYA-XZZ	Myanmar (Union of)
YAA-YAZ	Afghanistan (Islamic State of)
YBA-YHZ	Indonesia (Republic of)
YIA-YIZ	Iraq (Republic of)
YJA-YJZ	Vanuatu (Republic of)
YKA-YKZ	Syrian Arab Republic
YLA-YLZ	Latvia (Republic of)
YMA-YMZ	Turkey
YNA-YNZ	Nicaragua
YOA-YRZ	Romania
YSA-YSZ	El Salvador (Republic of)
YTA-YUZ	Serbia (Republic of) (WRC-07)
YVA-YYZ	Venezuela (Republic of)
Y2A-Y9Z	Germany (Federal Republic of)
ZAA-ZAZ	Albania (Republic of)
ZBA-ZJZ	United Kingdom of Great Britain and Northern Ireland
ZKA-ZMZ	New Zealand
ZNA-ZOZ	United Kingdom of Great Britain and Northern Ireland
ZPA-ZPZ	Paraguay (Republic of)
ZQA-ZQZ	United Kingdom of Great Britain and Northern Ireland
ZRA-ZUZ	South Africa (Republic of)
ZVA-ZZZ	Brazil (Federative Republic of)
Z2A-Z2Z	Zimbabwe (Republic of)
Z3A-Z3Z	The Former Yugoslav Republic of Macedonia
2AA-2ZZ	United Kingdom of Great Britain and Northern Ireland
3AA-3AZ	Monaco (Principality of)
3BA-3BZ	Mauritius (Republic of)
3CA-3CZ	Equatorial Guinea (Republic of)
3DA-3DM	Swaziland (Kingdom of)
3DN-3DZ	Fiji (Republic of)
3EA-3FZ	Panama (Republic of)
3GA-3GZ	Chile
3HA-3UZ	China (People's Republic of)
3VA-3VZ	Tunisia
3WA-3WZ	Viet Nam (Socialist Republic of)
3XA-3XZ	Guinea (Republic of)
3YA-3YZ	Norway
3ZA-3ZZ	Poland (Republic of)
4AA-4CZ	Mexico
4DA-4IZ	Philippines (Republic of the)
4JA-4KZ	Azerbaijani Republic

4LA-4LZ	Georgia (Republic of)
4MA-4MZ	Venezuela (Republic of)
4OA-4OZ	Montenegro (Republic of) (WRC-07)
4PA-4SZ	Sri Lanka (Democratic Socialist Republic of)
4TA-4TZ	Peru
4UA-4UZ	United Nations
4VA-4VZ	Haiti (Republic of)
4WA-4WZ	Democratic Republic of Timor-Leste (WRC-03)
4XA-4XZ	Israel (State of)
4YA-4YZ	International Civil Aviation Organization
4ZA-4ZZ	Israel (State of)
5AA-5AZ	Libya (Socialist People's Libyan Arab Jamahiriya)
5BA-5BZ	Cyprus (Republic of)
5CA-5GZ	Morocco (Kingdom of)
5HA-5IZ	Tanzania (United Republic of)
5JA-5KZ	Colombia (Republic of)
5LA-5MZ	Liberia (Republic of)
5NA-5OZ	Nigeria (Federal Republic of)
5PA-5QZ	Denmark
5RA-5SZ	Madagascar (Republic of)
5TA-5TZ	Mauritania (Islamic Republic of)
5UA-5UZ	Niger (Republic of the)
5VA-5VZ	Togolese Republic
5WA-5WZ	Samoa (Independent State of)
5XA-5XZ	Uganda (Republic of)
5YA-5ZZ	Kenya (Republic of)
6AA-6BZ	Egypt (Arab Republic of)
6CA-6CZ	Syrian Arab Republic
6DA-6JZ	Mexico
6KA-6NZ	Korea (Republic of)
6OA-6OZ	Somali Democratic Republic
6PA-6SZ	Pakistan (Islamic Republic of)
6TA-6UZ	Sudan (Republic of the)
6VA-6WZ	Senegal (Republic of)
6XA-6XZ	Madagascar (Republic of)
6YA-6YZ	Jamaica
6ZA-6ZZ	Liberia (Republic of)
7AA-7IZ	Indonesia (Republic of)
7JA-7NZ	Japan
7OA-7OZ	Yemen (Republic of)
7PA-7PZ	Lesotho (Kingdom of)
7QA-7QZ	Malawi
7RA-7RZ	Algeria (People's Democratic Republic of)
7SA-7SZ	Sweden
7TA-7YZ	Algeria (People's Democratic Republic of)

7ZA-7ZZ	Saudi Arabia (Kingdom of)
8AA-8IZ	Indonesia (Republic of)
8JA-8NZ	Japan
8OA-8OZ	Botswana (Republic of)
8PA-8PZ	Barbados
8QA-8QZ	Maldives (Republic of)
8RA-8RZ	Guyana
8SA-8SZ	Sweden
8TA-8YZ	India (Republic of)
8ZA-8ZZ	Saudi Arabia (Kingdom of)
9AA-9AZ	Croatia (Republic of)
9BA-9DZ	Iran (Islamic Republic of)
9EA-9FZ	Ethiopia (Federal Democratic Republic of)
9GA-9GZ	Ghana
9HA-9HZ	Malta
9IA-9JZ	Zambia (Republic of)
9KA-9KZ	Kuwait (State of)
9LA-9LZ	Sierra Leone
9MA-9MZ	Malaysia
9NA-9NZ	Nepal
9OA-9TZ	Democratic Republic of the Congo
9UA-9UZ	Burundi (Republic of)
9VA-9VZ	Singapore (Republic of)
9WA-9WZ	Malaysia
9XA-9XZ	Rwandese Republic
9YA-9ZZ	Trinidad and Tobago

Third-Party Communications and Amateur Radio

If all of this information about ham radios is somewhat intimidating, do not despair. "You" can still use ham radios for communications without being a licensed operator. Yes, you do have to have a ham license in order to legally transmit by ham equipment (or be under the direct supervision of someone else who is licensed), but there is an alternative – third-party communication.

Third-party communications occur when a licensed operator sends either written or verbal messages on behalf of unlicensed persons or organizations. There are two "controls" on third-party communication.

First, the communication must be noncommercial and of a personal nature. Asking a ham operator to contact another ham operator located in an area just hit by tornados and, because of being without power, phones do not work in Grandma Sally's city so you can check up on her, is okay. Asking a ham to send a message out that you have an old Chevy for sale would not be okay.

Second, the message must be going to a permitted area. Transmitting from a US location to another US location is okay, but transmitting from the US to another country may not. Because third-party communications bypass a country's normal telephone and postal systems, many foreign governments forbid such communications. In order to transmit from one country to another, the other country must have signed a third-party agreement with the US. What follows is a list of those countries that do have third-party a communications agreement with the US.

V2	Antigua / Barbuda
LU	Argentina
VK	Australia
V3	Belize
CP	Bolivia
T9	Bosnia-Herzegovina
PY	Brazil
VE	Canada
CE	Chile
HK	Colombia
D6	Comoros (Federal Islamic Republic of)
TI	Costa Rica
CO	Cuba
HI	Dominican Republic
J7	Dominica
HC	Ecuador
YS	El Salvador
C5	Gambia, The
9G	Ghana
J3	Grenada
TG	Guatemala
8R	Guyana
HH	Haiti
HR	Honduras
4X	Israel
6Y	Jamaica
JY	Jordan
EL	Liberia
V7	Marshall Islands
XE	Mexico
V6	Micronesia, Federated States of
YN	Nicaragua
HP	Panama
ZP	Paraguay
OA	Peru
DU	Philippines
VR6	Pitcairn Island

V4	St. Christopher / Nevis
J6	St. Lucia
J8	St. Vincent and the Grenadines
9L	Sierra Leone
ZS	South Africa
3DA	Swaziland
9Y	Trinidad / Tobago
TA	Turkey
GB	United Kingdom
CX	Uruguay
YV	Venezuela
4U1ITUITU	Geneva
4U1VICVIC	Vienna

Remember, before TSHTF, keep your pantry well stocked, your powder dry, and your batteries fully charged. 73

APPENDIX A

American Radio Relay League

Affiliated Amateur Radio Clubs in

Arizona

ARRL Affiliated Club	Bill Williams Mountain Radio Club
City:	Ash Fork, AZ
Call Sign:	K7NAZ
Section:	AZ
Links:	billwilliamsradioclub.webuda.com/

ARRL Affiliated Club	Central Arizona DX Association
City:	Chandler, AZ
Call Sign:	K7UGA
Section:	AZ
Links:	www.cadxa.org

ARRL Affiliated Club	Hassayampa Amateur Radio Klub
City:	Congress, AZ
Section:	AZ
Links:	www.harkaz.org

ARRL Affiliated Club	Verde Valley Amateur Radio Assn., Inc.
City:	Cottonwood, AZ
Call Sign:	W7EI
Section:	AZ
Links:	www.vvara.org

ARRL Affiliated Club	Northern Arizona DX Assn.
City:	Flagstaff, AZ
Call Sign:	W7TB
Section:	AZ
Links:	www.nadxa.com

ARRL Affiliated Club	Coconino Amateur Radio Club
City:	Flagstaff, AZ
Call Sign:	KC7KCN
Section:	AZ
Links:	cocoradio.org/

ARRL Affiliated Club	Northern Arizona University
City:	Flagstaff, AZ
Call Sign:	K7NAU
Section:	AZ

ARRL Affiliated Club	Mohave Amateur Radio Club
City:	Golden Valley, AZ
Call Sign:	K7MPR
Section:	AZ
Links:	K7MPR.COM

ARRL Affiliated Club	Tri City Amateur Radio Association
City:	Goodyear, AZ
Call Sign:	W7GDY
Section:	AZ
Links:	www.tricityara.org

ARRL Special Service Club	Green Valley Amateur Radio Club
City:	Green Valley, AZ
Call Sign:	WE7GV
Section:	AZ
Links:	www.gvarc.us

ARRL Affiliated Club	Rim Country Amateur Radio Club
City:	Heber, AZ
Call Sign:	W7RIM
Section:	AZ
Links:	W7RIM.org

ARRL Affiliated Club	Hualapai Amateur Radio Club
City:	Kingman, AZ
Call Sign:	WB6RER
Section:	AZ
Links:	wb6rer.n7ffl.us

ARRL Affiliated Club	London Bridge Amateur Radio Assn.
City:	Lake Havasu City, AZ
Call Sign:	K7LHC
Section:	AZ
Links:	www.lbara.net

ARRL Affiliated Club	Thunderbird Amateur Radio Club
City:	Laveen, AZ
Call Sign:	W7TBC
Section:	AZ
Links:	www.w7tbc.org

ARRL Affiliated Club	Arizona Outlaws Contest Club
City:	Mesa, AZ
Call Sign:	N7AT
Services Offered:	Club Newsletter, Mentor
Section:	AZ
Links:	www.arizonaoutlaws.net

ARRL Affiliated Club	Sunlife Amateur Radio Club
City:	Mesa, AZ
Section:	AZ
Links:	www.sunlifearc.webs.com

ARRL Affiliated Club	Viewpoint Amateur Radio Club
City:	Mesa, AZ
Call Sign:	K7VPR
Section:	AZ

ARRL Affiliated Club	Superstition Amateur Radio Club
City:	Mesa, AZ
Call Sign:	WB7TJD
Section:	AZ
Links:	wb7tjd.org

ARRL Affiliated Club	Venture Out Amateur Radio Association
City:	Mesa, AZ
Call Sign:	N7VOC
Section:	AZ

ARRL Affiliated Club	Mesa Amateur Radio Club
City:	Mesa, AZ
Call Sign:	WM7RC
Section:	AZ
Links:	mesa-arc.org/

ARRL Affiliated Club	Oro Valley Amateur Radio Club
City:	Oro Valley, AZ
Call Sign:	WOHF
Section:	AZ
Links:	www.w0hf.com

ARRL Affiliated Club	Arizona Amateur Radio Club
City:	Phoenix, AZ
Call Sign:	W7IO
Section:	AZ
Links:	www.w7io.org

ARRL Affiliated Club	Maricopa Co. Sheriff's Comm. Posse, Inc.
City:	Phoenix, AZ
Call Sign:	K7MCS
Section:	AZ
Links:	www.posse.net

ARRL Affiliated Club	Amateur Radio Council of AZ
City:	Phoenix, AZ
Call Sign:	KC7TMA
Section:	AZ
Links:	www.arca-az.org

ARRL Affiliated Club	Cochise Amateur Radio Assn.
City:	Sierra Vista, AZ
Call Sign:	K7RDG
Section:	AZ
Links:	www.k7rdg.org

ARRL Affiliated Club	Eastern Arizona Amateur Radio Society
City:	Solomon, AZ
Call Sign:	K7EAR
Section:	AZ
Links:	www.EAARS.com

ARRL Affiliated Club	West Valley Amateur Radio Club
City:	Sun City, AZ
Call Sign:	NY7S
Section:	AZ
Links:	www.westvalleyarc.org

ARRL Affiliated Club	Amateur Radio Society at AZ State Univ.
City:	Tempe, AZ
Call Sign:	W7ASU
Section:	AZ
Links:	www.asu.edu/clubs/amateur_radio_society/

ARRL Affiliated Club	MARCA, Inc.
City:	Tempe, AZ
Call Sign:	W7MOT
Section:	AZ
Links:	www.w7mot.org

ARRL Affiliated Club	Tucson Repeater Association
City:	Tucson, AZ
Call Sign:	K7TRA
Section:	AZ

ARRL Affiliated Club	University of Arizona Amateur Radio Club
City:	Tucson, AZ
Call Sign:	K7UAZ
Section:	AZ
Links:	www.k7uaz.com

ARRL Affiliated Club	Western Wireless Contest Club
City:	Tucson, AZ
Call Sign:	KQ7M
Section:	AZ

ARRL Affiliated Club	Cholla Amateur Remote Base Association
City:	Tucson, AZ
Call Sign:	AK7Z
Section:	AZ
Links:	www.carba.net

ARRL Special Service Club	Radio Society of Tucson (RST CLUB)
City:	Tucson, AZ
Call Sign:	K7RST
Section:	AZ
Links:	www.k7rst.org, www.rstclub.org

ARRL Affiliated Club	Old Pueblo Radio Club
City:	Tucson, AZ
Call Sign:	W7GV
Section:	AZ
Links:	www.neighborhoodlink.com/org/tra/

ARRL Affiliated Club	Southern Arizona DX Association
City:	Tucson, AZ
Call Sign:	WS7DX
Section:	AZ
Links:	SADXA.ORG

ARRL Affiliated Club	Tucson Repeater Association
City:	Tucson, AZ
Call Sign:	K7TRA
Section:	AZ

ARRL Affiliated Club	Yuma DX Association
City:	Yuma, AZ
Call Sign:	N7YDX
Section:	AZ
Links:	www.ydxa.org/

ARRL Special Service Club	Yuma Amateur Radio Club
City:	Yuma, AZ
Call Sign:	K7YA
Section:	AZ
Links:	www.qsl.net/k7ya

APPENDIX B

Amateur Radio License Holders

in

Arizona: Colorado Plateau Region
(by City)

FCC Amateur Radio Licenses in Ajo

Call Sign: KC7QGI
Ellery M Horton
231 10th St
Ajo AZ 85321

Call Sign: KC7QGJ
Myrna F Horton
231 10th St
Ajo AZ 85321

Call Sign: N7YZV
Marilyn A Papier
400 7th St
Ajo AZ 85321

Call Sign: N7YZS
Maurice J Papier
400 7th St
Ajo AZ 85321

Call Sign: KE7RKS
Michael D Taylor
120 E 1st Ave
Ajo AZ 85321

Call Sign: KC7QGG
Shirley J Glasby
121 E 2nd Ave
Ajo AZ 85321

Call Sign: N7MWF
William W Glasby
121 E 2nd Ave
Ajo AZ 85321

Call Sign: WA5TFF
Douglas D Adkins
101 E 3rd Ave
Ajo AZ 85321

Call Sign: KA7YWG
B June Babcock
220 E 3rd Ave
Ajo AZ 85321

Call Sign: KC5CHM

Harley L Murray
240 E 4th Ave
Ajo AZ 85321

Call Sign: N0AJO
Harley L Murray
240 E 4th Ave
Ajo AZ 85321

Call Sign: KC7KRG
Wilmer L Huff
351 E Arroyo Ave
Ajo AZ 85321

Call Sign: N7YXU
William C Feld
621 Esperanza Ave
Ajo AZ 85321

Call Sign: KC7LDX
Paul S Smith Jr
550 Greenway Dr
Ajo AZ 85321

Call Sign: KL7GRK
Allen G Berry
1000 Lewis Rd
Ajo AZ 85321

Call Sign: KD7FJE
Warren F Stafford
721 Morondo Ave
Ajo AZ 85321

Call Sign: N7YZT
Bob E Bryant
2330 N Elliott Rd
Ajo AZ 85321

Call Sign: KC7QPS
Estelle Bryant
2330 N Elliott Rd
Ajo AZ 85321

Call Sign: KC7QPQ
Barbara N Silva
2331 N Elliott Rd
Ajo AZ 85321

Call Sign: KC7QGH
Marvin Z Silva
2331 N Elliott Rd
Ajo AZ 85321

Call Sign: N7YZU
Rex A Silva
2331 N Elliott Rd
Ajo AZ 85321

Call Sign: N7YZQ
Michael D Lane
2560 N Elliott Rd
Ajo AZ 85321

Call Sign: KC7QGK
Richard E Daniels
2710 N Elliott Rd
Ajo AZ 85321

Call Sign: KC7QPR
Evangeline A Walker
2911 N Elliott Rd
Ajo AZ 85321

Call Sign: KF7LA
Richard D Walker Jr
2911 N Elliott Rd
Ajo AZ 85321

Call Sign: W7AJO
Richard D Walker Jr
2911 N Elliott Rd
Ajo AZ 85321

Call Sign: KD7BJC
Barry D Estes
1200 N Kilbright Ave
Ajo AZ 85321

Call Sign: W6EZD
Edward T Martin
801 N McKinley
Ajo AZ 85321

Call Sign: WA7WFB
Alvin D Bausman
1061 N Rosedale Ave
Ajo AZ 85321

Call Sign: N7YZR
Dixie P Grissom
3061 N Rosser Rd
Ajo AZ 85321

Call Sign: KC7KCK
Bette L Whiting
110 North St
Ajo AZ 85321

Call Sign: KC7JPC
Wesley W Whiting
110 North St
Ajo AZ 85321

Call Sign: KC7QGE
Vernon L Rockwell
1241 Palm St
Ajo AZ 85321

Call Sign: N7YZO
Fannie L Couch
1420 Rasmussen Rd
Ajo AZ 85321

Call Sign: WB7FBC
Claude M Mason
530 Vananda
Ajo AZ 85321

Call Sign: KE7ALA
Joan B Riner
200 W 1st Ave
Ajo AZ 85321

Call Sign: K7AJO
Joan B Riner
200 W 1st Ave
Ajo AZ 85321

Call Sign: WD0BEO
Billie F Riner
200 W 1st Ave
Ajo AZ 853212114

Call Sign: KL7DSI
Billie F Riner
200 W 1st Ave

Ajo AZ 853212114

Call Sign: W5TJW
Clarence W Wenzel
340 W 2nd Ave
Ajo AZ 853212124

Call Sign: W9ILM
Clarence W Wenzel
340 W 2nd Ave
Ajo AZ 853212124

Call Sign: KE7KBC
Jack D Wesely
141 W 3rd Ave
Ajo AZ 85321

Call Sign: KD6RSO
Larry E Horton
301 W 3rd Ave
Ajo AZ 85321

Call Sign: KC7ROV
Sharon L Horton
301 W 3rd Ave
Ajo AZ 85321

Call Sign: K5AKF
Kenton S Ahrens Jr
420 W Arroyo
Ajo AZ 85321

Call Sign: W7AKF
Kenton S Ahrens Jr
420 W Arroyo
Ajo AZ 85321

Call Sign: KC7QGC
James M Decheine
210 W Arroyo Ave
Ajo AZ 85321

Call Sign: N7YZN
Donald O Stephens
340 W Arroyo Ave
Ajo AZ 85321

Call Sign: KE7ZDU
William L Doremus

400 W Arroyo Ave
Ajo AZ 85321

Call Sign: N7YZP
Roy A Brewster
1450 W Briggs Rd
Ajo AZ 85321

Call Sign: WN7E
Jerry E Grubbs
801 W Cholla Ave
Ajo AZ 85321

Call Sign: KF7RSN
Douglas R Brader
1580 W North St
Ajo AZ 85321

Call Sign: KC0YT
Albert H Fenn
Ajo AZ 85321

Call Sign: KE7KUP
Ron J Russell
Ajo AZ 85321

Call Sign: KA7HTQ
Terry Jones
Ajo AZ 85321

FCC Amateur Radio Licenses in Alpine

Call Sign: KA7ZHY
Storm E Luce
Blue River Rt
Alpine AZ 85920

Call Sign: WB7DKN
Julia M Luce
Blue River Rt
Alpine AZ 85920

Call Sign: WA8LFH
David G Akers
2 CR 2040
Alpine AZ 859200910

Call Sign: KC7MVY

Merle J Diggins
47 CR 2067
Alpine AZ 85920

Call Sign: WA1FSV
Ronald F Jacobs
46 CR 2140
Alpine AZ 859200094

Call Sign: N7EAQ
Byron F Simmons
38 CR 2147
Alpine AZ 85920

Call Sign: N6ZNS
Darwin B Crezee
CR 2150 N 17
Alpine AZ 85920

Call Sign: N7OIU
Barbara L Kofira
10 CR N 2148
Alpine AZ 859200814

Call Sign: N7OIO
Robert L Kofira
10 CR N 2148
Alpine AZ 859200814

Call Sign: KD7UVV
Noralee L Crezee
Alpine AZ 85290

Call Sign: KB6TTO
Joanne N L Bogdanski
Alpine AZ 85920

Call Sign: KD7GPL
James N Ransom
Alpine AZ 85920

Call Sign: KS6FF
Michael G Hitchcock
Alpine AZ 85920

Call Sign: KE7CLO
Eric L Krueger
Alpine AZ 859200076

Call Sign: AK7Y
Gregory J Farkas
Alpine AZ 859200226

Call Sign: WB6UDA
Joan M Hitchcock
Alpine AZ 859200398

Call Sign: WA6UDA
Michael G Hitchcock
Alpine AZ 859200398

Call Sign: KD7FDX
Jess C Hartman
Alpine AZ 859200623

Call Sign: KD7FDY
Susan J Hartman
Alpine AZ 859200623

FCC Amateur Radio Licenses in Amado

Call Sign: N7RYN
David J Bucciarelli
Box 6257
Amado AZ 85645

Call Sign: KE7SBP
Jordan D Juhlin
26507 S Coppers Hawk Rd
Amado AZ 85645

Call Sign: AB7VE
David P Sader
28300 S Foxwood Way
Amado AZ 85645

Call Sign: KC7TAC
Susan D Sader
28300 S Foxwood Way
Amado AZ 85645

Call Sign: WD5IUD
Ernest M Madison
26851 S Purple Finch Ln
Amado AZ 85645

Call Sign: KE4BX

Jewell W Thompson
4561 Tumacacori Dr
Amado AZ 856459763

Call Sign: KC7ANH
Lloyd E Brown
2000 W Eagle Way
Amado AZ 85645

Call Sign: KC7ANI
Sherry C Brown
2000 W Eagle Way
Amado AZ 85645

Call Sign: KC7BHY
Mike T Hoye
575 W Hawk
Amado AZ 85645

Call Sign: W7PD
Thomas J Donahue
15 Whitehead Ln
Amado AZ 85645

Call Sign: KB7VKA
Stephen J Criswell
Amado AZ 85645

Call Sign: KF7MXO
Edward P Eisenhauer
Amado AZ 85645

Call Sign: KF6PPM
James F Cochran
Amado AZ 85645

Call Sign: KB7WQV
James R Peters
Amado AZ 85645

FCC Amateur Radio Licenses in Arivaca

Call Sign: AB7WU
Charles H Abercrombie
37030 6th Ave
Arivaca AZ 856010188

Call Sign: KD7DOJ

Darlene M Minear
15585 Cota Rd
Arivaca AZ 85601

Call Sign: W7UO
Marion W Minear
Arivaca AZ 85601

Call Sign: N7HAP
Obe Sweetwater
Arivaca AZ 85601

Call Sign: KE7VJS
Anna L Gilbert
Arivaca AZ 85601

Call Sign: KC7HND
Carlyle A Martin
Arivaca AZ 85601

Call Sign: KC7UNB
Darlene D Shaffer
Arivaca AZ 85601

Call Sign: KC7PRZ
Donald E Honnas
Arivaca AZ 85601

Call Sign: KC7SZW
Gordon E Rife
Arivaca AZ 85601

Call Sign: KD7MZZ
Jen M Taylor
Arivaca AZ 85601

Call Sign: KC7ZXN
Jesse E Casey
Arivaca AZ 85601

Call Sign: KC7PRW
Lavona E Howe
Arivaca AZ 85601

Call Sign: KC7PRY
Lowell E Robinson
Arivaca AZ 85601

Call Sign: KF7GFH

Marcia N Olney
Arivaca AZ 85601

Call Sign: KE7VJR
Marshall J Gilbert Sr
Arivaca AZ 85601

Call Sign: KC7PRV
Milo D Turnpaugh
Arivaca AZ 85601

Call Sign: KC7PRX
Russell C Howe
Arivaca AZ 85601

Call Sign: KB7BVU
Ted H Noon
Arivaca AZ 85601

Call Sign: KC7OEA
Theodore E Seitz
Arivaca AZ 85601

Call Sign: AL0F
Timothy S Brown
Arivaca AZ 85601

Call Sign: KA7YNB
Owen E Gibson
Arivaca AZ 85601

Call Sign: WB7OTU
Ralph F Griffin Sr
Arivaca AZ 856010066

Call Sign: KE7COX
Terry W Tompkins
Arivaca AZ 856010240

Call Sign: AD7EL
Terry W Tompkins
Arivaca AZ 856010240

FCC Amateur Radio Licenses in Arizona City

Call Sign: KE7MRL
Dean Hill
9733 La Paz Ln

Arizona City AZ 85223

Call Sign: KB8LQY
Gregory L Poehlman
8977 Raven
Arizona City AZ 85123

Call Sign: N7HCI
Brian D Finney
15180 S Amado Blvd
Arizona City AZ 852230726

Call Sign: WA2UBE
Frederick J Wiedemann
15109 S Lamb Rd
Arizona City AZ 852232523

Call Sign: KC7PLV
Douglas S Fiore
10020 Sasabe Dr
Arizona City AZ 85223

Call Sign: AD5H
Gary L Petersen
8497 Swansea
Arizona City AZ 85123

Call Sign: WD6DZO
Jon R Greene
8446 W Altos Dr
Arizona City AZ 852233516

Call Sign: KC8IJW
Cynthia A Pogue
8262 W Concordia A
Arizona City AZ 85223

Call Sign: KJ6MOX
John Pinches
9054 W Coronado
Arizona City AZ 85123

Call Sign: NF7F
Donald E Meyer
8257 W Milligan Rd
Arizona City AZ 852232313

Call Sign: K8BVY
Sean T O Callaghan

10089 W Sasabe
Arizona City AZ 85123

Call Sign: KE7BVJ
Lee A Mertesdorf
8591 W Valdez Dr
Arizona City AZ 85123

Call Sign: K8GRN
Herbert F Selbach
Arizona City AZ 85223

Call Sign: KC7JVG
Brianne Washburn
Arizona City AZ 85123

Call Sign: KF7MHT
Gary Gardner
Arizona City AZ 85123

Call Sign: KD7PEM
Lori L Christensen
Arizona City AZ 85123

Call Sign: KF7NMD
Rex A Turvin
Arizona City AZ 85123

Call Sign: WA6ZOS
Russell W Stein
Arizona City AZ 85123

Call Sign: KK7YP
Russell W Stein
Arizona City AZ 85123

Call Sign: K8ERR
Steven A Kerr
Arizona City AZ 85123

Call Sign: KD7OUY
Wayne Brown
Arizona City AZ 85123

Call Sign: KA0NPI
Carl E Goodrich
Arizona City AZ 85223

Call Sign: WA7ROT

Eldon W Dixon
Arizona City AZ 85223

Call Sign: WB6EWK
James G Sevick Jr
Arizona City AZ 85223

Call Sign: KD7SFV
John E Wooten
Arizona City AZ 85223

Call Sign: KC7EJY
John L Lee
Arizona City AZ 85223

Call Sign: KC7KMU
Karen L Lindgren
Arizona City AZ 85223

Call Sign: KB7UCT
Kathy J Lee
Arizona City AZ 85223

Call Sign: KE7OYP
Lawanda C Hill
Arizona City AZ 85223

Call Sign: KC7KMV
Mark S Lindgren
Arizona City AZ 85223

Call Sign: KC2AXD
Michael T Kersnowski
Arizona City AZ 85223

Call Sign: WB0KUD
Richard F Rose
Arizona City AZ 852230624

Call Sign: AC6SF
Beverly J Mc Cune
Arizona City AZ 852231624

Call Sign: AC6SG
Ralph K Mc Cune
Arizona City AZ 852231624

**FCC Amateur Radio
Licenses in Bellemont**

Call Sign: KF7RCV
Kaci A Heins
4490 Bellemont Springs
Bellemont AZ 86015

Call Sign: KF7QWV
National Weather Service
Flagstaff
Bellemont AZ 86015

Call Sign: WX7FGZ
National Weather Service
Flagstaff
Bellemont AZ 86015

Call Sign: KF7EIU
Aaron W Ake
Bellemont AZ 86015

Call Sign: KG6HWJ
Charles M Wilkins
Bellemont AZ 86015

Call Sign: AB7SC
Gregory R Baker
Bellemont AZ 860156179

Call Sign: AC7OM
Gregory R Baker
Bellemont AZ 860156179

**FCC Amateur Radio
Licenses in Benson**

Call Sign: KB7TLI
Mark B Lesniak
Box 3226
Benson AZ 85602

Call Sign: W7MBU
Thornton E Benson
Box 4245
Benson AZ 85602

Call Sign: KC7HWM
Kevin J Bouchard
Box 8001
Benson AZ 85602

Call Sign: AA7OY
Dale M Jensen
24112 Chickasha Tr
Benson AZ 85602

Call Sign: WA7GGF
Jack R Gallagher
3143 Clark Rd
Benson AZ 85602

Call Sign: KB7SKX
Pamela J Straughn
566 E 6th St
Benson AZ 85602

Call Sign: W7QGU
Jack S Mc Quown
298 E 7th St
Benson AZ 85602

Call Sign: N7CK
Michael R Bucciarelli
210 E 8th St
Benson AZ 85602

Call Sign: KB7QLL
Audie R Holbert
895 E McNeil
Benson AZ 85602

Call Sign: KD7DO
John J Vanaglash Jr
867 E McNeil Rd
Benson AZ 85602

Call Sign: N6BHY
Charles N Bradley
600 E Saguaro Dr 199
Benson AZ 856027055

Call Sign: KA8GEU
Edward W Elliott
600 E Saguaro Dr 272
Benson AZ 85602

Call Sign: KK7XV
Edward W Elliott
600 E Saguaro Dr 272

Benson AZ 85602

Call Sign: KA5TLT
Donald White
600 E Saguaro Dr 289
Benson AZ 856027097

Call Sign: KB4YPR
Barbra A Bailey
600 E Saguaro Dr 69
Benson AZ 85602

Call Sign: W4DHV
Oakley Bailey
600 E Saguaro Dr 69
Benson AZ 85602

Call Sign: N4BJX
Charles B Hoelzel
600 E Saguaro Dr Lot 196
Benson AZ 85602

Call Sign: KB1RSE
Andrew B Cornwall
600 E Saguaro Dr No 66
Benson AZ 85602

Call Sign: K6OFH
Edna P Lando
600 E Saguaro Dr Unit 138
Benson AZ 85602

Call Sign: K6OFI
Zane A Lando
600 E Saguaro Dr Unit 138
Benson AZ 85602

Call Sign: W7AFC
William O Grieve
3185 Evani Ave
Benson AZ 85602

Call Sign: WB7TJO
Fred W Berndt
Hcr Box 1915
Benson AZ 85602

Call Sign: N7UGO
Gloria G Berndt

Hcr Box 1915
Benson AZ 85602

Call Sign: N7VGH
Evelyn R Green
Hcr Box 2518
Benson AZ 85602

Call Sign: WB1DPI
George A Thompson
Hcr Box 301
Benson AZ 85602

Call Sign: WA7NYC
James W Grissom
Hcr Box 4330
Benson AZ 85602

Call Sign: KB7VJO
Ruth L Miller
481 Hillcrest Dr
Benson AZ 85602

Call Sign: N7XAT
Wallace S Miller
481 Hillcrest Dr
Benson AZ 85602

Call Sign: W7BAH
Albert F Rafferty
802 La Mesa Dr
Benson AZ 85602

Call Sign: KO5CSA
Bob A L Aloge
203 N Brandt Ave
Benson AZ 85602

Call Sign: WD6DVJ
Eleanor S Mideke
6025 N Cascabel Rd
Benson AZ 85602

Call Sign: WA6GFE
Lawrence A Beno
349 N Dusty Tyra Rd
Benson AZ 85602

Call Sign: N7QVK

Stephen J Stogsdill
227 N Evani Ave
Benson AZ 85602

Call Sign: WB7DBQ
John M Mac Kenzie
2510 N Mescal
Benson AZ 85602

Call Sign: KF7PES
Carey W Starzinger
622 N Mescal Rd
Benson AZ 85602

Call Sign: KD7BBQ
Carey W Starzinger
622 N Mescal Rd
Benson AZ 85602

Call Sign: WA7PIQ
Alan A Haines
3160 N No Way
Benson AZ 85602

Call Sign: K7VWI
Perry B Nance
185 N Park Ln Dr
Benson AZ 85602

Call Sign: KE7KSG
Clyde E Edwards
584 N Warren Rd
Benson AZ 85602

Call Sign: AB7JB
Gary K Pierce
266 N Well Drilling Rd
Benson AZ 85602

Call Sign: KI7UO
Harold R Lanman
232 Robin Rd Hc 2 Box 1797
Benson AZ 85602

Call Sign: AA1OV
Mark D Tetrault
1030 S Barrel Cactus Ridge
Lot 107
Benson AZ 85602

Call Sign: KA7AAS
Jacqueline K Talley
13741 S Bell Rd
Benson AZ 85602

Call Sign: WB7TVF
Lance A Talley
13741 S Bell Rd
Benson AZ 85602

Call Sign: KC7KGE
Billy L Hines
16200 S Choctaw Pl
Benson AZ 85602

Call Sign: KC2IQQ
Terry L Dietz
744 S Foothill Pl
Benson AZ 85602

Call Sign: N6RDB
Ronald A Brooks
647 S Huachuca St
Benson AZ 85602

Call Sign: K6PYP
Scott V Swanson
1063 S Limestone St
Benson AZ 85602

Call Sign: N7URJ
Xuan T Swanson
1063 S Limestone St
Benson AZ 85602

Call Sign: WB8LNG
Clifford M Marshall Jr
378 S Mimbres Pl
Benson AZ 85602

Call Sign: KE7CQJ
Butterfield ARC
251 S Ocotillo Ave
Benson AZ 85602

Call Sign: N7YGV
Martin D Jensen
735 S Shortino Ln

Benson AZ 85602

Call Sign: N0IUY
Mark L Sorensen
16241 S Whetstone Ave
Benson AZ 85602

Call Sign: KJ7CT
David A Lieber
16230 S Whetstone Ave 1
Benson AZ 85602

Call Sign: KB7GZR
Charles O Green Jr
11500 S Wrong Mountain Rd
Benson AZ 856027293

Call Sign: WB2DRJ
Louis M Amoroso
144 W 3rd St
Benson AZ 85602

Call Sign: KE7NQY
Mark B Lesniak
581 W 4th St 10
Benson AZ 85602

Call Sign: KB7TLI
Mark B Lesniak
995 W 4th St G 10
Benson AZ 85602

Call Sign: KE7OSW
Edward Islas
995 W 4th St G114
Benson AZ 85602

Call Sign: KB7PZM
Alan P Sloan Sr
238 W 5th
Benson AZ 85602

Call Sign: KB7TLC
Janine F Sloan
238 W 5th St
Benson AZ 85602

Call Sign: KD7CGQ
Thomas J Gacek

3101 W Cactus View Ln
Benson AZ 85602

Call Sign: KG7WN
Mary S Fournie
3145 W Citrus Rd
Benson AZ 85602

Call Sign: N7WBR
David L Fournie
3145 W Citrus Rd
Benson AZ 85602

Call Sign: N0WPC
Wayne E Perales
1111 W Jennella Dr
Benson AZ 85602

Call Sign: W7QQQ
Harold J Meadows
1396 W Sheep Wash Way
Benson AZ 85602

Call Sign: KC7CJX
Richard E Wilcox
3263 W Thunderbird Trl
Benson AZ 85602

Call Sign: W5ULL
Alexander P Mozden
550 W Union 16
Benson AZ 856026723

Call Sign: KJ7KR
James G Onifer
3158 W Verde Ave
Benson AZ 85602

Call Sign: W6LHL
James R Hostetter
3036 Williams Rd
Benson AZ 85602

Call Sign: N7ADP
David W Naas
Benson AZ 85602

Call Sign: KB7PZK
Donald C Nutt

Benson AZ 85602

Call Sign: KA7SPQ
Everett Cox
Benson AZ 85602

Call Sign: KA7PCI
James S Coston
Benson AZ 85602

Call Sign: K6RUX
Jay W Bemis Jr
Benson AZ 85602

Call Sign: W7HRB
Paul M Dickey Jr
Benson AZ 85602

Call Sign: N7UGM
Robert E Smith
Benson AZ 85602

Call Sign: K7SPV
San Pedro Valley ARC
Benson AZ 85602

Call Sign: W6CSM
Bual J Mead
Benson AZ 85602

Call Sign: W7LJY
Lowell P Gessert
Benson AZ 85602

Call Sign: N7HBG
Jack S Mc Quown
Benson AZ 85602

Call Sign: KB7TBI
Earl R Soth
Benson AZ 85602

Call Sign: KA3RKK
Allen T Reed
Benson AZ 85602

Call Sign: KC7DFF
Betty L White Eagle
Benson AZ 85602

Call Sign: N0HNC
Gary L Hunsaker
Benson AZ 85602

Call Sign: K7VVC
Harold G Sample
Benson AZ 85602

Call Sign: W7LDI
John E Schrengohst
Benson AZ 85602

Call Sign: KE7PUA
Max J Kartchner
Benson AZ 85602

Call Sign: K7MJK
Max J Kartchner
Benson AZ 85602

Call Sign: K7BMW
Paul Moreau
Benson AZ 85602

Call Sign: KF7QKH
Richard S De Shazo
Benson AZ 85602

Call Sign: N7ZBE
Thomas C Holbert Sr
Benson AZ 85602

Call Sign: K6UQ
Veteran Emerg Comm
Support Group
Benson AZ 85602

Call Sign: W6OZ
Palisades Emerg Ar Assn
Benson AZ 85602

Call Sign: KB7SMQ
Phyllis A Douglass
Benson AZ 856020483

Call Sign: KC7GEY
Mary L Hattala
Benson AZ 856020668

Call Sign: N7WJ
Winstan J Hattala
Benson AZ 856020668

**FCC Amateur Radio
Licenses in Bisbee**

Call Sign: KC7DWA
Sidney C Kelly
Arizona St
Bisbee AZ 85603

Call Sign: KE5DJ
Ransom W Burke
208 Arizona St
Bisbee AZ 85603

Call Sign: KC7NZH
Reece P Terrell
28 Black Knob View
Bisbee AZ 85603

Call Sign: KC7SZX
Leah J Terrell
28 Black Knob View
Bisbee AZ 85603

Call Sign: KC7SZY
Nathan J Terrell
28 Black Knob View
Bisbee AZ 85603

Call Sign: KC7TBP
Renee L Terrell
28 Black Knob View
Bisbee AZ 85603

Call Sign: KB7CWQ
Jamie L Terrell
28 Black Knob View
Bisbee AZ 856031902

Call Sign: KB7CYJ
Peter D Terrell
28 Black Knob View
Bisbee AZ 856031902

Call Sign: KB7ICH

James C Walker
625 Border Rd
Bisbee AZ 85603

Call Sign: K7LP
Lee T Propeck
306 Campbell St
Bisbee AZ 85603

Call Sign: KI7NW
Charles D Turner
315 Center Ave
Bisbee AZ 85603

Call Sign: KC7NXZ
Gay Turner
315 Center Ave
Bisbee AZ 85603

Call Sign: KE7YPD
Vincent W Creviston
9 Cochise Ln
Bisbee AZ 85603

Call Sign: W6NSC
Harold A Davis
77 Czar Ave
Bisbee AZ 85603

Call Sign: KE7LIY
Robert L Kappler
1487 Franklin St
Bisbee AZ 85603

Call Sign: K7NYR
Roger M Parnell
247 Hwy 80
Bisbee AZ 85603

Call Sign: KD7AYP
Russell J Anderson
4432 Hwy 80
Bisbee AZ 85603

Call Sign: KF7EWB
Timothy C Zimmerman
1415 Melody Ln D
Bisbee AZ 85603

Call Sign: KC7NYC
Earl D Power
101 N Lupine Rd
Bisbee AZ 85603

Call Sign: K3CIA
Wayne Badger
400 O Hara Ave
Bisbee AZ 85603

Call Sign: KC7RJS
David L Bixler
2174 S Bower St
Bisbee AZ 85603

Call Sign: KE7LIZ
Roy E Eaton
2142 S Kentucky St
Bisbee AZ 85603

Call Sign: KF7TXD
Kathleen J Hodges
3362 S Mesquite Ridge
Bisbee AZ 85603

Call Sign: KF7TXE
William R Hodges
3362 S Mesquite Ridge
Bisbee AZ 85603

Call Sign: KC7IQN
Richard W Hinckley
2136 S Naco Hwy
Bisbee AZ 85603

Call Sign: KB7TKZ
John W Sanders
103 San Jose Dr
Bisbee AZ 85603

Call Sign: KB7FYU
Douglas A Henry
125 San Jose Dr
Bisbee AZ 856033009

Call Sign: KA7TNW
Anthony J Finch
67 Spray Ave
Bisbee AZ 85603

Call Sign: KG7QM
William A Mc Nab
Bisbee AZ 85603

Call Sign: KE6UEC
Anthony S Rogers
Bisbee AZ 85603

Call Sign: WA7HL
Brendan J Wahl
Bisbee AZ 85603

Call Sign: KC7GLE
David A Mc Mullen
Bisbee AZ 85603

Call Sign: KD7TDM
Frederick M Brown
Bisbee AZ 85603

Call Sign: K7LGN
Frederick M Brown
Bisbee AZ 85603

Call Sign: KF7DYT
Gerald L Asher
Bisbee AZ 85603

Call Sign: KB7WOW
James D Clarkson
Bisbee AZ 85603

Call Sign: K7WOW
James D Clarkson Dr
Bisbee AZ 85603

Call Sign: AA1DH
John K Rimer
Bisbee AZ 85603

Call Sign: N6NTG
Kenneth B Oxx
Bisbee AZ 85603

Call Sign: KE6AHM
Lisa Kulp
Bisbee AZ 85603

Call Sign: KC7DGZ
Milo W Prince
Bisbee AZ 85603

Call Sign: KB7TEQ
Robert L Andrews
Bisbee AZ 85603

Call Sign: KF7OHJ
Steven S Mincher
Bisbee AZ 85603

Call Sign: KC5RKE
Vincent M Robel III
Bisbee AZ 85603

Call Sign: K6OFQ
Gilbert Warrenton Jr
Bisbee AZ 856035348

FCC Amateur Radio Licenses in Blue

Call Sign: K0MXC
Sam A Luce
Blue River
Blue AZ 85922

Call Sign: KD7VR
Elizabeth J Youse
Blue AZ 85922

Call Sign: N7GGE
James R Youse
Blue AZ 85922

Call Sign: N7CVM
Jon L Zimmerman
Blue AZ 85922

Call Sign: N7CDX
Matthew A Luce
Blue AZ 85922

FCC Amateur Radio Licenses in Blue Gap

Call Sign: KE7WUS
Louis St Germaine

Blue Gap AZ 86520

FCC Amateur Radio Licenses in Bouse

Call Sign: W9HAP
Donald I Mendenhall
25461 4 Wheel Dr
Bouse AZ 85325

Call Sign: WA7ONU
Duane A Verley
28080 Frame Ave
Bouse AZ 85325

Call Sign: KJ7OP
Robert L Roripaugh
44178 Palo Verde St
Bouse AZ 853250805

Call Sign: N7TMQ
Emory J Sandberg II
25293 Pendelton Way 6
Bouse AZ 85325

Call Sign: WB6EBB
Adam J Draugelis
Bouse AZ 85325

Call Sign: KA4NWB
Fred G Robertson
Bouse AZ 85325

Call Sign: KC7JGX
Amos H Burgess
Bouse AZ 85325

Call Sign: KF7CUV
David K Locke
Bouse AZ 85325

Call Sign: K7DKL
David K Locke
Bouse AZ 85325

Call Sign: W7KSF
Gordon R Kloster
Bouse AZ 85325

Call Sign: KD7AWO
Joyce A Helt
Bouse AZ 85325

Call Sign: WB7BTQ
Margaret E Kloster
Bouse AZ 85325

Call Sign: AB7ZG
Phylos E Lame
Bouse AZ 85325

Call Sign: KD7ART
Lois A Bonney
Bouse AZ 853250218

Call Sign: KD7AXU
Mepet M Bonney Clay
Bouse AZ 853250366

Call Sign: KC7JGY
William C Ashley
Bouse AZ 853250480

Call Sign: KE7BLX
David R Holm
Bouse AZ 853250660

Call Sign: N7DRH
David R Holm
Bouse AZ 853250660

FCC Amateur Radio Licenses in Bowie

Call Sign: KE5MF
David S Cole
Bowie AZ 85605

FCC Amateur Radio Licenses in Cactus Forest

Call Sign: WA2SJI
Anthony J La Joie
24400 E Cholla Rd
Cactus Forest AZ 85232

FCC Amateur Radio Licenses in Casa Grande

Call Sign: WA7YHO
Bruce C Smith
11 Mile Corner
Casa Grande AZ 85222

Call Sign: KD7RQA
John H Kainrath
1255 Avenida Isabella
Casa Grande AZ 85222

Call Sign: K7JHK
John H Kainrath
1255 Avenida Isabella
Casa Grande AZ 85222

Call Sign: W7GPQ
Charles W Staats
1132 E 12th St
Casa Grande AZ 85222

Call Sign: KB1DDI
Jerome J Erickson
1434 E Avenida Grande
Casa Grande AZ 85222

Call Sign: N7JAY
John E Wooten
1261 E Avenida Isabella
Casa Grande AZ 85222

Call Sign: W7GVT
Eugene H Falkner
1274 E Barcelona
Casa Grande AZ 85222

Call Sign: KD6HPT
Jerome S Ward
509 E Barrus Pl
Casa Grande AZ 85222

Call Sign: KD7GMK
Luis E Martinez
515 E Barrus Pl
Casa Grande AZ 85222

Call Sign: WD9HJP
John H Schroeder
1840 E Birch St

Casa Grande AZ 85122

Call Sign: KA7AMZ
Dennis C Johnson
1844 E Birch St
Casa Grande AZ 85222

Call Sign: WA2AAS
Lawrence B Lang
1747 E Bishop Pl
Casa Grande AZ 852222810

Call Sign: W8OES
Joshua A Harville
1140 E Bisnaga St
Casa Grande AZ 85122

Call Sign: KF7GUR
Richard L Dickson
1759 E Catalina St
Casa Grande az 85122

Call Sign: KA0ZHR
Ronald L Stroud
1620 E Clover St
Casa Grande AZ 851226083

Call Sign: N7IKS
Paul T Harrenstein
1191 E Cordova
Casa Grande AZ 85222

Call Sign: KF7MYE
Frankie L Hanna
1619 E Daisy St
Casa Grande AZ 85122

Call Sign: KF7HVW
Herbert J Boleyn
120 E Date Ave Apt 2
Casa Grande AZ 85222

Call Sign: KI6EWE
Donn W Holman
1207 E Delano Dr
Casa Grande AZ 85122

Call Sign: KI6FEH
Jeanette S Holman

1207 E Delano Dr
Casa Grande AZ 85122

Call Sign: W5CB
Raul M Martinez
1594 E Desert Breeze Dr
Casa Grande AZ 85222

Call Sign: KG2LF
Glenn T Cline
430 E Duke Dr
Casa Grande AZ 852221511

Call Sign: WA7QCX
Karen I Hall
513 E Florence Blvd
Casa Grande AZ 85222

Call Sign: WA7QCW
Leo Hall
513 E Florence Blvd
Casa Grande AZ 85222

Call Sign: KC7QKV
Dennis E Dillon
1377 E Florence Blvd Ste
147 Box 311
Casa Grande AZ 852225357

Call Sign: KE6GHS
Gary L Croll
1640 E Gardenia St
Casa Grande AZ 85222

Call Sign: KE6LCO
Gary W Croll
1640 E Gardenia St
Casa Grande AZ 85222

Call Sign: KE6RTT
Vickie L Croll
1640 E Gardenia St
Casa Grande AZ 85222

Call Sign: WD4KZI
Walter D Bradshaw
1639 E Jasmine St
Casa Grande AZ 85222

Call Sign: N7YAK
Walter D Bradshaw
1639 E Jasmine St
Casa Grande AZ 85222

Call Sign: AD7QS
Theodore J Donahue
1875 E Kachina Dr
Casa Grande AZ 851226449

Call Sign: N8XCF
Theodore J Donahue
1875 E Kachina Dr
Casa Grande AZ 852226449

Call Sign: KC7CF
William L Showers
1527 E Laurel Dr
Casa Grande AZ 85222

Call Sign: KE7ETM
Jack J Brashier
540 E Manor
Casa Grande AZ 85222

Call Sign: KA8FWL
Gerald G Bush
1385 E Martha Dr
Casa Grande AZ 85122

Call Sign: KC7SLQ
Dean W Davis
1204 E McMurray Blvd
Casa Grande AZ 85222

Call Sign: KF7SLN
Ranjit Sood
1260 E McMurray Blvd
Casa Grande AZ 85122

Call Sign: KD7RON
Ron A Pickell
1656 E Melissa St
Casa Grande AZ 85222

Call Sign: KD7FSK
Yvonne L Pickell
1656 E Melissa St
Casa Grande AZ 85222

Call Sign: KG7VON
Yvonne L Pickell
1656 E Melissa St
Casa Grande AZ 85222

Call Sign: WA7WA
James S Mays Jr
1569 E Melrose Dr
Casa Grande AZ 85122

Call Sign: WA7FQJ
Eugene L Evanoff
331 E Orange Dr
Casa Grande AZ 85222

Call Sign: W7GFK
George F Kick
216 E Pebble Ct
Casa Grande AZ 852226233

Call Sign: W7SLK
Susan L Kick
216 E Pebble Ct
Casa Grande AZ 852226233

Call Sign: WB0SHD
Mark L Chalcraft
668 E Rancho Viejo Loop
Casa Grande AZ 85222

Call Sign: WA9BOP
Kenneth D Krueger
700 E Rodeo Rd 173
Casa Grande AZ 85222

Call Sign: AB7UL
Orville R Williams
155 E Rodeo Rd 81
Casa Grande AZ 85222

Call Sign: WA0ROU
Glen E Chase
155 E Rodeo Rd Lot 15
Casa Grande AZ 85222

Call Sign: KC7MG
Alex G Weimer
1886 E Sandalwood Loop

Casa Grande AZ 85222

Call Sign: KA7PUO
Irmgard M Weimer
1886 E Sandalwood Loop
Casa Grande AZ 85222

Call Sign: KB9QY
William D May
2637 E Santa Maria Dr
Casa Grande AZ 851943833

Call Sign: WB7RJR
Raymon W Giles
1736 E Shasta St
Casa Grande AZ 85222

Call Sign: KB5HHT
James M Carter Jr
836 E Stonewood Dr
Casa Grande AZ 852221757

Call Sign: KB9BHA
Donald F Mc Mahon
1083 E Sunscape Way
Casa Grande AZ 85222

Call Sign: KB0USO
Charles E Pennington
1083 E Sunscape Way 11
Casa Grande AZ 85222

Call Sign: KA3RIC
Herbert J Bloxsom
1083 E Sunscape Way 273
Casa Grande AZ 85222

Call Sign: KA7WTY
Melvin Glaze
1083 E Sunscape Way Lot
408
Casa Grande AZ 85194

Call Sign: KC7TRF
Jared A Morton
1253 E Sunset Dr
Casa Grande AZ 85222

Call Sign: K7TPN

Richard W Phelps
1259 E Sunset Dr
Casa Grande AZ 85222

Call Sign: WB7TNW
Ann Dee K Graham
1288 E Sunset Dr
Casa Grande AZ 85222

Call Sign: WB0TOH
Duane E Roepke
1825 E Sycamore Rd
Casa Grande AZ 85222

Call Sign: KC7ZDQ
Christopher J Losey
1137 E Trinity Pl
Casa Grande AZ 85222

Call Sign: KC7OYQ
Tanya A Clevenger
10249 N Battle Ford
Casa Grande AZ 85222

Call Sign: K7GPD
Mark J Hill Sr
10091 N Battleford Dr
Casa Grande AZ 85122

Call Sign: KD7NAP
Lynette M Clevenger
10249 N Battleford Dr
Casa Grande AZ 85222

Call Sign: KJ7YM
Larry C Miller
10249 N Battleford Dr
Casa Grande AZ 85222

Call Sign: KE0DB
Donald P Adamavich
8256 N Belair Rd
Casa Grande AZ 85222

Call Sign: KF7FSK
Clayton E Freed
1833 N Briarcliff Rd
Casa Grande AZ 85122

Call Sign: KE7FZV
Jeffrey K Chervenka
10904 N Faldale Rd
Casa Grande AZ 85222

Call Sign: NR7Q
Jeffrey K Chervenka
10904 N Faldale Rd
Casa Grande AZ 85222

Call Sign: KE7LRT
Sherrlyn Seward
10904 N Faldale Rd
Casa Grande AZ 85222

Call Sign: N9QEB
Randy D Pifer
3654 N French Pl
Casa Grande AZ 85222

Call Sign: KC7WBC
Robert E Cecil
5757 N Fuchsia St
Casa Grande AZ 85222

Call Sign: KF7QFL
Robert L Andrae Jr
10533 N Geronimo Dr
Casa Grande AZ 85222

Call Sign: W7TPG
Chris W Steward
1110 N Henness Rd 368
Casa Grande AZ 85122

Call Sign: KC7MG
Alex G Weimer
1110 N Henness Rd 593
Casa Grande AZ 85222

Call Sign: W7AGW
Alex G Weimer
1110 N Henness Rd 593
Casa Grande AZ 85222

Call Sign: KE7PB
Herbert H Rode
1110 N Henness Rd Lot 1315
Casa Grande AZ 85122

Call Sign: N7BON
Bonnie L Rode
1110 N Henness Rd Lot 712
Casa Grande AZ 85222

Call Sign: N8FLJ
Gary J Sole
1785 N Hester Trl
Casa Grande AZ 85122

Call Sign: NI7O
William O Wright
10529 N Hillside Dr
Casa Grande AZ 85122

Call Sign: AC7FM
William O Wright
10529 N Hillside Dt
Casa Grande AZ 85222

Call Sign: KG6HPE
Ronald N Horton
88 N Nueva Ln
Casa Grande AZ 85222

Call Sign: KE7OHM
John M Hill
2022 N Parish Ln
Casa Grande AZ 85222

Call Sign: W7OVE
Frank T Winter
1497 N Poppy St
Casa Grande AZ 85222

Call Sign: N7UF
Frank T Winter
1497 N Poppy St
Casa Grande AZ 85222

Call Sign: KB7MOJ
Jack M Ovitt
1830 N Princeton Ave
Casa Grande AZ 85222

Call Sign: N9ZLL
Nathan A Nixon
2123 N Santiana Pl

Casa Grande AZ 85222

Call Sign: KC7PLU
Christopher J Shoemaker
9740 N Scott Dr
Casa Grande AZ 85222

Call Sign: KC7TZE
Ralph I Hamilton
2054 N Thornton Rd 102
Casa Grande AZ 85222

Call Sign: N7QMR
Donald W Smart
2228 S Calle Maria Juana
Casa Grande AZ 85222

Call Sign: KC7JGF
Steve D Robinette
1390 S Ethington Rd
Casa Grande AZ 85222

Call Sign: KF7BRQ
James E Johnson III
10556 S Hahn St
Casa Grande AZ 85293

Call Sign: K0DWZ
Fred M Betz Jr
1800 S Indiana Dr
Casa Grande AZ 85222

Call Sign: KC6WTL
Robert N Johnson Jr
7879 S Lamb Rd
Casa Grande AZ 85293

Call Sign: W9GQE
Charles F Kaiser
6938 S Lehr Rd
Casa Grande AZ 85293

Call Sign: KD7LMD
Michael D Craig
4547 S Mammoth Dr
Casa Grande AZ 85222

Call Sign: KD7ZBA
David D Gladden

73 S Overfield Rd
Casa Grande AZ 85222

Call Sign: K4KJT
Donald L Barnes
1734 S Pecos Dr
Casa Grande AZ 85222

Call Sign: KD7DZJ
Gerald L Mc Connell
1781 S Pecos Dr
Casa Grande AZ 85222

Call Sign: W0PHT
Gerald L Mc Connell
1781 S Pecos Dr
Casa Grande AZ 85222

Call Sign: W5TEJ
Taylor E Jones
7136 S Sunland Gin Rd
Casa Grande AZ 85222

Call Sign: N7TAY
Taylor E Jones
7136 S Sunland Gin Rd
Casa Grande AZ 85222

Call Sign: KC7OBK
Laura A Conaway
4028 S Whispering Sands Dr
Casa Grande AZ 85193

Call Sign: KF7FND
Thomas Kallberg
2419 Sandstone Pl
Casa Grande AZ 85222

Call Sign: KH6EF
Richard P Richards
450 Sun West Dr 61
Casa Grande AZ 85222

Call Sign: KE6TNQ
Victoria L Rosenbaum
14632 W Belmont Dr
Casa Grande AZ 85222

Call Sign: K1VIK

Lee W Winsor
817 W Cholla St
Casa Grande AZ 85230

Call Sign: KD7MOJ
Jonathan B Rogers
25510 W Clayton Rd
Casa Grande AZ 85222

Call Sign: KD7NAO
Heather D Rogers
25510 W Clayton Rd
Casa Grande AZ 85222

Call Sign: KI7R
H David Akers
932 W Crooked Stick Dr
Casa Grande AZ 852226148

Call Sign: KF7FAM
Kenneth E Brown
1216 W Del Monte Dr
Casa Grande az 85122

Call Sign: W2EFK
Robert D Baer
962 W Diamond Rim Dr
Casa Grande AZ 85222

Call Sign: K1GKM
Richard A Klepadlo
15188 W Earley Rd
Casa Grande AZ 85222

Call Sign: WA2TLN
David R Towle
12398 W Greystone Dr
Casa Grande AZ 85230

Call Sign: KA6HWB
Foster I Woods Jr
15807 W Hopi Dr
Casa Grande AZ 85122

Call Sign: WB8EDF
Vernon M Bishop
18756 W Jacqueline Ave
Casa Grande AZ 852228978

Call Sign: N8UVV
Donald T Duffy
11449 W Martin Rd
Casa Grande AZ 85222

Call Sign: N8UVU
Nancy J Duffy
11449 W Martin Rd
Casa Grande AZ 85222

Call Sign: WB7CXE
Anthony F Eberle
11555 W Martin Rd
Casa Grande AZ 85222

Call Sign: W0NGH
Alfred B Covert
221 W Montego Dr
Casa Grande AZ 85222

Call Sign: NQ7R
Thomas L Kramer
10900 W Paradise Ln
Casa Grande AZ 85193

Call Sign: KA0TUA
Judith S Kramer
10900 W Paradise Ln
Casa Grande AZ 85193

Call Sign: K0VSV
Thomas L Kramer
10900 W Paradise Ln
Casa Grande AZ 85222

Call Sign: KC7OIS
John J Fisher
19701 W Peters Rd
Casa Grande AZ 85222

Call Sign: KC7OIT
Will R Fishers
19701 W Peters Rd
Casa Grande AZ 85222

Call Sign: KE7HMN
Manti O Galbraith
661 W Prickly Pear Dr
Casa Grande AZ 85222

Call Sign: KE6TBB
Teresa L Ly
579 W Racine Loop
Casa Grande AZ 85222

Call Sign: KF7VAH
Dale C Nelson
280 W Seven Seas Dr
Casa Grande AZ 85122

Call Sign: KB5IYI
Libby Long
280 W Seven Seas Dr
Casa Grande AZ 85122

Call Sign: KB9RGA
Debra S Xifaras
26346 W Sherbundy Dr
Casa Grande AZ 85222

Call Sign: NJ7U
Ronald A Ryno
19435 W Sweet Acacia Dr
Casa Grande AZ 85222

Call Sign: KJ7VF
David E C Fowler
W Val Vista Blvd
Casa Grande AZ 85222

Call Sign: KC0CKR
Gene V Snyder
16680 W Val Vista Blvd 44
Casa Grande AZ 85222

Call Sign: W7RMC
Gene V Snyder
16680 W Val Vista Blvd 44
Casa Grande AZ 85222

Call Sign: KE7CAL
Paul G Thomas
4905 W Warren Dr
Casa Grande AZ 85222

Call Sign: K7PGT
Paul G Thomas
4905 W Warren Dr

Casa Grande AZ 85294

Call Sign: KB7TZF
Brian W Doughty
Casa Grande AZ 85230

Call Sign: KC6UWH
David M Hansen
Casa Grande AZ 85130

Call Sign: WA8ZUE
Frank J Travick
Casa Grande AZ 852300238

Call Sign: KD6HEI
Cathren A Hansen
Casa Grande AZ 852301265

FCC Amateur Radio Licenses in Catalina

Call Sign: KC7QMJ
Josh D Slaughter
3840 E Hawser St
Catalina AZ 85739

Call Sign: KI7ZZ
Donald A Hastings
4341 E Pinal St
Catalina AZ 85739

Call Sign: KA9QCF
Robert A Welch
3540 E Thornberry Ln
Catalina AZ 857380987

Call Sign: KD7NTC
Chris A Pedersen
4105 E Trotter Pl
Catalina AZ 85739

Call Sign: K0DMH
David M Hamilton
4240 E White Hill Way
Catalina AZ 857399293

Call Sign: KC7TEY
Nicholas F Thill
16510 N Elkins

Catalina AZ 85739

Call Sign: KK7XR
Charles E Cavanaugh
Catalina AZ 85738

Call Sign: KB9CQ
Ralph E Smith Jr
Catalina AZ 85738

FCC Amateur Radio Licenses in Central

Call Sign: KA7CLD
Glade M Smith
4738 W Central Rd Box 200
Central AZ 85531

Call Sign: KC7LYU
Bradley R Smith
Central AZ 85531

Call Sign: KC7JKW
Carmen R Smith
Central AZ 85531

Call Sign: KE7WRR
Joel R Layton
Central AZ 85531

Call Sign: KE7YUD
Justin R Layton
Central AZ 85531

Call Sign: KC7YDC
Karen R Whitmer
Central AZ 85531

Call Sign: KC7UDK
Lon A Whitmer
Central AZ 85531

Call Sign: K7LON
Lon A Whitmer
Central AZ 85531

Call Sign: KC7JKX
Talana S Hooper
Central AZ 85531

Call Sign: KD7EZJ
Corwin L Whitmer
Central AZ 85531

FCC Amateur Radio Licenses in Chinle

Call Sign: KA7MMF
Richard T Bowers
Chief Manuelito Blvd Cvs
Trailer 24
Chinle AZ 86503

Call Sign: KC7VML
Eric A Mitchell
Chinle AZ 86503

Call Sign: KC7WBZ
Micah S Young
Chinle AZ 86503

Call Sign: KC7WVL
Paul V Goodluck
Chinle AZ 86503

Call Sign: KD7ARM
Robert Toney
Chinle AZ 86503

FCC Amateur Radio Licenses in Cibola

Call Sign: KX7LDS
Wilma G Matlock
Box 102
Cibola AZ 85328

Call Sign: KD7SPN
Desert Waves ARC
Box 102
Cibola AZ 85328

Call Sign: KR7AZ
Desert Waves ARC
Box 102
Cibola AZ 85328

Call Sign: K7WM

Micheal W Matlock
Box 102
Cibola AZ 85328

Call Sign: KD6NOA
Mike W Matlock
Box 102
Cibola AZ 85328

Call Sign: KF7UVK
Matt P Farrar
Box 139
Cibola AZ 85328

Call Sign: KE7TRA
Bernard E Gaskill
Box 164
Cibola AZ 85328

FCC Amateur Radio Licenses in Clay Springs

Call Sign: WD8MHM
Dale L Kalchert
5612 Desert Breeze Rd
Clay Springs AZ 85923

Call Sign: N7DEE
Dale M White
5612 Desert Breeze Rd
Clay Springs AZ 85923

Call Sign: KE7LAI
Kenneth C Davis
Clay Springs AZ 85923

Call Sign: W7PRP
Paul R Potts
Clay Springs AZ 85923

Call Sign: KE7LAK
David B Hancock
Clay Springs AZ 85923

Call Sign: KE7YSO
Hubert B Brewer
Clay Springs AZ 85923

Call Sign: KE7LAL

Patricia A Hancock
Clay Springs AZ 85923

Call Sign: KE7LAM
Raymond D Brewer
Clay Springs AZ 85923

Call Sign: KE7LAJ
William D Bigler
Clay Springs AZ 85923

FCC Amateur Radio Licenses in Claypool

Call Sign: N7HHT
Charles W Terry
Claypool AZ 85532

Call Sign: KB7STL
Kenneth L Van Drome Sr
Claypool AZ 85532

Call Sign: KC7SBC
Sue A Edmiston
Claypool AZ 85532

Call Sign: K7UMU
Clyde L Richardson
Claypool AZ 85532

Call Sign: WA7HUH
Charles V Dodd
Claypool AZ 85532

Call Sign: KK7AR
Jim L Edmiston
Claypool AZ 85532

Call Sign: KA7DJI
Rosa L Dodd
Claypool AZ 85532

FCC Amateur Radio Licenses in Clifton

Call Sign: WB7EWK
Ethel L Ruzila
Box 289 Bobcat Dr
Clifton AZ 85533

Call Sign: KB7FQG
Harry Ruzila
Box 289 Bobcat Dr
Clifton AZ 85533

Call Sign: K5TYU
Louis Lehner Jr
Box 473 Calle Del Rio Lot
71
Clifton AZ 85533

Call Sign: KW7A
Robert G Powell
Box 474
Clifton AZ 85530

Call Sign: WB7UDP
Buryl F Short
256 N Calle Del Sol
Clifton AZ 85533

Call Sign: KD7JXA
Troy M Wyatt
149 Terrace Ln
Clifton AZ 85533

Call Sign: KB7AGW
Elden L Winkle
Clifton AZ 85533

Call Sign: KC0CJD
Daniel R Alvarez
Clifton AZ 855331612

FCC Amateur Radio Licenses in Cochise

Call Sign: KF7XU
James I Everett
46A
Cochise AZ 85606

Call Sign: W7HSR
Chester G Newman
Box 44A
Cochise AZ 85606

Call Sign: W7LBY

Raymond C Craig
Box 617 Arabian Ln
Cochise AZ 85606

Call Sign: KC7UDJ
Frank G Longo
Box 674 B
Cochise AZ 85606

Call Sign: W6VUE
Edgar L Esterwold
Box 747
Cochise AZ 85606

Call Sign: KC8FIV
Jason S Wallace
222 E Richland Way
Cochise AZ 85606

Call Sign: KB7RWV
Donald L Bezek
512 E Van Ness St
Cochise AZ 85606

Call Sign: K7GMF
Tom Lopez
683 E Van Ness St
Cochise AZ 85606

Call Sign: N7KCX
Thomas W Rice
878 W Eslick Ranch Rd
Cochise AZ 856068779

Call Sign: NO7T
Thomas W Rice
878 W Eslick Ranch Rd
Cochise AZ 856068779

FCC Amateur Radio Licenses in Concho

Call Sign: KC7KGH
Gene Reamer
Box 197
Concho AZ 85924

Call Sign: KB7QFJ
Anna S Keezer

Box 26
Concho AZ 85924

Call Sign: K3HHP
Charles E Bell Jr
Box 3008
Concho AZ 859248506

Call Sign: N7CTB
Jo Anne Brown
Box 3008
Concho AZ 85924

Call Sign: KA7FNW
Dennis B Pogue
Box 3231
Concho AZ 85924

Call Sign: KD7AHZ
Margaret F Pogue
Box 3231
Concho AZ 85924

Call Sign: W7GXH
Allen D Johnson
Box 34005
Concho AZ 859248515

Call Sign: KB7QBN
James D Johnston
Box 3467
Concho AZ 85924

Call Sign: KD7NCD
John D Fuhrmann
Box 527035
Concho AZ 859248512

Call Sign: N7SJL
James I Mc Kinnon Jr
Box 784
Concho AZ 85924

Call Sign: KC7MWP
Edward A Cifelli
36668 Hwy 61
Concho AZ 859240537

Call Sign: KD7ZWN

Crosson P Clevenger
Concho AZ 85924

Call Sign: W8DLC
Daymon L Campbell
Concho AZ 85924

Call Sign: W7FKP
Edward G Duggan
Concho AZ 85924

Call Sign: KI4ZLM
Ella P Campbell
Concho AZ 85924

Call Sign: KF7RQU
Lionel W Mcmaken
Concho AZ 85924

Call Sign: KE7AZU
Sandra M Cifelli
Concho AZ 85924

Call Sign: N1FW
Franklin L Woodward
Concho AZ 859240094

Call Sign: WA6KJN
Sheldon L Barrett
Concho AZ 859240662

Call Sign: KB0ZBX
David H Mc Clellan Sr
Concho AZ 859240741

FCC Amateur Radio Licenses in Coolidge

Call Sign: K0GNZ
Clayton L Hill
1925 Arizona Blvd Sp 119
Coolidge AZ 85228

Call Sign: K7VAV
Henry S Wang
377 Byrd Ave
Coolidge AZ 85228

Call Sign: KB7ISC

Jeffrey J Herrold
3665 E Coolidge Ave
Coolidge AZ 85128

Call Sign: N7ECZ
John A Palmer Jr
3422 E Randolph Rd
Coolidge AZ 85228

Call Sign: KC7KF
John T O Brien
413 N Macrae Rd
Coolidge AZ 85128

Call Sign: N7DAI
Luther H Light
11211 N Macrae Rd
Coolidge AZ 85228

Call Sign: WB7SZE
Donna M O Brien
11317 N Macrae Rd
Coolidge AZ 85228

Call Sign: KC7KBK
Timothy T Ovitt
601 N Main St
Coolidge AZ 85228

Call Sign: N1RLT
Hank F Collins
1012 N Navajo Ln
Coolidge AZ 85228

Call Sign: KC7DUA
Janel M Barnett
1161 N Palo Verde Ln
Coolidge AZ 85228

Call Sign: K0WHF
Robert L Miers
1175 N Palo Verde Ln
Coolidge AZ 85228

Call Sign: KB7RFG
Billie E Baldridge
3569 N Wheeler Rd
Coolidge AZ 85228

Call Sign: KC7HIE
Chris J Smith
739 Padre Kino Dr
Coolidge AZ 85228

Call Sign: N7ZCI
Kathleen A Smith
739 Padre Kino Dr
Coolidge AZ 85228

Call Sign: KC7HIF
Ryan T Smith
739 Padre Kino Dr
Coolidge AZ 85228

Call Sign: KC7KMM
Tony A Starns
616 Palo Verde Ave
Coolidge AZ 85228

Call Sign: KF7BBV
Larry B Espinoza
191 S 17th St
Coolidge AZ 85228

Call Sign: N7XSN
James A Munzer
781 S 1st St
Coolidge AZ 85228

Call Sign: AB3B
Edward B Leviton
1501 S 7th St
Coolidge AZ 852284148

Call Sign: KC5ACM
Lora E Charvoz
501 S Arnold Way
Coolidge AZ 85228

Call Sign: WA7KEG
Nathan C Charvoz
501 S Arnold Way
Coolidge AZ 85228

Call Sign: AD7RO
Bryce A Denker
182 S Chapman Rd
Coolidge AZ 85228

Call Sign: AB7HN
Gene E Lee
556 Spruell Ave
Coolidge AZ 851285911

Call Sign: KE7OQD
Kevin B Todd
2125 W Broadway Ave
Coolidge AZ 85228

Call Sign: KC7RLY
Thomas A Palmer
610 W Central
Coolidge AZ 85228

Call Sign: K7HYW
Melvin L Harrison
743 W Central
Coolidge AZ 85228

Call Sign: WA7HJN
Melvin L Harrison
743 W Central
Coolidge AZ 85228

Call Sign: W0TXJ
Sumner D Rasmussen
783 W Central Ave
Coolidge AZ 85228

Call Sign: N7EBA
Ardyce M Shaw
830 W Dewey
Coolidge AZ 85228

Call Sign: AD7KM
Lloyd Shaw
830 W Dewey
Coolidge AZ 85228

Call Sign: KE5RAT
John D Dorsey
707 W Gibson Ave
Coolidge AZ 85128

Call Sign: WA7OIO
Jerry W Luttrell
253 W Lindbergh Ave

Coolidge AZ 85228

Call Sign: KB7LSN
Allen W Harrison
921 W Martin Rd
Coolidge AZ 85128

Call Sign: KB7OAI
Alan S Carpenter
316 W Northern
Coolidge AZ 85228

Call Sign: KB7PUD
Crystal K Carpenter
316 W Northern
Coolidge AZ 85228

Call Sign: KD7IKT
Allen S Holden
1205 W Northern
Coolidge AZ 85228

Call Sign: KF7KOQ
Jacob A Carpenter
316 W Northern Ave
Coolidge AZ 85128

Call Sign: KF7NJG
Wyatt L Carpenter
316 W Northern Ave
Coolidge az 85128

Call Sign: KC7FJS
Christopher H Marley
747 W Padre Kino Dr
Coolidge AZ 85228

Call Sign: N7XVC
Melvin A Helmick
429 W Pima
Coolidge AZ 85228

Call Sign: KC7WEY
Dennis T Gillespie
865 W Pima
Coolidge AZ 85228

Call Sign: N7QVM
Julius A Rogers

865 W Pinkley
Coolidge AZ 85228

Call Sign: WB0FGK
John H Freels
675 W Pinkley Ave
Coolidge AZ 85228

Call Sign: KB7LXL
Auvie R Lee
556 W Spruell Ave
Coolidge AZ 85128

Call Sign: KE7GRK
George H Kinnison
612 W Verde Ln
Coolidge AZ 85228

Call Sign: W0AYE
Robert M Schumacher
543 Whitlow Cir
Coolidge AZ 852285017

Call Sign: KC7YSL
Gloria A Schumacher
543 Whitlow Cr
Coolidge AZ 85228

Call Sign: WB7SAE
Dennis W Cox
Coolidge AZ 85228

Call Sign: KB7OOY
Garth D Goodrich
Coolidge AZ 85228

Call Sign: N6GV
Thomas L Dixon
Coolidge AZ 85128

Call Sign: WU7T
Cynthia B Varnay
Coolidge AZ 85228

Call Sign: KA2APP
Douglas J Kipphut
Coolidge AZ 85228

Call Sign: WA6FYV

Irvin M Ferguson
Coolidge AZ 85228

Call Sign: WA7OJR
Jack J Ovitt
Coolidge AZ 85228

Call Sign: KC7JRH
Scott J Henley
Coolidge AZ 85228

Call Sign: N7AQY
Dennis E Cox
Coolidge AZ 852281587

FCC Amateur Radio Licenses in Corona

Call Sign: KC7VBN
Peter L Keys
10420 E Observatory Dr
Corona AZ 85641

Call Sign: WA3TGC
Ben P Fisher Jr
281 S Atlanta Dr
Corona AZ 856412315

Call Sign: K3ITN
Walter D Voelker Jr
132 W Andrew Potter
Corona AZ 85641

Call Sign: KD7LUP
Timothy J Gugliotta
158 W William Carey St
Corona AZ 85641

FCC Amateur Radio Licenses in Corona De Tucson

Call Sign: N7YGW
Daniel M Jensen
619 E Macon Dr
Corona De Tucson AZ 85641

Call Sign: KF7OOO
Jerry Scrivano

10495 E Observatory Dr
Corona De Tucson AZ 85641

Call Sign: KB7OWF
Patricia L Finger
300 S Melpomene Way
Corona De Tucson AZ
856412312

Call Sign: W7ZT
Ronald J Finger
300 S Melpomene Way
Corona De Tucson AZ
856412312

Call Sign: KE7KRH
Wren A Keller
102 W William Carey St
Corona De Tucson AZ 85641

Call Sign: W0REN
Wren A Keller
102 W William Carey St
Corona De Tucson AZ 85641

FCC Amateur Radio Licenses in Cortaro

Call Sign: N9AHY
Charles E Warren
Cortaro AZ 85652

Call Sign: KD6CCM
Richard D Tompkins
Cortaro AZ 85652

Call Sign: N6PKT
Richard M Pierce
Cortaro AZ 85652

Call Sign: W5UAB
William J Ward Jr
Cortaro AZ 85652

Call Sign: AA7MY
Edward J Nicewander
Cortaro AZ 856521083

Call Sign: KC7MLP

Gail J Nicewander
Cortaro AZ 856521083

FCC Amateur Radio Licenses in Davis Monthan

Call Sign: KD4HAW
Michael B Breen
Talon Dr
Davis Monthan AFB AZ
85708

FCC Amateur Radio Licenses in Douglas

Call Sign: KB7PCQ
George De La Torre
1244 11th St
Douglas AZ 85607

Call Sign: KB7NEG
John C De La Torre
1244 11th St
Douglas AZ 85607

Call Sign: W7LBZ
Richard E Depweg
1651 12th St
Douglas AZ 85607

Call Sign: W0PKQ
George A Wangelin
2520 12th St
Douglas AZ 85607

Call Sign: KB7JMR
Manny R Teran
2525 13th St
Douglas AZ 85607

Call Sign: K7EFN
Stephen Y Tsuya
3010 13th St
Douglas AZ 85607

Call Sign: W7NDR
Tom C Millican
2201 15 St
Douglas AZ 85607

Call Sign: KA7ELM
Jesus C Moreno
634 15th St
Douglas AZ 85607

Call Sign: KA7TUG
Ruth C Millican
2201 15th St
Douglas AZ 85607

Call Sign: KD7SNY
Ivan Marquez
1041 16th St
Douglas AZ 85607

Call Sign: WB7WQH
David J Eiting
1262 19th St
Douglas AZ 85607

Call Sign: KC7NHY
Janet Lopez
1380 23rd St
Douglas AZ 85607

Call Sign: KC7EJZ
Julie Lopez
2302 6th St
Douglas AZ 85607

Call Sign: NS7G
Rodrigo Lopez
2302 6th St
Douglas AZ 85607

Call Sign: KE7FPP
Pablo R Duarte
2506 7th St
Douglas AZ 85607

Call Sign: KA7TUF
Nina K Thomasson
1554 8th St
Douglas AZ 85607

Call Sign: N7BEO
Richard L Thomasson
1554 8th St

Douglas AZ 85607

Call Sign: W7SMS
Albert W Bartel
1955 8th St Apt 5
Douglas AZ 85607

Call Sign: K6JQA
Robert A Easterbrooks
637 9th St
Douglas AZ 85607

Call Sign: K7DV
John L Kurdeka
2501 9th St
Douglas AZ 856072709

Call Sign: N7WWZ
Solmon J Rye Jr
1761 Baker Ave
Douglas AZ 85607

Call Sign: KG7QP
Gabor K Leidenfrost
Box 190
Douglas AZ 85607

Call Sign: KB5FNU
Glenn O Tutt
Box 58
Douglas AZ 85607

Call Sign: KC7EYR
James E Foppe
1501 Cochise Dr
Douglas AZ 85607

Call Sign: KC7UMY
Carl R Thornton
1900 E 13th St
Douglas AZ 85607

Call Sign: KF7HKY
Ernesto R Almada
2051 E 14th St
Douglas AZ 85607

Call Sign: KB7ZYA
Dee A Homer

1231 E 23rd St
Douglas AZ 85607

Call Sign: W7GED
Pete B Dillman
2600 E 7th St
Douglas AZ 85607

Call Sign: KE7DDP
John W Cryar
724 E Cordova St
Douglas AZ 85607

Call Sign: KE7DHG
Larry L Clough
2521 E Dahlia Dr
Douglas AZ 85607

Call Sign: KA0ERZ
Larry D Erland
1201 E Fairway Dr Ste 111
Douglas AZ 856075267

Call Sign: KB7JWS
Clayton L Douglas
1103 G Ave
Douglas AZ 85607

Call Sign: KD7YOY
Aaron M Mendle
3796 Northwestern Dr
Douglas AZ 85607

Call Sign: KC7ZND
Barbara A Heck
3796 Northwestern Dr
Douglas AZ 85607

Call Sign: KD7YOZ
Barbara A Heck
3796 Northwestern Dr
Douglas AZ 85607

Call Sign: KC7RLR
Warren D Griffin
4657 Paul Spur Rd
Douglas AZ 85607

Call Sign: W4AMM

Alberto M Melis
1733 Rogers Ave
Douglas AZ 85607

Call Sign: W7INN
Ellen R Dees
1537 San Antonio Dr
Douglas AZ 85607

Call Sign: W7DZG
Robert E Glasscock
1537 San Antonio Dr
Douglas AZ 85607

Call Sign: KD7NP
James D Luce
3505 W El Sol Dr
Douglas AZ 85607

Call Sign: N7UGN
Mary E Fogleman
3771 W Michigan State Dr
Douglas AZ 85607

Call Sign: KF7YT
Steven J Fogleman
3771 W Michigan State Dr
Douglas AZ 85607

Call Sign: W7JSL
Milan G Fogleman
3781 W Michigan State Dr
Douglas AZ 85607

Call Sign: KD7JUN
Rosalind A Fogleman
3781 W Michigan State Dr
Douglas AZ 85607

Call Sign: KB7WXH
Eloisa C Schwamm
Douglas AZ 85607

Call Sign: N7MAJ
Jack M Whidden
Douglas AZ 85607

Call Sign: N7DLY
Carlton R Mc Junkins

Douglas AZ 85608

Call Sign: W7NZB
Norman L Robb
Douglas AZ 85608

Call Sign: KB7ZQG
William H Kieckhefer
Douglas AZ 85608

Call Sign: WC7H
Ivan L Griswold
Douglas AZ 85608

FCC Amateur Radio Licenses in Dragoon

Call Sign: W6CGV
Robert E Erickson
1937 Lee
Dragoon AZ 85609

Call Sign: WA6WSI
William C Graham Jr
Dragoon AZ 85609

FCC Amateur Radio Licenses in Duncan

Call Sign: N7FAH
Constance R Griggs
Box 116
Duncan AZ 85534

Call Sign: KB7FCJ
Karen L Hamilton
Box 117
Duncan AZ 85534

Call Sign: KF7LIU
Anthony R Rodriguez
Box 172
Duncan AZ 85534

Call Sign: N7GP
Jacks Peak ARA Guthrie
Peak
Box 176
Duncan AZ 85534

Call Sign: KE7DVB
Milton B Jensen
Box 238
Duncan AZ 85534

Call Sign: KB7IVV
James Q Segraves Jr
Box 410
Duncan AZ 85534

Call Sign: N7NNH
Danny F Richins
Box 419
Duncan AZ 85534

Call Sign: N7UHD
Timothy E Bigelow
Box 423
Duncan AZ 85534

Call Sign: KF7SOO
Anna B Davis
422 La Canada Rd
Duncan AZ 85534

Call Sign: W7KQZ
Stephen C Ernst
355 Stevens Loop
Duncan AZ 85534

Call Sign: N7LNM
Bradley E Boyd
Duncan AZ 85534

Call Sign: KB7IWD
Donald C Smith
Duncan AZ 85534

Call Sign: W7VMN
Gerald L Crotts
Duncan AZ 85534

Call Sign: N7UHE
Joann M Boyd
Duncan AZ 85534

Call Sign: KB7EZD
John M Payne

Duncan AZ 85534

Call Sign: KB7HPD
Max J Rapier Jr
Duncan AZ 85534

Call Sign: K5ZIA
Zia Connection Repeaters
Duncan AZ 85534

Call Sign: K7KRL
Steeple Rock ARC
Duncan AZ 85534

Call Sign: KC5OCR
James A Reid
Duncan AZ 85534

Call Sign: N7UHF
Valadee W Crotts
Duncan AZ 85534

Call Sign: N7XEU
Richard O Billingsley
Duncan AZ 855340207

FCC Amateur Radio Licenses in Eagar

Call Sign: WA7FPO
Glen R Stewart
475 E 4th St
Eagar AZ 85925

Call Sign: W7KNA
Darval H Nelson
479 E 4th St
Eagar AZ 85925

Call Sign: N7XDO
James E Tieman
171 E 5th St
Eagar AZ 85925

Call Sign: KC7OYR
Micky L Tieman
171 E 5th St
Eagar AZ 85925

Call Sign: WA6SUS
Thomas H Price
777 N Main St
Eagar AZ 85925

Call Sign: WA0KZG
Bob J Marek
977 S Safari Dr
Eagar AZ 85925

Call Sign: W7ZK
Allan C Kruger
1316 S Skyline Dr
Eagar AZ 85925

Call Sign: KC7QMD
Olga E Kruger
1316 S Skyline Dr
Eagar AZ 85925

Call Sign: W4NHA
Andrew S Knox
1570 W 10th St
Eagar AZ 85925

Call Sign: WA4YGH
Claire W Knox
1570 W 10th St
Eagar AZ 85925

Call Sign: WA4YGE
Gary S Knox
1570 W 10th St
Eagar AZ 85925

Call Sign: KB7YIJ
Raymond D Rice
1724 W 26 Bar Ranch Rd
Eagar AZ 85925

Call Sign: KE7BQH
Seth D Copeland
1570 W Sable Way
Eagar AZ 85925

Call Sign: KG7QH
Steven C Harbison
1498 W Seventh Ln
Eagar AZ 85925

Call Sign: KA7OPT
Asa D Palmer
Eagar AZ 85925

Call Sign: KB7VVU
Elizabeth A Lund
Eagar AZ 85925

Call Sign: W7INK
Homer O Jarrel
Eagar AZ 85925

Call Sign: KB7MPT
Lynn E Ellsworth
Eagar AZ 85925

Call Sign: KB7VVW
William G Lund
Eagar AZ 85925

Call Sign: KG7CJ
Jim Tyler
Eagar AZ 85925

Call Sign: KC7M
Glenn Jacobs
Eagar AZ 85925

Call Sign: KE7DGF
Bernetta N Eagar
Eagar AZ 85925

Call Sign: WA7WPG
Charles A Gerbens
Eagar AZ 85925

Call Sign: N7ZRA
Don K Thibodeaux
Eagar AZ 85925

Call Sign: KF7OLQ
Gary A Ciminski
Eagar AZ 85925

Call Sign: KA4TTT
John B Haynie Jr
Eagar AZ 85925

Call Sign: KE7DGE
Karl B Eagar
Eagar AZ 85925

Call Sign: KA7YOS
Patricia A Harbison
Eagar AZ 85925

Call Sign: KF7KVR
Rockford L Adair
Eagar AZ 85925

Call Sign: KF7OLP
Stanley B Ciminski
Eagar AZ 85925

Call Sign: KF7QJN
Thomas N White
Eagar AZ 85925

Call Sign: WA7KLA
Royce P Adams
Eagar AZ 85925

Call Sign: WB7RJV
Walter W Hochuli
Eagar AZ 859250565

FCC Amateur Radio Licenses in Eden

Call Sign: NR7Q
Benjamin Smith
Box 3248
Eden AZ 85535

Call Sign: N7HRV
Neil A Smith
Box 3248
Eden AZ 85535

Call Sign: KA7WCQ
Nyla S Smith
Box 3248
Eden AZ 85535

FCC Amateur Radio Licenses in Ehrenberg

Call Sign: W3GJR
Charles Stein
Ehrenberg AZ 85334

Call Sign: KF7HGT
John R Hoge
Ehrenberg AZ 85334

Call Sign: KE6HWZ
Johnny R Waterman
Ehrenberg AZ 85334

Call Sign: KD7LYF
Michael B Lauborough
Ehrenberg AZ 85334

Call Sign: K9MBL
Michael B Lauborough
Ehrenberg AZ 85334

Call Sign: K7MBL
Michael B Lauborough
Ehrenberg AZ 85334

Call Sign: KD7HXW
Ronald M Sturbaum
Ehrenberg AZ 85334

Call Sign: KD7RS
Ronald M Sturbaum
Ehrenberg AZ 85334

**FCC Amateur Radio
Licenses in Elfrida**

Call Sign: W5JJO
John J O' Neil
11101 N High Lonesome Rd
Elfrida AZ 85610

Call Sign: KD1ON
Joel B Levin
11290 N High Lonesome Rd
Elfrida AZ 85610

Call Sign: N1OYY
Kathleen W Levin
11290 N High Lonesome Rd
Elfrida AZ 85610

Call Sign: KC7UZR
Robert E Learned
11583 N Silver Bill Rd
Elfrida AZ 85610

Call Sign: KC1DE
Raymond E O Neal
6346 W Quiet Country Rd
Elfrida AZ 85610

Call Sign: KF0GC
Jeffrey K Schaa
3960 W Trails End
Elfrida AZ 85610

Call Sign: KD5WCQ
Cindi Leist
4723 W Webb Rd
Elfrida AZ 856109032

Call Sign: KD5WCP
Rodney L Leist
4723 W Webb Rd
Elfrida AZ 856109032

Call Sign: N7UGH
Carolyn A Cazee
Elfrida AZ 85610

Call Sign: W7TOA
Arthur B Dunn
Elfrida AZ 85610

Call Sign: K7MJJ
Elizabeth A Dunn
Elfrida AZ 85610

**FCC Amateur Radio
Licenses in Elgin**

Call Sign: KD7FKB
Mark A Shepard
Box 433
Elgin AZ 856119725

Call Sign: N7COB
Philip E Callahan
Box 670

Elgin AZ 85611

Call Sign: WB7DZU
Ramona M Dow
Box 677
Elgin AZ 85611

Call Sign: KB7OIA
Douglas M Petersen
Box 678
Elgin AZ 85611

Call Sign: KC7HHT
Edward J Vander Laan
Box 702
Elgin AZ 856119728

Call Sign: W6SCD
Arthur C Lynch
Box 746
Elgin AZ 85611

Call Sign: N7LFG
Michael M Boy
Sr 406
Elgin AZ 85611

Call Sign: KB7OHZ
Eric S Petersen
Elgin AZ 85611

**FCC Amateur Radio
Licenses in Eloy**

Call Sign: KG5EN
Charles R Zimmer
4468 E Pinto Dr
Eloy AZ 85231

Call Sign: N9NMI
Douglas J Anderson
4215 N Granada Dr 8
Eloy AZ 85231

Call Sign: N9PFN
Mary L Anderson
4215 N Granada Dr 8
Eloy AZ 85231

Call Sign: N7DJR
David K Bohmke Jr
4220 N Granada Dr Apt 12
Eloy AZ 85131

Call Sign: W7TEJ
Taylor E Jones
7136 S Sunland Gin Rd
Eloy AZ 85231

Call Sign: N6IDU
Dennis P Schneider
7136 S Sunland Gin Rd 40
Eloy AZ 85131

Call Sign: N6NDQ
Olga A Carnahan
5388 W Gulch Dr
Eloy AZ 85131

Call Sign: N6WQM
Stephen P Carnahan
5388 W Gulch Dr
Eloy AZ 85131

Call Sign: KC7OJL
Christine R Sanders
14372 W Hydrus
Eloy AZ 85231

Call Sign: KC7OJK
Ronald M Sanders
14372 W Hydrus Ave
Eloy AZ 85231

Call Sign: W8ED
Clarence E Polmanteer
14900 W Libra Dr
Eloy AZ 852313336

Call Sign: KA0SXF
Gloria J Smith
3110 W Solano Dr
Eloy AZ 852319458

Call Sign: W0BGF
Vernon S Dollar
14755 W Zodiac Dr
Eloy AZ 85231

Call Sign: K7QAT
David G Akers
14013 W Zodiac Dr
Eloy AZ 851313226

Call Sign: K8QAT
David G Akers
Eloy AZ 85131

Call Sign: N6QWA
Stephen D Austin
Eloy AZ 85231

Call Sign: WA6TBI
Stephen D Austin
Eloy AZ 85231

FCC Amateur Radio Licenses in Flagstaff

Call Sign: WB7TPL
Walter J Tucker
3309 Ascona
Flagstaff AZ 86001

Call Sign: KC7ZIV
Timothy Dolan
10255 Aurora
Flagstaff AZ 86004

Call Sign: KF7NPT
Stacy L Petro
1887 Ax Handle Way
Flagstaff AZ 86001

Call Sign: KC7FAK
Donna Baird
700 Blackbird Roost Apt 122
Flagstaff AZ 86001

Call Sign: KE7CMQ
Patricia A Reimer
Box 137
Flagstaff AZ 86004

Call Sign: KD7YCE
Daniel M Mcdonald
Box 39

Flagstaff AZ 86004

Call Sign: KB7YXE
Frances M Koger
Box 61 Leupp Rd
Flagstaff AZ 80004

Call Sign: KC7MNC
Deborah A Wolf
Box 716
Flagstaff AZ 86001

Call Sign: KC7JAF
David L Wolf
Box 716
Flagstaff AZ 860019301

Call Sign: W2RVS
G Henry Boyce
Box 734 Schultz Pass Rd
Flagstaff AZ 86001

Call Sign: KB7UMM
Craig S Newman
Box 749
Flagstaff AZ 86001

Call Sign: KD7CUW
Jeffrey A Ingelse
Box 800
Flagstaff AZ 86001

Call Sign: KD7CVC
Kathy M Ingelse
Box 800
Flagstaff AZ 86001

Call Sign: KF7NPY
Andrew M Foss
4268 Broken Rock Loop
Flagstaff AZ 86004

Call Sign: KF7NPX
David A Foss
4268 Broken Rock Loop
Flagstaff AZ 86004

Call Sign: KB9UCK
Eric A TRUE

249 Buffalo Trl
Flagstaff AZ 86001

Call Sign: KC7FHL
Richard A Mc Cort
255 Buffalo Trl
Flagstaff AZ 86001

Call Sign: KC7YWQ
Stephen W Fehr
9410 Burone Dr
Flagstaff AZ 86004

Call Sign: KB7NKF
Hugh E Stamper
23 Campbell Ave
Flagstaff AZ 86004

Call Sign: KB7DAA
Donald R Garrett Sr
303 Campbell Ave
Flagstaff AZ 86004

Call Sign: N7NPK
Anthony L Wheat
506 Campus Heights
Flagstaff AZ 86001

Call Sign: KD7RDG
Timothy Goya
504 Campus Hgts
Flagstaff AZ 86001

Call Sign: KL7OS
Mark C Enerson
4101 Canyon Loop
Flagstaff AZ 86001

Call Sign: KB1C
Robert M Hemm M D
3528 Captain Colton Ln
Flagstaff AZ 86001

Call Sign: N7ZFX
Jacqueline Mc Michael
8972 Carefree Ave
Flagstaff AZ 86004

Call Sign: KE7ITK

Perry D Shirley
9118 Carefree Ave
Flagstaff AZ 86004

Call Sign: AD7LZ
Perry D Shirley
9118 Carefree Ave
Flagstaff AZ 86004

Call Sign: N7YIQ
Daniel M Shearer Jr
2624 Chaco Trl
Flagstaff AZ 86001

Call Sign: KD7NNW
Gordon C Fox
57 Chof Trl
Flagstaff AZ 86001

Call Sign: KE7DNV
Michael E Miller
6401 Christmas Tree Ln Apt
11
Flagstaff AZ 86004

Call Sign: KB7CFV
Arwin E Sturnacle
322 Comanche
Flagstaff AZ 86001

Call Sign: KB7LOI
Deirdre C Scott
5404 Cortland 284
Flagstaff AZ 86004

Call Sign: KE7LRI
Eugene W Kazup
8580 Crystal View Ln
Flagstaff AZ 86004

Call Sign: K7KAZ
Eugene W Kazup
8580 Crystal View Ln
Flagstaff AZ 86004

Call Sign: KC7GWA
Walter G Hopkins III
523 Deanna Dr
Flagstaff AZ 86001

Call Sign: AC7IW
Walter G Hopkins III
523 Deanna Dr
Flagstaff AZ 86001

Call Sign: KD7CPF
Allan D Isenberg
12890 Dunlap Dr
Flagstaff AZ 860045406

Call Sign: AC7JA
Allan D Isenberg
12890 Dunlap Dr
Flagstaff AZ 860045406

Call Sign: KB7KVD
Jarret L Campbell
218 Dunnam
Flagstaff AZ 86001

Call Sign: AA7AC
Barbara J Reed
215 Dunnam St
Flagstaff AZ 86001

Call Sign: KE4AVY
Daniel G Neary
3530 Dylan St
Flagstaff AZ 86001

Call Sign: KE7TYL
Andrew T Moore
1731 E Arrowhead Ave Unit
4
Flagstaff AZ 86004

Call Sign: KF7PTG
Andrew T Moore
1731 E Arrowhead Ave Unit
4
Flagstaff AZ 86004

Call Sign: KB7TQZ
Leonard E Cummings
3341 E Ascona Way
Flagstaff AZ 86004

Call Sign: KB7KCD

Robert D Marsh
748 E Cherry Ave
Flagstaff AZ 86001

Call Sign: K7RJP
Richard J Polukort
5303 E Cortland Blvd S8
Flagstaff AZ 86004

Call Sign: KC7YYI
Karen L Gustafson
209 E Cottage Ave
Flagstaff AZ 86001

Call Sign: N7FVK
Robert W Braatz
4855 E Crestview St
Flagstaff AZ 86004

Call Sign: KJ4BQS
Derek J Hansen
7515 E Dalton Rd
Flagstaff AZ 86004

Call Sign: KJ4ETD
Melissa O Hansen
7515 E Dalton Rd
Flagstaff AZ 86004

Call Sign: N7IHJ
William F Lesko
5210 E Daphne Ln
Flagstaff AZ 86001

Call Sign: KF7IZW
John Montgomery
830 E David Dr
Flagstaff AZ 86001

Call Sign: W3JBQ
Marjorie K Sinton
850 E David Dr
Flagstaff AZ 86001

Call Sign: KI7LS
William M Sinton
850 E David Dr
Flagstaff AZ 86001

Call Sign: N7JQB
Ernest R Ryan
1822 E Dortha
Flagstaff AZ 86004

Call Sign: AA3UP
Darrel E Anthony
3920 E El Paso Dr
Flagstaff AZ 86004

Call Sign: KE7DEZ
Phillip J Hornyak
7845 E Gemini Dr
Flagstaff AZ 86004

Call Sign: N7YKU
Patrick A Tarr
1207 E Harmony Way
Flagstaff AZ 86004

Call Sign: KA7TVM
Alan W Ake
4845 E Indian Dr
Flagstaff AZ 86004

Call Sign: KD7OSW
Jason D Ake
4854 E Indian Dr
Flagstaff AZ 86004

Call Sign: N7HQI
Lucile C Moore
2 E Juniper Ave
Flagstaff AZ 86001

Call Sign: KA7WNY
Charles D Moore
2 E Juniper Ave
Flagstaff AZ 860011425

Call Sign: N7SRF
Steven P Allen
27 E Juniper Ave
Flagstaff AZ 86001

Call Sign: KE7IXW
Bruce W Belman
6465 E Leisure Ln
Flagstaff AZ 86004

Call Sign: KB7PXW
Dean L Hatch
3024 E Lewis
Flagstaff AZ 86004

Call Sign: WB7CDO
Joseph L Remy
2808 E Lewis Dr
Flagstaff AZ 86004

Call Sign: N7SRG
James D Silverman
1700 E Linda Vista
Flagstaff AZ 86004

Call Sign: KB7PWG
Michael R Sprinzl
2155 E Maple 17
Flagstaff AZ 86004

Call Sign: KE7DEY
Jack C Petersen
2540 E Matterhorn Dr
Flagstaff AZ 86004

Call Sign: KB7MVL
Benjamin J Crysler
2655 E Matterhorn Dr
Flagstaff AZ 86004

Call Sign: N5KFP
Gayla J Lusk
8545 E Mercury Dr
Flagstaff AZ 86004

Call Sign: N5HRA
Myron C Lusk
8545 E Mercury Dr
Flagstaff AZ 86004

Call Sign: KC7EYF
David F Pemberton
2708 E Miller Dr
Flagstaff AZ 86004

Call Sign: KC7BPM
Willard N Gilbert
4652 E Northwood Way

Flagstaff AZ 86004

Call Sign: KB7YQG
Nelson D Hochberg
825 E Ponderosa Pky
Flagstaff AZ 86004

Call Sign: KB7FEO
Larry E Watkins
9595 E Rabbit Ridge Rd
Flagstaff AZ 86004

Call Sign: KD7YLO
Larry E Watkins
9595 E Rabbit Ridge Rd
Flagstaff AZ 86004

Call Sign: KB7ZTE
Roxanne Stell
9595 E Rabbit Ridge Rd
Flagstaff AZ 86004

Call Sign: W6MJH
Bill Young
4403 E Rustie Knolls Ln
Flagstaff AZ 86004

Call Sign: KB7FEK
Val J Paleski
4890 E Snowshoe Way
Flagstaff AZ 86004

Call Sign: N1RUM
John E Goodwin
4015 E Soliere Ave
Flagstaff AZ 86004

Call Sign: KG6ILC
Bridget A Hoffman
4255 E Soliere Ave 157
Flagstaff AZ 86004

Call Sign: KF7BRW
Michael T Blair
4015 E Soliere Ave Apt 155
Flagstaff AZ 86004

Call Sign: KC2KLQ
John M Ciccone

4211 E Spring Meadows Cir
Flagstaff AZ 86004

Call Sign: KC7JAG
James B Hartzog
3929 E Summer Run Dr
Flagstaff AZ 86004

Call Sign: KY2KJM
James W Mc Cord Jr
3359 E Swiss Rd
Flagstaff AZ 86004

Call Sign: KB7GIQ
Robert J Pinnick Sr
3809 E Thrush Ln
Flagstaff AZ 86004

Call Sign: KF7TQT
Bill Schuchman Radiosport
Association
6315 E Townsend Winona
Rd
Flagstaff AZ 86004

Call Sign: W7YS
Bill Schuchman Radiosport
Association
6315 E Townsend Winona
Rd
Flagstaff AZ 86004

Call Sign: NF7E
Robert C Wertz
6315 E Townsend Winona
Rd
Flagstaff AZ 86004

Call Sign: WJ0F
Lee Amoroso
9825 E Townsend Winona
Rd
Flagstaff AZ 86004

Call Sign: KC7ZQQ
David W Foss
6612 E Vail
Flagstaff AZ 86004

Call Sign: KB7HIB
Lorinda F Collier
205 E Zuni
Flagstaff AZ 86001

Call Sign: N7LQT
Robert R Mcphetridge
205 E Zuni
Flagstaff AZ 86001

Call Sign: KD7QET
Fredric H Sartorius
7825 Easy St
Flagstaff AZ 86004

Call Sign: KF7PLF
Jill M Rundall
2835 Echo Cave Ovi
Flagstaff AZ 86001

Call Sign: N7EJE
William G Ruge
193 Elk Ovi
Flagstaff AZ 86001

Call Sign: KE7NGC
Mark A Decker
2424 Eva Loop
Flagstaff AZ 86004

Call Sign: KF7PDY
Adolfo O Astorga
4054 Fallen Oak Way
Flagstaff AZ 86004

Call Sign: NA7CJ
Craig J Johnson
5415 Foster Rd
Flagstaff AZ 86004

Call Sign: KC7AJR
Vernon D Cernusak
1082 Hano Trl
Flagstaff AZ 860019676

Call Sign: KC7BPL
Rowena M Cernusak
1082 Hano Trl
Flagstaff AZ 860019676

Call Sign: AA7JD
Judith A Young
2166 Hano Trl
Flagstaff AZ 86001

Call Sign: KF7LMS
Mark D Dauer
11415 Homestead Ln
Flagstaff AZ 86004

Call Sign: N7TUG
Royce G Buckley Jr
7795 Hummingbird Ln
Flagstaff AZ 86004

Call Sign: KJ7WY
Peter A Koehler
7825 Hummingbird Ln
Flagstaff AZ 86004

Call Sign: KB7HFX
Charles G Moore
498 Hutcheson Dr
Flagstaff AZ 86001

Call Sign: KB7QAV
John H Eubank
416 James St
Flagstaff AZ 86001

Call Sign: KB7DCH
Tom J Motsenbocker
8085 Jupiter Ln
Flagstaff AZ 86004

Call Sign: KB7ZIF
Jason G Hatchett
162 Kachina Trl 3
Flagstaff AZ 86004

Call Sign: NN7D
Richard W Ferguson
7460 Koch Field Rd
Flagstaff AZ 86004

Call Sign: KB7LOO
Thomas L Ryan Sr
7735 Koch Field Rd

Flagstaff AZ 86004

Call Sign: N7SQW
Keith E Vogler
474 Lake Mary Rd
Flagstaff AZ 86001

Call Sign: KB3EOK
Marci J Mullen
4619 Lake Mary Rd 3
Flagstaff AZ 86001

Call Sign: KB7TBK
John W Smelser
7285 Larson Ln
Flagstaff AZ 86004

Call Sign: KD7DVK
Bryce Bearchell
8695 Leah Ln
Flagstaff AZ 86004

Call Sign: KD7DVL
Roslyn J Bearchell
8695 Leah Ln
Flagstaff AZ 86004

Call Sign: KD7QAB
Joshua A Sprinkle
9708 Legacy Ln
Flagstaff AZ 86004

Call Sign: KC7WJM
Jan E Borrud
39 Leupp Rd
Flagstaff AZ 86004

Call Sign: KF7PLE
Jinnifer L Rister
43 Leupp Rd
Flagstaff AZ 86004

Call Sign: WW7R
James M Buford
4303 Lynch Ave
Flagstaff AZ 860042314

Call Sign: KE7FXF
Michael C Wertz

11050 Margaret Way
Flagstaff AZ 86004

Call Sign: KF7PJE
Amy J Martin
8620 Marys Dr
Flagstaff AZ 86004

Call Sign: KE7BIT
Roderick S Martin
8620 Marys Dr
Flagstaff AZ 86004

Call Sign: KY7A
Roderick S Martin
8620 Marys Dr
Flagstaff AZ 86004

Call Sign: KE6DO
Frederick M Sammis
1820 Meadow Lark Dr
Flagstaff AZ 86001

Call Sign: KD7KEJ
Judith C Gonzalez
760 Mesa Trl
Flagstaff AZ 86001

Call Sign: KB7NKM
Felix Haeuptle
762 Mesa Trl
Flagstaff AZ 86001

Call Sign: W7LUX
Joseph R Hobart
2570 Mesa Trl
Flagstaff AZ 860013648

Call Sign: W1MQT
Gerald J San Giacomo
9880 Mesquite Loop
Flagstaff AZ 86004

Call Sign: K7YVS
Marvin A Bansbach Jr
9162 Moonbeam Ave
Flagstaff AZ 86004

Call Sign: KB7QNV

Ronald L Pearsall
3302 N 4th St
Flagstaff AZ 86004

Call Sign: AD6UT
Joseph L Becker
1401 N 4th St 230
Flagstaff AZ 86004

Call Sign: AC7OC
Joseph L Becker
1401 N 4th St 230
Flagstaff AZ 86004

Call Sign: W7TB
Northern Arizona Dx
Association
8210 N Aspen Glen Ln
Flagstaff AZ 86004

Call Sign: KD7ZGZ
David M Brown
8210 N Aspen Glen Ln
Flagstaff AZ 860043242

Call Sign: W7FYW
David M Brown
8210 N Aspen Glen Ln
Flagstaff AZ 860043242

Call Sign: KC7EBO
Leslie G Ripps
7 N Aztec St
Flagstaff AZ 86001

Call Sign: KC7DQU
Thaddeus R Edel
319 N Beaver St
Flagstaff AZ 86001

Call Sign: KA7SZV
Duart M Martin
1819 N Beaver St
Flagstaff AZ 86001

Call Sign: WB7EUJ
Robert L Gilbert
3808 N Bern
Flagstaff AZ 86001

Call Sign: KC7NHI
Carole A Gilbert
3808 N Bern
Flagstaff AZ 86004

Call Sign: KC7OYB
Mount Elden Middle School
Ham Radio Club
3808 N Bern
Flagstaff AZ 86004

Call Sign: W7EYG
William S Webster
2333 N Beth Way
Flagstaff AZ 86001

Call Sign: N7LQS
Kenneth D Gardner
4329 N Bonner St
Flagstaff AZ 86004

Call Sign: KF7SFK
Ryan L Cannell
4419 N Bonner St
Flagstaff AZ 86004

Call Sign: W8MIF
David B Shaffer
7355 N Bright Leaf Ln
Flagstaff AZ 86001

Call Sign: KC7QMB
Andrew L Rockhold
9285 N Bryant Rd
Flagstaff AZ 86004

Call Sign: KC7QMA
Melinda M Rockhold
9285 N Bryant Rd
Flagstaff AZ 86004

Call Sign: K2AZW
Charles F Cram
3516 N Captain Colton Ln
Flagstaff AZ 860010728

Call Sign: N1LLL
Robert W Burroughs

1913 N Center St
Flagstaff AZ 86004

Call Sign: KA7PVD
Douglas E Simmons
1724 N Center St Apt C
Flagstaff AZ 86004

Call Sign: KB7XG
A Philip Gall
7055 N Chambers Dr
Flagstaff AZ 86001

Call Sign: WB7QAD
Fannie C Williams
3306 N Childress St
Flagstaff AZ 86004

Call Sign: N7HW
Howard A Williams
3306 N Childress St
Flagstaff AZ 86004

Call Sign: WB7OWW
Flagstaff Middle School
ARC
3306 N Childress St
Flagstaff AZ 86004

Call Sign: KF7AYO
John B Mcgowan
6428 N Conrad Ln
Flagstaff AZ 86004

Call Sign: KB1LZ
William C Smith
5712 N Cosnino Rd
Flagstaff AZ 860049731

Call Sign: KQ1S
William C Smith
5712 N Cosnino Rd
Flagstaff AZ 860049731

Call Sign: KC6UJJ
Stephen W Woolard
2525 N Eddy Dr
Flagstaff AZ 86001

Call Sign: KF6ROO
Erik A Hardman
3420 N Eiger Mountain Rd
Flagstaff AZ 86004

Call Sign: KE7ELR
John A Paplow
1701 N Falcon Rd
Flagstaff AZ 86004

Call Sign: K7PAP
John A Paplow
1701 N Falcon Rd
Flagstaff AZ 86004

Call Sign: KC7GVZ
Michael C Harvey
1706 N Fort Valley Rd 19
Flagstaff AZ 86001

Call Sign: KK7WM
Peter A Blakey
966 N Fox Hill Rd
Flagstaff AZ 86004

Call Sign: KD3EY
Frederic I Solop
2646 N Fox Run Dr
Flagstaff AZ 86004

Call Sign: KC7FYN
James A Divine
2822 N Fremont Blvd
Flagstaff AZ 86001

Call Sign: KE7QFE
Lina H Wallen
3716 N Grandview Dr
Flagstaff AZ 86004

Call Sign: KC7WJH
John D Breckon
4175 N Grindelwald
Flagstaff AZ 86004

Call Sign: KE7JVZ
Marvin G Mansfield
3380 N Harris Way
Flagstaff AZ 86004

Call Sign: KE7YDN
Amanda K Loveless
10439 N Hopi Rd
Flagstaff AZ 86004

Call Sign: KE7YDO
Bryan G Loveless
10439 N Hopi Rd
Flagstaff AZ 86004

Call Sign: KB7GUI
Bryan A Ramsey
9000 N Hwy 89 Sp 5
Flagstaff AZ 86004

Call Sign: W7KWL
Donald D Helm
3212 N Jamison
Flagstaff AZ 86004

Call Sign: KD7OKB
Stacy J Camp
12580 N John Wayne Blvd
Flagstaff AZ 86004

Call Sign: KE7QFH
Edward B Smith
1813 N Katchina Rd
Flagstaff AZ 86001

Call Sign: KF7BRU
Joseph R Davidson
2328 N Keystone Dr
Flagstaff AZ 86004

Call Sign: KD7KET
Richard E Nepple
1630 N Lakeview Ln
Flagstaff AZ 86004

Call Sign: AC7RM
Richard E Nepple
1630 N Lakeview Ln
Flagstaff AZ 86004

Call Sign: KD7OZJ
John T Stilley
17 N Leroux St

Flagstaff AZ 86001

Call Sign: WA7HUR
Erwin K Isbrecht
659 N Locust St
Flagstaff AZ 86001

Call Sign: AB7SN
Roland B Voellmer
659 N Locust St
Flagstaff AZ 86001

Call Sign: N0VFT
Douglas D Swenson
678 N Lone Oak Way
Flagstaff AZ 860047621

Call Sign: KD7JID
Clinton E Sharp
3435 N Manor
Flagstaff AZ 86004

Call Sign: KB7YQC
Tom L Elzey
3365 N Manor Rd
Flagstaff AZ 86004

Call Sign: N7WIC
Arline R Martens
1927 N Marion Dr
Flagstaff AZ 86001

Call Sign: N7PNL
Charles F Martens III
1927 N Marion Dr
Flagstaff AZ 86001

Call Sign: N1CI
Charles F Martens III
1927 N Marion Dr
Flagstaff AZ 86001

Call Sign: KC9GQ
Richard C Oliver
3519 N Monte Vista Dr
Flagstaff AZ 86004

Call Sign: K7MQ
Louis Wilson

9900 N Natchez Trl
Flagstaff AZ 86004

Call Sign: KC7HAJ
Steve V Nebel
2353 N Oakmont Dr
Flagstaff AZ 86004

Call Sign: N7KTH
Christopher R Horn
3859 N Paradise Rd
Flagstaff AZ 86004

Call Sign: KE7ODU
Jeremy P Edgar
3335 N Park Dr
Flagstaff AZ 86004

Call Sign: KE7CDI
Anthony W Vanwey II
5301 N Parson Ranch Rd 1
Flagstaff AZ 86004

Call Sign: KA7TWW
Charles A Butler
2939 N Prescott Rd
Flagstaff AZ 86001

Call Sign: KC7FKS
Joshua Colvin
2801 N Prescott Rd
Flagstaff AZ 86001

Call Sign: AE7OH
Philip W Brunner
4955 N Primrose Cir
Flagstaff AZ 86001

Call Sign: KF7QPH
Barbara D Brunner
4955 N Primrose Cir
Flagstaff AZ 86001

Call Sign: W6HQJ
Barbara D Brunner
4955 N Primrose Cir
Flagstaff AZ 86001

Call Sign: KC7OIE

James K Neverman
2007 N Rain Tree Rd
Flagstaff AZ 86004

Call Sign: WB7SJC
Kent J Luttrell
1821 N Raintree Rd
Flagstaff AZ 86004

Call Sign: KB7YXI
Robert E Belton
1901 N Raintree Rd
Flagstaff AZ 86004

Call Sign: KF7NPV
Dylan A Baxter
2800 N Roberta Dr
Flagstaff AZ 86001

Call Sign: WB7FCS
Ray E Teague
8450 N Round Tree Rd
Flagstaff AZ 86001

Call Sign: WB7FBN
Mary M Teague
8450 N Roundtree Rd
Flagstaff AZ 86001

Call Sign: KC7YAH
Richard L Downey
10880 N Sage Rd
Flagstaff AZ 860041040

Call Sign: KB7IRG
Marie Wilson
100 N San Francisco St
Flagstaff AZ 86001

Call Sign: KF7PLN
Kevin R Daly
930 N San Franciso 8
Flagstaff AZ 86001

Call Sign: WB7WXR
Ronald J Dovzak
3021 N Schevene
Flagstaff AZ 86004

Call Sign: KF7PLG
Ben E Ullyot
3311 N Schevene Blvd
Flagstaff AZ 86004

Call Sign: KD7FGV
Richard M Lake
905 N Sinagua Heights Dr
Flagstaff AZ 86004

Call Sign: KA7ZHT
Craig A Stoneberger
5750 N Smokerise
Flagstaff AZ 86004

Call Sign: KD7SHY
James H Gibson
1708 N Sunset Dr
Flagstaff AZ 86001

Call Sign: W7THG
Thomas H Gewecke
3907 N Swiss Rd
Flagstaff AZ 86004

Call Sign: KI6WCK
Janice D Enloe
900 N Switzer Canyon Dr
116
Flagstaff AZ 86001

Call Sign: KE7INK
Teresa R Cummins
900 N Switzer Canyon Dr
219
Flagstaff AZ 86001

Call Sign: KF7PJD
Steven L Duaime
900 N Switzer Canyon Dr
236
Flagstaff AZ 86001

Call Sign: KI6SGV
Jeffrey A Hoover
900 N Switzer Canyon Dr
Apt 116
Flagstaff AZ 86001

Call Sign: KD7HVP
Anthony W Brollini
900 N Switzer Canyon Dr
Apt 136
Flagstaff AZ 86001

Call Sign: N7SRB
John E Nolting
2316 N Talkington Dr
Flagstaff AZ 86001

Call Sign: AA7LN
Vladimir P Sannikov
1400 N Wakonda St
Flagstaff AZ 86004

Call Sign: W7YS
William G Schuchman
1400 N Wakonda St
Flagstaff AZ 86004

Call Sign: N4LCT
Sonya M Epperson
1506 N West St
Flagstaff AZ 86004

Call Sign: KC7RVC
John H Weckback
2213 N West St
Flagstaff AZ 86004

Call Sign: KC7LVC
Kevin J Thomas
2382 N Whispering Pine
Way
Flagstaff AZ 86004

Call Sign: KB7CFE
Edward F Dallago
3987 N Zurich St
Flagstaff AZ 86004

Call Sign: KB7VDC
Peter D Jansen
17 Onondaga St
Flagstaff AZ 86001

Call Sign: WQ7J
Peter J Horn

3859 Paradise Rd
Flagstaff AZ 86004

Call Sign: KM6LD
Janet F Brickey
7224 Patriot Dr
Flagstaff AZ 86004

Call Sign: KB7SKQ
Norbert L Langbecker
5 Pine Ridge Dr
Flagstaff AZ 86001

Call Sign: KB7SKP
Susan B Langbecker
5 Pine Ridge Dr
Flagstaff AZ 86001

Call Sign: NF7C
Bruce H Johnson
6845 Pintail Dr
Flagstaff AZ 86004

Call Sign: KD7XM
Danye L Turner
6845 Pintail Dr
Flagstaff AZ 86004

Call Sign: KA7UXG
Judith F Doerfler
741 Polacca Trl
Flagstaff AZ 86001

Call Sign: KD7DVN
Eon V Friesen
2498 Polacca Trl
Flagstaff AZ 86001

Call Sign: KE7NAK
Rebecca L Cooke
13150 Red Mountain Rd
Flagstaff AZ 86004

Call Sign: KD6YBN
Kyle D Jones
1200 Riordan Ranch 44
Flagstaff AZ 86001

Call Sign: KD7MEQ

Philip A Fowler
601 Riordan Rd 315
Flagstaff AZ 86001

Call Sign: KC7AJQ
Carl F Howerton
10280 Roan Rd
Flagstaff AZ 86004

Call Sign: KB7YQK
Patricia L Meridith
10335 Roan Rd
Flagstaff AZ 86004

Call Sign: KB7RGH
Ted O Meredith
10335 Roan Rd
Flagstaff AZ 86004

Call Sign: KF7NJF
Cynthia L Riley
3507 S Amanda
Flagstaff AZ 86001

Call Sign: KF7JRT
Michael J Riley
3507 S Amanda Dr
Flagstaff AZ 86001

Call Sign: KD7DVO
Theresa A Warr
102 S Beaver
Flagstaff AZ 86001

Call Sign: KE7QFQ
Robert M Hernandez
4827 S Bright Angel Trl
Flagstaff AZ 86001

Call Sign: N8KIQ
Carol Ann Bradfield
3640 S Cheryl Dr
Flagstaff AZ 860019028

Call Sign: KE7QFJ
Marti C Blad
3671 S Cheryl Dr
Flagstaff AZ 86001

Call Sign: KE7FFP
Paul T Flanagan
2464 S Cliffview St
Flagstaff AZ 86001

Call Sign: KE7TYM
Victor S Walco
4708 S Dorty Tr
Flagstaff AZ 86001

Call Sign: KE7IXR
John D Schaub
2406 S Highland Mesa Rd
Flagstaff AZ 86001

Call Sign: KC7TRE
Daniel R Fierro
3990 S Holland Rd
Flagstaff AZ 86001

Call Sign: KF6IXL
Richard A Fierro
3990 S Holland Rd
Flagstaff AZ 86001

Call Sign: KF7RIA
Cindy M Mcarthur
4816 S House Rock Trl
Flagstaff AZ 86001

Call Sign: KC7SKN
Douglas H Johnson
3601 S Lake Mary Rd Apt
244
Flagstaff AZ 86001

Call Sign: KD7HIT
David E Evans
516 S Leroux St
Flagstaff AZ 86001

Call Sign: KC8BGV
Craig C Williams
2181 S Linmar Ct
Flagstaff AZ 86001

Call Sign: AD7NN
Craig C Williams
2181 S Linmar Ct

Flagstaff AZ 86001

Call Sign: KM5UI
Dennis R Kimbell
3264 S Little Dr
Flagstaff AZ 86001

Call Sign: AA7DK
Dennis R Kimbell
3264 S Little Dr
Flagstaff AZ 86001

Call Sign: KD5JIW
Irene L Kimbell
3264 S Little Dr
Flagstaff AZ 86001

Call Sign: KF6DXU
Perry J S Crampton
3274 S Little Dr
Flagstaff AZ 86001

Call Sign: KE7VNQ
Curtis A Boushley
3250 S Litzler Dr
Flagstaff AZ 85308

Call Sign: K9DMS
David M Speer
3834 S Marble Canyon Trl
Flagstaff AZ 860016956

Call Sign: N7NLW
Michael E Young
51 S Maricopa St 802C
Flagstaff AZ 860016734

Call Sign: KE7NAN
Timothy F Sapio
51 S Maricopa St Apt 601
Flagstaff AZ 86001

Call Sign: N7KIE
David T Ursin
3340 S Moore Cir
Flagstaff AZ 860018500

Call Sign: KC7NHK
Robert W Gonzales

102 S Oleary
Flagstaff AZ 86001

Call Sign: KB7UMI
Stacey L Brewer
1200 S Reardan Ranch St 5
Flagstaff AZ 86001

Call Sign: KD7LHQ
Gregory T Long
1600 S River Valley Rd
Flagstaff AZ 86004

Call Sign: KE7DYO
Christpher W Moore
2545 S Sonoran Ln
Flagstaff AZ 86001

Call Sign: KC7GDY
Adam W Lewis
2700 S Woodlands Village
Blvd 300 108
Flagstaff AZ 86001

Call Sign: KC7HAL
Sarah E Lewis
2700 S Woodlands Village
Blvd 300 108
Flagstaff AZ 86001

Call Sign: KE7QFK
Jayne T Abraham
2700 S Woodlands Village
Blvd So 300 304
Flagstaff AZ 86001

Call Sign: N8GRT
Robert J Gerlak
2450 S Woody Mountain Rd
Flagstaff AZ 86001

Call Sign: KC7TPN
Robert L Lund
1515 S Yale Apt 7 2
Flagstaff AZ 86001

Call Sign: KF7DUN
Kenneth T Sager
1515 S Yale St Apt 1 1A

Flagstaff AZ 86001

Call Sign: KG6KUM
Clayton T Abbott
3554 S Zachary Way
Flagstaff AZ 86001

Call Sign: N9DA
Daniel A Adamovich
76 Seneca Dr
Flagstaff AZ 86001

Call Sign: WA7KTF
James D Koreltz
3279 Shonto Trl
Flagstaff AZ 86001

Call Sign: N6DFQ
Thomas A Mc Kinney
1301 Shullenbarger Dr
Flagstaff AZ 86001

Call Sign: KC7SJI
Ryan W Hales
5860 Silver Saddle Rd
Flagstaff AZ 86004

Call Sign: KC6SHA
Javier M Melendez
8885 Slayton Ranch Rd
Flagstaff AZ 86004

Call Sign: KA7WFJ
David L Garrison
8990 Slayton Ranch Rd
Flagstaff AZ 86004

Call Sign: KB0DBP
Konrad Kaserer
3920 Summer Run
Flagstaff AZ 86004

Call Sign: KB5ZH
Julian G Menard
900 Switzer Canyon Dr Apt
141
Flagstaff AZ 86001

Call Sign: KC7SLM

Richard L Crain
1175 Teastoh Ovl
Flagstaff AZ 86001

Call Sign: K8AFN
Jon Q Groth
904 Tishepi Trl
Flagstaff AZ 860019616

Call Sign: KF7GCL
David S Schaubert
2103 Toboggan Ct
Flagstaff AZ 86001

Call Sign: NJ0W
David S Schaubert
2103 Toboggan Ct
Flagstaff AZ 86001

Call Sign: N7LUY
John J Tewes
951 Tolani Trl
Flagstaff AZ 86001

Call Sign: KD7OEL
Wesley D Gaither
5325 Townsend Winona Rd
Flagstaff AZ 86004

Call Sign: KE7HPK
Jeffrey J Kosmicki
10080 Townsend Winona Rd
Flagstaff AZ 86004

Call Sign: N7KOZ
Jeffrey J Kosmicki
10080 Townsend Winona Rd
Flagstaff AZ 86004

Call Sign: KE7HPM
Owen N Kosmicki
10080 Townsend Winona Rd
Flagstaff AZ 86004

Call Sign: N7KOS
Owen N Kosmicki
10080 Townsend Winona Rd
Flagstaff AZ 86004

Call Sign: KC0EDI
Evan C Thomason
11515 Valley View
Flagstaff AZ 86004

Call Sign: KE7HPL
Joseph M Thomason
11515 Valley View
Flagstaff AZ 86004

Call Sign: KE7GIM
John M Lindsey
14280 Ventoso Ct
Flagstaff AZ 86004

Call Sign: K7FLG
John M Lindsey
14280 Ventoso Ct
Flagstaff AZ 86004

Call Sign: NO7AZ
John M Lindsey
14280 Ventoso Ct
Flagstaff AZ 86004

Call Sign: N6JOY
Douglas T Miyatake
1111 W Azure Dr
Flagstaff AZ 86001

Call Sign: KB7QAW
Matthew T Gilbert
614 W Beal Rd
Flagstaff AZ 86001

Call Sign: KE7ETC
Erin K O'Brien
2381 W Blue Willow Rd
Flagstaff AZ 86001

Call Sign: N7SKR
Betty L Smith
3265 W Brenda Loop
Flagstaff AZ 86001

Call Sign: WE7S
Robert I Smith
3265 W Brenda Loop
Flagstaff AZ 86001

Call Sign: KF7BRV
Kay H Perelstein
5160 W Cassandra
Flagstaff AZ 86001

Call Sign: KE7QFI
Erwin S Perelstein
5160 W Cassandra Blvd
Flagstaff AZ 86001

Call Sign: KC7KCN
Coconino ARC
5160 W Cassandra Blvd
Flagstaff AZ 86001

Call Sign: N7PNP
Carl R Schwimmer
612 W Cherry
Flagstaff AZ 86001

Call Sign: KC7AVF
Daniel B Hulls
120 W Columbus
Flagstaff AZ 86001

Call Sign: KF7JCD
Larry D Ward
939 W Coy Dr
Flagstaff AZ 86001

Call Sign: W7GST
Larry D Ward
939 W Coy Dr
Flagstaff AZ 86001

Call Sign: AC7HA
Michael J Pleasants
1221 W Coy Dr
Flagstaff AZ 86001

Call Sign: KC7JGD
Shelly A Pleasants
1221 W Coy Dr
Flagstaff AZ 86001

Call Sign: KC7NVO
Carol H Blann
1211 W Davis Wy

Flagstaff AZ 86001

Call Sign: KD7ODX
Paul G Flikkema
303 W Fir Ave
Flagstaff AZ 86001

Call Sign: KB7ASH
Edward J Reineberg
3009 W Foothills Way
Flagstaff AZ 86001

Call Sign: AB2CD
William S Hogin
800 W Forest Meadows St
101
Flagstaff AZ 86001

Call Sign: K7DHF
William S Hogin
800 W Forest Meadows St
101
Flagstaff AZ 86001

Call Sign: K7BUG
William S Hogin
800 W Forest Meadows St
101
Flagstaff AZ 86001

Call Sign: W0XAZ
William S Hogin
800 W Forest Meadows St
101
Flagstaff AZ 86001

Call Sign: KE7GEN
Weston Scow
1000 W Forest Meadows St
Apt 102
Flagstaff AZ 86001

Call Sign: KF7PLK
Megan C Schwitzer
800 W Forest Meadows St
Apt 294
Flagstaff AZ 86001

Call Sign: N7PVB

Benjamin C Butler
4880 W Hwy 66
Flagstaff AZ 86001

Call Sign: WA7UHK
Jerry A Bravo Jr
2401 W Hwy 66 46
Flagstaff AZ 86001

Call Sign: KC7ZLZ
Guy J Giglio
1450 W Kaibab 15
Flagstaff AZ 86001

Call Sign: WL7CBO
John W Broecher
1450 W Kaibab Ln 169
Flagstaff AZ 86001

Call Sign: KC7NEW
Joseph W Eilo
1450 W Kaibab Ln 24
Flagstaff AZ 86001

Call Sign: KC7QME
Matthew S Swain
1450 W Kaibab Ln 24
Flagstaff AZ 86001

Call Sign: KC7QLZ
Lisa R Swain
1450 W Kaibaf Ln 24
Flagstaff AZ 86001

Call Sign: KC7ZIT
Wayne E Mclellan
2415 W Kiltie Ln
Flagstaff AZ 86001

Call Sign: N6ZVE
David C Jessen
3575 W Kiltie Loop
Flagstaff AZ 896002670

Call Sign: KF7QQZ
Daniel A Painter
3425 W Lois Ln
Flagstaff AZ 86001

Call Sign: KD7IC
Jonathan P Koger
2801 W Lynette
Flagstaff AZ 86001

Call Sign: N7YIU
Christopher V Michels
1450 W Melissa Dr
Flagstaff AZ 86001

Call Sign: K7MTH
Mark T Hawthorne
112 W Mexican Hat Trl
Flagstaff AZ 86001

Call Sign: KF7BRT
Aaron B Dick
3435 W Mountain Dr
Flagstaff AZ 86001

Call Sign: KF7LEH
David C Coy
8545 W Mtn Shadows
Flagstaff AZ 86001

Call Sign: KB7WMY
David T Sanders
413 W Navajo Rd
Flagstaff AZ 86001

Call Sign: KC7SBF
Gregg D Suter
499 W Philomena
Flagstaff AZ 86001

Call Sign: K7SUT
John W Suter
499 W Philomena
Flagstaff AZ 860011333

Call Sign: KB7XN
Charles E Upton
309 W Pine
Flagstaff AZ 86001

Call Sign: KD7VYV
Lori Ann Lane
2331 W Rio Grande
Flagstaff AZ 86001

Call Sign: KD7UJJ
David A Lane
2331 W Rio Grande Ct
Flagstaff AZ 86001

Call Sign: KA6YDF
Mary Janice Wallace
2101 W Rt 66
Flagstaff AZ 86001

Call Sign: KD7MWR
Steve E Camp
1801 W Rt 66 Ste 117
Flagstaff AZ 86001

Call Sign: KC7PRC
Albert D Boone
1223 W Saturn Way
Flagstaff AZ 86001

Call Sign: KC7DWX
Toni M Zuercher
1767 W Sequoia Dr
Flagstaff AZ 86001

Call Sign: KA7FCE
John M Dunford Jr
1110 W Shullenbarger
Flagstaff AZ 86001

Call Sign: KE7QFF
Alice M Dunford
1110 W Shullenbarger Dr
Flagstaff AZ 86001

Call Sign: KC7COI
Steven W Loritz
1803 W Soft Wind Ln
Flagstaff AZ 86001

Call Sign: N7SWL
Steven W Loritz
1803 W Soft Wind Ln
Flagstaff AZ 86001

Call Sign: N7BBI
Daniel R Edel
3120 W Tami Ln

Flagstaff AZ 86001

Call Sign: KB7UMJ
Mary M Edel
3120 W Tami Ln
Flagstaff AZ 86001

Call Sign: KD7IVN
Robert D Edel
3120 W Tami Ln
Flagstaff AZ 86001

Call Sign: KF7PLH
Nathan R Vince
1990 W Topeka Ave
Flagstaff AZ 86001

Call Sign: KC6RQT
Mario G Cardinaletti
1185 W University Ave 153
Flagstaff AZ 86001

Call Sign: K7GG
George J Gosch
1421 W University Heights
Dr N
Flagstaff AZ 86001

Call Sign: N7TXW
Vaughn S Mc Guire II
1880 W University Heights
Dr N
Flagstaff AZ 86001

Call Sign: WA7GGB
Kevin A Rogers
2401 W Us 66 36
Flagstaff AZ 86001

Call Sign: KD7GGY
William A Loucks
8235 Wendys Way
Flagstaff AZ 860043339

Call Sign: KB2IQW
Les D Rubenstein
7175 Whispering Pines Rd
Flagstaff AZ 86003

Call Sign: KL2DD
David G Vonderheide
3014 White Cone Trl
Flagstaff AZ 86001

Call Sign: N7CEE
Bruce O Grubbs
Flagstaff AZ 86002

Call Sign: N7NUR
Diedre Weage
Flagstaff AZ 86002

Call Sign: N7EEO
Douglas C Acuff
Flagstaff AZ 86002

Call Sign: KA7KZR
H Jeffrey Coker
Flagstaff AZ 86002

Call Sign: N7YZI
Robert L Hansen
Flagstaff AZ 86002

Call Sign: KB7YQQ
William K Spriggs
Flagstaff AZ 86002

Call Sign: N7XXF
Cortney E Smith
Flagstaff AZ 86003

Call Sign: KB7TKN
Foster T Hoover
Flagstaff AZ 86003

Call Sign: KB7FEM
Kathleen M Keenan
Flagstaff AZ 86003

Call Sign: KB7HBV
Larry K Wright
Flagstaff AZ 86003

Call Sign: WA0LIW
Lee R Hopson
Flagstaff AZ 86003

Call Sign: N7UCQ
Robert E Goodin
Flagstaff AZ 86003

Call Sign: KB7WFN
Stanley F Verusio
Flagstaff AZ 86003

Call Sign: N7UGZ
Finn T Agenbroad
Flagstaff AZ 86001

Call Sign: K7NAU
Northern Arizona Univ ARC
Flagstaff AZ 86001

Call Sign: N7SQZ
Stan L Mish
Flagstaff AZ 86002

Call Sign: KD7PII
Andrew B Berman
Flagstaff AZ 86002

Call Sign: KE7YDM
David A Hazlett
Flagstaff AZ 86002

Call Sign: KD7LHR
David J Dechambre
Flagstaff AZ 86002

Call Sign: KF7DUQ
Erin C Steddom
Flagstaff AZ 86002

Call Sign: KD2UY
James F Sladky
Flagstaff AZ 86002

Call Sign: WR3C
John P Bittner
Flagstaff AZ 86002

Call Sign: KF7PDZ
Scott K Kuhr
Flagstaff AZ 86002

Call Sign: KC7EYG

Billy J Parish
Flagstaff AZ 86003

Call Sign: KG7BG
James D Pickard
Flagstaff AZ 86003

Call Sign: WB7CRH
James M Rutherford
Flagstaff AZ 86003

Call Sign: KF7BWX
Jon D Rabinovitz
Flagstaff AZ 86003

Call Sign: KF7RCU
Lauren Petro
Flagstaff AZ 86003

Call Sign: KB7KKF
Leslie M Pickard
Flagstaff AZ 86003

Call Sign: W7ZIP
Philip Burrington
Flagstaff AZ 86003

Call Sign: KA7EEI
Sara L Hartzler
Flagstaff AZ 86003

Call Sign: AB6TM
Yoshiharu Horio
Flagstaff AZ 86003

Call Sign: KJ6KUV
Kyle R Crockett
Flagstaff AZ 86004

Call Sign: KI9L
Kyle R Crockett
Flagstaff AZ 86004

Call Sign: K6JJB
John J Bruckner
Flagstaff AZ 860020490

Call Sign: KE6EZO
Mark A Steddom

Flagstaff AZ 860020762

Call Sign: KC6MOH
Betsy L Bingham
Flagstaff AZ 860021962

Call Sign: KC7YWJ
Richard R Fritz
Flagstaff AZ 860021962

Call Sign: N7ZGS
Andrew D Miller
Flagstaff AZ 860023555

Call Sign: WB7QDQ
Robert W Schmitt
Flagstaff AZ 860030145

Call Sign: KE6AKY
Nicholas E Roach
Flagstaff AZ 860030193

Call Sign: KD7QGE
Mary A Ireland
Flagstaff AZ 860032072

Call Sign: N6MA
D Paul Gagnon
Flagstaff AZ 860032265

Call Sign: KD7DVQ
Verlinda G Milton
Flagstaff AZ 860032727

Call Sign: W7GOQ
Sheldon W Gates
Flagstaff AZ 860033570

FCC Amateur Radio Licenses in Florence

Call Sign: KB7RXK
Daniel R Lizarraga
675 Adamsville Rd
Florence AZ 85232

Call Sign: KB7HAR
J L Rueve
Box 165 Fg

Florence AZ 85232

Call Sign: KB7MYR
Kenneth K Kraushaar
Box 548
Florence AZ 85232

Call Sign: KF7CJN
Michael K Blackstock
200225 Cacf 1037
Florence AZ 85132

Call Sign: K1HOT
Michael K Blackstock
200225 Cacf 1037
Florence AZ 85232

Call Sign: WA0ZPJ
Roy L Horton
494 Chollo Ln
Florence AZ 85232

Call Sign: AD7ID
Darrel E Anthony
10573 E Cliffrose Ln
Florence AZ 85132

Call Sign: KL2FD
Mark L Stephens
26617 E Desert Hills Rd
Florence AZ 85132

Call Sign: N4ZYC
Roland O Leeman
19400 E Diversion Dam Rd
Florence AZ 85232

Call Sign: KN6TE
Charles R Kelly
5712 E Helios Dr
Florence AZ 85132

Call Sign: KA0JHM
Alton A Cobb
800 E MacFarland Blvd Msc 44
Florence AZ 85232

Call Sign: K7KAY

Kay D Matson
129 E Maricopa Blvd
Florence AZ 85132

Call Sign: KL7AKB
Andrew K Brumbaugh
211 E Mesa Dr
Florence AZ 85132

Call Sign: KA7CYP
Oma J Spillman
216 E Ocotillo Dr
Florence AZ 85232

Call Sign: KF7ULL
Catherine D Yates
6760 E Stacy St
Florence AZ 85132

Call Sign: KF7LRR
Michael A Yates
6760 E Stacy St
Florence AZ 85132

Call Sign: KA3NCR
Jaime E Sanchez
401 E Stewart St 504
Florence AZ 85132

Call Sign: KF7HGP
Isaac W Bridge
5618 E Sunrise Cir
Florence AZ 85132

Call Sign: KF7HGR
Nikki W Bridge
5618 E Sunrise Cir
Florence AZ 85132

Call Sign: KF7KZS
Joshua J Wright
6816 E Superstition Way
Florence AZ 85132

Call Sign: W7GPO
Kenneth E Shaffer
413 Echo Ln
Florence AZ 85232

Call Sign: WA7FTP
Robert J Rennie Jr
418 Fiesta Del Sol
Florence AZ 85132

Call Sign: KB7UOL
Richard E Hofmann
112 Florance Gdns
Florence AZ 85232

Call Sign: WB9OQX
Donald E Liedl
3609 Florence Blvd 262
Florence AZ 85232

Call Sign: N7QBN
Haywood A Gilbert
560 Mesa Dr
Florence AZ 85232

Call Sign: KA8VZT
Arthur H Tober
7825 N Diffin Rd
Florence AZ 85232

Call Sign: KI6SZN
Jerilyn F Atnip
9668 N Hwy 79
Florence AZ 85232

Call Sign: N7KWJ
Virgil R Carrell
3925 N Idaho
Florence AZ 852328033

Call Sign: WA0OZD
Richard J Kelley
3805 N Illinois Ave
Florence AZ 852328418

Call Sign: AB7UT
Harvey B Zilm Jr
3600 N Iowa Ave
Florence AZ 852328522

Call Sign: W0YHE
Marvin P Holmes
3729 N Kansas Ave
Florence AZ 85232

Call Sign: N0UEO
Karl S Albrink
3916 N Lancaster Cir
Florence AZ 85232

Call Sign: W9DRO
Vernon L Hayes
3729 N Montana Ave
Florence AZ 852328766

Call Sign: KF7TQH
Edward Cundiff
12674 N Osito St
Florence AZ 85132

Call Sign: KF7RTJ
Lloyd Frizzell
8312 N Palo Verde
Florence AZ 85132

Call Sign: KC7SUE
Donna J Crawford
3910 N Santa Cruz Dr
Florence AZ 85232

Call Sign: KC7FPZ
Larry L Harrison
10240 N Sidewinder Cir
Florence AZ 852329559

Call Sign: KD7WPA
Constantine Lapidakis
4784 N St Josephs Way
Florence AZ 852329399

Call Sign: KF7OVL
David L Rinehart
6810 W Sandpiper Way
Florence AZ 85132

Call Sign: K8IEL
Derrick L George
8050 W Sonoma Way
Florence AZ 85132

Call Sign: WB6THH
William E Wisto
6942 W Trenton Way

Florence AZ 85132

Call Sign: W6SML
Stephen M Spencer
7402 W Trenton Way
Florence AZ 85232

Call Sign: KB7SVO
William R Revis
5988 W Yorktown Way
Florence AZ 85132

Call Sign: KD7NAQ
Larson B Bennett
6084 W Yorktown Way
Florence AZ 85132

Call Sign: N2QPT
Lawrence L La Joie
12507 Wildwood Rd
Florence AZ 85232

Call Sign: KB7PP
James F Stevenson
3818 Wisconsin Ave 289
Florence AZ 85232

Call Sign: KB7QHW
Herbert J Chapman
Florence AZ 85232

Call Sign: KF7PCI
Fred E Appel
Florence AZ 85132

Call Sign: KF7RZE
William A Foster
Florence AZ 85132

Call Sign: KB7LSV
William M Mc Limore
Florence AZ 85232

Call Sign: KC7GFD
David D Cluff Sr
Florence AZ 85232

Call Sign: KB7PZJ
Herbert J Chapman Jr

Florence AZ 85232

Call Sign: KB7WQX
John W Amos
Florence AZ 85232

Call Sign: N7NUK
John W Baker
Florence AZ 85232

Call Sign: KC7BEN
Kenneth W Robinson
Florence AZ 85232

Call Sign: KC7KNE
Frank Meeks
Florence AZ 85232

Call Sign: K7CQW
Matthew L Kipp
Florence AZ 851321380

Call Sign: KC7SSS
Emil F Snyder
Florence AZ 852322924

FCC Amateur Radio Licenses in Forest Lakes

Call Sign: KC7NWQ
David W Holt
837 Wildcat Rd
Forest Lakes AZ 85931

Call Sign: W7NAZ
David W Holt
1829 Wildcat Rd
Forest Lakes AZ 85931

Call Sign: KB7WGV
Lowell G Moss
Forest Lakes AZ 85931

Call Sign: KD7JMK
Richard L Sowell
Forest Lakes AZ 85931

Call Sign: KC7ELR
Robert J Vebber

Forest Lakes AZ 85931

Call Sign: W7PVE
Robert J Vebber
Forest Lakes AZ 85931

Call Sign: KD7LQH
Mogollon Rim Collins
Collectors Club
Forest Lakes AZ 859311597

FCC Amateur Radio Licenses in Fort Defiance

Call Sign: N1IZW
John A Garson
2095 Cedar Cir
Fort Defiance AZ 86504

Call Sign: N7XVN
Larry B Dunn
Fort Defiance AZ 86504

Call Sign: N7ZNG
May Yuan
Fort Defiance AZ 86504

Call Sign: KC7BLF
Jennifer A Murga
Fort Defiance AZ 86504

Call Sign: KD7LEN
Patrick R Willie
Fort Defiance AZ 86504

Call Sign: KC7BLG
Ricardo Murga
Fort Defiance AZ 86504

Call Sign: KB7LTK
Kellamay Kelly
Fort Defiance AZ 86504

FCC Amateur Radio Licenses in Fort Grant

Call Sign: WA7TFY
Walter C Cox
Fort Grant AZ 85644

FCC Amateur Radio Licenses in Fort Huachuca

Call Sign: KC7WEM
Christopher W Reed
209th Sig Co Bldg 52108
Fort Huachuca AZ 85613

Call Sign: KE6KCS
Michael P O Bryon
504th Sig Bn 11th Sig Bde
Fort Huachuca AZ 85613

Call Sign: KD7YJW
John T Green
86th Sig Bn Box 84
Fort Huachuca AZ 85613

Call Sign: KC7WLB
Robert H Darling
Brown Ct
Fort Huachuca AZ 85613

Call Sign: KJ4RVT
John W Watters Jr
101 Dove Ave
Fort Huachuca AZ 85613

Call Sign: KG4LIB
Matthew A Wallace
108 Dove Ave
Fort Huachuca AZ 85613

Call Sign: AB0JK
Charles C Dodd
109 Grierson Ave
Fort Huachuca AZ 85613

Call Sign: W4DRM
Daniel R Matchette
Grierson Ave
Fort Huachuca AZ 85613

Call Sign: KC7WKR
Thomas P Swatloski
105 Grierson Rd
Fort Huachuca AZ 85613

Call Sign: KD7MAO
Robert E Brown
Hall Cir
Fort Huachuca AZ 85613

Call Sign: KC7VQH
Murrill P Ware Jr
Hall Cir
Fort Huachuca AZ 85613

Call Sign: KI4DOQ
Matthew K Hinshaw
Hughes St
Fort Huachuca AZ 85613

Call Sign: KC7WER
Howard E Crebo
Jeffords Nbu 97J
Fort Huachuca AZ 85613

Call Sign: KB7VYC
Bernardus J Pol
Jeffords St
Fort Huachuca AZ 85613

Call Sign: K1KBO
Usa Intelligence Center Fort
Huachuca
Jim Ave
Fort Huachuca AZ 85613

Call Sign: KC7CKA
Dale W Maxwell
Mason St
Fort Huachuca AZ 85613

Call Sign: KD7FKA
Kristoffer A Hart
Meyer Ave
Fort Huachuca AZ 85613

Call Sign: KD7MAG
Jonathan D Todd
Meyer Ave
Fort Huachuca AZ 85613

Call Sign: KE7UJA
Michael C Smith
Meyer Ave

Fort Huachuca AZ 85613

Call Sign: KB7LLE
Francis P Goss
Meyer Ave Nbu 51 0
Fort Huachuca AZ 85613

Call Sign: KB7GBY
Raymond D Kellogg
Meyer St Nbu 54M
Fort Huachuca AZ 85613

Call Sign: KD7MAP
Amataga Tiafala
Mott Cir
Fort Huachuca AZ 85613

Call Sign: KC7VQN
Jesse L Berain
141 Royal St
Fort Huachuca AZ 85613

Call Sign: KD7MAJ
Kevin R Thompson
Rucker St
Fort Huachuca AZ 85613

Call Sign: KB7YRH
Robert J Mc Murtry
Fort Huachuca AZ 85613

Call Sign: KC7WEO
Christopher W Hanovic
Fort Huachuca AZ 85613

Call Sign: KD7MAH
Aaron C Taylor
Fort Huachuca AZ 85613

Call Sign: N2RHF
Joel J Mason
Fort Huachuca AZ 85670

Call Sign: KE5PQI
Jonathan S Gholson
Fort Huachuca AZ 85670

Call Sign: KB0MVP
Lawrence R Greene

Fort Huachuca AZ 85670

Call Sign: WA7GNV
Lawrence R Greene
Fort Huachuca AZ 85670

Call Sign: KC7THV
Marc A Smelser
Fort Huachuca AZ 85670

Call Sign: KE7WWT
Maurice A Mitchell
Fort Huachuca AZ 85670

Call Sign: KC7VQL
Nicholas J George Jr
Fort Huachuca AZ 85670

Call Sign: KC7QXK
Paul O Dietrich
Fort Huachuca AZ 85670

Call Sign: KF7JUQ
William L Sweeney
Fort Huachuca AZ 85670

Call Sign: WA6GAQ
William L Sweeney
Fort Huachuca AZ 85670

Call Sign: KC7EXK
Margaret M Cady
Fort Huachuca AZ
856131019

Call Sign: KC7FMD
Gayla B Burns
Fort Huachuca AZ
856702233

Call Sign: KA5BEZ
Daniel Q Bradford
Fort Huachuca AZ
856702235

Call Sign: WA7SLD
James H Skjervem
Fort Huachuca AZ
856702400

Call Sign: W7GLN
Lloyd C Hill
Fort Huachuca AZ
856702506

Call Sign: KC7VQI
Michael J Schuman
Fort Huachuca AZ
856702731

Call Sign: W7SPR
Scott P Soukup
Fort Huachuca AZ
856702972

FCC Amateur Radio Licenses in Fort Thomas

Call Sign: KB7RJS
Leo R Monchamp
Fort Thomas AZ 85536

Call Sign: KB7TNT
Leo P Kriley
Fort Thomas AZ 85536

Call Sign: KB7TNU
Dolores T Monchamp
Fort Thomas AZ 85536

Call Sign: KC7FQN
Ellis R Black
Fort Thomas AZ 85536

Call Sign: KC7SOQ
Roxsanna L Black
Fort Thomas AZ 85536

Call Sign: KC6TRS
Thomas W Lucatorta
Fort Thomas AZ 855360219

FCC Amateur Radio Licenses in Fredonia

Call Sign: N6LRG
Ralph D Magee
Box 451

Fredonia AZ 86022

Call Sign: KE1KJ
Colin M Strong
Box 5
Fredonia AZ 860229600

Call Sign: KC7IKB
Dixon L Baron
65 E Brown St
Fredonia AZ 86022

Call Sign: KD7EXC
George Skroblus
175 W Jensen St
Fredonia AZ 860220505

Call Sign: KC7AOT
Bobett Ray
Fredonia AZ 86022

Call Sign: K7PNR
Fred B Griswold
Fredonia AZ 86022

Call Sign: KF7CIN
Clare L Poulsen
Fredonia AZ 86022

Call Sign: KC7EDI
Edith R Williams
Fredonia AZ 86022

Call Sign: KC7VSL
Ross A Ray
Fredonia AZ 86022

FCC Amateur Radio Licenses in Globe

Call Sign: WB2HZX
Morton Farmer Sr
18 Basham Dr
Globe AZ 85501

Call Sign: N7GJE
Robert L Hilker
1410 Birch St
Globe AZ 85501

Call Sign: KA7UPQ
Michael R Minton
111 Blazer Dr
Globe AZ 85501

Call Sign: WA2TD
Anthony T Dell
Box 454 Sp 39
Globe AZ 85501

Call Sign: W7ATD
Anthony T Dell
Box 454 Sp 39
Globe AZ 85501

Call Sign: KB2RSU
Patricia I Dell
Box 454 Sp 39
Globe AZ 85501

Call Sign: KF7YM
Larry A Evans
8019 Derringer Dr
Globe AZ 85501

Call Sign: WB7RZX
Keith E Murray
1151 E Bailey
Globe AZ 85501

Call Sign: KB7RWF
Richard H Blazer
555 E Cedar St
Globe AZ 85501

Call Sign: KF7MVT
William G Sypult
651 E Kline St
Globe AZ 85501

Call Sign: N9PDR
John C Hampton
7949 E Pueblo St
Globe AZ 85501

Call Sign: WA7UPN
Robert D Tunis
8088 E Savage

Globe AZ 85501

Call Sign: KC7WOT
Paula M Erkens
855 E Skyline Dr
Globe AZ 85501

Call Sign: KF7MVS
Linda A Mclennan
937 N Bancroft St
Globe AZ 85501

Call Sign: KB7UQI
Frank L Guerin
492 N Broad St
Globe AZ 85501

Call Sign: N7UYZ
David F Burke
247 N High St
Globe AZ 855012226

Call Sign: KB7TNY
Jay L Shoemaker Sr
500 N Main St 88
Globe AZ 85501

Call Sign: KB7UQE
Alice T Shoemaker
500 N Main St 88
Globe AZ 85501

Call Sign: KD7ETB
Ellis D Pettigrew
7935 Pinal View
Globe AZ 85502

Call Sign: KF7MVU
Thomas H Homan
730 S 10th St
Globe AZ 85501

Call Sign: KG7XB
William H Howes
770 S 11th St
Globe AZ 85501

Call Sign: AB5RY
Jesus M Falquez III

530 S Bradley Ln
Globe AZ 85501

Call Sign: WB7QMU
Jeanette L Bronson
8200 S Cherokee Dr
Globe AZ 85501

Call Sign: WA7HOP
Teddy J Bronson
8200 S Cherokee Rd
Globe AZ 85501

Call Sign: KB7DLR
Carmen C Corso
475 S East St
Globe AZ 85501

Call Sign: KB7DJE
Michael H Volckmann
1243 S Holy Spirit Ln
Globe AZ 855011969

Call Sign: KF7LUO
Marilyn Medearis
7834 S Hopi Ave
Globe AZ 85501

Call Sign: N7CQM
Richard M Weddle
9359 S Kellner Canyon Rd
Globe AZ 85501

Call Sign: KB7SST
Billy J Drake
5571 S McKinney Ave
Globe AZ 85501

Call Sign: N7IBB
Linda C Corso
1340 S Monterey Dr
Globe AZ 85501

Call Sign: KD7POX
Daniel G Tope
611 S Prickly Pear Dr
Globe AZ 855012421

Call Sign: AE7CW

Charles R Wyatt
8747 S Sharps Rd
Globe AZ 85501

Call Sign: WA7KUM
Ingo Radicke
8346 S Springfield Rd
Globe AZ 855020611

Call Sign: WB7DRD
Kenneth W Simpson
106 W Ash St
Globe AZ 85501

Call Sign: N7ZBU
David D Lockard
Globe AZ 85502

Call Sign: WA7QZU
Doris J Obermeyer
Globe AZ 85501

Call Sign: KF7MVV
Carmen I Kiss
Globe AZ 85502

Call Sign: KC5CXQ
Charles R Visockis
Globe AZ 85502

Call Sign: KB7YEH
Darrell R Hornsby
Globe AZ 85502

Call Sign: KD7OEE
John S Bliss Jr
Globe AZ 85502

Call Sign: KF7GOH
Rodger W Hardy
Globe AZ 85502

Call Sign: K7ENM
Rodger W Hardy
Globe AZ 85502

Call Sign: KC7SON
Ronald D Baroldy
Globe AZ 85502

FCC Amateur Radio Licenses in Gold Canyon

Call Sign: K7OHM
Larry S Roth
7356 Desert Honey Suckle
Gold Canyon AZ 85218

Call Sign: N1YMK
David W Lindquist
8114 E Birdie Ln
Gold Canyon AZ 85218

Call Sign: KD7YEN
Zak K Fargo
6550 E Casa De Leon Ln
Gold Canyon AZ 85218

Call Sign: KF7KFY
Brett M Gonsowski
18244 E El Amancer
Gold Canyon az 85118

Call Sign: N6UTI
James D Porter
9808 E Fortuna Ave
Gold Canyon AZ 85118

Call Sign: KL7BCH
Leo E Olendorff Jr
7151 E Hwy 60 Pmb 210
Gold Canyon AZ 85218

Call Sign: WB6SAB
Angelo Valenti
8704 E Jumping Cholla Dr
Gold Canyon AZ 85219

Call Sign: KB7RRH
John E Fendrick
10751 E Maverick Trl
Gold Canyon AZ 85218

Call Sign: KB0NT
Jeffrey A Liedl
7845 E Opuntia Path
Gold Canyon AZ 85218

Call Sign: W7SCP
C Olheiser II
10436 E Peralta Canyon Dr
Gold Canyon AZ 85218

Call Sign: WB7LRV
P Bernard
10436 E Peralta Canyon Dr
Gold Canyon AZ 85218

Call Sign: KF7MNA
Lawrence Cain
10057 E Prospector Dr
Gold Canyon AZ 85118

Call Sign: N0ZFN
Joseph H Urban
10041 E Prospector Dr
Gold Canyon AZ 851185975

Call Sign: KA0GWW
Ginger K Urban
10041 E Prospector Dr
Gold Canyon AZ 852185975

Call Sign: N2ZLC
Scott Skinner
10153 E Rising Sun Pl
Gold Canyon AZ 85118

Call Sign: KB3MJE
Robert E Turner Jr
7513 E Rugged Ironwood Rd
Gold Canyon AZ 85218

Call Sign: KK7RT
Robert E Turner Jr
7513 E Rugged Ironwood Rd
Gold Canyon AZ 85218

Call Sign: N6EUL
Wells A Hutchins
8807 E Saguaro Blossom Rd
Gold Canyon AZ 852197005

Call Sign: KE7VZE
Richard D Allred
8501 E Sunrise Sky Dr
Gold Canyon AZ 85218

Call Sign: KE7VZD
Noraly A Allred
8501 E Sunrise Sky Dr
Gold Canyon AZ 85218

Call Sign: K7CLK
Chester L Kitchens
10233 E Superstition Range Rd
Gold Canyon AZ 851184927

Call Sign: KB9PIP
Chester L Kitchens
10233 E Superstition Range Rd
Gold Canyon AZ 852184927

Call Sign: KA7ACK
Willard J Zerbe
10587 E Superstition Range Rd
Gold Canyon AZ 85218

Call Sign: KE7ZZH
Brent R Harper
8132 E Sweet Acacia Dr
Gold Canyon AZ 85218

Call Sign: KD7AWQ
Janet R Pengelly
10511 E Tortilla Creek Ct
Gold Canyon AZ 85118

Call Sign: KG8NC
Michael A Pengelly
10511 E Tortilla Creek Ct
Gold Canyon AZ 85118

Call Sign: N8IMO
Robert A Cash
10553 E Tortilla Creek Ct
Gold Canyon AZ 852185107

Call Sign: N7CNI
Thomas M Garneski
7151 E US Hwy 60
Gold Canyon AZ 85218

Call Sign: WA4LCA
Fred Kuykendall Jr
7373 E US Hwy 60 235
Gold Canyon AZ 85218

Call Sign: KC7RK
Boone A Barker
7729 E Usery Pass Trl
Gold Canyon AZ 851181731

Call Sign: N7DON
Donald E Wilson
7096 E Veracruz Way
Gold Canyon AZ 85118

Call Sign: K7PEG
Margaret E Wilson
7096 E Veracruz Way
Gold Canyon AZ 85118

Call Sign: KC6JHS
Arthur O Bridgeforth
6571 S Alameda Rd
Gold Canyon AZ 852196891

Call Sign: N2MDJ
Salvatore Ardizzone
4229 S Avenida De Angeles
Gold Canyon AZ 85118

Call Sign: N7KEI
Donald L Cline
4189 S Hackberry Trl
Gold Canyon AZ 85218

Call Sign: KB6WXF
Paul A Contreras
6708 S Haunted Canyon Rd
Gold Canyon AZ 85118

Call Sign: K7YUZ
Larry W Starr
5476 S Indigo Dr
Gold Canyon AZ 852185363

Call Sign: N7HAH
David D Hop
6268 S Kings Ranch Rd
Gold Canyon AZ 85219

Call Sign: W3WTF
Jeffrey S Cook
6832 S Kings Ranch Rd Ste 2
25
Gold Canyon AZ 85118

Call Sign: N7MOF
Harold G Scholz
5187 S Marble Dr
Gold Canyon AZ 85219

Call Sign: KE7FQP
Larry G Day
8177 S Mountain Air Ln
Gold Canyon AZ 85218

Call Sign: N7DFV
David P Knight
5663 S Pinnacle Ln
Gold Canyon AZ 85219

Call Sign: KC7JSB
Michele A Booskay
3675 S Pottery Rd
Gold Canyon AZ 85219

Call Sign: KC7AEH
Robert J Bocskay Jr
3675 S Pottery Rd
Gold Canyon AZ 85219

Call Sign: AE7FS
Arnold A Zoutte
2644 S Prickly Point Dr
Gold Canyon AZ 85118

Call Sign: KA1ZIL
James G Soler
4627 S Primrose Dr
Gold Canyon AZ 85218

Call Sign: K7JQ
Robert P Olschwang
4766 S Primrose Dr
Gold Canyon AZ 85118

Call Sign: KF7IHV
Austin W Miller

4771 S Primrose Dr
Gold Canyon AZ 85118

FCC Amateur Radio Licenses in Grand Canyon

Call Sign: KL7XI
Ross Rice
1620 Barry Hance Cir
Grand Canyon AZ
860230489

Call Sign: KB7WZK
William F Russell
Desert View
Grand Canyon AZ 86023

Call Sign: N0RZN
Michael A Mchenry
Havasupai St
Grand Canyon AZ
860230236

Call Sign: KC7SRQ
Barbara G Nelson
Havasupai St
Grand Canyon AZ 86023

Call Sign: KB7WFM
James W King
Grand Canyon AZ 86023

Call Sign: KB7ZEP
Jerry D Shinkle
Grand Canyon AZ 86023

Call Sign: KB7ZEQ
Milton J Wright
Grand Canyon AZ 86023

Call Sign: K5ALE
Cris G Cordova
Grand Canyon AZ 86023

Call Sign: W7ORT
Cris G Cordova
Grand Canyon AZ 86023

Call Sign: KD6IJG

Donald A Mc Clelland
Grand Canyon AZ 86023

Call Sign: KD5JNO
Jacqueline M Berbaum
Grand Canyon AZ 86023

Call Sign: KL1MF
Malinda S Fielding
Grand Canyon AZ 86023

Call Sign: KE7MWW
Michael J Weaver
Grand Canyon AZ 86023

Call Sign: N7ZQN
Robert L Sands
Grand Canyon AZ 86023

Call Sign: KL1SF
Sean R Fielding
Grand Canyon AZ 86023

Call Sign: WB6JAA
Paul B Glazer
Grand Canyon AZ
860231105

FCC Amateur Radio Licenses in Green Valley

Call Sign: N7XXQ
Dean E Mac Donald
1570 Agave Ln
Green Valley AZ 85614

Call Sign: WB6TYP
Santiago L Navarro
17805 Ave Valle Verde Del
Norte
Green Valley AZ 85614

Call Sign: K2AHF
Andrew L Lane
380 Brujo N B U 2216
Green Valley AZ 85614

Call Sign: N7TVH
Thomas H Gibbons

908 Calle De Emilia
Green Valley AZ 85614

Call Sign: KC7ODZ
Patricia Signoretti
902 Calle De Marzo
Green Valley AZ 85614

Call Sign: W2JUI
Aaron Traiger
390 Calle Del Brujo
Green Valley AZ 85614

Call Sign: KC7HWD
Joyce Traiger
390 Calle Del Brujo
Green Valley AZ 85614

Call Sign: N2ART
Joseph J Spiller
386 Calle Del Chancero
Green Valley AZ 85614

Call Sign: KC7BHT
Dorothy M Brust
1674 Calle Del Grajo
Green Valley AZ 85614

Call Sign: KC7DFB
Claude M Bobilya
1633 Calle Hacienda
Green Valley AZ 85614

Call Sign: KC7MF
Roy L Mc Callum
1241 Calle Ramiro
Green Valley AZ 85614

Call Sign: KC7URZ
Mary F Youngblood
1365 Camino De La Ola
Green Valley AZ 85614

Call Sign: KE7QKQ
Sidney E Hickman Jr
1665 Camino Del Sol
Green Valley AZ 85614

Call Sign: KE7SFB

Sidney E Hickman Jr
1665 Camino Del Sol
Green Valley AZ 85614

Call Sign: WB4DBH
James W Swanson
236 Camino Del Vate Nbu
2412
Green Valley AZ 85614

Call Sign: WA9ELG
John W Swanson
236 Camino Del Vate Nbu
2412
Green Valley AZ 85614

Call Sign: NR7I
Kenneth H Newbury
2777 Camino Selva
Green Valley AZ 85614

Call Sign: KE7COU
Linda J Epstein
812 Dessert Hills Dr
Green Valley AZ 85614

Call Sign: AD7FP
Linda J Epstein
812 Dessert Hills Dr
Green Valley AZ 85614

Call Sign: KE7COV
Robert Epstein
812 Dessert Hills Dr
Green Valley AZ 85614

Call Sign: AD7FQ
Robert Epstein
812 Dessert Hills Dr
Green Valley AZ 85614

Call Sign: K6HLY
Mervyn C Beaumont
2574 E Alger Dr
Green Valley AZ 85614

Call Sign: KF7JZB
H Richard Jones
2620 E Arica Way

Green Valley AZ 85614

Call Sign: W4PRB
Allan T Mense
1052 E Baldy Spring Pl
Green Valley AZ 85614

Call Sign: AD7FB
Allan T Mense
1052 E Baldy Spring Pl
Green Valley AZ 85614

Call Sign: KF7NZC
Elliott M Klahr
1073 E Baldy Springs
Green Valley AZ 85614

Call Sign: AB0A
Thomas F Purdon
706 E Bent Branch Pl
Green Valley AZ 85614

Call Sign: K6OCW
Richard J Halmos
2215 E Bluejay Vista Ln
Green Valley AZ 85614

Call Sign: KA7OCW
Richard J Halmos
2215 E Bluejay Vista Ln
Green Valley AZ 85614

Call Sign: KC7YFP
James Y Tong III
183 E Camino De Diana
Green Valley AZ 85614

Call Sign: WN7U
Donald T Flood
1956 E Desert Lark Pass
Green Valley AZ 85614

Call Sign: KC7AMW
Edward Crump III
131 E El Naranjo
Green Valley AZ 85614

Call Sign: KC7PSA
Eugene W Friesen

204 E El Valle
Green Valley AZ 85614

Call Sign: KE7SBQ
Robert W Call
140 E El Viento
Green Valley AZ 856142222

Call Sign: KA0IKI
John E Long Jr
2699 E Heber Way
Green Valley AZ 85614

Call Sign: KC0FGT
Walter W Harsch
2474 E Hilbar Ln
Green Valley AZ 85614

Call Sign: W0ALT
Walter W Harsch
2474 E Hilbar Ln
Green Valley AZ 85614

Call Sign: KF7ANL
John H Stauffer
110 E La Soledad
Green Valley AZ 85614

Call Sign: KD7FRS
Leonard F Defendorf
140 E La Soledad
Green Valley AZ 856142426

Call Sign: K0FCM
Francis C Mayo
357 E Las Milpas
Green Valley AZ 85614

Call Sign: K0RAM
Ruth A Mayo
357 E Las Milpas
Green Valley AZ 85614

Call Sign: KD7KDQ
Norman B Jennings
25 E Los Arcos
Green Valley AZ 85614

Call Sign: N7XJU

Thomas M Moore
81 E Los Mangos
Green Valley AZ 856142238

Call Sign: WA2YPJ
Albert Rottell
411 E Mariposa
Green Valley AZ 85614

Call Sign: KC7USA
Nicholas J Lay
367 E Mariposa St
Green Valley AZ 85614

Call Sign: KE7EGT
Karen K Wallace
901 E Mt Wrightston Loop
Green Valley AZ 85614

Call Sign: KE7DQJ
Kellie R Wallace
901 E Mt Wrightston Loop
Green Valley AZ 85614

Call Sign: KE7DUE
Andrew J Lichtsinn
920 E Mt Wrightston Loop
Green Valley AZ 85614

Call Sign: N7ZIJ
Charles M Milne
2655 E Nathan Way
Green Valley AZ 856146263

Call Sign: W3DHF
Donald S Jarvis
353 E Paseo Azul
Green Valley AZ 85614

Call Sign: KC7THT
Patricia H Garrett
352 E Paseo Verde
Green Valley AZ 856144134

Call Sign: WB3FNW
Erica L Piersol
42 E Placita Jazmin
Green Valley AZ 85614

Call Sign: W7DMT
Theodore C Rosenberg
83 E San Vincent Dr
Green Valley AZ 85614

Call Sign: N6KO
Northe K Osbrink
109 E Santa Belia
Green Valley AZ 85614

Call Sign: KC7LVR
Harley J Fee
151 E Santa Rebecca
Green Valley AZ 85741

Call Sign: KC7VDB
Evelyn B Fee
151 E Santa Rebecca Dr
Green Valley AZ 85614

Call Sign: KD7VBL
David L Fuelleman
908 E Sawmill Canyon Pl
Green Valley AZ 85614

Call Sign: KE7QKU
Callum J Farrell
913 E Sylvester Pl
Green Valley AZ 856146064

Call Sign: WA6VWJ
Norman L Kibby
805 E Sylvester Spring Pl
Green Valley AZ 85614

Call Sign: KE7QKV
Colin T Farrell
913 E Sylvester Spring Pl
Green Valley AZ 856146064

Call Sign: KB7LCU
Ivan M Boyer
161 El Naranjo
Green Valley AZ 85614

Call Sign: W7IFS
Ward W Watrous
372 El Valle
Green Valley AZ 85614

Call Sign: KF7ANJ
Patricia Pember
349 El Viento
Green Valley AZ 85614

Call Sign: KE7AUO
Stephen E Quinn
4191 Emelita
Green Valley AZ 85614

Call Sign: KF7LMU
Joseph Misinski
3983 Golden Lynx Rd
Green Valley AZ 85614

Call Sign: K4ILP
Paul W Sturm
777 La Huerta
Green Valley AZ 85614

Call Sign: W7PU
Hubert J Martin
306 Las Hamacas
Green Valley AZ 85614

Call Sign: KC7HSK
William P Ehinger
342 Los Rincones
Green Valley AZ 85614

Call Sign: KC7TYY
Fred H Bigelow
745 Los Topacios
Green Valley AZ 856142314

Call Sign: KC7JLG
Eliot D Blass
1200 Mtn View
Green Valley AZ 85614

Call Sign: KB7SXB
Frederick W Wedekind
917 N Abrego Dr
Green Valley AZ 85614

Call Sign: KE4MII
Kenneth G Clark
941 N Abrego Dr

Green Valley AZ 85614

Call Sign: KB0YVR
Brian R Corner
2124 N Avenida Fina
Green Valley AZ 85614

Call Sign: KD7ISB
Brent E Hofstra
632 N Avenida Tortuga
Green Valley AZ 85614

Call Sign: WX9G
Kenneth E Hofstra
632 N Avenida Tortuga
Green Valley AZ 856143459

Call Sign: K6WWH
William W Hooper
1391 N Boyce Ave
Green Valley AZ 85614

Call Sign: KA1VX
Ted J Zazeski
1619 N Buttes Dr
Green Valley AZ 85614

Call Sign: N7SX
Ted J Zazeski
1619 N Buttes Dr
Green Valley AZ 85614

Call Sign: KI4SQQ
James W Gaw Jr
404 N Calle De Lumbre
Green Valley AZ 85614

Call Sign: WA6FUV
Raymond A Newman
1161 N Canon Del Cajon
Green Valley AZ 85614

Call Sign: WB6FVB
Thelma J Newman
1161 N Canon Del Cajon
Green Valley AZ 85614

Call Sign: WA0KDL
Le Roy C Krsiean

286 N Cape Royal Dr
Green Valley AZ 856145920

Call Sign: KC7RMV
Philip D Wenstrand
80 N Cape Rpyal Dr
Green Valley AZ 85614

Call Sign: N7XF
Willard H Du Bord
692 N Cedar Bend Ave
Green Valley AZ 85614

Call Sign: KE7QKR
Ned K Bleuer
317 N Cobalt Dr
Green Valley AZ 85614

Call Sign: W0KAD
Gene D Schouweiler
214 N Crocodile Rock Dr
Green Valley AZ 85614

Call Sign: KE7KUD
Green Valley ARC
601 N La Canada Dr
Green Valley AZ 85614

Call Sign: WE7GV
Green Valley ARC
601 N La Canada Dr
Green Valley AZ 85614

Call Sign: KC7OEF
Fred Lukas
1919 N La Canada Dr 1008
Green Valley AZ 85614

Call Sign: AD7NJ
Ronald G Phillips
505 N Michelangelo Dr
Green Valley AZ 85614

Call Sign: AA7RP
Ronald G Phillips
505 N Michelangelo Dr
Green Valley AZ 85614

Call Sign: KC7OEG

Raymond E Brown
1601 N Pacana Way
Green Valley AZ 85614

Call Sign: KF7RJZ
Paul D Boyle
1816 N Pacana Way
Green Valley AZ 85614

Call Sign: KR0J
Jeffrey D Vecbastiks
1590 N Paseo La Tinaja
Green Valley AZ 856143988

Call Sign: W0RSP
Adrian Weiss
810 N Placita De La Canoa
Green Valley AZ 85614

Call Sign: KD7HPM
Cristen E Olds
1421 N Placita Real
Green Valley AZ 85614

Call Sign: KF7PUU
Robert E Harmon
1441 N Placita Real
Green Valley AZ 85614

Call Sign: KI3K
Barry O Cruise
1768 N Rio Mayo
Green Valley AZ 856143975

Call Sign: W0YFB
Donald N Smith
1436 N Rio Santa Cruz
Green Valley AZ 85614

Call Sign: KC7WIH
Richard J Zimmerman
1400 N Rio Sonora
Green Valley AZ 85614

Call Sign: WB7RDW
Benjamin C Cleveland
1871 N Rio Yaqui
Green Valley AZ 85614

Call Sign: KB7VKM
Robert B Hyslop
272 N Royal Bell Dr
Green Valley AZ 85614

Call Sign: AK6C
Patrick W Wong
1576 N Rush Creek Ct
Green Valley AZ 85614

Call Sign: KE7UUX
Terry L Tubb
1576 N Rush Creek Ct
Green Valley AZ 85614

Call Sign: KA7TLT
Terry L Tubb
1576 N Rush Creek Ct
Green Valley AZ 85614

Call Sign: W7AKR
Alan K Roehl
1264 N Sun Catcher Way
Green Valley AZ 85614

Call Sign: KA7QEV
Velvalea L Roehl
1264 N Sun Catcher Way
Green Valley AZ 85614

Call Sign: KE7QKP
Robert D Shaub
1954 N Terra Cotta Dr
Green Valley AZ 856144272

Call Sign: KC7TJJ
William C Keedy
1891 N Via Carrizal
Green Valley AZ 85614

Call Sign: KJ7FS
William H Clary
1720 N Via Frondosa
Green Valley AZ 85614

Call Sign: KD7CFB
Henry A Hain
344 Paseo Chico
Green Valley AZ 85614

Call Sign: N7SQB
Duane E Stordahl
224 Paseo Churea
Green Valley AZ 856143335

Call Sign: WA2OCF
Kenneth C Hazen
601 Paseo De Amigos
Green Valley AZ 85614

Call Sign: W2EAV
Fred R Herr
122 Paseo De Chino
Green Valley AZ 85614

Call Sign: KA7YXA
Lawrence W Meyer
100 Paseo De Golf
Green Valley AZ 85614

Call Sign: N6DDR
Richard Wells
180 Paseo De Golf
Green Valley AZ 85614

Call Sign: N6JTS
Henry H Brodsky
1384 Paseo De Golf
Green Valley AZ 85614

Call Sign: K2CVT
Lloyd S Eberhart
1520 Paseo Del Cervato
Green Valley AZ 856144144

Call Sign: N7XJV
Welland A Christenson
1082 Paseo Iris
Green Valley AZ 85614

Call Sign: KB7VKK
Richard Van Horne
Paseo Pena
Green Valley AZ 85614

Call Sign: KD7LUE
Evan A Edwards
781 Placita Cotonia

Green Valley AZ 85614

Call Sign: N0XIR
Edward J Kaufman
1300 Placita De La Cotonia
Green Valley AZ 85614

Call Sign: WB7SCH
John H Rielag
3300 Placita De La Fabula
Green Valley AZ 85614

Call Sign: KB7SWP
Dinah J Lewis
18001 Placita Junio
Green Valley AZ 85614

Call Sign: KB7UCW
Ronald G Lewis
18001 Placita Junio
Green Valley AZ 85614

Call Sign: KB7VKC
Jeanette G Brown
18042 Placita Junio
Green Valley AZ 85614

Call Sign: W8SXX
Robert L Brown
18042 Placita Junio
Green Valley AZ 85614

Call Sign: W7SY
Nelson L Raymond
1706 Retorno De Manana
Green Valley AZ 85614

Call Sign: N8AFS
Norman R Keck
714 Rio San Pedro
Green Valley AZ 856143928

Call Sign: KD6FA
Ted B Litchfield
301 S Abrego Dr
Green Valley AZ 85614

Call Sign: KC7USB
Patricia W Harp

640 S Abrego Dr
Green Valley AZ 85614

Call Sign: N2BIR
George D Walker
725 S Abrego Dr
Green Valley AZ 856142206

Call Sign: K7GXD
Maynard C Richardson
1031 S Abrego Dr
Green Valley AZ 85614

Call Sign: KF7HYT
Daniel E Dyvig
1550 S Abrego Dr
Green Valley AZ 85614

Call Sign: K7DED
Daniel E Dyvig
1550 S Abrego Dr
Green Valley AZ 85614

Call Sign: W0OX
Leslie W Bruce
1181 S Alpine Cir
Green Valley AZ 85614

Call Sign: N5ORN
Clayton J Chamberlain
1184 S Alpine Cir
Green Valley AZ 85614

Call Sign: KJ7OF
Barbara J Peters
3754 S Avenida De Los
Solmos
Green Valley AZ 85614

Call Sign: KE7AUM
George E Clark
1067 S Calle De Las Casitas
Green Valley AZ 856141984

Call Sign: KD4QKZ
Alice M Loring Paquin
3917 S Calle Viva
Green Valley AZ 85614

Call Sign: KE7YKW
Jerome F Franklin
3773 S Camino Comica
Green Valley AZ 85614

Call Sign: K7JFF
Jerome F Franklin
3773 S Camino Comica
Green Valley AZ 85614

Call Sign: W8BDR
Orville D Underwood
2710 S Camino Diaz
Green Valley AZ 85614

Call Sign: KF7UGU
William R Symons
490 S Camino Golgado
Green Valley AZ 85614

Call Sign: WA0JUZ
Richard A Delmonico
2351 S Cliff Dr
Green Valley AZ 85614

Call Sign: N9NOY
Perry W Young
500 S Corpino De Pecho
Green Valley AZ 85614

Call Sign: WB6EHN
William A Albrektsen
858 S Corte Monte Cristo
Green Valley AZ 85614

Call Sign: N7YUJ
Barbara J Foster
2671 S Desert Hills Dr
Green Valley AZ 85614

Call Sign: KE4XK
James H Mauldin
4372 S Desert Jewel Loop
Green Valley AZ 85614

Call Sign: KF7IZI
Laurens R Halsey
1092 S Dutch John Spring Ct
Green Valley AZ 85614

Call Sign: AA4SH
Vincent T Henry
4141 S Emelita Dr
Green Valley AZ 85614

Call Sign: KJ7ON
Ann E Davis
2759 S Fade Dr
Green Valley AZ 85614

Call Sign: KJ7OM
Gerald E Davis
2759 S Fade Dr
Green Valley AZ 85614

Call Sign: KC7OGP
John D Otto Jr
639 S Fremont Cir
Green Valley AZ 85614

Call Sign: AD7GS
John D Otto Jr
639 S Fremont Cir
Green Valley AZ 85614

Call Sign: KC7OGS
Rey J Otto
639 S Fremont Cir
Green Valley AZ 85614

Call Sign: WA7WEJ
Clifford C Marrs
4967 S Gloria View Ct
Green Valley AZ 85614

Call Sign: KH6VJ
Carl L Mellberg
4400 S Golf Est Dr
Green Valley AZ 85614

Call Sign: W6PGK
Robert F Lindstaedt
18211 S I 19 Frontage Rd
Green Valley AZ 856144911

Call Sign: KJ7ZI
Alice A Roy
949 S La Bellota

Green Valley AZ 85614

Call Sign: KC7OEC
Gordon L Parker
S La Canada
Green Valley AZ 85614

Call Sign: N7YMN
Imogene J Ross
1490 S La Canada Dr
Green Valley AZ 85622

Call Sign: WA7UGS
Mario F Alexay Sr
1490 S La Canada Dr
Green Valley AZ 856223313

Call Sign: N3KCJ
Foster L Baker
S La Canada Dr
Green Valley AZ 85614

Call Sign: KC7ANR
Alfred E Thayer
1704 S La Posada Cir 685
Green Valley AZ 85614

Call Sign: W0ROD
Harvey S Steele
501 S La Posada Cir Apt 301
Green Valley AZ 856145107

Call Sign: WA2BTB
Alice G Tannenbaum
685 S La Posada Cir G H
1204
Green Valley AZ 85614

Call Sign: K2BN
Michael D Tannenbaum
685 S La Posada Cir G H
1204
Green Valley AZ 85614

Call Sign: WA7NPD
Walter L Bown
685 S La Posada Cir Unit
3201
Green Valley AZ 85614

Call Sign: KC7KKT
Robert J Hoeckelberg
601 S Los Robies Cir
Green Valley AZ 85614

Call Sign: KF7UGT
Bryan D Goldsmith
27150 S Madera Vista Pl
Green Valley AZ 85614

Call Sign: KF7UGS
Reagan P Goldsmith
27150 S Madera Vista Pl
Green Valley AZ 85614

Call Sign: KC7ZXM
Clyde L Burton
4937 S Meadow Ridge Dr
Green Valley AZ 85614

Call Sign: KX7J
Philip D Doersam
2372 S Orchard View Dr
Green Valley AZ 856141400

Call Sign: K8TXT
Stuart M Hughes
635 S Park Centre Ave
Green Valley AZ 85614

Call Sign: K9FZU
Robert D Berry
835 S Paseo De La Lira
Green Valley AZ 85614

Call Sign: N1MVO
John T Driscoll
S Paseo Madera
Green Valley AZ 85614

Call Sign: KE7YKY
Debby J Lundell
S Paseo Pena
Green Valley AZ 85614

Call Sign: KE7LKY
Kenneth R Hall
2464 S Pecan Vista Jdr

Green Valley AZ 85614

Call Sign: K9GMC
James W Ariana
3381 S Pla Del Esconces
Green Valley AZ 85614

Call Sign: KC7JTH
Louis Goodman
3890 S Placita De La
Moneda
Green Valley AZ 856145060

Call Sign: N7UXT
David T Appleton
3911 S Placita De La
Moneda
Green Valley AZ 85614

Call Sign: WB0ZGA
Roger E Hubbard
3920 S Placita De La
Moneda
Green Valley AZ 85614

Call Sign: KB7VKO
Kelley P Smith
17840 S Placita Junio
Green Valley AZ 85614

Call Sign: KC7CJY
William E Deeg
17949 S Placita Mayo
Green Valley AZ 85614

Call Sign: KA4AAZ
Alonzo J Stotler
633 S Placita Prosperidad
Green Valley AZ 85614

Call Sign: KD7FQW
John F Adderley
2699 S Ridge Top Dr
Green Valley AZ 85614

Call Sign: KA1NVE
Ralph B Trueblood
1600 S San Ray
Green Valley AZ 85614

Call Sign: AB7KC
Carolyn S Miller
1612 S San Ray
Green Valley AZ 85614

Call Sign: N7GV
Lloyd G Miller
1612 S San Ray
Green Valley AZ 85614

Call Sign: WA2IWD
Bruce A Tewksbury
2060 S San Ray
Green Valley AZ 85614

Call Sign: KF7DZA
Catherine A Tewksbury
2060 S San Ray Dr
Green Valley AZ 85614

Call Sign: KE7SBR
Charles H Elder
1924 S San Vincent Dr
Green Valley AZ 85614

Call Sign: K7CHE
Charles H Elder
1924 S San Vincent Dr
Green Valley AZ 85614

Call Sign: KE7YKX
Dennis P Kynion
2305 S Via Amerigo
Green Valley AZ 85614

Call Sign: N4FEL
Robert A Gatterer
24150 S Via Cielo Azul
Green Valley AZ 85614

Call Sign: N7WBW
Kreg C Vergith
2821 S Via Del Bac
Green Valley AZ 856141073

Call Sign: NU7AA
George A Schwartz
2353 S Via Espinosa

Green Valley AZ 856141490

Call Sign: KE7GUQ
Monica M Voorhees
25775 S Via Montana Vista
Green Valley AZ 85614

Call Sign: N0VVH
Ronald E Mc Afee
2299 S Via Pompilo
Green Valley AZ 85614

Call Sign: W3JSN
Paul Hoffman Jr
1491 S Walnut Spring Pl
Green Valley AZ 85614

Call Sign: N7SQL
Ophelia Navarro
17805 Valle Verde
Green Valley AZ 85614

Call Sign: KB7VJV
Ofelia Navarro
17805 Valle Verde Del Norte
Green Valley AZ 85614

Call Sign: WW7JR
Jack D Reeder
1622 Vuelta Salva Tierra
Green Valley AZ 85614

Call Sign: W6NGZ
Jack D Reeder
1622 Vuelta Salva Tierra
Green Valley AZ 85614

Call Sign: KF4WQO
David G Ellerbrake
1769 W Acacia Bluffs Dr
Green Valley AZ 85614

Call Sign: KF4WQP
Laura M Ellerbrake
1769 W Acacia Bluffs Dr
Green Valley AZ 85614

Call Sign: WB6WJC
Edward J Peters Jr

1525 W Acala St
Green Valley AZ 85614

Call Sign: KC7JTI
Richard R Oslund
1527 W Baltusrol Dr
Green Valley AZ 85614

Call Sign: KC7PRU
Daniel H Holter
1493 W Belfry Ct
Green Valley AZ 856145632

Call Sign: K7JPM
David A Mocabee
1041 W Belltower Dr
Green Valley AZ 85614

Call Sign: KC7KKS
Martha A Quimby
1393 W Calle Altamira
Green Valley AZ 85614

Call Sign: KE7KCT
Linda A Cadell
2292 W Calle Balaustre
Green Valley AZ 85614

Call Sign: KE7GUS
Frank C Cadell
2292 W Calle Balaustre
Green Valley AZ 856148049

Call Sign: AC7JM
John A Mitchell
2364 W Calle Cacillo
Green Valley AZ 85622

Call Sign: W7ETM
Evelyn T Mitchell
2364 W Calle Cacillo
Green Valley AZ 85622

Call Sign: W1RII
Robert S Townend
1159 W Calle De Emiua
Green Valley AZ 85614

Call Sign: KA7KEU

Rosemary D Ormond
70 W Calle Del Chance Rd
Green Valley AZ 85614

Call Sign: N7WUI
Lester A Higgins
170 W Calle Del Chancero
Green Valley AZ 85614

Call Sign: KC7OEE
Robert E Johnson
1542 W Calle Del Ducado
Green Valley AZ 85614

Call Sign: WB7TYQ
Annette C Ogren
891 W Calle Del Regalo
Green Valley AZ 85614

Call Sign: W7IZH
Larry A Ogren
891 W Calle Del Regalo
Green Valley AZ 856142805

Call Sign: WD4NSW
John T Nettling
2235 W Calle Guatemote
Green Valley AZ 85614

Call Sign: N1LS
Nils R Holmes
1530 W Calle Hacienda
Green Valley AZ 85614

Call Sign: WA7BWQ
Raymond C Malone
272 W Calle Hogal
Green Valley AZ 85614

Call Sign: W6LAN
Vincent W Stimmel
132 W Calle Manantial Kent
Green Valley AZ 85614

Call Sign: N7IQS
Kenneth K Hillmon
120 W Calle McCleary
Green Valley AZ 85614

Call Sign: KB7SKR
John B Shannon
151 W Calle Montana Jack
Green Valley AZ 85614

Call Sign: KD7ZRF
Harold W Glover
35 W Calle Nogal
Green Valley AZ 85614

Call Sign: KJ7JX
Mervin H Glover
35 W Calle Nogal
Green Valley AZ 85614

Call Sign: KD7QOZ
Alexis N Heimback
4059 W Calle Ocho
Green Valley AZ 85614

Call Sign: KC7ANJ
George K Latch
1200 W Calle Ramiro
Green Valley AZ 85614

Call Sign: KD7QPB
Stephen Myers
3881 W Calle Seis
Green Valley AZ 85614

Call Sign: KE7PEK
Ethan N Beneze
4125 W Calle Seis
Green Valley AZ 85614

Call Sign: W9NGA
Donald G Bergmark
3939 W Calle Siete
Green Valley AZ 85622

Call Sign: KF7HYR
Joel A Dent
4301 W Calle Siete
Green Valley AZ 85622

Call Sign: KF7HYQ
Patricia A Dent
4301 W Calle Siete
Green Valley AZ 85622

Call Sign: K2UFW
Seymour B Kramer
1407 W Camino De La Oca
Green Valley AZ 85614

Call Sign: AA0TF
William V Kulawske
1332 W Camino Del Pato
Green Valley AZ 85614

Call Sign: KF7HYU
Ben C Duncan
5775 W Camino Del Sol
Green Valley AZ 85622

Call Sign: WA6GEF
Bernard T Jeavons
917 W Camino Delicias
Green Valley AZ 85614

Call Sign: KE7COW
Philip L Brooke
500 W Camino Encanto Apt
189
Green Valley AZ 85614

Call Sign: KC7TJH
Diane J Ernest
1501 W Camino Estelar
Green Valley AZ 856225053

Call Sign: K6IZZ
Jack O Ernest
1501 W Camino Estelar
Green Valley AZ 856225053

Call Sign: KF7STO
Glenn A Steinacker
1442 W Camino Lucientes
Green Valley AZ 85622

Call Sign: KB0KP
James S Brown
980 W Camino Sagasta
Green Valley AZ 856144540

Call Sign: WB7ONS
Michael G Herndon

1830 W Camino Urbano
Green Valley AZ 85614

Call Sign: WB5ZJO
Alfred Ely Jr
1842 W Camino Urbano
Green Valley AZ 85614

Call Sign: KA7KET
Allen Ormond
70 W Chance Rd
Green Valley AZ 85614

Call Sign: NX2L
Joseph Schienberg
985 W Cimeno Tierre Libre
Green Valley AZ 85614

Call Sign: KE7FZY
Sigmund Friedman
1143 W Circulo Del Sur
Green Valley AZ 85614

Call Sign: KE7KCU
Edward W Lord Sr
1161 W Circulo Del Sur
Green Valley AZ 85614

Call Sign: W2RS
Raphael Soifer
190 W Continental Rd 220
186
Green Valley AZ 85622

Call Sign: K3YGW
Clyde F Stryker
282 W Continental Vista Pl
Green Valley AZ 85614

Call Sign: KF7NZA
Richard A Hengst
493 W Deerwood Ln
Green Valley AZ 85614

Call Sign: KD7VBK
Ronald A Woodrow
737 W Desert Hills Dr
Green Valley AZ 85614

Call Sign: WA8GTY
Eugene C Torrey
860 W Desert Hills Dr
Green Valley AZ 85614

Call Sign: KC7OED
Roger Q Barnard
25 W Duval Rd 7
Green Valley AZ 85614

Call Sign: WA7QZK
Thorvald W Christiansen
65 W El Indio
Green Valley AZ 85614

Call Sign: WA8ENX
Raymond O Swensen
101 W El Indio
Green Valley AZ 85614

Call Sign: N8RKJ
Shirley J Swensen
101 W El Indio
Green Valley AZ 85614

Call Sign: W7JWR
Gordon M Dunning
140 W El Indio
Green Valley AZ 85614

Call Sign: KF7UGV
Jack J Herman
788 W Firehawk
Green Valley AZ 85614

Call Sign: KB0NN
Donald L Hawley
744 W Fountain Creek Dr
Green Valley AZ 85614

Call Sign: KB9EKD
Alfred W Wichmann
841 W La Calandria
Green Valley AZ 85614

Call Sign: KB9OIQ
Bruce A Roberts
106 W La Pintura
Green Valley AZ 856141927

Call Sign: KC7HSL
James H Carr
1320 W Mariquita St
Green Valley AZ 85614

Call Sign: N3EBG
Rudolph W Sweisfurth Jr
1990 W Mintbush Srive
Green Valley AZ 85614

Call Sign: KC7OEB
Lisa E Newman
121 W Montana Jack
Green Valley AZ 85614

Call Sign: N0TPF
Robert G Lehrke
747 W Moorwood
Green Valley AZ 85614

Call Sign: KA7NBM
John A Washburne
200 W Mora Dr
Green Valley AZ 85614

Call Sign: K3RN
Robert P Newkirk Jr
278 W Mora Dr
Green Valley AZ 856144318

Call Sign: K6UZP
James W Stephens
1151 W Mtn Nugget Dr
Green Valley AZ 85614

Call Sign: KE7KCX
James D Powell
922 W Mtn Stone Dr
Green Valley AZ 85614

Call Sign: AF7L
Lyle B Hocking
1097 W Mtn Stone Dr
Green Valley AZ 85614

Call Sign: WA3UFY
Richard C Thomson Jr
2511 W Music Mountains Dr

Green Valley AZ 856228122

Call Sign: K0JWJ
John W Johnston
283 W Palma Dr
Green Valley AZ 85614

Call Sign: KA5NNR
Carl E Colman
712 W Paraiso Pl
Green Valley AZ 85614

Call Sign: KF7OHK
Alice Mckenzie
565 W Paseo Del Canto
Green Valley AZ 85622

Call Sign: KF7NZD
Robert O Blanton
2 W Paseo Del Chino
Green Valley AZ 85614

Call Sign: KF7HYS
Donald M Davies
142 W Paseo Del Chino
Green Valley AZ 85614

Call Sign: AE7QB
Donald M Davies
142 W Paseo Del Chino
Green Valley AZ 85614

Call Sign: KC7IVD
William H H Hart III
890 W Paseo Del Cilantro
Green Valley AZ 85614

Call Sign: W7LAL
Robert R Morris
12 W Pinon Dr
Green Valley AZ 85614

Call Sign: KB3GUT
George E Birch
2031 W Placita De Enero
Green Valley AZ 856145433

Call Sign: W7IRL
Anne O Birch

2031 W Placita De Enero
Green Valley AZ 856225433

Call Sign: AD7DH
George E Birch
2031 W Placita De Enero
Green Valley AZ 856225433

Call Sign: KG4LCT
Robert E Wright Jr
2241 W Placita De Los
Anillos
Green Valley AZ 85614

Call Sign: WE7PB
Philip L Brooke
1841 W Placita Del Zacaton
Green Valley AZ 85614

Call Sign: KM7T
Randall E Mc Kay
606 W Placita Nueva
Green Valley AZ 85614

Call Sign: KC7YFQ
Doug W Spain
231 W Placita Sin Fin
Green Valley AZ 85614

Call Sign: KC7HSJ
Duane C Kaufman
1476 W Prestwick Dr
Green Valley AZ 85614

Call Sign: KA3ZDL
Dionne G Frank
909 W Quail Dr
Green Valley AZ 85614

Call Sign: W9RZ
Richard B Frank
909 W Quail Dr
Green Valley AZ 85614

Call Sign: WS1X
Carole D Kissinger
641 W Redondo Pl
Green Valley AZ 85614

Call Sign: WS1W
Gary W Kissinger
641 W Redondo Pl
Green Valley AZ 85614

Call Sign: AE7FG
Frank T Supan
393 W Rio Altar
Green Valley AZ 85614

Call Sign: NZ0D
Armin R Diestler
900 W Rio Altar
Green Valley AZ 85614

Call Sign: K7DOD
Donald O Doehring
1041 W Rio Magdalena
Green Valley AZ 85614

Call Sign: WA2UCY
Charles V Lundstedt
622 W Rio San Pedro
Green Valley AZ 85614

Call Sign: KB7BJC
Joseph J Tornatore
317 W Rio Santa Cruz
Green Valley AZ 856143933

Call Sign: KE7GUT
Evelyn T Mitchell
451 W Rio Sinaloa
Green Valley AZ 85614

Call Sign: AD4DG
John A Mitchell
451 W Rio Sinaloa
Green Valley AZ 85614

Call Sign: KE7AUN
James F Galford Jr
141 W Rosa Dr
Green Valley AZ 85614

Call Sign: WA9TKK
Michael A Bass
407 W San Ignacio
Green Valley AZ 85614

Call Sign: KE7YKV
Douglas L Macintyre
956 W Tenniel Dr
Green Valley AZ 85614

Call Sign: N7SPZ
James H Knudson
205 W Tuna Dr
Green Valley AZ 85614

Call Sign: KE7CCS
John R Roquet
1002 W Union Bell Dr
Green Valley AZ 85614

Call Sign: KC7GTN
Richard D Palmer
1022 W Union Bell Dr
Green Valley AZ 856145945

Call Sign: KJ7TF
Russell J Boteilho
1829 W Via De La Gloria
Green Valley AZ 85614

Call Sign: KF7PZ
Judson L Moore
1900 W Via De La Gloria
Green Valley AZ 85614

Call Sign: KE7VTW
Kenneth G Vanhorn
611 W Via De Suenos
Green Valley AZ 85622

Call Sign: N1HN
Hector A Nadreau
1991 W Via Del Picamaderos
Green Valley AZ 85614

Call Sign: NN1V
Howard E Morgan
2148 W Via Nuevo Leon
Green Valley AZ 85614

Call Sign: W1IDP
Gerald E Brooks
742 W Vista Hermosa Dr

Green Valley AZ 85614

Call Sign: KB7CCQ
Donald L Bohannan
Green Valley AZ 85622

Call Sign: K7TNS
Gerald P Winder
Green Valley AZ 85622

Call Sign: W6AH
Lawrence E Black
Green Valley AZ 85622

Call Sign: W0EVL
Roy E Youngblood
Green Valley AZ 85622

Call Sign: KD7VBM
Andrew Pryne
Green Valley AZ 85622

Call Sign: KB1PG
Bert R Klett
Green Valley AZ 85622

Call Sign: KC7TJI
Delnette A Clark
Green Valley AZ 85622

Call Sign: KC7JDV
Hilliard T Tidmore
Green Valley AZ 85622

Call Sign: KC7TJG
Norris L West
Green Valley AZ 85622

Call Sign: KC7HSH
Richard G Molland
Green Valley AZ 85622

Call Sign: KA0TTW
Sheryl K Atterberg
Green Valley AZ 85622

Call Sign: K9UL
Steven E Atterberg
Green Valley AZ 85622

Call Sign: K8VIR
Edwin H Hartz
Green Valley AZ 856220480

FCC Amateur Radio Licenses in Greenehaven

Call Sign: KE6VUK
Brian T Bussey
Greenehaven AZ 86040

FCC Amateur Radio Licenses in Greer

Call Sign: WC7R
Alan K Unangst
10 Off CR 1007
Greer AZ 859270181

Call Sign: KE7BQL
David C Woods Jr
Greer AZ 85927

FCC Amateur Radio Licenses in Happy Jack

Call Sign: KD7ZXB
Delbert A Chase
2547 Blue Ridge Dr
Happy Jack AZ 86024

Call Sign: N7HOG
Perry D Arnold
Box 1300
Happy Jack AZ 860249721

Call Sign: WB7RZV
James C Koontz
Box 478
Happy Jack AZ 86024

Call Sign: KB6LRV
Gladys M Garner
Box 921
Happy Jack AZ 86024

Call Sign: KB6LRU
Richard A Garner

Box 921
Happy Jack AZ 86024

Call Sign: KD7JBS
Northern Arizona Dx
Association
Box 987
Happy Jack AZ 86024

FCC Amateur Radio Licenses in Heber

Call Sign: KC7YAY
Aaron E Haneline
1878 Artists Draw
Heber AZ 85928

Call Sign: KD7AHX
Leroy Bates
2976 Canary Ln
Heber AZ 859280212

Call Sign: N7KDN
Robert L Rice
3323 Stone Bridge Trl
Heber AZ 85928

Call Sign: KC7DHL
Nancy E Rice
3323 Stonebridge Trl
Heber AZ 85928

Call Sign: N7ZBW
Henry W Haffa
Heber AZ 85928

Call Sign: W7RST
Robert S Telfer
Heber AZ 85928

Call Sign: K7TNX
Susan D Witt
Heber AZ 85928

Call Sign: K7ANT
Coda W Witt
Heber AZ 85928

Call Sign: KD7KOT

Coda P Witt
Heber AZ 85928

Call Sign: KE7FRP
Diane D Collins
Heber AZ 85928

Call Sign: KA7VUW
Dianna M Bracke
Heber AZ 85928

Call Sign: K7WPB
Douglas B Fraser
Heber AZ 85928

Call Sign: KE7CBV
Mary A Kartchner
Heber AZ 85928

Call Sign: KC7JGB
Robert E Collins
Heber AZ 85928

Call Sign: W7REC
Robert E Collins
Heber AZ 85928

Call Sign: KE7CBW
Vernon E Kartchner
Heber AZ 85928

Call Sign: W7RIM
Rim Country ARC
Heber AZ 85928

Call Sign: KF6JLX
James R Wirth
Heber AZ 859280369

Call Sign: KC7SAW
George J Gollick Jr
Heber AZ 859280849

FCC Amateur Radio Licenses in Hereford

Call Sign: NL7FC
John M Waller
6877 Apache Plume Rd

Hereford AZ 85615

Call Sign: KB7DDY
Arthur J Cornellier
Box 28E
Hereford AZ 85615

Call Sign: KB7ELC
Milton C Lundin
Box 65B
Hereford AZ 85615

Call Sign: N4GJE
Jimmy L Rittenhouse
5550 Brickey Dr
Hereford AZ 85615

Call Sign: AA7EW
David L Hartzell
6039 Burro Dr
Hereford AZ 85615

Call Sign: KD7PEH
Brian R Dews
5535 Calle Coyote
Hereford AZ 85615

Call Sign: KD7RJF
Gay E Dews
5535 Calle Coyote
Hereford AZ 85615

Call Sign: KB9MNA
Timothy A Gord
5948 Calle De La Tierra
Hereford AZ 85615

Call Sign: KB7YHT
David T Owen
9633 Cana St
Hereford AZ 85615

Call Sign: WX7B
Paul H Winslow
7523 Chippewa St
Hereford AZ 85615

Call Sign: AB2BH
David B Partington Sr

7934 Circle S Dr
Hereford AZ 85615

Call Sign: KC7ZRH
Robert F Hochman
5293 Corral Dr
Hereford AZ 85615

Call Sign: WO6V
James T Scudella
8286 Dakota St
Hereford AZ 85615

Call Sign: WA7NHU
Walter R Wan Sr
5087 Davis St
Hereford AZ 85615

Call Sign: K7WAN
Walter R Wan Sr
5087 Davis St
Hereford AZ 85615

Call Sign: WA7NHU
Walter R Wan Sr
5087 Davis St
Hereford AZ 85615

Call Sign: KF7BIY
John N Herrod
5236 E Ash Canyon Rd
Hereford AZ 85615

Call Sign: KE7YPH
Dennis B Richardson
3499 E Astro St
Hereford AZ 85615

Call Sign: W1LYT
Raymond G Berger
9730 E Baileys Trl
Hereford AZ 856159016

Call Sign: KD7QNQ
Keith R Stone
5500 E Calle Coyote
Hereford AZ 85615

Call Sign: KE7AKZ

Loretta Stone
5500 E Calle Coyote
Hereford AZ 85615

Call Sign: KE4ZZS
Daniel R Riley
5922 E Calle Linda
Hereford AZ 85615

Call Sign: KC7JKY
Karen L Gold
9840 E Cana St
Hereford AZ 85615

Call Sign: KB7RVF
Kevin J Gold
9840 E Cana St
Hereford AZ 85615

Call Sign: KC7WKW
Geoffrey T Bohrer
11463 E Dixon Ln
Hereford AZ 85615

Call Sign: KD7JZE
Jack M Malone
9305 E Hereford Rd
Hereford AZ 85615

Call Sign: W7EJJ
Jack M Malone
9305 E Hereford Rd
Hereford AZ 85615

Call Sign: KN6QQ
Raymond E Fraze
5922 E Hickory Ct
Hereford AZ 85615

Call Sign: KB7TTI
Norman H Wiseman
9036 E Hwy 92
Hereford AZ 85615

Call Sign: KB7HCD
Daniel M Roos
12291 E Hwy 92
Hereford AZ 83864

Call Sign: N0NTO
Malcolm S Wise
5527 E La Paloma Ln
Hereford AZ 85615

Call Sign: KD6QM
James W Lamb
6119 E Lippizan Way
Hereford AZ 85615

Call Sign: KC6EBR
Judith A Lamb
6119 E Lippizan Way
Hereford AZ 85615

Call Sign: N7LNP
Michael E Dickinson
8977 E Nevada Dr
Hereford AZ 85615

Call Sign: KE7NGP
Paul D Jackson
8226 E Nevado Dr
Hereford AZ 85615

Call Sign: KE7FSH
William K Taylor
9475 E Olive Ave
Hereford AZ 85615

Call Sign: KC7WKT
Thomas P Huntoon
5274 E Polly Dr
Hereford AZ 856150102

Call Sign: KF7ITE
Catherine M Fix
6156 E Ramsey Rd
Hereford AZ 85615

Call Sign: KF7ITF
Verlon J Land Jr
6156 E Ramsey Rd
Hereford AZ 85615

Call Sign: KF7ATP
Clarinda S Asato
10425 E Tierra Del Sol
Hereford AZ 85615

Call Sign: KF7ATQ
Ryan M Asato
10425 E Tierra Del Sol
Hereford AZ 85615

Call Sign: KC8TUG
Randy S Powers
5726 E Wade Ln
Hereford AZ 85615

Call Sign: KB6JAV
Charles B Plummer
4818 Green Oak Ln
Hereford AZ 85615

Call Sign: WB7OZB
Vincent P Moreau
5418 Hereford Rd
Hereford AZ 85615

Call Sign: KD7MOK
Richard J Newton
Hereford Rd
Hereford AZ 85615

Call Sign: KF5O
A David Melvin
6754 Jaxel Rd
Hereford AZ 85615

Call Sign: W6DZU
Carlton L Porep
8133 Keeling Rd
Hereford AZ 85615

Call Sign: KC7TAA
Johnny J Lankford
5826 La Donna Ln
Hereford AZ 85615

Call Sign: KK7VE
Dewayne Smith
6570 Ladonna Ln
Hereford AZ 85615

Call Sign: W7BLR
Ray E Heikes
4584 Miller Canyon Rd

Hereford AZ 85615

Call Sign: WB7BGQ
Stanley D Davidson
5068 Muheim
Hereford AZ 85615

Call Sign: KD7QZG
Thomas A Fry
100 Ramsey Canyon Rd
Hereford AZ 85615

Call Sign: N0CAR
Bruce Prince
6250 S Alvarado Pl
Hereford AZ 85615

Call Sign: N7XJL
James R Gunnell
6571 S Arabian Dr
Hereford AZ 85615

Call Sign: KB7TTH
Robert Pisaneschi
9280 S Bryerly Dr
Hereford AZ 85615

Call Sign: N7OO
Jack R Taylor
6267 S Burro Dr
Hereford AZ 85615

Call Sign: N7RN
Rollin F Pettingill
6537 S Calle De La Naranja
Hereford AZ 85615

Call Sign: KD7BZE
Andreas Haensel
8037 S Coyote Song Ln
Hereford AZ 85615

Call Sign: W7DOG
Thomas L Roberts
8037 S Coyote Song Ln
Hereford AZ 86515

Call Sign: KC7LCD
Margaret F Allen

5999 S De Mello
Hereford AZ 85615

Call Sign: KC7GUJ
Billy R Allen
5999 S Demello
Hereford AZ 85615

Call Sign: K7AIM
Billy R Allen
5999 S Demello
Hereford AZ 85615

Call Sign: KF6EHX
David A Adams
8121 S Downey St
Hereford AZ 856159675

Call Sign: KE6UPW
Paul D Adams
8121 S Downey St
Hereford AZ 856159675

Call Sign: KB7ZAU
Paul L Jones
10088 S Grey Fox Trl
Hereford AZ 85615

Call Sign: KB7WXG
Arthur H Thompson
7502 S Hereford Rd
Hereford AZ 85615

Call Sign: WD4NOM
Robert D Shaw
8099 S High Rd
Hereford AZ 85615

Call Sign: KE7DLH
Robert W Norquist
10022 S Hwy 92
Hereford AZ 85615

Call Sign: KC7RCQ
Anthony C Barton
S Hwy 92
Hereford AZ 85615

Call Sign: N7FRL

Randall H Wilson
6983 S Jaxel Rd
Hereford AZ 85615

Call Sign: KB7ELD
Curtis J Vincent
6130 S Kino Rd
Hereford AZ 86516

Call Sign: KC7GUD
David A Lease
6356 S Kino Rd
Hereford AZ 85615

Call Sign: KD7AIM
Gwendolyn M Smith
6570 S La Donna Ln
Hereford AZ 85615

Call Sign: KC7OYN
Carol A Pool
5846 S Mesquite Tree Ln
Hereford AZ 85615

Call Sign: KE7CBS
Jason M Cotton
5868 S Mountain Side Ln
Hereford AZ 85615

Call Sign: KE7LJB
Mark R Nichols
6561 S Natoma Trl
Hereford AZ 85615

Call Sign: KF7TJ
Robert L Warren
6658 S Pintek Ln
Hereford AZ 85615

Call Sign: N7UZX
Barbara E Siemens
6301 S Ranch Rd
Hereford AZ 85615

Call Sign: N7KGK
Leslie A Siemens
6301 S Ranch Rd
Hereford AZ 85615

Call Sign: KF7GBA
Keith D Latam
9009 S Rio Santiago
Hereford AZ 85615

Call Sign: KF7PSP
James H Akridge
9287 S Springtail Dr
Hereford AZ 85615

Call Sign: K7TLA
James H Akridge
9287 S Springtail Dr
Hereford AZ 85615

Call Sign: K9HJO
George E Merrihew II
9407 S Springtail Dr
Hereford AZ 85615

Call Sign: AB7E
David M Gilbert
10623 S Stone Ridge Rd
Hereford AZ 85615

Call Sign: KF7BJE
Kirsten J Kimbler
5696 S Wild Rose Rd
Hereford AZ 85615

Call Sign: KB7TLE
Scott T Harvey
6251 S Y Lightning Ranch
Rd
Hereford AZ 85615

Call Sign: KC7LBZ
Danny R Brown
4557 Vista Granda Rd
Hereford AZ 85615

Call Sign: KD7FJZ
Suzanne Ollano Mayer
4443 Wickersham Rd
Hereford AZ 85615

Call Sign: KD7VVP
Michael S King
5746 Wild Rose Rd

Hereford AZ 85615

Call Sign: K1NGZ
Michael S King
5746 Wild Rose Rd
Hereford AZ 85615

Call Sign: NJ7P
William A Beech
6567 Y Lightning Rd
Hereford AZ 85615

Call Sign: WA6RAC
Mark C Ritter
Hereford AZ 85615

Call Sign: KE7IPW
South Eastern Arizona Radio
Society
Hereford AZ 85615

Call Sign: KD7AIL
Dewayne Smith
Hereford AZ 85615

Call Sign: KC7WKS
Kim R Harvey
Hereford AZ 85615

Call Sign: W1RRT
Richard A Pomroy
Hereford AZ 85615

Call Sign: KC7YUO
Thomas A Harvey
Hereford AZ 85615

Call Sign: KF7CKC
Vernon W Martin II
Hereford AZ 85615

Call Sign: K5OPL
Shirl E Cook
Hereford AZ 856150748

**FCC Amateur Radio
Licenses in Holbrook**

Call Sign: KD7HHX

Donald W Ohlson
901 1st Ave
Holbrook AZ 86025

Call Sign: N6DDU
Neal L Fritchey
109 Court Ln Apt 15
Holbrook AZ 86025

Call Sign: KC7GAD
Jerry H Hunt
201 Desert View Dr
Holbrook AZ 86025

Call Sign: KA7VTM
Daniel Simper
704 E Florida
Holbrook AZ 86025

Call Sign: KA7VTL
Evan J Simper
704 E Florida
Holbrook AZ 86025

Call Sign: KA0MNK
Reginald C Hicks
918 E Hampshire St
Holbrook AZ 86025

Call Sign: KD7BUB
Tauv J Kelley
318 E Hopi Dr
Holbrook AZ 86025

Call Sign: K7SVK
Clifford S Towers Sr
308 Encanto Dr
Holbrook AZ 86025

Call Sign: KC7REM
Joseph E Slade
1207 Hey Wood Ave
Holbrook AZ 86025

Call Sign: KC7REN
Hellen E Slade
1207 Heywood
Holbrook AZ 86025

Call Sign: KD7ZBI
Robert F Mc Carthy
815 N 5th Ave
Holbrook AZ 86025

Call Sign: WB7RYS
Charles R Cullison
9219 Northern Star Rd
Holbrook AZ 860259744

Call Sign: KF7DYV
Jeffery D Lineberry
9373 Prairie Dog Rd
Holbrook AZ 86025

Call Sign: K7JDL
Jeffery D Lineberry
9373 Prairie Dog Rd
Holbrook AZ 86025

Call Sign: KF7IPZ
Lane F Farr
1519 Sacaton Dr
Holbrook AZ 86025

Call Sign: KE4JKC
Lucia V Sparks
203 W Buffalo
Holbrook AZ 86025

Call Sign: KA7ARZ
Alver W Rogers
1207 W Buffalo
Holbrook AZ 86025

Call Sign: KA7VUY
Leo G Hunt
1107 W Buffalo St
Holbrook AZ 86025

Call Sign: KB7YZX
Gayle M Carbonneau
1307 W Erie
Holbrook AZ 86025

Call Sign: N7MGX
Gregory R Carbonneau
1307 W Erie St
Holbrook AZ 86025

Call Sign: KB7TQF
Stuart A Szink
819 W Florida
Holbrook AZ 86025

Call Sign: KB7FAD
Danett Pierson
Holbrook AZ 86025

Call Sign: KB7EZJ
Gains E Murray
Holbrook AZ 86025

Call Sign: W6IJZ
Robert A Cerasuolo
Holbrook AZ 86025

Call Sign: KB7FFE
Ronald C G Fox Jr
Holbrook AZ 86025

Call Sign: KB7FDH
Wendie L Raeder
Holbrook AZ 86025

Call Sign: KB7EYS
William O Erkkila II
Holbrook AZ 86025

Call Sign: WU7X
William O Erkkila
Holbrook AZ 86025

Call Sign: KC7JDC
Donald W Gardner
Holbrook AZ 86025

Call Sign: WA6WDC
Robert J Diodati
Holbrook AZ 86025

Call Sign: N8SBO
Janet R Young
Holbrook AZ 860250820

Call Sign: N8RUU
Richard G Young
Holbrook AZ 860250820

FCC Amateur Radio Licenses in Hotevilla

Call Sign: KD7VWH
Barry Poleyumptewa
Hotevilla AZ 86030

Call Sign: KD7IVH
Jeremy R Toews
Hotevilla AZ 86030

Call Sign: KD7IAQ
Russell G Toews
Hotevilla AZ 86030

FCC Amateur Radio Licenses in Houck

Call Sign: WA7HRV
Richard G Baumann
Houck AZ 86506

FCC Amateur Radio Licenses in Huachuca City

Call Sign: WA7VRT
Harvey W Jackson
107 2nd St
Huachuca City AZ 85616

Call Sign: KF7HKZ
Justin L Moore
102 3rd St
Huachuca City AZ 85616

Call Sign: N7SQD
George M Lloyd
9 Ash St
Huachuca City AZ 85616

Call Sign: N1SKL
Paul J Grillo
2515 Calle Quarto
Huachuca City AZ 85616

Call Sign: W7JTF
Jerry T Floyd
2566 Calle Quarto

Huachuca City AZ 85616

Call Sign: KD6OJL
Edward C Gamble
2520 Calle Seis
Huachuca City AZ 85616

Call Sign: N7QEK
Dorothy A Dybvig
149 E Ash St
Huachuca City AZ 85616

Call Sign: NZ7Z
Paul H Dybvig
149 E Ash St
Huachuca City AZ 85616

Call Sign: WB0WVS
Richard N Baxter
339 E Camino De Mesa
Huachuca City AZ 85616

Call Sign: W7WBZ
Avon K Anderson
474 E K C Williams Ln
Huachuca City AZ 85616

Call Sign: W7LQT
Kenneth C Williams
474 E K C Williams Ln
Huachuca City AZ 85616

Call Sign: K7SDD
Stanley D Davidson
1455 E Landers Rd
Huachuca City AZ 85616

Call Sign: KF7HLD
Terrance A Bastian
1461 E Lincoln Rd
Huachuca City AZ 85616

Call Sign: KF7HLA
Samuel J Bastian
1461 E Lincoln Rd
Huachuca City AZ 85616

Call Sign: KD7HAB
Patricia J Thies

102 E Via Corta
Huachuca City AZ 85616

Call Sign: WB4VAM
David A Moore
1921 E Zachary Way
Huachuca City AZ 85616

Call Sign: KI4FKH
Nancy W Moore
1921 E Zachary Way
Huachuca City AZ 85616

Call Sign: KE6LXI
Kenneth D Fox
203 Grant St
Huachuca City AZ 85616

Call Sign: K7LIR
Richard E Nurss
Hamel Rd
Huachuca City AZ 85616

Call Sign: KB7RDE
Edwin G Pittsley
15 Holly Pl
Huachuca City AZ 85616

Call Sign: N8PLC
Michael S Van Nattan
2525 N Calle Segundo
Huachuca City AZ 85616

Call Sign: KD7IIR
Gerald W Cotner
2090 N Laurel Pl
Huachuca City AZ 85616

Call Sign: KD7FKF
George W Morris
2338 N Mustang Hts Rd
Huachuca City AZ 85616

Call Sign: KD7CJG
Joshua R Leavitt
2721 N Sheila Ln
Huachuca City AZ 85616

Call Sign: KA7PCJ

Donald L Armstrong
130 Via Guamuchil
Huachuca City AZ 85616

Call Sign: KC7GUB
Emory S Lawson
W Hwy 82
Huachuca City AZ 85616

Call Sign: K9TED
Edward C Weaver
252 W Hwy 82 Sp 5
Huachuca City AZ 85616

Call Sign: KF7GBC
Keith A Moore
955 W Stephens Ranch Rd
Huachuca City AZ 85616

Call Sign: KD7MXI
James F Weisbeck
99 W Vista Ln
Huachuca City AZ 85616

Call Sign: AA7JB
Vincent D Fero
864 W Yucca Springs Trl
Huachuca City AZ 85616

Call Sign: W7FSJ
Otis C Barber
Huachuca City AZ 85616

Call Sign: KC7YDG
Cecilia R Barron
Huachuca City AZ 85616

Call Sign: KC7PGP
John L Barron
Huachuca City AZ 85616

Call Sign: AB4EU
Mitchell G Hohstadt
Huachuca City AZ 85616

Call Sign: KF7HKW
Thomas J O'Brien
Huachuca City AZ 85616

Call Sign: W7MU
Thomas R Dewey
Huachuca City AZ 85616

Call Sign: KB7RVJ
Carley L Milam
Huachuca City AZ 85616

FCC Amateur Radio Licenses in Haulapai

Call Sign: KB7TON
Jerry L Shook
Hualapai AZ 86412

Call Sign: KB7VWQ
Patricia A Shook
Hualapai AZ 86412

Call Sign: KA9KRX
Chris A Stayton
Hualapai AZ 86412

Call Sign: AF5G
Chris G Brill
Hualapai AZ 86412

Call Sign: KD7RUG
Iona Kaye Kennard
Hualapai AZ 86412

Call Sign: KF7MRJ
Terry A Lee
Hualapai AZ 86412

FCC Amateur Radio Licenses in Joseph City

Call Sign: KC7QL
David R Legg
4520 4th N
Joseph City AZ 86032

Call Sign: AE7EW
David R Legg
4520 4th N
Joseph City AZ 86032

Call Sign: KC6MEU

Lhindah L Straw
4423 Fish Ln
Joseph City AZ 86032

Call Sign: KA7VEC
Deborah M Mc Curdy
8102 Frontage Rd
Joseph City AZ 86032

Call Sign: KB7YCQ
Duane E Mc Curdy
8102 Frontage Rd
Joseph City AZ 86032

Call Sign: KB7MUB
Merle J Kissling
Joseph City AZ 86032

Call Sign: KD7WIT
Dirk H Baker
Joseph City AZ 86032

FCC Amateur Radio Licenses in Kaibeto

Call Sign: KC7BCK
Benedict Henry
Kaibeto AZ 86053

Call Sign: KC7BCG
Mike N Benally
Kaibeto AZ 86053

FCC Amateur Radio Licenses in Kayenta

Call Sign: N7LIC
Scott E Braden
Kayenta AZ 86033

FCC Amateur Radio Licenses in Kearny

Call Sign: N7EXL
Robert W Evans
308 Croydon Rd
Kearny AZ 85237

Call Sign: KF7TKK

Craig A Hall
Kearny AZ 85137

Call Sign: KB7FDF
Richard A Morris
Kearny AZ 85237

Call Sign: KJ7VK
Kevin N Wheeler
Kearny AZ 85237

FCC Amateur Radio Licenses in Kykotsmovi

Call Sign: KB7UPY
Robin C Jelle
Kykotsmovi AZ 86039

FCC Amateur Radio Licenses in Lakeside

Call Sign: KD7CVF
Thomas L Lenz
1029 Apache Ln
Lakeside AZ 85929

Call Sign: KC7VCT
Paul H Wisniewski
1490 Apache Ln
Lakeside AZ 85929

Call Sign: W7KDG
John P Howard
Box 150
Lakeside AZ 85929

Call Sign: KC7CPG
Sharon L Manor Roberts
Box 1882
Lakeside AZ 85929

Call Sign: KA6KTL
June C Wilkerson
Box 2251
Lakeside AZ 85929

Call Sign: KA6KTM
Ray L Wilkerson
Box 2251

Lakeside AZ 85929

Call Sign: W7ANC
John Crofford
Box 2260
Lakeside AZ 85929

Call Sign: KB7ZIK
John H Kinney
5503 Darren Dr
Lakeside AZ 85929

Call Sign: KB7ZIL
Julie A Kinney
5503 Darren Dr
Lakeside AZ 85929

Call Sign: KE7AZV
William R Morales
5160 East St
Lakeside AZ 85929

Call Sign: KE7NOI
Donna L Stanger
5418 Elk Pkwy
Lakeside AZ 85929

Call Sign: KB5TBA
Ian J Fleming
1801 Fir Dr
Lakeside AZ 859292422

Call Sign: W7LHP
Eugene A Wiseman
2622 Hidden Pines Dr
Lakeside AZ 85929

Call Sign: K7LHP
Donna L Wiseman
2622 Hidden Pines Dr
Lakeside AZ 859296170

Call Sign: N7MXR
Raymond A James
1960 Homestead Rd
Lakeside AZ 85929

Call Sign: AD7W
Michael R Elders

3152 Lazy River Ln
Lakeside AZ 85929

Call Sign: KD7TET
Michael R Elders Jr
3152 Lazy River Ln
Lakeside AZ 85929

Call Sign: KA7QPK
Archie L Prust
6629 Lower Ridge Dr
Lakeside AZ 85929

Call Sign: KA7IDE
David A Russell
4140 Maricopa Dr
Lakeside AZ 85929

Call Sign: K7YCO
James D Porter
4932 Mogollon Rim Dr
Lakeside AZ 85929

Call Sign: WB7QON
Robert L Moore
370 Mtn View Dr
Lakeside AZ 859295648

Call Sign: KQ7Y
Shirlee J Moore
370 Mtn View Dr
Lakeside AZ 859296435

Call Sign: KF7LJS
Kayle V Mcneil
2761 Navajo Way
Lakeside AZ 85929

Call Sign: KB7RXE
Craig L Jackson
2639 Parkinson Rd
Lakeside AZ 85929

Call Sign: KD7DEB
John A Taylor Jr
3321 Petes Retreat Rd
Lakeside AZ 85929

Call Sign: KB7QNK

Wallace R Selby
3854 Porter Creek Ln
Lakeside AZ 85929

Call Sign: N7DPX
Stephen C Luenz
232 Riverside Dr
Lakeside AZ 85929

Call Sign: KE7KO
Paul F Reed
1826 Shoreline Dr
Lakeside AZ 85929

Call Sign: K7ZOV
Harry L Latterman
2590 Summer Dr
Lakeside AZ 85929

Call Sign: KD7TNZ
Jeffrey L Moffat
3088 Sunset Ln
Lakeside AZ 85929

Call Sign: KE7GVB
Clark Halls
1875 W Settlers Ln
Lakeside AZ 85929

Call Sign: KE7IID
Emily C Carpenter
6695 Wagon Wheel Ln
Lakeside AZ 85929

Call Sign: KE7ELV
Evan A Carpenter
6695 Wagon Wheel Ln
Lakeside AZ 85929

Call Sign: N7ZMO
Susan L Carpenter
6695 Wagonwheel Ln
Lakeside AZ 85929

Call Sign: KA7SXU
Richard K Franklin Jr
4386 White Mountain Rd
Lakeside AZ 85929

Call Sign: KB7LTG
David L Hegmann
Lakeside AZ 85929

Call Sign: WA7SAM
Scott A Midkiff
Lakeside AZ 85929

Call Sign: WT7X
Troy E Waters
Lakeside AZ 85929

Call Sign: KC7OWM
Nanette S Geringer
Lakeside AZ 85929

Call Sign: KA7YQY
Shane A Atwell
Lakeside AZ 85929

FCC Amateur Radio Licenses in Lukachukai

Call Sign: KC7VMJ
Adam L Baldwin
Lukachukai AZ 86507

FCC Amateur Radio Licenses in Mammoth

Call Sign: KB7PXV
Clarence M Baugher
106 N Hwy 77 Box 578
Mammoth AZ 85618

Call Sign: K8GJZ
Harold E Detwiler
611 Rolfs Ave
Mammoth AZ 856180858

Call Sign: KB7TLF
Donald O Wright
Mammoth AZ 85618

Call Sign: KB7WFP
James L Taylor
Mammoth AZ 85618

Call Sign: WB7NPM

Isaac M Mikels
Mammoth AZ 85618

Call Sign: K7FRY
Steve P Fry
Mammoth AZ 85618

Call Sign: KF7ITH
Steven P Fry
Mammoth AZ 85618

Call Sign: KD7DCK
Nancy K Wright
Mammoth AZ 856180264

FCC Amateur Radio Licenses in Many Farms

Call Sign: KC7VMK
Gorlando A Claw
Many Farms AZ 86538

FCC Amateur Radio Licenses in Marana

Call Sign: KB7UMW
Edward D Kacura
12122 Blacktail Rd A
Marana AZ 85653

Call Sign: N7YPB
Victor L Carter
30239 E Little Crow Rd
Marana AZ 85653

Call Sign: KC7TOG
Felix H Bessler Jr
24641 E Pinal Airpark
Marana AZ 85653

Call Sign: KD7FKI
Delroy N Guild
17019 Gold Bell Rd
Marana AZ 85653

Call Sign: KI4MYZ
John R Wilde
17760 Lickskillet Ln
Marana AZ 85653

Call Sign: KF7LZX
David L Beauchesne
11366 N Adobe Village Pl
Marana AZ 856584736

Call Sign: AK2L
David L Beauchesne
11366 N Adobe Village Pl
Marana AZ 856584736

Call Sign: KE7TXW
Stefanie L Mellott
12120 N Antelope Rd
Marana AZ 85653

Call Sign: N7ZBD
Timothy E Mellott
12120 N Antelope Rd
Marana AZ 85653

Call Sign: W5LLD
Lynn L Drury
12520 N Anway Rd
Marana AZ 85653

Call Sign: KC7SIN
James A Gummer
12021 N Blacktail Rd
Marana AZ 85653

Call Sign: KC7SIP
Thomas A Gummer
12021 N Blacktail Rd
Marana AZ 85653

Call Sign: N7EDK
Edward D Kacura
12122 N Blacktail Rd A
Marana AZ 85653

Call Sign: KC6DYH
Bonnie L Coe
7485 N Blanco Wash Trl
Marana AZ 85653

Call Sign: WA0RTO
Fred E Coe
7485 N Blanco Wash Trl

Marana AZ 85653

Call Sign: KG6ATP
Martin O Adriaanse
12912 N Cenozoic Dr
Marana AZ 85658

Call Sign: KC7CJZ
Albert W Kern Sr
12602 N Derringer
Marana AZ 85653

Call Sign: WA7RYH
Edward W Dungan
12211 N Derringer Rd
Marana AZ 85238

Call Sign: KC6EVL
Alan D Swensen
12328 N Fallen Shadows Dr
Marana AZ 85658

Call Sign: KD6RJG
Vivien L Provost
12619 N Fallen Shadows Dr
Marana AZ 85658

Call Sign: AC6NA
William B Provost
12619 N Fallen Shadows Dr
Marana AZ 85658

Call Sign: KD7ECN
Annette Sostarich
13350 N Flintlock Rd
Marana AZ 85653

Call Sign: KF6QGE
Warren E Clark
12377 N Globe Mallow Pl
Marana AZ 85653

Call Sign: KE7BXI
J T Dameron
13392 N Hertitage Club Pl
Marana AZ 85653

Call Sign: KB8DZB
Gerald D Peters Jr

13612 N Jane Ave
Marana AZ 85653

Call Sign: KC5NOF
Daniel B Carman
13595 N Lon Adams Rd
Marana AZ 85653

Call Sign: KD7INX
Melanie K Shroyer
10740 N Longview Ave
Marana AZ 85653

Call Sign: KJ7WX
Michael J O Sullivan
12402 N Luckett Rd
Marana AZ 85653

Call Sign: KA7BBD
Denelda M Skramstad
10501 N Maybrook Ave
Marana AZ 85653

Call Sign: KA7APA
Larry D Skramstad
10501 N Maybrook Ave
Marana AZ 85653

Call Sign: KC7QYH
Darrell D Milstead
4421 N Musket Rd
Marana AZ 85653

Call Sign: KC7WXY
Duane C Kenny
12595 N New Reflecton Dr
Marana AZ 85658

Call Sign: KD7DKB
Lorna A Kenny
12595 N New Reflecton Dr
Marana AZ 85658

Call Sign: N9NCV
Earl D Shuman
12988 N Ocotillo Bluff Pl
Marana AZ 85658

Call Sign: KF6PGG

David S Adriaanse
12465 N Owl Head Canyon
Rd
Marana AZ 85658

Call Sign: W4OEP
Stephen K Park
12426 N Paseo Penuela
Marana AZ 85658

Call Sign: KF7DRR
Christopher P Hizny
12435 N Pinnacle Vista Ct
Marana AZ 85658

Call Sign: KF7KRX
John Re
14377 N Pipestone Pl
Marana az 85658

Call Sign: KF7MYF
Christopher S Burnett
12807 N Pocatella Dr
Marana AZ 85653

Call Sign: K7ICU
James S Redding
12825 N Ponderay Dr
Marana AZ 85653

Call Sign: KE7VLE
Steven D Beyer
13305 N Red Hill Rd
Marana AZ 85653

Call Sign: KF7ATO
James H Hill
4987 N Sabi
Marana AZ 85653

Call Sign: KF7TGS
Gary W Pester
13377 N Sandario Rd 9
Marana AZ 85653

Call Sign: WA6CVL
Jerry N Sharp
13377 N Sandario Sp 4
Marana AZ 85653

Call Sign: W7ZXQ
Alvin Merten
10335 N Tall Cotton Dr
Marana AZ 85653

Call Sign: WA7Y
Marty Martinson
7703 N Via Atascadero
Marana AZ 85743

Call Sign: KC6MWZ
Veryl J Nelson
9767 N Volk
Marana AZ 85652

Call Sign: KC7NCA
Eugene F Fink
11060 N Waite Rd
Marana AZ 856530398

Call Sign: WA4OXR
Robert J Sales
13449 N Warfield Cir
Marana AZ 85653

Call Sign: KG4KFJ
Jacob M Wardrip
13500 N Warfield Cir
Marana AZ 85658

Call Sign: KA4NGW
Paul C Stromberg Jr
12523 New Reflection Dr
Marana AZ 85658

Call Sign: W7LSU
Charles L Amy
31890 S Galena Dr
Marana AZ 85653

Call Sign: NB0S
Larry W Hulsker
37883 S Jacy Trl
Marana AZ 85658

Call Sign: KF7ATS
John G Browning III
35419 S Longhorn Trl

Marana AZ 85658

Call Sign: KD5AJI
Toni J Davis
35259 S Marylynne Ln
Marana AZ 85653

Call Sign: K5LBT
Frank C Davis
35259 S Marylynne Ln
Marana AZ 85658

Call Sign: N9RXO
Stan D Kennaugh
11582 Vanderbilt Farms Way
Marana AZ 85653

Call Sign: KA3TUI
Mark T Simpson
11085 W Aplomado Dr
Marana AZ 85653

Call Sign: KC7CPB
Cortney T Ellis
18701 W Avra Valley Rd
Marana AZ 85653

Call Sign: KE6GTS
Steve W Collins
5117 W Bass Butte Ln
Marana AZ 85653

Call Sign: KB7WFO
Gregory W Michels
4720 W Cactus Bluff Dr
Marana AZ 856534242

Call Sign: KE7EKD
Nathan A Prather
17040 W Calle Carmela
Marana AZ 85653

Call Sign: KC7WTN
Mac W Murray
16642 W Calle Gravilla
Marana AZ 85653

Call Sign: KR4IW
Kenneth R Nichols

5885 W Clear Brook Ln
Marana AZ 85653

Call Sign: W8OFC
James H Grams
5441 W Cochie Springs St
Marana AZ 85653

Call Sign: KC2CPZ
Michael A Sherwood
5491 W Cochie Springs St
Marana AZ 85653

Call Sign: KC7MLR
Andrea L Cooper
16480 W El Tiro Rd
Marana AZ 85653

Call Sign: KD7SIT
Nicholas G Cooper
16480 W El Tiro Rd
Marana AZ 85653

Call Sign: K7SIT
Nicholas G Cooper
16480 W El Tiro Rd
Marana AZ 85653

Call Sign: KC7MLS
Steve M Cooper
16480 W El Tiro Rd
Marana AZ 85653

Call Sign: KE7OLJ
Jason R Bowman
16901 W Falcon Ln
Marana AZ 85653

Call Sign: KE7OYM
Robert A Bowman
16901 W Falcon Ln
Marana AZ 85653

Call Sign: KF7JGH
Craig S Brewer
3403 W Hawk View Dr
Marana AZ 85658

Call Sign: W8JBT

Brian W Handy
17380 W Jaguar Ln
Marana AZ 85653

Call Sign: N7BXV
Doris J Fruth
16275 W Lambert Ln
Marana AZ 856539233

Call Sign: KB7NB
John E Fruth
16275 W Lambert Ln
Marana AZ 856539233

Call Sign: KF7PSY
Jonathan E Wheeler
12052 W Makenna Ln
Marana AZ 85653

Call Sign: KE7DHH
Warren P Mc Quiggan
20615 W Mullins Ln
Marana AZ 85653

Call Sign: W3EYD
Warren P Mc Quiggan
20615 W Mullins Ln
Marana AZ 85653

Call Sign: WH6CXN
John M Ladd
5075 W New Shadow Way
Marana AZ 85658

Call Sign: KE7BYP
Rebecca D Hashman
17600 W Oatman Rd
Marana AZ 85653

Call Sign: KC5EGC
Terry E Hashman
17600 W Oatman Rd
Marana AZ 85653

Call Sign: KB5B
Terry E Hashman
17600 W Oatman Rd
Marana AZ 85653

Call Sign: KF7CEJ
Timothy P Mcguire
5565 W Painted Cliff Dr
Marana AZ 85658

Call Sign: KD7TLI
Robert L Jones
17401 W Picacho Rd
Marana AZ 85653

Call Sign: KD7ZNB
Robert W Jones
17401 W Picacho Rd
Marana AZ 85653

Call Sign: KA7FTZ
Kathleen E Lafferty
16835 W Placita La Junta
Marana AZ 85653

Call Sign: KE7VKI
Janet F Mclay
11272 W Ruddy Dr
Marana AZ 85653

Call Sign: KB7BNY
Marvin R Brown
16250 W Sandy Sy
Marana AZ 85653

Call Sign: KE7OEC
James R Dunn
5066 W Spoon Plant Ct
Marana AZ 85658

Call Sign: KE7IQV
Vanyel L Amenhauser
16193 W Spurbell Ln
Marana AZ 85050

Call Sign: KE7INF
Edward N Patino
11496 W Stone Mound Dr
Marana AZ 85653

Call Sign: KI0PB
Darryl W Arnold
9015 W Tangerine Farms 23
Marana AZ 85653

Call Sign: KD7SIQ
Albert Bright
Marana AZ 85653

Call Sign: N7CVG
Daniel C Erdman
Marana AZ 85653

Call Sign: KI7HF
Daun R Suarez
Marana AZ 85653

Call Sign: KE7NOY
Larry W Kimber Sr
Marana AZ 85653

Call Sign: KD7CXR
Richard J Mazur
Marana AZ 85653

Call Sign: KE7RIA
Robert L Johnson
Marana AZ 85653

Call Sign: N7TVD
Rubena J Suarez
Marana AZ 85653

Call Sign: KD7SWT
Wyndom J Newman
Marana AZ 85653

Call Sign: WD8NIS
Michael G Schnell
Marana AZ 856530247

Call Sign: KD7AGS
George M Nellis
Marana AZ 856530718

FCC Amateur Radio Licenses in Maricopa

Call Sign: KF7HMF
Steve D Miller
636 Blacktrail Trl
Maricopa AZ 85139

Call Sign: KD7AOK
Robert R Lyle
Box 679 G
Maricopa AZ 85239

Call Sign: KC7EUM
Dieter H Geibel
4947 N Arabian Rd
Maricopa AZ 85239

Call Sign: W7DHG
Dieter H Geibel
4947 N Arabian Rd
Maricopa AZ 85239

Call Sign: KG9JC
Curtis J Steger
9441 N Bottle Brush Rd
Maricopa AZ 85239

Call Sign: NA7CS
Curtis J Steger
9441 N Bottle Brush Rd
Maricopa AZ 85239

Call Sign: W9LEO
Leo J Deckelmann Sr
1871 N Brower Ln
Maricopa AZ 85239

Call Sign: KL0ZN
Jerome E Painter
18488 N Celis St
Maricopa AZ 85138

Call Sign: WA6YVA
Fred J Fichman
20466 N Cloud Nine Ln
Maricopa AZ 85138

Call Sign: W6YTT
Carol A Dulay
20814 N Dries Rd
Maricopa AZ 85138

Call Sign: KF7DYD
E Marie Murray
7282 N Escondido Rd
Maricopa az 85139

Call Sign: WB9SYL
E Marie Murray
7282 N Escondido Rd
Maricopa AZ 85139

Call Sign: KC0OVV
Mark R Gumto
22784 N Kennedy Dr
Maricopa AZ 85238

Call Sign: KD7FSI
Seth A Pickell
6395 N La Burma Rd
Maricopa AZ 85239

Call Sign: KD7FSJ
Valarae Pickell
6395 N La Burma Rd
Maricopa AZ 85239

Call Sign: N0PQW
Jeffrey P Price
21103 N Mac Neil
Maricopa AZ 85138

Call Sign: W7WET
Jeffrey P Price
21103 N Mac Neil
Maricopa AZ 85138

Call Sign: KC7NFH
Scott J Reece
19147 N Meghan Dr
Maricopa AZ 85239

Call Sign: KF7OJW
Duane P Meinen
17131 N Nicoles Pl
Maricopa AZ 851393201

Call Sign: KD7XH
Cary D Mammen
14621 N Palo Verde Dr
Maricopa AZ 85239

Call Sign: W7KOK
Russell E Shouse
12288 N Ralston Rd

Maricopa AZ 85239

Call Sign: KD7GHA
Ruth E Sweeney
12288 N Ralston Rd
Maricopa AZ 85239

Call Sign: N9MMC
Pamela A Andrew
22239 N Reinbold Dr
Maricopa AZ 85138

Call Sign: AD7BH
Glenn C Gabriel
19152 N San Juan St
Maricopa AZ 85138

Call Sign: KG6QQF
Sasha Gabriel
19152 N San Juan St
Maricopa AZ 85138

Call Sign: N3OYM
Anita D Donelson
21688 N Sunset Dr
Maricopa AZ 851395480

Call Sign: N3LDH
Fabian B Chapman
21688 N Sunset Dr
Maricopa AZ 851395480

Call Sign: KD0EEZ
Robert D Singer
20996 N Sweet Dreams Dr
Maricopa AZ 85138

Call Sign: KB7NUS
Carol E Mc Bride
11398 N Thunderbird Rd
Maricopa AZ 852390927

Call Sign: WA7VVA
Donald A Mc Bride
11398 N Thunderbird Rd
Maricopa AZ 852390927

Call Sign: K7DAE
Richard K Welsh

12760 N Thunderbird Rd
Maricopa AZ 85239

Call Sign: N7NRT
Blaine K Briggs
20252 N Toledo Ave
Maricopa AZ 852385381

Call Sign: KD7HLU
Michael A Elsberry
22290 N Vargas Dr
Maricopa AZ 85138

Call Sign: KB7PYI
Jo Anne Bell
10137 N White Rd
Maricopa AZ 85239

Call Sign: KG4MKX
Andrew J Hunter Non
21080 N Wilford Ave
Maricopa AZ 85239

Call Sign: KF7QOV
Chris P Ehrbright
22238 O Sullivan Dr
Maricopa AZ 85138

Call Sign: W6SDM
Steve D Miller
636 S Blacktail Trl
Maricopa AZ 85139

Call Sign: KC1BB
James W Charboneau
856 S Blacktail Trl
Maricopa AZ 85239

Call Sign: KA7QKB
John W Anderson
572 S Deer Trl
Maricopa AZ 85239

Call Sign: K7JWA
John W Anderson
572 S Deer Trl
Maricopa AZ 85239

Call Sign: KD7KK

Stephan Schreiner
209 S Hidden Valley Rd
Maricopa AZ 852396905

Call Sign: N6JZH
Carl F Pierce
1824 S Indiansummer St
Maricopa AZ 85239

Call Sign: N7NNJ
Susan L Wright
860 S John Wayne Pkwy
Maricopa AZ 85239

Call Sign: KE7JVX
Monty H Dana
1720 S Ralston Rd
Maricopa AZ 85139

Call Sign: KG7ML
Edward F Stoffa
32261 San Lorenzo Dr
Maricopa AZ 85239

Call Sign: KE7NWK
Dylan B Martin
36455 Velasquez Dr
Maricopa AZ 85239

Call Sign: N7DYL
Dylan B Martin
36455 Velasquez Dr
Maricopa AZ 85239

Call Sign: KF7SJB
Richard F Tworek
44126 W Adobe Cir
Maricopa AZ 85139

Call Sign: N7LQR
John R Timmons
45415 W Alamendras St
Maricopa AZ 852398790

Call Sign: KC7OGJ
James M Towner
42766 W Anne Ln
Maricopa AZ 85239

Call Sign: N7FAN
David M French
43669 W Arizona Ave
Maricopa AZ 85138

Call Sign: KE7EES
Joseph J La Russa
41680 W Avella Dr
Maricopa AZ 85239

Call Sign: N0ELM
Frederick R Troeh
36399 W Barcelona Ln
Maricopa AZ 852385383

Call Sign: KG7IW
Ford L Willman
36650 W Barcelona Ln
Maricopa AZ 85238

Call Sign: N5FW
Ford L Willman
36650 W Barcelona Ln
Maricopa AZ 85238

Call Sign: N7NRT
Blaine K Briggs
40132 W Bonneau St
Maricopa AZ 851385189

Call Sign: K7BKB
Blaine K Briggs
40132 W Bonneau St
Maricopa AZ 852385189

Call Sign: N7OXF
Dale T Taylor
40930 W Brandt Dr
Maricopa AZ 85138

Call Sign: K7JLH
James L Hick
42450 W Candyland Pl
Maricopa AZ 85239

Call Sign: K7RM
David N Ellis
36307 W Cartegna Ln
Maricopa AZ 85138

Call Sign: K9ZHJ
Robert S Howard
35881 W Catalan St
Maricopa AZ 85138

Call Sign: W8RH
Robert S Howard
35881 W Catalan St
Maricopa AZ 85138

Call Sign: KR4LU
David E Wimmer
42457 W Chimayo Dr
Maricopa AZ 85138

Call Sign: KB2OZQ
Lawrence E Ruback
43384 W Chisolm Dr
Maricopa AZ 85238

Call Sign: KB1WWW
Jerome J Erickson
42284 W Colby
Maricopa AZ 85238

Call Sign: KG6RCB
Matthew V Huffaker
41605 W Corvalis Ln
Maricopa AZ 85239

Call Sign: WO0Z
Larry W Loen
43632 W Cydnee Dr
Maricopa AZ 85138

Call Sign: KF7EIF
Stephen M Andert
45067 W Desert Garden Rd
Maricopa AZ 85139

Call Sign: WD8PMH
George H Pulk
56015 W Desert Vly Rd
Maricopa AZ 85239

Call Sign: N7RFC
Robert F Conaway Jr
48761 W Dune Shadow Rd

Maricopa AZ 85239

Call Sign: KE7PZO
Christopher T Dreher
56071 W Fulcar Ln
Maricopa AZ 85239

Call Sign: W0SDD
Christopher T Dreher
56071 W Fulcar Ln
Maricopa AZ 85239

Call Sign: KD7KMC
Tamara A Lara
49785 W Gail Ln
Maricopa AZ 85239

Call Sign: KD7KUG
Tianna M Lara
49785 W Gail Ln
Maricopa AZ 85239

Call Sign: KD7KMB
James D Lara III
49785 W Gail Ln
Maricopa AZ 85239

Call Sign: KD7KMD
Rachel R Lara
49785 W Gail Ln
Maricopa AZ 85239

Call Sign: KD7OBQ
Jerry L Jensen
50209 W Gail Ln
Maricopa AZ 85239

Call Sign: W5BBD
Norman D Vickers
44062 W Granite Dr
Maricopa AZ 85239

Call Sign: WA6FQW
John L Bernstein Sr
54544 W Granite Dr
Maricopa AZ 852398890

Call Sign: KF7DIT
Randy N Miller Jr

40826 W Hayden Dr
Maricopa az 85238

Call Sign: KC7HAR
Walter A Bishoff Jr
43571 W Hillman Dr
Maricopa AZ 85239

Call Sign: KE7MMU
Brian D Shaw
45105 W Horse Mesa Rd
Maricopa AZ 85139

Call Sign: K1WNM
Steven F Farwell
45096 W Jack Rabbit Tr
Maricopa AZ 85239

Call Sign: K3LQ
James V Henry
45112 W Jackrabbit Tr
Maricopa AZ 85239

Call Sign: K6BZZ
Richard W Dabney
42561 W Jailhouse Rock Ct
Maricopa AZ 85138

Call Sign: W5UFZ
Richard W Dabney
42561 W Jailhouse Rock Ct
Maricopa AZ 85238

Call Sign: W9PQO
Donna M Parrish
42528 W Jailhouse Rock Ct
Maricopa AZ 85138

Call Sign: KA9SZU
Donna M Parrish
42528 W Jailhouse Rock Ct
Maricopa AZ 851383124

Call Sign: KC7JIH
Judith S Walp
49005 W Julie Ln
Maricopa AZ 85239

Call Sign: N4AUR

David R Ellis
49495 W Julie Ln
Maricopa AZ 85239

Call Sign: KE7BRP
William E Cope
43211 W Magnolia Rd
Maricopa AZ 85138

Call Sign: KC7YVX
Elisabeth M Moe
50219 W Mayer Blvd
Maricopa AZ 85239

Call Sign: KC7NOK
James K Moe
50219 W Mayer Blvd
Maricopa AZ 85239

Call Sign: KD7KIF
James R Dickes
44208 W McCord Dr
Maricopa AZ 85138

Call Sign: KF7HHM
Raymond W Zalanka III
43243 W Neely Dr
Maricopa az 85138

Call Sign: N2ELK
Raymond W Zalanka III
43243 W Neely Dr
Maricopa AZ 85138

Call Sign: KF7UKV
Jeffrey C Ostler
43542 W Neely Dr
Maricopa AZ 85138

Call Sign: KF7UKT
Amanda O Ostler
43542 W Neely Dr
Maricopa AZ 85138

Call Sign: KD7FVA
Michelle Allcott Mills
52115 W Peters
Maricopa AZ 85139

Call Sign: KB2EBA
James J Crawford
44703 W Portabello Rd
Maricopa AZ 85239

Call Sign: KE6COT
Marcelino C Monegas
40772 W Pryor Ln
Maricopa AZ 85138

Call Sign: KD7ETF
Norman W Fasoletos
44621 W Redrock Rd
Maricopa AZ 85139

Call Sign: N7VKL
Emory V Chase
54142 W Ridoway Rd
Maricopa AZ 85239

Call Sign: WD9JCI
William J Garrigan
42184 W Rummy Rd
Maricopa AZ 85138

Call Sign: W7JCI
William J Garrigan
42184 W Rummy Rd
Maricopa AZ 85138

Call Sign: KD7IPZ
Thomas R Pacific
41194 W Sanders Way
Maricopa AZ 85238

Call Sign: KF7DZG
Josh T Taylor
45538 W Sky Ln
Maricopa AZ 85239

Call Sign: KE7KUR
David J Mckinley
46169 W Sky Ln
Maricopa AZ 85239

Call Sign: KC7CYB
Richard A Kelly
43576 W Sparks Ct
Maricopa AZ 85239

Call Sign: KF7LEI
Nathan K Lussier
42426 W Sparks Dr
Maricopa az 85138

Call Sign: KE7TPF
Eric D Somerville
54143 W Stallion Rd
Maricopa AZ 85239

Call Sign: KC7ZUW
Karl E Jensen
46126 W Tulip Ln
Maricopa AZ 85239

Call Sign: WB3HXU
Harry L Hughes III
49588 W Val Vista
Maricopa AZ 85239

Call Sign: KE6OAT
Steven J Martin
36455 W Velaquez Dr
Maricopa AZ 85239

Call Sign: AC7CA
Mckay L Monson
35691 W Velazquez Dr
Maricopa AZ 851385854

Call Sign: KF7MIO
Kevin A Hall
44290 W Vineyard St
Maricopa AZ 85139

Call Sign: W7RDC
Robert D Cleaver
50525 W Whirly Bird Rd
Maricopa AZ 85239

Call Sign: NI7R
Phillip H Brown
42875 W Whispering Wind
Ln
Maricopa AZ 851388519

Call Sign: N7HTB
Carol A Casarow

50820 W Wildwood Rd
Maricopa AZ 85239

Call Sign: N7NJ
David L Casarow
50820 W Wildwood Rd
Maricopa AZ 85239

Call Sign: KD7KEB
Kay D Williams
50820 W Wildwood Rd
Maricopa AZ 85239

Call Sign: AD5VG
Kevin W Beverage
46094 W Windmill Dr
Maricopa AZ 85239

Call Sign: KF7KKR
Ryan D Sutherland
44004 W Yucca Ln
Maricopa AZ 85138

Call Sign: W7TFO
Dennis D Gilliam
Maricopa AZ 85139

Call Sign: KF7EUK
Robert S Howard
Maricopa AZ 85139

Call Sign: KD7CXU
Brad D Butz
Maricopa AZ 85239

Call Sign: AD7YP
Dennis D Gilliam
Maricopa AZ 85239

Call Sign: KD7VCF
Jonathan G Simmonds
Maricopa AZ 85239

Call Sign: KF6WBU
Kenneth W Rowe
Maricopa AZ 85239

Call Sign: KF7UCD
Kenneth W Vance

Maricopa AZ 85239

Call Sign: KD7ZBC
Mary E Simmonds
Maricopa AZ 85239

Call Sign: KC7WJC
Stephanie L Smith
Maricopa AZ 85239

Call Sign: KE7IOO
Steven T Hodges
Maricopa AZ 85239

**FCC Amateur Radio
Licenses in McNeal**

Call Sign: KC7FLE
Hugh Pendergrass
Box 66L
McNeal AZ 85617

Call Sign: KE7AOO
Andrew T O Dwyer
3870 Davis Rd
McNeal AZ 85617

Call Sign: KC7GUA
Christine M Grotendiek
3870 Davis Rd
McNeal AZ 85617

Call Sign: KE7AOS
Daniel W Bohling
3870 Davis Rd
McNeal AZ 85617

Call Sign: KE7AOQ
Dwight R Brown
3870 Davis Rd
McNeal AZ 85617

Call Sign: KE7AON
Eric C Zimmerman
3870 Davis Rd
McNeal AZ 85617

Call Sign: KE7DNF
Jeffry J Werley

3870 Davis Rd
McNeal AZ 85617

Call Sign: KE7AOU
Johnathan D Van Wormer
3870 Davis Rd
McNeal AZ 85617

Call Sign: KE7DNG
Julie B Harkins
3870 Davis Rd
McNeal AZ 85617

Call Sign: KE7AOR
Linda K Bohling
3870 Davis Rd
McNeal AZ 85617

Call Sign: KE7AOT
Maria J Van Wormer
3870 Davis Rd
McNeal AZ 85617

Call Sign: KE7AOP
Todd L Harkins
3870 Davis Rd
McNeal AZ 85617

Call Sign: KA9RGB
Brett W Randolph
3870 Davis Rd
McNeal AZ 85617

Call Sign: KE7KAL
Joel L Rich
3870 Davis Rd
McNeal AZ 85617

Call Sign: KC8UTV
Michael P Jackson
4012 Davis Rd
McNeal AZ 85617

Call Sign: KC8ANI
Randey M Bell
3069 Leyte
McNeal AZ 85617

Call Sign: KB7FLX

Edna M Fifer
7271 McBride Rd
McNeal AZ 85617

Call Sign: N7VJV
Neale B Fifer
7271 McBride Rd
McNeal AZ 85617

Call Sign: KB7IN
John T Hellyer
8393 Mescalero Pl
McNeal AZ 85617

Call Sign: KB7VKN
Michelle Haynie
9033 N Coffman Rd
McNeal AZ 85617

Call Sign: KC7LCS
Charles A Hebron
7390 N McBride Rd
McNeal AZ 85617

Call Sign: W6RLL
Joseph W E Young
6807 N Rockhouse Rd
McNeal AZ 856179504

Call Sign: KD7LUO
Kevin L Lewis
3870 W Davis Rd
McNeal AZ 85617

Call Sign: KE7AOW
Cynthia K Spence
3870 W Davis Rd
McNeal AZ 85617

Call Sign: KE7AOV
Daren K Spence
3870 W Davis Rd
McNeal AZ 85617

Call Sign: KC8KMM
Arthur Glidewell
3870 W Davis Rd
McNeal AZ 85617

Call Sign: KE7QFU
Bart D Haines
3870 W Davis Rd
McNeal AZ 85617

Call Sign: KE7QFX
Brian J Pruett
3870 W Davis Rd
McNeal AZ 85617

Call Sign: KE7QFV
Bryan M Abbott
3870 W Davis Rd
McNeal AZ 85617

Call Sign: KE7KAN
Carlos Chala Espinosa
3870 W Davis Rd
McNeal AZ 85617

Call Sign: KE7QFW
Joel N Davis
3870 W Davis Rd
McNeal AZ 85617

Call Sign: KE7KAM
Preston I Huntting
3870 W Davis Rd
McNeal AZ 85617

Call Sign: KB5RJW
Johnnie B Cutts
3870 W Davis Rd
McNeal AZ 85617

Call Sign: W3CIV
John P Super
4155 W Double Adobe Rd
McNeal AZ 85617

Call Sign: W2CRS
John P Super
4155 W Double Adobe Rd
McNeal AZ 85617

Call Sign: W7WEB
Paul E Davis
5057 W Double Adobe Rd
McNeal AZ 85617

Call Sign: KD7OGS
Laura L Randolph
4255 W Heart Ln
McNeal AZ 85617

Call Sign: KB6UYD
Billy J Haslam
4175 W Hopkins Rd
McNeal AZ 856179660

Call Sign: WA6STP
Anna E Petersen
McNeal AZ 85617

Call Sign: WB6NGU
George E W Petersen
McNeal AZ 85617

Call Sign: KE7ARZ
Adam L Brown
McNeal AZ 85617

Call Sign: KD7VWL
Lurah Magee
McNeal AZ 85617

Call Sign: KB4FHO
Alvin L Brown
McNeal AZ 85617

Call Sign: KC6NUG
David L Newgen
McNeal AZ 856170161

FCC Amateur Radio Licenses in Miami

Call Sign: N2AZY
James C Oberst
30 Chapparal Loop
Miami AZ 85539

Call Sign: KB7UQG
Jay C Shoemaker
802 Cypress
Miami AZ 85539

Call Sign: KB7UQF

Pat D Shoemaker
802 Cypress
Miami AZ 85539

Call Sign: KA7LSX
Don W Zobel
52235 E Black Jack Rd
Miami AZ 85539

Call Sign: K7UAN
James D Guy
406 Indian Ave
Miami AZ 85539

Call Sign: WB7NOS
Donald E Guy
Indian Ave
Miami AZ 85539

Call Sign: WB7NLC
Georgina Guy
Indian Ave
Miami AZ 85539

Call Sign: WB7OBY
Irene V Guy
Indian Ave
Miami AZ 85539

Call Sign: KA7HSW
Dale D Rickabaugh
5714 Miami Gardens Dr
Miami AZ 85539

Call Sign: KA7HSX
Mary L Rickabaugh
5714 S Miami Gardens Dr
Miami AZ 85539

Call Sign: KB7UQV
Gary M Venturelli
53463 Sutton Pl
Miami AZ 85539

Call Sign: KI7HB
Robert A Lewis
949 W Cypress
Miami AZ 855391086

Call Sign: KA7MDY
Robert A Lewis
949 W Cypress
Miami AZ 855391086

Call Sign: W3IEL
James F Craib
Miami AZ 85539

FCC Amateur Radio Licenses in Morenci

Call Sign: KF7VBQ
Errol R Olson
106 Acacia Rd
Morenci AZ 85540

Call Sign: KC7BHR
Antonio S Escalante
92 Gila
Morenci AZ 85540

Call Sign: KJ7LH
John M Tysoe
House 2 Eagle
Morenci AZ 85540

Call Sign: KC7GHB
Larry A Scott
Morenci AZ 85540

Call Sign: KE7CDM
Gilbert R Hilpert
Morenci AZ 85540

Call Sign: N7FGO
Laura L Aroz
Morenci AZ 85540

Call Sign: KE7CDL
Lee C Hilpert
Morenci AZ 85540

Call Sign: KC7VOU
Quentin C Hilpert
Morenci AZ 85540

FCC Amateur Radio Licenses in Mount Lemmon

Call Sign: KD7AWT
Extreme Team Contest Club
Mount Lemmon AZ
856190835

FCC Amateur Radio Licenses in Munds Park

Call Sign: WB7SMT
Jackie F Neve
640 Crestline
Munds Park AZ 86017

Call Sign: WB7SMU
Robert H Neve
640 Crestline
Munds Park AZ 86017

Call Sign: KA7MGO
Richard W Nix
506 E Meadowview
Munds Park AZ 86017

Call Sign: W7KEX
Donald R Cross
17930 Lake Odell Pl
Munds Park AZ 86017

Call Sign: KB7VMB
Kevin E Carpenter
390 Pinewood Blvd
Munds Park AZ 86017

Call Sign: AA7JA
John E Van Such
17120 S Elk Pl
Munds Park AZ 86017

Call Sign: KC7HES
Ryan Oler
17375 S Oak
Munds Park AZ 86017

Call Sign: KC7CHM
Madelon S Anderson
Munds Park AZ 86017

Call Sign: KF7HSD

Allen J Traber
Munds Park AZ 86017

Call Sign: N7LAV
Danny C Anderson
Munds Park AZ 86017

Call Sign: KC7FYO
David E Hawkins
Munds Park AZ 86017

Call Sign: KD6VYH
Deborah A Lorenz
Munds Park AZ 86017

Call Sign: KF7WE
James M Thomas
Munds Park AZ 86017

Call Sign: KF7DUR
Kenneth J Held
Munds Park AZ 86017

Call Sign: W7DVC
Larry W Young Sr
Munds Park AZ 86017

Call Sign: KE7QFG
Patricia L Traber
Munds Park AZ 86017

Call Sign: WB7RLM
William J Kuemper
Munds Park AZ 86017

Call Sign: KF6LCB
Lucinda K Derango
Munds Park AZ 860177544

Call Sign: N7TAD
Thomas A Derango
Munds Park AZ 860177544

FCC Amateur Radio Licenses in Naco

Call Sign: KE7TXZ
Michael K Lavallee
Naco AZ 85620

FCC Amateur Radio Licenses in Nazlini

Call Sign: KD7EFZ
Edison M Gorman
Nazlini AZ 86540

FCC Amateur Radio Licenses in Nogales

Call Sign: KA7UPR
Daniel L Vanata
50 Apache Way
Nogales AZ 85621

Call Sign: N7FA
Matthew J Campbell
230 E Thelma St 1
Nogales AZ 856211592

Call Sign: N7HAJ
Edd C Parker
322 Mesquite Dr
Nogales AZ 85621

Call Sign: KD7CQV
Christian D Guevara
2731 N Camino Vista Del
Cielo
Nogales AZ 85621

Call Sign: N7ECG
Janis D Bell
182 N Court St
Nogales AZ 85621

Call Sign: N7ECF
Thomas J Bell
182 N Court St
Nogales AZ 85621

Call Sign: KE6THR
Jacques Elbert
1777 N Frank Reed Rd Ste C
Nogales AZ 85621

Call Sign: KE7CDN
Vicente U Martinez

577 N Grand Ave
Nogales AZ 85621

Call Sign: KL0BB
Jon W Carroll
581 N Grand Ave
Nogales AZ 85621

Call Sign: KB7LLV
Gilbert C Soto
2133 N Grand Ave 1 A
Nogales AZ 85621

Call Sign: K7SM
Stephen J Marstall
563 S River Rd
Nogales AZ 85621

Call Sign: KE7TXT
Roberto C Medina
35 S River Rd Trl 33
Nogales AZ 85621

Call Sign: KC7HWK
Michael M R Crabtree
1181 W Cimarron St
Nogales AZ 85621

Call Sign: W6SKC
James A Scharfe Jr
Nogales AZ 85628

Call Sign: N2IY
Vicente U Martinez
Nogales AZ 85628

Call Sign: KA6TLT
Bill R Nicholas
Nogales AZ 856281725

FCC Amateur Radio Licenses in North Rim

Call Sign: KB7PXJ
James C Jackson Jr
North Rim AZ 86052

FCC Amateur Radio Licenses in Nutrioso

Call Sign: KE7BQJ
David A Line Dengli
Nutrioso AZ 859320107

Call Sign: K5DLD
David A Line Dengli
Nutrioso AZ 859320107

Call Sign: KC7YBU
Mark A Mandile
Nutrioso AZ 859320400

FCC Amateur Radio Licenses in Oracle

Call Sign: KF7ERU
Gerald A Bond
939 Calle Futura
Oracle AZ 85623

Call Sign: KD7SH
Alice M Epperson
1610 El Paseo Cir
Oracle AZ 85623

Call Sign: NH6U
John V Epperson
1610 El Paseo Cir
Oracle AZ 85623

Call Sign: KC0CUN
Judy S Conover
33351 High Jinks Rd
Oracle AZ 85623

Call Sign: NQ7B
Charles R Jaffe
1150 N Estill
Oracle AZ 85623

Call Sign: N6AUD
James E Norine
815 N Evergreen
Oracle AZ 85623

Call Sign: KC7PUI
Sheila M Norine
815 N Evergreen

Oracle AZ 85623

Call Sign: KE7YTY
Steven E Anderson
845 N John Adams St
Oracle AZ 85623

Call Sign: KB7ID
Lee W Mc Cutchen
721 N Timerline Rd
Oracle AZ 85623

Call Sign: N7KHK
Thomas H Beeston
2805 N Triangle L Ranch Rd
Oracle AZ 856230900

Call Sign: AB2IP
William R Jones
2691 W Linda Vista
Oracle AZ 856231684

Call Sign: AD7EX
William R Jones
2691 W Linda Vista
Oracle AZ 856231684

Call Sign: W7DCD
Ray L Winiecke
480 W Robles Pl
Oracle AZ 865230205

Call Sign: KB7KRC
Benjamin N Finch
Oracle AZ 85623

Call Sign: W7CS
Charles S Smallhouse
Oracle AZ 85623

Call Sign: KC4BRA
Jason F Baer
Oracle AZ 85623

Call Sign: W7NNS
Nancy N Smallhouse
Oracle AZ 85623

Call Sign: KB7KRB

Neil M Finch
Oracle AZ 85623

Call Sign: KB7OCF
Roy C Serody
Oracle AZ 85623

Call Sign: KB7OCE
Sarah J Fazakerley
Oracle AZ 85623

Call Sign: WA7ELN
Troy O Hall Jr
Oracle AZ 85623

Call Sign: N7KZ
Oracle Ridge ARA
Oracle AZ 85623

Call Sign: KD7MPS
David W Kelly
Oracle AZ 85623

Call Sign: N7WEK
Floyd D Fitzgerald
Oracle AZ 85623

Call Sign: KC7IXP
Howard A Hawes
Oracle AZ 85623

Call Sign: KB5DPT
James C Baldwin III
Oracle AZ 85623

Call Sign: N6VGL
James T Austin
Oracle AZ 85623

Call Sign: KE7OYI
Lorin P Mcrae
Oracle AZ 85623

Call Sign: KD7JZD
Ronald D Niswander
Oracle AZ 85623

Call Sign: KC7SSG
Sharlene D Hall

Oracle AZ 85623

Call Sign: KD7GGV
Susan S Finelsen Glenn
Oracle AZ 85623

Call Sign: KF7CEH
Vivien D Mayer
Oracle AZ 85623

Call Sign: KC7ZMV
James D Cadien
Oracle AZ 85623

Call Sign: KM6IX
Suzan L Austin
Oracle AZ 856230581

Call Sign: W2INQ
Don Schricker
Oracle AZ 856235365

FCC Amateur Radio Licenses in Oro Valley

Call Sign: KD7TMZ
David C Cook
611 E Bridal Veil Falls Rd
Oro Valley AZ 85737

Call Sign: KC0BBV
Thomas M Simpson
340 E Cambridge Dr
Oro Valley AZ 85704

Call Sign: W6KZZ
Marvin B Luke
1212 E Camino Diestro
Oro Valley AZ 85704

Call Sign: W7RHB
Theodore Kelpinski
2207 E Cargondera Canyon
Dr
Oro Valley AZ 85755

Call Sign: KB0ZMH
Dale A Knudson

2342 E Cargondera Canyon
Dr
Oro Valley AZ 85755

Call Sign: KC7OVI
Robert C Kley Jr
1104 E Crown Ridge Dr
Oro Valley AZ 85755

Call Sign: K7LEY
Robert C Kley Jr
1104 E Crown Ridge Dr
Oro Valley AZ 85755

Call Sign: AL7HD
Larry Cast
310 E Fieldcrest Ln
Oro Valley AZ 85737

Call Sign: K7RML
Peter A Cento
425 E Hardy Rd
Oro Valley AZ 857047406

Call Sign: KG7OV
Lowell L O Connor
290 E Highcourte Ln
Oro Valley AZ 85737

Call Sign: KF7SEA
Scott D Ingram
504 E Marshall Peak Dr
Oro Valley AZ 85755

Call Sign: W7WSO
Scott D Ingram
504 E Marshall Peak Dr
Oro Valley AZ 85755

Call Sign: WB2MJC
Stephen H Dobbs
2354 E Mortar Pestle Dr
Oro Valley AZ 857551903

Call Sign: KD7YNJ
Glenn H Luglan Jr
270 E Oro Valley Dr
Oro Valley AZ 85737

Call Sign: K0WLS
Randall S Malick
2479 E Spring Pioneer Ln
Oro Valley AZ 85755

Call Sign: KF0X
Randall S Malick
2479 E Spring Pioneer Ln
Oro Valley AZ 85755

Call Sign: N7KVR
John L Hunsperger
1810 E Starmist Pl
Oro Valley AZ 85737

Call Sign: W7EXP
John L Hunsperger
1810 E Starmist Pl
Oro Valley AZ 85737

Call Sign: W1HRZ
Harry K Roseberry
1171 E Sunset Ridge Pl
Oro Valley AZ 857378861

Call Sign: KF7DDJ
Andrew R Prochniak
12136 Jarren Canyon Way
Oro Valley AZ 85755

Call Sign: KH6LEM
Lem W Nash
14095 N Biltmore Dr
Oro Valley AZ 85755

Call Sign: KC7QVV
James L Kinzie
10973 N Black Cyn Ct
Oro Valley AZ 85737

Call Sign: AE7JQ
James L Kinzie
10973 N Black Cyn Ct
Oro Valley AZ 85737

Call Sign: WB0TUF
Fredrich A Clarkson
13245 N Booming Dr
Oro Valley AZ 857370021

Call Sign: W0SKI
Fredrich A Clarkson
13245 N Booming Dr
Oro Valley AZ 857370021

Call Sign: KD7MZY
Richard Gilbert Jr
13905 N Buckingham Dr
Oro Valley AZ 857375852

Call Sign: KC7HWN
William H Graff
9201 N Calle Buena Vista
Oro Valley AZ 857374901

Call Sign: N7JXS
Walter H Williams
11351 N Charoleau Dr
Oro Valley AZ 85737

Call Sign: AL7KE
Walter S Brophy
14420 N Choctaw Dr
Oro Valley AZ 85755

Call Sign: KE7NDM
Zachary P May
11491 N Civano Pl
Oro Valley AZ 85737

Call Sign: WB7NUY
Joseph B Barr
9711 N Cliff View Pl
Oro Valley AZ 85704

Call Sign: KC7DPM
Doug R Haynes
11746 N Desert Holly Dr
Oro Valley AZ 85737

Call Sign: KF7MQM
James R Garrity Sr
11048 N Divot Dr
Oro Valley AZ 85737

Call Sign: WA1KFI
James R Garrity Sr
11048 N Divot Dr

Oro Valley AZ 85737

Call Sign: KE7RYT
Ralph S Richards
12485 N Echo Valley Dr
Oro Valley AZ 85755

Call Sign: K7SRL
Ralph S Richards
12485 N Echo Valley Dr
Oro Valley AZ 85755

Call Sign: KE7UVN
Patrick E Fleming
11730 N Edi Pl
Oro Valley AZ 85737

Call Sign: KF7SEF
Marilyn N Smoler
13917 N Embassy Dr
Oro Valley AZ 85755

Call Sign: AD6KI
David E Smoler
13917 N Embassy Dr
Oro Valley AZ 857555849

Call Sign: KC7FNV
Norman W Gardner
12851 N Genesee Dr
Oro Valley AZ 85755

Call Sign: N5TDD
Neil E Hejny
10702 N Glen Abbey Dr
Oro Valley AZ 85737

Call Sign: N7AMJ
Vicki L Merley
13262 N Hammerstone Ln
Oro Valley AZ 857551901

Call Sign: WA2WLX
Robert C Molczan
13731 N High Mountain
View Pl
Oro Valley AZ 85737

Call Sign: KA7VPR

Robert C Molczan
13731 N High Mountain
View Pl
Oro Valley AZ 857398844

Call Sign: KE7FSI
David W Cornelius
10176 N Invverrary Pl
Oro Valley AZ 85737

Call Sign: KD7NVK
Ronald K Thevenot
11940 N Joi Dr
Oro Valley AZ 857379570

Call Sign: WA2ITA
Kenneth J Cottrell
10261 N Krauswood Ln
Oro Valley AZ 857376937

Call Sign: KB7URS
Joseph E Ferdyn
11602 N Kriscott Ct
Oro Valley AZ 85737

Call Sign: KK6IF
Gary J Schmitz
11000 N La Canada Pd
Oro Valley AZ 85737

Call Sign: KT7AZ
Gary J Schmitz
11000 N La Canada Pd
Oro Valley AZ 85737

Call Sign: WA8OXS
Robert H Nickel
10701 N La Reserve Dr
Oro Valley AZ 85737

Call Sign: KD5ZCX
Timothy S Newton
10700 N La Reserve Dr
14102
Oro Valley AZ 85737

Call Sign: W4RXT
John C Pomeroy

10701 N La Reserve Dr Apt 359
Oro Valley AZ 85737

Call Sign: K7MAP
Mark A Pagel
10700 N La Reserve Dr Apt 9201
Oro Valley AZ 85737

Call Sign: KD6RE
Bruce Freifeld
12760 N Lantern Way
Oro Valley AZ 85755

Call Sign: KD7IIT
Ed Miner
14570 N Lost Arrow Dr
Oro Valley AZ 857377128

Call Sign: K7EDM
Ed Miner
14570 N Lost Arrow Dr
Oro Valley AZ 857557128

Call Sign: KC5PGW
Andrew J Hinsdale
11547 N Monika Leigh Pl
Oro Valley AZ 85737

Call Sign: KE7ZPH
Bruce H Andres
11158 N Mountain Breeze Dr
Oro Valley AZ 85737

Call Sign: KE7ILV
Donald L Malick
12318 N New Dawn Ave
Oro Valley AZ 85755

Call Sign: K7DON
Donald L Malick
12318 N New Dawn Ave
Oro Valley AZ 85755

Call Sign: KE2VB
Larry Reader
11099 N Olympic Pl
Oro Valley AZ 85737

Call Sign: KC7GDV
Christina L Wiley
8851 N Oracle 159
Oro Valley AZ 85737

Call Sign: N6YXM
James P Barba
9901 N Oracle Rd 1101
Oro Valley AZ 85737

Call Sign: KD7UUP
Dale L Swesey
10333 N Oracle Rd 21105
Oro Valley AZ 85737

Call Sign: KE6YRX
Matt J Mazurek
12590 N Piping Rock Rd
Oro Valley AZ 85737

Call Sign: KB7GNX
Marvin G Stafford
9941 N Placita Papalote
Oro Valley AZ 85737

Call Sign: KC7MXF
Philippe H Coursodon
8305 N Rancho Catalina Dr
Oro Valley AZ 85704

Call Sign: K7KGB
A J Kruger
8420 N Rancho Catalina Dr
Oro Valley AZ 857047256

Call Sign: K7TDC
A J Kruger
8420 N Rancho Catalina Dr
Oro Valley AZ 857047256

Call Sign: K7KGB
A J Kruger
8420 N Rancho Catalina Dr
Oro Valley AZ 857047256

Call Sign: N7DJM
Patrick D Silva

13401 N Rancho Vistoso Blvd
Oro Valley AZ 85755

Call Sign: K7GPS
David S Dobbins
13401 N Rancho Vistoso Blvd 211
Oro Valley AZ 85755

Call Sign: KF6DEM
Rosalie I Wright
12289 N Reflection Ridge Dr
Oro Valley AZ 85755

Call Sign: KF6DEL
Warren H Wright
12289 N Reflection Ridge Dr
Oro Valley AZ 85755

Call Sign: WV6Y
Warren H Wright
12289 N Reflection Ridge Dr
Oro Valley AZ 85755

Call Sign: KF7A
James P Mandaville Jr
11638 N Ribbonwood Dr
Oro Valley AZ 85737

Call Sign: KE4EBN
Gregory A Johnson
11330 N Seven Falls Dr
Oro Valley AZ 85737

Call Sign: N7UBK
Thomas M Jordan
14289 N Silver Cloud Dr
Oro Valley AZ 857554755

Call Sign: KC7JHY
Gregory C Franklin
14725 N Silver Hawk Dr
Oro Valley AZ 85755

Call Sign: W7GCF
Gregory C Franklin
14725 N Silver Hawk Dr
Oro Valley AZ 85755

Call Sign: KE7UVK
Bryan S Reese
11301 N Silver Pheasant
Loop
Oro Valley AZ 85737

Call Sign: KE7UVJ
Gordon S Reese
11301 N Silver Pheasant
Loop
Oro Valley AZ 85737

Call Sign: KB9JMD
William P Griffith
13021 N Singh Dr
Oro Valley AZ 85755

Call Sign: K0EVC
Andrew R Lamb
10925 N St Georges Loop
Oro Valley AZ 857378926

Call Sign: K0EVD
Mary K Lamb
10925 N St Georges Loop
Oro Valley AZ 857378926

Call Sign: N7ZZM
Mary K Lamb
10925 N St Georges Loop
Oro Valley AZ 857378926

Call Sign: AA9MX
Donald R Rhodes
10710 N Stargazer Dr
Oro Valley AZ 857377211

Call Sign: N6GDO
Dwight L Small
13901 N Steprock Canyon
Oro Valley AZ 85755

Call Sign: W0MPH
Richard A Hyde Jr
10855 N Summer Moon Pl
Oro Valley AZ 85737

Call Sign: N5NYM

Allen D Moore
12387 N Tall Grass Dr
Oro Valley AZ 85737

Call Sign: KE7OP
James E Olson
10613 N Thunderhill Pl
Oro Valley AZ 85737

Call Sign: K7MMN
Laurence A Arps
13960 N Trade Winds Way
Oro Valley AZ 857379087

Call Sign: KE7WIP
Jeffrey N Zerbe
11437 N Verch Way
Oro Valley AZ 85737

Call Sign: K7JNZ
Jeffrey N Zerbe
11437 N Verch Way
Oro Valley AZ 85737

Call Sign: KD7SPV
Michael A Collett
13469 N Wide View Dr
Oro Valley AZ 85737

Call Sign: KF7PC
Larry K Clark
14052 N Willow Bend Dr
Oro Valley AZ 85755

Call Sign: N9MQS
Harold Feldman
281 Sacaton Canyon Dr
Oro Valley AZ 85755

Call Sign: KC7CJS
Stanley Weintraub
1320 Starship Pl
Oro Valley AZ 85737

Call Sign: WR7P
Gregory T Kishi
861 W Annandale Way
Oro Valley AZ 85737

Call Sign: N7LFP
Melanie C Kishi
861 W Annandale Way
Oro Valley AZ 85737

Call Sign: WB6BFW
John S Sides
1043 W Breezy Pine Ct
Oro Valley AZ 857378706

Call Sign: KB5JLK
Angela L Addison
1140 W Calle Concordia
Oro Valley AZ 85704

Call Sign: KB5LHU
Marion S Addison
1140 W Calle Concordia
Oro Valley AZ 85704

Call Sign: W8GT
Michael J Rauh
1890 W Canada Hills Dr
Oro Valley AZ 85737

Call Sign: K7EMM
Harold P Koenig
W Caroline Ln
Oro Valley AZ 857046620

Call Sign: N3BYW
Neal Obert
1254 W Casentino Pass
Oro Valley AZ 85755

Call Sign: N3BYX
Patricia H Obert
1254 W Casentino Pass
Oro Valley AZ 85755

Call Sign: WA7JBE
William M Matsukado
1217 W Cordia Pl
Oro Valley AZ 85755

Call Sign: N7GNH
Robert G Black Jr
1920 W Desert Highland Dr
Oro Valley AZ 85737

Call Sign: KE7HFL
Henry B Cribbs III
1901 W Desert Highlands Dr
Oro Valley AZ 85737

Call Sign: KE7UVL
Kevin F Kinghorn
1080 W Dragoon Springs Pl
Oro Valley AZ 85737

Call Sign: KE7UVM
Sandi L Kinghorn
1080 W Dragoon Springs Pl
Oro Valley AZ 85737

Call Sign: KD7CLC
Christopher D Ingraham
140 W Drover Pl
Oro Valley AZ 85737

Call Sign: KD7OVT
William D Gay
301 W Golf View Dr
Oro Valley AZ 857379701

Call Sign: K7ISF
Ian S Friedlander
283 W Greys Rd
Oro Valley AZ 85737

Call Sign: W2IAN
Ian S Friedlander
283 W Greys Rd
Oro Valley AZ 85737

Call Sign: K7IAN
Ian S Friedlander
283 W Greys Rd
Oro Valley AZ 85737

Call Sign: WB4FUZ
Sherry Friedlander
283 W Greys Rd
Oro Valley AZ 85737

Call Sign: KD7BIC
Tracy L Kranz
435 W Klinger Canyon

Oro Valley AZ 85755

Call Sign: WA6CFS
John W Douglas
363 W Klinger Canyon Dr
Oro Valley AZ 85755

Call Sign: KB8WBB
Joseph D Rother
937 W Leatherleaf Dr
Oro Valley AZ 85755

Call Sign: KC7WWM
Gerald L Chadbourn
57 W Oro Pl
Oro Valley AZ 85737

Call Sign: KA2IYU
Donald J Fork
80 W Oro Valley Dr
Oro Valley AZ 85737

Call Sign: KA2IYV
Nadine L Fork
80 W Oro Valley Dr
Oro Valley AZ 85737

Call Sign: KA7AUM
Paul R Coltrin
1510 W Placita Corto
Oro Valley AZ 85737

Call Sign: KE7CVP
Tucson ARA
1633 W Placita Montuoso
Oro Valley AZ 857373677

Call Sign: KD7SEA
Explorer Post 73
1633 W Placita Montuoso
Oro Valley AZ 857373677

Call Sign: KC7GEW
Alicia A Pagel
440 W Rolling Hills Pl
Oro Valley AZ 85737

Call Sign: KD7SWU
Cheyenne H Pagel

440 W Rolling Hills Pl
Oro Valley AZ 85737

Call Sign: N6NZO
Mark A Pagel
440 W Rolling Hills Pl
Oro Valley AZ 85737

Call Sign: N9MJS
Jeffrey S Feldman
305 W Sacaton Canyon Dr
Oro Valley AZ 857371782

Call Sign: KD7VI
Quinton A Gleason
1881 W Serenade
Oro Valley AZ 85737

Call Sign: WA7QG
Quinton A Gleason
1881 W Serenade St
Oro Valley AZ 85737

Call Sign: KC6NNU
Anthony D Calabrese
930 W Silver Hills St
Oro Valley AZ 85737

Call Sign: KE7VKH
Leopold Gutierrez
350 W Tara Danette Dr
Oro Valley AZ 85704

Call Sign: KE4NBT
Francisco G Castillo
1189 W Wild Dune Ln
Oro Valley AZ 85737

Call Sign: KK7AC
Andrew H Smith
Oro Valley AZ 85737

Call Sign: W7RLC
Randy L Carlson
Oro Valley AZ 85737

**FCC Amateur Radio
Licenses in Overgaard**

Call Sign: KF7DJ
Jack D Snyder Sr
2932 Breezy Pine Dr
Overgaard AZ 85933

Call Sign: KC7DQF
Laureline M Watson
2874 Cattle Trl Rd
Overgaard AZ 85933

Call Sign: N7XVJ
Roger D Takvam
3651 Grn Frst Dr
Overgaard AZ 85933

Call Sign: K8NMZ
Clarence W Albanese
2893 Lazy Bear Trl
Overgaard AZ 85933

Call Sign: WA7ZIM
Doyle C Cool
2889 Le Jo Rd
Overgaard AZ 85933

Call Sign: AA7IG
Thomas Dovi
2873 Moose Trl Box 219
Overgaard AZ 85933

Call Sign: W7GM
Ira G Miller
2011 Running Elk
Overgaard AZ 859332073

Call Sign: N7AIA
Betty L Kelley
Overgaard AZ 85933

Call Sign: KB7VVR
John P Creach
Overgaard AZ 85933

Call Sign: KK7HR
Charles S Clark Jr
Overgaard AZ 85933

Call Sign: WA7VMY
Arleen E Settle

Overgaard AZ 85933

Call Sign: KC7TWC
Harold L Kelley
Overgaard AZ 85933

Call Sign: KC7EZY
Harry M Hoppe Jr
Overgaard AZ 85933

Call Sign: WB7UAN
Hermann I Kakucsi
Overgaard AZ 85933

Call Sign: KD7GPM
Jerry D Blackert
Overgaard AZ 85933

Call Sign: KF7PHT
Johnnie R Perry
Overgaard AZ 85933

Call Sign: KE7BTM
Jon A Weigen
Overgaard AZ 85933

Call Sign: KE7CBX
Kathleen A Vosburgh
Overgaard AZ 85933

Call Sign: KE7CBZ
Robert M Dalsanto
Overgaard AZ 85933

Call Sign: K7YTL
Rolland V Watson
Overgaard AZ 85933

Call Sign: KE7EDO
Wayne M Mead
Overgaard AZ 85933

Call Sign: KE7CBY
Wes N Vosburgh
Overgaard AZ 85933

Call Sign: K7XZ
Retirement Dx Club
Overgaard AZ 85933

Call Sign: N7QVU
Jerry A Wyatt
Overgaard AZ 859330465

Call Sign: KF7LXD
Efrain M Quihuis III
Overgaard AZ 859331932

Call Sign: WN4GUS
Efrain M Quihuis III
Overgaard AZ 859331932

FCC Amateur Radio Licenses in Page

Call Sign: N6ZOI
Bret B Axlund
7 16th Ave
Page AZ 860404304

Call Sign: KE7EHN
Acil B Jones
154 5th Ave Box 3761
Page AZ 86040

Call Sign: KC7CAV
Albert L Vogel
200 Antelope Dr
Page AZ 86040

Call Sign: N7OQM
David E Rankin
18 Marble
Page AZ 860401017

Call Sign: KC7ENI
Bryan T Hill
231 Morgan
Page AZ 860402126

Call Sign: KA7ZLE
Lehaman J Burrow Jr
916 S Navajo
Page AZ 86040

Call Sign: N6XEX
Eve Oppedisano
112 S Navajo Dr

Page AZ 86040

Call Sign: WB7UWW
Vincent J Oppedisano
112 S Navajo Dr
Page AZ 86040

Call Sign: KC6EMO
Erik S Axlund
291 S Wahweal Dr
Page AZ 86040

Call Sign: KA0KSU
Robert L Hartzell
825 Spruce Ave
Page AZ 860400643

Call Sign: KA7HEI
Brian P Wheeler
Page AZ 86040

Call Sign: N7ROW
Caroline Christensen
Page AZ 86040

Call Sign: KB7VPL
Jeffery L Hickman
Page AZ 86040

Call Sign: KB7MUO
Kevin J Henry
Page AZ 86040

Call Sign: N7XYQ
Lenita K Burrow
Page AZ 86040

Call Sign: KA7MRH
Mary L Wheeler
Page AZ 86040

Call Sign: KB7TEP
Maurice W Gossner
Page AZ 86040

Call Sign: N7XXW
Susan C Jones
Page AZ 86040

Call Sign: KQ7RP
Page Lake Powell Qrp Group
Page AZ 86040

Call Sign: KB7PBH
Patrick L Black
Page AZ 86040

Call Sign: KC7BCH
Michelle L Woodcock
Page AZ 86040

Call Sign: N7ZRB
Cynthia A Kobel
Page AZ 86040

Call Sign: KC7FVN
Anthony J Barney
Page AZ 86040

Call Sign: N7ZRE
Michael J Bergner
Page AZ 86040

Call Sign: KB7QXC
Dennis D Crane
Page AZ 86040

Call Sign: KE7JUW
Abraham D Tucker
Page AZ 86040

Call Sign: KB6YTR
Cathy M Bell
Page AZ 86040

Call Sign: KE7MVR
Christine L Kirchner
Page AZ 86040

Call Sign: KA7BAG
Dan K Lindemann
Page AZ 86040

Call Sign: KE7OZE
Donna F Chapman
Page AZ 86040

Call Sign: KA7LHW

Evelyn L Roberts
Page AZ 86040

Call Sign: KD7VUN
Gero Meyer
Page AZ 86040

Call Sign: N0GUH
James L Bloomfield
Page AZ 86040

Call Sign: N7ZRD
Jessica L Brown
Page AZ 86040

Call Sign: KF7ANU
Jimmie T Yazzie
Page AZ 86040

Call Sign: NA7DB
John D Brown
Page AZ 86040

Call Sign: KD7KBX
Kendall P Knudsen
Page AZ 86040

Call Sign: KA7DNZ
Mary M Teig
Page AZ 86040

Call Sign: KA7IFW
Orrin V La Rue Sr
Page AZ 86040

Call Sign: KD7LWP
Pushpa W Caldwell
Page AZ 86040

Call Sign: KC7NIV
Rance S Makuch
Page AZ 86040

Call Sign: N6EKF
Robert L Bell
Page AZ 86040

Call Sign: KE7MVQ
Steve M Kirchner

Page AZ 86040

Call Sign: KC7KHJ
Temple A Reynolds
Page AZ 86040

Call Sign: KC7BPK
Thomas C Caldwell
Page AZ 86040

Call Sign: KD7YCJ
Wayne A Chapman
Page AZ 86040

Call Sign: W7WAC
Wayne A Chapman
Page AZ 86040

Call Sign: KA2GGN
William J Burnaz
Page AZ 86040

Call Sign: W7DRR
Joe G Roberts
Page AZ 860400670

Call Sign: N7XYR
Sarah L Brown
Page AZ 860401774

Call Sign: KD7AGP
Paul E Smith
Page AZ 860404871

FCC Amateur Radio Licenses in Palominas

Call Sign: N7BIL
William A Mc Nab
11017 E Calle Gavilan
Palominas AZ 85615

FCC Amateur Radio Licenses in Parker

Call Sign: WA6AA
Michael J Frue
37398 Bayview Dr
Parker AZ 85344

Call Sign: KD7GS
Duncan Mac Leod
Box 711B
Parker AZ 85344

Call Sign: K7GOX
Edward L White
14 Cienega Springs Rd
Parker AZ 85344

Call Sign: WB7NOU
Louis H Plunkett Sr
31817 Cienega Springs Rd
Parker AZ 853448428

Call Sign: WA6AGH
George E Hall
10894 Crystal Canyon Dr
Parker AZ 85344

Call Sign: N7TMO
Russell E Dawkins
1318 Desert Ave
Parker AZ 85344

Call Sign: WA6KDV
Julius J Schmidt
903 E Linger Dr
Parker AZ 85344

Call Sign: KF7AMP
Paddy E Messersmith
508 Laguna Ave
Parker AZ 853444440

Call Sign: AD7ZX
Paddy E Messersmith
508 Laguna Ave
Parker AZ 853444440

Call Sign: KD7NKB
Connie L Mclaren
937 Linger Dr
Parker AZ 85344

Call Sign: KF6ZF
Laurance A Ward
61124 Linger Dr

Parker AZ 85344

Call Sign: KA6GAL
Marjorie J Ward
61124 Linger Dr
Parker AZ 85344

Call Sign: N7UAI
Gail A Richards
10167 Marina Loop
Parker AZ 853447802

Call Sign: KA7WSK
George D Abbe
410 Misty Ln
Parker AZ 85344

Call Sign: N6HYB
Paul E Lazelle
412 Misty Ln
Parker AZ 85344

Call Sign: KB7NYZ
Derik W Wooddell
1412 Mohave
Parker AZ 85344

Call Sign: WA6OFT
James W Wooddell
1412 Mohave
Parker AZ 85344

Call Sign: K7WFR
James W Wooddell
1412 Mohave
Parker AZ 85344

Call Sign: N7UAO
Janet R Hayes
1113 Navajo Ave
Parker AZ 85344

Call Sign: KA7MVF
Theodore E Lamb
495 Riverfront Dr
Parker AZ 85344

Call Sign: AF6JJ
Randolph H Brown

1016 S Hopi Ave 184
Parker AZ 85344

Call Sign: KD4RWM
Wanda L Brown
1016 S Hopi Ave 184
Parker AZ 85344

Call Sign: KA6HMG
Wendy S Wooddell
1412 S Mohave Ave
Parker AZ 85344

Call Sign: N7LXS
Eugene T Garrett
33915 Smoketree Ln
Parker AZ 85344

Call Sign: KF7RNT
Joseph E Merrill
326 Stardust Ln
Parker AZ 85344

Call Sign: N7UAN
Lois M Mendenhall
Parker AZ 85344

Call Sign: K7LDP
William J Stephenson
Parker AZ 85344

Call Sign: N7BMW
Joseph H Durrer
Parker AZ 85344

Call Sign: KD6OEF
Cara M Fay
Parker AZ 85344

Call Sign: AB7KD
Carl W Noah
Parker AZ 85344

Call Sign: KC7VUF
Dottie M High
Parker AZ 85344

Call Sign: KD6ZWN
Emily L Fay

Parker AZ 85344

Call Sign: KD6UII
J Michael Fay
Parker AZ 85344

Call Sign: KB6JCQ
James E High
Parker AZ 85344

Call Sign: K7FAY
John A Fay
Parker AZ 85344

Call Sign: KC7ESZ
Marilyn N Fay
Parker AZ 85344

Call Sign: WA7RAT
California Arizona River Rat
Radio Amateurs
Parker AZ 85344

Call Sign: KA7ZUD
William J Stephenson Jr
Parker AZ 85344

Call Sign: KD7JWT
Gregory C Lewis
Parker AZ 85344

Call Sign: KA9IQZ
Douglas G Burkland
Parker AZ 85344

FCC Amateur Radio Licenses in Parks

Call Sign: KB5SQT
Chris A Magley
Boy Scout Camp Rd
Parks AZ 860180493

Call Sign: N7IEU
Gordon S Miller Sr
19 Juniper
Parks AZ 86018

Call Sign: KD7GJZ

Laurel L Strongmuehl
7 Kaibab Ln Pine Aire
Parks AZ 860180127

Call Sign: K7BTB
James E Leathem
83 Kings Deer Rd
Parks AZ 86018

Call Sign: WB7NLD
James F Winschel
4163 Mountainview Way
Parks AZ 86018

Call Sign: WB8VWC
Mark W Christian
526 W Park Rd
Parks AZ 86018

Call Sign: AK6Y
Cletis R Boan
Parks AZ 86018

Call Sign: N7UGU
Homer L Wright
Parks AZ 86018

Call Sign: KF7CYC
Arizona Microwave Users
Group
Parks AZ 86018

Call Sign: W7GBI
Arizona Microwave Users
Group
Parks AZ 86018

Call Sign: KD7IRY
Charles H Smith Jr
Parks AZ 86018

Call Sign: KF7SFJ
Diane M Christian
Parks AZ 86018

Call Sign: KF7QZI
John W Davis
Parks AZ 86018

Call Sign: KD7GKA
Philip Strongmuehl
Parks AZ 86018

Call Sign: KE7RBD
William S Bouchard
Parks AZ 86018

Call Sign: N7ARI
Laurel L Strongmuehl
Parks AZ 860180127

FCC Amateur Radio Licenses in Patagonia

Call Sign: K7TOW
Edward C Fleder
450 W Costello Dr
Patagonia AZ 85624

Call Sign: W9DDP
William J Stange
Patagonia AZ 85624

Call Sign: W3FZV
Philip E Battey
Patagonia AZ 85624

Call Sign: KF7LLF
Robert A Smith
Patagonia AZ 85624

Call Sign: WW7RAS
Robert A Smith
Patagonia AZ 85624

Call Sign: KC7LSE
Michael L Wold
Patagonia AZ 856240312

FCC Amateur Radio Licenses in Payson

Call Sign: N7BUB
Gary D Barker
212 Airline
Payson AZ 85547

Call Sign: AE7OV

Gary Lust
908 Bavarian Way
Payson AZ 85541

Call Sign: AA7UI
James P Livingood
407 Black Forest Ln
Payson AZ 85541

Call Sign: KB7WGT
Edward E Griffin
Box 100
Payson AZ 85541

Call Sign: KK7BJ
Philip L Phillips
Box 1062J
Payson AZ 85541

Call Sign: K7RGB
Sandra J Phillips
Box 1062J
Payson AZ 85541

Call Sign: KD7FOO
Vernon E Harrison
Box 1065C
Payson AZ 855419801

Call Sign: KE7PKQ
Joseph J Celauro
Box 1104
Payson AZ 85541

Call Sign: KF7BWY
George E Demack
Box 1197
Payson AZ 85541

Call Sign: KC7VJZ
Gordon L Hauptman
Box 1199 G
Payson AZ 85541

Call Sign: KC7REF
Gregory D Barsness
Box 1370
Payson AZ 85541

Call Sign: N7LS
Louis W Staalberg
Box 1401 E
Payson AZ 85541

Call Sign: KC7OIH
Josephina C Staalberg
Box 1401E
Payson AZ 85541

Call Sign: KC7REH
Benjamin K Hitzhusen
Box 1403
Payson AZ 85541

Call Sign: KC7REB
Rochelle L Hitzhusen
Box 1403
Payson AZ 85541

Call Sign: N6BGZ
Doris J Green
Box 1413
Payson AZ 85541

Call Sign: KC7MMJ
Aaron J Birchak
Box 1454
Payson AZ 85541

Call Sign: KC7HAF
Ian A Birchak
Box 1454
Payson AZ 85541

Call Sign: KC7HAE
Susan A Birchak
Box 1454
Payson AZ 85541

Call Sign: KB7VFG
John E Birchak
Box 1454
Payson AZ 85541

Call Sign: KD7FOS
Cindy K Sabo
Box 153 T
Payson AZ 85541

Call Sign: KD7FOX
Lance R Sabo
Box 153 T
Payson AZ 85541

Call Sign: KC7TGS
Gloria L Alliger
Box 181 E
Payson AZ 85541

Call Sign: KC7FPV
James R Alliger Jr
Box 181 E
Payson AZ 85541

Call Sign: KD7SKB
Dewey K Boone II
Box 20 23
Payson AZ 85541

Call Sign: WK7J
Vernon L Craw
Box 23 B
Payson AZ 85541

Call Sign: AI7R
David J Kelley
Box 271 K
Payson AZ 85541

Call Sign: KE7VPS
John H Logan
Box 3 W
Payson AZ 85541

Call Sign: KD0LD
Timothy L Hines
Box 30t
Payson AZ 85541

Call Sign: KB7VCT
George A Fiala
Box 330 J
Payson AZ 85541

Call Sign: KC7SAI
Eugene R Watts
Box 330 K

Payson AZ 85541

Call Sign: KD7MRF
Christopher M Babb
Box 40R
Payson AZ 85541

Call Sign: KD7GJK
John F Hetherington
Box 41 48
Payson AZ 85541

Call Sign: KD7UKY
Wayne G Rowland
Box 41 52
Payson AZ 85541

Call Sign: KB7PHQ
Jacob A Goble
Box 46K
Payson AZ 85541

Call Sign: W7PSN
Steven D Bingham
Box 4C
Payson AZ 85541

Call Sign: N7OPQ
J Johnson
Box 508
Payson AZ 855419708

Call Sign: KE7WRZ
Jeff Johnson
Box 508
Payson AZ 855419708

Call Sign: KE7ESO
David R Knauer Jr
Box 512 N
Payson AZ 85541

Call Sign: KC7OIF
Larry D Shelton
Box 513 F
Payson AZ 85541

Call Sign: KC7OIG
Sandra F Shelton

Box 513 F
Payson AZ 85541

Call Sign: N7AQO
Lorenz H Bauer
Box 518B
Payson AZ 85541

Call Sign: KC7REE
Gary G Walton
Box 568 J
Payson AZ 85541

Call Sign: KD7SKA
Shirley E Armstrong
Box 579C
Payson AZ 85541

Call Sign: KB7PHR
Larry R Paul
Box 582
Payson AZ 85541

Call Sign: K7ERB
Robert H Rhoades
Box 590
Payson AZ 85541

Call Sign: KC7LVX
Frank J Silcock
Box 78H
Payson AZ 85541

Call Sign: N7FVT
William A Mc Tyre
Box 93F
Payson AZ 85541

Call Sign: KD7RL
Gerald D Moody
1300 Camelot Ln
Payson AZ 85541

Call Sign: KB7WGO
James F Wilson Sr
1503 Cessna Cir
Payson AZ 85541

Call Sign: N7PZX

Merrill White
1007 Chalet Cir
Payson AZ 85541

Call Sign: WB7VRS
Robert A Dodds
2088 Crown Ct
Payson AZ 855472341

Call Sign: W7DDJ
Erwin W Tustison
200 E Aero
Payson AZ 85541

Call Sign: KB7WGW
Charles Farmer Jr
216 E Airline
Payson AZ 85541

Call Sign: WA7PGW
Robert M Ely
406 E Bonita Dr
Payson AZ 85541

Call Sign: K2KXG
Robert M Norman
1102 E Cedar Ln
Payson AZ 85541

Call Sign: KF7UJJ
Guy L Lanahan
1111 E Cedar Ln
Payson AZ 85541

Call Sign: N7VAP
Gregory L Lemoine
1500 E Cedar Ln
Payson AZ 85541

Call Sign: W1XU
James H Gray
210 E Chateau Cir
Payson AZ 85541

Call Sign: KD7BWJ
Richard C Gomber
609 E Continental Dr
Payson AZ 855415628

Call Sign: N7XVI
Philip E Gerard
600 E Drowsey Cir
Payson AZ 85541

Call Sign: KA7ETC
Joseph W Pepera
503 E Eckles
Payson AZ 85541

Call Sign: KA7ETD
Marvel P Pepera
503 E Eckles
Payson AZ 85541

Call Sign: KX7O
George A Lewis
216 E Eidelweiss Cir
Payson AZ 85541

Call Sign: KA7VFN
Idris M Davies
407 E Evergreen
Payson AZ 85541

Call Sign: WB7QNM
William V Campbell
608 E Evergreen St
Payson AZ 85541

Call Sign: WA7JTL
Peter J Scola
211 E Forest Dr
Payson AZ 85541

Call Sign: W6BVA
Richard W Dickson
302 E Forest Dr
Payson AZ 85541

Call Sign: N7CVL
Neloa A Beeler
608 E Frontier
Payson AZ 85541

Call Sign: WA7PUT
Barbara M Van Pelt
800 E Frontier
Payson AZ 855415707

Call Sign: K7KNP
Stanton D Van Pelt
800 E Frontier
Payson AZ 855415707

Call Sign: KC7WOM
Dacey L Taylor
704 E Frontier St
Payson AZ 85541

Call Sign: KC7HAA
Stanley A Miller
901 E Frontier St
Payson AZ 85541

Call Sign: WA6TML
John R Clyde
1301 E Frontier St
Payson AZ 855415814

Call Sign: KC7OIJ
Charles H Small
604 E Gila Ln
Payson AZ 85547

Call Sign: KB7LWY
Bernie E House
901 E Granite Dells Rd
Payson AZ 85541

Call Sign: KD7NMU
Jonathan R Simmons
1401 E Granite Dells Rd
Payson AZ 85541

Call Sign: N7BCM
Don R Frazier
413 E Idle Cir
Payson AZ 85541

Call Sign: KB7IPA
Daniel S Bramble
502 E Jura Cir
Payson AZ 85541

Call Sign: KA7HRB
Robert E Berger
503 E Jura Cir

Payson AZ 85541

Call Sign: W7UTO
John J Foy Jr
504 E Lorene St
Payson AZ 85541

Call Sign: KA7QWF
Barbara W Martin
705 E Miller Rd 31
Payson AZ 85541

Call Sign: N7HYO
Paul B Martin
705 E Miller Rd 31
Payson AZ 85541

Call Sign: KD7FOU
Elizabeth J Monte
205 E Phoenix St
Payson AZ 85541

Call Sign: KD7FOT
Charles A Calkins
710 E Phoenix St
Payson AZ 85541

Call Sign: KA6BKL
Thomas W Benson
1002 E Phoenix St
Payson AZ 85541

Call Sign: KD7ODJ
Ramona T Coppelli
1006 E Phoenix St
Payson AZ 85541

Call Sign: K7NVY
Kenneth W Kowaliski
1106 E Phoenix St
Payson AZ 85541

Call Sign: WB7UUL
Jack B Sheahan
320 E Ridge Ln
Payson AZ 85541

Call Sign: N1CK
Robert P Nichols

673 E Sycamore Ln
Payson AZ 85541

Call Sign: KF7SFI
Grant E Smith
601 E Tahoe Vista Cir
Payson AZ 85541

Call Sign: KD7IFM
Steven R Feistner
213 E Wade Ln
Payson AZ 85541

Call Sign: KB7WGY
Frank L Carr
402 E Wade Ln
Payson AZ 85541

Call Sign: KB7WGZ
Jane C Medlock
402 E Wade Ln
Payson AZ 85541

Call Sign: KB0UTO
Janice Nash
804 E Wagon Wheel Cir
Payson AZ 85541

Call Sign: KB7PLP
Arnold B Northwick
Echerry St
Payson AZ 85541

Call Sign: KC7RPC
Carlton L Burns
800 Graham Ranch Rd
Payson AZ 85541

Call Sign: KD7RSX
Waunetta D Chandler
Hci Box 1099 K
Payson AZ 85541

Call Sign: KA6FIX
Palmer T Wade
Hcr 27B4
Payson AZ 85541

Call Sign: KB7IOX

Petra B Arellano
Hcr 330M
Payson AZ 85541

Call Sign: KB7WGM
Donald A Gagnon
Hcr 579B
Payson AZ 85541

Call Sign: KB7TZW
Mary A Mc Tyre
Hcr 93F
Payson AZ 85541

Call Sign: N6BGY
Warren L Green
Hcr Box 1413
Payson AZ 85541

Call Sign: KB7WGQ
Dorothy A Murphy
Hcr Box 165 0
Payson AZ 85541

Call Sign: WB7QPU
Jim Murphy
Hcr Box 165 0
Payson AZ 85541

Call Sign: KB7WGP
James L Widger
Hcr Box 191D
Payson AZ 85541

Call Sign: KB7WGN
Steven M Kamp
Hcr Box 191D
Payson AZ 85541

Call Sign: KB7IOY
Anneke K Arellano
Hcr Box 330M
Payson AZ 85541

Call Sign: KB7IQM
Linda K Porter
Hcr Box 73
Payson AZ 85541

Call Sign: KB7WGS
Arthur E Lloyd
Hcr Box 81L
Payson AZ 85541

Call Sign: KJ7GB
Robert Z Muggli
157 Lion Sp Rd Hc 5 Box
77E
Payson AZ 85541

Call Sign: AC7HY
Robert Z Muggli
157 Lion Sp Rd Hc 5 Box
77E
Payson AZ 85541

Call Sign: KD7BWG
Charles J Heron
260 Mount View Rd Hc 5
75F
Payson AZ 855419804

Call Sign: KO6ZW
Clifford E De Magri
1304 N Alpine Heights Dr
Payson AZ 855413325

Call Sign: KE6NEW
Susan K De Magri
1304 N Alpine Heights Dr
Payson AZ 855413325

Call Sign: KC6SIY
Terry W Hayes
1412 N Alpine Heights Dr
Payson AZ 85541

Call Sign: N7CSY
Robert L Ehrhardt
1503 N Alpine Heights Dr
Payson AZ 855413331

Call Sign: KD7FOR
Eugene W Briss
1101 N Arrowhead Dr
Payson AZ 85541

Call Sign: N7JOJ

Diane C Waldrop
1112 N Bavarian Way
Payson AZ 85541

Call Sign: KE7WA
Mark C Waldrop
1112 N Bavarian Way
Payson AZ 85541

Call Sign: KF7ALU
Ernest H Sambrano
1000 N Beeline Hwy 103
Payson AZ 85541

Call Sign: W7EHS
Ernest H Sambrano
1000 N Beeline Hwy 103
Payson AZ 85541

Call Sign: KF7BWZ
Cynthia L Sambrano
1000 N Beeline Hwy 103
Payson AZ 85541

Call Sign: N7QPR
Nadine S Schendel
604 N Blue Spruce Rd
Payson AZ 85541

Call Sign: W7KOH
Donald D Schendel Jr
604 N Blue Spruce Rd
Payson AZ 855416662

Call Sign: KD7JTC
Arthur D Pirtle
508 N Bobby Jones Dr
Payson AZ 85541

Call Sign: W7UC
Arthur E Lux
107 N Bryce Cir
Payson AZ 85541

Call Sign: WB7BXN
La Rue E Pierce
300 N Budweiser Cir
Payson AZ 85541

Call Sign: KB7IPW
Eden J Zang
1109 N Camelot
Payson AZ 85541

Call Sign: KB7IPD
Tiana J Zang
1109 N Camelot
Payson AZ 85541

Call Sign: KD7BWD
J Todd Bramlet
1102 N Carefree Cir
Payson AZ 85541

Call Sign: KF6SPR
Robert M Holmes
356 N Deer Creek Rd
Payson AZ 85541

Call Sign: K6SPR
Robert M Holmes
356 N Deer Creek Rd
Payson AZ 85541

Call Sign: K7FBM
Harold J Kintner Jr
992 N Deer Creek Rd
Payson AZ 85541

Call Sign: KB7IPE
Colby A Ledbetter
504 N Doubletree
Payson AZ 85541

Call Sign: WB7TJS
Marjorie K Cushman
1305 N Easy St
Payson AZ 85541

Call Sign: WB7ASU
Tracy L Cushman
1305 N Easy St
Payson AZ 85541

Call Sign: N7DMF
Ralph R Ross
1320 N Easy St
Payson AZ 85541

Call Sign: K7DRI
Maurice F Peterson
1510 N Easy St
Payson AZ 85541

Call Sign: KB7TUG
Brad E Petry
1308 N Easy St Way
Payson AZ 85541

Call Sign: KD7BFR
Richard A Uskat
102 N Foothill Dr
Payson AZ 85541

Call Sign: KB7PHP
Richard D Lundholm
504 N Graham Ranch Rd
Payson AZ 85541

Call Sign: W7CER
Arthur M Walters
601 N Graham Ranch Rd
Payson AZ 85541

Call Sign: KC7OIM
Paul B Johnson
808 N Granite Dr
Payson AZ 85541

Call Sign: KD7HZB
Kim M Nees
1101 N Heather Cir
Payson AZ 85541

Call Sign: KJ7K
Robert L Green
1101 N Heather Cir
Payson AZ 85541

Call Sign: KK7QL
James S Cambier
243 N Helen Dr
Payson AZ 855412872

Call Sign: KC7RDW
Mary L Cambier
243 N Helen Dr

Payson AZ 855412872

Call Sign: KZ2X
Robert A Wilgus
600 N Hideaway Cir
Payson AZ 85541

Call Sign: KC7MMT
Carole J White
1214 N Hillcrest Dr
Payson AZ 85541

Call Sign: KD7BWE
Lorraine L White
1214 N Hillcrest Dr
Payson AZ 85541

Call Sign: KK7IB
George R White
1214 N Hillcrest Dr
Payson AZ 855413322

Call Sign: KB7IPG
Brent S Calkins
209 N Kodz Rd
Payson AZ 85541

Call Sign: KB7IPF
Chadd R Calkins
209 N Kodz St
Payson AZ 85541

Call Sign: KB7QKZ
Patricia L Lenon
708 N Madison
Payson AZ 85541

Call Sign: KB7QLC
Steve L Lenon
708 N Madison
Payson AZ 85541

Call Sign: N7EZE
Steve L Lenon
708 N Madison
Payson AZ 85541

Call Sign: N7XVK
John D Lenon

708 N Madison Dr
Payson AZ 85541

Call Sign: KB7QKW
George H Bloomfield
805 N Matterhorn
Payson AZ 85541

Call Sign: KB7HNY
Albert Campeas
1106 N Matterhorn Rd
Payson AZ 85541

Call Sign: KC7ZVJ
Aaron L Svendsen
1111 N Matterhorn Rd
Payson AZ 85541

Call Sign: KC7UZB
Lynn W Godfrey
1600 N Maverick Cir
Payson AZ 85541

Call Sign: KB7IPB
Colleen N Hale
805 N McLane Rd
Payson AZ 85541

Call Sign: KB7IPC
Terry D Hale
805 N McLane Rd
Payson AZ 85541

Call Sign: KD7MRH
Kristin Remonda
2005 N McLane Rd
Payson AZ 85541

Call Sign: KB7QKR
Harold R Rush
313 N Mogollon Trl
Payson AZ 85541

Call Sign: KE7FJH
Virginia L Nyman
114 N Parkwood Ln
Payson AZ 85541

Call Sign: W7KTY

Doyle B Ross
213 N Parkwood Rd
Payson AZ 85541

Call Sign: KE7FDA
David M Durfee
220 N Parkwood Rd
Payson AZ 85541

Call Sign: KC7LVY
Harry L Evers
1106 N Ponderosa Cir
Payson AZ 85541

Call Sign: WA6VHB
Frederick W Franz
1204 N Ponderosa Cir
Payson AZ 855413843

Call Sign: K2YAW
Edward L Bugliarelli
1108 N Rhone Cir
Payson AZ 85541

Call Sign: KB7TUH
Scott A Tustison
1909 N Saddle Blanket
Payson AZ 85541

Call Sign: KK7UL
Charles H Juenger
211 N Stagecoach Pass
Payson AZ 855416242

Call Sign: KE7ZNU
Eric E Randau
1416 N Sunrise Ct
Payson AZ 85541

Call Sign: KC7REG
Archie R Johnson
1311 N Sunshine Ln
Payson AZ 85541

Call Sign: KC7RDY
Patricia Ann Johnson
1311 N Sunshine Ln
Payson AZ 85541

Call Sign: K0AYU
Robert L Froehling
305 N Titel
Payson AZ 85541

Call Sign: KA7HQW
Douglas S Waldrop
202 N Trailwood Rd
Payson AZ 85541

Call Sign: N1LSF
John Rukstalis
1105 N Tyrolean Dr
Payson AZ 85541

Call Sign: KD7FOM
Thomas A Butler
260 N Walnut Ln
Payson AZ 855412760

Call Sign: KD7OEG
John A Swenson
302 N Whitetail Dr
Payson AZ 855413557

Call Sign: W7VNO
John A Swenson
302 N Whitetail Dr
Payson AZ 855413557

Call Sign: WA7BGK
Paul A Swenson
302 N Whitetail Dr
Payson AZ 855413557

Call Sign: KB7WGU
William Lockman
207 N Whiting Dr
Payson AZ 85541

Call Sign: K6DLE
Dana L Elliott
212 N Whiting Dr
Payson AZ 855414252

Call Sign: KR7P
Dana L Elliott
212 N Whiting Dr
Payson AZ 855414252

Call Sign: KF7BXA
Michael L Wood
802 N William Tell Cir
Payson AZ 85541

Call Sign: W7BNN
Walter W Carlson
1206 N William Tell Cir
Payson AZ 85541

Call Sign: K0CSA
William D Powers
1316 N Woodland Dr
Payson AZ 855413246

Call Sign: W7ETL
Eric T Lunden
1413 Northeasy St
Payson AZ 85541

Call Sign: KA7IRT
Marie D Davis
305 S Bassett Ln
Payson AZ 855414903

Call Sign: K7RIM
Marie D Davis
305 S Bassett Ln
Payson AZ 855414903

Call Sign: N7IOH
Allen S Turner
703 S Bootleg Alley
Payson AZ 85541

Call Sign: KE7BXX
Franklin N Karnes
302 S Brassie Dr
Payson AZ 85541

Call Sign: N6HGK
Gerald Bessler
209 S Canpar Way
Payson AZ 85541

Call Sign: KB6NTC
Joanne M Bessler
209 S Canpar Way

Payson AZ 85541

Call Sign: KD7FON
Paul W Andrews
305 S Canpar Way
Payson AZ 85541

Call Sign: KL7CKC
Robert H Perry
609 S Colcord St
Payson AZ 85541

Call Sign: KC7WOO
John A Wenzel
905 S Coronado Way
Payson AZ 85541

Call Sign: KK6B
Robert E Dye
1107 S Deer Born Dr
Payson AZ 85541

Call Sign: KM4FA
James P Hunt
1101 S Elk Ridge Pt
Payson AZ 85541

Call Sign: KD7JSW
Eduard A Vos
107 S Forest Park Dr
Payson AZ 85541

Call Sign: KC7OII
Veronica A Reynolds
209 S Granite
Payson AZ 85541

Call Sign: KB7PHS
Rayne W R Rohrbach
709 S Hermosillo
Payson AZ 85541

Call Sign: KB7IPU
Roger W Rohrbach
709 S Hermosillo Dr
Payson AZ 85541

Call Sign: KE7CN
Robert H Lloyd

109 S Kodz Rd
Payson AZ 85541

Call Sign: KD7JTE
Ernest A Francisco Jr
907 S Pincecone St
Payson AZ 85541

Call Sign: KE7AMV
Scot V Proudfoot
906 S Pineview St
Payson AZ 85541

Call Sign: KD7ZKH
Louis E Mendibles
405 S Ponderosa
Payson AZ 85541

Call Sign: KC2EAT
Asa E Boehme
604 S Ponderosa St
Payson AZ 85541

Call Sign: KC7HAB
Charles M Panian
907 S Santa Fe Cir
Payson AZ 85541

Call Sign: KD7FOQ
Edward R Torres
813 S St Philip St
Payson AZ 85541

Call Sign: KC7PFR
David T Humphries
512 S Stetson Dr
Payson AZ 85541

Call Sign: KC7QMG
Julia R Humphries
512 S Stetson Dr
Payson AZ 85541

Call Sign: N0BBH
Drusilla J Thompson
120 S Tonto St 7
Payson AZ 85541

Call Sign: KD7TJH

Tommy R Ball
249 S Valley View
Payson AZ 85541

Call Sign: AE7GJ
Frank W Ahern
225 S Valley View Rd
Payson AZ 85541

Call Sign: KD7QAA
Robert W Feistner
285 S Valley Vw
Payson AZ 85541

Call Sign: AF8W
Frank W Ahern
225 S Valley Vw
Payson AZ 85541

Call Sign: KB7QNI
Neil E Landers
807 S Westerly Rd 305
Payson AZ 85541

Call Sign: KM0P
Judy A Shafferkoetter
414 S Whisper Ridge Ln
Payson AZ 855415876

Call Sign: K7MLE
Raymond F Adams
348 S Zane Meadows Rd
Payson AZ 85541

Call Sign: KB7TUI
Shanda M Vaught
603 Solitude Cir
Payson AZ 85541

Call Sign: N0ZIL
Richard A Fentzlaff
121 Tonto St 22
Payson AZ 85541

Call Sign: WA0SXB
Russell M Hustead
1301 W Aviator Cir
Payson AZ 85541

Call Sign: WB6EGU
Walter S Hart
1712 W Bonita St
Payson AZ 855414500

Call Sign: N7HQO
Larry C Hanson
1311 W Bravo Taxiway
Payson AZ 85541

Call Sign: KF7JLN
Don R Johnson Jr
813 W Bridle Path
Payson AZ 85541

Call Sign: KB7QKX
Walter B Prychodnik
500 W Bridle Path Ln
Payson AZ 85541

Call Sign: KB7ZKO
Lawrence J Pirtle
2807 W Bulla Dr
Payson AZ 85541

Call Sign: KD7VLF
James J Chase
2808 W Bulla Dr
Payson AZ 85541

Call Sign: W7YOF
Melvin H Crain
2909 W Bulla Dr
Payson AZ 85541

Call Sign: KF7FGN
Jim J Ross
903 W Chatham
Payson AZ 85541

Call Sign: AE7IX
Jim J Ross
903 W Chatham
Payson AZ 85541

Call Sign: KD7ODK
Robert B Mcdougall
909 W Chatham Dr
Payson AZ 85541

Call Sign: KB1FTJ
Ned F Hines
1501 W Cloud Nine Pkwy
Payson AZ 85541

Call Sign: WA8SUJ
George P Mootsey Jr
918 W Colt Dr
Payson AZ 855413024

Call Sign: KD7IQA
Robert J Youtz
312 W Corral Dr
Payson AZ 85541

Call Sign: KL7DWB
Ernest E Smith
813 W Country Ln
Payson AZ 855416642

Call Sign: N7FMT
Willard E Cox
1903 W Fairway Ln
Payson AZ 855414527

Call Sign: KE7AMW
David J Martindale
432 W Frontier St
Payson AZ 85541

Call Sign: KB7QLB
Donn B Martin
1205 W Gold Nugget
Payson AZ 85541

Call Sign: W0RQJ
Claude W Callaghan
507 W Jones Dr
Payson AZ 85541

Call Sign: AA7UG
Brian K Cassens
914 W Landmark Trl
Payson AZ 85541

Call Sign: K6SIU
Selden Mitchell
509 W Laredo Loop

Payson AZ 85541

Call Sign: KC7RKF
Barry H Smith
506 W Locust
Payson AZ 85541

Call Sign: KB7IPV
Shaya M Smith
506 W Locust
Payson AZ 85547

Call Sign: KC7SAY
Curtice J Smith
506 W Locust
Payson AZ 855413646

Call Sign: KC5TWG
Joanne K Van Cleve
926 W Madera Ln
Payson AZ 85541

Call Sign: KF7QFN
Todd W Longfellow
408 W Main St Ste 5
Payson AZ 85541

Call Sign: N7TWL
Todd W Longfellow
408 W Main St Ste 5
Payson AZ 85541

Call Sign: KA7SDB
Gerard P Bergeron
410 W Main St Ste A
Payson AZ 85541

Call Sign: KB7LK
Dennis A Pribbenow
1504 W Mooney Pkwy
Payson AZ 85541

Call Sign: W7DAP
Dennis A Pribbenow
1504 W Mooney Pkwy
Payson AZ 85541

Call Sign: KC7CCA
Milo R Durfee

2709 W Palmer
Payson AZ 85541

Call Sign: KC7REA
Dennis C Satterfield
2603 W Palmer Dr
Payson AZ 85541

Call Sign: KC7FGX
Dallin J Durfee
2709 W Palmer Dr
Payson AZ 85541

Call Sign: KC7DGS
Renee Durfee
2709 W Palmer Dr
Payson AZ 85541

Call Sign: N7WTS
Frank L Christopher
146 W Patriot Dr
Payson AZ 85541

Call Sign: W6JOG
Lee Elswood
1706 W Point Dr
Payson AZ 85541

Call Sign: KF7VC
Ray J Kleinberg
1204 W Random Way
Payson AZ 85541

Call Sign: K2MAT
Marika E Meixner
1205 W Random Way
Payson AZ 85541

Call Sign: N7ACP
Arne P Koch
1300 W Random Way
Payson AZ 85541

Call Sign: N7BII
Joyce I Koch
1300 W Random Way
Payson AZ 85541

Call Sign: KD7BWC

Terry L Murray
912 W Rim View Rd
Payson AZ 85541

Call Sign: KC7WOR
George H Spears
910 W Rimview
Payson AZ 85541

Call Sign: KD7JTA
Michael E Brown
275 W Round Valley Rd
Payson AZ 85541

Call Sign: KD7JSZ
Vicki L Brown
275 W Round Valley Rd
Payson AZ 85541

Call Sign: KB7TUJ
Angelia M Segletes
1102 W Saddle
Payson AZ 85541

Call Sign: K7OLP
Wilbert Butcher
603 W Saddle Ln
Payson AZ 85541

Call Sign: KD7NMV
Teresa F Baldwin
411 W Sherwood Dr
Payson AZ 85541

Call Sign: KB7PJA
William S Baldwin
411 W Sherwood Dr
Payson AZ 85541

Call Sign: KC7LVH
Carl F Wiesner
500 W Sherwood Dr
Payson AZ 85541

Call Sign: KC7LVI
Carol L Wiesner
500 W Sherwood Dr
Payson AZ 85541

Call Sign: N4XWE
Daniel J Babcock
819 W Sherwood Dr
Payson AZ 85541

Call Sign: KB7UOK
Steve Vaught
603 W Solito De Cir
Payson AZ 85541

Call Sign: KD7MSS
Bill B Hutchinson
619 W St Moritz Dr
Payson AZ 85541

Call Sign: W7WBH
Bill B Hutchinson
619 W St Moritz Dr
Payson AZ 85541

Call Sign: KE7JHF
Lon C Thomas
408 W Summit St
Payson AZ 85541

Call Sign: WB5GUB
Gary E Hampsch
601 W Summit St
Payson AZ 85541

Call Sign: WA7HHM
Gary E Hampsch
601 W Summit St
Payson AZ 85541

Call Sign: KB7LMA
Randy S Taylor
111 W Vera Ln
Payson AZ 85541

Call Sign: KD7BWF
Donald E Hocker
907 W Wagon Trl
Payson AZ 85541

Call Sign: KE7OOO
Neil E Landers
708 Westley
Payson AZ 85541

Call Sign: W7NEL
Neil E Landers
708 Westley
Payson AZ 85541

Call Sign: KD7JTB
Judith R Nichols
1114 Yodel Cir
Payson AZ 85541

Call Sign: WA7AAH
Boyd D Walker
Payson AZ 85541

Call Sign: KA7CNI
Clyde L Staveness
Payson AZ 85541

Call Sign: KB7WHB
Anita L Barker
Payson AZ 85547

Call Sign: KB7HNZ
Bryan A Hoernke
Payson AZ 85547

Call Sign: N7CVT
Gerald A Mimnaugh
Payson AZ 85547

Call Sign: KB7IOZ
James R Bramble
Payson AZ 85547

Call Sign: W7KX
Stanley H Kenyon
Payson AZ 85541

Call Sign: KC7HAO
Philip J Taylor
Payson AZ 85541

Call Sign: KD7MRC
Thomas M Plets
Payson AZ 85541

Call Sign: KD7JTG
Larry J Maniag

Payson AZ 85541

Call Sign: KD7JSY
Patricia A Walker
Payson AZ 85541

Call Sign: KB7ZXM
Luis A Coppelli
Payson AZ 85541

Call Sign: KD7JTF
Delbert E Newland
Payson AZ 85541

Call Sign: KE7NZY
Samuel H Bomyea
Payson AZ 85541

Call Sign: KD7ETM
Andrew S Kofile
Payson AZ 85547

Call Sign: KA7CNJ
Ann H Staveness
Payson AZ 85547

Call Sign: K7FFN
Donald L Cline
Payson AZ 85547

Call Sign: KJ7JE
Gary E Harkins
Payson AZ 85547

Call Sign: KC7FKW
Harry W Troutman
Payson AZ 85547

Call Sign: KD7QPQ
James H Bolt
Payson AZ 85547

Call Sign: KD7OOL
Mark J Plets
Payson AZ 85547

Call Sign: KC7RDX
Martha J Meadows
Payson AZ 85547

Call Sign: N0QAN
Michael J Alexander
Payson AZ 85547

Call Sign: KC7HAQ
Michael L Chittick
Payson AZ 85547

Call Sign: KD7BWB
Paul B Pollock
Payson AZ 85547

Call Sign: KD7DMB
Peri C Cline
Payson AZ 85547

Call Sign: KA2SQJ
Peter J Havens
Payson AZ 85547

Call Sign: N0RYL
Robert C Pena
Payson AZ 85547

Call Sign: WB7ERO
Terry H Hudgens
Payson AZ 85547

Call Sign: KC7OIK
Todd A Watson
Payson AZ 85547

Call Sign: KK7LD
Warren D Meadows
Payson AZ 85547

Call Sign: KC7WOQ
William M Webb
Payson AZ 85547

Call Sign: KC7YYM
Tonto Amateur Radio Assn
Inc
Payson AZ 85547

Call Sign: N7TAR
Tonto ARA Inc
Payson AZ 85547

Call Sign: KA7PNX
Lorne J Cory Sr
Payson AZ 855470116

Call Sign: AC7EP
Darde G De Roulhac
Payson AZ 855470422

Call Sign: KD7IJG
Rex G De Roulhac
Payson AZ 855470422

Call Sign: AC7MT
Selma L De Roulhac
Payson AZ 855470422

Call Sign: KD7KJN
Selma L De Roulhac
Payson AZ 855470422

Call Sign: K6HHV
Philip B Ittel
Payson AZ 855470600

Call Sign: K7GGG
Gary R Miller
Payson AZ 855471346

Call Sign: KC7ELQ
John J Varljen
Payson AZ 855471800

Call Sign: KD7MRE
Jarissa M Kirkpatrick
Payson AZ 855472265

Call Sign: KD7QZN
Susan M Plets
Payson AZ 855472383

Call Sign: KE7ROZ
George A Fiala
Payson AZ 855472552

Call Sign: K7ROZ
George A Fiala
Payson AZ 855472552

Call Sign: KD7YVN
Inc Gila County Emergeny
Communications
Payson AZ 855473124

Call Sign: WR7GC
Inc Gila County Emergency
Communications
Payson AZ 855473124

FCC Amateur Radio Licenses in Pearce

Call Sign: KD6IVP
Donald W Fraser
Box 354
Pearce AZ 85625

Call Sign: KJ7WM
Darrell E Baker
1011 Christmas Tree Ln
Pearce AZ 85625

Call Sign: W7LBQ
Walter C Hieber Jr
1118 Christmas Tree Ln
Pearce AZ 85625

Call Sign: W7GVG
David O Reichlein
1203 Christmas Tree Ln
Pearce AZ 85625

Call Sign: WB7RZZ
Larry L Mingus
1166 E Desert Rose Dr
Pearce AZ 85625

Call Sign: KF7JUR
Jacqueline E Rule
1024 E Geneva St
Pearce AZ 85625

Call Sign: N8DNQ
Anne C Greene
1141 E Goldminers Cir
Pearce AZ 85625

Call Sign: KG7EO

Laurence C Strout
1000 E Mescal Dr
Pearce AZ 85625

Call Sign: KC7YDA
Paul S Meyer
6075 E San Carlos Dr
Pearce AZ 856250311

Call Sign: W7MBT
James A Mowery
318 Flynn Jans Ct
Pearce AZ 85625

Call Sign: KF7GRS
Robert J Rule
1024 Geneva St
Pearce AZ 85625

Call Sign: KC7TGD
Victor G Templer Jr
6 Goldminers Rv Resort
Pearce AZ 85625

Call Sign: N7ONJ
Dorothy M Stephens
1116 Justin St
Pearce AZ 85625

Call Sign: AA7DY
Walter Stephens
1116 Justin St
Pearce AZ 85625

Call Sign: WB6NBN
Eileen M Cliburn
1211 Justin St
Pearce AZ 85625

Call Sign: WB6NBO
James E Cliburn
1211 Justin St
Pearce AZ 85625

Call Sign: K4MOE
Gary S Moe
212 N Sage St
Pearce AZ 856254008

Call Sign: KE6HKF
Thomas M Mc Gaffey
101 N Sage St
Pearce AZ 85625

Call Sign: KE6IKI
Laura Mc Gaffey
101 N Sage St
Pearce AZ 85625

Call Sign: KJ7ZH
Paul G Dunn
13600 S Chato Rd
Pearce AZ 85625

Call Sign: KD7HJ
Claude K Wright
Pearce AZ 85625

Call Sign: K0LGW
Merum L Simpson
Pearce AZ 85625

Call Sign: KD7PPM
Beate Eberspaecher
Pearce AZ 85625

Call Sign: KC7BCL
Mark S Spencer
Pearce AZ 85625

Call Sign: KC7QVT
Patricia L O Connor
Pearce AZ 85625

Call Sign: KD7MCY
Thomas O Butts
Pearce AZ 85625

Call Sign: KD7TZX
William B Garrett
Pearce AZ 85625

Call Sign: W7WBG
William B Garrett
Pearce AZ 85625

Call Sign: KE6VBF
Gordon J Soflin
Picacho AZ 852410160

Call Sign: KF7LVD
Claude E Martin
Box 4002
Pima AZ 85543

Call Sign: KA7UGF
Donna M Wiedmeyer
Box 4101
Pima AZ 85543

Call Sign: N7VQG
Wendell G Winter
Box 4199
Pima AZ 855439709

Call Sign: W7WGW
Wendell G Winter
Box 4199
Pima AZ 855439709

Call Sign: N7GXC
Howard E Jenkins
Box 5237
Pima AZ 85543

Call Sign: KA7BCE
Lynn W Skinner
134 N 1000 W
Pima AZ 85543

Call Sign: KC7ZGJ
Jessie E Pylican
186 S 200 W
Pima AZ 85543

Call Sign: KJ7FJ
Jerry J Foard
355 S 400E
Pima AZ 85543

Call Sign: KD7LPQ

William C Smith
355 S Spear Ranch Rd
Pima AZ 855439740

Call Sign: KA7HBE
Donald R Cluff
4762 Tripp Canyon Rd
Pima AZ 85543

Call Sign: N7IHA
Robin Cluff
4762 Tripp Canyon Rd Nbu 7
Pima AZ 85543

Call Sign: W2RJZ
Ronald R Avery
11444 W Cottonwood Wash
Rd
Pima AZ 855439501

Call Sign: N7XL
Ben N Bryce
Pima AZ 85543

Call Sign: KA7LJX
Gregg D Cluff
Pima AZ 85543

Call Sign: KC7GIX
Bud Hawkins
Pima AZ 85543

Call Sign: WB7ONJ
David E Wells
Pima AZ 85543

Call Sign: W7ONJ
David E Wells
Pima AZ 85543

Call Sign: N7AM
David E Wells
Pima AZ 85543

Call Sign: KF7SPE
Donald B Carter
Pima AZ 85543

Call Sign: KF7UFK

Elmer L Prophet
Pima AZ 85543

Call Sign: KB7CSE
Grace E Wells
Pima AZ 85543

Call Sign: KE7IOY
Jerry R Nelson
Pima AZ 85543

Call Sign: KC7OBZ
Patricia A Bryce
Pima AZ 85543

Call Sign: N7CCQ
Stephen L Cluff
Pima AZ 85543

Call Sign: KA7BFG
Ladd A Bryce
Pima AZ 855430219

FCC Amateur Radio Licenses in Pine

Call Sign: KF7SWA
Herbert J Dwyer
3336 Bobcat Cir
Pine AZ 855440504

Call Sign: AA7WK
Joseph M Drummond
6670 Jan Dr
Pine AZ 85544

Call Sign: N6ZEV
William H Harless Jr
3602 Mistletoe Dr
Pine AZ 855441301

Call Sign: KG7XI
David H Buchholz
6685 W Ridge Rd
Pine AZ 855442371

Call Sign: N7TVG
Carol A Wurzell
Pine AZ 85544

Call Sign: N7HVP
Jack P Barnhart
Pine AZ 85544

Call Sign: N7AJQ
Kenneth C Hollemon
Pine AZ 85544

Call Sign: KB7WHA
Mari Jean Crossman
Pine AZ 85544

Call Sign: KB7QLA
Michael S Crossman
Pine AZ 85544

Call Sign: N7AUX
William R Steinberg
Pine AZ 85544

Call Sign: KF7FGO
Alan P Zabarsky
Pine AZ 85544

Call Sign: N7XYA
Barbara A Hall
Pine AZ 85544

Call Sign: N7TVA
Barbara S Smith
Pine AZ 85544

Call Sign: KE7TYQ
Clifford L Sage
Pine AZ 85544

Call Sign: KF7SFG
David C Brockman
Pine AZ 85544

Call Sign: KF7SFH
David J Burkhart
Pine AZ 85544

Call Sign: KN7AWH
Dennis M Howe
Pine AZ 85544

Call Sign: W7AWH
Dennis M Howe
Pine AZ 85544

Call Sign: KA7IOI
Jonathan A Andrews
Pine AZ 85544

Call Sign: KE7TYP
Joseph Oravec
Pine AZ 85544

Call Sign: KD7PMR
Kevin R Murphy
Pine AZ 85544

Call Sign: WA7RPY
Robert F Hall
Pine AZ 85544

Call Sign: KJ7I
Robert H Branch
Pine AZ 85544

Call Sign: WB8RDY
Joseph J Johnson
Pine AZ 85544

Call Sign: K0CNT
George F Bruzenak
Pine AZ 855440386

Call Sign: W4ITQ
Daniel F Mc Kinney
Pine AZ 855440472

Call Sign: KC7UXU
Gila Repeater Group
Pine AZ 855440472

Call Sign: KC7WJB
Charles R Simpson
Pine AZ 855441493

Call Sign: W1APZ
Alan P Zabarsky
Pine AZ 855441870

FCC Amateur Radio Licenses in Pinedale

Call Sign: N6GTB
Marjorie L Fox
1588 Eagle Rest Rd
Pinedale AZ 859341220

Call Sign: KA6QFQ
Melvin E Taunt
1588 Eagle Rest Rd
Pinedale AZ 859341220

Call Sign: KB0QAX
Norman W Kalat III
5406 Oak Ave
Pinedale AZ 85934

Call Sign: KC7DQD
Gerald W Butler
Pinedale AZ 85934

Call Sign: KD7VIA
Jason K Butler
Pinedale AZ 85934

Call Sign: KE7LAH
Jonathan D Crookston
Pinedale AZ 85934

Call Sign: KF7EPE
Kevin D Puckett
Pinedale AZ 85934

Call Sign: KE7LAG
Paul O'Dair
Pinedale AZ 85934

Call Sign: KB7ZIH
Paul D Crookston
Pinedale AZ 85934

Call Sign: KD7WMF
Rachel A Crookston
Pinedale AZ 85934

Call Sign: KD7WME
Stephen B O'Dair
Pinedale AZ 85934

Call Sign: KF7EOV
Tanya B Puckett
Pinedale AZ 85934

Call Sign: KD7VIB
Tonya H Butler
Pinedale AZ 85934

Call Sign: W7OPS
Thomas W James
Pinedale AZ 859341274

FCC Amateur Radio Licenses in Pinetop

Call Sign: KA7EQD
David J Nolan
3195 Bison Cir
Pinetop AZ 85935

Call Sign: N7IBA
Milas P Larson
Blue Grass Ranch
Pinetop AZ 85935

Call Sign: KA7PPM
Raymond G Harris Jr
Box 14966
Pinetop AZ 85935

Call Sign: KC7WTT
Karen W Carter
Box 39732
Pinetop AZ 85935

Call Sign: KA7APE
David A Boles
Box 63711
Pinetop AZ 85935

Call Sign: N6KQL
Dean P Reed
Box 90158
Pinetop AZ 85935

Call Sign: KD7JRS
Robert K Flake
Box 90230
Pinetop AZ 85935

Call Sign: KD7QPP
Mark C Binnie
8239 Bucksprings Rd
Pinetop AZ 85935

Call Sign: KD7WMG
Shelley J Sackett
6309 Dun Cir
Pinetop AZ 85935

Call Sign: KE7QBZ
David M Lucas
474 E Woodland Ln
Pinetop AZ 85935

Call Sign: K6BRD
John E Gerlach
2209 Jackrabbit Dr
Pinetop AZ 859354929

Call Sign: KF7RIR
Christopher C Cannon
4949 Night Hawk Loop
Pinetop AZ 85935

Call Sign: KA6WKK
Rodolfo A Steger
5059 Night Hawk Loop
Pinetop AZ 85935

Call Sign: K7VUK
Arnold Redford
6092 Pitchfork Ln
Pinetop AZ 85935

Call Sign: W7LEN
John G Belt III
625 S Evergreen Dr
Pinetop AZ 859352428

Call Sign: KB7VPZ
Peggy K Belt
625 S Evergreen Dr
Pinetop AZ 859352428

Call Sign: KE7SBO
William M Peoples

2752 S Pine Wood Ln
Pinetop AZ 859357188

Call Sign: KB7QXQ
Cris D Mc Bride
1858 S Woodland Ln
Pinetop AZ 85935

Call Sign: KE7NOJ
Virginia E Mc Bride
1858 S Woodland Ln
Pinetop AZ 85935

Call Sign: W5TTV
Peter B George
2809 Sports Village Loop
Pinetop AZ 859358101

Call Sign: WB0TXR
Michael R Elders
324 Westway Ln
Pinetop AZ 85935

Call Sign: KB7TZR
Dolly T Greer
6444 Wildcat Way
Pinetop AZ 85935

Call Sign: W6YPI
James B Greer
6444 Wildcat Way
Pinetop AZ 85935

Call Sign: N7UKG
Stephen F Roark
1051 Woodland Lake Rd
Pinetop AZ 85935

Call Sign: WA7YRR
Wayne B Hughes
1859 Woodland Ln
Pinetop AZ 85935

Call Sign: N7RBZ
Grady L Cauthron
Pinetop AZ 85935

Call Sign: N7VLJ
Thomas F Knight Jr

Pinetop AZ 85935

Call Sign: KD7QPT
Alan G Madrid
Pinetop AZ 85935

Call Sign: K5AGM
Alan G Madrid
Pinetop AZ 85935

Call Sign: KE7SCP
Donald D Caverly
Pinetop AZ 85935

Call Sign: KF7OBV
Gary G Miller
Pinetop AZ 85935

Call Sign: KB7ZRN
James M Betts
Pinetop AZ 85935

Call Sign: KF7TIS
Lijun Shan
Pinetop AZ 85935

Call Sign: K7MNV
Mark C Binnie
Pinetop AZ 85935

Call Sign: W3NYC
Mark C Binnie
Pinetop AZ 85935

Call Sign: WB6ZXY
Matthew C Williamson
Pinetop AZ 85935

Call Sign: KA7SWP
Robert C Iles
Pinetop AZ 85935

Call Sign: KE7FRM
Suzie L Hansen
Pinetop AZ 85935

Call Sign: KD7SIG
Terri L Madrid
Pinetop AZ 85935

Call Sign: KD7SUO
Valerie L Binnie
Pinetop AZ 85935

Call Sign: KA7JOI
Vincent J Cattolica
Pinetop AZ 85935

Call Sign: N7QYF
David A Demetri
Pinetop AZ 859353693

Call Sign: KE6SBQ
William F Neel
Pinetop AZ 859353948

FCC Amateur Radio Licenses in Polacca

Call Sign: W2FF
Timothy J Petersen
Polacca AZ 86042

Call Sign: KX7J
Timothy J Petersen
Polacca AZ 86042

FCC Amateur Radio Licenses in Pomerene

Call Sign: KG6MQL
Gregory Loring
Pomerene AZ 85627

Call Sign: KF7GPU
Lane A Ciminski
Pomerene AZ 85627

FCC Amateur Radio Licenses in Portal

Call Sign: KB5OQH
Kenneth D Joens
8399 E Blacktail Rd
Portal AZ 85632

Call Sign: N5WSI
Lydia M Joens

8399 E Blacktail Rd
Portal AZ 85632

Call Sign: KE7KRE
Dennis J Mcavoy
2340 S McAvoy Rd
Portal AZ 85632

Call Sign: W8OX
Paul J Van Wie
Portal AZ 85632

Call Sign: N6FHC
Gilbert A Clark
Portal AZ 85632

Call Sign: KE6OIS
Richard D Beno
Portal AZ 85632

Call Sign: KE7KRF
Richard P Schreiber
Portal AZ 85632

Call Sign: KA7FTC
Lloyd T Dorsey
Portal AZ 856320410

Call Sign: KL7UE
Maurice L Ward
Portal AZ 856320421

Call Sign: K7HDV
William D Queen
Portal AZ 856326177

FCC Amateur Radio Licenses in Quartzsile

Call Sign: WB7VWA
Elbert M Jones
52862 Century Dr
Quartzsile AZ 85346

Call Sign: WD6ERM
Rose B Martin
49600 Topaz Ave
Quartzsile AZ 85346

Call Sign: KE5EUE
Frank E Anner
Quartzsile AZ 85346

Call Sign: KD7HXV
Dwayne D Farmer
Quartzsile AZ 85359

Call Sign: KE7VL
Grant A Anderson
Quartzsile AZ 85359

Call Sign: KE7GGZ
Daniel Horvath
Quartzsile AZ 85359

FCC Amateur Radio Licenses in Quartzsite

Call Sign: KB7WBL
Michael H A Jewitt
6900 E Mockingbird St
Quartzsite AZ 853460450

Call Sign: KB8KML
James W Schultz Jr
635 E Quail Trl
Quartzsite AZ 85359

Call Sign: KB7PZH
Jill L Schultz
635 E Quail Trl
Quartzsite AZ 88534

Call Sign: KC8KVK
Helen M Marlo
3278 Garden
Quartzsite AZ 85359

Call Sign: KC7BUH
Fred G Oatman
22160 Moon Mt Rd N
Quartzsite AZ 85346

Call Sign: KE8WW
James A Mueller
1615 Quail Trl Dr Apt 6
Quartzsite AZ 85359

Call Sign: KF6HBI
Patricia A Weiss
49740 Topaz Ave
Quartzsite AZ 85359

Call Sign: N6YRV
William C Weiss
49740 Topaz Ave
Quartzsite AZ 85359

Call Sign: KD7JXE
Robert Novak
110 Washington St
Quartzsite AZ 85346

Call Sign: KB7HQI
Beverly L Peterson
Quartzsite AZ 85346

Call Sign: WB6UWK
Herman T Bruck
Quartzsite AZ 85346

Call Sign: WB7WUI
Lowell W Farrington
Quartzsite AZ 85346

Call Sign: KB7QAI
Marvin C Fowler
Quartzsite AZ 85346

Call Sign: W7BUE
Verlyn L Michel
Quartzsite AZ 85346

Call Sign: N0CDG
Alexander B Dannenberg
Quartzsite AZ 85359

Call Sign: KC7BUK
Dean L Stebbins
Quartzsite AZ 85359

Call Sign: KC7CDO
Elizabeth A Stebbins
Quartzsite AZ 85359

Call Sign: W8DTP
Harold Knoll Sr

Quartzsite AZ 85346

Call Sign: KC7YU
Harlow W Tonheim
Quartzsite AZ 85346

Call Sign: KF7BPJ
Alvin E Johnson
Quartzsite AZ 85346

Call Sign: KF7SYK
Andrew D Combs
Quartzsite AZ 85346

Call Sign: KF7UJE
Andrew D Combs
Quartzsite AZ 85346

Call Sign: KC7UJK
Anne A Clemons
Quartzsite AZ 85346

Call Sign: KC7POP
Betty V Michel
Quartzsite AZ 85346

Call Sign: KC7PDQ
Charlie L Clemons
Quartzsite AZ 85346

Call Sign: KD7LYB
David A Erekson
Quartzsite AZ 85346

Call Sign: K7DEE
Dee K Lindsay
Quartzsite AZ 85346

Call Sign: KC7PIC
Douglas A Ross
Quartzsite AZ 85346

Call Sign: KE7ZEP
Dwight H Cantley
Quartzsite AZ 85346

Call Sign: KD7LYE
Earl K Jaycox
Quartzsite AZ 85346

Call Sign: K7EKJ
Earl K Jaycox
Quartzsite AZ 85346

Call Sign: KB7TEO
Francis D Moore
Quartzsite AZ 85346

Call Sign: WB6WYT
Gracie G Zellers
Quartzsite AZ 85346

Call Sign: KE7YOW
Janet L Mcelwain
Quartzsite AZ 85346

Call Sign: KC7IZO
John D Langston
Quartzsite AZ 85346

Call Sign: KE7GQM
Joseph A Kachmar
Quartzsite AZ 85346

Call Sign: K7JAK
Joseph A Kachmar
Quartzsite AZ 85346

Call Sign: KD7AYS
Larry E Kester
Quartzsite AZ 85346

Call Sign: KE7YOX
Lawrence R Vierra
Quartzsite AZ 85346

Call Sign: KE0AC
Le Roy E Lahti
Quartzsite AZ 85346

Call Sign: KD7LYC
Lynda D Erekson
Quartzsite AZ 85346

Call Sign: KE7YOY
Marilyn E Green
Quartzsite AZ 85346

Call Sign: W7FCG
Martha M Moore
Quartzsite AZ 85346

Call Sign: KD7ARP
Michael S Adams
Quartzsite AZ 85346

Call Sign: KC7FTE
Paul D Staudt
Quartzsite AZ 85346

Call Sign: KB7AVI
Philip D Cushman
Quartzsite AZ 85346

Call Sign: W3RF
Robert R Finn
Quartzsite AZ 85346

Call Sign: KE7YOV
Ronald C Green
Quartzsite AZ 85346

Call Sign: KC7PDO
Ronald E Koehler
Quartzsite AZ 85346

Call Sign: KD7AXT
Scott A Adams
Quartzsite AZ 85346

Call Sign: KC7TTN
Sergio Sarzo
Quartzsite AZ 85346

Call Sign: KD7AYT
Terry L Kester
Quartzsite AZ 85346

Call Sign: KF7DBU
Thomas L Audet
Quartzsite AZ 85346

Call Sign: WB6WYU
William C Zellers
Quartzsite AZ 85346

Call Sign: W7FBO

William P Moore
Quartzsite AZ 85346

Call Sign: KA7DSC
Melvin H Ball
Quartzsite AZ 85359

Call Sign: KC7JQS
Ardie P Jones
Quartzsite AZ 85359

Call Sign: KF7NRL
Betty J Hause
Quartzsite AZ 85359

Call Sign: KD7LYD
Carolyn D Guthrie
Quartzsite AZ 85359

Call Sign: KC7UJL
Charles Watson
Quartzsite AZ 85359

Call Sign: KF7IXE
Dale A Crowe
Quartzsite AZ 85359

Call Sign: W6PIE
Dale A Crowe
Quartzsite AZ 85359

Call Sign: KC7BUD
Debra J Metzger
Quartzsite AZ 85359

Call Sign: KA0JTX
Elaine O Dannenberg
Quartzsite AZ 85359

Call Sign: N0BSE
George R Caron Jr
Quartzsite AZ 85359

Call Sign: KD7KGD
Howard H Smith
Quartzsite AZ 85359

Call Sign: W6TBA
John R Larson

Quartzsite AZ 85359

Call Sign: KD7PPI
Kritchuree Anderson
Quartzsite AZ 85359

Call Sign: NF0Z
Lawrence E Feick
Quartzsite AZ 85359

Call Sign: W8BHS
Lawrence E Feick
Quartzsite AZ 85359

Call Sign: KC7PON
Lila R Patten
Quartzsite AZ 85359

Call Sign: KD7OJT
Merton L Thomas
Quartzsite AZ 85359

Call Sign: KA7YVZ
Buck Burdette
Quartzsite AZ 853460001

Call Sign: KC7BUG
Arlie C Moore
Quartzsite AZ 853460902

Call Sign: KD7EET
Charles J Phinney
Quartzsite AZ 853461308

Call Sign: KD7EES
Geraldine A Phinney
Quartzsite AZ 853461308

Call Sign: KD7ARQ
James A Troeger Sr
Quartzsite AZ 853461539

Call Sign: KD7MFB
Thomas Demelker
Quartzsite AZ 853462416

Call Sign: KC7QWO
Gary L Armstrong
Quartzsite AZ 853462669

Call Sign: KD7ARR
John L Baird
Quartzsite AZ 853469000

Call Sign: KF7BDE
James E Tyler
Quartzsite AZ 853469999

Call Sign: K6ANZ
Michael A Pianga
Quartzsite AZ 853593128

Call Sign: KC7OIC
Barbara L Jones
Quartzsite AZ 853593967

Call Sign: N0DPB
Craig B Shackelford
Quartzsite AZ 853594201

Call Sign: W7FM
Craig B Shackelford
Quartzsite AZ 853594201

Call Sign: KD7ARS
Donald W Pepper
Quartzsite AZ 853595215

Call Sign: KD7ASZ
Mary E Pepper
Quartzsite AZ 853595215

FCC Amateur Radio Licenses in Queen Creek

Call Sign: KF7EBH
Walter H Hitchcock
21240 E Alyssa Rd
Queen Creek AZ 85242

Call Sign: KE7OWL
Steven J Connet
20319 E Appaloosa Dr
Queen Creek AZ 85242

Call Sign: KF7SLQ
Janet K Cooper
20343 E Appaloosa Dr

Queen Creek AZ 85142

Call Sign: N2QOJ
Joseph A Sammartino Sr
18863 E Arrowhead Trl
Queen Creek AZ 85142

Call Sign: KF7FNV
David K Mclennan II
4324 E Ascot Dr
Queen Creek az 85140

Call Sign: KF7FNW
Kerri L Mclennan
4324 E Ascot Dr
Queen Creek az 85140

Call Sign: WB7OSR
Kenn Burnell
21159 E Aspen Valley Dr
Queen Creek AZ 85142

Call Sign: KE7TPM
Rusdon A Ray
19520 E Aster Dr
Queen Creek AZ 85242

Call Sign: KE7YII
George A Perez
21427 E Avenida Del Valle
Queen Creek AZ 85242

Call Sign: KC7QGY
Brandon E Lowe
21164 E Bonanza Way
Queen Creek AZ 85242

Call Sign: KF7RZR
Yancy E Littler
21421 E Bonanza Way
Queen Creek AZ 85142

Call Sign: KE7TOG
Allen C Blaine
643 E Bradstock Way
Queen Creek AZ 85240

Call Sign: N0RFN
Gary P Rice

359 E Brook St
Queen Creek AZ 85240

Call Sign: KE7ZZG
Roger B Beecroft
20131 E Calle De Flores
Queen Creek AZ 85242

Call Sign: NA7AA
Robert G Soltys
19722 E Camina Plata
Queen Creek AZ 85242

Call Sign: KD7SFU
Joseph D Bouvier
19820 E Camina Plata
Queen Creek AZ 85142

Call Sign: KA7FLY
John H Mc Nary
21419 E Camina Plata Ct
Queen Creek AZ 85242

Call Sign: KF6EZT
Bruce K Barnes
18478 E Carriage Way
Queen Creek AZ 85142

Call Sign: KF6RSM
Billy J Barnes
18478 E Carriage Way
Queen Creek AZ 85242

Call Sign: KF6ODI
Karen J Barnes
18478 E Carriage Way
Queen Creek AZ 85242

Call Sign: KF7RZQ
Tracy L Riley
18438 E Cattle Dr
Queen Creek AZ 85142

Call Sign: KB7SHM
Dean J Palmer
19725 E Chestnut Dr
Queen Creek AZ 852427211

Call Sign: KE7ENU

Edwin G Allred
1297 E Christopher St
Queen Creek AZ 85242

Call Sign: KE7IVI
Kara F Allred
1297 E Christopher St
Queen Creek AZ 85242

Call Sign: KE7VYY
Perie L Bigler
19324 E Cloud Rd
Queen Creek AZ 85242

Call Sign: KE7JBL
Curtis H Horton Jr
18727 E Cloud Rd
Queen Creek AZ 85242

Call Sign: AA7K
Curtis H Horton Jr
18727 E Cloud Rd
Queen Creek AZ 85242

Call Sign: N7EL
Elmer J Harger Jr
20451 E Colt Dr
Queen Creek AZ 851426028

Call Sign: KD5YW
David N Ellis
212 E Desert Holly Dr
Queen Creek AZ 85242

Call Sign: K1EC
Conrad H Sheldon
1014 E Desert Springs Way
Queen Creek AZ 85243

Call Sign: AK7M
Kevin N Maurer
2478 E Dry Head Ln
Queen Creek AZ 85242

Call Sign: KE7RHF
David A Moeller Jr
1680 E Dust Devil Dr
Queen Creek AZ 85243

Call Sign: WB6FIC
Donald W Jakubowski
17528 E Flintlock Dr
Queen Creek AZ 85242

Call Sign: KC7CTP
Benjamin F Baker Sr
5764 E Fox Hollow Ln
Queen Creek AZ 85242

Call Sign: KC7SMG
Rick Gomez Jr
6210 E Fox Hollow Ln
Queen Creek AZ 85242

Call Sign: KF7AOV
Edward M Eastman
2085 E Friesian Dr
Queen Creek AZ 85140

Call Sign: KD7YMD
Dolly M Sperry
1150 E Geona St
Queen Creek AZ 85242

Call Sign: KB0ZUE
Elvin D Byers
437 E Germann Rd Lot 135
Queen Creek AZ 85242

Call Sign: KF7LVB
Carl Allred
20624 E Happy Rd
Queen Creek AZ 85142

Call Sign: KF7FNR
James C Stalder
4546 E Hash Knife Draw Rd
Queen Creek az 85140

Call Sign: KE7JYU
Glenn E Tooley
736 E Horizon Heights Dr
Queen Creek AZ 85243

Call Sign: K7GET
Glenn E Tooley
736 E Horizon Heights Dr
Queen Creek AZ 85243

Call Sign: KF7PVG
Nathan G Peterson
17904 E Hunt Hwy
Queen Creek AZ 83142

Call Sign: KF7CYP
Jacob W Shumway
270 E Hunt Hwy Ste 16 140
Queen Creek AZ 85243

Call Sign: KF7RZI
Myron C Checketts
18718 E Kingbird Dr
Queen Creek AZ 85142

Call Sign: KF7RZJ
David J Rich
18658 E Lark Dr
Queen Creek AZ 85142

Call Sign: KC7UHV
Alfred T Berry
854 E Lovegrass Dr
Queen Creek AZ 85242

Call Sign: KC7GMX
David L Perlman
18523 E Mary Ann Way
Queen Creek AZ 85242

Call Sign: KF7RYX
Dennis H Lawrence
19718 E Mayberry Rd
Queen Creek AZ 85142

Call Sign: N7HHG
George R Garrett Jr
4173 E Meadow Creek Way
Queen Creek AZ 85240

Call Sign: WB2YJS
Michael L Tarnowsky
2797 E Mineral Park Rd
Queen Creek AZ 85243

Call Sign: KK6IA
Lloyd E Lawrence
446 E Navajo Trl

Queen Creek AZ 85243

Call Sign: KA7FQW
Gene B Williams
19333 E Ocotillo Rd
Queen Creek AZ 85242

Call Sign: KE7FEB
Aaron R Smith
18637 E Old Beau Trl
Queen Creek AZ 85242

Call Sign: KF6NCQ
Richard W Jensen
2409 E Olivine Rd
Queen Creek AZ 85243

Call Sign: KF7RZM
Alfred R Jamison III
19195 E Oriole Way
Queen Creek AZ 85142

Call Sign: KB8MCC
Lawrence W Portell
20518 E Palm Beach Dr
Queen Creek AZ 852427456

Call Sign: KC7TXM
Matthew D Karls
2113 E Paso Fino Dr
Queen Creek AZ 85242

Call Sign: WL7CEY
Roger W Cooper
21693 E Pegasus Pkwy
Queen Creek AZ 85242

Call Sign: KC7QPI
Calvin J Millyard
18517 E Pheasant Run Rd
Queen Creek AZ 85242

Call Sign: N0ELT
Richard L Lonn
640 E Pheasant Run Rd Sp 56
Queen Creek AZ 85240

Call Sign: KF6GUG

Daniel H Carroll
198 E Piccolo Ct
Queen Creek AZ 851437512

Call Sign: KF7MAV
Nicole Mcghan
4359 E Pony Track Ln
Queen Creek AZ 85140

Call Sign: KF7FNJ
Logan J Mcghan
4359 E Ponytrack Ln
Queen Creek az 85240

Call Sign: KF7NOT
Garrett W Harrison
18525 E Purple Sage Dr
Queen Creek az 85142

Call Sign: KD7DUW
Jim Cherryholmes
654 E Ranch Rd 39
Queen Creek AZ 85240

Call Sign: KD7DUV
Patricia A Cherryholmes
654 E Ranch Rd 39
Queen Creek AZ 85240

Call Sign: KF7QNX
Andrew V Kap
19339 E Reins Rd
Queen Creek AZ 85142

Call Sign: N7KAP
Andrew V Kap
19339 E Reins Rd
Queen Creek AZ 85142

Call Sign: KE7YUE
Erik C Morse
1923 E Renegade Trl
Queen Creek AZ 85243

Call Sign: KF7RZO
Scott A Smith
21771 E Rosa Rd
Queen Creek AZ 85142

Call Sign: N7LZD
Bradley A Heck
21128 E Round Up Way
Queen Creek AZ 85242

Call Sign: N7NT
Richard R Kendrick Jr
19911 E San Tan Blvd
Queen Creek AZ 85142

Call Sign: KB7ZAM
Jared M Canova
4980 E Sandwick Dr
Queen Creek AZ 85242

Call Sign: WA7PNO
Edward J Young Jr
1232 E Santa Fiore St
Queen Creek AZ 85242

Call Sign: KC7KUS
Anthony S West
4715 E Santa Rita Dr
Queen Creek AZ 85242

Call Sign: KE7FQM
Nathaniel S West
4715 E Santa Rita Dr
Queen Creek AZ 85242

Call Sign: W0CTR
Leon S Cluff
3758 E Sierrita Rd
Queen Creek AZ 85243

Call Sign: KD7RPX
Alan L Lagerhausen
4320 E Silverbell Rd
Queen Creek AZ 85243

Call Sign: KD7ELL
Wayne A Dancer
4699 E Silverbell Rd
Queen Creek AZ 85243

Call Sign: N6VRZ
Keith D Mc Lean
3516 E Superior Rd
Queen Creek AZ 85243

Call Sign: KF7RZP
Rachelle R Scott
18526 E Swan Dr
Queen Creek AZ 85142

Call Sign: KF7RZC
Elizabeth N Lee
18603 E Swan Dr
Queen Creek AZ 85142

Call Sign: KF7SAA
Rebekah A Lee
18603 E Swan Dr
Queen Creek AZ 85142

Call Sign: KF7RZD
Terry J Lee III
18603 E Swan Dr
Queen Creek AZ 85142

Call Sign: KB7IQE
Terry J Lee Jr
18603 E Swan Dr
Queen Creek AZ 85142

Call Sign: KF7RZG
Ronald J Flewellen
18851 E Swan Dr
Queen Creek AZ 85142

Call Sign: KE7JBJ
Joe E Cooperrider
933 E Taylor Trl
Queen Creek AZ 85243

Call Sign: KF7VAM
Gordon L Fulton
19657 E Thornton Rd
Queen Creek AZ 85142

Call Sign: KC8KKP
Martin R Baker
1442 E Trellis Pl
Queen Creek AZ 85240

Call Sign: KF7RYY
Anthony Martorana
21610 E Twin Acres Dr

Queen Creek AZ 85142

Call Sign: N7BBL
Michael P Costello
19102 E Via De Arboles
Queen Creek AZ 85242

Call Sign: KC7NFI
J D Glaess
19212 E Via De Olivas
Queen Creek AZ 85242

Call Sign: KD7FHU
Tom O Cox
20363 E Via Del Oro
Queen Creek AZ 85242

Call Sign: KF7E
James L Henderson
18601 E Via Del Rancho
Queen Creek AZ 85242

Call Sign: W0EDC
Robert A Jannereth
20835 E Via Del Rancho
Queen Creek AZ 85142

Call Sign: N8AGQ
Leonard L Rulason
19080 E Via Park St
Queen Creek AZ 85142

Call Sign: KE7EJA
Charles R Kollett
8546 E Waterford Cir
Queen Creek AZ 85242

Call Sign: W7CRK
Charles R Kollett
8546 E Waterford Cir
Queen Creek AZ 85242

Call Sign: NU7P
Zbigniew Baranski
17841 E Watford Dr
Queen Creek AZ 85142

Call Sign: KA6EOW
Sherman S Francisco

34836 N Bargona Tr
Queen Creek AZ 85243

Call Sign: KC7ERW
Elaine D Frisbie
36610 N Bushwacker Pass 31
Queen Creek AZ 85242

Call Sign: KE7BMH
Wyoming Dx Association
39764 N Country Ln
Queen Creek AZ 85242

Call Sign: KE7VZB
Jason A St Gelais
28087 N Desert Native
Queen Creek AZ 85243

Call Sign: KD7MAT
Jonathon C Mccommack
41300 N Desert Thistle Tr
Queen Creek AZ 85242

Call Sign: KD7WOZ
Robert A Nyberg
42517 N Friend Ave
Queen Creek AZ 85242

Call Sign: KC6MRI
Sherree L Chapman
28234 N Jade St
Queen Creek AZ 85143

Call Sign: KF7OJR
Oyate Mcghan
39215 N Kelley Cir
Queen Creek AZ 85140

Call Sign: N4BRB
William R Billington
39089 N Kelley Ln
Queen Creek AZ 85240

Call Sign: KD7VXX
Michael A Dougher
32111 N Larkspur Dr
Queen Creek AZ 852435823

Call Sign: W7YBY

Brian E Thorn
30098 N Little Leaf Dr
Queen Creek AZ 85243

Call Sign: N8EMT
Robert A Flowers
29528 N Little Leaf Dr
Queen Creek AZ 85242

Call Sign: KC7SXM
Jacob A James
28983 N Shannon Dr
Queen Creek AZ 85242

Call Sign: KC7SAJ
Dale M White
42657 N Suburban Ave
Queen Creek AZ 85242

Call Sign: KF7FNH
John A Erickson
36480 N Texas Ranger Rd
Queen Creek az 85240

Call Sign: W6OVE
Frank T Winter
28381 N Welton Pl
Queen Creek AZ 85243

Call Sign: KF7FJR
James P Carter
40103 N Zampino St
Queen Creek AZ 85140

Call Sign: KD7FFJ
Darcine M Kishpaugh
39097 N Zampino St
Queen Creek AZ 85240

Call Sign: KG6OZR
Luis G Escaner
41577 Palm Spring Trl
Queen Creek az 85240

Call Sign: KC7UHR
Joseph W Gledhill
20697 S 184th Pl
Queen Creek AZ 85242

Call Sign: KF7SEG
Janice A Seever
20256 S 186th St
Queen Creek AZ 85142

Call Sign: KC7RDD
John E Clayton Jr
25507 S 190th Pl
Queen Creek AZ 85242

Call Sign: KB7FJN
Clint J Rapier
25706 S 196th St
Queen Creek AZ 85242

Call Sign: W6OCL
Osiel Rodriguez
26330 S 204th Way
Queen Creek AZ 85142

Call Sign: KD7HUU
Terry L Pendergrass
22550 S 208th St
Queen Creek AZ 85242

Call Sign: KD7GAG
Jerome D Carter
24527 S 210th Pl
Queen Creek AZ 85242

Call Sign: KD7FSG
Luke A Johnson
24711 S 210th Pl
Queen Creek AZ 85242

Call Sign: KF7RZB
Aaron C Thompson
21923 S 214th St
Queen Creek AZ 85142

Call Sign: KI6ZDX
John A Jevahirjian
22414 S 214th St
Queen Creek AZ 85142

Call Sign: KF7RZK
Brent L Vernon
21525 S 217th St
Queen Creek AZ 85142

Call Sign: KF7SEI
Scott M Piper
21863 S 219th Pl
Queen Creek AZ 85142

Call Sign: KF7SEH
William H Neville III
21863 S 219th Pl
Queen Creek AZ 85142

Call Sign: KF7RZZ
Krystall M Lawlor
21011 S 220th Pl
Queen Creek AZ 85142

Call Sign: KF7DPA
Charles S Quist
23293 S 220th St
Queen Creek AZ 85242

Call Sign: KF7RZL
Edward G Clark
22350 S Ellsworth Rd
Queen Creek AZ 85142

Call Sign: W7DEZ
Frank D Galas
20018 S Emperor Blvd
Queen Creek AZ 85242

Call Sign: KF7HGO
Carolyn Bridge
25407 S Grape Fruit Dr
Queen Creek AZ 85242

Call Sign: KF7HWI
John R Sundelin
26126 S Grapefruit Dr
Queen Creek AZ 85142

Call Sign: KE7JYS
Robert A Brooks
25615 S Lemon Ln
Queen Creek AZ 85242

Call Sign: KF7GDL
Daniel B Kuefner
26214 S Mandarin Dr

Queen Creek AZ 85242

Call Sign: KE7WHA
Ralph A Cuillo
23844 S Power Rd Ste 102
420
Queen Creek AZ 85242

Call Sign: KF7JKM
Ryan L Harder
21924 S Reina Dr
Queen Creek AZ 85142

Call Sign: KF7ULG
Kurt Licence
20825 S Tiberius Dr
Queen Creek AZ 85142

Call Sign: KF7TIR
Lloyd C Licence
20825 S Tiberius Dr
Queen Creek AZ 85142

Call Sign: AE7QY
Lloyd C Licence
20825 S Tiberius Dr
Queen Creek AZ 85142

Call Sign: NU0Z
Lloyd C Licence
20825 S Tiberius Dr
Queen Creek AZ 85142

Call Sign: AA7PE
Kenneth V Gledhill
19503 Via De Arboles
Queen Creek AZ 85242

Call Sign: KD7FNI
Charles D Countryman
23041 Via Del Arroyo
Queen Creek AZ 85242

Call Sign: KC7TZH
Chris Monk
23412 Via Del Arroyo
Queen Creek AZ 852424052

Call Sign: W8YFN

Earl W Joyner
18721 Via Del Rancho
Queen Creek AZ 852424070

Call Sign: N7XVR
Mary F Kilborn
1452 W Bonnie Ln
Queen Creek AZ 85242

Call Sign: KD6IJZ
George C Fischer
21390 W Camina Plata
Queen Creek AZ 85242

Call Sign: KC6DKX
Roger A Powell
631 W Corriente Ct
Queen Creek AZ 85242

Call Sign: KD6AZD
Ryan W Powell
631 W Corriente Ct
Queen Creek AZ 85242

Call Sign: KC7ZMI
Alfred M Cardenas III
1126 W Desert Basin Dr
Queen Creek AZ 85143

Call Sign: N7EEF
Richard L Lemons
1248 W Desert Hollow Dr
Queen Creek AZ 852433445

Call Sign: KB7ERN
Nancy J Martineau
2132 W Desert Seasons Dr
Queen Creek AZ 85242

Call Sign: WB7PZH
Tony C Martineau
2132 W Desert Seasons Dr
Queen Creek AZ 85242

Call Sign: KF7DIZ
Ian Somes
1047 W Desert Valley Dr
Queen Creek AZ 85243

Call Sign: KT7C
Douglas L Amos
2080 W Dixon Ln
Queen Creek AZ 85242

Call Sign: KD7COZ
Ellery K Watkins
291 W Gascon Rd
Queen Creek AZ 852435466

Call Sign: K7AZS
Steven R Simmons
2322 W Goldmine Mountain
Dr
Queen Creek AZ 85142

Call Sign: KA1NUM
Vincent M Sousa
3417 W Hayden Peak Dr
Queen Creek AZ 85242

Call Sign: WB7NEQ
Ellenor J Schimel
295 W Red Fern Rd
Queen Creek AZ 852426244

Call Sign: K7WYY
Jon M Schimel Sr
295 W Red Fern Rd
Queen Creek AZ 852426244

Call Sign: N7JYD
Douglas J Wolf
2458 W Skyline Ln
Queen Creek AZ 85242

Call Sign: KB7KSX
Ricky A Kilborn
1436 W Virgil Dr
Queen Creek AZ 85242

Call Sign: WB7SHM
Dale R Eckhardt
2251 W Virgil Dr
Queen Creek AZ 85242

Call Sign: AB8FY
Jeremy A Watkins
3859 W Yellow Peak Dr

Queen Creek AZ 85242

Call Sign: KF7DYI
Amy S Karstetter
Queen Creek az 85142

Call Sign: KF7PCJ
Brittany A Switzer
Queen Creek AZ 85142

Call Sign: KF7OKA
Christopher A Switzer
Queen Creek AZ 85142

Call Sign: W7ZWT
Christopher A Switzer
Queen Creek AZ 85142

Call Sign: KE7WES
G W Debeaux
Queen Creek AZ 85142

Call Sign: KF7RTQ
Paul K Barnes
Queen Creek AZ 85142

Call Sign: AD7PD
Paul R Estes
Queen Creek AZ 85142

Call Sign: KF7RZX
Preston J Strebeck
Queen Creek AZ 85142

Call Sign: KE7VYQ
Sandi Neus
Queen Creek AZ 85142

**FCC Amateur Radio
Licenses in Queen Valley**

Call Sign: W9MHD
Eugene E Costello
524 E Donna Dr
Queen Valley AZ 85218

Call Sign: W9NM
Russell C Hoffman
947 E Macleod Dr

Queen Valley AZ 85219

Call Sign: N7ANK
Laurus W Lehwalder
642 E Phyllis Pl
Queen Valley AZ 852189066

Call Sign: KC7ION
Rena M Miglore
485 E Queen Creek Dr
Queen Valley AZ 85218

Call Sign: KC7FUI
Roger A Miglore
485 E Queen Creek Dr
Queen Valley AZ 85218

Call Sign: KB7TZS
Ron D King
181 Kirk Dr
Queen Valley AZ 85219

Call Sign: KD7DJA
Sten G Linnander
2400 N Elephant Butte Rd
Queen Valley AZ 85219

Call Sign: K5VW
Clarence V Weekley
320 W Morris Dr
Queen Valley AZ 85219

Call Sign: KA7TTI
Philip R Bernacke
50 W Oro Viejo Dr 180
Queen Valley AZ 85118

Call Sign: K7TTI
Philip R Bernacke
50 W Oro Viejo Dr 180
Queen Valley AZ 85118

Call Sign: WA7ZQY
Neal A Matheson
782 W Silver King Rd
Queen Valley AZ 85218

**FCC Amateur Radio
Licenses in Red Rock**

Call Sign: KF7CNS
Chad C Gerber
21069 E Prospector Pl
Red Rock AZ 85245

Call Sign: KE7SZU
Donald P Erickson
21378 E Reunion Rd
Red Rock AZ 85245

Call Sign: K7PRO
Donald P Erickson
21378 E Reunion Rd
Red Rock AZ 85245

Call Sign: KE7UVO
Riley Heflin
33863 S Colony Dr
Red Rock AZ 85245

Call Sign: KF7KKQ
Paul H Houdyshelt
34375 S Spirit Ln
Red Rock AZ 85145

**FCC Amateur Radio
Licenses in Rillito**

Call Sign: KF7BQM
Gary L Taylor
Rillito AZ 85654

**FCC Amateur Radio
Licenses in Rio Rico**

Call Sign: N7VO
Victor M Ortiz
339 Ambrosia Ct
Rio Rico AZ 85648

Call Sign: KE7QKT
David A Slagg
204 Angel Ct
Rio Rico AZ 85648

Call Sign: WD9ADT
Mark A Pecenka
1161 Avenida Gandara

Rio Rico AZ 85648

Call Sign: KD7ZNC
Ferdinand E Farrish
412 Bury Ct
Rio Rico AZ 85648

Call Sign: W6RHJ
John S Wanzer
293 Calle Cappela
Rio Rico AZ 85648

Call Sign: N7DXX
Charles L Sellman
999 Calle Carmona
Rio Rico AZ 85648

Call Sign: KA7JAO
Carl F Jefferson Jr
2824 Calle Osito
Rio Rico AZ 85621

Call Sign: KA7KOT
Daniel M Chitwood
2824 Calle Osito
Rio Rico AZ 85621

Call Sign: W7WSU
Patricia L Clark
293 Camino Apolena
Rio Rico AZ 85648

Call Sign: KF7UGN
Peter V Ashcraft
347 Camino Canoa
Rio Rico AZ 85648

Call Sign: W0YJX
Fred M Chitwood
467 Camino Osito
Rio Rico AZ 85648

Call Sign: KA7AOZ
Margaret R Chitwood
467 Camino Osito
Rio Rico AZ 85648

Call Sign: KB2SKQ
Jesus M Matos

1720 Circulo Alameda
Rio Rico AZ 85648

Call Sign: N7LHR
Erich A Draeger
773 Dorotea Ct
Rio Rico AZ 856485601

Call Sign: KD7PIA
Arthur F Defazio
1174 Emilio Ct
Rio Rico AZ 85648

Call Sign: KA7YDK
Steve L Ewing
687 Heritage Ct
Rio Rico AZ 85648

Call Sign: KD7YGG
Heriberto Alanis
89 Highland Cir
Rio Rico AZ 85648

Call Sign: K7HAB
Heriberto Alanis
89 Highland Cir
Rio Rico AZ 85648

Call Sign: KD7YMA
Gabriela Y Valencia
89 Highland Cir
Rio Rico AZ 85648

Call Sign: WB7TSU
Vernal J Cassady
488 Pacana Ct
Rio Rico AZ 85648

Call Sign: N7MDT
Thomas M Nolan
374 Papagayo
Rio Rico AZ 85648

Call Sign: KC7TKK
Pedro Hernandez
825 Pendelton Dr
Rio Rico AZ 85648

Call Sign: WB1AFK

Laurence R Myers
381 Placita Baca
Rio Rico AZ 85648

Call Sign: KC7TJK
Pamela M Ewing
393 Placita Baca
Rio Rico AZ 85648

Call Sign: KE7QKS
Rachel M Ewing
393 Placita Baca
Rio Rico AZ 85648

Call Sign: KE7KCY
Sara J Lang
362 Rio Rico Dr
Rio Rico AZ 85648

Call Sign: AD7NR
Sara J Lang
362 Rio Rico Dr
Rio Rico AZ 85648

Call Sign: AA1SZ
Dale H Lang
362 Rio Rico Dr
Rio Rico AZ 85648

Call Sign: W8ZYV
Billy Sellman
2485 Rio Rico Dr
Rio Rico AZ 85621

Call Sign: KB7MWI
Robert L Mc Broom
114 Vereda Patria
Rio Rico AZ 85648

Call Sign: KE7DVN
Jason D Sene
1847 Via Tapachula
Rio Rico AZ 85648

Call Sign: W7JDS
Jason D Sene
1847 Via Tapachula
Rio Rico AZ 85648

Call Sign: KK6HG
James David Hathaway
1060 Yavapai Dr 2B 229
Rio Rico AZ 85648

Call Sign: KF7KEQ
Julie A Hathaway
1060 Yavapai Dr 2B 229
Rio Rico AZ 85648

Call Sign: KF7KEP
Rebekah E Hathaway
1060 Yavapai Dr 2B 229
Rio Rico AZ 85648

Call Sign: KF7KER
Sarah K Hathaway
1060 Yavapai Dr 2B 229
Rio Rico AZ 85648

Call Sign: KE7TXU
Roberto H Gil Sr
184 Zebu Ct
Rio Rico AZ 85648

Call Sign: K5JAS
Jorge A Sotelo
Rio Rico AZ 85648

Call Sign: K5SMS
Susan M Sotelo
Rio Rico AZ 85648

Call Sign: K4KID
Terry A Ketron
Rio Rico AZ 85648

Call Sign: N4ANF
Virginia H Ketron
Rio Rico AZ 856484886

**FCC Amateur Radio
Licenses in Roosevelt**

Call Sign: KB7OBT
Julianne Harston
Box 4236
Roosevelt AZ 85545

Call Sign: KD7DV
Allen A Lehman
Box 5034
Roosevelt AZ 85545

Call Sign: W6ZUL
Eldon C Berneathy
Roosevelt AZ 85545

FCC Amateur Radio Licenses in Sacaton

Call Sign: W1OKC
Mark J Hill Sr
669 W Seed Farm Rd
Sacaton AZ 85247

FCC Amateur Radio Licenses in Saddlebrooke

Call Sign: W6ZQ
Ronald R Cade
39676 Winding Trl Dr
Saddlebrooke AZ 857392252

FCC Amateur Radio Licenses in Safford

Call Sign: KA7YMT
Betty M Worden
964 12th Ave
Safford AZ 85546

Call Sign: N7BBD
Lawrence R Worden
964 12th Ave
Safford AZ 85546

Call Sign: KC7JKU
Lee W Russell
1505 12th Ave
Safford AZ 85546

Call Sign: KC7QCZ
Thomas T Clonts
1620 14th Ave
Safford AZ 85546

Call Sign: KC7VOQ

James L Saline
801 20th Ave
Safford AZ 85546

Call Sign: N7PCJ
Howard C Allen
1901 20th Ave Apt 104B
Safford AZ 85546

Call Sign: KC7IKC
Lynn E Malloque
1556 25th St
Safford AZ 85546

Call Sign: W7RKG
Earl G Ridlon
628 5th Ave
Safford AZ 85546

Call Sign: N9FL
Frank Lauter
220 7th Ave
Safford AZ 85546

Call Sign: N7GNO
Royce G Thomas
1123 8th Ave
Safford AZ 85546

Call Sign: KB7TNW
Walter E Seale II
2016 9th Ave
Safford AZ 85546

Call Sign: KD7PID
Robert L Starks
204 Apache St
Safford AZ 85546

Call Sign: KC7JKZ
Sharon L Elmer
Box 1003 4
Safford AZ 85546

Call Sign: KC7DLH
Adam D Marble
Box 197
Safford AZ 85540

Call Sign: KD7LMZ
David M Lines
355 Cochise Cir
Safford AZ 85546

Call Sign: KB7YIF
Warren B Francisco Jr
1412 Cuatro Cerros Rd
Safford AZ 85546

Call Sign: KI7ZL
Oby A Dunn
109 E 19th Pl
Safford AZ 85546

Call Sign: KC7NJT
Randy L Micetich
114 E 4th St
Safford AZ 85546

Call Sign: KC7DLN
Leann Hancock
5900 E Hancock Pl
Safford AZ 85546

Call Sign: KC7DLG
Richard N Hancock
5900 E Hancock Pl
Safford AZ 85546

Call Sign: KC7DQC
Emily K Hancock
5911 E Hancock Pl
Safford AZ 85546

Call Sign: KB7RMF
Eric F Hancock
5911 E Hancock Pl
Safford AZ 85546

Call Sign: KD7LMV
Robert E Chapman
3201 E Hwy 70 11
Safford AZ 85546

Call Sign: KC7FQS
Ryan F Jarvis
1622 E Hwy 70 44
Safford AZ 85546

Call Sign: KD7LMY
Luis A Rivera
2056 E Hwy 70 48
Safford AZ 85546

Call Sign: KD7LMX
Leroy E Schneidewent
3201 E Hwy 70 Sp 113
Safford AZ 85546

Call Sign: KB7QLS
Harold S Clark
3201 E Hwy 70 Sp 178
Safford AZ 85546

Call Sign: KC7VOP
Randy L Lucas
762 E Morningdove Ln
Safford AZ 85546

Call Sign: KD7LNA
Harlan Fry
2586 E Nelson Pl
Safford AZ 85546

Call Sign: WB7DNT
Wayne E Lisonbee
224 E Nor Jean Way
Safford AZ 85546

Call Sign: KF7SOP
Barbara J Rains
3178 E Skyline View Dr
Safford AZ 85546

Call Sign: WA5YLV
James L Voelker
3201 E US Hwy 70 Trlr 145
Safford AZ 85546

Call Sign: KC7DT
Dale J Holladay
429 Main St
Safford AZ 85546

Call Sign: N7OAZ
Janice Holladay
429 Main St

Safford AZ 85546

Call Sign: KC7NJU
Claude E Martin
1852 N Safford Bryce Rd
Safford AZ 85546

Call Sign: KE7EDQ
Penny M Stewart
708 S 11th Ave
Safford AZ 85546

Call Sign: N7IUH
Vernon M Roudebush
2605 S 14th Ave
Safford AZ 85546

Call Sign: KL7AO
John N Morris
1855 S 20th Ave
Safford AZ 85546

Call Sign: KC7DLO
Jeffrey T Bingham
6702 S 20th Ave
Safford AZ 85546

Call Sign: KD7JBJ
Jay C Higgins Sr
1775 S 20th Ave Apt B208
Safford AZ 85546

Call Sign: ND7C
Wendell M Hughes
515 S 2nd Ave
Safford AZ 85546

Call Sign: KF7SOQ
Brenda K Brown
2523 S Barney Ln
Safford AZ 85546

Call Sign: KF7SOU
Michael R Brown
2523 S Barney Ln
Safford AZ 85546

Call Sign: K7KAV
Linda J Kavanaugh

7648 S Chuckwagon Loop
Safford AZ 85546

Call Sign: KC7UMZ
Nicholas C Kavanaugh
7648 S Chuckwagon Loop
Safford AZ 85546

Call Sign: K7SOO
Quentin M Kavanaugh
7648 S Chuckwagon Loop
Safford AZ 85546

Call Sign: N7QK
Quentin M Kavanaugh
7648 S Chuckwagon Loop
Safford AZ 85546

Call Sign: KD7GPG
Erin M Kavanaugh
7648 S Chuckwagon Loop
Safford AZ 85546

Call Sign: K3EMK
Erin M Kavanaugh
7648 S Chuckwagon Loop
Safford AZ 85546

Call Sign: KB7QLR
John D Franklin
610 S Gila Ave Apt B
Safford AZ 85546

Call Sign: KC7VON
Mark D Brinkley
6910 S Hwy 191
Safford AZ 85546

Call Sign: K7VON
Mark D Brinkley
6910 S Hwy 191
Safford AZ 85546

Call Sign: KF7SOT
Janna Montierth
2250 S Montierth Ln
Safford AZ 85546

Call Sign: K7JEM

Joseph E Montierth
2250 S Montierth Ln
Safford AZ 85546

Call Sign: KD7IYG
James A Reid
3413 S US 191 Unit 10
Safford AZ 85546

Call Sign: W1EYE
James A Reid
3413 S US 191 Unit 10
Safford AZ 85546

Call Sign: KD7LMW
William D Wilcoxson
6894 S US Hwy 191
Safford AZ 85546

Call Sign: KA7PXB
Mike Holguin
723 S Valley Ave
Safford AZ 85546

Call Sign: KC7VOT
Don F Hart
1023 Santa Fe
Safford AZ 85546

Call Sign: KF7LVC
Erica D Parnell
1025 Santa Fe St
Safford AZ 85546

Call Sign: KF7JCJ
John F Parnell
1025 Santa Fe St
Safford AZ 85546

Call Sign: KD7JIN
William W Martin
835 Stirrup Dr
Safford AZ 85546

Call Sign: K7WIL
William W Martin
835 Stirrup Dr
Safford AZ 85546

Call Sign: K7RJG
Carl C Boden
547 Swift Tr E
Safford AZ 85546

Call Sign: WA7ZCO
Elvin G Thompson
610 Valley Ave
Safford AZ 85546

Call Sign: KC7ACU
Sharon L Arkon
1815 W 14th Dr
Safford AZ 85546

Call Sign: KJ7KX
Alfred M Lorenz
111 W 15th St
Safford AZ 85546

Call Sign: KK7SJ
Mary G Lorenz
111 W 15th St
Safford AZ 85546

Call Sign: KB7YID
David C De Spain
1380 W 27th St
Safford AZ 85546

Call Sign: AB7ES
Frank Lauter
710 W 3rd St
Safford AZ 85546

Call Sign: WD5KGE
Patricia A Cooper
1970 W 45th St
Safford AZ 85546

Call Sign: KB7WI
David W Green
520 W 5th St
Safford AZ 85546

Call Sign: KC7FQU
Dixie L Powell
1833 W Cactus Rd
Safford AZ 85546

Call Sign: KC7FQO
Daniel E Larson
1936 W Cactus Rd
Safford AZ 85546

Call Sign: KC7DLJ
Joel R Bingham
2110 W Cactus Rd
Safford AZ 85546

Call Sign: KC7JKV
Paula Bingham
2110 W Cactus Rd
Safford AZ 85546

Call Sign: KC7FMX
Jared M Wilhelm
1041 W Cactus St
Safford AZ 85546

Call Sign: KB7YII
Alcuin P Theisen
1103 W Cactus St
Safford AZ 85546

Call Sign: KD7TZV
Delbert L Humphries
1055 W Cholla St
Safford AZ 85546

Call Sign: K7UYZ
Boyd T Elmer
1677 W Elmer Ln
Safford AZ 85546

Call Sign: KD7LMU
Ross D Abner
1190 W Ocotilla St
Safford AZ 85546

Call Sign: K7RDA
Ross D Abner
1190 W Ocotilla St
Safford AZ 85546

Call Sign: KD7WEP
Doug P Schulz
738 W Puma Dr

Safford AZ 85546

Call Sign: KC6NJX
Philip Madsen
1725 W Relation
Safford AZ 85546

Call Sign: KF7LIV
Janice M Tysoe
909 W Relation St
Safford AZ 85546

Call Sign: KC7OBY
Jeff Glenn Tysoe
909 W Relation St
Safford AZ 85546

Call Sign: KJ7LG
John W Tysoe
909 W Relation St
Safford AZ 85546

Call Sign: KC7VOR
Jacob J Neff
1409 W Relation St
Safford AZ 85546

Call Sign: KD6IXR
Charles G Tresselt
1725 W Relation St
Safford AZ 85546

Call Sign: KD6BEL
Jean F Madson
1725 W Relation St
Safford AZ 85546

Call Sign: W7TOP
Patrick E Fleming
2886 W Sunnyview Ln
Safford AZ 855469586

Call Sign: WA0WIF
Wilford N Clemens
1535 W Thatcher Blvd Sp 67
Safford AZ 85546

Call Sign: KD7JIO
Sam J Showers

1713 W Vista Dr
Safford AZ 85546

Call Sign: N7FIW
Robert M Vasquez
1772 W Vista Dr
Safford AZ 855469370

Call Sign: KF7SOR
Ilene Church
Safford AZ 85548

Call Sign: KE7AVO
John M Canady
Safford AZ 85548

Call Sign: K7AVO
John M Canady
Safford AZ 85548

Call Sign: KR7RR
John N Morris
Safford AZ 85548

Call Sign: KD7NAA
Kenneth K Kelly
Safford AZ 85548

Call Sign: KC7FQP
Reed P Larson
Safford AZ 85548

Call Sign: KC7FQR
Roy G Powell
Safford AZ 85548

Call Sign: KC7ACS
Sandi J Blair
Safford AZ 85548

Call Sign: KC7ACT
Stoney E Blair
Safford AZ 85548

Call Sign: W7KKK
Kenneth K Kelly
Safford AZ 855480186

FCC Amateur Radio Licenses in Sahaurita

Call Sign: KE5MEL
David W Laity
17850 S Camino De Loreto
Sahaurita AZ 85629

Call Sign: N7SQN
Albert R Minker
Box 3212
Sahuarita AZ 85629

Call Sign: N7TIA
Jani S Minker
Box 3212
Sahuarita AZ 85629

Call Sign: KF7CT
James W Hartwell
Box 3601
Sahuarita AZ 85629

Call Sign: KB7EYA
Karen L Hartwell
Box 3601
Sahuarita AZ 85629

Call Sign: KA7ZJW
James E Hartwell
Box 3601
Sahuarita AZ 85629

Call Sign: KC7MGS
Jeffrey W Thornsberry
Box 3617
Sahuarita AZ 85629

Call Sign: KC7LVQ
Teralyn K Thornsberry
Box 3617
Sahuarita AZ 85629

Call Sign: KF7NZG
Natalie G Mcgee
Box 4607
Sahuarita AZ 85629

Call Sign: W7LAT

George D Johnson
1351 Calle De La Plaza
Sahuarita AZ 85629

Call Sign: KC7HSG
Gary R Richardson
1221 Calle Ensayador
Sahuarita AZ 85629

Call Sign: KF7UGR
Rick L Perry
18188 Camino De Las
Quintas
Sahuarita AZ 85629

Call Sign: KB0TEV
James E Avers
87 E Calle Del Rondador
Sahuarita AZ 85629

Call Sign: W9YYS
Steven L Makowski
509 E Camino Crystal Azul
Sahuarita AZ 85629

Call Sign: KB7CRH
Kenneth A Harrison
515 E Camino Del Abeto
Sahuarita AZ 85629

Call Sign: KF7PHU
Zachary J Palmer
6340 E Camino Emmanuel
Sahuarita AZ 85629

Call Sign: KE7VKT
Roberto A Torres
194 E Corte Rancho Dorado
Sahuarita AZ 85629

Call Sign: KE7UKZ
David L Medearis
3651 E Dawson Rd
Sahuarita AZ 85629

Call Sign: KE7KCS
Delores J Gross
6459 E Grace Ln
Sahuarita AZ 85629

Call Sign: AD7NM
Delores J Gross
6459 E Grace Ln
Sahuarita AZ 85629

Call Sign: KE7DQK
Ronald T Gross
6459 E Grace Ln
Sahuarita AZ 85629

Call Sign: AD7FV
Ronald T Gross
6459 E Grace Ln
Sahuarita AZ 85629

Call Sign: KE7KCQ
Barbara L Taylor
6577 E Kryshann
Sahuarita AZ 85629

Call Sign: KB7QKS
Mac P Powas Jr
251 E Mtn Alder
Sahuarita AZ 85629

Call Sign: KD5CSL
Jason M Cole
434 E Placita Amuleto
Sahuarita AZ 85629

Call Sign: KF7EWQ
Michael L Iuzzolino
56 E Placita Vista Alegre
Sahuarita AZ 85629

Call Sign: N8ELA
Eugene M Short
344 E River Birch Pl
Sahuarita AZ 85629

Call Sign: KE7WJE
Stephen S Baker
309 E Via Puente De La
Lluvia
Sahuarita AZ 85629

Call Sign: KE7QID
Nathan D Powell

274 E Via Teresita
Sahuarita AZ 85629

Call Sign: N7XJG
Charles J Birbeck
17732 Placita De Laton
Sahuarita AZ 85629

Call Sign: KR6W
Joseph R Ravella
14631 S Avenida Cucana
Sahuarita AZ 85629

Call Sign: KF7UGQ
Teri D Perry
18188 S Camino De Las
Quintas
Sahuarita AZ 85629

Call Sign: KF7UGP
Luke A Perry
18210 S Camino De Las
Quintas 2
Sahuarita AZ 85629

Call Sign: N7GXP
Steven B Elwood
14350 S Camino Vallado
Sahuarita AZ 85629

Call Sign: KC7USC
Scott M Burke
16531 S Delgado Rd
Sahuarita AZ 85629

Call Sign: KB7VKG
George W Stratton
17445 S La Canada Dr
Sahuarita AZ 85629

Call Sign: KE7VMK
Gugler Family ARC
18475 S Mann Ave
Sahuarita AZ 85629

Call Sign: KE7QVB
Abigail K Gugler
18475 S Mann Ave
Sahuarita AZ 85629

Call Sign: KE7VJO
Annalisa E Gugler
18475 S Mann Ave
Sahuarita AZ 85629

Call Sign: KC7OVN
Douglas P Gugler
18475 S Mann Ave
Sahuarita AZ 85629

Call Sign: NA6RA
Gary K Jue
16283 S Petrified Forest Dr
Sahuarita AZ 85629

Call Sign: N7NJ
Gary K Jue
16283 S Petrified Forest Dr
Sahuarita AZ 85629

Call Sign: KC5EAN
Darell W New
16352 S Petrified Forest Dr
Sahuarita AZ 856299284

Call Sign: KF7UGO
James A Boeck
17774 S Placita Cocinera
Sahuarita AZ 85629

Call Sign: KD7IKN
Karen A Hanson
14157 S Placita La Veronica
Sahuarita AZ 85629

Call Sign: KG6CMI
Michael D Abeyta
16551 S Sahuarita Pl
Sahuarita AZ 85629

Call Sign: KF7NZB
Mark E Watkins
14607 S Sumac Dr
Sahuarita AZ 85629

Call Sign: KF7EAL
Charlotte Krebs
16533 S Sycamore Run Ln

Sahuarita AZ 85629

Call Sign: KD7SNX
Robbie R Craver
15082 S Theodore Roosevelt
Way
Sahuarita AZ 85629

Call Sign: K8YVU
Gerald C Cermak
16268 S Three Wells Ct
Sahuarita AZ 85629

Call Sign: KE7BGL
Thomas J Curley
16656 S Three Wells Ct
Sahuarita AZ 85629

Call Sign: K8NRT
Robert E Junke
14229 S Via Del Farolito
Sahuarita AZ 85629

Call Sign: KF7GVQ
Justin P Isley
14320 S Via Del Moro
Sahuarita AZ 85629

Call Sign: KI6GBK
Daniel F Addington
733 W Calle Marojo
Sahuarita AZ 85629

Call Sign: K7INN
Richard L Boyles
291 W Calle Montero
Sahuarita AZ 856298544

Call Sign: KF7NZE
John P Aslan Jr
526 W Calle Montero
Sahuarita AZ 85629

Call Sign: KC7TNQ
Joshua M Gibson
303 W Calle Paso Suave
Sahuarita AZ 85629

Call Sign: WB4YPA

William H Maurer
168 W Calle Patio Lindo
Sahuarita AZ 85629

Call Sign: KC7OEH
Tom T Donahue
1026 W Camino Hombre
Viejo
Sahuarita AZ 85629

Call Sign: KC7UGN
Roger F Wheaton
18 W Camino Rancho Felice
Sahuarita AZ 85629

Call Sign: KB7YIE
Kerry L Mitchell
3820 W Curly Horn Rd
Sahuarita AZ 85629

Call Sign: KE7NID
Kerry L Mitchell
3820 W Curly Horn Rd
Sahuarita AZ 85629

Call Sign: K7VOA
Thomas W Lang
1085 W El Toro Rd
Sahuarita AZ 85629

Call Sign: KF7IGP
Glen L Ballard
7160 W Lost Silver Ln
Sahuarita AZ 85629

Call Sign: K3TIN
Lawrence R Bailey III
1260 W Paseo Del Compadre
Sahuarita AZ 85629

Call Sign: K7LRB
Lawrence R Bailey III
1260 W Paseo Del Compadre
Sahuarita AZ 85629

Call Sign: KE7UXE
Richard L Mccallum
1280 W Paseo Del Compadre
Sahuarita AZ 85629

Call Sign: WA2KPW
Raymond L Kraley
1640 W Placita Abreojos
Sahuarita AZ 85629

Call Sign: KF7NUA
Nicolo Sciortino
1554 W Placita Lluvia De
Oro
Sahuarita AZ 85629

Call Sign: KD6CDP
Robert A Wallace
1200 W Via Cerro Colorado
Sahuarita AZ 85629

Call Sign: KD7YHP
John R Sparks
99 W Via Costilla
Sahuarita AZ 85629

Call Sign: K7FLI
Adam S Mercier
943 W Via De Gala
Sahuarita AZ 85629

Call Sign: K6AOX
Leland E Irvin
1248 W Via De Santo Tomas
Sahuarita AZ 85629

Call Sign: W7AOX
Leland E Irvin
1248 W Via De Santo Tomas
Sahuarita AZ 85629

Call Sign: W3BFM
Roger L Beamon
1559 W Via Muleje
Sahuarita AZ 85629

Call Sign: K7GUG
Gugler Family ARC
Sahuarita AZ 85629

Call Sign: WA4DSD
Cornelius E Easterling
Sahuarita AZ 85629

Call Sign: KC7DPO
Jack E Mc Gowan
Sahuarita AZ 85629

Call Sign: AD7NK
Jack E Mc Gowan
Sahuarita AZ 85629

Call Sign: KE7VTR
Raymond A Draves
Sahuarita AZ 85629

Call Sign: KD7CZB
Richard G Zachary
Sahuarita AZ 85629

Call Sign: KD7GPI
Shawnna R Gugler
Sahuarita AZ 85629

Call Sign: KD7FMC
Dimitri Tsalabounis
Sahuarita AZ 856290163

Call Sign: WA4TKU
John F Praytor
Sahuarita AZ 856290700

Call Sign: KE7KCR
Dora M Mcgowan
Sahuarita AZ 856290737

FCC Amateur Radio Licenses in Saint David

Call Sign: WB7WSY
Edward S Ingalsbe
Box 175
Saint David AZ 85630

Call Sign: KQ7O
Norman E Cook
Box 187B
Saint David AZ 85630

Call Sign: KD7RWX
Russell J Hunter
212 Chihaverty Trl

Saint David AZ 85630

Call Sign: KC7GUL
Mary A Merrill
126 E Patton
Saint David AZ 85630

Call Sign: KC7DFJ
Daison G Merrill
126 E Patton
Saint David AZ 85630

Call Sign: KE7BRR
Trevar A Janke
238 E Pederson
Saint David AZ 85630

Call Sign: KE7BNJ
Brandon V Estrella
1088 E Summers Ln
Saint David AZ 85630

Call Sign: KD7JQK
Dustin O Merrill
324 N Syble
Saint David AZ 85630

Call Sign: KE7FJB
Michael A Mcneill
3981 S Curtis Flats Rd
Saint David AZ 85630

Call Sign: AD7HZ
Michael A Mcneill
3981 S Curtis Flats Rd
Saint David AZ 85630

Call Sign: W8ZRD
Jill A Atherton
413 S Flynn Rd
Saint David AZ 85630

Call Sign: KA6SAJ
Ray D Burgess
510 Vail Ln
Saint David AZ 85630

Call Sign: WA0UHT
Fredric J White

2455 W Quail Hollow Trl
Saint David AZ 85630

Call Sign: KF7LOO
John A Trotter
1400 W Turtle Trl
Saint David AZ 85630

Call Sign: W8AGQ
Arthur S Townsend
Saint David AZ 85630

Call Sign: KA7WYK
Donald E Hoffman
Saint David AZ 85630

Call Sign: W6MQL
Billy W Killian
Saint David AZ 85630

Call Sign: KC7EYT
Elaine M Panczak
Saint David AZ 85630

Call Sign: KA5EPG
Garry W Phillips
Saint David AZ 85630

**FCC Amateur Radio
Licenses in Saint Johns**

Call Sign: N7ZBM
Kathryn A Jolley
1495 7th N 15th W
Saint Johns AZ 85936

Call Sign: NR7G
Bobby J Curry
8 Blue Sage Rd
Saint Johns AZ 85936

Call Sign: N7KAS
Virginia M Curry
8 Blue Sage Rd
Saint Johns AZ 85936

Call Sign: KF7EOS
Benjamin J Dugdale
Box 33A

Saint Johns AZ 85936

Call Sign: KF7EOT
Kimberly D Dugdale
Box 33A
Saint Johns AZ 85936

Call Sign: KA7MDT
Laura Humphreys
Hc 50
Saint Johns AZ 85936

Call Sign: NV7F
Robert W Lundahl
Lot 97
Saint Johns AZ 85936

Call Sign: KB9QZF
James E Walsh
294 River Springs Ranch
Saint Johns AZ 859360946

Call Sign: K9ARO
James E Walsh
River Springs Ranch
Saint Johns AZ 859360946

Call Sign: NT9B
James E Walsh
River Springs Ranch
Saint Johns AZ 859360946

Call Sign: KA7LPA
Myrna J Mc Grath
Rt 1 Box 51
Saint Johns AZ 85936

Call Sign: AA7PT
Darrell R Perkins
525 S 1 W
Saint Johns AZ 85936

Call Sign: K7EWS
Wesley C Shreeve
465 S 3rd W
Saint Johns AZ 85936

Call Sign: N7QHE
Stephen K Rogers

165 S 4th W
Saint Johns AZ 85936

Call Sign: N7SZC
Billy G Maquet
470 S Water St
Saint Johns AZ 859361527

Call Sign: KG6CMO
Harold Henson
Salk Lake Rd Apacahe Co 60
Saint Johns AZ 85936

Call Sign: N7ZBJ
Ferris L Jolley
330 W 4th N
Saint Johns AZ 85936

Call Sign: N7VXO
Derek M Davis
2010 W 4th N
Saint Johns AZ 85936

Call Sign: KB7RGI
Donald A Dargie
Saint Johns AZ 85936

Call Sign: KB7QXX
Berta A Rogers
Saint Johns AZ 85936

Call Sign: KB7MLM
Bruce K Redford
Saint Johns AZ 85936

Call Sign: N7VLT
Charles R Jensen
Saint Johns AZ 85936

Call Sign: N7ZBP
Craig W Bloomfield
Saint Johns AZ 85936

Call Sign: KB7MLN
James H Badger
Saint Johns AZ 85936

Call Sign: KB7CKS
Jeff S Richins

Saint Johns AZ 85936

Call Sign: KB7MHC
Jerry D Warren
Saint Johns AZ 85936

Call Sign: KA7DSM
Jesse M Broadbent
Saint Johns AZ 85936

Call Sign: KB7QXS
John W Gill
Saint Johns AZ 85936

Call Sign: N7ZBK
Mary A Perkins
Saint Johns AZ 85936

Call Sign: KB7QXV
Melissa G Koski
Saint Johns AZ 85936

Call Sign: WB7DYK
Robert B Badger
Saint Johns AZ 85936

Call Sign: N7ZBL
Russell E Bloomfield
Saint Johns AZ 85936

Call Sign: N7ZBO
Timothy M Lesperance Sr
Saint Johns AZ 85936

Call Sign: KB7JZY
Wesley A Womack
Saint Johns AZ 85936

Call Sign: N7ZBN
Wayne A Lesperance
Saint Johns AZ 85936

Call Sign: W7CSW
Carroll S Wilhelm
Saint Johns AZ 85936

Call Sign: N7QHD
Elynn P Badger
Saint Johns AZ 85936

Call Sign: WB6SPA
Gwen Robinson
Saint Johns AZ 85936

Call Sign: WB6RFT
Herb K Robinson
Saint Johns AZ 85936

Call Sign: KD7KZ
Howard E Vorpahl
Saint Johns AZ 85936

Call Sign: KF7SZW
Howard N Lee
Saint Johns AZ 85936

Call Sign: N7VXN
John B Richardson
Saint Johns AZ 85936

Call Sign: N7VXM
Linda A Richardson
Saint Johns AZ 85936

Call Sign: KD7IGO
Mark P Madrid
Saint Johns AZ 85936

Call Sign: NF7G
Robert B Badger
Saint Johns AZ 85936

Call Sign: AB7ZF
Robert W Lundahl
Saint Johns AZ 85936

Call Sign: KC7QZA
Shirley A Jensen
Saint Johns AZ 85936

Call Sign: KB7MRO
Terry G Maher Sr
Saint Johns AZ 85936

Call Sign: N7VXP
Tim C Raban
Saint Johns AZ 85936

Call Sign: KD7IPY
Allen D Johnson
Saint Johns AZ 85936

Call Sign: KD6SBQ
Christine Carnett
Saint Johns AZ 85936

Call Sign: KF7KVS
Frank J Finnie
Saint Johns AZ 85936

Call Sign: KC7YWE
Merlin A Peterson
Saint Johns AZ 85936

Call Sign: KD7PVW
Raymond L Mell
Saint Johns AZ 85936

Call Sign: W6SJR
Ronald J Carnett
Saint Johns AZ 85936

Call Sign: KB7LZE
William T Wallace Jr
Saint Johns AZ 85936

FCC Amateur Radio Licenses in Saint Michaels

Call Sign: KD7ULA
Cavan C Holliday
Saint Michaels AZ 86511

Call Sign: KD7NSU
Clifford S Sangster
Saint Michaels AZ 86511

Call Sign: KE7LFZ
Lucy Slim
Saint Michaels AZ 86511

Call Sign: KE7KUC
Wilfred E Keeto
Saint Michaels AZ 86511

FCC Amateur Radio Licenses in Salome

Call Sign: WB6NSG
Kenneth S Comer
46125 127 E Hwy 60 70
Salome AZ 85348

Call Sign: KE6TVJ
Pamela J Comer
46125 127 E Hwy 60 70
Salome AZ 85348

Call Sign: KC7IZQ
James E Dorsey
Box 200 62
Salome AZ 853489801

Call Sign: KF7NPA
Olga Potter
Desert Gold 46628 E Hwy 60
Salome AZ 85348

Call Sign: AE7LQ
Olga Potter
Desert Gold 46628 E Hwy 60
Salome AZ 85348

Call Sign: KA5VHL
Albert C Nord Sr
66931 E B Ave
Salome AZ 85348

Call Sign: N6EZZ
Jay Koch
46751 E Hwy 60 70 160
Salome AZ 85348

Call Sign: WA6SBE
Arthur C Lutus
46251 E Hwy 60 70 178
Salome AZ 85348

Call Sign: KL7OM
Lewis K Mc Clendon
46628 E Hwy 60 C56
Salome AZ 85348

Call Sign: KF7HGG
Ron Potter
46628 E Hwy 60 Sp D40

Salome AZ 85348

Call Sign: AE7XX
Ron Potter
46628 E Hwy 60 Sp D40
Salome AZ 85348

Call Sign: NA6E
Mary K Cherry
46628 E Hwy 60 Sp F80
Salome AZ 85348

Call Sign: KC7YRZ
Mary L Jones
46251 E Hwy 60 Unit 57
Salome AZ 85348

Call Sign: KS7B
Calvin E Jones
46251 E Hwy 60 Unit 57
Salome AZ 85348

Call Sign: AB8IL
Thomas F Hager
46125 E Hy 60 33
Salome AZ 85348

Call Sign: K6TIB
Donald W Roland
46025 E Roland Ln
Salome AZ 85348

Call Sign: KF6IDL
Don B Jarman
54504 Hwy 60
Salome AZ 85348

Call Sign: KG7ST
Robert D Black
46628 Hwy 60 E
Salome AZ 85348

Call Sign: KF7LKP
Na6E Memorial ARC
46628 Hwy 60 F80
Salome AZ 85348

Call Sign: KD7ZVJ
Robert Kunzmann

46387 Ironwood Ln
Salome AZ 85348

Call Sign: K7RUK
Robert U Kunzmann
46387 Ironwood Ln
Salome AZ 85348

Call Sign: KQ6ED
Robert F Comer
43980 S Ave 46E
Salome AZ 85348

Call Sign: KD7LXZ
Dean W Tedford
40725 S Kelles Ave
Salome AZ 85348

Call Sign: N7BEG
John F Lippincott Jr
Salome AZ 85348

Call Sign: KE7KLR
James Edmunds
Salome AZ 85348

Call Sign: KC7UTB
Clifford M Olson
Salome AZ 85348

Call Sign: KB6QQV
Don P Hagen
Salome AZ 85348

Call Sign: KY6W
Donald H Rainwater
Salome AZ 85348

Call Sign: W7HHR
Donald H Rainwater
Salome AZ 85348

Call Sign: KY6W
Donald H Rainwater
Salome AZ 85348

Call Sign: KE7KLT
Emogene M Randall
Salome AZ 85348

Call Sign: KE7PQY
James S Lyman
Salome AZ 85348

Call Sign: K6TPX
Jerold R Bradbury
Salome AZ 85348

Call Sign: KC7MRH
Larry M Tipton
Salome AZ 85348

Call Sign: KE7KLS
Leo G Cauley
Salome AZ 85348

Call Sign: KE7PQX
Neva E Lyman
Salome AZ 85348

Call Sign: KF6UZO
Susan E Dewar
Salome AZ 85348

Call Sign: KJ7RR
Susan E Dewar
Salome AZ 85348

Call Sign: W7TH
Clinton H Stevenson
Salome AZ 853480279

Call Sign: KB7LHW
Milton L Bailes
Salome AZ 853481500

Call Sign: NZ7E
Erik H Dewar
Salome AZ 853482708

**FCC Amateur Radio
Licenses in San Manuel**

Call Sign: N7NMI
Richard D Alexander
1016 2nd Ave
San Manuel AZ 85631

Call Sign: K7TYB
Carol F Marshall
920 3rd Ave
San Manuel AZ 85631

Call Sign: KC7HDH
George K Gallaher
215 4th St
San Manuel AZ 85631

Call Sign: WB2EIS
David R Litwiler
907 5th Ave
San Manuel AZ 85631

Call Sign: KC7WLV
Paul E Fuller
12050 Airport Rd
San Manuel AZ 85631

Call Sign: KB7ZJF
Jaime A Ortiz Jr
205 Ave A
San Manuel AZ 85631

Call Sign: N7LNZ
John T Williams
225 Ave A
San Manuel AZ 85631

Call Sign: W7TZG
James E Carender
111 Ave B
San Manuel AZ 85631

Call Sign: KA7TZG
James E Carender
111 Ave B
San Manuel AZ 85631

Call Sign: W6UYH
Joseph M Boyer
235 Ave B
San Manuel AZ 85631

Call Sign: KC7VAN
Paul C Matthews Jr
202 Ave I
San Manuel AZ 85631

Call Sign: KD6VM
Ralph L Perry
289 E Main St
San Manuel AZ 85631

Call Sign: KC7SLJ
James L Perry
303 Main St
San Manuel AZ 85631

Call Sign: KE7NPA
Jesse A Fleming
910 N 2nd Ave
San Manuel AZ 85631

Call Sign: KC7CYV
Paul J Wadusky
201 S 5th Pl
San Manuel AZ 85631

Call Sign: N7MWH
Henry R Thompson
110 W 5th Ave
San Manuel AZ 85631

Call Sign: KC7RDZ
Morris Courtright Jr
612 W 6th Ave
San Manuel AZ 856311105

Call Sign: W1JTS
Jon T Shannon
914 W Webb Dr
San Manuel AZ 85631

Call Sign: KB7QLI
Emmett S Miller Sr
San Manuel AZ 85631

**FCC Amateur Radio
Licenses in San Tan Valley**

Call Sign: KF7NIV
Timothy F Thompson
1178 E Anastasia St
San Tan Valley AZ 85140

Call Sign: AA7OO

Norman E Johnson
4007 E Ascot Dr
San Tan Valley AZ 85140

Call Sign: W7MOT
Motorola ARC Of Arizona
4007 E Ascot Dr
San Tan Valley AZ 85140

Call Sign: KB7LMI
David L Cornell
323 E Bradstock Way
San Tan Valley AZ 85140

Call Sign: KF7RZT
Van C Summers
4040 E Brae Joe Way
San Tan Valley AZ 85140

Call Sign: KE7VZC
Adam R Mcghan
1455 E Christopher St
San Tan Valley AZ 85140

Call Sign: WA7HBN
Jerry R Wright
1947 E Cowboy Cove Trl
San Tan Valley AZ 85143

Call Sign: K7EIT
Jerry R Wright
1947 E Cowboy Cove Trl
San Tan Valley AZ 85143

Call Sign: K7WWM
William W Mclean
803 E Denim Trl
San Tan Valley AZ
851436132

Call Sign: KF7NOS
Christopher White
1952 E Desert Moon Trl
San Tan Valley az 85143

Call Sign: K7QCX
Christopher White
1952 E Desert Moon Trl
San Tan Valley AZ 85143

Call Sign: KJ6EZR
Paul V Knapp
2733 E Desert Rose Trl
San Tan Valley AZ 85143

Call Sign: KD0MVC
Walter L Marshall
1300 E Ferrara Ct
San Tan Valley AZ 85140

Call Sign: KF7RZF
Cameron D Flewellen
873 E Geona St
San Tan Valley AZ 85140

Call Sign: KF7PJR
Riley C Kimball
980 E Harold Dr
San Tan Valley AZ 85140

Call Sign: KE7OQB
Lisa L Romney
1324 E Kelsi Ave
San Tan Valley AZ 85140

Call Sign: KF7RZY
Elisa Bond
1223 E March St
San Tan Valley AZ 85140

Call Sign: KF7LEB
Michael S Dessaint
2574 E Meadow Creek Way
San Tan Valley AZ 85140

Call Sign: KF7SEJ
David O Thorvaldsen
4826 E Meadow Land Dr
San Tan Valley AZ 85140

Call Sign: KF7GJT
Hermilo D Pabalan
1148 E Oak Rd
San Tan Valley az 85140

Call Sign: KF7HWG
Brandon P Hathcock
922 E Penny Ln

San Tan Valley AZ 85140

Call Sign: KF7SVZ
Jessica Hathcock
922 E Penny Ln
San Tan Valley az 85140

Call Sign: KD7RJA
Jarvis L Carter Sr
4273 E Pony Track Ln
San Tan Valley AZ
851404927

Call Sign: KF7RTV
Andres A Barreto
896 E Quentin Ln
San Tan Valley AZ 85140

Call Sign: KF7RTW
Kristy A Barreto
896 E Quentin Ln
San Tan Valley AZ 85140

Call Sign: KF7LUX
Zachary W Gougar
2333 E Renegade Trl
San Tan Valley AZ 85143

Call Sign: KF7CUQ
Michael T Rogers
4976 E Rogers Ln
San Tan Valley AZ 85140

Call Sign: KF7CUP
Starleen A Rogers
4976 E Rogers Ln
San Tan Valley AZ 85140

Call Sign: KC8BT
Gary M Townsend Sr
1069 E Saddleback Pl
San Tan Valley AZ
851436790

Call Sign: KF7LUR
Jared Whitfield
1050 E Shari St
San Tan Valley AZ 85140

Call Sign: KF7SYE
Thomas M Hurst
4544 E Sierrita Rd
San Tan Valley az 85143

Call Sign: KF7OZC
Douglas M Rohrer
2745 E Southwood Rd
San Tan Valley AZ 85140

Call Sign: KF7RYZ
Adam R Sessions
819 E Sun Valley Farms Ln
San Tan Valley AZ 85140

Call Sign: KF7VAK
Nancy J Williamson
3776 E Superior Rd
San Tan Valley AZ 85143

Call Sign: KB6PPF
Richard J Speedy Sr
40876 N Cambria Ln
San Tan Valley AZ 85140

Call Sign: KD7HVA
C Robert Allred
39441 N Carolina Ave
San Tan Valley AZ 85140

Call Sign: WB6CNX
Donald O Harrison
28090 N Crystal Ln
San Tan Valley AZ 85143

Call Sign: N7ASK
Amy S Barriga
35838 N Desert Ln
San Tan Valley AZ 85140

Call Sign: KF7NBB
Jeffrey G Anderson
30232 N Desert Willow Blvd
San Tan Valley AZ 85143

Call Sign: N7XYP
Nancy J Christ
32144 N Dog Leg Ct
San Tan Valley AZ 85143

Call Sign: KF7HGN
Aaron L Bridge
39739 N Lynmills Dr
San Tan Valley AZ 85140

Call Sign: KF7RZV
Laurel S Leavitt
42516 N Murphy Ave
San Tan Valley AZ 85140

Call Sign: KF7OJM
Andrew Devito
42664 N Murphy Ave
San Tan Valley AZ 85140

Call Sign: KB0JOK
Donna E Goering
40367 N Orkney Way
San Tan Valley AZ 85140

Call Sign: N7AZ
Jon F Goering
40367 N Orkney Way
San Tan Valley AZ 85140

Call Sign: KF7RTK
Matthew D Palmer
41687 N Rabbit Brush Trl
San Tan Valley AZ 85140

Call Sign: KE7SWI
Brandon J Weeks
41204 N Salix Dr
San Tan Valley AZ 85140

Call Sign: N5USE
Robert W Bryan
33843 N Slate Creek Dr
San Tan Valley AZ 85143

Call Sign: KC8YQY
Lyssa N Rickard
30409 N Spur Way
San Tan Valley AZ 85143

Call Sign: KF7RZA
John R White
85 W Combs Rd Ste 113

San Tan Valley AZ 85140

Call Sign: K7HID
James L Serkowski
35 W Cooper Canyon Rd
San Tan Valley AZ
851436243

Call Sign: WA2CZX
Charles V Wakefield
1358 W Danish Red Trl
San Tan Valley AZ 85143

Call Sign: K3GA
Edmund S Gabryelski
714 W Desert Seasons Dr
San Tan Valley AZ 85143

Call Sign: KB9JTN
Scott C Moran
3144 W Five Mile Peak Dr
San Tan Valley AZ 85142

Call Sign: WQ5Q
Kelly L Brown
1218 W Gascon Rd
San Tan Valley AZ 85143

Call Sign: W9KMI
Stephen G Revell
3789 W Goldmine Mountain
Dr
San Tan Valley AZ 85142

Call Sign: KB7MLJ
Benjamin M Lee
906 W Holstein Tr
San Tan Valley AZ
851434898

Call Sign: KF7EJA
Roger A Lewis
4371 W Kirkland Ave
San Tan Valley AZ 85142

Call Sign: K7MSD
Michael S Dessaint
3163 W Mineral Butte Dr
San Tan Valley AZ 85142

Call Sign: KC7WTL
Sean W Cubberley
710 W Witt Ave
San Tan Valley AZ 85140

FCC Amateur Radio Licenses in Sanders

Call Sign: KC7RIZ
Larry L Hill
134 Prairie Ln
Sanders AZ 86512

Call Sign: KC7FVC
Carl V Call
137 Prarie Ln
Sanders AZ 86512

Call Sign: N7BEI
Peter Bonigut
Sanders AZ 86512

Call Sign: KB7OAW
Karen A Snow
Sanders AZ 86512

Call Sign: KC7DZC
Albert R Van Deaver
Sanders AZ 86512

Call Sign: KB4YAT
Randall B Wilson
Sanders AZ 86512

FCC Amateur Radio Licenses in Sedona

Call Sign: KE7GVW
Kristina L Hall
110 Abbott Rd
Sedona AZ 86336

Call Sign: KE7GVY
Pasquale Benedetto
110 Abbott Rd
Sedona AZ 86336

Call Sign: KB7EOX

Raphael C Courtney
55 Adobe Trl
Sedona AZ 86336

Call Sign: W3TZ
John W Hamblen
925 Andante Dr
Sedona AZ 86336

Call Sign: W2GAS
Richard G Munson
335 Apache Trl
Sedona AZ 86336

Call Sign: KD5GPO
Frank J Fowsky
405 Arroyo Pinon Dr
Sedona AZ 86336

Call Sign: KC2EN
Arthur C Rissberger Jr
125 Blackjack Dr
Sedona AZ 863517540

Call Sign: W6RXP
Francis C Osborn
140 Blue Jay Dr
Sedona AZ 86336

Call Sign: KA0FKI
Donald D Hall
130 Broken Arrow Way S
Sedona AZ 86351

Call Sign: N9ORI
Bernard A Sakowicz
3030 Calle Del Montana
Sedona AZ 86336

Call Sign: KA7FEB
Peter G Fish
20 Calle Feliz
Sedona AZ 86336

Call Sign: W7DHD
William J Byron
240 Canyon Dr
Sedona AZ 86336

Call Sign: KP2CB
Robert D Stimson
130 Castle Rock Rd 74
Sedona AZ 86351

Call Sign: WD9JLE
David A Whisner
230 Cathedral Rock Dr
Sedona AZ 86351

Call Sign: K7DAW
David A Whisner
230 Cathedral Rock Dr
Sedona AZ 86351

Call Sign: W8AD
Don R Tyrrell
90 Colinas
Sedona AZ 86351

Call Sign: KC7NSU
George D Yance
495 Color Cove Rd
Sedona AZ 86336

Call Sign: KC7NVA
Marjorie K Yance
495 Color Cove Rd
Sedona AZ 86336

Call Sign: KE7ZGO
Kevin J O'Connor
770 Concho Dr
Sedona AZ 86351

Call Sign: W6QOI
Rodney J Olsen
160 Copper Canyon Dr
Sedona AZ 86336

Call Sign: N4GZR
Melvin R Larsen
10 Cord Cir
Sedona AZ 86351

Call Sign: KA0IAV
Scott L Wilcox
25 Cove Dr
Sedona AZ 86351

Call Sign: N6XLQ
Ralph S Granchelli Jr
790 Dry Creek Rd
Sedona AZ 86336

Call Sign: KE7TYO
Richard F Roda
185 E Big Horn Ct
Sedona AZ 86351

Call Sign: KK6SD
James R Mc Kee
107 E Mallard
Sedona AZ 86336

Call Sign: KC6UTR
Joseph L Garner
200 El Camino Grande
Sedona AZ 863365098

Call Sign: KE3KR
Charles D Murcko
220 El Camino Rd
Sedona AZ 863365169

Call Sign: KD5BHY
Michael K Mc Kinney Md
315 El Camino Rd
Sedona AZ 86336

Call Sign: KB7FEL
Donald D Shanks
670 Elmersville Rd
Sedona AZ 86336

Call Sign: N7HNB
Carl M Givens
680 Elysian Dr
Sedona AZ 86336

Call Sign: W1HWT
Robert E Mc Manus
55 Fairway Oaks Dr
Sedona AZ 863518827

Call Sign: KD7MEN
Allen C Cornell
46 Fawn Spur

Sedona AZ 86336

Call Sign: W7RNA
Stephen H Blodgett
375 Harmony Dr
Sedona AZ 86336

Call Sign: W2TKO
Roy W Weise
45 Homestead Rd
Sedona AZ 86336

Call Sign: N7SPV
Arthur C Edwards
60 Homestead Rd
Sedona AZ 86336

Call Sign: NU6X
Mark J Mumaw
138 Horse Ranch Rd
Sedona AZ 86351

Call Sign: K7QV
John J Schueler
405 Jacks Canyon Rm 115
Sedona AZ 86351

Call Sign: KF7GCM
Andy P Glanz
60 Jones Ln
Sedona AZ 86336

Call Sign: KF7GCK
Kristine A Damico
60 Jones Ln
Sedona AZ 86336

Call Sign: KD6VUP
Drew G Trabish
265 Juniper Dr
Sedona AZ 86336

Call Sign: KE6AGY
Janice K Trabish
265 Juniper Dr
Sedona AZ 86336

Call Sign: KC7HY
James J Nemeth Jr

280 Madole Dr
Sedona AZ 86336

Call Sign: K8BCB
David L Brumback Sr
506 Manzanita Dr
Sedona AZ 86336

Call Sign: N7ZFY
Charles J Swartwout
703 Manzanita Dr
Sedona AZ 86336

Call Sign: W9GLA
Charles F Wittkop
15 Merry Go Round Rock Rd
Sedona AZ 863518601

Call Sign: KB7FA
Lester A Earnshaw
60 Mingus Rd
Sedona AZ 86339

Call Sign: N6GQC
Jack F Randall
45 Moonlight Cir
Sedona AZ 86336

Call Sign: KD7ZXC
John L Baugh
90 Moons View
Sedona AZ 86351

Call Sign: WD8CHF
Arthur J Challis
91 Morning Sun Dr
Sedona AZ 86336

Call Sign: KC7LKT
Kenneth J Romm
655 Mtn Shadows Dr
Sedona AZ 86336

Call Sign: AE7PX
Kenneth J Romm
655 Mtn Shadows Dr
Sedona AZ 86336

Call Sign: KC7LKS

Laurel A Romm
655 Mtn Shadows Dr
Sedona AZ 86336

Call Sign: K2KIM
Salvatore M Pietrofitta
845 Mtn Shadows Dr
Sedona AZ 863363927

Call Sign: KC7OFZ
John P Young II
4200 N Hwy 89 A
Sedona AZ 86336

Call Sign: KC7OGA
John P Young III
4200 N Hwy 89A
Sedona AZ 86336

Call Sign: N6YY
Alfred W Hugueny
305 Oak Creek Blvd
Sedona AZ 86336

Call Sign: W7KWP
George B Walker Sr
401 Oak Creek Cliffs Dr Rr 4
Sedona AZ 86336

Call Sign: N9DJA
Betty M Schottland
260 Oak Ridge Ln
Sedona AZ 86336

Call Sign: KB7YZW
James B Buehler
275 Oaktree Dr
Sedona AZ 86351

Call Sign: KA6ERE
Cecelia Marvin
140 Palo Verde Cir
Sedona AZ 86351

Call Sign: KE7VWM
James W Breen
405 Panorama Blvd
Sedona AZ 86336

Call Sign: WB9GVO
Roswell N Wert
60 Panorama Ln
Sedona AZ 86336

Call Sign: KD7CJK
Brandon G Vaughn
85 Pebble Dr
Sedona AZ 86351

Call Sign: W0RID
James W Patterson
25 Pine Ct
Sedona AZ 86351

Call Sign: N7HYH
Donald F Rader
70 Pinewood Dr
Sedona AZ 86336

Call Sign: KB7JGY
Ralph E Worsham
205 Pinon Dr
Sedona AZ 86336

Call Sign: KB7EBN
Willard A Greiner
180 Pony Soldier Rd
Sedona AZ 86336

Call Sign: WB0URJ
Delwyn J Watt
215 Quail Hollow Dr
Sedona AZ 86351

Call Sign: K2ASR
William H Lyons
340 Rainbow Ln
Sedona AZ 86351

Call Sign: KB1MG
Richard E Racicot
65 Rainbow Rock Rd
Sedona AZ 86351

Call Sign: WB7RR
Richard E Racicot
65 Rainbow Rock Rd
Sedona AZ 86351

Call Sign: K0RSO
Donald L Schaefer
210 Ridge Rock Rd
Sedona AZ 86351

Call Sign: KJ7MEL
James E Richards
120 Ridgecrest Dr
Sedona AZ 863519541

Call Sign: KD7YHU
Michael A Lagomarsino
145 Ross Rd
Sedona AZ 86336

Call Sign: WA7KFC
John S Norman
205 S Sunset Dr 87
Sedona AZ 86336

Call Sign: KE6QIQ
John L Brown
680 Saddle Horn Rd
Sedona AZ 86351

Call Sign: KE7EVT
Michael F Vitek
550 Saddlerock Cir
Sedona AZ 86336

Call Sign: K6KDB
Kelvin D Borcoman
290 San Miguel
Sedona AZ 86330

Call Sign: W6HHJ
William G Tuers
230 San Miguel Dr
Sedona AZ 86336

Call Sign: W8WBV
Louis W Camp III
55 Sitgreaves Ct
Sedona AZ 86351

Call Sign: KC7HET
Gene L Mason
20 Spur Ct

Sedona AZ 86351

Call Sign: KE7BIE
Edward A Foster
205 Sunset Dr 92
Sedona AZ 86336

Call Sign: WB7RSX
Virginia G Rogers
31 Sunset Hills Cir
Sedona AZ 863369791

Call Sign: KE7ENG
Jessica L Martini
40 Symphony Way
Sedona AZ 86336

Call Sign: KC7TNF
Charles S Malinowski
50 Symphony Way
Sedona AZ 863363761

Call Sign: KD7HIW
Lilianna Kaufmanis
1895 Upper Red Rock Loop
Rd
Sedona AZ 86340

Call Sign: KD7CGG
Lilianna Kaufmanis
1895 Upper Red Rock Loop
Rd
Sedona AZ 863369123

Call Sign: KA2REM
John C Zier
1415 Verde Valley School
Rd
Sedona AZ 86351

Call Sign: KD7CFL
Ralph H Clark
1485 Verde Valley School
Rd
Sedona AZ 86351

Call Sign: KD7NXX
James E Richards

3511 Verde Valley School
Rd
Sedona AZ 863519541

Call Sign: KC7GVD
Elmer P Van Denburgh
175 View Dr
Sedona AZ 86336

Call Sign: W7LPV
Michael V Schmitt
6 Vista Bonita Dr
Sedona AZ 86336

Call Sign: N6ZBP
William R Williams
1360 Vista Montana Dr
Unit27
Sedona AZ 86336

Call Sign: W6LPR
Gary M Paster
1380 Vista Montana Rd Unit
23
Sedona AZ 86336

Call Sign: WH6PH
Thomas J Skene
6770 W Hwy 89 A 141
Sedona AZ 863369503

Call Sign: NM7C
Gail A Hill
3058 W Hwy 89A
Sedona AZ 86336

Call Sign: KE7SWL
David Wile
2370 W Hwy 89A 11
Sedona AZ 86336

Call Sign: AJ6B
Jonathan Wood
2370 W Hwy 89A 11 139
Sedona AZ 86336

Call Sign: KF7SK
John R Crane
6770 W Hwy 89A 14

Sedona AZ 86336

Call Sign: N3NPM
Charlotte G Gourley
90 Whitetail Ln
Sedona AZ 86336

Call Sign: KE3BF
Earle D Gourley Jr
90 Whitetail Ln
Sedona AZ 86336

Call Sign: K0AZA
Azaya Mccoy
115 Wild Horse Mesa Dr
Sedona AZ 86351

Call Sign: N6QXR
Edwin R Greene
65 Windsong Dr
Sedona AZ 863364435

Call Sign: KB7XW
Harner Selvidge
Sedona AZ 86336

Call Sign: N7XFB
Ian A Lewis
Sedona AZ 86336

Call Sign: WB7VNH
Robert C Clemenz
Sedona AZ 86336

Call Sign: N7NFZ
Robert T Jaffe
Sedona AZ 86336

Call Sign: W2EJ
Robert W Mc Carty
Sedona AZ 86336

Call Sign: N7SZO
Eric Sacher
Sedona AZ 86339

Call Sign: KB6LAK
Craig W Dible
Sedona AZ 86341

Call Sign: KC9EK
Robert A Schottland Jr
Sedona AZ 863392848

Call Sign: N7SSI
Eric Sacher
Sedona AZ 86339

Call Sign: W6RLA
Gary S Rasmussen
Sedona AZ 86339

Call Sign: W7TB
Lewis L Wilhelm
Sedona AZ 86339

Call Sign: KA6DSD
Peter R Korzaan
Sedona AZ 86339

Call Sign: WA2OVR
Carl Galletti
Sedona AZ 86340

Call Sign: KJ7NW
James S Beck
Sedona AZ 86340

Call Sign: W6RTN
Philip K Cole
Sedona AZ 86340

Call Sign: N2IQF
Daniel H Hochstein
Sedona AZ 86341

Call Sign: KB7VNO
Frederick G Donahue
Sedona AZ 86341

Call Sign: W1UGX
Joel L Ekstrom
Sedona AZ 86341

Call Sign: KG6AKH
Lonnie Reed
Sedona AZ 86341

Call Sign: KF7TZS
Tad Coyner
Sedona AZ 86341

Call Sign: N6XRX
Ronald L Loper
Sedona AZ 863391492

Call Sign: KD7UUR
Christopher D Reeves
Sedona AZ 863410487

Call Sign: NW2F
Steven Berkule
Sedona AZ 863411085

FCC Amateur Radio Licenses in Sells

Call Sign: N0USL
Thomas Delikat
Mile 74
Sells AZ 85634

Call Sign: KB7IDL
Lorrie T Lott
Sells AZ 85634

Call Sign: KF7DRS
Joseph G Salcido
Sells AZ 85634

FCC Amateur Radio Licenses in Shonto

Call Sign: KC7APH
Shonnie Reese
Shonto AZ 86054

Call Sign: KC7BCF
David Fuller
Shonto AZ 86054

FCC Amateur Radio Licenses in Show Low

Call Sign: KE6YTB
William G Ness
389 Acr 3076

Show Low AZ 85901

Call Sign: KE7ETN
William G Ness
389 Acr 3076
Show Low AZ 85901

Call Sign: WB7OHG
John R Bostick Jr
485 Acr 3144
Show Low AZ 85901

Call Sign: N9YJJ
Bruce A Schaffer
18 Acr 3161
Show Low AZ 85901

Call Sign: KB9ZMH
Sarah B Schaffer
18 Acr 3161
Show Low AZ 85901

Call Sign: NA6NA
Kenneth T Barnes
6280 Apache Trl
Show Low AZ 85901

Call Sign: KA7HOD
Robert H Burmeister
6763 Arizona Hwy 260
Show Low AZ 85901

Call Sign: N7VRP
Shirley A Cossey
8534 Big Bear Dr
Show Low AZ 85901

Call Sign: KB7UPZ
Edwin A Roach
Box 2496
Show Low AZ 85901

Call Sign: N7GXY
William J Knapman Jr
Box 533
Show Low AZ 85901

Call Sign: W9UBG
Clifford C Hatcher

Box 7589
Show Low AZ 85901

Call Sign: N7QQR
David P Ascenzo
148 Bull Elk Run
Show Low AZ 85901

Call Sign: KD7LEM
Cindy L Overbey
8508 Canyon Dr
Show Low AZ 85901

Call Sign: AB7NQ
Dan R Neeley
6756 Circle C Ln
Show Low AZ 85901

Call Sign: KE6DSL
Matthew G Mainwaring
8500 Dragon Rd
Show Low AZ 859023809

Call Sign: W5JCG
John E Drexler
130 E Savage
Show Low AZ 85901

Call Sign: KB7OHU
Sarah K Hatcher
2415 Indian Trl
Show Low AZ 85901

Call Sign: KD7ETC
Roland E D Entremont
8423 Javelina Dr
Show Low AZ 85901

Call Sign: KD7YGY
Russell G Smith
2501 Jicarilla Dr
Show Low AZ 85901

Call Sign: WA2DQH
Philip Sienkiewicz
300 Juniper Ridge Resort
Show Low AZ 85901

Call Sign: K7DQH

Philip Sienkiewicz
300 Juniper Ridge Resort
Show Low AZ 85901

Call Sign: K7BHQ
Donald E Fogle
2034 Maryanne Rd
Show Low AZ 85901

Call Sign: KB7BRF
Robert R Palmer
4280 Meadow Grove Dr
Show Low AZ 85901

Call Sign: KD7YXZ
Robert R Palmer
4280 Meadow Grove Dr
Show Low AZ 85901

Call Sign: N7FSR
Norman L Gray Sr
41 N 14th Dr
Show Low AZ 85901

Call Sign: N7GBX
Thelma R Gray
41 N 14th Dr
Show Low AZ 85901

Call Sign: KD7LYQ
Donald K Corum
250 N 18th Ave
Show Low AZ 85901

Call Sign: KF7DGU
Laura J Gurk
1020 N 22nd Ave
Show Low AZ 85901

Call Sign: KE7EDP
Richard L Gurk
1020 N 22nd Ave
Show Low AZ 85901

Call Sign: KB7FRM
Patrick K Sipes
1461 N 22nd Dr
Show Low AZ 859013551

Call Sign: AE7OY
Patrick K Sipes
1461 N 22nd Dr
Show Low AZ 859013551

Call Sign: KE6EOB
James Majeski
1510 N 22nd Dr
Show Low AZ 859013511

Call Sign: KB6OWL
Thomas J Majewski
1510 N 22nd Dr
Show Low AZ 859013511

Call Sign: KD7YVR
Leslie S Fletcher
1191 N 27th Ave
Show Low AZ 85901

Call Sign: KF7LJQ
Patricia A Wright
440 N 34th Dr
Show Low AZ 85901

Call Sign: K6GJD
William T Salter
1641 N 39th Dr
Show Low AZ 85901

Call Sign: KB7YUU
Harold L Pierce
437 N 6th Ave
Show Low AZ 85901

Call Sign: WB7CDR
Conrad N Black
121 N 6th Dr
Show Low AZ 859022140

Call Sign: KB7SJW
Shirley L Black
121 N 6th Dr
Show Low AZ 859022140

Call Sign: KB7DPC
Michael R Carpenter
151 N Central Ave
Show Low AZ 85901

Call Sign: KC7JMU
Brian K Peterson
1001 N Central Sp D8
Show Low AZ 85901

Call Sign: KB7VVQ
James R Miolli
8427 Ortega Dr
Show Low AZ 85901

Call Sign: KD5JNR
Neva J Doub
1967 Passage Dr
Show Low AZ 85901

Call Sign: N5ZBO
John M Doub
1967 Passage Dr
Show Low AZ 85901

Call Sign: KE7ETX
Elizabeth A Mc Carty
860 Pine Oaks Dr
Show Low AZ 85901

Call Sign: KD7QPS
Melinda L Halsall
241 S 14th Dr
Show Low AZ 85901

Call Sign: KD7LYS
Theodore E Halsall
241 S 14th Dr
Show Low AZ 85901

Call Sign: AB7FK
Lea A Delzer
661 S 29 Dr
Show Low AZ 85901

Call Sign: AB7CM
Robert C Delzer
661 S 29th Dr
Show Low AZ 85901

Call Sign: N7HLZ
Michael L Sipes
11 S 9th Ave

Show Low AZ 85901

Call Sign: AE7OZ
Michael L Sipes
11 S 9th Ave
Show Low AZ 85901

Call Sign: AC7HS
Charles C Briery
1931 S Alpine Dr
Show Low AZ 85901

Call Sign: AL0H
David S Hunt
520 S Rockridge Dr
Show Low AZ 85901

Call Sign: WB7SAR
Jerome F Schrunk
1610 S Sierra Park Trl
Show Low AZ 85282

Call Sign: KD7VIC
Ellen F Brewer
2800 S White Mountain Rd
83
Show Low AZ 85901

Call Sign: N7RA
Conrad S Monroe
280 Sierra Pines Dr
Show Low AZ 85901

Call Sign: KD5ALY
Anthony L Moreland
8618 Silver Creek Dr
Show Low AZ 85901

Call Sign: KD7QPR
Eric E Cottrell
4257 Silver Fox Way
Show Low AZ 85901

Call Sign: KB7UGO
Elaine S Selby
8470 W Antelope Dr
Show Low AZ 85901

Call Sign: KB7QNL

Steven S Selby
8470 W Antelope Dr
Show Low AZ 85901

Call Sign: KB7SJT
Donald F Trewartha
1781 W Huning
Show Low AZ 85901

Call Sign: KB7QXR
Goldie F Trewartha
1781 W Huning
Show Low AZ 85901

Call Sign: KG6ORQ
Michael Ruiz
1620 W Mcneil
Show Low AZ 85901

Call Sign: KE7WXA
William K Mcquillan
4220 W Mogollon Dr
Show Low AZ 85901

Call Sign: KD7NEE
Heidi M Shipitalo
1300 W Nikolaus
Show Low AZ 85901

Call Sign: KD7JJY
William R Shipitalo
1300 W Nikolaus St
Show Low AZ 85901

Call Sign: KF7NFT
Kenneth D Smith
3400 W Old Linden Rd
Show Low AZ 85901

Call Sign: W7DCA
Omer D Robbins
2281 W Savage Cir
Show Low AZ 85901

Call Sign: N7NVT
William V Craig
2375 W Sylvester Cir
Show Low AZ 85901

Call Sign: N7MJJ
John F Jarrett
3921 W Thornton
Show Low AZ 85901

Call Sign: AA7UC
Judith K Roush
2940 W Young St
Show Low AZ 85901

Call Sign: N7SQU
Kenneth E Roush
2940 W Young St
Show Low AZ 85901

Call Sign: KB7ZIG
Dale T Winders
Show Low AZ 85901

Call Sign: KB7TZP
Diana L Born
Show Low AZ 85901

Call Sign: N7ENS
Donald W Letcher
Show Low AZ 85901

Call Sign: KB7ONN
Glennis Mitchell
Show Low AZ 85901

Call Sign: KB7VVT
Lenora M Whiting
Show Low AZ 85901

Call Sign: KB7SJV
Nell R Wise
Show Low AZ 85901

Call Sign: N7POB
Richard E Born
Show Low AZ 85901

Call Sign: KB7SJU
Robert J Wise
Show Low AZ 85901

Call Sign: KB7SJX
Shirlee M Peterson

Show Low AZ 85901

Call Sign: KB7WDH
Susan L Pectol
Show Low AZ 85901

Call Sign: KB7HJB
Wayne N Robeson
Show Low AZ 85901

Call Sign: KA7LQS
Clifford W Meister
Show Low AZ 85901

Call Sign: KA7YYK
Frank W Daily
Show Low AZ 85901

Call Sign: KC7ATX
John U Pectol
Show Low AZ 85901

Call Sign: KC7MLL
Steven M Tallent
Show Low AZ 85901

Call Sign: KA7KUU
Lois C Welsh
Show Low AZ 85901

Call Sign: KB7QXW
Charles E Whiting
Show Low AZ 85901

Call Sign: W7OTA
Donald W Letcher
Show Low AZ 85901

Call Sign: KC7NZI
Marlene L Amos
Show Low AZ 85901

Call Sign: N7VLK
Merlin W Peterson
Show Low AZ 85901

Call Sign: KC7CPD
Mickie Colvin
Show Low AZ 85901

Call Sign: KB7IZN
Robert W Conner
Show Low AZ 85901

Call Sign: KC7MRC
Ronald M Tallent
Show Low AZ 85901

Call Sign: KA7QMR
Virginia L Heiman
Show Low AZ 85901

Call Sign: KB7VVS
Walter J Colvin
Show Low AZ 85901

Call Sign: N7OCG
Larry V Amos
Show Low AZ 85901

Call Sign: K7BDY
Martin H Heiman
Show Low AZ 85901

Call Sign: KF7CC
Robert De Carvalho
Show Low AZ 85901

Call Sign: KC7JMV
Scott Colvin
Show Low AZ 85901

Call Sign: KE6PQT
Robert M Doerr
Show Low AZ 85902

Call Sign: KD7CL
Charles E Whiting
Show Low AZ 85902

Call Sign: KE7FRO
Clark Hockabout
Show Low AZ 85902

Call Sign: KF7QXG
Dallin R Jones
Show Low AZ 85902

Call Sign: K7MBJ
Howard L Fouts
Show Low AZ 85902

Call Sign: KE7UKY
Jason M Owens
Show Low AZ 85902

Call Sign: KE7ZZA
Jerry K Johnson
Show Low AZ 85902

Call Sign: KE7QCA
John J Savino
Show Low AZ 85902

Call Sign: KE7HCD
Norlis C Mckay
Show Low AZ 85902

Call Sign: W7GL
Robert J Schwartz
Show Low AZ 85902

Call Sign: KD7WJK
Russell Rova
Show Low AZ 85902

Call Sign: KE7QBY
Stephen P Wenger
Show Low AZ 85902

Call Sign: W7EH
Kachina ARC
Show Low AZ 85902

Call Sign: N7AAZ
Gary R Downing
Show Low AZ 859010475

Call Sign: KC7NUZ
Lorna J Downing
Show Low AZ 859010475

Call Sign: N7DPH
Virgil T Churchill
Show Low AZ 859012223

Call Sign: KC7MRB

Paul L Tallent
Show Low AZ 859012284

Call Sign: W6WKP
Barbara S Bell
Show Low AZ 859020181

Call Sign: KC7LJD
Joyce Peterson
Show Low AZ 859020358

Call Sign: N7LJD
Lorna J Downing
Show Low AZ 859020475

Call Sign: KE7DDQ
James A Schallmann
Show Low AZ 859020878

Call Sign: WA9SKA
John W Nantelle
Show Low AZ 859023149

Call Sign: KD7QPU
Gabrielle N Zornes
Show Low AZ 859023460

Call Sign: N7VLH
Reese Loveless
Show Low AZ 859029285

FCC Amateur Radio Licenses in Sierra Vista

Call Sign: KC7GUG
Henry A Werchan
1247 Acacia
Sierra Vista AZ 85635

Call Sign: W7ETT
Jack A Chewning
202 Andrea Dr
Sierra Vista AZ 856352040

Call Sign: KB7KRJ
Micah R Stanley
1380 Andrea Dr
Sierra Vista AZ 85613

Call Sign: W7MDJ
Harry L Mossor
1601 Andrea Dr
Sierra Vista AZ 85635

Call Sign: WA0OEB
Donald L Thomas
1632 Andrea Dr
Sierra Vista AZ 85635

Call Sign: N7FLX
Lawrence W O Brien
5425 Apache Ave
Sierra Vista AZ 85635

Call Sign: KB8LMA
Charles E Kline
2615 Arroyo Verde
Sierra Vista AZ 85650

Call Sign: KB7ELB
Richard C Whipple
980 Ashley Pl
Sierra Vista AZ 85635

Call Sign: N7UZY
Robert L Sutton
3166 Atsina Dr
Sierra Vista AZ 85650

Call Sign: WA4VBP
William A Rierson
3383 Atsina Dr
Sierra Vista AZ 85650

Call Sign: KC7QXH
James D Reed
668 Avenida Del Sol
Sierra Vista AZ 85635

Call Sign: KC6YMJ
Elizabeth M Schwartz
Avenida Palermo
Sierra Vista AZ 85635

Call Sign: KE7GUM
Leland L Lehr
2718 Avondale Rd
Sierra Vista AZ 85650

Call Sign: N7MAW
Warren A Bovee
2048 Baywood Ln
Sierra Vista AZ 85635

Call Sign: KC7RM
Loren L De Witt
2132 Baywood Ln
Sierra Vista AZ 85635

Call Sign: K7LOH
John J Murray
82 Bel Aire MHP
Sierra Vista AZ 85635

Call Sign: KB7LOH
John J Murray
82 Bel Aire MHP
Sierra Vista AZ 85635

Call Sign: AB7SO
Richard T Harris
96 Bel Aire Pl 11
Sierra Vista AZ 85635

Call Sign: KA7THO
William R Freeman
1064 Bella Vista Dr
Sierra Vista AZ 85635

Call Sign: KA7SOC
Delbert R Himes
1132 Bella Vista Dr
Sierra Vista AZ 85635

Call Sign: KA7RBG
Robert B Bailey Sr
1148 Bella Vista Dr
Sierra Vista AZ 85635

Call Sign: W1FQF
Donald F Austin
1632 Bella Vista Dr
Sierra Vista AZ 85635

Call Sign: KB7RDH
Charles H Rutherford III
1664 Bella Vista Dr

Sierra Vista AZ 85635

Call Sign: KD7FJX
Christine R Pate
700 Blue Jay Cir
Sierra Vista AZ 85635

Call Sign: KA5CDO
James A Luster
3101 Brae Burn St
Sierra Vista AZ 85635

Call Sign: AA1MZ
Andrew V Berresford
1811 Brentwood Pl
Sierra Vista AZ 85635

Call Sign: KE7YPN
Lincoln J Daynes
2737 Brewer Dr
Sierra Vista AZ 85650

Call Sign: WB5NOG
Hans Clahsen
7211 Brumby Ln
Sierra Vista AZ 85635

Call Sign: N5KVJ
Joan C Clahsen
7211 Brumby Ln
Sierra Vista AZ 85635

Call Sign: WD6AWR
Robert Schwartz
2003 Brushwood Dr
Sierra Vista AZ 85650

Call Sign: KE4UQG
Philip Lydon
860 Buckhorn Cir
Sierra Vista AZ 85635

Call Sign: KC7GTY
Michael C Bales
823 Buckhorn Pl
Sierra Vista AZ 856351360

Call Sign: KB7VYG
Georgia M Foster

4250 Busby Dr 103
Sierra Vista AZ 85635

Call Sign: KC7VQJ
Keith A Richard
4250 Busby Dr 601
Sierra Vista AZ 85635

Call Sign: KC7SWJ
Stephen W Bieda Jr
650 Busby Dr Lot 156
Sierra Vista AZ 85635

Call Sign: KF7SHE
Mark B Manwaring
5053 Calle Cumbre
Sierra Vista AZ 85635

Call Sign: KF7BIX
Greg H Byington
5140 Calle Cumbre
Sierra Vista AZ 85635

Call Sign: K7GHB
Greg H Byington
5140 Calle Cumbre
Sierra Vista AZ 85635

Call Sign: KB7ICI
William V Nicholson
5187 Calle Cumbre
Sierra Vista AZ 85635

Call Sign: N5LOC
Rolf J Kvamme
5133 Calle Encina
Sierra Vista AZ 856358903

Call Sign: KE7WWU
Richard L Goldschmidt
932 Calle Gardenia
Sierra Vista AZ 85635

Call Sign: WB5VNT
Robert M Larson
5165 Calle Granada
Sierra Vista AZ 85635

Call Sign: KB7SKW

Gordon M Miller Sr
905 Calle Jinete
Sierra Vista AZ 85635

Call Sign: KC7WFI
James H Roach
4200 Calle Ladero Apt G
Sierra Vista AZ 85635

Call Sign: W6RMB
James N Heller Jr
925 Calle Virada
Sierra Vista AZ 85635

Call Sign: KA7TBW
Charles F Campbell
5157 Calle Virada
Sierra Vista AZ 85635

Call Sign: K4AFN
Charles F Campbell
5157 Calle Virada
Sierra Vista AZ 85635

Call Sign: KB7TFC
Paul E Kelly II
5182 Calle Virada
Sierra Vista AZ 85635

Call Sign: KD7SDV
Michael E Aloise
3914 Camino Arroyo
Sierra Vista AZ 85650

Call Sign: KB7LG
William C Neuendorff
590 Camino Majapo
Sierra Vista AZ 856353145

Call Sign: KD7AYN
Dennis G Stewart
1836 Camino Montana
Sierra Vista AZ 85635

Call Sign: KF7RIM
John S Downey
3058 Candlewood Way
Sierra Vista AZ 85650

Call Sign: W7JSD
John S Downey
3058 Candlewood Way
Sierra Vista AZ 85650

Call Sign: W5OBT
Robert D Lee
3097 Candlewood Way
Sierra Vista AZ 85650

Call Sign: KD7YOX
Robert E Nolte Jr
3126 Candlewood Way
Sierra Vista AZ 85650

Call Sign: K7MIT
Richard D Mitterlehner
401 Canterbury Dr
Sierra Vista AZ 856354634

Call Sign: N0LUW
Neil C Anderson
5485 Canteria Ct
Sierra Vista AZ 85635

Call Sign: KB7NED
Paul J Hartman
2800 Cardinal Dr
Sierra Vista AZ 85635

Call Sign: KE7CQE
Karl M Rogers
2917 Cardinal Dr
Sierra Vista AZ 85635

Call Sign: KB7RDG
Richard G Hotchkiss
2932 Cardinal Dr
Sierra Vista AZ 85635

Call Sign: AA7RH
Richard G Hotchkiss
2932 Cardinal Dr
Sierra Vista AZ 85635

Call Sign: KE7YPO
Scott D Bramwell
2948 Cardinal Dr
Sierra Vista AZ 85635

Call Sign: KA7AKJ
John W Mees
3000 Cardinal Dr
Sierra Vista AZ 856354227

Call Sign: KC7ANV
Kim C Breitwieser
3049 Cardinal Dr
Sierra Vista AZ 85635

Call Sign: AA7MV
Richard E Breitwieser
3049 Cardinal Dr
Sierra Vista AZ 85635

Call Sign: KB7NEH
Verlin Z Cronn
3065 Cardinal Dr
Sierra Vista AZ 85635

Call Sign: KF7SYC
Victor A Aviles Rivera
1033 Carmelita Dr
Sierra Vista AZ 85635

Call Sign: KB7ND
Kenton C Gassaway
1932 Carmelita Dr
Sierra Vista AZ 85635

Call Sign: W7LPJ
Floyd B Sharp Jr
2065 Carmelita Dr
Sierra Vista AZ 85635

Call Sign: KE7PCY
David N Cook
500 Carmichael Ave 310
Sierra Vista AZ 85635

Call Sign: KC7VQG
James E Young
4697 Cedar Dr
Sierra Vista AZ 85635

Call Sign: KB7VYD
Walter M Blackburn
4875 Chaparral Loop

Sierra Vista AZ 85635

Call Sign: KE7YPI
Russell L Zufelt
1741 Chaplain Carter Dr
Sierra Vista AZ 85613

Call Sign: W7MPL
Peter Maireder
4600 Charleston Rd Apt 103
Sierra Vista AZ 85635

Call Sign: KE7HBU
Peter Maireder
4600 Charleston Rd Apt 220
Sierra Vista AZ 85635

Call Sign: W6EZF
Edward G Delaney
2564 Cherry Hills Dr
Sierra Vista AZ 85650

Call Sign: W5DBU
Melvin D Wright
2637 Chevy Ct
Sierra Vista AZ 85650

Call Sign: AA7F
Don L Goertz
1770 Choctaw Dr
Sierra Vista AZ 85635

Call Sign: W6SGF
Jonathan J Watson
3224 Choctaw Dr
Sierra Vista AZ 85635

Call Sign: K7JHC
Joseph H Cardin
5010 Cielo Cir
Sierra Vista AZ 85635

Call Sign: W7JLA
Earl C Parkhurst
4496 Citadel Dr
Sierra Vista AZ 85635

Call Sign: WB7AOF
Nadine M Parkhurst

4496 Citadel Dr
Sierra Vista AZ 85635

Call Sign: N9HNT
Carl J Lamonica Jr
4985 Colina Way
Sierra Vista AZ 85635

Call Sign: KE7AL
Fredrick T Fitzpatrick
5103 Colina Way
Sierra Vista AZ 85635

Call Sign: KG7LC
Charles E Darrow
3076 Copper Pointe Dr
Sierra Vista AZ 85635

Call Sign: KD7TXL
Ernest S Kile
2530 Copper Sunrise Dr
Sierra Vista AZ 85635

Call Sign: KE7YOZ
Matthew H Lund
2663 Copper Sunrise Dr
Sierra Vista AZ 85635

Call Sign: K2OC
Charles E Glenn
2413 Coral Brooke Dr
Sierra Vista AZ 85650

Call Sign: N2QWF
James E Pitts III
8 Corral Rd
Sierra Vista AZ 85635

Call Sign: AA7JC
Kenneth C Lotts
823 Corte Rey
Sierra Vista AZ 85635

Call Sign: KA9EDC
William F Mc Ivor
4826 Corte Vista
Sierra Vista AZ 85635

Call Sign: KI6QDO

Lawrence T Dorn Jr
4967 Corte Vista
Sierra Vista AZ 85635

Call Sign: WA7ZXW
Elmer P Sangbush
970 Cottonwood Dr
Sierra Vista AZ 85635

Call Sign: KB7SKT
Juan J Rivera
1311 Cottonwood Dr
Sierra Vista AZ 85613

Call Sign: KA3UCP
David A Reinert
2144 Crestview Way
Sierra Vista AZ 85635

Call Sign: K7ZXY
David A Reinert
2144 Crestview Way
Sierra Vista AZ 85635

Call Sign: KE7YPM
Paul J Fritz
2111 Cristina Ave
Sierra Vista AZ 85635

Call Sign: KF7BJG
Sean M Robertson
35 Danser Dr
Sierra Vista AZ 85635

Call Sign: KA7GFT
Jesse D Schmerfeld
50 De Palma
Sierra Vista AZ 85635

Call Sign: KD7DZ
Jacqueline J Kelly
5349 Desert Shadows Dr
Sierra Vista AZ 85635

Call Sign: AB7NP
Jack A Johnson
2017 Devonshire Dr
Sierra Vista AZ 85635

Call Sign: KE7HUM
William J Simotti
445 Duchess Dr
Sierra Vista AZ 85635

Call Sign: K7WJS
William J Simotti
445 Duchess Dr
Sierra Vista AZ 85635

Call Sign: KE7EUZ
Getulio M Brewer
2750 E Atsina Dr
Sierra Vista AZ 85650

Call Sign: N6YS
Getulio M Brewer
2750 E Atsina Dr
Sierra Vista AZ 85650

Call Sign: KE7EVA
John B Brewer
2750 E Atsina Dr
Sierra Vista AZ 85650

Call Sign: W8KLT
Richard L Orzechowski
3032 E Atsina Dr
Sierra Vista AZ 85650

Call Sign: WA6MJN
David W James
8750 E Barataria Blvd
Sierra Vista AZ 85650

Call Sign: N7LYL
Kirk R Cazee
1448 E Bella Vista Dr
Sierra Vista AZ 85635

Call Sign: KC7WEQ
Frederick W Dalton
1461 E Buckhorn Dr
Sierra Vista AZ 85635

Call Sign: KB0LPN
Chris D Wright
4250 E Busby Dr 520
Sierra Vista AZ 85635

Call Sign: KA5TWM
Joseph C Stroup
4400 E Busby Dr Apt 1122J
Sierra Vista AZ 85635

Call Sign: WD8DOM
Harold R Thomas
1555 E Busby Dr Apt 139
Sierra Vista AZ 85635

Call Sign: KC7UMW
Jamieson A Christian
1555 E Busby Dr Apt 212
Sierra Vista AZ 85635

Call Sign: KF7VDR
Jesse L Brewington
4400 E Busby Dr Apt 2145
Sierra Vista AZ 85635

Call Sign: KB7RDD
Regina M Kvamme
4250 E Busby Dr Apt 509
Sierra Vista AZ 85635

Call Sign: KC7CQT
Thomas H Shibe
4313 E Camino Principal
Sierra Vista AZ 856359436

Call Sign: KM5EA
Gordon B Carpenter
8173 E Canda Dr
Sierra Vista AZ 85650

Call Sign: KK7XF
Gordon B Carpenter
8173 E Canda Dr
Sierra Vista AZ 85650

Call Sign: AC7YM
Gordon B Carpenter
8173 E Canda Dr
Sierra Vista AZ 85650

Call Sign: KC6WXZ
Eric C Sundius
2901 E Cardinal Dr

Sierra Vista AZ 85635

Call Sign: WK7T
Eric C Sundius
2901 E Cardinal Dr
Sierra Vista AZ 85635

Call Sign: WB7SGS
Glen T Emmons
1608 E Chantilly Dr
Sierra Vista AZ 85635

Call Sign: KE7IUE
Glen T Emmons
1608 E Chantilly Dr
Sierra Vista AZ 85635

Call Sign: KC7GPK
Irwin J Robinson III
1937 E Chantilly Dr
Sierra Vista AZ 85635

Call Sign: KC7GNM
Gregory L Thompson
600 E Charles Dr 225
Sierra Vista AZ 85635

Call Sign: KF7HKX
Martha E Mayberry
2230 E Cherokee Way
Sierra Vista AZ 85650

Call Sign: N7DQS
Charles H Morris Jr
5126 E Evergreen Dr
Sierra Vista AZ 85635

Call Sign: KC7LCE
Peggy J Morris
5126 E Evergreen Dr
Sierra Vista AZ 85635

Call Sign: N0IGO
David T Bly
2011 E Foothills Dr
Sierra Vista AZ 856354144

Call Sign: K7DTB
David T Bly

2011 E Foothills Dr
Sierra Vista AZ 856354144

Call Sign: N7SFQ
Harold E Pearson
1636 E Fry Blvd
Sierra Vista AZ 85635

Call Sign: KB7JDI
Charles R Heselton
3300 E Fry Blvd 12
Sierra Vista AZ 85635

Call Sign: KB7QZT
Sebastian Y Halyard
2160 E Fry Blvd 192
Sierra Vista AZ 85635

Call Sign: K7EFC
Floyd D Glenn
4210 E Glenn Rd
Sierra Vista AZ 856509483

Call Sign: KF7SHG
David B Gose
100 E Golf Links Rd Apt 113
Sierra Vista AZ 856356105

Call Sign: KB7DZW
Samuel A Mugford
100 E Golflinks 509
Sierra Vista AZ 85635

Call Sign: KB7VJZ
Eugene E Mahoney
3571 E Greenwood Dr
Sierra Vista AZ 85635

Call Sign: KD7JJV
Charles E Braffett
980 E Hwy 90
Sierra Vista AZ 85635

Call Sign: KA7BOM
Charles E Braffett
9800 E Hwy 90
Sierra Vista AZ 85635

Call Sign: AC7IK

Charles E Braffett
9800 E Hwy 90
Sierra Vista AZ 85635

Call Sign: AJ4UU
Timothy J Millea
6201 E Karen Dr
Sierra Vista AZ 85635

Call Sign: K7KS
Richard V Mc Colley
1955 E Kasti Trl
Sierra Vista AZ 85650

Call Sign: KE7YPB
Marilyn J Godfrey
6425 E Kendall Ln
Sierra Vista AZ 85650

Call Sign: KE7YPA
Robert V Godfrey
6425 E Kendall Ln
Sierra Vista AZ 85650

Call Sign: NA7F
John W Pitkin
7773 E Lower Ranch Rd
Sierra Vista AZ 85650

Call Sign: KX6X
Kenneth L Roth
7537 E Madera Dr
Sierra Vista AZ 85650

Call Sign: W7JOZ
Paul C Winter
8151 E Madera Dr
Sierra Vista AZ 85635

Call Sign: KE7JNB
Donald E Savill
8751 E Madera Dr
Sierra Vista AZ 85650

Call Sign: KE7YPE
Stephen M Baker
9120 E Madera Dr
Sierra Vista AZ 85650

Call Sign: KF6BRB
Karl J Emilio
9355 E Magic Dr
Sierra Vista AZ 85650

Call Sign: KF7TLA
Nathan R Hodges
18 E Martin Dr
Sierra Vista AZ 85635

Call Sign: AE7RC
Nathan R Hodges
18 E Martin Dr
Sierra Vista AZ 85635

Call Sign: N7ZGT
Richard E Cox
2697 E Meadowlark Dr
Sierra Vista AZ 85635

Call Sign: N2CKN
Paul W Harwood Sr
3401 E Navaho St
Sierra Vista AZ 85650

Call Sign: KA7TBZ
Richard W Besselman
3325 E Oak Hill St
Sierra Vista AZ 85635

Call Sign: WB7WMP
Patrick T Besselman
3325 E Oak Hill St
Sierra Vista AZ 85650

Call Sign: N7GJG
William F Wright Jr
2913 E Oakhill St
Sierra Vista AZ 85635

Call Sign: KB0EVX
Robert D Cass
2917 E Oakmont Dr
Sierra Vista AZ 85650

Call Sign: KD7SOA
Robert D Cass
2917 E Oakmont Dr
Sierra Vista AZ 85650

Call Sign: AC7XA
Robert D Cass
2917 E Oakmont Dr
Sierra Vista AZ 85650

Call Sign: AF4ZN
David L Cunningham
3605 E Ojibwa St
Sierra Vista AZ 856509609

Call Sign: WH6KC
Timothy J Woodard
2622 E Papago Trl
Sierra Vista AZ 85650

Call Sign: N4NRK
Robert C Miller
582 E Phillip Dr
Sierra Vista AZ 85635

Call Sign: WA7UIM
Ken H Carpenter
2218 E Sierra View Ln
Sierra Vista AZ 856508760

Call Sign: N7KAZ
Linda A Carpenter
2218 E Sierra View Ln
Sierra Vista AZ 856508760

Call Sign: K7HVV
Robert B Rice Sr
3722 E Trevino Dr
Sierra Vista AZ 85650

Call Sign: KG6DNX
Michael R Gerard
6859 E Valley Dr
Sierra Vista AZ 856509184

Call Sign: KF7VS
James S Edwards
3048 E Wilcox Dr
Sierra Vista AZ 85635

Call Sign: WB7VNF
Everett E Wittig Jr
2367 E Yaqui St

Sierra Vista AZ 85650

Call Sign: KF7CYD
Jonathan F Andrew
1901 E Yavapai Ct
Sierra Vista AZ 85650

Call Sign: KC7NHU
Chris R Harriman
3339 Eagle Ridge Dr
Sierra Vista AZ 85635

Call Sign: KB7TCP
Collin K Hill
3405 Eagle Ridge Dr
Sierra Vista AZ 85635

Call Sign: WD6GHJ
Wilmer L Jones
3405 Eagle Ridge Dr
Sierra Vista AZ 85650

Call Sign: KC4BTI
Sandra J Cowan
3459 Eagle Ridge Dr
Sierra Vista AZ 85650

Call Sign: WF4P
Roland Cowan
3459 Eagle Ridge Dr
Sierra Vista AZ 85650

Call Sign: KD7UOP
Jeffrey M Covert
3461 Eagle Vista Dr
Sierra Vista AZ 85650

Call Sign: KC5AHB
Jeffrey M Covert
3461 Eagle Vista Dr
Sierra Vista AZ 85650

Call Sign: W7KAD
Wayne Hester
463 Earl Dr
Sierra Vista AZ 85635

Call Sign: KC7IM
John A Lanza Sr

1109 El Sonoro Dr
Sierra Vista AZ 85635

Call Sign: W7JL
John A Lanza Sr
1109 El Sonoro Dr
Sierra Vista AZ 85635

Call Sign: KC7YDD
Arlen P Isaak
1104 El Sonoro Dr
Sierra Vista AZ 85635

Call Sign: KC7WKZ
Brenda L Isaak
1104 El Sonoro Dr
Sierra Vista AZ 85635

Call Sign: N4PDR
David G Isaak
1104 El Sonoro Dr
Sierra Vista AZ 85635

Call Sign: KD7OBE
Travis W Isaak
1104 El Sonoro Dr
Sierra Vista AZ 85635

Call Sign: W7SVD
Sierra Vista Contesting Club
3707 Elder Ct
Sierra Vista AZ 85650

Call Sign: WB6OTS
Lawrence G Hays
3707 Elder Ct
Sierra Vista AZ 85650

Call Sign: KC7XT
Gordon H Freick
1849 Elmwood Ln
Sierra Vista AZ 85635

Call Sign: KG5HC
Donald R Ditmore
1084 Escondido Dr
Sierra Vista AZ 85635

Call Sign: K1YSE

Lloyd D Ford
617 Essex
Sierra Vista AZ 85635

Call Sign: KA7UPA
Marianne Ford
617 Essex
Sierra Vista AZ 85635

Call Sign: WB5QDY
Paul G Cooper
924 Essex Dr
Sierra Vista AZ 85635

Call Sign: WB7EAA
Donald F Pettit
2000 Foothills Pl
Sierra Vista AZ 85635

Call Sign: N0DSQ
Troy D Chung
840 Fort Ave 5
Sierra Vista AZ 85635

Call Sign: KB7ZKU
John K Feuerbach
35 Freihage Dr Ne
Sierra Vista AZ 85635

Call Sign: KD7QZY
William C Mayberry
2160 Fry Blvd 300
Sierra Vista AZ 85635

Call Sign: W0LJL
Philip M Taylor
2763 Glengarry Way
Sierra Vista AZ 85650

Call Sign: KC7OVL
Kim L Sliper
Glenn Rd
Sierra Vista AZ 85635

Call Sign: W0OGN
Walter J Prill
2349 Glenview Dr
Sierra Vista AZ 85650

Call Sign: KD7QOS
Arthur J Montgomery
3011 Glenview Dr
Sierra Vista AZ 85650

Call Sign: KD7FKE
William J Morris
1301 Golf Links Rd
Sierra Vista AZ 85635

Call Sign: KC7HUZ
Judith E Gustavson
3416 Greenbriar Rd
Sierra Vista AZ 85635

Call Sign: KC7EAO
Roy C Gustavson
3416 Greenbriar Rd
Sierra Vista AZ 85635

Call Sign: WA7ISG
Appie R King
217 Hayden Dr Ne
Sierra Vista AZ 85635

Call Sign: W7EZV
Jerry W King
217 Hayden Dr Ne
Sierra Vista AZ 85635

Call Sign: KV4DW
Bradley F Hardin
3327 Herba De Maria
Sierra Vista AZ 85650

Call Sign: KE6OJV
Brian C Degn
5373 Highland Shadows Dr
Sierra Vista AZ 85635

Call Sign: KC0JHM
Robert T Norton
808 Homestead Rd
Sierra Vista AZ 85635

Call Sign: KA7ULA
Tanya O Tongue
1990 Homestead Rd
Sierra Vista AZ 85635

Call Sign: KE7YPK
Allen E Bingham
986 Horner Dr
Sierra Vista AZ 85635

Call Sign: WA7JJP
Vincent A Siebenrock
495 Howard Dr
Sierra Vista AZ 85635

Call Sign: KQ7H
Everett A Trezise
1415 Hummingbird Ln
Sierra Vista AZ 85635

Call Sign: N7ZQJ
Jeff D Porter
3750 Ironwood Cir
Sierra Vista AZ 85635

Call Sign: WA7UVS
Rodney G Frazier
2663 Isla Bonita Dr
Sierra Vista AZ 856504280

Call Sign: KE7DVM
Thad S Strange Jr
3062 Jacklin Ave
Sierra Vista AZ 85650

Call Sign: W7IKF
Frank B Mc Laughlin
232 James Dr Ne
Sierra Vista AZ 85635

Call Sign: KB3LJP
Nathan B Gray
1380 Joshua Tree
Sierra Vista AZ 85635

Call Sign: KD7AYO
Charles F Carr
296 Judd St
Sierra Vista AZ 85635

Call Sign: KA9USO
Richard W Cushing
2778 Kalispell

Sierra Vista AZ 85635

Call Sign: KK7KE
Arnold J Lane
6059 Karen Dr
Sierra Vista AZ 85635

Call Sign: KC7DVM
Barbara A Lane
6059 Karen Dr
Sierra Vista AZ 85635

Call Sign: KC7JCV
Kenneth R Bacon
7125 Kendall Ln
Sierra Vista AZ 85650

Call Sign: W5EOF
Richard E Griffin
3828 Kiowa St
Sierra Vista AZ 85635

Call Sign: KD7HRC
Glenwood E Bradley
2769 Knollridge Dr
Sierra Vista AZ 85650

Call Sign: KD7HRB
Julie M Bradley
2769 Knollridge Dr
Sierra Vista AZ 85650

Call Sign: KC7GUM
Timothy J Simmons
2200 Las Brisas Way 103
Sierra Vista AZ 85635

Call Sign: KF7ITA
Kedric M Clark
2200 Las Brisas Way Apt
505
Sierra Vista AZ 85635

Call Sign: KD7FKC
David J Penrod
2033 Laurel Ln
Sierra Vista AZ 85635

Call Sign: KF7RSO

Dennis G Jones Jr
1201 Lea St
Sierra Vista AZ 85635

Call Sign: WA7MQE
Earl W Hocker
500 Lenzner Apt A8
Sierra Vista AZ 85635

Call Sign: N7EHQ
Ray C Benites Jr
1821 Lexington Dr
Sierra Vista AZ 85635

Call Sign: KC7UNC
William R Jordan
1649 Loma Ct
Sierra Vista AZ 85635

Call Sign: KF7PSO
William R Jordan
1649 Loma Ct
Sierra Vista AZ 85635

Call Sign: K7WRJ
William R Jordan
1649 Loma Ct
Sierra Vista AZ 85635

Call Sign: KL1WO
Roch A Cabler
4864 Loma Loop
Sierra Vista AZ 85635

Call Sign: KD7NEG
Jeffrey A Denton
4949 Loma Loop
Sierra Vista AZ 85635

Call Sign: WA1VGM
Douglas J Jacques
1668 Loma Pl
Sierra Vista AZ 85635

Call Sign: K5BGG
Leonard A Morgan
4827 Los Reyes Dr
Sierra Vista AZ 85635

Call Sign: KD7CUQ
William J Harris
4936 Los Reyes Dr
Sierra Vista AZ 85635

Call Sign: N3NEW
William J Harris
4936 Los Reyes Dr
Sierra Vista AZ 856357105

Call Sign: KB7SVJ
Gary T Cheatham
372 Magdalena Ct
Sierra Vista AZ 85635

Call Sign: WB7SPU
Walter W Smith
196 Martin Dr Ne
Sierra Vista AZ 85635

Call Sign: W7YVY
Gerald W Hudson
208 Martin Dr Ne
Sierra Vista AZ 85635

Call Sign: KF7BJD
Douglas T Henderson
2701 Meadowlark Dr
Sierra Vista AZ 85635

Call Sign: KF7BJB
Michael W Sisson
2733 Meadowlark Dr
Sierra Vista AZ 85635

Call Sign: KB6AEK
Kenneth S Luchini
3033 Meadowlark Dr
Sierra Vista AZ 85635

Call Sign: W8UXD
Peter M La Count
3064 Meadowlark Dr
Sierra Vista AZ 85635

Call Sign: KF7JUS
Jeffrey W Twilley
217 Meadows Dr
Sierra Vista AZ 85635

Call Sign: KD7GXT
Juanita F Portz
265 Meadows Dr
Sierra Vista AZ 85635

Call Sign: KK7WA
Juanita F Portz
265 Meadows Dr
Sierra Vista AZ 85635

Call Sign: KB7RVI
Stephen L Felts Jr
1155 Meadows Dr
Sierra Vista AZ 85635

Call Sign: N6YMD
Joseph E Lepine Jr
602 Milky Way
Sierra Vista AZ 85635

Call Sign: KE7MMP
Christopher S Reynolds
1759 Mission Viejo Dr
Sierra Vista AZ 85635

Call Sign: KD7FWH
C Lex Herron
2682 Misty View Way
Sierra Vista AZ 85650

Call Sign: KD7FWG
Suzanne G Herron
2682 Misty View Way
Sierra Vista AZ 85650

Call Sign: KA7UOY
Charles A Williams
2916 Mockingbird
Sierra Vista AZ 85635

Call Sign: KD7IP
Michael L Mowrey
2797 Mockingbird Dr
Sierra Vista AZ 85635

Call Sign: KD7OED
Lee F Ilse
3785 Mohawk Dr

Sierra Vista AZ 85650

Call Sign: KG7CA
Bernard J Mc Gill Jr
4697 Monarch Dr
Sierra Vista AZ 85635

Call Sign: N7ZGN
Gertraud Mc Gill
4697 Monarch Dr
Sierra Vista AZ 85635

Call Sign: KE7DZG
Gayle D Pisani
1600 Moonflower Way
Sierra Vista AZ 85635

Call Sign: KF7IYO
Cheryl M Jackson
N 1st St
Sierra Vista AZ 85635

Call Sign: KA6BXC
Jon S Standing Bear
218 N 1st St A
Sierra Vista AZ 85635

Call Sign: KD7QQS
Melvin D Wright
355 N 7th St
Sierra Vista AZ 85635

Call Sign: KB9BQL
Peter M Becola
555 N 7th St Apt 516
Sierra Vista AZ 85635

Call Sign: KE7YPF
Lloyd E Howden
1233 N Catalina Dr
Sierra Vista AZ 85635

Call Sign: N7DMD
Lester N Wilmarth
205 N Central Ave
Sierra Vista AZ 85636

Call Sign: K9RX
Gary L Myers

1460 N Clanton Ave
Sierra Vista AZ 85635

Call Sign: KC7RBY
Justin D Hess
1201 N Colombo Ave 12104
Sierra Vista AZ 85635

Call Sign: KE7YPC
Paul F Woolston
1201 N Colombo Ave Apt
11191
Sierra Vista AZ 85635

Call Sign: WA0JTD
Dennis J Kunkel
780 N Nanas Trl
Sierra Vista AZ 85635

Call Sign: W5SBG
Douglas G Waltz
1588 N San Francisco Cir
Sierra Vista AZ 856359262

Call Sign: WA7RJG
Dennis W Richardson
2091 N San Marcos De Niza
Dr
Sierra Vista AZ 856359277

Call Sign: KE7GUK
Kerry D Thurber
709 N Schraeder Rd
Sierra Vista AZ 85635

Call Sign: WB7WMQ
Richard A Besselman
2925 Oakmont Dr
Sierra Vista AZ 856505151

Call Sign: KE7GUJ
Craig D Gardner
1009 Ocotillo Dr
Sierra Vista AZ 85635

Call Sign: W6SEL
Salustiano S Wong Jr
1449 Ocotillo Dr
Sierra Vista AZ 85635

Call Sign: KG7BY
Edwin H Iriye
3606 Ojibwa St
Sierra Vista AZ 85635

Call Sign: KB7FLZ
George A Lavis
2261 Orchid Dr
Sierra Vista AZ 85635

Call Sign: W7CI
Stephen F Wagner
2833 Oriole Dr
Sierra Vista AZ 85635

Call Sign: W7LU
Oleg G Kolen
2916 Oriole Dr
Sierra Vista AZ 856354215

Call Sign: AA7D
Robert Pettijohn
2932 Oriole Dr
Sierra Vista AZ 856354215

Call Sign: KB7OHJ
Bruno R Talerico Sr
3001 Oriole Dr
Sierra Vista AZ 85635

Call Sign: KC7WKQ
Ruel T Blagg
1359 Overlook Dr
Sierra Vista AZ 85635

Call Sign: KD7JZA
Walter J Vidinski Jr
2853 Palmer Dr
Sierra Vista AZ 85650

Call Sign: KJ7WU
Edwin E Goethe
709 Pampas Pl
Sierra Vista AZ 85635

Call Sign: KC7NHV
Phillip G Orth
2615 Papago Tr

Sierra Vista AZ 85635

Call Sign: KE7CJX
James P Barba
4634 Paseo Brazos
Sierra Vista AZ 85635

Call Sign: N7GJF
Helen N Beckwith
2696 Paseo Media
Sierra Vista AZ 85635

Call Sign: WA7JHH
John T Beckwith
2696 Paseo Media
Sierra Vista AZ 85635

Call Sign: KA0RKW
Marwin H Brown
3202 Pebble Beach Dr
Sierra Vista AZ 85650

Call Sign: N7ZGM
Elizabeth G Kelly
348 Peterson St
Sierra Vista AZ 85635

Call Sign: KB7JFD
Janet L Kelly
348 Peterson St
Sierra Vista AZ 85635

Call Sign: W5FWE
Charles M Stanley Jr
1948 Picadilly Dr
Sierra Vista AZ 85635

Call Sign: KE7U
Francis D Ivey
1648 Piccadilly Dr
Sierra Vista AZ 85635

Call Sign: W7KAE
Lily M Hester
2048 Piccadilly Dr
Sierra Vista AZ 85635

Call Sign: KB1CUT
Robert F Stevens Jr

4532 Pine Tree Dr
Sierra Vista AZ 85635

Call Sign: KF6TY
Carlo Sanfilippo
3041 Player Ave
Sierra Vista AZ 856356605

Call Sign: WB0VYH
James L Lewis
3617 Plaza De La Yerba
Sierra Vista AZ 856509278

Call Sign: N0NBH
Paul L Herrman
3678 Plaza De La Yerba
Sierra Vista AZ 85650

Call Sign: KF7SNG
Scott B Schneeweis
2732 Plaza De Viola
Sierra Vista AZ 85650

Call Sign: KC7GUE
Charles J Biere
1465 Plaza Dominguin
Sierra Vista AZ 85635

Call Sign: KC7WKY
Matthew L Bridges
Plaza Oro Loma
Sierra Vista AZ 85635

Call Sign: N7FIO
Lester B Holmes
Plaza Oro Loma
Sierra Vista AZ 85635

Call Sign: KC7WLA
Karen S Gunn
365 Prairie
Sierra Vista AZ 85635

Call Sign: KE7FDK
Sean Y Henry
4645 Pueblo Ave
Sierra Vista AZ 85650

Call Sign: KC7LJM

Jeffrey C Hendy
4659 Pueblo Ave
Sierra Vista AZ 85635

Call Sign: KC7LJL
Lora B Hendy
4659 Pueblo Ave
Sierra Vista AZ 85635

Call Sign: KC7KVI
Theodore A Hendy
4659 Pueblo Ave
Sierra Vista AZ 85635

Call Sign: KS7S
James H Skjervem
3048 Quail Run Dr
Sierra Vista AZ 856353455

Call Sign: KF6BMV
Eugene W Simpson
3832 Quail Run Dr
Sierra Vista AZ 85635

Call Sign: N7XAV
Nicholas A Chizewsky
4564 Queens Way
Sierra Vista AZ 856353633

Call Sign: KE4CJR
Kieran Curtiss
2610 Raven Dr
Sierra Vista AZ 85650

Call Sign: W7LCI
Edward N Morrell
583 Raymond Dr
Sierra Vista AZ 85635

Call Sign: KF7HLC
James R Callahan
1450 Redrock Dr
Sierra Vista AZ 85650

Call Sign: KF7BIZ
George L Castle
1855 Regency Dr
Sierra Vista AZ 85635

Call Sign: KC7NHW
Denise B De La Cruz
3223 Ridge Crest St
Sierra Vista AZ 85650

Call Sign: KD7MOL
Harold H Miles
3302 Ridge Crest St
Sierra Vista AZ 85650

Call Sign: KH6RY
Mark C Carnett
10540 Rocky Rd
Sierra Vista AZ 85635

Call Sign: AD7BG
Mark C Carnett
10540 Rocky Rd
Sierra Vista AZ 85635

Call Sign: KE7IBD
Megan C Carnett
10540 Rocky Rd
Sierra Vista AZ 85635

Call Sign: KE7VJP
Scott C Carnett
10540 Rocky Rd
Sierra Vista AZ 85635

Call Sign: N9GZC
Teresa S Carnett
10540 Rocky Rd
Sierra Vista AZ 85635

Call Sign: KE7IAA
Daniel M Carnett
10540 Rocky Rd
Sierra Vista AZ 85635

Call Sign: KC7RLQ
Jeffrey T Gunn
2037 Roselie Way
Sierra Vista AZ 85635

Call Sign: N3HAL
Dale H Chidester
5053 S Apache Ave
Sierra Vista AZ 85650

Call Sign: NJ7C
Dale H Chidester
5053 S Apache Ave
Sierra Vista AZ 85650

Call Sign: KE7PCX
Nancy A Chidester
5053 S Apache Ave
Sierra Vista AZ 856509706

Call Sign: WL7ASK
Alan J Humphrey
4934 S Bannock Ave
Sierra Vista AZ 85650

Call Sign: K7ALN
Alan J Humphrey
4934 S Bannock Ave
Sierra Vista AZ 85650

Call Sign: KE7DVO
Michael B Christie
4235 S Bodie Ct
Sierra Vista AZ 85650

Call Sign: KF7BLE
James E Taylor
4866 S Calle Encina
Sierra Vista AZ 85650

Call Sign: KF7BJC
Wendy L Taylor
4866 S Calle Encina
Sierra Vista AZ 85650

Call Sign: KJ7KZ
Larry L Crouch
4903 S Calle Encina
Sierra Vista AZ 85650

Call Sign: KE7JNA
Jaime M Figueroa
800 S Carmichael Ave Apt
114B
Sierra Vista AZ 85635

Call Sign: KE7FPQ
Jodi L Meere

500 S Carmichael Ave Apt
333
Sierra Vista AZ 85635

Call Sign: N9XGI
Charlie W Shaffer Jr
303 S Chase St
Sierra Vista AZ 85635

Call Sign: KB9MDS
Patricia A Shaffer
303 S Chase St
Sierra Vista AZ 85635

Call Sign: KD7MAL
Edward R Jones
4630 S Cherokee Ave
Sierra Vista AZ 85650

Call Sign: K7ERJ
Edward R Jones
4630 S Cherokee Ave
Sierra Vista AZ 85650

Call Sign: KD7MAK
Linda H Jones
4630 S Cherokee Ave
Sierra Vista AZ 85650

Call Sign: W7LHJ
Linda H Jones
4630 S Cherokee Ave
Sierra Vista AZ 85650

Call Sign: KE7YPJ
Kevin R Goates
5016 S Cherokee Ave
Sierra Vista AZ 85650

Call Sign: K7KRG
Kevin R Goates
5016 S Cherokee Ave
Sierra Vista AZ 85650

Call Sign: KA7VBC
Carl J Lawrence
4199 S Comanche Dr
Sierra Vista AZ 85650

Call Sign: KD7MAF
Paul A Curtis Jr
520 S Coronado Dr Apt E
241
Sierra Vista AZ 85635

Call Sign: KE7UXD
Gabriel E Jaramillo
471 S Deer Creek Ln
Sierra Vista AZ 85636

Call Sign: W5EOR
Allen B Fortenberry
698 S Deer Creek Ln
Sierra Vista AZ 856358532

Call Sign: KC7JLH
Brian T Janssens
405 S Garden Ave 177
Sierra Vista AZ 85635

Call Sign: K7BTJ
Brian T Janssens
405 S Garden Ave 177
Sierra Vista AZ 85635

Call Sign: KC7JDP
Christopher M Van Vleet
405 S Garden Ave 61
Sierra Vista AZ 85635

Call Sign: KA7IQV
Dale W Tongue
1990 S Homestead Rd
Sierra Vista AZ 85635

Call Sign: KD7FTD
Christopher A Acheson
2404 S Homestead Rd
Sierra Vista AZ 85635

Call Sign: AA1BP
Donald J Marquis
4732 S Hopi Ave
Sierra Vista AZ 85650

Call Sign: N1KSH
Louise B Marquis
4732 S Hopi Ave

Sierra Vista AZ 85650

Call Sign: N0HLC
James R Hazen
289 S Hwy 92 10102
Sierra Vista AZ 85635

Call Sign: KD5OMJ
Boyd S Sharp
4575 S Kino Rd
Sierra Vista AZ 85650

Call Sign: KD7FUV
Raymond M Huebner
4975 S Kino Rd
Sierra Vista AZ 856509143

Call Sign: KE7GHX
Michael R Cox
5005 S Kino Rd
Sierra Vista AZ 85650

Call Sign: N7SFP
David L Kelly
2638 S La Donna Ln
Sierra Vista AZ 85650

Call Sign: KF7GBB
James A Sills
5043 S Laguna Ave
Sierra Vista AZ 85650

Call Sign: KE7VPK
Michael J Elyea
409 S Lenzner Ave Apt
10208
Sierra Vista AZ 85635

Call Sign: KF7CX
Joseph A Loposzko
409 S Lenzner Ave Apt
12207
Sierra Vista AZ 85635

Call Sign: KC7EQW
Mgt Memorial Club
409 S Lenzner Ave Apt 7207
Sierra Vista AZ 85635

Call Sign: N7TY
Bruce C Thompson
409 S Lenzner Ave Apt 7207
Sierra Vista AZ 85635

Call Sign: N2GTS
Gabrielle T Steinau
409 S Lenzner Ave Apt 7207
Sierra Vista AZ 85635

Call Sign: KE7NGQ
Charles V Hedgpeth
414 S Moorman Ave
Sierra Vista AZ 856353392

Call Sign: N7XJK
Glen A Peters
5326 S Moson Rd
Sierra Vista AZ 85650

Call Sign: N7ASR
Neoma P Stewart
5461 S Moson Rd
Sierra Vista AZ 856509156

Call Sign: N7ARC
John W Stewart
5461 S Moson Rd
Sierra Vista AZ 856509156

Call Sign: W7JWS
John W Stewart
5461 S Moson Rd
Sierra Vista AZ 856509156

Call Sign: N7ARC
John W Stewart
5461 S Moson Rd
Sierra Vista AZ 856509156

Call Sign: K7HHG
Lyle C Painter Sr
5091 S Natoma Trl
Sierra Vista AZ 85650

Call Sign: KD7SSN
Barbara A Beckner
496 S Nature Way
Sierra Vista AZ 85635

Call Sign: K7ZIO
Donald L Sywassink
554 S Nature Way
Sierra Vista AZ 856358518

Call Sign: KE7RPZ
Oliver C Stokes
4960 S Nez Perce Ave
Sierra Vista AZ 85650

Call Sign: W7OCS
Oliver C Stokes
4960 S Nez Perce Ave
Sierra Vista AZ 85650

Call Sign: KE7IEP
David L Seitz
5122 S Night Hawk Tr
Sierra Vista AZ 85650

Call Sign: KE7DZF
Kelsey A Neese
3015 S Player Ave
Sierra Vista AZ 85635

Call Sign: NV3W
Daniel E Schmidli
4551 S Pueblo Ave
Sierra Vista AZ 856508130

Call Sign: KA3RMO
Katharine W Schmidli
4551 S Pueblo Ave
Sierra Vista AZ 856508130

Call Sign: W9ZGM
Emil J Bovich
3322 S Ridge Crest St
Sierra Vista AZ 85650

Call Sign: N7IVV
Bradley P Risk
4916 S San Juan Ave
Sierra Vista AZ 85650

Call Sign: N7INK
Robert L Hollister
5457 S San Juan Ave

Sierra Vista AZ 856509340

Call Sign: KC7HHA
Jason J Hutchinson
5251 S San Pedro
Sierra Vista AZ 85635

Call Sign: KE7WRJ
Michael Chasse
5431 S San Pedro Ave
Sierra Vista AZ 85650

Call Sign: W7WRJ
Michael Chasse
5431 S San Pedro Ave
Sierra Vista AZ 85650

Call Sign: KF7SHF
Robert J Drake
4842 S Santa Anna Ave
Sierra Vista AZ 85650

Call Sign: N7XAS
James R Thies
5041 S Santa Aurelia
Sierra Vista AZ 85635

Call Sign: W4MX
Stewart C Hoeper
5135 S Santa Lucia
Sierra Vista AZ 85635

Call Sign: W8DEW
Jerry J Petranek
5056 S Santa Lucia Ave
Sierra Vista AZ 85635

Call Sign: KC7LIN
Raymond D Shough
4249 S Sauk Ave
Sierra Vista AZ 85650

Call Sign: KB7YZP
Peter H De Rosa
4074 S Seminole Pl
Sierra Vista AZ 85635

Call Sign: N1XFD
Fred E Thomas

482 S Taylors Trl
Sierra Vista AZ 85635

Call Sign: KH2CH
Leroy F Heitz Jr
4919 S Whitening Rd
Sierra Vista AZ 85650

Call Sign: KC7EAL
Zachary W Lea
1009 Sahuaro Dr
Sierra Vista AZ 856351259

Call Sign: K1GLJ
Gregory L Johnson
4632 San Cristobal
Sierra Vista AZ 85635

Call Sign: KA5JPC
Roger W Bayes
4664 San Cristobal
Sierra Vista AZ 85635

Call Sign: ND7E
William H Wright
2523 San Xavier Rd
Sierra Vista AZ 85635

Call Sign: KC7ZMD
William M Vetzel
1730 Santa Clara Cir
Sierra Vista AZ 85635

Call Sign: WB6BNE
Gary A Hinton
1616 Santa Clara Cr
Sierra Vista AZ 85635

Call Sign: KF7HLB
Zachary W Brown
2173 Santa Fe Trl
Sierra Vista AZ 85635

Call Sign: KC7GUH
Winford E Gullett
2115 Santa Maria Dr
Sierra Vista AZ 85635

Call Sign: KA7WSA

Michael L Douglas
2040 Santa Rosa Dr
Sierra Vista AZ 85635

Call Sign: W2JRT
Jeffrey R Thomas
1955 Santa Teresa Dr
Sierra Vista AZ 85635

Call Sign: K7WIN
Jeffrey R Thomas
1955 Santa Teresa Dr
Sierra Vista AZ 85635

Call Sign: K2AK
Jeffrey R Thomas
1955 Santa Teresa Dr
Sierra Vista AZ 85635

Call Sign: KF7BTZ
Sierra Vista D-Star Club
1955 Santa Teresa Dr
Sierra Vista AZ 85635

Call Sign: N7XCP
Roy K Abel
774 Savanna Dr
Sierra Vista AZ 85635

Call Sign: KC7GUF
William R Paulson
43 School Dr
Sierra Vista AZ 85635

Call Sign: KC7EAP
Paul M Hotzel
59 School Dr
Sierra Vista AZ 85635

Call Sign: AC7IZ
Paul M Hotzel
59 School Dr
Sierra Vista AZ 85635

Call Sign: KA7WSB
Edward N Janecki
99 School Dr
Sierra Vista AZ 85635

Call Sign: KC7HWI
Ricardo Zelaya
41 Se Brown Dr
Sierra Vista AZ 85635

Call Sign: KD7GQY
Susan K Lorenz
2908 Shawnee Dr
Sierra Vista AZ 85650

Call Sign: N8IOG
George L Roberts
3515 Shawnee Dr
Sierra Vista AZ 85635

Call Sign: K7TFS
Thomas L Maunu
4632 Shoshoni Ave
Sierra Vista AZ 85635

Call Sign: KF4KPJ
Kevin P Murdock
2446 Sierra Bermeja Dr
Sierra Vista AZ 85650

Call Sign: KE7HUN
Mark C Bangle
2673 Sierra Bermesa Dr
Sierra Vista AZ 85650

Call Sign: W7EZA
Robert F Kelly
1296 Sierra Dr
Sierra Vista AZ 85635

Call Sign: KC7LCH
Thomas L Stuckey Jr
5501 Sioux
Sierra Vista AZ 85635

Call Sign: KD6EGS
John R Braden
2200 Sonoita Dr
Sierra Vista AZ 85635

Call Sign: KD6EGT
Leatha J Braden
2200 Sonoita Dr
Sierra Vista AZ 85635

Call Sign: KK7RV
James E Banks
2785 Southridge St
Sierra Vista AZ 85635

Call Sign: KB7GR
Raymond Quillen
3532 Sparrow Dr
Sierra Vista AZ 85635

Call Sign: WA7SQL
Michael D Crista
3532 Sparrow Dr
Sierra Vista AZ 856352918

Call Sign: KC7EAJ
Don C Abata
3549 Sparrow Dr
Sierra Vista AZ 85635

Call Sign: K4GRU
Robert G Galloway
647 Steppe Pl
Sierra Vista AZ 856354027

Call Sign: W0PAF
Edward J Kalkbrenner Jr
2779 Stonehenge Dr
Sierra Vista AZ 85650

Call Sign: KF7SNF
Stephen A Saway
533 Suffolk Dr
Sierra Vista AZ 85635

Call Sign: KA7GFC
David S Oishi
549 Suffolk Dr
Sierra Vista AZ 85635

Call Sign: N7NWY
Raymond M Miller
717 Suffolk Dr
Sierra Vista AZ 85635

Call Sign: KD7TDL
Paul E Angelo
2455 Sun Crest Dr

Sierra Vista AZ 85650

Call Sign: KF7SHB
Matthew J Stoffolano
2924 Sun Crest Dr
Sierra Vista AZ 85650

Call Sign: KB7ZWZ
Matthew J Stoffolano
2924 Sun Crest Dr
Sierra Vista AZ 85650

Call Sign: KC7WTK
Adam D Bielicki
2140 Sunburst Dr
Sierra Vista AZ 85635

Call Sign: KC7VDH
Ted J Adamczyk
2150 Sunburst Dr
Sierra Vista AZ 85636

Call Sign: N4HUS
Arthur E Frantz
1212 Sunflower Way
Sierra Vista AZ 85635

Call Sign: KB7VYB
Nicholas G Rostas
3201 Swan Dr
Sierra Vista AZ 85635

Call Sign: W7NIC
Nicholas G Rostas
3201 Swan Dr
Sierra Vista AZ 85635

Call Sign: WA0CIF
Donald E Wyatt
3407 Swan Dr
Sierra Vista AZ 85636

Call Sign: N7CAR
Carl E Kelchner
116 Terra Dr
Sierra Vista AZ 85635

Call Sign: KB7NEI
Robert G Moon

1133 Terra Dr
Sierra Vista AZ 85635

Call Sign: N3NAK
Lynn C Heishman
2735 Thornwood Dr
Sierra Vista AZ 856505774

Call Sign: KF7SHA
Joshua D Rummerfield
2773 Thunderbird
Sierra Vista AZ 85650

Call Sign: N7XAQ
Douglas A Griswold
3084 Thunderbird Dr
Sierra Vista AZ 85635

Call Sign: KC7GUK
Karen A Griswold
3084 Thunderbird Dr
Sierra Vista AZ 85635

Call Sign: KB7YPF
Richard A Padgette
3722 Toltec Ct
Sierra Vista AZ 85635

Call Sign: K7CCL
James F Martin
432 Treetop Ave
Sierra Vista AZ 85635

Call Sign: KH6IHA
William S Carnett
3651 Trevino Dr
Sierra Vista AZ 85635

Call Sign: KE7ARY
William S Carnett
3651 Trevino Dr
Sierra Vista AZ 85635

Call Sign: KH6JKL
Jeffrey L Carnett
3651 Trevnio Dr
Sierra Vista AZ 85650

Call Sign: KD7WGX

Wally-Wally ARS
Twilight Dr
Sierra Vista AZ 856353768

Call Sign: WW7OO
Raymond J Yakesh
Twilight Dr
Sierra Vista AZ 856353768

Call Sign: WW7FM
Wally Wally Amateur Radio
Network
Twilight Dr
Sierra Vista AZ 856353768

Call Sign: W7SNS
Raymond J Yakesh
Twilight Dr
Sierra Vista AZ 856353768

Call Sign: KK7JK
Raymond J Yakesh
Twilight Dr
Sierra Vista AZ 856353768

Call Sign: K7PIG
Raymond J Yakesh
Twilight Dr
Sierra Vista AZ 856353768

Call Sign: KK7JK
Raymond J Yakesh
Twilight Dr
Sierra Vista AZ 856353768

Call Sign: KC7GO
John W Reddix
315 Valerie Ln
Sierra Vista AZ 85635

Call Sign: N7SQO
Bob G Blair
4950 Vespucci
Sierra Vista AZ 85635

Call Sign: KE7TXX
Deborah A Griffin
1645 Via Cuerno
Sierra Vista AZ 85635

Call Sign: KE7LJA
James E Griffin
1645 Via Cuerno
Sierra Vista AZ 85635

Call Sign: KD7MAN
Marie B Epperson
485 Via Luna
Sierra Vista AZ 85635

Call Sign: K7MBE
Marie B Epperson
485 Via Luna
Sierra Vista AZ 85635

Call Sign: KK7NO
William O Epperson
485 Via Luna
Sierra Vista AZ 85635

Call Sign: NC7VU
William O Epperson
485 Via Luna
Sierra Vista AZ 85635

Call Sign: N7CVU
William O Epperson
485 Via Luna
Sierra Vista AZ 85635

Call Sign: W7OL
William O Epperson
485 Via Luna
Sierra Vista AZ 85635

Call Sign: W7RJF
Randall Federico
1680 Via Riata
Sierra Vista AZ 85635

Call Sign: KE7TYA
Randall J Federico
1680 Via Riata
Sierra Vista AZ 85635

Call Sign: N7CYK
Frederick L Allard
1623 Via Socorro

Sierra Vista AZ 85635

Call Sign: N7NYG
Bruce R Johnson
1784 Via Socorro
Sierra Vista AZ 85635

Call Sign: KC7FMF
Willard A Turner
4720 Via Viento
Sierra Vista AZ 85635

Call Sign: N7ZGO
Dwight M Arnold
3496 Village Dr
Sierra Vista AZ 85635

Call Sign: W7KRI
Richard J Furlong Jr
1833 Viola Dr
Sierra Vista AZ 856352149

Call Sign: KF7PSQ
Robert C Irwin
1916 Viola Dr
Sierra Vista AZ 85635

Call Sign: AA7NZ
John H Yates
538 W Mallard Cir
Sierra Vista AZ 85635

Call Sign: W7END
Val J Schmitt Jr
3569 Wheelan Loop
Sierra Vista AZ 85635

Call Sign: N7ZGL
Paul D Plumb
4919 Whitewing
Sierra Vista AZ 85635

Call Sign: KC7LCF
Ronnie J Turnpaugh Jr
332 Whitton St
Sierra Vista AZ 85635

Call Sign: KB7IIS
Amy D Edwards

3048 Wilcox Dr
Sierra Vista AZ 85635

Call Sign: KF7SNL
Shari S Rice
1650 Wildflower Dr
Sierra Vista AZ 85635

Call Sign: KC7EEE
Marvin K Otto
3448 Willow Dr
Sierra Vista AZ 85635

Call Sign: KE7YPG
Alexander Berry
3595 Willow Dr
Sierra Vista AZ 85635

Call Sign: WH6CUN
Aaron P Graff
2358 Willowbrook Pl
Sierra Vista AZ 85650

Call Sign: AE7PN
Aaron P Graff
2358 Willowbrook Pl
Sierra Vista AZ 85650

Call Sign: KC7MK
Linda J Skjervem
3654 Windmill Ct
Sierra Vista AZ 85650

Call Sign: K3BRH
Conrad L Welch
2331 Woodland Ct
Sierra Vista AZ 85635

Call Sign: N7OYX
Stephen A Saway
1768 Yaqui St
Sierra Vista AZ 85635

Call Sign: W7TKI
John E Stanis
Sierra Vista AZ 85635

Call Sign: WD0EZO
Warren S Kirkland

Sierra Vista AZ 85635

Call Sign: N7SQK
Alexandra L Blair
Sierra Vista AZ 85636

Call Sign: KC7CAZ
Bruce R Mc Colley
Sierra Vista AZ 85636

Call Sign: KB7NEC
Harold W Garwood
Sierra Vista AZ 85636

Call Sign: N7XAW
James J Billingsley
Sierra Vista AZ 85636

Call Sign: KB7TCO
John F Seckman
Sierra Vista AZ 85636

Call Sign: N7DBY
Robert P Cotner
Sierra Vista AZ 85636

Call Sign: K3BPC
Robert J Heintz
Sierra Vista AZ 856360543

Call Sign: W7ACI
Donald H Morgan
Sierra Vista AZ 85635

Call Sign: W7DYP
Peter H Glisch
Sierra Vista AZ 85635

Call Sign: K7RDG
Cochise Amateur Radio Assn
Inc
Sierra Vista AZ 85635

Call Sign: N9DXC
Barry A Rietz
Sierra Vista AZ 85636

Call Sign: KE7AQ
Harold L Burch

Sierra Vista AZ 85636

Call Sign: W7SSU
Melvin A Naegle
Sierra Vista AZ 85636

Call Sign: KC7EAG
Brenda F Lewis
Sierra Vista AZ 85636

Call Sign: KE7TXV
George A Melnick
Sierra Vista AZ 85636

Call Sign: WB8CII
James M Huffman
Sierra Vista AZ 85636

Call Sign: AB7PD
James T Hinkle
Sierra Vista AZ 85636

Call Sign: W7BHZ
Janice L Fuller
Sierra Vista AZ 85636

Call Sign: KF7SHD
John B Clayton
Sierra Vista AZ 85636

Call Sign: KF7ITD
Jonathan V Fero
Sierra Vista AZ 85636

Call Sign: N7RCC
Jonathan V Fero
Sierra Vista AZ 85636

Call Sign: KE7GUI
Joseph C Wetherington
Sierra Vista AZ 85636

Call Sign: N7BNA
Kenneth A Norgren
Sierra Vista AZ 85636

Call Sign: KF7IYQ
Kenneth P Allen
Sierra Vista AZ 85636

Call Sign: KC7EAM
Lyle L Ross
Sierra Vista AZ 85636

Call Sign: KF7SHC
Melissa Clayton
Sierra Vista AZ 85636

Call Sign: KD7ELZ
Pauline A Cameron
Sierra Vista AZ 85636

Call Sign: KA9RSB
Robert K Rietz
Sierra Vista AZ 85636

Call Sign: W3IEZ
Robert L Flesch
Sierra Vista AZ 85636

Call Sign: KD4SIM
Wanda L Flesch
Sierra Vista AZ 85636

Call Sign: AB4LE
Wendell L Carter
Sierra Vista AZ 85636

Call Sign: KF6SPO
William I Bennett
Sierra Vista AZ 85636

Call Sign: KB7JGV
Marlene E Young
Sierra Vista AZ 85636

Call Sign: KD7PZV
Annie Webster
Sierra Vista AZ 856360142

Call Sign: KD7GXS
Lawrence S Chase
Sierra Vista AZ 856361107

Call Sign: KD7RHH
Betty L Simon
Sierra Vista AZ 856362692

**FCC Amateur Radio
Licenses in Snowflake**

Call Sign: N7IOC
Earl E Schneider
Box 5715
Snowflake AZ 85937

Call Sign: KF7SAD
Donald L Alexander
4946 Buckskin Trl
Snowflake AZ 85937

Call Sign: KF7SAC
Joyce A Alexander
4946 Buckskin Trl
Snowflake AZ 85937

Call Sign: KF7ANQ
Tom W Humes Sr
420 Center St
Snowflake AZ 85937

Call Sign: KB5YBO
Peter E Ellis
5142 Churchill Rd
Snowflake AZ 85937

Call Sign: KC7LVB
Ronald K Stowe
331 Concho Hwy
Snowflake AZ 85937

Call Sign: K7FQ
Jack L Otterson
10 CR N9228
Snowflake AZ 85937

Call Sign: W7UKK
Harvey G Wilhelm
67 E 1st S
Snowflake AZ 85937

Call Sign: KF7DGV
Nikolaus J Smeh
101 E 4th N
Snowflake AZ 85937

Call Sign: WA7NHQ

Mary A Gonsalves
106 E Ballard
Snowflake AZ 85937

Call Sign: WA7ICC
Robert W Gonsalves
106 E Ballard Box 73
Snowflake AZ 85937

Call Sign: KJ7UD
Alfred A Garcia
895 Greer Ave
Snowflake AZ 85937

Call Sign: K7VBH
Carl F Rieck
3879 Hidden Ranch Rd
Snowflake AZ 85937

Call Sign: N7YJJ
Philip A Caster
4959 Horseshoe Rd
Snowflake AZ 85937

Call Sign: W6NJO
Philip A Caster
4959 Horseshoe Rd
Snowflake AZ 85937

Call Sign: KF7HTK
Ursula C Summers
9532 Miller Trl
Snowflake AZ 85937

Call Sign: N6WGF
Ursula C Summers
9532 Miller Trl
Snowflake AZ 85937

Call Sign: KF7DBT
Gerald Smeh
301 N 1st E
Snowflake AZ 85937

Call Sign: AG7U
Alfred A Garcia
1962 N Mountain Highlands
Blvd
Snowflake AZ 85937

Call Sign: KC5HED
Don E Purcell
2525 N View Rd
Snowflake AZ 85937

Call Sign: AD1N
Ted C Vawter
8498 Navajo Ln
Snowflake AZ 859372136

Call Sign: KD7HHY
Christine D Sheaffer
3840 Petersen Rd
Snowflake AZ 85937

Call Sign: N7CMT
Wallace E Sheaffer III
3840 Petersen Rd
Snowflake AZ 85937

Call Sign: AE7H
Marvin D Taylor
696 Pkwy Dr
Snowflake AZ 85937

Call Sign: KD7PZY
Amos W Bairn
1160 S Highland Dr
Snowflake AZ 85937

Call Sign: KD7PZZ
Boyd O Bairn
1160 S Highland Dr
Snowflake AZ 85937

Call Sign: KA7BUN
Francis B Champlin
131 S Stinson
Snowflake AZ 85937

Call Sign: KD7KEK
Eleanor D Gardei
2535 Short Cir Dr
Snowflake AZ 85937

Call Sign: KB7YVL
Mark A Poole
8775 Stray Burro Trl

Snowflake AZ 85937

Call Sign: KD7URA
Michael D Marr
8182 Uttrecht Rd
Snowflake AZ 85937

Call Sign: KE7BTL
Quince C Amos
45 W 3rd N Box A
Snowflake AZ 85937

Call Sign: KD7YHT
Cole B Packard
412 W 8th S
Snowflake AZ 85937

Call Sign: KD7LEK
James A Mortensen
3119 W Bryant
Snowflake AZ 85937

Call Sign: W7AZY
James A Mortensen
3119 W Bryant
Snowflake AZ 85937

Call Sign: KD7LEJ
Marie E Mortensen
3119 W Bryant
Snowflake AZ 85937

Call Sign: W2AZY
Marie E Mortensen
3119 W Bryant
Snowflake AZ 85937

Call Sign: WA7LZF
Francis W Ericksen
129 W Center
Snowflake AZ 85937

Call Sign: KD7TG
James A Bailey
728 W Reidhead Ave
Snowflake AZ 85937

Call Sign: W7QWI
Alan J Gardiner

Snowflake AZ 85937

Call Sign: KB7TQG
Betsey L Clemens
Snowflake AZ 85937

Call Sign: KB7RRG
Caysie L Gardei
Snowflake AZ 85937

Call Sign: KB7OLS
Harry J Gunther
Snowflake AZ 85937

Call Sign: W7DLZ
James B Hagelstein
Snowflake AZ 85937

Call Sign: KB7GAE
Jo An R Washburn
Snowflake AZ 85937

Call Sign: KB7GAD
Jonathan R Washburn
Snowflake AZ 85937

Call Sign: KB7VMG
Michael S Lackey
Snowflake AZ 85937

Call Sign: WA7CGH
Kenneth A Webb
Snowflake AZ 85937

Call Sign: WD6BUJ
Carl E Kelchner
Snowflake AZ 85937

Call Sign: KD1MT
Chester M Humphrey
Snowflake AZ 85937

Call Sign: KG6MYI
Clint T Rounsavall
Snowflake AZ 85937

Call Sign: KE7JLP
Clint T Rounsavall
Snowflake AZ 85937

Call Sign: KE7YSP
Dana Myatt
Snowflake AZ 85937

Call Sign: KB7UEZ
Delores A Caster
Snowflake AZ 85937

Call Sign: KC7IFV
Dianne M Kienlen
Snowflake AZ 85937

Call Sign: KD7SOC
Elma L Walker
Snowflake AZ 85937

Call Sign: N7KZH
George F Gardei
Snowflake AZ 85937

Call Sign: KC7YAZ
Gerald A Delsasso
Snowflake AZ 85937

Call Sign: WU3P
Gordon G Griffo
Snowflake AZ 85937

Call Sign: KE7BMB
Jessica L Bloomer
Snowflake AZ 85937

Call Sign: KD7FZF
John C Walker
Snowflake AZ 85937

Call Sign: KF7KVV
June M Apedaile
Snowflake AZ 85937

Call Sign: KF7KVT
Karen L Stokes
Snowflake AZ 85937

Call Sign: KD7SUP
Kenneth B Willis
Snowflake AZ 85937

Call Sign: KD7NMK
Margaret A Herring
Snowflake AZ 85937

Call Sign: KE7YSQ
Mark Ziemann
Snowflake AZ 85937

Call Sign: KE7TD
Paul W Prenovost
Snowflake AZ 85937

Call Sign: KC7LUZ
Randolph W Turner
Snowflake AZ 85937

Call Sign: KG4FIY
Randy E Housel
Snowflake AZ 85937

Call Sign: KF7LXE
Richard P Vroome
Snowflake AZ 85937

Call Sign: KE7AZT
Scott A Hveem
Snowflake AZ 85937

Call Sign: KD7GFC
Timothy J Watson
Snowflake AZ 85937

Call Sign: N6OAH
W Brent Bogdanski
Snowflake AZ 85937

Call Sign: KF4DNU
Alan J Burger
Snowflake AZ 85937

Call Sign: N7MQP
Marque L French
Snowflake AZ 859370280

Call Sign: W7ARE
Marque L French
Snowflake AZ 859370280

Call Sign: KD7FSH

Harry S Price IV
Snowflake AZ 859371013

Call Sign: N7ABS
John C Walker
Snowflake AZ 859371227

Call Sign: KD7CKH
Nicholas L Gardei
Snowflake AZ 859371888

Call Sign: KD7ONQ
Galen L Hicks
Snowflake AZ 859371974

Call Sign: KE7IDB
George G Hatch
Snowflake AZ 859372406

FCC Amateur Radio Licenses in Solomon

Call Sign: K7EAR
Eastern Arizona Amateur
Radio Society Inc
Solomon AZ 85551

FCC Amateur Radio Licenses in Sonoita

Call Sign: K7OCM
Eugene L Stringer
40 Apache Trl
Sonoita AZ 85637

Call Sign: KC7NPT
Henry J Leblanc
66 Apache Trl
Sonoita AZ 85637

Call Sign: KE7COY
Charles G Hammond
Box 10008
Sonoita AZ 85637

Call Sign: W7AG
John S Bodey
99 Mustang Trl
Sonoita AZ 856371249

Call Sign: WA6QMQ
Albert A Leonardini Jr
34 Palomino Trl
Sonoita AZ 856370053

Call Sign: KB7WFH
Victoria L Murray
28240 S Sonoita Hwy
Sonoita AZ 85637

Call Sign: KF6TXD
Arnold J Adriaanse
200 Santa Rita Ct
Sonoita AZ 85637

Call Sign: W7OTJ
Charles G Hammond
13400 Singing Valley N
Sonoita AZ 85637

Call Sign: KC7ACZ
Daniel L Enos
Sonoita AZ 85637

Call Sign: KC7AVH
Joe M Silk
Sonoita AZ 85637

Call Sign: KB7OHY
Kathleen M Ervin
Sonoita AZ 85637

Call Sign: WA7JBQ
Keith W Casiraghi
Sonoita AZ 85637

Call Sign: W7JPI
Leo P Swatloski
Sonoita AZ 85637

Call Sign: N7XFN
Sr Beverly G Aitken
Sonoita AZ 85637

Call Sign: KC7ESG
Brad A Haber
Sonoita AZ 85637

Call Sign: KF7PDW
David A Lordi
Sonoita AZ 85637

Call Sign: KC7ESC
Debra R Haber
Sonoita AZ 85637

Call Sign: KC7WWL
Drexel D Jones
Sonoita AZ 85637

Call Sign: KK7VF
Edward C Fleder
Sonoita AZ 85637

Call Sign: KC7VQK
Erik J Powell
Sonoita AZ 85637

Call Sign: AE7KZ
Jake Wolfe
Sonoita AZ 85637

Call Sign: KA7CEB
James A Rath
Sonoita AZ 85637

Call Sign: KD6TPC
Karen L Manger
Sonoita AZ 85637

Call Sign: KC7ZKR
Kathleen K Jones
Sonoita AZ 85637

Call Sign: N7MCL
Kenneth L Van Kirk
Sonoita AZ 85637

Call Sign: KC7FFL
Lesia C George
Sonoita AZ 85637

Call Sign: KN6US
Michael C Manger
Sonoita AZ 85637

Call Sign: KF7IYP

Michael J Frede
Sonoita AZ 85637

Call Sign: KC7NYA
Michael R Stefanowicz
Sonoita AZ 85637

Call Sign: KE7AZR
Raymond V Russell
Sonoita AZ 85637

Call Sign: KB7ITT
Ruth A Vankirk
Sonoita AZ 85637

Call Sign: KC7VQM
Teresa L Elkins
Sonoita AZ 85637

Call Sign: N7QPC
Thomas H Hardin III
Sonoita AZ 85637

Call Sign: W7KTH
Thomas H Hardin III
Sonoita AZ 85637

Call Sign: KD7RPO
Julie S Firos
Sonoita AZ 856370128

Call Sign: K7JSF
Julie S Firos
Sonoita AZ 856370128

Call Sign: N7PF
Peter M Firos
Sonoita AZ 856370128

Call Sign: KD4KOC
Steven A Johnson
Sonoita AZ 856370281

Call Sign: KB4DXV
James W M Carson
Sonoita AZ 856370311

Call Sign: N7LDI
Richard A Ide

Sonoita AZ 856370566

Call Sign: N7AEY
Jessie L Cude
Sonoita AZ 856371221

FCC Amateur Radio Licenses in Springerville

Call Sign: KA7SCI
Robert H Hersey
Box 1460
Springerville AZ 85938

Call Sign: KE7FRN
Romel S Mac Leod
464 S El Cajon Cir
Springerville AZ 85938

Call Sign: K7FRN
Romel S Mac Leod
464 S El Cajon Cir
Springerville AZ 85938

Call Sign: KD7SIE
Daryl T Madrid
519 S Voight St
Springerville AZ 85938

Call Sign: KC7OZW
Mickey Hamilton Jr
231 S Voigt St
Springerville AZ 85938

Call Sign: N7VLI
Douglas A Henderson
15 S Williams Dr
Springerville AZ 85938

Call Sign: KB7WDG
Calvin E Smith II
Springerville AZ 85938

Call Sign: KD7PPS
Shawn S Dishman
Springerville AZ 85541

Call Sign: KE7BQK
Carlos G Quihuis Jr

Springerville AZ 85938

Call Sign: KF6EJK
Christina J Ivanoff
Springerville AZ 85938

Call Sign: KE7BQI
Jonathan M Hill
Springerville AZ 85938

Call Sign: KE7CLP
Savannah Mullins
Springerville AZ 85938

Call Sign: KE7CLQ
Steven Palmateer
Springerville AZ 85938

Call Sign: KE7EDN
Robert A Mackenzie
Springerville AZ 859380712

FCC Amateur Radio Licenses in Stanfield

Call Sign: KC7QPG
W Jeff Fleming
7773 S Skylark Trl
Stanfield AZ 85272

Call Sign: K7AE
Victor E Johnson
Stanfield AZ 85272

Call Sign: KC7HDW
Pamela L Johnson
Stanfield AZ 85272

Call Sign: K7ON
Brian K Short
Stanfield AZ 85272

Call Sign: KI7QR
Russell A Stillman
Stanfield AZ 85272

FCC Amateur Radio Licenses in Star Valley

Call Sign: N9LNF
Mark P Kirch
Box 16 236
Star Valley AZ 85541

Call Sign: N7FND
Gilbert O Woods
Star Vale Mhp Sp 40
Star Valley AZ 85547

FCC Amateur Radio Licenses in Strawberry

Call Sign: KD7BWK
John E Fischback
Box 1129
Strawberry AZ 85544

Call Sign: KE7OOS
Eddy A Floyd
Box 1226
Strawberry AZ 85544

Call Sign: W7EDF
Eddy A Floyd
Box 1226
Strawberry AZ 85544

Call Sign: KC7ECH
James B West
Box 1347
Strawberry AZ 85544

Call Sign: KC7NOJ
William H Daily
Box 1396
Strawberry AZ 85544

Call Sign: KD7EYE
Nazman R Schmitt
Box 1528
Strawberry AZ 85544

Call Sign: KC7HAH
Rudy Richard
Box 661
Strawberry AZ 85544

Call Sign: KC6OPC

Bob R Darland
Box 677
Strawberry AZ 85544

Call Sign: KC7MMX
Curtis G Standage
Box 912
Strawberry AZ 85544

Call Sign: KD7JSV
William B Elfeldt
Strawberry AZ 85544

FCC Amateur Radio Licenses in Sun Valley

Call Sign: KB7VVX
Elizabeth R Nicholson
Sun Valley AZ 86029

Call Sign: KC7EBS
Danny C Robbins
Sun Valley AZ 860294013

FCC Amateur Radio Licenses in Sunsites

Call Sign: WB7ODB
Theodore R Scott
Sunsites AZ 85625

FCC Amateur Radio Licenses in Superior

Call Sign: WA7JYR
Clarence J Cook
576 Gibbs
Superior AZ 85273

Call Sign: N7MHO
Karl L Deffenbaugh
154 Lime St
Superior AZ 852735031

Call Sign: W7ABS
Edward L Watson
296 Magma Ave
Superior AZ 85273

Call Sign: NU7R
Curtis A Rossow
240 N Kellner Ave
Superior AZ 85273

FCC Amateur Radio Licenses in Taylor

Call Sign: KA7EEJ
Brian A Carpenter
223 E Willow Ln
Taylor AZ 85939

Call Sign: KJ7AG
Mark D Davis
817 Glenrosa Blvd
Taylor AZ 85939

Call Sign: KC7FBT
Roberta R Lake
202 N 600 W Box 566
Taylor AZ 85939

Call Sign: KD7DWZ
James D Lara Jr
1200 Plum Ct
Taylor AZ 85939

Call Sign: W7LTW
Robert D Bertelle
104 Power Ln
Taylor AZ 859390131

Call Sign: KD6MUZ
Dennis A Preston
Taylor AZ 85939

Call Sign: W7MIO
Ermon G Lewis
Taylor AZ 85939

Call Sign: KE7CBU
Julianna M Kartchner
Taylor AZ 85938

Call Sign: AB7ID
Kenneth R Lake
Taylor AZ 85939

Call Sign: KB7GAG
John B Lea
Taylor AZ 85939

Call Sign: KB7ZII
Clint G Burden
Taylor AZ 85939

Call Sign: N7FUT
David P Desch
Taylor AZ 85939

Call Sign: KF7EOU
Joshua T Lara
Taylor AZ 85939

Call Sign: KF7RQV
Marcus Scott Mckinnis
Taylor AZ 85939

Call Sign: KF7RQW
Scott L Mckinnis
Taylor AZ 85939

Call Sign: KF7HIB
Tamra P Toner
Taylor AZ 85939

Call Sign: KC7JVH
Vicki S Davis
Taylor AZ 85939

Call Sign: W7PLX
Clyde W Rogers
Taylor AZ 859390206

Call Sign: W7LVE
James W Bruce
Taylor AZ 859390422

Call Sign: KD7ETN
Kelly Lara
Taylor AZ 859390902

Call Sign: W7ARZ
William R Smith
Taylor AZ 859391309

Call Sign: KB7YCY
Richard J Nininger
Teec Nos Pos AZ 86514

**FCC Amateur Radio
Licenses in Thatcher**

Call Sign: KA7BAR
Eugene V Cope
223 Church St
Thatcher AZ 85552

Call Sign: N7HRN
Lawrence E Harbison
3381 Mesa Flat Dr
Thatcher AZ 85552

Call Sign: KB7YIC
Willard E Harbison
3381 Mesa Flat Dr
Thatcher AZ 85552

Call Sign: N7ERP
Carl D Simmons
446 N Stadium Ave
Thatcher AZ 85552

Call Sign: KD7EZH
Curtis O Rossiter
3915 Pace
Thatcher AZ 85552

Call Sign: K7COR
Curtis O Rossiter
3915 Pace
Thatcher AZ 85552

Call Sign: KC7FQQ
Carol A Elders
1180 S 1st Ave
Thatcher AZ 85552

Call Sign: KC7DLM
Edward D Elders
1180 S 1st Ave
Thatcher AZ 85552

Call Sign: KC7OCA
Paul L Cole
3484 S Robinson Ave
Thatcher AZ 85552

Call Sign: KA7BJI
Riley E Warner
3894 W Allred St
Thatcher AZ 85552

Call Sign: KE7SYD
Elizabeth P James
3941 W Angle Dr
Thatcher AZ 85552

Call Sign: W7OPS
Elizabeth P James
3941 W Angle Dr
Thatcher AZ 85552

Call Sign: AA7NW
Elizabeth A James
3941 W Angle Dr
Thatcher AZ 85552

Call Sign: KD7GNA
Steven G Eaton
3941 W Angle Dr
Thatcher AZ 85552

Call Sign: KC7DLK
Donald H Carlin
3934 W Brinkerhoff St
Thatcher AZ 855525122

Call Sign: N7EBR
Charles M Morris
3205 W Church St
Thatcher AZ 85552

Call Sign: K7JWD
John W Dean Jr
4066 W Frye Creek Rd
Thatcher AZ 85552

Call Sign: NI5L
John W Dean Jr
4066 W Frye Creek Rd

Thatcher AZ 85552

Call Sign: KD7LSE
John W Dean Jr
4094 W Frye Creek Rd
Thatcher AZ 85552

Call Sign: N7HRQ
Cyril H Teague
3796 W Kimball St
Thatcher AZ 85552

Call Sign: KC7VOS
Steven J Black
3338 W Mullins Ln
Thatcher AZ 85552

Call Sign: AB6JY
Arnold A Williams
3833 W Valley View Rd
Thatcher AZ 855525141

Call Sign: KB7UKM
Lauralea H Bott
Thatcher AZ 85552

Call Sign: KC7ACW
Robert R Priest
Thatcher AZ 85552

Call Sign: KC7VOO
Dennis J Martin
Thatcher AZ 85552

Call Sign: KB7DZZ
Scott D Overall
Thatcher AZ 85552

Call Sign: KC7DLL
Scott W Howell
Thatcher AZ 85552

Call Sign: KC7FQM
Robert W Pascoe
Thatcher AZ 855520813

Call Sign: KD7EZF
Matthew O Jordahl
Thatcher AZ 855520906

Call Sign: KB7ZWF
James D Clark
14th St
Tombstone AZ 85638

Call Sign: NU7V
Christopher R Townsend
160 Avenida Hermosa
Tombstone AZ 85638

Call Sign: KB7NK
Rodger B Hallen
2431 Buckskin Frank Rd
Tombstone AZ 85638

Call Sign: AB7KB
Jack W Wright
132 Calle Escondida
Tombstone AZ 85638

Call Sign: N9BKJ
Robert W Krueger
565 Cortez Dr
Tombstone AZ 85638

Call Sign: N7BOO
Robert W Krueger
565 Cortez Dr
Tombstone AZ 85638

Call Sign: KE7TXY
George M Fauber
2477 E El Trigo Ln
Tombstone AZ 85638

Call Sign: AA7GE
B Bruce Bluemel
193 Front St
Tombstone AZ 85638

Call Sign: N6QAT
Dorothy M Rogers
Hc 1 3707
Tombstone AZ 85638

Call Sign: KB7QLH
Richard L Homer
1576 N Orante Rd
Tombstone AZ 856386120

Call Sign: KC7BHX
Nancy J Clark
118 S 14th St
Tombstone AZ 85638

Call Sign: KD7KV
Clarence R Cazee
468 Saddleback Rd
Tombstone AZ 856389793

Call Sign: KE7EUP
Sidney H Reed Jr
495 Saddleback Rd
Tombstone AZ 85638

Call Sign: KC7PUF
Del F Roach Sr
322 W Allen St
Tombstone AZ 85638

Call Sign: KA6WOB
George L Turner Jr
Tombstone AZ 85638

Call Sign: N7WIS
Billy G Honea
Tombstone AZ 85638

Call Sign: WD4CLQ
Carmen K C Mercer
Tombstone AZ 85638

Call Sign: KC7NHX
Darren W Jessop
Tombstone AZ 85638

Call Sign: KC7WPL
Evard L Mc Donald
Tombstone AZ 85638

Call Sign: KE7OLP
George E Barnes
Tombstone AZ 85638

Call Sign: AD7SU
George E Barnes
Tombstone AZ 85638

Call Sign: WA7KYZ
Gerald D Ford
Tombstone AZ 85638

Call Sign: N4DMS
James M Browning
Tombstone AZ 85638

Call Sign: KE7ASX
Judith K Miller
Tombstone AZ 85638

Call Sign: K7ASK
Judith K Miller
Tombstone AZ 85638

Call Sign: W7RJS
Robert J Schwartz
Tombstone AZ 85638

Call Sign: W7TN
Robert J Schwartz
Tombstone AZ 85638

Call Sign: KC7GUI
Sally A Milliken
Tombstone AZ 85638

Call Sign: KE7ACJ
Jeffrey P Miller
Tombstone AZ 85639

Call Sign: K7JZK
Jeffrey P Miller
Tombstone AZ 85639

Call Sign: K2PDC
William F Kelly
Tombstone AZ 856380208

Call Sign: K7OVR
Raymond J Mitchell Jr
Tombstone AZ 856380992

FCC Amateur Radio Licenses in Tonalea

Call Sign: KC7ZUT
Bobby Bizardi
Tonalea AZ 86044

Call Sign: KF7TQV
Dennis O Whiterock
Tonalea AZ 86044

FCC Amateur Radio Licenses in Tonto Basin

Call Sign: AD7VS
Judith L Frank
282 Burtons Ln
Tonto Basin AZ 855530564

Call Sign: KA7KSV
Sharon A Burmeister
261 Javalina Pl
Tonto Basin AZ 85553

Call Sign: KD7ZBD
Harold J Kintner
Lot 9
Tonto Basin AZ 85553

Call Sign: N7VAC
Bert G Cheney III
Tonto Basin AZ 85553

Call Sign: KB7UJX
Larry R Tallerday
Tonto Basin AZ 85553

Call Sign: KF7MVW
Dan W Cheek
Tonto Basin AZ 85553

Call Sign: KB7CSN
James B Compton
Tonto Basin AZ 85553

Call Sign: KC7FVL
Mark L Benshoof
Tonto Basin AZ 85553

Call Sign: N1ZG
Richard J Frank
Tonto Basin AZ 85553

Call Sign: KC7OIL
Rosemary Goff
Tonto Basin AZ 85553

Call Sign: KF7LMV
Thor E Nudson
Tonto Basin AZ 85553

FCC Amateur Radio Licenses in Tsaile

Call Sign: KC7VMM
Joseph W Sullivan
Tsaile AZ 86556

Call Sign: KE5ABO
Mark A Richards
Tsaile AZ 86556

FCC Amateur Radio Licenses in Tuba City

Call Sign: KB7FUM
Barbara A Nagy
Tuba City AZ 86045

Call Sign: KD7KRA
Dennis W Goldtooth
Tuba City AZ 86045

Call Sign: KE7KUB
Rita B Francisco
Tuba City AZ 86045

Call Sign: KC7YWC
William H Orman
Tuba City AZ 860450989

Call Sign: KD7CKQ
Bryan D Goldtooth
Tuba City AZ 860453188

Call Sign: N7BDG
Bryan D Goldtooth
Tuba City AZ 860453188

Call Sign: KE7KHL
Charles W Paarlberg
Tuba City AZ 860453241

Call Sign: KE7KHK
Jon W Paarlberg
Tuba City AZ 860453241

FCC Amateur Radio Licenses in Tubac

Call Sign: W0DGY
Dale A Devick
Cerro Peron Ln
Tubac AZ 85646

Call Sign: KC0RBA
James E Knight
132 Circulo Vespucci
Tubac AZ 85646

Call Sign: KG7OT
Hal H Empie
242 Tubac Rd
Tubac AZ 85646

Call Sign: KE7IR
Patti L Donahue
Tubac AZ 85646

Call Sign: N0QCT
Gracie A Jex
Tubac AZ 85646

Call Sign: KC7QVZ
Kenneth H Cox
Tubac AZ 85646

Call Sign: W7ODP
Louis H Frische
Tubac AZ 85646

Call Sign: KC7QVX
Martha T Cox
Tubac AZ 85646

Call Sign: KC7QVY
Michael A Cox

Tubac AZ 85646

Call Sign: KA7WNS
Ralph L Hare
Tubac AZ 85646

Call Sign: N0NMN
William D Jex
Tubac AZ 85646

Call Sign: W8GQW
Wray E Dudley
Tubac AZ 85646

Call Sign: N7NWX
Karl Miller
Tubac AZ 856461493

Call Sign: KE7GPI
Andrew R Roy
Tubac AZ 856464742

FCC Amateur Radio Licenses in Tucson

Call Sign: KB7HSL
Walter B Goedecke
1414 Allen Rd
Tucson AZ 85719

Call Sign: KD7HVK
Anthony E Fogle
1709 Ave Del Sol
Tucson AZ 85710

Call Sign: W7LFX
Ellis R Romer
119 Avenida Carolina
Tucson AZ 85711

Call Sign: WM7M
Art H Ripsky
1602 Avenida De
Maximillian
Tucson AZ 85704

Call Sign: WT7I
Gerald W Brandsma
35 Avenida Dela Madero

Tucson AZ 85710

Call Sign: N7SQQ
John A Clor
1934 Avenida Planeta
Tucson AZ 85710

Call Sign: KF7EAO
James E Sherman
1503 Avenida Sirio
Tucson AZ 85710

Call Sign: W7OPY
Abele E Polluconi
1717 Avenida Sirio
Tucson AZ 85710

Call Sign: KD4UXG
Gerald E Buckmaster Jr
2803 Bennet Ct
Tucson AZ 85708

Call Sign: KC7QYA
Roy T Dennis
3844 Blacklidge Dr
Tucson AZ 857161270

Call Sign: K7NOF
Billy A Bloomhuff
6661 Blue Blvd
Tucson AZ 85743

Call Sign: K7NOR
Roberta M Bloomhuff
6661 Blue Blvd
Tucson AZ 85743

Call Sign: KB0QLO
Robert W Lenz
5825 Bonney Rd
Tucson AZ 85706

Call Sign: KF7ODK
Joe Bidwell
Box 1043
Tucson AZ 85739

Call Sign: KA7FRY
Harry G Anderson

Box 1597D
Tucson AZ 85736

Call Sign: KD7CXJ
Bernard H Trombetta
Box 1597M
Tucson AZ 85736

Call Sign: AB7WG
Antonio G Basurto
Box 432
Tucson AZ 85735

Call Sign: KA7IVB
Vernon E Dupee
Box 452
Tucson AZ 857359749

Call Sign: KD7RS
Ivo W Toneck
Box 645
Tucson AZ 85706

Call Sign: K6BXT
Martel Firing
Box 756
Tucson AZ 85735

Call Sign: KF7FIX
Cathy L Owen
Box 782
Tucson AZ 85735

Call Sign: KD7CNK
Thomas V Peper
Box 803
Tucson AZ 85735

Call Sign: KD7AGQ
Bert G Mellish
Box 97 D
Tucson AZ 85736

Call Sign: KC7VVE
Jimmie F Anderson
Box 97 D
Tucson AZ 85736

Call Sign: KC7ZKQ

Geraldine R Anderson
Box 97D
Tucson AZ 85736

Call Sign: K7YKD
George W Falter
Box 984
Tucson AZ 857399801

Call Sign: KE7QII
Aaron L Herring
5711 Cactus Garden Dr
Tucson AZ 85742

Call Sign: N7SQG
Doris M Craig
6618 Calle Alegria C
Tucson AZ 85715

Call Sign: WA7JGW
Leland R Baker
7351 Calle Cabo
Tucson AZ 857502612

Call Sign: K7JWK
Gerald A Walinski
6562 Calle Castor
Tucson AZ 85710

Call Sign: K7JTJ
Charles J Soulliard
6391 Calle Cavillo
Tucson AZ 85750

Call Sign: W7JEA
James B Rowe
7058 Calle Centuri
Tucson AZ 85710

Call Sign: WA7NIX
Bryan Cowan
330 Calle De Madrid
Tucson AZ 857114135

Call Sign: N7FID
Richard E Donohue
2440 Calle De Maurer
Tucson AZ 85749

Call Sign: KC7DPP
Richard D Revis
6362 Calle De Mirar
Tucson AZ 85715

Call Sign: KB9WKD
Renelle L Schaffer
6631 Calle De San Alberto
Tucson AZ 85710

Call Sign: KC7FNI
Elizabeth Matty
2752 Calle Del Huerto
Tucson AZ 85741

Call Sign: KG7Z
Elizabeth Matty
2752 Calle Del Huerto
Tucson AZ 85741

Call Sign: K7RJJ
Richard J Jank
6942 Calle Denebola
Tucson AZ 85710

Call Sign: KC6NDV
Shawn B Wymer
6710 Calle Dened
Tucson AZ 85710

Call Sign: KC7LIO
Louis G Moran
450 Calle Garcia
Tucson AZ 85706

Call Sign: N7ZZE
Warren L Eyer
3733 Calle Guaymas
Tucson AZ 85716

Call Sign: WA7PAC
Johnnie E January
6926 Calle Marte
Tucson AZ 85710

Call Sign: W7AIY
Sam A Westmoreland
6568 Calle Mercurio
Tucson AZ 85710

Call Sign: KA7IQJ
Alta J Nicolai
2300 Calle Mesa Del Oso
Tucson AZ 85748

Call Sign: KC7S
Henry T Nicolai
2300 Calle Mesa Del Oso
Tucson AZ 85748

Call Sign: N7NVL
Michael G Pohanic
910 Calle Milu
Tucson AZ 85706

Call Sign: WB7NEX
Kenneth E Fredstrom
9059 Calle Norlo
Tucson AZ 857107345

Call Sign: KC7GLM
William H Brown
65 Calle Primorosa
Tucson AZ 857164934

Call Sign: WB0LFT
Gregory M Becker
9811 Calle Solano
Tucson AZ 85737

Call Sign: KB7QAH
Charles L Trepanier
4840 Calle Tobosa
Tucson AZ 85749

Call Sign: KD7THA
Arnold L Robles
2601 Calle Tonala
Tucson AZ 85745

Call Sign: WB7WBN
Leo L Prescott Jr
10401 Calle Trece
Tucson AZ 857486805

Call Sign: W7JQM
Reginald G Armstrong
314 Cambridge Dr

Tucson AZ 85704

Call Sign: N0DCT
Robert R Hause
7285 Caminito Feliz
Tucson AZ 85710

Call Sign: K6PPT
Paul P Tretiakoff
3821 Camino Blanco
Tucson AZ 85718

Call Sign: W7GJF
John L Bowden
7341 Camino De Cima
Tucson AZ 85715

Call Sign: KC7KFL
Norma E Bowden
7341 Camino De Cima
Tucson AZ 85715

Call Sign: KC7ZOA
Barbara R Wood
7351 Camino De Cima
Tucson AZ 857502212

Call Sign: KC7ZOB
Billie D Wood
7351 Camino De Cima
Tucson AZ 857502212

Call Sign: KK7NV
Nobuo Okazaki
850 Camino De Fray Marcos
Tucson AZ 85718

Call Sign: KC7KJV
Charlotte M Keating
5256 Camino De La Cumbre
Tucson AZ 85750

Call Sign: WA7JHA
Kenneth L Keating
5256 Camino De La Cumbre
Tucson AZ 85750

Call Sign: W7ISJ
Blase J Furfaro

10332 Camino De La Placita
Tucson AZ 85748

Call Sign: WL7SE
Ronald E Broden
4325 Camino De Oeste
Tucson AZ 85746

Call Sign: K7BCW
Charles H Ware
4217 Camino De Palmas
Tucson AZ 85711

Call Sign: KC7BER
Andrew M Hudor Jr
3566 Camino De Vista
Tucson AZ 85745

Call Sign: W1HIR
John A Wick
5749 Camino Del Celador
Tucson AZ 85750

Call Sign: WB7QJL
Alex H Woods
5805 Camino Escalante
Tucson AZ 85718

Call Sign: N6LBN
David A Wilcox
4710 Camino Feliz
Tucson AZ 85705

Call Sign: KB5AD
Larry E Gillihan
2711 Camino Llano
Tucson AZ 85742

Call Sign: WB7OHF
Raymond C Baldwin
6980 Camino Namara
Tucson AZ 85715

Call Sign: KB7CRT
Vourneen M Baldwin
6980 Camino Namara
Tucson AZ 85750

Call Sign: KB5YR

Milo R Hardenbrook
1610 Cathay Pl
Tucson AZ 85748

Call Sign: KA7J
Theodore Gersten
5870 Cerrada Circa
Tucson AZ 85741

Call Sign: N7OVU
Earl H Atkinson
4418 Cerrada Del Charro
Tucson AZ 85718

Call Sign: KD7CXI
Gerald A Tumarkin
6738 Chapultepec Cr
Tucson AZ 85750

Call Sign: KC7JVD
Anne B Watson
2600 Clay Alley
Tucson AZ 85716

Call Sign: KF7MQ
Benjamin L W Dong
4636 Coachlight Ln
Tucson AZ 85718

Call Sign: N7LJV
Brian B Dong
4636 Coachlight Ln
Tucson AZ 85718

Call Sign: N7LHS
Mary H Q Dong
4636 Coachlight Ln
Tucson AZ 85718

Call Sign: W7PSW
Paul S Warren
7390 Cobblestone Rd
Tucson AZ 85718

Call Sign: KC7RCT
Connie Doerty
8427 Coral Ridge Loop
Tucson AZ 85704

Call Sign: KB7AYJ
Stanley W Trachta
13077 Corsair Dr
Tucson AZ 85704

Call Sign: N0EYV
Edwin R Wesley
2424 Cottonwood Ln
Tucson AZ 85713

Call Sign: KL7KN
Lester L Robinson
10169 Coyote Ln
Tucson AZ 85742

Call Sign: N0YGE
Thomas H Broersma
10169 Coyote Ln
Tucson AZ 85742

Call Sign: KF7CIJ
Salvador D Fonseca
5347 Crown Bench Cir
Tucson AZ 85757

Call Sign: KF7YV
Wayne R Ferris
5510 Cumberland Dr
Tucson AZ 85704

Call Sign: KA8LEH
Shirley B Mark
1500 Daybreak Cir
Tucson AZ 85704

Call Sign: KL7DJD
Ralph W Alonis
14680 Del Webb Blvd
Tucson AZ 85737

Call Sign: N7QDG
John L French
8021 Della Robia Pl
Tucson AZ 85741

Call Sign: KC7TIJ
Robert S Toperzer
790 Desert Glen
Tucson AZ 85737

Call Sign: KA7RUT
Horace Williams
5501 Diamond K
Tucson AZ 85713

Call Sign: KD7LFW
Mark T Hawthorne
463 Dogstar Mountain Dr
Tucson AZ 85745

Call Sign: KD7YCP
Mark T Hawthorne
463 Dogstar Mountain Dr
Tucson AZ 85745

Call Sign: W7XP
Carl L Waterhouse Jr
9298 Dolores St
Tucson AZ 85730

Call Sign: W3ZUL
Harold E Wright
2370 Donatello Way
Tucson AZ 85704

Call Sign: N7WML
David A Tolman
1250 E 10th St Apt 202B
Tucson AZ 85719

Call Sign: KC7PGN
Adrian Noriega
1020 E 12th St
Tucson AZ 85719

Call Sign: KB7JM
Joseph V Pierson
4525 E 12th St
Tucson AZ 85711

Call Sign: KD7CTS
Michael R Ori
4934 E 12th St
Tucson AZ 85711

Call Sign: KD7CTH
Natalie A Doetsch
4934 E 12th St

Tucson AZ 85711

Call Sign: KC6WDK
George B Rosenberg
1644 E 12th St 2
Tucson AZ 85719

Call Sign: N7VGF
Walter H Mellors
4625 E 15th St
Tucson AZ 85711

Call Sign: KB7PNA
David R Dean
6051 E 15th St
Tucson AZ 85711

Call Sign: WA7RVU
Mottie J Hjerpe
6122 E 15th St
Tucson AZ 85711

Call Sign: K7DHD
Darrell J Hjerpe
6122 E 15th St
Tucson AZ 85711

Call Sign: N7BHS
William A Tekniepe
6021 E 16th Pl
Tucson AZ 857114609

Call Sign: KD7POJ
Martha Mcclements
336 E 16th St
Tucson AZ 85701

Call Sign: W7LHF
Leroy L Galhouse
6026 E 16th St
Tucson AZ 85711

Call Sign: KC7FRS
Kendel M Mc Carley
2903 E 17th St
Tucson AZ 85716

Call Sign: KE7AZP
Christine M Martin

4702 E 17th St
Tucson AZ 85711

Call Sign: KE7GAN
James J Moffett
5970 E 17th St
Tucson AZ 85711

Call Sign: KC7KFM
Jeffrey A Mead
6641 E 17th St
Tucson AZ 857104601

Call Sign: KE6SYE
Chad E Mayer
3927 E 17th St B
Tucson AZ 85711

Call Sign: KE7BTD
Jane Larkindale
4826 E 18th St
Tucson AZ 85711

Call Sign: KD7SNZ
James R Holmes
4826 E 18th St
Tucson AZ 85711

Call Sign: KD7SKT
Temple S Robinson
5961 E 18th St
Tucson AZ 85717

Call Sign: N7OUY
Christian W Adams
5204 E 19th St
Tucson AZ 85711

Call Sign: KA4RTA
Edward H Wilson III
7342 E 19th St
Tucson AZ 85710

Call Sign: KD7SMF
Edward H Wilson III
7342 E 19th St
Tucson AZ 85710

Call Sign: K7RTA

Edward H Wilson III
7342 E 19th St
Tucson AZ 85710

Call Sign: WA7RTA
Edward H Wilson III
7342 E 19th St
Tucson AZ 85710

Call Sign: KA7CYO
Martin E Belden
7351 E 19th St
Tucson AZ 85710

Call Sign: W7JTN
Edward M Shunk
7426 E 19th St
Tucson AZ 85710

Call Sign: WA7UBS
Charles W Polzer
2844 E 1st St
Tucson AZ 85716

Call Sign: WA7P
Edward G Stiles
3324 E 1st St
Tucson AZ 85716

Call Sign: KA7GTJ
Frank G Cannella
4025 E 1st St
Tucson AZ 857111003

Call Sign: KF7CNR
Lin C Hearn-Donnelly
4031 E 1st St
Tucson AZ 85711

Call Sign: KC7VDA
Daniel P Donnelly
4031 E 1st St
Tucson AZ 85711

Call Sign: K7WIP
J Lester Hearn
4031 E 1st St
Tucson AZ 85711

Call Sign: KD7FRQ
Linda C Hearn Donnelly
4031 E 1st St
Tucson AZ 857111003

Call Sign: KE7VJL
John Macgregor
4124 E 1st St
Tucson AZ 85711

Call Sign: W1TNB
John Macgregor
4124 E 1st St
Tucson AZ 85711

Call Sign: N7IOK
Clyde M Sakir
4243 E 1st St
Tucson AZ 85711

Call Sign: KB7ISS
Arthur J Mullins
4761 E 1st St
Tucson AZ 85711

Call Sign: W2EMB
Jean A Robinson
5324 E 1st St 278
Tucson AZ 85711

Call Sign: KB7QEW
Vernon W Hull III
6241 E 20th St
Tucson AZ 85711

Call Sign: N7ZQU
Jack C Herron
8118 E 20th St
Tucson AZ 85710

Call Sign: AE7GP
Gary R Pierce
8531 E 20th St
Tucson AZ 85710

Call Sign: KF7MEK
Susan G Pierce
8531 E 20th St
Tucson AZ 85710

Call Sign: W7BJC
William W Hempel Sr
7025 E 21st St
Tucson AZ 85710

Call Sign: KA7LML
Michael T Addis
11020 E 22nd St
Tucson AZ 85748

Call Sign: KB7VKH
Lloyd H Moffet
5641 E 23rd St
Tucson AZ 85711

Call Sign: N7JGB
Cherryl D Christian
8416 E 23rd St
Tucson AZ 85710

Call Sign: KA4VGI
John G Mac Nutt
6271 E 24th St
Tucson AZ 85711

Call Sign: N7PUX
Henry N Dluehosh
7512 E 24th St
Tucson AZ 85710

Call Sign: KB7TLD
Wesley C Mc Mahon
2325 E 24th St
Tucson AZ 857132038

Call Sign: KC7HGZ
Brian A Jacobson
6141 E 25th St
Tucson AZ 85711

Call Sign: KC7RXU
Robert J Koselow
8342 E 25th St
Tucson AZ 857107208

Call Sign: KC7BVA
John A Roberts
8445 E 25th St

Tucson AZ 85710

Call Sign: KC7BVB
William F Roberts
8445 E 25th St
Tucson AZ 85710

Call Sign: KF7IGV
William F Roberts
8445 E 25th St
Tucson AZ 85710

Call Sign: N7MEM
Martin R Linsenbigler
2925 E 26th St
Tucson AZ 85713

Call Sign: W7EPH
Edward P Hutchinson
2941 E 26th St
Tucson AZ 85713

Call Sign: KE7BOJ
Nathanial P Hendler
6022 E 26th St
Tucson AZ 85711

Call Sign: WB5LVW
Charles A Cudahy
8734 E 26th St
Tucson AZ 85710

Call Sign: N7PAF
Manuel Correia
3507 E 27th St
Tucson AZ 85713

Call Sign: KA6GDO
Timothy W Stucky
3620 E 27th St
Tucson AZ 85713

Call Sign: KC7MVW
Carl L Fish
3730 E 27th St
Tucson AZ 85713

Call Sign: W7AE
Louis F Ermi

5357 E 27th St
Tucson AZ 85711

Call Sign: N7KRA
Ethel M Haines
9234 E 27th St
Tucson AZ 85710

Call Sign: NX7G
Harold E Haines
9234 E 27th St
Tucson AZ 85710

Call Sign: KE7YO
Anthony San Angelo
9242 E 27th St
Tucson AZ 85710

Call Sign: WB7QKD
David G Odom
9330 E 27th St
Tucson AZ 85710

Call Sign: KB7HON
James W Chasteen
3209 E 28th St
Tucson AZ 85713

Call Sign: KE7WIR
Patrick M Fritton
3710 E 28th St
Tucson AZ 85713

Call Sign: KD7CAQ
David L Propst Jr
4826 E 28th St
Tucson AZ 85711

Call Sign: N7ZBF
Arthur Q Ruffner Jr
5645 E 28th St
Tucson AZ 85711

Call Sign: KC7OVR
Dorothy G Parsley
8801 E 28th St
Tucson AZ 85710

Call Sign: KC7LVM

Paul E Parsley
8801 E 28th St
Tucson AZ 85710

Call Sign: KC7RXV
William R Mac Vittie
5936 E 29th St
Tucson AZ 85711

Call Sign: N7LCN
Donald K Dow
6048 E 29th St
Tucson AZ 85711

Call Sign: KC7GLL
Robert I Mason
7349 E 29th St
Tucson AZ 85710

Call Sign: KE7FSJ
Daryl K Koch
7349 E 29th St
Tucson AZ 85710

Call Sign: W7XX
Daryl K Koch
7349 E 29th St
Tucson AZ 85710

Call Sign: KE7HJH
Georgeann Koch
7349 E 29th St
Tucson AZ 85710

Call Sign: KA8RFM
Robert S Peck Jr
9272 E 29th St
Tucson AZ 857108014

Call Sign: KE7WSV
Arthur B Havemeyer
9338 E 29th St
Tucson AZ 85710

Call Sign: KE7WIT
Janice A Lemon
9571 E 29th St
Tucson AZ 85748

Call Sign: KE7ZGS
Robert V Ludwick
9571 E 29th St
Tucson AZ 85748

Call Sign: W7MPP
Robert V Ludwick
9571 E 29th St
Tucson AZ 85748

Call Sign: K7GVQ
Harold A Williams Jr
2249 E 2nd St
Tucson AZ 85719

Call Sign: KD7AQU
Jurgen J Seidel
3008 E 2nd St
Tucson AZ 857164113

Call Sign: W7KXH
James M Gates
3025 E 2nd St
Tucson AZ 85716

Call Sign: W7WKM
William W Munsil
4043 E 2nd St
Tucson AZ 85711

Call Sign: N2OSC
John A Smith
4601 E 2nd St
Tucson AZ 85711

Call Sign: N7XKE
Theodore S Gould
4850 E 2nd St
Tucson AZ 85711

Call Sign: KD7JUJ
Jeffrey A Berringer
5708 E 2nd St
Tucson AZ 85711

Call Sign: KF7UBB
David A Bliss
5936 E 2nd St
Tucson AZ 85711

Call Sign: KD7VO
James E Lynch
6270 E 2nd St
Tucson AZ 85711

Call Sign: KE7NOM
Gilberto Valenzuela
135 E 30th St
Tucson AZ 85713

Call Sign: KB7RVH
Barbara L Mathews
4535 E 30th St
Tucson AZ 85711

Call Sign: KB7SWL
Robert R Mathews
4535 E 30th St
Tucson AZ 85711

Call Sign: KD7JZC
Lori S Walker
5609 E 30th St
Tucson AZ 85711

Call Sign: KD7JZB
William U Walker
5609 E 30th St
Tucson AZ 85711

Call Sign: WV7G
William U Walker
5609 E 30th St
Tucson AZ 85711

Call Sign: W5ZIO
William U Walker
5609 E 30th St
Tucson AZ 85711

Call Sign: KE5BX
Carl W Neihart
7102 E 30th St
Tucson AZ 85710

Call Sign: WA4NFX
Carroll A Jackson
9149 E 30th St

Tucson AZ 85710

Call Sign: KE7SK
Charles R Wellner
9225 E 30th St
Tucson AZ 85710

Call Sign: KE7GVZ
David B Wolf
9561 E 30th St
Tucson AZ 85748

Call Sign: KB7POW
Rebekah R Zum Brunnen
4318 E 31st St
Tucson AZ 85711

Call Sign: KA7GXU
Kathleen D Zumbrunnen
4318 E 31st St
Tucson AZ 85711

Call Sign: WB6UOL
John Zum Brunnen
4318 E 31st St
Tucson AZ 85711

Call Sign: KC7LIK
Edward C L Green
4562 E 31st St
Tucson AZ 85711

Call Sign: KF7SGV
Justin M Bundock
4672 E 31st St
Tucson AZ 85711

Call Sign: KB7PDZ
Dawn E Collier
5649 E 32nd St
Tucson AZ 85711

Call Sign: AA7HX
Henry T Willis
5649 E 32nd St
Tucson AZ 85711

Call Sign: N7PNS
Ian B Collier

5649 E 32nd St
Tucson AZ 85711

Call Sign: W7LFN
Clayton F Ifflander
7301 E 32nd St
Tucson AZ 857106036

Call Sign: KE7FZJ
David L Foreman
5811 E 33rd St
Tucson AZ 857116715

Call Sign: KC7FSC
Jeanne K Wearly
7602 E 33rd St
Tucson AZ 85710

Call Sign: KC7EDX
Michael E Wearly
7602 E 33rd St
Tucson AZ 85710

Call Sign: KC7OPL
Paul D Borquez
5709 E 34th St
Tucson AZ 85711

Call Sign: W6TPK
Virgil A Knox Jr
6125 E 34th St
Tucson AZ 85711

Call Sign: ND7H
Louis Aclin
7145 E 34th St
Tucson AZ 85710

Call Sign: N7USM
David E Gauf
7541 E 34th St
Tucson AZ 85710

Call Sign: KB7LKV
Larry M Holick
5717 E 35th St
Tucson AZ 85711

Call Sign: KE7LOT

Andrew J Keefer Jr
6050 E 35th St
Tucson AZ 85711

Call Sign: N5TMH
Gordon L Elkins
7308 E 35th St
Tucson AZ 85710

Call Sign: W7KVG
Kenneth J Leland
7324 E 35th St
Tucson AZ 85710

Call Sign: AB7NO
William D Jansen
7408 E 35th St
Tucson AZ 85716

Call Sign: KC7FZV
Anne C Lopez
7617 E 35th St
Tucson AZ 85710

Call Sign: KF7MZX
Gary S Goldberg
7718 E 35th St
Tucson AZ 85710

Call Sign: KE7GYQ
Douglas W Todd
7278 E 38th St
Tucson AZ 85730

Call Sign: KB7TBH
Steve W Clor
6625 E 39th St
Tucson AZ 85730

Call Sign: WA4NXZ
Randell G Sands
9341 E 39th St
Tucson AZ 85730

Call Sign: KC7LVP
Richard A Collins
5511 E 3rd Pl
Tucson AZ 85711

Call Sign: KF7UNX
William J Wagner III
8261 E 3rd Pl
Tucson AZ 85710

Call Sign: KC7EAT
William S Bickel
3340 E 3rd St
Tucson AZ 85716

Call Sign: KA7HEQ
Michael D White
4912 E 3rd St
Tucson AZ 85711

Call Sign: KA7HER
Tama H White
4912 E 3rd St
Tucson AZ 85711

Call Sign: W7BWP
Roger C Jones
5809 E 3rd St
Tucson AZ 85711

Call Sign: N8CWA
Charles M Gammie
8021 E 3rd St
Tucson AZ 85710

Call Sign: KB7VJY
Carol A Walts
9442 E 3rd St
Tucson AZ 85710

Call Sign: NH7FU
Gary D Lundlee
6944 E 42nd St
Tucson AZ 85730

Call Sign: N7YJD
Susan Mead Larssen
7440 E 42nd St
Tucson AZ 85730

Call Sign: KB7NFQ
Garnet G Morris III
9411 E 42nd St
Tucson AZ 85730

Call Sign: KC7XZ
Richard J Jank
9564 E 42nd St
Tucson AZ 85730

Call Sign: WA5PPO
Brian M Chesire
6848 E 45th St
Tucson AZ 85730

Call Sign: AD7WX
Brian M Chesire
6848 E 45th St
Tucson AZ 85730

Call Sign: N7SQC
Jerry D Johnston
6950 E 45th St
Tucson AZ 85730

Call Sign: KC7DVF
C Adam G Grose
7002 E 45th St
Tucson AZ 85730

Call Sign: KD7ZDF
Gracie Grose
7002 E 45th St
Tucson AZ 85730

Call Sign: KA7UOX
Michael C Williams
7022 E 45th St
Tucson AZ 857302304

Call Sign: KD7THB
John P Laughlin
7710 E 45th St
Tucson AZ 857302402

Call Sign: N7GIJ
David E Miller
4226 E 4th Pl
Tucson AZ 85711

Call Sign: K7QYN
Robert W Wise
8117 E 4th Pl

Tucson AZ 87510

Call Sign: KC7IOF
Ian M Guagliardo
725 E 4th St
Tucson AZ 85719

Call Sign: KD7OBJ
Jason W Worrell
3020 E 4th St
Tucson AZ 85716

Call Sign: KD7CQT
Robert A Offerle
3420 E 4th St
Tucson AZ 857164664

Call Sign: KA7BWZ
Clarence E Mow
4413 E 4th St
Tucson AZ 85711

Call Sign: KF7GPX
Craig W Sternberg
5608 E 4th St
Tucson AZ 85711

Call Sign: WB7DIW
Roger R Schroeder
5728 E 4th St
Tucson AZ 85711

Call Sign: KC7B
Louis Woofenden
5744 E 4th St
Tucson AZ 85711

Call Sign: WA7YVM
Edward K Ryan Sr
8344 E 4th St
Tucson AZ 85710

Call Sign: KC7VDD
Dana L Irvin
1420 E 5th Apt 201
Tucson AZ 85719

Call Sign: KA7WMB
Langdon Hill

628 E 5th St
Tucson AZ 85705

Call Sign: K7GIH
Walter H Evans
2026 E 5th St
Tucson AZ 85719

Call Sign: WA7STK
Jane M Becksted
2123 E 5th St
Tucson AZ 85719

Call Sign: WA7JYI
Roger G Becksted
2123 E 5th St
Tucson AZ 85719

Call Sign: W8HTX
Paul D Hartmann
2617 E 5th St
Tucson AZ 85716

Call Sign: N7KTE
Terry N Hartmann
2617 E 5th St
Tucson AZ 85716

Call Sign: KC7ERZ
James E Van Olphen
3355 E 5th St
Tucson AZ 85716

Call Sign: KC7CNV
Jane M Orient
3615 E 5th St
Tucson AZ 85716

Call Sign: KA7PQK
John W Gault
4602 E 5th St
Tucson AZ 85711

Call Sign: N7EMT
Delmar A Smith
9306 E 5th St
Tucson AZ 85710

Call Sign: N7QVI

Judy Smith
9306 E 5th St
Tucson AZ 85710

Call Sign: N6KIV
Edward S Sherlock
9433 E 5th St
Tucson AZ 85710

Call Sign: WA2BJS
Philip Elkind
9501 E 5th St
Tucson AZ 85710

Call Sign: KC7FXF
Martha Elkind
9501 E 5th St
Tucson AZ 85748

Call Sign: W2AZD
Donald A Chappell
9551 E 5th St
Tucson AZ 857483302

Call Sign: KB9VOM
Stephen E Davis
9932 E 5th St
Tucson AZ 85748

Call Sign: K0EEH
Emma Harder
10090 E 5th St
Tucson AZ 85748

Call Sign: K7GBH
Gabrielle Harder
10090 E 5th St
Tucson AZ 85748

Call Sign: K6RWH
Robert W Harder
10090 E 5th St
Tucson AZ 85748

Call Sign: KJ7YZ
Brian D Caillet
12150 E 5th St
Tucson AZ 85748

Call Sign: N7LIE
Robert T Griggs
4900 E 5th St 2012
Tucson AZ 85705

Call Sign: KD7CYB
Alan G Aversa
825 E 5th St Apt 255A
Tucson AZ 857195040

Call Sign: KA1PNZ
Andrew D Gorski
2544 E 6th St
Tucson AZ 85716

Call Sign: KA7O
Philip J Potter
4301 E 6th St
Tucson AZ 857112901

Call Sign: KC7PSF
Janet F Rabin
5650 E 6th St
Tucson AZ 85711

Call Sign: KB7GOW
Kirk C Wheeler
8157 E 6th St
Tucson AZ 85710

Call Sign: KC7FXE
Gary C Copus
8791 E 6th St
Tucson AZ 85710

Call Sign: KC7JWF
Karen S Copus
8791 E 6th St
Tucson AZ 85710

Call Sign: KC7RMS
Daniel R Sanderman
2929 E 6th St 211
Tucson AZ 85716

Call Sign: KA3QCK
Jack H Vaughn Jr
2820 E 6th St 220
Tucson AZ 85716

Call Sign: KC7QMK
David R Jacobsen
2820 E 6th St Unit 107
Tucson AZ 857164816

Call Sign: KC7RMC
Erik W Brown
1815 E 7th Apt B
Tucson AZ 85719

Call Sign: N7CXY
Carey A Bunker
2234 E 7th St
Tucson AZ 857195607

Call Sign: KC7JTJ
John Sims
4656 E 7th St
Tucson AZ 85711

Call Sign: KF7LTY
John D Sims
4656 E 7th St
Tucson AZ 85711

Call Sign: KC7ESD
David P Sliffe
5121 E 7th St
Tucson AZ 85711

Call Sign: KD7KDR
William C Kershaw
8712 E 7th St
Tucson AZ 857103002

Call Sign: KE7PMM
Simon C Dalzell
718 E 8th St
Tucson AZ 85719

Call Sign: KC7BHW
Andrew F Tubbiolo
1608 E 8th St
Tucson AZ 85719

Call Sign: K7CC
Hobart J Paine
4631 E 8th St

Tucson AZ 85711

Call Sign: N7SPW
Ronald J Kalish
5402 E 8th St
Tucson AZ 85711

Call Sign: KA7CBW
Charles R Seeger
5409 E 8th St
Tucson AZ 85711

Call Sign: KC7JTL
Frank A Wolf
5636 E 8th St
Tucson AZ 85711

Call Sign: K7SSN
Frank A Wolf
5636 E 8th St
Tucson AZ 85711

Call Sign: AH6PU
Scott H Ketcher
9005 E 8th St
Tucson AZ 85710

Call Sign: KC8BZD
Elton C Twork
9016 E 8th St
Tucson AZ 857103009

Call Sign: W6WMG
Robert J Lesser
1345 E 9th St
Tucson AZ 85719

Call Sign: KC7OVM
Richard E Corbett
2230 E 9th St
Tucson AZ 85719

Call Sign: WA7CVI
Henrietta Mc Donald
2250 E 9th St
Tucson AZ 85719

Call Sign: KF7CNK
Stephen J Furlong

2839 E 9th St
Tucson AZ 85716

Call Sign: KF7KRY
Zachary Jarrett
4555 E 9th St
Tucson AZ 85711

Call Sign: KC7RXQ
Amy L Leasure
5809 E Academy St Dmfab
Tucson AZ 85708

Call Sign: N6AWB
Anthony W Brollini
10125 E Achi St
Tucson AZ 85748

Call Sign: NS6N
Van R Brollini
10125 E Achi St
Tucson AZ 85748

Call Sign: W4ES
Brian L Stamper
4095 E Adams Rib Pl
Tucson AZ 85739

Call Sign: KE7QIL
Samrat M Clements
333 E Adams St
Tucson AZ 85705

Call Sign: AB7AR
James M Palmer
2342 E Adams St
Tucson AZ 85719

Call Sign: W1RER
Dustin D Lauth-Clements
333 E Adams St
Tucson AZ 85705

Call Sign: K7VAY
Dennis P Pugh
9582 E Adare Ln
Tucson AZ 85747

Call Sign: N7TXL

Robert B Dye
1071 E Aero Park Blvd
Tucson AZ 85706

Call Sign: KC7CJV
Jeffrey T Kartheiser
8931 E Alderpoint Way
Tucson AZ 85730

Call Sign: KD7YLY
Barbara A Godfrey
E Allen Rd
Tucson AZ 85719

Call Sign: W0BRH
Barbara A Godfrey
E Allen Rd
Tucson AZ 85719

Call Sign: KB5B
Albert K Godfrey
E Allen Rd
Tucson AZ 857191458

Call Sign: KB7NE
Murt W Weitzel
2642 E Alta Vista
Tucson AZ 85716

Call Sign: WA7SCG
Richard J Rotundo
5541 E Alta Vista
Tucson AZ 85712

Call Sign: W4LVC
Charles D Mount
8041 E Alteza Vista
Tucson AZ 857502848

Call Sign: K5RR
Richard C Fenwick Sr
8000 E Alvin Rd
Tucson AZ 85750

Call Sign: KA6TBM
Ralph S Richards
9880 E Amarosa Ln
Tucson AZ 85748

Call Sign: KB8HTO
Hector J Munoz
62473 E Amberwood Dr
Tucson AZ 85739

Call Sign: KE6UYP
Richard G Embom
11601 E Andalusian Pl
Tucson AZ 85748

Call Sign: N7YMG
John J Dupee
5359 E Andrew
Tucson AZ 85711

Call Sign: KC7QYG
Holly A Marcott
5217 E Andrews St
Tucson AZ 85711

Call Sign: W6BCZ
Joseph W Morgan
42132 E Anya Way
Tucson AZ 85738

Call Sign: W7JWM
Joseph W Morgan
42132 E Anya Way
Tucson AZ 85738

Call Sign: KE7YTD
Regina Swift
12565 E Arbor Vista Blvd
Tucson AZ 85749

Call Sign: KC7LIJ
Russell W Hewlett
10890 E Armada Ln
Tucson AZ 85749

Call Sign: KE7HJB
Leigh A Thrasher
3150 E Arroyo Chico
Tucson AZ 85716

Call Sign: KE7ZZT
Lawrence B Icely
1821 E Arroyo Vista Dr
Tucson AZ 85746

Call Sign: WA2YHP
Martin Dennis
9470 E Asoleada Dr
Tucson AZ 85710

Call Sign: AC7JD
Joe L Theobald
12481 E Ave Vista Verde
Tucson AZ 85749

Call Sign: KM6MV
Dorothy N Fagg
12440 E Avenida De La
Vista Verde
Tucson AZ 85749

Call Sign: WA6WPM
Willis L Fagg
12440 E Avenida De La
Vista Verde
Tucson AZ 85749

Call Sign: N3SRU
Joseph R Thompson
2651 E Avenida De Maria
Tucson AZ 85718

Call Sign: K7ZFV
Doyle J Kelly Sr
2645 E Avenida De Pueblo
Tucson AZ 85718

Call Sign: KC4YKA
Roger K Brubaker
2702 E Avenida De Pueblo
Tucson AZ 85718

Call Sign: KD7PLW
Roger K Brubaker
2702 E Avenida De Pueblo
Tucson AZ 85718

Call Sign: KB7AZ
Roger K Brubaker
2702 E Avenida De Pueblo
Tucson AZ 85718

Call Sign: KC7WLN

Tim B Hunter
4571 E Avenida Shelly
Tucson AZ 85718

Call Sign: KD7AQS
Diane E Mayhew
5250 E Baker St
Tucson AZ 857112307

Call Sign: KK7HC
Jeffrey S Mayhew
5250 E Baker St
Tucson AZ 857112307

Call Sign: AE7HL
Jan Kraus
5328 E Baker St
Tucson AZ 85711

Call Sign: W7LHI
William J English
5936 E Baker St
Tucson AZ 857112412

Call Sign: KA7ARX
Eugene H Pepper
6902 E Baker St
Tucson AZ 85710

Call Sign: KA7KLJ
Sally E Grieve Duncan
9216 E Baker St
Tucson AZ 85710

Call Sign: KF7KRV
James E Malmberg
9641 E Baker St
Tucson AZ 85748

Call Sign: AJ7AA
James E Malmberg
9641 E Baker St
Tucson AZ 85748

Call Sign: W7OQR
William Corbett
1742 E Bantam Rd
Tucson AZ 85706

Call Sign: KF7ITC
Cornelius Jongsma
12035 E Barbary Coast Rd
Tucson AZ 85749

Call Sign: AD7RZ
Michael J Lindsay
12401 E Barbary Coast Rd
Tucson AZ 85749

Call Sign: N9TDG
Jason J Pototsky
9600 E Barrudean Hills St
Tucson AZ 857482720

Call Sign: NH6BF
Peter G Pototsky
9600 E Barrudean Hills St
Tucson AZ 857482720

Call Sign: WR7A
Edward W Laconto
9935 E Basque Pl
Tucson AZ 85748

Call Sign: K7RKC
Acree S Shreve
6337 E Baylor Dr
Tucson AZ 85710

Call Sign: KD7VUE
Louis F Sellyei
9031 E Bear Cir
Tucson AZ 85749

Call Sign: KE7GHZ
Robert G Wright
8910 E Bear Creek Dr
Tucson AZ 85749

Call Sign: KF7ECP
Diana J Ebbert
8864 E Bear Paw Pl
Tucson AZ 85749

Call Sign: KC7CJW
Richard A Rice
6100 E Belleview 13
Tucson AZ 85712

Call Sign: AB7HU
Matthew J Zamora
3237 E Bellevue St
Tucson AZ 85716

Call Sign: KB8OEH
Michael T Leonard
3819 E Bellevue St
Tucson AZ 85716

Call Sign: N7FFE
Dennis M Shepard
4551 E Bellevue St
Tucson AZ 85712

Call Sign: KE7NGA
Robert M Brewer
6101 E Bellevue St 143
Tucson AZ 85712

Call Sign: KF7TKI
Justin C Ashler
3535 E Bellevue St 2
Tucson AZ 85716

Call Sign: KD7FHB
Baltazar R Castillo
3344 E Bellevue St Apt A
Tucson AZ 85716

Call Sign: N2GJF
Gabriel L Agardi
9750 E Bennett Dr
Tucson AZ 857475103

Call Sign: W7WIA
Oliver A Larsen
7860 E Bensen Hwy 149
Tucson AZ 85706

Call Sign: N6ETA
Peter F Sheakley
4444 E Benson Hwy 151
Tucson AZ 85706

Call Sign: KC7HWJ
William H Cook
4444 E Benson Hwy 216

Tucson AZ 85706

Call Sign: KC7FXM
Terry E Weeks
4444 E Benson Hwy 270
Tucson AZ 85706

Call Sign: WA2RIH
Dan L Graham Jr
305 E Benson Hwy Apt 204
Tucson AZ 85713

Call Sign: KX7E
Ronald E Harvey
7220 E Benson Hwy Lot P
Tucson AZ 857069039

Call Sign: KD7LLM
Joseph P Seymour III
7412 E Benson Hwy Rural Rt
136
Tucson AZ 85756

Call Sign: N7GFI
William C Wittkoff
3652 E Bermuda St
Tucson AZ 85716

Call Sign: W6MKF
William K Wittkoff
3652 E Bermuda St
Tucson AZ 85716

Call Sign: KB6IRC
Elizabeth A Wittkoff
3652 E Bermuda St
Tucson AZ 857162361

Call Sign: KC7LVV
Karl A Nielsen
9301 E Betsey Pl
Tucson AZ 85710

Call Sign: AC7NG
Karl A Nielsen
9301 E Betsey Pl
Tucson AZ 85710

Call Sign: KC7QXZ

Teresa A Nielsen
9301 E Betsey Pl
Tucson AZ 85710

Call Sign: W7IBM
Tucson Ibm ARC
9301 E Betsey Pl
Tucson AZ 85710

Call Sign: KB7GAN
Adrian A Baxter
5834 E Beverly Dr
Tucson AZ 85711

Call Sign: KE7WIS
Robert A Critch
6161 E Beverly Dr
Tucson AZ 85711

Call Sign: KD7DXZ
Karl E Rifenbark
7441 E Beverly Dr
Tucson AZ 857105017

Call Sign: KC7RXT
C Eugene Cole
7448 E Beverly Dr
Tucson AZ 85710

Call Sign: K7CEC
C Eugene Cole
7448 E Beverly Dr
Tucson AZ 85710

Call Sign: N7DME
John H Bryson
8555 E Beverly Dr
Tucson AZ 85710

Call Sign: W9NRX
Lawrence I Presler
9318 E Bidahochi Dr
Tucson AZ 85749

Call Sign: KC6AHF
James C Hinkle
8242 E Big Horn Trl
Tucson AZ 85715

Call Sign: W7VAV
Henry R Bauer
1201 E Bilby Rd 4
Tucson AZ 85706

Call Sign: WB0DZU
Glen L Bohnke
10513 E Black Willow Dr
Tucson AZ 85747

Call Sign: KE7EUX
Spencer K Edgerton
1406 E Blacklidge Dr
Tucson AZ 85719

Call Sign: KC7AON
Lowell Curtis
2262 E Blacklidge Dr
Tucson AZ 85719

Call Sign: KB7TVL
Charles D Bertelsen
2503 E Blacklidge Dr
Tucson AZ 85716

Call Sign: KD7WJF
Todd H Hawthorne
2726 E Blacklidge Dr
Tucson AZ 85716

Call Sign: K7THH
Todd H Hawthorne
2726 E Blacklidge Dr
Tucson AZ 85716

Call Sign: KE7WIY
Thomas A Woodrow
3650 E Blacklidge Dr
Tucson AZ 85716

Call Sign: N5GTO
Thomas A Woodrow
3650 E Blacklidge Dr
Tucson AZ 85716

Call Sign: KK7EJ
James L Rodger
3646 E Blacklidge Dr 3
Tucson AZ 85716

Call Sign: WB9TPD
Lee J Benson
4001 E Blacklidge Dr 74
Tucson AZ 85712

Call Sign: KE7FZI
Joel M Brodsky
1719 E Blacklidge Dr Apt J
Tucson AZ 85719

Call Sign: WA7KEF
Francis C Bauer
1115 E Blanton Dr
Tucson AZ 85719

Call Sign: KE7VTT
Richard W Adams
2549 E Blanton Dr
Tucson AZ 85716

Call Sign: N0FAQ
Richard W Adams
2549 E Blanton Dr
Tucson AZ 85716

Call Sign: KE7YLY
Zachary W Jones
11055 E Blue Grama Dr
Tucson AZ 85748

Call Sign: KE7VKU
Mark E Ekstum
9015 E Bluefield St
Tucson AZ 85710

Call Sign: KE7ZPI
Elizabeth M Fagan
10650 E Bridgeport St
Tucson AZ 85747

Call Sign: KE7LHY
Marjorie A Fagan
10650 E Bridgeport St
Tucson AZ 85747

Call Sign: WB7NXH
Thomas J Fagan
10650 E Bridgeport St

Tucson AZ 85747

Call Sign: K7DF
Thomas J Fagan
10650 E Bridgeport St
Tucson AZ 85747

Call Sign: KE7IDC
James T Fagan
10650 E Bridgeport St
Tucson AZ 857475925

Call Sign: KA7EGF
Andrew N Barry
10480 E Bridgestone Pl
Tucson AZ 857305001

Call Sign: AD7DM
Andrew N Barry
10480 E Bridgestone Pl
Tucson AZ 857305001

Call Sign: WF7H
Henry Kaldenbaugh
1132 E Broadway
Tucson AZ 85719

Call Sign: KC7INO
Paul E Garrison
4533 E Broadway
Tucson AZ 85711

Call Sign: W7GJN
Foster A Hall
9600 E Broadway
Tucson AZ 85748

Call Sign: KC7OKG
Scott H Barkley
4702 E Broadway 110
Tucson AZ 85711

Call Sign: KC7PUG
Michael A Watts
6979 E Broadway 119
Tucson AZ 85710

Call Sign: WD6EYW
James W Richards

2203 E Broadway 150
Tucson AZ 85719

Call Sign: KB7RXW
Delancy R Scrivner
8880 E Broadway 181
Tucson AZ 85710

Call Sign: KC7ZPF
Phyliss A Davis
6901 E Broadway 247
Tucson AZ 85710

Call Sign: KB7ZRA
Lynn B Neal
7353 E Broadway 328
Tucson AZ 85710

Call Sign: KF7SNI
Wesley A Glogner
7739 E Broadway 43
Tucson AZ 85710

Call Sign: AH6GH
Robert C Sweet
6901 E Broadway Apt 141
Tucson AZ 85710

Call Sign: W0NUB
James D Mc Clanahan
6639 E Broadway Apt 239
Tucson AZ 85710

Call Sign: W2GRQ
Anita M Wardell
8477 E Broadway Bl
Tucson AZ 857104005

Call Sign: KC6SDI
Jeff Benge
3849 E Broadway Blvd
Tucson AZ 85716

Call Sign: AB6TO
Jeff Benge
3849 E Broadway Blvd
Tucson AZ 85716

Call Sign: KF7FTT

Marlon W Oliver
5425 E Broadway Blvd
Tucson AZ 85711

Call Sign: W7PLR
Peter L Rabin
7739 E Broadway Blvd
Tucson AZ 85710

Call Sign: KF7LNC
Jeff Benge
3849 E Broadway Blvd 103
Tucson AZ 85716

Call Sign: KD7OBH
Michael J Grammond
7739 E Broadway Blvd 135
Tucson AZ 85710

Call Sign: KF7MQL
Emily Robinson
3849 E Broadway Blvd 173
Tucson AZ 85716

Call Sign: KD7LHL
Owen L Watson
5425 E Broadway Blvd Pmb
111
Tucson AZ 85711

Call Sign: AD7PP
Owen L Watson
5425 E Broadway Blvd Pmb
111
Tucson AZ 85711

Call Sign: AK7AR
Owen L Watson
5425 E Broadway Blvd Pmb
111
Tucson AZ 85711

Call Sign: KF7GQA
Rst Contest Sig
5425 E Broadway Blvd Pmb
111
Tucson AZ 85711

Call Sign: AK7AZ

Rst Contest Sig
5425 E Broadway Blvd Pmb
111
Tucson AZ 85711

Call Sign: N7SCC
George M Collenberg
6821 E Broadway Blvd Unit
250
Tucson AZ 857102821

Call Sign: AA7QQ
George M Collenberg
6821 E Broadway Blvd Unit
250
Tucson AZ 857102821

Call Sign: KC7LIA
Terry K Winslow
434 E Bromley St
Tucson AZ 857045707

Call Sign: AB7IC
Thomas G Britton
8410 E Brookwood Dr
Tucson AZ 857502468

Call Sign: KC7VDC
Paul B Rhatigan
4422 E Brott St
Tucson AZ 857121102

Call Sign: AC7WZ
Robert D Mumme
4352 E Bryn Mawr Rd
Tucson AZ 857112928

Call Sign: KC7OKH
Joseph E Hayes
3829 E Buoy Pl
Tucson AZ 85739

Call Sign: KF7ANK
George Economidis
9685 E Burnett St
Tucson AZ 85730

Call Sign: WA7RKI
L W Pronneke

4659 E Burns
Tucson AZ 85711

Call Sign: W7VC
Spencer E Leifheit
9700 E Bush Hill Pl
Tucson AZ 85749

Call Sign: KA7OPG
Joyce K O Neill
9700 E Bush Hill Pl
Tucson AZ 857499590

Call Sign: KB0UYK
Dale E Brech
9661 E Caldwell Dr
Tucson AZ 85747

Call Sign: KC0AXY
Tami M Brech
9661 E Caldwell Dr
Tucson AZ 85747

Call Sign: KB7ZBG
Eric J Burns
E Calle Arizona
Tucson AZ 85705

Call Sign: W3SCV
Robert D Schnaufer
4326 E Calle Aurora
Tucson AZ 85711

Call Sign: KD7JFF
Robert D Schnaufer
4326 E Calle Aurora
Tucson AZ 85711

Call Sign: KF7DDG
Cliff D Cannon
11460 E Calle Aurora
Tucson AZ 85748

Call Sign: KE7QM
James D Cannon
11460 E Calle Aurora
Tucson AZ 85748

Call Sign: KD7YVI

Stanley J Braun
8830 E Calle Bolivar
Tucson AZ 85715

Call Sign: N3ENB
Carl A Jensen
9458 E Calle Bolivar
Tucson AZ 85715

Call Sign: KE7IHX
Andrew J Wickhorst
7632 E Calle Cabo
Tucson AZ 85750

Call Sign: KD7GWW
Ronald H Wickhorst
7632 E Calle Cabo
Tucson AZ 857502123

Call Sign: N7ZTP
Angelo S Tirambulo
6418 E Calle Cappela
Tucson AZ 85710

Call Sign: KC7UNA
Robert L Schlottman
9581 E Calle Casada
Tucson AZ 85715

Call Sign: W7LAF
William F Harrison
9219 E Calle Cascada
Tucson AZ 85715

Call Sign: KE7UYI
Pantano Christian Church
ARC
9581 E Calle Cascada
Tucson AZ 85715

Call Sign: K7PCC
Pantano Christian Church
ARC
9581 E Calle Cascada
Tucson AZ 85715

Call Sign: KE7VAB
Bradley Schlottman
9581 E Calle Cascada

Tucson AZ 85715

Call Sign: KB7RAD
Bradley Schlottman
9581 E Calle Cascada
Tucson AZ 85715

Call Sign: KF7DUL
Jason A Schlottman
9581 E Calle Cascada
Tucson AZ 85715

Call Sign: KR7JAS
Jason A Schlottman
9581 E Calle Cascada
Tucson AZ 85715

Call Sign: KR7RK
Keith D Schlottman
9581 E Calle Cascada
Tucson AZ 85715

Call Sign: KB5UEU
Pamela L Schlottman
9581 E Calle Cascada
Tucson AZ 85715

Call Sign: KR7PAM
Pamela L Schlottman
9581 E Calle Cascada
Tucson AZ 85715

Call Sign: KD7YDH
Ryan A Schlottman
9581 E Calle Cascada
Tucson AZ 85715

Call Sign: KR7YAN
Ryan A Schlottman
9581 E Calle Cascada
Tucson AZ 85715

Call Sign: KC7MLX
Signacom ARC
9581 E Calle Cascada
Tucson AZ 85715

Call Sign: KB7RG
John J Kelly

6616 E Calle Cavalier
Tucson AZ 85715

Call Sign: N4QOA
Harvey O J Small
980 E Calle De La Cabra
Tucson AZ 85718

Call Sign: KD5OBZ
Marquette Mc Ardle
3200 E Calle De La Punta
Unit 1
Tucson AZ 85718

Call Sign: KM7ARK
Marquette Mc Ardle
3200 E Calle De La Punta
Unit 1
Tucson AZ 85718

Call Sign: KU7T
Randy L Carlson
6325 E Calle De Mirar
Tucson AZ 85750

Call Sign: N7RMD
Lynn P Revis
6362 E Calle De Mirar
Tucson AZ 85715

Call Sign: KF7HYF
Deborah E Shelton
6424 E Calle De Mirar
Tucson AZ 85750

Call Sign: KC7VVD
Bruce Pferdeort
11720 E Calle De Samuel
Tucson AZ 85749

Call Sign: KC7LWH
Andrew J Centofanti
11725 E Calle De Samuel
Tucson AZ 85749

Call Sign: KE7JDH
Stephen D French
11805 E Calle De Samuel
Tucson AZ 85749

Call Sign: N8HOV
Klaus J Buchenrieder
3720 E Calle Del Cacto
Tucson AZ 857183340

Call Sign: N7KHL
Frederick M Beeston
1850 E Calle Del Cielo
Tucson AZ 85718

Call Sign: KE7UR
Henry J Melosh IV
4400 E Calle Del Conde
Tucson AZ 85718

Call Sign: KD7MRD
Alex J Williamson
4675 E Calle Del Pantera
Tucson AZ 85718

Call Sign: KA9CWJ
Charles G Chambers
11461 E Calle Del Valle
Tucson AZ 85749

Call Sign: WB6YSB
Eldon D Lahr
11721 E Calle Del Valle
Tucson AZ 85749

Call Sign: W7YSB
Eldon D Lahr
11721 E Calle Del Valle
Tucson AZ 85749

Call Sign: KD7BTI
Michael A Martinez
11751 E Calle Del Valle
Tucson AZ 85749

Call Sign: KA1TY
George W Lynch
6950 E Calle Denebola
Tucson AZ 85710

Call Sign: WB7WFQ
Paul L Schneider
6334 E Calle Dened

Tucson AZ 85710

Call Sign: KB7SVN
Matthew M Parrett
6741 E Calle Dened
Tucson AZ 85710

Call Sign: KB7SWM
Michael L Parrett Sr
6741 E Calle Dened
Tucson AZ 85710

Call Sign: K7SVV
John W Mc Clain
10701 E Calle Desierto
Tucson AZ 85748

Call Sign: WB7TTJ
Virginia F Mc Clain
10701 E Calle Desierto
Tucson AZ 85748

Call Sign: KE7VTH
Stephen J Lew
3813 E Calle Fernando
Tucson AZ 85716

Call Sign: KI7KO
Hiroyuki Kurita
6580 E Calle Herculo
Tucson AZ 85710

Call Sign: W0EA
Lloyd M Kelley
6682 E Calle Herculo
Tucson AZ 85710

Call Sign: KB7SVM
Eugene K Oppen
6718 E Calle Herculo
Tucson AZ 85710

Call Sign: W7LOQ
Thomas F Whitehead
7021 E Calle Hermosa
Tucson AZ 85715

Call Sign: W7HUO
John P Kelsey

4960 E Calle Jabali
Tucson AZ 85711

Call Sign: WD8LMN
John F Didham
9244 E Calle Kuehn
Tucson AZ 85715

Call Sign: KA7TYN
Harvey E Gussow
E Calle La Paz
Tucson AZ 85715

Call Sign: KF7UNW
Brian N Webb
2224 E Calle Los Altos
Tucson AZ 85718

Call Sign: N6AG
Arthur R Gillentine
2350 E Calle Los Altos
Tucson AZ 857182065

Call Sign: W7SWL
Robert J Coomler
7322 E Calle Los Arboles
Tucson AZ 85750

Call Sign: KC2TX
Spencer F Ritchie
6302 E Calle Luna
Tucson AZ 85710

Call Sign: N7ZD
Espee Dx Association
6302 E Calle Luna
Tucson AZ 85710

Call Sign: KD7YLZ
James H Russell
6310 E Calle Luna
Tucson AZ 85710

Call Sign: KA7KTI
Lawrence T Diehl Jr
6614 E Calle Luna
Tucson AZ 85710

Call Sign: KK7TI

Cheryl A Fitzwater
7433 E Calle Maicoba
Tucson AZ 85710

Call Sign: KE7VTU
Ronald L Edwards
7442 E Calle Maicoba
Tucson AZ 85710

Call Sign: KC7FSB
George D Ross
6958 E Calle Neptuno
Tucson AZ 85710

Call Sign: KD7PZT
Michael J Comeau
10600 E Calle Nopalito
Tucson AZ 85748

Call Sign: KA2IMD
Kristopher Peterson
10641 E Calle Nopalito
Tucson AZ 85748

Call Sign: N2DXC
Raymond Peterson
10642 E Calle Nopalito
Tucson AZ 85748

Call Sign: KF7EAQ
Foster E Powers
10681 E Calle Nopalito
Tucson AZ 85748

Call Sign: KE7VSJ
Miriam B Fawcett
10681 E Calle Nopalito
Tucson AZ 85748

Call Sign: KE7FBO
Sean W Fawcett
10681 E Calle Nopalito
Tucson AZ 85748

Call Sign: KN2SNC
Sean W Fawcett
10681 E Calle Nopalito
Tucson AZ 85748

Call Sign: WA0GUF
William R Clark
6100 E Calle Ojos Verde
Tucson AZ 857501945

Call Sign: KF7NRN
Gerald M Melino
7018 E Calle Orion
Tucson AZ 85710

Call Sign: W9AGT
Michael S Kroot
7441 E Calle Perpetuo
Tucson AZ 857152809

Call Sign: KF7OYV
John B Witter
9036 E Calle Playa
Tucson AZ 85715

Call Sign: NV7M
Richard S Sparrold
9045 E Calle Playa
Tucson AZ 85715

Call Sign: KE7VKF
Alan I Levenson
75 E Calle Resplendor
Tucson AZ 85716

Call Sign: KF7IGQ
Marco A Vidal
2402 E Calle Sierra Del
Manantial
Tucson AZ 85706

Call Sign: W6TGC
Stephen G Brown
2432 E Calle Sin
Controversia
Tucson AZ 85718

Call Sign: KF7CUG
Tanque Verde Contest Club
12589 E Calle Tango
Tucson AZ 85749

Call Sign: W7XI
Tanque Verde Contest Club

12589 E Calle Tango
Tucson AZ 85749

Call Sign: W9TWM
Carole A Wothe
12589 E Calle Tango
Tucson AZ 85749

Call Sign: W9TWM
Clifford W Andersen
12589 E Calle Tango
Tucson AZ 85749

Call Sign: W6XI
Jerry D Wothe
12589 E Calle Tango
Tucson AZ 85749

Call Sign: WB7B
James M Jacobs
12581 E Calle Tatita
Tucson AZ 85749

Call Sign: KG7IZ
Qro Dx Club
12581 E Calle Tatita
Tucson AZ 85749

Call Sign: KE7EGS
Jerry A Hain
12661 E Calle Tatita
Tucson AZ 85749

Call Sign: KE7AUL
Sean M Vanover
255 E Calle Zafiro
Tucson AZ 85704

Call Sign: KA4TKQ
Antonio T Watkins
7620 E Callisto Cir 109
Tucson AZ 85715

Call Sign: KF7ISZ
Michael J Curley
1545 E Camino Cielo
Tucson AZ 85718

Call Sign: KJ7OG

L Stephen Bell
1702 E Camino Cielo
Tucson AZ 85718

Call Sign: KC7POL
John W Manka
4579 E Camino De Cancon
Tucson AZ 85718

Call Sign: KC7POJ
Eileen R Stamer
4579 E Camino De Cancun
Tucson AZ 85718

Call Sign: KC7GPM
James B Gillis
725 E Camino De Los Padres
Tucson AZ 85718

Call Sign: KD7CGR
Tracy J Castell
3907 E Camino De Palmas
Tucson AZ 85711

Call Sign: N0RSE
Jim D Goedhart
11544 E Camino Del
Desierto
Tucson AZ 85747

Call Sign: KE7PMH
Deblen C Oke
10332 E Camino Dela Placita
Tucson AZ 85748

Call Sign: K7ISJ
Deblen C Oke
10332 E Camino Dela Placita
Tucson AZ 85748

Call Sign: KC4KGF
John D Wey Jr
1123 E Camino Diestro
Tucson AZ 85704

Call Sign: N6FLL
Mary Luke
1212 E Camino Diestro
Tucson AZ 85737

Call Sign: N7OBX
Warren B Johnson
11060 E Camino Mira Monte
Tucson AZ 85749

Call Sign: KD7WXU
Charles N Cardinell
10901 E Camino Miramonte
Tucson AZ 85749

Call Sign: KD7WCE
Charles S Cardinell
10901 E Camino Miramonte
Tucson AZ 85749

Call Sign: KD7VGI
Elena Cardinell
10901 E Camino Miramonte
Tucson AZ 85749

Call Sign: WB0UEH
Ronald J Ash
10991 E Camino Miramonte
Tucson AZ 857158765

Call Sign: N7CFV
Curtis E Brewington
7741 E Camino Montaraz
Tucson AZ 85715

Call Sign: KE7ZZU
Michael T Kidd
10535 E Camino Quince
Tucson AZ 85748

Call Sign: KE7IIZ
Christina S Grossman
2231 E Camino Rio
Tucson AZ 85718

Call Sign: KD7JVI
Matthew J Grossman
2231 E Camino Rio
Tucson AZ 85718

Call Sign: KD7JBO
Rita A Mc Farlin
7060 E Camino Tenerife

Tucson AZ 85715

Call Sign: KY7P
Charles M Kearns
7239 E Camino Vecino
Tucson AZ 85715

Call Sign: KD9JM
Oscar J Tuttle
65445 E Canyon Dr
Tucson AZ 85739

Call Sign: K6SJS
Stanley J Strebig
65510 E Canyon Dr
Tucson AZ 85739

Call Sign: KF7FTU
Brian J Boll
10174 E Canyon Meadow Dr
Tucson AZ 85747

Call Sign: KF7QQH
Michael B Deyoung
575 E Canyon View Dr
Tucson AZ 85704

Call Sign: KC6WFU
Jeffrey L Vollin
580 E Canyon View Dr
Tucson AZ 85704

Call Sign: WD6N
Carl C Pitts
12431 E Cape Horn Dr
Tucson AZ 857499103

Call Sign: KB6EKY
Gail C Pitts
12431 E Cape Horn Dr
Tucson AZ 857499103

Call Sign: W7AQK
Thomas D Yarnes
12630 E Cape Horn Dr
Tucson AZ 85749

Call Sign: KE7ODY
Brandon W Holman

9269 E Carmel Dr
Tucson AZ 85747

Call Sign: KE3HF
David A Holman
9269 E Carmel Dr
Tucson AZ 85747

Call Sign: AC7DS
David A Holman
9269 E Carmel Dr
Tucson AZ 85747

Call Sign: N6VPY
Douglas S Richmond
9332 E Carmel Dr
Tucson AZ 85747

Call Sign: N3QVK
Brenda P Holman
9269 E Carmel Dr
Tucson AZ 85747

Call Sign: N3UTF
Mark R Bowles
9318 E Carmel Dr
Tucson AZ 85747

Call Sign: KC5TMI
William D Tanksley
10508 E Carolina Willow Ln
Tucson AZ 85747

Call Sign: KB7RHV
Daniel O Howard
6653 E Carondelet Dr 317
Tucson AZ 85710

Call Sign: N6LUV
Camille T Sweet
6770 E Carondelet Dr Apt
118
Tucson AZ 857102134

Call Sign: WB5RZJ
Merlin J Benningfield II
63451 E Cat Claw Ln
Tucson AZ 85739

Call Sign: KD5BJS
Julie R Benningfield
63451 E Cat Claw Ln
Tucson AZ 85739

Call Sign: KD7CYW
Wendy E Niehaus
9055 E Catalina Hwy 18203
Tucson AZ 85749

Call Sign: KB7ZBP
Victor Shdanov
4882 E Cecelia
Tucson AZ 85711

Call Sign: KE7YTE
Thomas L Andrews
10385 E Cele Peterson Ln
Tucson AZ 85747

Call Sign: KF7JYX
K Robert P Klug
2421 E Cerrada De Promesa
Tucson AZ 85718

Call Sign: NA6AF
K Robert P Klug
2421 E Cerrada De Promesa
Tucson AZ 85718

Call Sign: KF7IYK
Kevin J Klug
2421 E Cerrada De Promesa
Tucson AZ 85718

Call Sign: KD7VGL
Tyler L Kilian
2100 E Cerrado Brio
Tucson AZ 85718

Call Sign: W7FF
James E Swafford
8951 E Chauncey St
Tucson AZ 85715

Call Sign: KB7INH
Maria T Swafford
8951 E Chauncey St
Tucson AZ 85715

Call Sign: KE7VKP
Tyler A Cornell
11235 E Chuckwagon Cir
Tucson AZ 85749

Call Sign: N7EDM
Bruce E Coddington
12575 E Chukut Tr
Tucson AZ 85749

Call Sign: KF7UBA
John T Rompel
1131 E Chula Vista Rd
Tucson AZ 85718

Call Sign: WB7PUY
James R Taylor
1805 E Chula Vista Rd
Tucson AZ 85718

Call Sign: WA8HUL
Bruce E Wilson
2130 E Circulo Solaz
Tucson AZ 85718

Call Sign: KE7SGF
Stanley C Ross
9852 E Cisco Ct
Tucson AZ 85748

Call Sign: KD7QHE
David E Hill
9895 E Cisco Ct
Tucson AZ 85748

Call Sign: W0HTM
David E Hill
9895 E Cisco Ct
Tucson AZ 85748

Call Sign: WB7DTX
Gordon C Kordas
7759 E Clarence Pl
Tucson AZ 857154508

Call Sign: KE7WIN
Nancy L Florez
7262 E Clayridge

Tucson AZ 85750

Call Sign: KT7D
Michael N Parker
8525 E Cloud Rd
Tucson AZ 85750

Call Sign: KD7LHM
Teodoro L Rodriguez
2918 E Coconino Vista
Tucson AZ 85713

Call Sign: K7MUF
Lee R Kerr
2933 E Coconino Vista
Tucson AZ 85713

Call Sign: KC7LUS
Daniel D Kaufman
7913 E Colette Cir 43
Tucson AZ 85710

Call Sign: WA7CSN
Theodore G Smith Jr
8124 E Colette Pl
Tucson AZ 85710

Call Sign: N7RMF
Lawrence B Allan
8358 E Colette St
Tucson AZ 85710

Call Sign: KF7JYZ
Angela K Schilb
8432 E Colette St
Tucson AZ 85710

Call Sign: W9VHN
Dennis N Widdows
9658 E Colette St
Tucson AZ 85748

Call Sign: KC7FNM
Wallace E Burlingame
E Colette St
Tucson AZ 85710

Call Sign: KC7EDZ
Larry R Mc Whorter

3701 E Columbia
Tucson AZ 85714

Call Sign: KJ7UM
Grayson W Evans
10355 E Conservation Ln
Tucson AZ 85747

Call Sign: W7QBG
Stephen T Portell
4065 E Cooper St
Tucson AZ 85711

Call Sign: KD7CGO
Guy K Mc Arthur
4145 E Cooper St
Tucson AZ 85714

Call Sign: N7OPZ
John H Putney
5751 E Cooper St
Tucson AZ 85711

Call Sign: AF4JT
Robert B Gillette
3900 E Coronado Sunset Dr
Tucson AZ 85739

Call Sign: WA7LLB
Thomas H Merrill
415 E Coronard Sp 31
Tucson AZ 857067571

Call Sign: K8MUF
Henry N Testa Jr
9672 E Corte Arcos Del Sol
Tucson AZ 85748

Call Sign: KD6DIY
Richard A Peck
9180 E Corte Arroyo Oeste
Tucson AZ 85710

Call Sign: KK5OH
Charles E Noe
8771 E Corte Caida Del Sol
Tucson AZ 85715

Call Sign: W7LTL

John R Sundberg
5451 E Craycroft Cir
Tucson AZ 85718

Call Sign: KR8A
Arlo B Brakel
7541 E Crested Saguaro Pl
Tucson AZ 85750

Call Sign: KC7FNL
Ron A Foster
2627 E Crosby Vista
Tucson AZ 85713

Call Sign: W2UNV
Gordon W Daniels
826 E Crown Ridge Dr
Tucson AZ 85737

Call Sign: KD7CNV
A Lee Seidler
2610 E Croyden St
Tucson AZ 857165502

Call Sign: KE7QIE
Deborah L Heilig
10173 E Danbury Pl
Tucson AZ 85748

Call Sign: N7SCG
Mark A Paye
6396 E David Dr
Tucson AZ 85730

Call Sign: KC7EYW
Robert J Mitchell
6616 E David Dr
Tucson AZ 85730

Call Sign: KB7ZKQ
Terrence L Brown
6625 E David Dr
Tucson AZ 85730

Call Sign: N3LBX
James S Van Scoyk
7512 E David Dr
Tucson AZ 857301809

Call Sign: KD7OR
Herbert C Breckon
7760 E David Dr
Tucson AZ 85730

Call Sign: KA4RCJ
Donald J Benchoff
1701 E Deer Hollow Loop
Tucson AZ 87537

Call Sign: KC7DVH
Jeanette G Davis
1773 E Deer Hollow Loop
Tucson AZ 85737

Call Sign: KD7SPY
Steven J Anderson
470 E Deers Rest Pl
Tucson AZ 85704

Call Sign: KC7GPN
Paul J Dounn
9942 E Desert Aire
Tucson AZ 85730

Call Sign: KE7VJU
John W Bradfield
8874 E Desert Lavender
Tucson AZ 85715

Call Sign: KF7KF
Thomas A Bunner
8581 E Desert Palm St
Tucson AZ 85730

Call Sign: KB7DQZ
Virginia K Hess
63646 E Desert Peak Dr
Tucson AZ 85739

Call Sign: KA2REZ
Robert L Perez
65187 E Desert Sands Ct
Tucson AZ 857391509

Call Sign: NY7Y
Harold W Deppe
8661 E Desert Spring St
Tucson AZ 85730

Call Sign: KB7SLH
Robert P Hubbard
8520 E Desert Steppes Dr
Tucson AZ 85710

Call Sign: KF7IZH
Aida Lacarra
4842 E Desert Thorn Dr
Tucson AZ 85756

Call Sign: K7HEY
Aida Lacarra
4842 E Desert Thorn Dr
Tucson AZ 85756

Call Sign: WA7WYV
Andrew J Griffith
3926 E Desmond Ln
Tucson AZ 85712

Call Sign: KC7INZ
Ione I Bishop
8721 E Dexter Dr
Tucson AZ 85715

Call Sign: KC7INQ
Walker K Bishop
8721 E Dexter Dr
Tucson AZ 85715

Call Sign: WA7MSK
Larry C Wilson
3818 E Diablo Canyon
Tucson AZ 857182305

Call Sign: NK7E
Larry C Wilson
3818 E Diablo Canyon
Tucson AZ 857182305

Call Sign: KD7IEZ
Joseph D Branson
3880 E Diablo Canyon Pl
Tucson AZ 85718

Call Sign: KF7XR
Richard G Molchan
6097 E Diablo Sunrise Rd

Tucson AZ 85706

Call Sign: WA7MOW
Harrison A Berger
6771 E Dorado Ct
Tucson AZ 85715

Call Sign: N7ED
Edward Murphy
6789 E Dorado Ct
Tucson AZ 85715

Call Sign: KB7YRK
Martin P Pokorny
497 E Downtown St
Tucson AZ 85701

Call Sign: KB1DVJ
Alexander E Murphy
2514 E Drachman St
Tucson AZ 857163848

Call Sign: KD7TII
Raza K Lodhi
1201 E Drachman St Apt 143
Tucson AZ 85719

Call Sign: W0PGC
William R Tickner
8842 E Driftwood Tr
Tucson AZ 85749

Call Sign: KE7CVC
Andrea Zuccolo
1315 E Duke Dr
Tucson AZ 85719

Call Sign: N5GFR
Brian J Mc Clung
8614 E Dunbar Way
Tucson AZ 85747

Call Sign: KD7RHF
Laura A Zumwalde
9546 E Dunnigan Dr
Tucson AZ 85747

Call Sign: KE6DLY
Thomas W Zumwalde

9546 E Dunnigan St
Tucson AZ 857471920

Call Sign: KE7YTF
Robert B Frett Jr
8778 E Eagle Creek Dr
Tucson AZ 85730

Call Sign: K2ENN
Michael I Neidich
60917 E Eagle Heights Dr
Tucson AZ 85739

Call Sign: N7JKI
Robert R Durand
4333 E Eastland
Tucson AZ 85711

Call Sign: KA7WSE
Stuart H Hancock
4809 E Eastland
Tucson AZ 85711

Call Sign: W7SWN
Arthur Davison
4874 E Eastland
Tucson AZ 85711

Call Sign: WB7VMY
Marvin Roesch
5734 E Eastland
Tucson AZ 85711

Call Sign: WB5VHZ
Charles E Abernethy
956 E Edison St
Tucson AZ 85719

Call Sign: K7KYP
David L Middleton
1387 E Edison St
Tucson AZ 85719

Call Sign: KD7QHF
Jill L Carrigg
1387 E Edison St
Tucson AZ 85719

Call Sign: W9OSN

James C Noonan
2015 E Edison St
Tucson AZ 85719

Call Sign: AA7WA
Scott E Spickard
3726 E Edison St
Tucson AZ 85716

Call Sign: WT7P
Charles N Edwards Sr
7535 E Edison St
Tucson AZ 85715

Call Sign: N7ZQW
Grayce B Edwards
7535 E Edison St
Tucson AZ 85715

Call Sign: K7IZ
David S Eckert
7661 E Edison St
Tucson AZ 85715

Call Sign: N7SMU
Donald K Iozia
10312 E Edna Pl
Tucson AZ 85748

Call Sign: KC7FXI
Erich K Kehl
9402 E El Cajon Dr
Tucson AZ 85710

Call Sign: KC7FNA
Leroy E Kehl
9402 E El Cajon Dr
Tucson AZ 85710

Call Sign: KG7XH
Melody D Kehl
9402 E El Cajon Dr
Tucson AZ 85710

Call Sign: KC7FXL
Karla D Weeks
9402 E El Cajon Dr
Tucson AZ 85710

Call Sign: KB7RVC
Robert J Kemp
3326 E El Tovar Ave
Tucson AZ 85705

Call Sign: KF7DYW
Marcia M Burcham
7025 E Elbow Bay Dr
Tucson AZ 85710

Call Sign: KD7KEQ
Randall C Burcham
7025 E Elbow Bay Dr
Tucson AZ 85710

Call Sign: KC5VCW
Brendon R Holt
9102 E Elderberry St
Tucson AZ 85747

Call Sign: K0JFR
Raymond V Bishop
8508 E Eli Sreet
Tucson AZ 85710

Call Sign: KD7OVU
David C Dean
6041 E Eli St
Tucson AZ 85711

Call Sign: W7KDT
Marion L Parrish
27861 E Elida
Tucson AZ 85715

Call Sign: KC7HVA
Durward S Dragger
3627 E Elida St
Tucson AZ 85716

Call Sign: KE7VTK
Phillip Gutt
7744 E Elk Creek Rd
Tucson AZ 85750

Call Sign: WB7FAO
Clyde B Bornhurst
1259 E Ellis St
Tucson AZ 85719

Call Sign: KA6DTY
Peter G Schmerl
1428 E Elm St
Tucson AZ 85719

Call Sign: WF7S
William L Dalrymple
9650 E Elmtree Cir
Tucson AZ 85749

Call Sign: K6OVF
John W Montgomery
4026 E Elmwood St
Tucson AZ 85711

Call Sign: AC7IL
Matthew J Grossman
10020 E English Woods Rd
Tucson AZ 85748

Call Sign: KF7IGU
Rolland J Sicard
10072 E Eric Alan Pl
Tucson AZ 85748

Call Sign: KW7RS
Rolland J Sicard
10072 E Eric Alan Pl
Tucson AZ 85748

Call Sign: KA6AUY
John R Wood
8989 E Escalante 255
Tucson AZ 857302899

Call Sign: N5PZ
Thomas R Plunkett
8989 E Escalante Rd 208
Tucson AZ 85730

Call Sign: W0PSN
Donald L Krentzel
8989 E Escalente
Tucson AZ 85730

Call Sign: KC7JWO
Richard E White
8131 E Estes Ln

Tucson AZ 85710

Call Sign: WB6NXM
Ray L Miles
9987 E Eugenia
Tucson AZ 85730

Call Sign: N0UCT
Heinz P Wasielewski
9959 E Eugenia Dr
Tucson AZ 85730

Call Sign: KA7MSN
Nancy J Miles
9987 E Eugenia Dr
Tucson AZ 85730

Call Sign: KB7RF
Roy H Martens
9959 E Eugenia Dr
Tucson AZ 85730

Call Sign: KF7EAN
Victoria Omori
2733 E Exeter St
Tucson AZ 85716

Call Sign: KC7QYE
Kenneth L Mc Daniel
5432 E Fairmont
Tucson AZ 85712

Call Sign: KC7CLZ
Nancy A Rogers
3728 E Fairmount
Tucson AZ 85716

Call Sign: KB7CI
Norman A Buck
5656 E Fairmount
Tucson AZ 85712

Call Sign: KD6GPN
David C Kinn
3402 E Fairmount 16
Tucson AZ 85712

Call Sign: KB0BYV
Randal Wasser

8888 E Fairway Groves Dr
Tucson AZ 857308751

Call Sign: KF7LRG
Thomas W Quigley
6020 E Fangio Pl
Tucson AZ 85750

Call Sign: KA7UKF
Trever S Brown
5824 E Farmridge Dr
Tucson AZ 85706

Call Sign: KC6VLE
Mark A Varney
5906 E Farmstead
Tucson AZ 857069788

Call Sign: N2FM
Mark A Varney
5906 E Farmstead
Tucson AZ 857069788

Call Sign: KC6ZRQ
Gina L Gershwin Varney
5906 E Farmstead Dr
Tucson AZ 857569788

Call Sign: KD7CRC
Kenneth F Block
270 E Fieldcrest Ln
Tucson AZ 85937

Call Sign: KF7TUE
Richard L Transue II
3726 E Fjord Pony Rd
Tucson AZ 85739

Call Sign: KF7SAQ
John T Rompel Jr
10461 E Flintlock Trl
Tucson AZ 85749

Call Sign: KE7VTQ
Thomas F Luckow
4790 E Flower
Tucson AZ 85712

Call Sign: KI6BAQ

Richard H Stevenson
62710 E Flower Ridge Dr
Tucson AZ 85739

Call Sign: WA7RWY
George D Shaffer
8517 E Fond Du Lac Dr
Tucson AZ 85730

Call Sign: WA2UCZ
Ronald Gould
5950 E Fort Crittendon Trl
Tucson AZ 85750

Call Sign: KB7JPL
Roy A Schneider
5950 E Fort Crittendon Trl
Tucson AZ 85750

Call Sign: KD7ZGP
Mona L Johnson
1515 E Fort Lowell Rd
Tucson AZ 85719

Call Sign: AA7UB
Robert E Lintner
3374 E Fort Lowell Rd
Tucson AZ 85716

Call Sign: WB6EGJ
Paul E Clinco
5495 E Fort Lowell Rd
Tucson AZ 85712

Call Sign: KF7EAK
Patrick F Gallagher
10700 E Fort Lowell Rd
Tucson AZ 85749

Call Sign: N0EWZ
Bruce N Jenks
4840 E Fort Lowell Rd Unit
G
Tucson AZ 857121264

Call Sign: W7LBW
John D Rather IV
7019 E Fox Sparrow Pl
Tucson AZ 857500933

Call Sign: W6SWE
Robert D Nielsen
7050 E Fox Sparrow Pl
Tucson AZ 85715

Call Sign: N7UBM
Stephen Y Felker
10225 E Foxmoor Dr
Tucson AZ 85748

Call Sign: KC7KMK
Claude J Owen
10273 E Foxmoor Dr
Tucson AZ 85748

Call Sign: KB4YD
Kenneth E Barry
1505 E Frazier
Tucson AZ 85706

Call Sign: KC7EVR
David J Repath
445 E Ft Lowell 17
Tucson AZ 85705

Call Sign: N7APT
Larry C Martin
8030 E Ft Lowell Rd
Tucson AZ 85715

Call Sign: KE7WIW
George F Herget
8156 E Galinda Dr
Tucson AZ 85750

Call Sign: N2LUQ
Patricia K Scott
64339 E Galveston Ln
Tucson AZ 85739

Call Sign: N2LUR
Stuart D Scott Jr
64339 E Galveston Ln
Tucson AZ 85739

Call Sign: KC7WTM
Kenneth C Salber
7201 E Gambel Cir

Tucson AZ 85750

Call Sign: WB6FIH
Donald K Knight
1590 E Ganymede Dr
Tucson AZ 85704

Call Sign: KB7ISR
David A Mason II
3621 E Garden St
Tucson AZ 85713

Call Sign: N7JXA
Dennis E Hoyt
8656 E Getsinger Ln
Tucson AZ 85747

Call Sign: KB7TVO
Warren E Faidley Jr
6598 E Ghost Flower Dr
Tucson AZ 85715

Call Sign: W7MHC
Allan W Hoskins
3590 E Gibbon Mt Pl
Tucson AZ 85718

Call Sign: WB5OAO
James C Harris
1038 E Gifford Dr
Tucson AZ 85719

Call Sign: KB2TJR
Anthony F Demma
9018 E Glenmont Dr
Tucson AZ 85730

Call Sign: N7KCD
Michael C Schmitt
3635 E Glenn E3
Tucson AZ 85716

Call Sign: KA7YSZ
Earl J Horley
832 E Glenn St
Tucson AZ 85719

Call Sign: W6KYL
Michael P Higgins

1540 E Glenn St
Tucson AZ 85719

Call Sign: W7IOE
Elver G Grimm Sr
3126 E Glenn St
Tucson AZ 85716

Call Sign: KE7CVE
Brian R Walker
3635 E Glenn St F4
Tucson AZ 85716

Call Sign: N7CRS
Saul M Chorost
64255 E Golden Spur Ct
Tucson AZ 857391030

Call Sign: K7INO
Kino School ARC
11445 E Golf Links
Tucson AZ 85730

Call Sign: KF7MQK
Peter Philippe
9420 E Golf Links 140
Tucson AZ 85730

Call Sign: W3TUC
Peter Philippe
9420 E Golf Links 140
Tucson AZ 85730

Call Sign: WE7DOG
Stanley C Ross
9420 E Golf Links 226
Tucson AZ 85730

Call Sign: KB1MDO
Steven F Krause
6091 E Golf Links Apt 3
Tucson AZ 85711

Call Sign: KC7KKW
Robert L Carnevale
7400 E Golf Links Rd
Tucson AZ 85730

Call Sign: N2MGL

Joel M Statkevicus
11538 E Golf Links Rd
Tucson AZ 85730

Call Sign: K3TYE
Joseph R Statkevicus
11538 E Golf Links Rd
Tucson AZ 85730

Call Sign: KC7ANT
Craig E Simons
6710 E Golf Links Rd 2080
Tucson AZ 85730

Call Sign: KD7WNH
Jennifer R Rehwinkle
6450 E Golf Links Rd Nr
2114
Tucson AZ 85730

Call Sign: NH6IE
Ernest T Cabuslay
6502 E Golf Links Rd Nr 234
Tucson AZ 85730

Call Sign: KB7ZVV
Robert E Fee
4501 E Grant
Tucson AZ 85712

Call Sign: KB7HFO
Jacqueline L Lieberman
3938 E Grant Rd 138
Tucson AZ 85712

Call Sign: KD6NN
Stanley Lieberman
3939 E Grant Rd 138
Tucson AZ 85712

Call Sign: KD7AL
John L Zeigler
5000 E Grant Rd 159
Tucson AZ 85712

Call Sign: KB7FDB
Lloyd R Smith Sr
6161 E Grant Rd 1605
Tucson AZ 85712

Call Sign: W9EFP
Bernard E Mayer
5000 E Grant Rd 43
Tucson AZ 857122753

Call Sign: KA7UYF
Delbert G Sutton
5000 E Grant Rd 80
Tucson AZ 85712

Call Sign: KF7SEB
Thomas M Kelly Jr
6161 E Grant Rd Apt 16206
Tucson AZ 85712

Call Sign: N7UBL
Richard J Toups
5000 E Grant Rd Sp 31
Tucson AZ 85712

Call Sign: KD6YUH
Sharon C Smalley
4951 E Grant Rd Ste 105 247
Tucson AZ 85712

Call Sign: KI7GS
William L Olson
925 E Grass Meadow Pl
Tucson AZ 85737

Call Sign: KF7CNJ
Paul H Comins Jr
8650 E Green Acres Dr
Tucson AZ 85715

Call Sign: W1GHF
Paul H Comins Jr
8650 E Green Acres Dr
Tucson AZ 85715

Call Sign: N7DGO
Frank A Kandt Jr
64255 E Greenbelt Ln
Tucson AZ 85739

Call Sign: N7FKT
Maxine G Kandt
64255 E Greenbelt Ln

Tucson AZ 85739

Call Sign: WX9H
Ronald C Melzer
63737 E Greenbelt Ln
Tucson AZ 857391244

Call Sign: W7DME
Richard W Oaks
2530 E Greenlee Pl
Tucson AZ 85716

Call Sign: W7JGU
Clement K Chase
1351 E Greenlee Rd
Tucson AZ 85719

Call Sign: KB7QLM
Kent L Ardle
3202 E Greenlee Rd 82
Tucson AZ 85716

Call Sign: K7EVZ
Cecil L Buchanan
3919 E Guayman Pl
Tucson AZ 857111925

Call Sign: K7KZE
James C Buchanan
3920 E Guaymas Pl
Tucson AZ 85711

Call Sign: WB7WLS
William W Hempel Jr
11420 E Gunsmith Dr
Tucson AZ 85749

Call Sign: KE7BPY
Samuel K Horner
3739 E Guthrie Mountain Pl
Tucson AZ 85718

Call Sign: KB7YPQ
Mark A Templin
430 E Hadley St
Tucson AZ 85705

Call Sign: KD7GQE
Matthew J O'Brien

802 E Halcyon Rd
Tucson AZ 85719

Call Sign: N7GAI
Ellen L Price
821 E Halcyon Rd
Tucson AZ 85719

Call Sign: N7BPH
Leila S Gillette
821 E Halcyon Rd
Tucson AZ 85719

Call Sign: WD9BEH
Randall L Pierson
1059 E Halcyon Rd
Tucson AZ 85719

Call Sign: KC7ZYK
William Casey Townsend
6002 E Hampton St
Tucson AZ 85712

Call Sign: KA7ZES
Dennis H Cowsky
6122 E Hampton St
Tucson AZ 85712

Call Sign: KA4CBK
Robert J Johnson
5666 E Hampton St
Tucson AZ 857122926

Call Sign: KF7OHM
William T Reitze
1104 E Hampton St Apt A
Tucson AZ 85719

Call Sign: WB7OSY
George W King
2917 E Hardy
Tucson AZ 85716

Call Sign: KA7CKS
John A Cramer
3241 E Hardy Pl
Tucson AZ 85716

Call Sign: KD7LVH

409Th Asa Hogs On Amateur
Radio
3241 E Hardy Pl
Tucson AZ 85716

Call Sign: N7ASA
409Th Asa Hogs On Amateur
Radio
3241 E Hardy Pl
Tucson AZ 85716

Call Sign: WA9QYC
James A Jindrick
9455 E Harrison Park Dr
Tucson AZ 85749

Call Sign: KC7BN
Lee H Brown
4245 E Havasu Rd
Tucson AZ 85718

Call Sign: KD7KJY
Barry M Tucker
4413 E Haven Ln
Tucson AZ 85712

Call Sign: KC7PGQ
Dale A Slaughter
3840 E Hawser St Apt 1
Tucson AZ 85739

Call Sign: KC7NYV
Christopher A Lewicki
2128 E Hawthorne St
Tucson AZ 857194938

Call Sign: KA7ZTX
Charles T Morriss
2222 E Hawthorne St
Tucson AZ 857194940

Call Sign: KD7QWC
Michael L Gavelek
4158 E Hawthorne St
Tucson AZ 85719

Call Sign: KC7JWG
James B De Veny
5307 E Hawthorne St

Tucson AZ 85711

Call Sign: KC7JWK
Maureen M De Veny
5307 E Hawthorne St
Tucson AZ 85711

Call Sign: W7PEY
Nathaniel W Mc Kelvey
5901 E Hawthorne St
Tucson AZ 85711

Call Sign: KC7POC
Susan D Dick
5948 E Hawthorne St
Tucson AZ 85711

Call Sign: N7EKT
Harold B Wetzel
7735 E Hawthorne St
Tucson AZ 85710

Call Sign: NX7KL
Dirk Den Baars
6318 E Hayne St
Tucson AZ 85710

Call Sign: W9ZKE
Edward H Roland
1128 E Hedrick Dr
Tucson AZ 85719

Call Sign: KI7BA
V Alexander S Mc Cord
2202 E Hedrick Dr
Tucson AZ 85719

Call Sign: KC7PLR
Nathan E Van Den Berg
802 E Hedrick Dr Unit A
Tucson AZ 85719

Call Sign: KC7TZS
Edward E Davis
2228 E Helen St
Tucson AZ 85719

Call Sign: KC7UIG
Eleanor M Davis

2228 E Helen St
Tucson AZ 85719

Call Sign: KE7TAY
Seymour Shapiro
4826 E Helen St
Tucson AZ 85712

Call Sign: KA5NNO
Terry J Erisman
5817 E Helen St
Tucson AZ 85712

Call Sign: WA7IHM
Duane B Miller
9021 E Henry Pl
Tucson AZ 85710

Call Sign: KC7HGW
Shawn L Schroeder
5550 E Hermans Rd
Tucson AZ 85706

Call Sign: KF7VDW
Daniel F Smith
9334 E Hermosa Hills Dr
Tucson AZ 85710

Call Sign: N7THV
Ali E Guvenoz
7801 E Highview Pl
Tucson AZ 85715

Call Sign: KF4HOJ
James M Gampper
12261 E Hill Crest Cir
Tucson AZ 85747

Call Sign: KA7SGH
Joshua J Tofield
5221 E Hill Place Dr
Tucson AZ 85712

Call Sign: KC5DWB
Robert E O Connell
370 E Hillcrest Pl
Tucson AZ 85704

Call Sign: KF7EMD

Keith P Arnold
8370 E Hillwood Ct
Tucson AZ 85750

Call Sign: KE7KA
Keith P Arnold
8370 E Hillwood Ct
Tucson AZ 85750

Call Sign: KV7B
Daniel Morrison
4301 E Holmes
Tucson AZ 85711

Call Sign: KV7D
Margaret S Morrison
4301 E Holmes
Tucson AZ 85711

Call Sign: KB7JAQ
Charles S Henning
4411 E Holmes St
Tucson AZ 85711

Call Sign: KF7EZJ
Robert A Henning
4411 E Holmes St
Tucson AZ 85711

Call Sign: KE7KSH
James W Franklin
9002 E Holmes St
Tucson AZ 857103033

Call Sign: K4TMJ
James W Franklin
9002 E Holmes St
Tucson AZ 857103033

Call Sign: N4JZD
Albert J Banks Jr
3831 E Hopseed Ln
Tucson AZ 85718

Call Sign: KE7VKD
Frederick C Schroder
9161 E Indian Canyon Rd
Tucson AZ 85749

Call Sign: KQ6WJ
Raymond Z Villalobos
9282 E Indio Pl
Tucson AZ 85749

Call Sign: KC7KNZ
Kevin C Abercrombie
1527 E Iowa Dr
Tucson AZ 85706

Call Sign: KA7WXI
Benjamin J Venema
2004 E Irvington 91
Tucson AZ 85714

Call Sign: KC7HNG
Megan M Milam
2004 E Irvington Box 310
Tucson AZ 85714

Call Sign: N7BZY
Alton F Harrison Sr
2004 E Irvington Rd
Tucson AZ 85714

Call Sign: KK7JJ
Dale F Regelman
11200 E Irvington Rd
Tucson AZ 85747

Call Sign: KE7WIV
Jerry B Simmons
11670 E Irvington Rd
Tucson AZ 85747

Call Sign: KE7WJF
Wayne P Coyne
2004 E Irvington Rd 104
Tucson AZ 85714

Call Sign: KC7OPH
Sharon E Miller
9855 E Irvington Rd 271
Tucson AZ 85730

Call Sign: KE7ID
Arnold G Miller
9855 E Irvington Rd 271
Tucson AZ 85730

Call Sign: KF7ODM
William R Miller
1340 E Ishtaria Pl
Tucson AZ 85737

Call Sign: AE7MD
William R Miller
1340 E Ishtaria Pl
Tucson AZ 85737

Call Sign: N7WBT
William C Seligman
8800 E Jacaranda Way
Tucson AZ 85749

Call Sign: N7OTR
William B Baxter
402 E Jacinto St
Tucson AZ 85705

Call Sign: WA6UAR
John E Leonard Jr
6991 E Jagged Canyon Pl
Tucson AZ 857506196

Call Sign: K7UAZ
University Of Arizona ARC
1127 E James E Rogers Way
Rm 303
Tucson AZ 85721

Call Sign: KF7IYL
Diana C Knyazeva
12030 E Jefsumark Cir
Tucson AZ 85749

Call Sign: KF7LIL
Diana C Knyazeva
12030 E Jefsumark Cir
Tucson AZ 85749

Call Sign: K7ZBG
William P Gorman
8005 E Jennifer Anne Dr
Tucson AZ 85730

Call Sign: KC7IOD
Keith W Everill

508 E Joan St
Tucson AZ 85705

Call Sign: N7UTU
Eric L Vastine
10577 E John Mcnair Pl
Tucson AZ 85747

Call Sign: W4WXB
George L Hafkemeyer
7840 E Joshua Pl
Tucson AZ 85730

Call Sign: KR7N
Bonal Downing
5931 E Juarez
Tucson AZ 85711

Call Sign: KB7JFJ
John H Hauschildt
3973 E Justin Ln
Tucson AZ 85712

Call Sign: KI4CHU
Timothy R Medeiros
5455 E Kachina St Unit 312
Tucson AZ 85707

Call Sign: KB7ZBH
Robert H Buecher
7050 E Katchina Ct
Tucson AZ 85715

Call Sign: KD7CQU
Debbie C Buecher
7050 E Katchine Ct
Tucson AZ 85715

Call Sign: WA7CDO
Wilbur L Daniels
9400 E Kayenta Dr
Tucson AZ 85749

Call Sign: W7GH
Charles Q Bufe
249 E Kelso
Tucson AZ 85705

Call Sign: N6SPT

James R Huston
8220 E Kenyon Dr
Tucson AZ 857104226

Call Sign: KE7CVB
Steven C Lane
8242 E Kenyon Dr
Tucson AZ 85710

Call Sign: N7SCL
Steven C Lane
8242 E Kenyon Dr
Tucson AZ 85710

Call Sign: KY7K
Steven C Lane
8242 E Kenyon Dr
Tucson AZ 85710

Call Sign: KD7SDW
Ryan K Guthrie
127 E King Rd
Tucson AZ 85705

Call Sign: KD7AQT
James W Mc Crady
6809 E Kingston Pl
Tucson AZ 85710

Call Sign: NN7AA
Devon G Crowe
12522 E Kit Carson Pl
Tucson AZ 85749

Call Sign: N7XJP
Carmen Garcia Downing
1402 E Kleindale Rd
Tucson AZ 85719

Call Sign: W7KEY
Theodore E Downing
1402 E Kleindale Rd
Tucson AZ 857191914

Call Sign: KF6CBM
Alice F Terry
2124 E Kleindale Rd
Tucson AZ 85719

Call Sign: N6DGT
Dail G Terry
2124 E Kleindale Rd
Tucson AZ 85719

Call Sign: W7DGT
Dail G Terry
2124 E Kleindale Rd
Tucson AZ 85719

Call Sign: KE7ONZ
William A Vallejo
3143 E Kleindale Rd 4
Tucson AZ 85716

Call Sign: AE7KB
William A Vallejo
3143 E Kleindale Rd 4
Tucson AZ 85716

Call Sign: W7HIJ
Maurice G Free
3344 E Kliendale Rd S3
Tucson AZ 85716

Call Sign: KD7CNE
Rondi W Carter
8154 E Knollwood Ter
Tucson AZ 85750

Call Sign: W0PZD
Richard M Jones
9509 E Kokopelli Cir
Tucson AZ 857487407

Call Sign: NR7S
Louis J Nicolosi
6558 E Koralee
Tucson AZ 85710

Call Sign: NN8O
Stephen L Nicolosi
6566 E Koralee Dr
Tucson AZ 857101029

Call Sign: WA7DLR
John B Theiss
8265 E Koralee Pl
Tucson AZ 85710

Call Sign: W7CHG
Everette P Reeves
2526 E La Cienega
Tucson AZ 85716

Call Sign: N7BT
George Boross
4159 E La Cienega Dr
Tucson AZ 857121423

Call Sign: KC7QDW
P Otis Phillips
4638 E La Cienega St
Tucson AZ 85712

Call Sign: W7AYF
Russell F Dorsch Sr
7441 E La Clenega Dr
Tucson AZ 85715

Call Sign: KF6MSH
Jeffrey P Hutmacher
8794 E La Palma Dr
Tucson AZ 85747

Call Sign: KF7HYH
Robert E Weiland
8991 E La Palma Dr
Tucson AZ 85747

Call Sign: KC7CG
David N Wade Jr
7461 E Lakeside Dr
Tucson AZ 857303320

Call Sign: N7VGL
Richard E Monson
8030 E Lakeside Pkwy
Tucson AZ 85730

Call Sign: N7VGJ
Kirk L Krentzel
8030 E Lakeside Pkwy 6104
Tucson AZ 85730

Call Sign: KC0RR
Jon C Richins
8711 E Lancaster

Tucson AZ 85715

Call Sign: KA0UBY
Shauna L Richins
8711 E Lancaster
Tucson AZ 85715

Call Sign: KK7OK
Barry L Richards
9655 E Laurel Ridge Dr
Tucson AZ 85748

Call Sign: KF7AOJ
Shawn M Hermann
9006 E Laurie Ann Dr
Tucson AZ 85747

Call Sign: KC7GNJ
Richard G Hicks
301 E Lawton
Tucson AZ 85704

Call Sign: KI6NIZ
Peter W Hall
3308 E Lee St
Tucson AZ 85716

Call Sign: KD7QYR
Edward O Kirkby
3526 E Lee St
Tucson AZ 85716

Call Sign: KB7VKL
William J Spanburgh
4240 E Lee St
Tucson AZ 85712

Call Sign: W7BPR
Richard R La Vigne
4549 E Lee St
Tucson AZ 857123948

Call Sign: KA7OFC
Carlos M Gates
4747 E Lee St
Tucson AZ 85712

Call Sign: KA7OFB
Carol A Gates

4747 E Lee St
Tucson AZ 85712

Call Sign: KA0INQ
Brooks J Fitzpatrick
4873 E Lee St
Tucson AZ 85712

Call Sign: N7ADQ
Robert P Ortiz
5067 E Lee St
Tucson AZ 85712

Call Sign: KB7QEX
Robert H Kimpland
601 E Lee St 12
Tucson AZ 85705

Call Sign: KC7HPG
Kiyoshi Miyagawa
715 E Lee St Apt 26
Tucson AZ 85719

Call Sign: KA4GUH
Bettye J Childers
11845 E Lenher Schwerin
Tucson AZ 85749

Call Sign: KA4CKJ
Thomas A Childers
11845 E Lenher Schwerin Trl
Tucson AZ 85749

Call Sign: KR7U
John Perrotta
7633 E Lerma Pl
Tucson AZ 857106321

Call Sign: WA7PEO
Cratis H Inman
2909 E Lester
Tucson AZ 85716

Call Sign: KF7EAI
John D Williams
7821 E Lester
Tucson AZ 85715

Call Sign: KE7OEB

Brian S Janezic
1106 E Lester St
Tucson AZ 85719

Call Sign: KC7RMB
Paul D Tynan
7761 E Lester St
Tucson AZ 85715

Call Sign: WA7YNE
Wayne D Sanaghan
930 E Limberlost
Tucson AZ 85719

Call Sign: KC7ZPE
Larry L Cunningham
11550 E Limberlost
Tucson AZ 85749

Call Sign: KD7BFO
Staci M Newsom
1102 E Limberlost Apt E
Tucson AZ 85719

Call Sign: KB7QLK
Mark R Romero
1111 E Limberlost Dr 62
Tucson AZ 85719

Call Sign: K7WTW
Delores Emmons
332 E Lincoln
Tucson AZ 85714

Call Sign: K7CRN
William C Schussler
1316 E Lind Rd
Tucson AZ 857192242

Call Sign: W7FEY
Peter B Pichetto
2015 E Lind Rd
Tucson AZ 85719

Call Sign: KC7HSI
Ann M Kersten
2225 E Lind Rd
Tucson AZ 85719

Call Sign: KC7HWH
Clyde W Kersten
2225 E Lind Rd
Tucson AZ 85719

Call Sign: KC7RXS
Brent C Anderson
2551 E Lind Rd
Tucson AZ 85716

Call Sign: WA7NES
Michael J Marum
1819 E Linden
Tucson AZ 85719

Call Sign: KF7IYM
Jeffrey J Zappia
2730 E Linden
Tucson AZ 85715

Call Sign: N7HND
Henry K Zappia
7730 E Linden
Tucson AZ 85715

Call Sign: KA7ZPX
Francesca Balistreri
9012 E Linden
Tucson AZ 85715

Call Sign: KE7DVC
David T Montgomery
1621 E Linden 2
Tucson AZ 85719

Call Sign: KC7FRY
Robert L Hall
5314 E Linden Pl
Tucson AZ 85712

Call Sign: W8LQE
Frederick Durham
3005 E Linden St
Tucson AZ 85716

Call Sign: KE7OLN
Darrell J Stewart
3322 E Linden St
Tucson AZ 85716

Call Sign: KF7OHL
David A Wright
4142 E Linden St
Tucson AZ 85712

Call Sign: KE7KQ
Angelo Ienna Balistreri
9012 E Linden St
Tucson AZ 85715

Call Sign: KD7AYQ
Gary L Bruins
11041 E Linden St
Tucson AZ 85749

Call Sign: N7RMH
Kirk T Wingrove
9325 E Lochnay Ln
Tucson AZ 85747

Call Sign: KB7WDJ
John W Cook
7810 E Locust St
Tucson AZ 85730

Call Sign: KB7PXF
Luna A Cook
7810 E Locust St
Tucson AZ 85730

Call Sign: KB7LLP
Vince E Cook
7810 E Locust St
Tucson AZ 85730

Call Sign: KB7RFK
Stephen M Stewart
9110 E Loma Linda Pl
Tucson AZ 85749

Call Sign: K0ETD
Ronald E Watkins
3280 E Lone Coyote Trl
Tucson AZ 85739

Call Sign: N0EOV
Roger B Lee
1836 E Lone Rider Way

Tucson AZ 85737

Call Sign: KB7USM
Ivan R Settle
217 E Los Reales Rd
Tucson AZ 85706

Call Sign: KC7WJO
David O Eddington
8598 E Louhelen Way
Tucson AZ 85747

Call Sign: N7OJG
Carol A Galati
8318 E Louise Dr
Tucson AZ 85730

Call Sign: KF7QG
Vincent M Galati
8318 E Louise Dr
Tucson AZ 85730

Call Sign: KE7TZA
Ryan E Gebhart
8333 E Louise Dr
Tucson AZ 85730

Call Sign: KB7ZKV
Paula D Campbell
8365 E Louise Dr
Tucson AZ 85730

Call Sign: WB7WOI
Patricia A Schuler
7700 E Lurene Dr
Tucson AZ 85730

Call Sign: K7UNZ
James P Mc Nichols
7741 E Lurlene Dr
Tucson AZ 85730

Call Sign: KC7OVK
Robert J Krauth
2316 E Mabel
Tucson AZ 85719

Call Sign: N7XJR
Mark C Boccaccio Parker

1010 E Mabel 217
Tucson AZ 85719

Call Sign: KE7WJB
Harry R Eckes
7930 E Mabel Dr
Tucson AZ 85715

Call Sign: KB7YLU
Theodore M Forgach
8621 E Mabel Pl
Tucson AZ 85715

Call Sign: KA7IAL
John Y Cordell II
1249 E Mabel St
Tucson AZ 85719

Call Sign: KA4YLH
Sophia M Coleman
9599 E Magdalena Rd
Tucson AZ 857486612

Call Sign: N7THP
Ralph P Mersiowsky
8046 E Maguey Dr
Tucson AZ 857509614

Call Sign: NF6G
Marvin E Hayes
8082 E Maguey Dr
Tucson AZ 85750

Call Sign: N6FZY
Mary E Hayes
8082 E Maguey Dr
Tucson AZ 85750

Call Sign: KC7IIU
Vincent C Jenkins
3695 E Mainsail Blvd
Tucson AZ 85739

Call Sign: KD7RYW
Alexander M Davis
12360 E Makohoh Trl
Tucson AZ 857499595

Call Sign: W1IE

James Zellon
2626 E Malvern
Tucson AZ 85719

Call Sign: KD7SSO
Stephen J Apperson
7931 E Malvern Pl
Tucson AZ 85710

Call Sign: K7YJF
David H Sandrock
2741 E Malvern St
Tucson AZ 85716

Call Sign: KB7JRO
Charles B Mers
6342 E Malvern St
Tucson AZ 85710

Call Sign: W7KGY
Bernis J Estrem
8914 E Maple Leaf Dr
Tucson AZ 85710

Call Sign: N7BBF
Gene S Sandusky
8964 E Maple Leaf Dr
Tucson AZ 85710

Call Sign: N7EH
Erich J Holzer
3526 E March Pl
Tucson AZ 85713

Call Sign: KE7SGB
Donald E Smith
4248 E Marion Trl
Tucson AZ 85711

Call Sign: KW7AA
John D Newton
7475 E Maritime Dr
Tucson AZ 85756

Call Sign: N6MWL
Steven G Harlow
8813 E Martha Root Ct
Tucson AZ 85747

Call Sign: KA7PMV
Sarah L Staggers
8945 E Martha Root Ct
Tucson AZ 85747

Call Sign: N7ADT
Ernest F Lavalley
3248 E Masterson Pl
Tucson AZ 85706

Call Sign: NH6CI
Dale E Hazelwood
8822 E Maxwell Dr
Tucson AZ 85747

Call Sign: K7BWB
Bruce W Bescript
8858 E Maxwell Dr
Tucson AZ 85747

Call Sign: KD7JGQ
Mary Ann F Bescript
8858 E Maxwell Dr
Tucson AZ 85747

Call Sign: K7MAB
Mary Ann F Bescript
8858 E Maxwell Dr
Tucson AZ 85747

Call Sign: KI7TK
Bernard L Seward
8979 E Maxwell Dr
Tucson AZ 85747

Call Sign: KD7KXJ
Lawrence D Guerrero
8957 E Mayberry Dr
Tucson AZ 85730

Call Sign: WA6HPV
Robert W Hahn
64074 E Meander Dr
Tucson AZ 857391051

Call Sign: N7WER
Yehoyadah J Johnson
9991 E Merrill Way
Tucson AZ 85749

Call Sign: KC7PGR
Matthew D Keppel
10 E Mills Apt B
Tucson AZ 85705

Call Sign: N7XJQ
James R Sierra
1956 E Minorka
Tucson AZ 85706

Call Sign: KD7ZUR
Steven T Crean
5821 E Mitchell Ave
Tucson AZ 85708

Call Sign: W6TZN
Allan L Anderson
9142 E Moenkopi Trl
Tucson AZ 85749

Call Sign: K7IG
Thomas C Jarvis III
9184 E Moenkopi Trl
Tucson AZ 85749

Call Sign: KD7JMH
Erik R Baker
9201 E Moenkopi Trl
Tucson AZ 85749

Call Sign: N7EOJ
Joseph H Turner Jr
349 E Mohave Rd
Tucson AZ 85705

Call Sign: WB7SAN
Earl F Montgomery
560 E Monaco Pl
Tucson AZ 85737

Call Sign: KA7WRL
Michael J Elliott
3961 E Monte Vista Dr Apt
203
Tucson AZ 85712

Call Sign: KA7BRI
James L Ivans

4518 E Montecito Ave
Tucson AZ 85711

Call Sign: KD7QDY
Gerald D Bach
4757 E Montecito Ave
Tucson AZ 85711

Call Sign: N7OUG
John R Rhodes
4926 E Montecito Ave
Tucson AZ 85711

Call Sign: KE7GKF
Dirk J Harris
4327 E Montecito St
Tucson AZ 85711

Call Sign: W7YZY
Leroy J Mack Sr
4710 E Montecito St
Tucson AZ 85711

Call Sign: KK7EV
Bodo Bartocha
1305 E Moonridge Rd
Tucson AZ 857181191

Call Sign: WA7JEI
Donald A Bulau
1633 E Moonshroud Dr
Tucson AZ 85737

Call Sign: KF4GES
David P Owens
8538 E Mormon Dr
Tucson AZ 85730

Call Sign: KB7UPS
Joel Johnson
9991 E Morrill Way
Tucson AZ 85749

Call Sign: KC7FXH
Gloria A Johnson
9991 E Morrill Way
Tucson AZ 85749

Call Sign: KB7KRL

Josiah S Johnson
9991 E Morrill Way
Tucson AZ 85749

Call Sign: KF7QQB
Lewis L Tenney
9991 E Morrill Way
Tucson AZ 85749

Call Sign: WA7GXD
Lyle V Johnson
9991 E Morrill Way
Tucson AZ 85749

Call Sign: KC7QMM
Micaiah P Johnson
9991 E Morrill Way
Tucson AZ 85749

Call Sign: KC7QQU
Ian C Truex
10001 E Morrill Way
Tucson AZ 85749

Call Sign: KB7KMQ
Karen R Parks
1051 E Mossman
Tucson AZ 85706

Call Sign: KF7IGR
Katheryn L Edward
3230 E Mountainaire Dr
Tucson AZ 85739

Call Sign: WA2JJW
Norman Elton
633304 E Mountainwood Dr
Tucson AZ 85739

Call Sign: KC7AIV
Bryan S Koch
9990 E Mt Pleasant Dr
Tucson AZ 85749

Call Sign: KF4BSA
Jason R Engholm
9252 E Muleshoe St
Tucson AZ 85747

Call Sign: KD5SHP
Kimberly A Canfield
6721 E Nasumpta Dr
Tucson AZ 85715

Call Sign: WB2YWW
Jay J Cohen
937 E Navajo Rd
Tucson AZ 85719

Call Sign: KD7LNL
Dwight C Knox
7156 E Navigator Ln
Tucson AZ 857569023

Call Sign: W7JRG
Jack R Green
7336 E Navigator Ln
Tucson AZ 85706

Call Sign: KD7RNK
Elaine M Glynn
7498 E Navigator Ln
Tucson AZ 85706

Call Sign: KE7ASW
Thomas A Fox
6408 E Nelson Dr
Tucson AZ 85730

Call Sign: N7HAG
John D Daniel
6501 E Nelson Dr
Tucson AZ 85730

Call Sign: KB7PWY
Sharon C Daniel
6501 E Nelson Dr
Tucson AZ 85730

Call Sign: KD7FEB
Rick M Sturgeon
6872 E Nelson Dr
Tucson AZ 85730

Call Sign: KC7NYX
Gary L Ross
2230 E Nevada
Tucson AZ 85706

Call Sign: KF7PTA
Mike J Conner
6810 E New Hampshire Dr
Tucson AZ 85710

Call Sign: KA7ABN
Roy D Iley
6555 E Nicaragua Dr
Tucson AZ 857302234

Call Sign: KC7AV
Richard D Scheier
7741 E Nicaragua Dr
Tucson AZ 85730

Call Sign: N7YOU
Verne A Kennedy
8255 E Nicaragua Dr
Tucson AZ 857303529

Call Sign: W7GZ
David A Phillips
5824 E North Wilshire Dr
Tucson AZ 857114532

Call Sign: N7XXS
Karen K Lindsay
62151 E Northwood Rd
Tucson AZ 85739

Call Sign: N7RDK
Richard L Lindsay
62151 E Northwood Rd
Tucson AZ 85739

Call Sign: KE7QVC
John R Wallace
3529 E Nugget Canyon Pl
Tucson AZ 85718

Call Sign: N7KOO
Darrell J Eide
3548 E Nugget Canyon Pl
Tucson AZ 85718

Call Sign: KB8IQL
Tony C Ewing
6102 E Oak St

Tucson AZ 85711

Call Sign: KD7LOL
Tony C Ewing
6102 E Oak St
Tucson AZ 85711

Call Sign: KL2AP
Scott Stewart
5141 E Oakmont Dr
Tucson AZ 85718

Call Sign: K7PUM
John S Neufeldt
10560 E Oakwood Dr
Tucson AZ 857499485

Call Sign: WD6CYL
James A Boaz
9350 E Old Pellegrino Rd
Tucson AZ 85749

Call Sign: N7YMH
Rita I Boaz
9350 E Old Pellegrino Rd
Tucson AZ 857498198

Call Sign: AB7DL
William S Johnston
11235 E Old Spanish Trl
Tucson AZ 85748

Call Sign: N7ERG
David R Tulloss
11255 E Old Spanish Trl
Tucson AZ 85748

Call Sign: K7DRT
David R Tulloss
11255 E Old Spanish Trl
Tucson AZ 857488305

Call Sign: K7OPX
Joe Wong
11450 E Old Spanish Trl
Tucson AZ 85730

Call Sign: N7ZQR
Marion Wong

11450 E Old Spanish Trl
Tucson AZ 85730

Call Sign: N7MJE
Sanford Wong
11450 E Old Spanish Trl
Tucson AZ 85730

Call Sign: WB7SCI
Kenneth W Isham
1250 E Old Vail Rd Sp F
Tucson AZ 85706

Call Sign: W7JQE
Kenneth D Smith
6861 E Opatas St
Tucson AZ 85715

Call Sign: K7YBF
Robert F Lewis
11 E Orange Grove Apt 2512
Tucson AZ 85704

Call Sign: W7GRB
Robert C Wolford
11 E Orange Grove Rd 1123
Tucson AZ 85704

Call Sign: KB7PRI
Richard Steensma
11 E Orange Grove Rd Apt
526
Tucson AZ 85704

Call Sign: KD7YNK
Melinda S Luglan
270 E Oro Valley Dr
Tucson AZ 85737

Call Sign: W7KMV
Dennis W Nendza
4219 E Oxford Dr
Tucson AZ 85711

Call Sign: KF7EZG
Austin M Brown
2701 E Ozona Pl
Tucson AZ 85718

Call Sign: KF7EZH
David M Brown
2701 E Ozona Pl
Tucson AZ 857181279

Call Sign: KF7PDX
Ashley L Schneider
9042 E Palm Springs Pl
Tucson AZ 85730

Call Sign: WB7WQJ
Neil E King
9361 E Palm Tree Dr
Tucson AZ 85710

Call Sign: N7JND
Christopher Buchanan
9500 E Palm Tree Dr
Tucson AZ 85748

Call Sign: KE7JHX
M Angelica Buchanan
9500 E Palm Tree Dr
Tucson AZ 85748

Call Sign: N7EMB
M Angelica Buchanan
9500 E Palm Tree Dr
Tucson AZ 85748

Call Sign: N7POH
Ronald A Ohm
8909 E Palms Park Dr
Tucson AZ 85715

Call Sign: N7SRM
Bert R Webb
9371 E Palmtree Dr
Tucson AZ 85710

Call Sign: KC7LIC
Frank T Williams
10440 E Pantano Trl
Tucson AZ 85730

Call Sign: KE7PEA
Steven A Yaple
10650 E Pantano Trl
Tucson AZ 85730

Call Sign: N7JXQ
Richard L Aufmuth
5675 E Paseo Cimarron
Tucson AZ 85750

Call Sign: KE7VTL
Renee M Payton
5701 E Paseo Cimarron
Tucson AZ 85750

Call Sign: KC9MH
Gerald C Stombaugh
5749 E Paseo Cimarron
Tucson AZ 85715

Call Sign: KD7YQH
Harry J Steinnecker
5909 E Paseo Cimarron
Tucson AZ 85750

Call Sign: N7HJS
Harry J Steinnecker
5909 E Paseo Cimarron
Tucson AZ 85750

Call Sign: KB7NIE
Henry R Knoepfle
10128 E Paseo De Mejia
Tucson AZ 85747

Call Sign: KE7WD
James C Bailey
5610 E Paseo De Tampico
Tucson AZ 85715

Call Sign: KB7PXD
Frederick A Convery
4852 E Paseo Del Bac
Tucson AZ 85718

Call Sign: N9DRG
Ronald P Mc Donald
9910 E Paseo Juan Tabo
Tucson AZ 85747

Call Sign: N3SNL
Joshua M Chastain

2582 E Paseo La Terria
Buena
Tucson AZ 85706

Call Sign: W7HLG
Edward K Moore
4837 E Paseo Luisa
Tucson AZ 85711

Call Sign: N7DXA
Barry Fruchtman
6620 E Paseo San Andres
Tucson AZ 85710

Call Sign: W7FVD
Robert L La Roche
6625 E Paseo San Andres
Tucson AZ 85710

Call Sign: KE7ZZS
Brian M Page
9582 E Paseo San Ardo
Tucson AZ 85747

Call Sign: KE7VKQ
Jonathan S Hamnett
10060 E Paseo San Ardo
Tucson AZ 85747

Call Sign: KS7TAN
Jonathan S Hamnett
10060 E Paseo San Ardo
Tucson AZ 85747

Call Sign: KE7ZZV
Alicia J Mckean
9628 E Paseo San Bernardo
Tucson AZ 85747

Call Sign: KD6MMN
Charles T Reeves II
9689 E Paseo San Bernardo
Tucson AZ 85747

Call Sign: KF7EAR
Alice Mckean
9628 E Paseo San Bernardo
St
Tucson AZ 85747

Call Sign: KF7EAS
James D Mckean
9628 E Paseo San Bernardo
St
Tucson AZ 85747

Call Sign: KE7WIZ
Aaron G Sechrist
10070 E Paseo San Bruno
Tucson AZ 85747

Call Sign: WA7BHO
George B Sands Jr
6402 E Paseo San Ciro
Tucson AZ 85710

Call Sign: KE7EUY
Steven C West
9370 E Paseo Tierra Verde
Tucson AZ 85749

Call Sign: KI5WL
Jeffrey C Wadsworth
6126 E Paseo Ventoso
Tucson AZ 85750

Call Sign: KA7NFP
Joseph M Nickerson
3243 E Patricia St
Tucson AZ 85716

Call Sign: KD7NBM
Frederick A West
9201 E Patrick Dr
Tucson AZ 85730

Call Sign: K7JUB
Frederick A West
9201 E Patrick Dr
Tucson AZ 85730

Call Sign: KD7CDH
Joseph A Dalmas
7659 E Pearson St
Tucson AZ 85715

Call Sign: K7AI
Tori R Basford

4809 E Pima 108
Tucson AZ 85712

Call Sign: KC7JTJ
John D Sims
6001 E Pima 56
Tucson AZ 85712

Call Sign: N1KVO
Thomas D Silliman
3403 E Pima St
Tucson AZ 85716

Call Sign: KB7QHL
David S Hall
4808 E Pima St
Tucson AZ 85712

Call Sign: N7NYP
Jacob C Rogers
7900 E Pima St
Tucson AZ 85715

Call Sign: WB7DKO
Mark E Luce
8263 E Pima St
Tucson AZ 85715

Call Sign: N7SCH
David A Fruchtman
6001 E Pima St Apt 11
Tucson AZ 85701

Call Sign: N7XEX
James F Mc Cormack
3350 E Pinal
Tucson AZ 85739

Call Sign: KD7KXI
Arthur L Bergey Jr
10520 E Pinal Vista
Tucson AZ 85730

Call Sign: KB7LBJ
Vincent J Locascio
10902 E Pinal Vista
Tucson AZ 85730

Call Sign: N7IUC

John R Lamont
8840 E Pine Valley
Tucson AZ 85710

Call Sign: WA0LIT
Mark C Spear
7855 E Pinon Cir
Tucson AZ 85750

Call Sign: KF7MZW
George A Welch
4066 E Pinto Ln
Tucson AZ 85739

Call Sign: KG7XK
James R Mc Knight
4230 E Pinto Ln
Tucson AZ 85739

Call Sign: KI4BTM
Sean P Lynch
4923 E Placita Abrevadero
Tucson AZ 85712

Call Sign: WD8KRV
G David Burnett
7301 E Placita Antigua
Tucson AZ 85710

Call Sign: KF7CEK
Jonathon Harvey
5400 E Placita Apan
Tucson AZ 85718

Call Sign: WA4CEW
Christopher K Walker
5321 E Placita Bosque
Tucson AZ 85718

Call Sign: K7CKW
Christopher K Walker
5321 E Placita Bosque
Tucson AZ 85718

Call Sign: KE7RPY
Donald S Smith
10215 E Placita Cresta Feliz
Tucson AZ 857499534

Call Sign: KD7JYY
David W Meyer
10236 E Placita Cresta Feliz
Tucson AZ 85749

Call Sign: KB7PJ
David W Adams
7595 E Placita De La Poesia
Tucson AZ 85750

Call Sign: KB7TV
Franklin W Mc Pherson
7593 E Placita De La Vina
Tucson AZ 857507205

Call Sign: KF7LIK
Robert D Millikin
5491 E Placita Del Mesquite
Tucson AZ 85712

Call Sign: KC7EAK
Xinming A Lin
11670 E Placita Del Rincon
Tucson AZ 85749

Call Sign: KC7YZN
Jeffrey L Bozarth
10055 E Placita Del Timbre
Tucson AZ 85747

Call Sign: KA0BIU
Dale M Crockatt
10149 E Placita Del Timbre
Tucson AZ 85747

Call Sign: KF7KH
Charles S Goldman
6355 E Placita Divina
Tucson AZ 85718

Call Sign: KA1BJ
Charles S Goldman
6355 E Placita Divina
Tucson AZ 857500954

Call Sign: KB7TRX
William M Hutchinson
13316 E Placita El Algodon
Tucson AZ 85749

Call Sign: K7IOU
David J Stanford
9140 E Placita Huajillo
Tucson AZ 85749

Call Sign: K8IOU
Cecilia M Stanford
9140 E Placita Huajillo
Tucson AZ 85749

Call Sign: KD7KIB
Joseph S Gordon
10561 E Placita Loma Verde
Tucson AZ 85748

Call Sign: WB6RAO
David J De Grado
6276 E Placita Lozana
Tucson AZ 85750

Call Sign: K7HIL
Michael K Perrett
11442 E Placita Madre
Tucson AZ 85749

Call Sign: KB7QLJ
Thomas R Birkholz
10801 E Placita Metate
Tucson AZ 85749

Call Sign: N7XJN
James F Garliepp III
10821 E Placita Metate
Tucson AZ 85749

Call Sign: KD7JUP
James F Garliepp IV
10821 E Placita Metate
Tucson AZ 85749

Call Sign: KB7UCX
Melanie D Garliepp
10821 E Placita Metate
Tucson AZ 85749

Call Sign: NS4Q
Gregory A Masse
5065 E Placita Salud

Tucson AZ 85718

Call Sign: KB7NQI
James E Cushing
9161 E Placita Violeta
Tucson AZ 85749

Call Sign: KI7LA
Elizabeth J Hardaway
10401 E Plumeria
Tucson AZ 85749

Call Sign: KY7B
Bruce E Wilson
4229 E Pontatoc Dr
Tucson AZ 85718

Call Sign: K7ODO
Kathrine L Wilson
4229 E Pontatoc Dr
Tucson AZ 85718

Call Sign: KC7EJX
Thomas J Zawada
3334 E Popinac Loop
Tucson AZ 85716

Call Sign: KO7J
Darwin E Campbell
10141 E Prairie Dog Ln
Tucson AZ 85749

Call Sign: K7SE
John B Irwin
2879 E Presidio Rd
Tucson AZ 85716

Call Sign: N7ZQX
Irene K Watkins
7911 E Presidio Rd
Tucson AZ 85715

Call Sign: N7VVF
Norman Watkins
7911 E Presidio Rd
Tucson AZ 85750

Call Sign: KE7OEE
Mark A Paquette

7931 E Presidio Rd
Tucson AZ 85750

Call Sign: KE7OED
Karen Paquette
7931 E Presidio Rd
Tucson AZ 857502842

Call Sign: KB7ZGB
Robert P Rai
438 E Prince Rd 236
Tucson AZ 85705

Call Sign: KC7EJW
Michael E Smith
405 E Prince Rd 317
Tucson AZ 85705

Call Sign: KD7EZI
Matthew L Smith
405 E Prince Rd 422
Tucson AZ 85705

Call Sign: KD5RSG
Henry L Gray
438 E Prince Rd Apt 112
Tucson AZ 85705

Call Sign: KF7ADN
Rick C Aaberg
7410 E Princeton Dr
Tucson AZ 85710

Call Sign: N7HMN
Scott B Clemans
11262 E Prospect Ln
Tucson AZ 85749

Call Sign: KC7IOA
Amy K Clemans
11262 E Prospect Ln
Tucson AZ 85749

Call Sign: KC7POE
Sue M Clemans
11262 E Prospect Ln
Tucson AZ 85749

Call Sign: W9NUO

Albert F Verthein
11380 E Prospect Ln
Tucson AZ 85749

Call Sign: KF7ADO
Dena C Jones
9661 E Quail Pl
Tucson AZ 85748

Call Sign: N7SVV
Barbara Joseph
7130 E Quail Run
Tucson AZ 85715

Call Sign: W8PEE
Donald Clouse
4440 E Quivira Pl
Tucson AZ 857181679

Call Sign: WN8PEE
Donald Clouse
4440 E Quivira Pl
Tucson AZ 857181679

Call Sign: KF6ZLC
Karen M Hager
7969 E Ragweed Dr
Tucson AZ 85710

Call Sign: KC7RYX
Marcia I Aurand
10125 E Rainbow Meadow
Dr
Tucson AZ 85747

Call Sign: WW5R
William R Aurand
10125 E Rainbow Meadow
Dr
Tucson AZ 85747

Call Sign: W7MQ
William R Aurand
10125 E Rainbow Meadow
Dr
Tucson AZ 85747

Call Sign: WB8RFD
Douglas A Cammel

10256 E Rainbow Meadow
Dr
Tucson AZ 857475502

Call Sign: KF7RNL
Matthew B Kent
8984 E Rainsage St
Tucson AZ 85747

Call Sign: KE7KID
Willem W Vankerk
10539 E Ralph Alvarez Pl
Tucson AZ 85747

Call Sign: KE7UVP
William A Heflin
1490 E Ram Canyon
Tucson AZ 85737

Call Sign: KE7UVQ
Norma J Heflin
1490 E Ram Canyon Dr
Tucson AZ 85737

Call Sign: KF7FTZ
Sean P Riley
8151 E Rawhide Tr
Tucson AZ 85750

Call Sign: W4NNR
Steve Cserpnyak
8170 E Rawhide Trl
Tucson AZ 85715

Call Sign: KB7HNL
Thomas M Prim
10001 E Ray Ann Pl
Tucson AZ 85749

Call Sign: K0CIX
Lloyd A Bartlett
4607 E Red Mesa Dr
Tucson AZ 85718

Call Sign: K7CIX
Lloyd A Bartlett
4607 E Red Mesa Dr
Tucson AZ 85718

Call Sign: W0NF
Palmyra L Leahy
61778 E Redwood Dr
Tucson AZ 85739

Call Sign: K0MP
William D Leahy
61778 E Redwood Dr
Tucson AZ 85739

Call Sign: KQ7M
Western Wireless Contest
Club
61778 E Redwood Dr
Tucson AZ 85739

Call Sign: KE7IBC
Michael E Bernstein
6780 E Resort View Pl
Tucson AZ 85750

Call Sign: KG7EG
Timothy R Howard
4580 E Rex St 8
Tucson AZ 85706

Call Sign: W7LBL
Leroy C Ingram
4580 E Rex St Lot 2
Tucson AZ 85706

Call Sign: WA7JCK
Merle K Hutton
2549 E Richards Pl
Tucson AZ 857161123

Call Sign: KC7ALI
Karl F Gast
8161 E Ridgebrook Dr
Tucson AZ 85750

Call Sign: KE7WJD
Craig A Freeman
5743 E Rio Verde Vista
Tucson AZ 85750

Call Sign: N7DU
Bernard M Augustyn
7503 E Rio Vista Cr

Tucson AZ 857153545

Call Sign: KF7RNO
Erik R Timmermann
10433 E Rita Ranch Crossing
Cir
Tucson AZ 85747

Call Sign: KF7FTW
Richard M Davis
8179 E Rivenoak Cir
Tucson AZ 85715

Call Sign: N8LLA
Earl W Fernelius
8144 E Rivenoak Dr
Tucson AZ 85715

Call Sign: KC7TAP
Gerard Anderson
2200 E River 124
Tucson AZ 85718

Call Sign: KB7NX
Carl C Anderson
7838 E River Forest Pl
Tucson AZ 85715

Call Sign: W7OFZ
Wallace S Platt
209 E River Rd
Tucson AZ 85704

Call Sign: KF7EMC
Todd D West
4161 E River Rd
Tucson AZ 85718

Call Sign: K7EI
Carle F Bumpus Sr
E River Rd
Tucson AZ 85740

Call Sign: KF7IYJ
Robert Laity
2550 E River Rd 16206
Tucson AZ 85718

Call Sign: KF4FTR

Christopher A Miller
5755 E River Rd 1907
Tucson AZ 85750

Call Sign: KR6CZ
Koji Shibata
5755 E River Rd 3809
Tucson AZ 85750

Call Sign: N3FW
Koji Shibata
5755 E River Rd 3809
Tucson AZ 85750

Call Sign: KF7KEU
Anthony J Miller
855 E River Rd 46
Tucson AZ 85718

Call Sign: W9CWK
Joseph H Kuranz
1550 E River Rd Apt 1
Tucson AZ 85718

Call Sign: KE7VJN
Ronald H Van Loan
5755 E River Rd Apt 1411
Tucson AZ 85750

Call Sign: KF7UAZ
Lee T Suring
5755 E River Rd Apt 2230
Tucson AZ 85750

Call Sign: W7LSO
Robert B Leech
5755 E River Rd Apt 3709
Tucson AZ 85715

Call Sign: KC7HWQ
Donald C Scott
5755 E River Rd Apt 4013
Tucson AZ 85750

Call Sign: W1WAN
Walter P Tefft
6974 E Rivercrest Rd
Tucson AZ 85750

Call Sign: K7KHO
R Mark Woodruff
4034 E Roberts Pl
Tucson AZ 85711

Call Sign: KA9WQF
Bernhardt J Outram
7150 E Rocky Ridge Dr
Tucson AZ 85750

Call Sign: KF7VDU
Travis B Polinger
3661 E Roger Rd
Tucson AZ 85718

Call Sign: KF7OHN
Paul R Howe
2000 E Roger Rd Apt H3
Tucson AZ 85719

Call Sign: W0PEQ
Dale R Hicks
7875 E Roget Dr
Tucson AZ 857106070

Call Sign: W2ZIF
Robert Juncosa
65329 E Rose Crest Ct
Tucson AZ 85739

Call Sign: KA7TSH
John E Strohmeyer
5362 E Rosewood Cir
Tucson AZ 85711

Call Sign: W7LIZ
Edith E Caldwell
6279 E Rosewood Cir
Tucson AZ 85711

Call Sign: KE7ZGW
Henry Fagg
6712 E Rosewood Cir
Tucson AZ 85710

Call Sign: KD5YG
Jeff K Steinkamp
6765 E Rosewood Cir
Tucson AZ 85710

Call Sign: KE4GDQ
Patricia L Steinkamp
6765 E Rosewood Cir
Tucson AZ 85710

Call Sign: K7YAK
Patricia L Steinkamp
6765 E Rosewood Cir
Tucson AZ 85710

Call Sign: KE7FPF
Flight Safety International
Radio Club
6765 E Rosewood Cir
Tucson AZ 85710

Call Sign: K7FSI
Flight Safety International
Radio Club
6765 E Rosewood Cir
Tucson AZ 85710

Call Sign: N7YG
Jeff K Steinkamp
6765 E Rosewood Cir
Tucson AZ 857101215

Call Sign: KB7WP
Russell B Love
7902 E Rosewood Cir
Tucson AZ 85710

Call Sign: KA7BXA
Gregory M Walker
9320 E Rosewood Cir
Tucson AZ 85710

Call Sign: KA7UZK
Rashid F Alrashid
6724 E Rosewood Pl
Tucson AZ 85710

Call Sign: N7DI
Jeffrey F Martensen
6733 E Rosewood Pl
Tucson AZ 85710

Call Sign: KE7W

Robert D Lively
9410 E Rosewood St
Tucson AZ 857101808

Call Sign: KB7ZKS
Beth V Pfeifer
9925 E Rosewood St
Tucson AZ 85748

Call Sign: W7US
Beth V Pfeifer
9925 E Rosewood St
Tucson AZ 85748

Call Sign: KB7ZKT
Peter P Pfeifer
9925 E Rosewood St
Tucson AZ 85748

Call Sign: N7OKI
Harold Asquith
7211 E Rosslare Dr
Tucson AZ 85715

Call Sign: WB9ROU
Joseph A Azzarello
1329 E Royal Ridge Dr
Tucson AZ 85737

Call Sign: KB7OUC
Robert G Patrick
5524 E S Wilshire
Tucson AZ 85711

Call Sign: KD6AMR
Alan K Brunelle
8180 E Sabino Dr
Tucson AZ 85750

Call Sign: KD6OGN
Katheryn L Brunelle
8180 E Sabino Dr
Tucson AZ 857509629

Call Sign: KF4PGM
James L Porter
7760 E Sabino Shadow Pl
Tucson AZ 85750

Call Sign: KD1TJ
Douglas G Jaffe
7976 E Sabino Sunrise Cir
Tucson AZ 85750

Call Sign: WA3ZXH
Joel R Huebner
7605 E Sabino Vista Dr
Tucson AZ 85750

Call Sign: KB7TLA
Lawrence E Fields
9893 E Sabrena Ln
Tucson AZ 85748

Call Sign: KB7YQD
Thomas P Freese
8935 E Saddleback Dr
Tucson AZ 85749

Call Sign: WB6OZP
Preston G Rubin
11566 E Saguaro Crest Pl
Tucson AZ 85747

Call Sign: WD6ERS
Leslie K Watson
12010 E Saguaro Sunrise Dr
Tucson AZ 85749

Call Sign: K2DT
Wayne C Carlson
4841 E Salida Del Sol Pl
Tucson AZ 85718

Call Sign: KG4IME
Ivan Collazo Dr
10756 E Salsabila Rd
Tucson AZ 85747

Call Sign: KG7KX
Rodney Stoddard
9676 E Salvatore Pl
Tucson AZ 85748

Call Sign: NN7BH
Bruce N Homer
62088 E Sandlewood Rd
Tucson AZ 85739

Call Sign: KH6FSX
Robert L Wilders
8341 E Sandstone Dr
Tucson AZ 85750

Call Sign: KE7VDE
Robert J Jacobs
10061 E Sarah Ann Pl
Tucson AZ 85748

Call Sign: W7JVT
Raymond S Howard
8410 E Sarnoff Pl
Tucson AZ 85715

Call Sign: KD7ELY
Jeffrey G Jaster
5602 E Scarlett St
Tucson AZ 85711

Call Sign: AJ7EF
Jeffrey G Jaster
5602 E Scarlett St
Tucson AZ 85711

Call Sign: KD7CNJ
Christopher J Dean
6813 E Scarlett St
Tucson AZ 85710

Call Sign: WY7W
Thomas P Dean
6813 E Scarlett St
Tucson AZ 85710

Call Sign: K7TPD
Thomas P Dean
6813 E Scarlett St
Tucson AZ 85710

Call Sign: W7TKR
James A Metzger
9305 E Sellarole
Tucson AZ 85730

Call Sign: N7CYW
Richard C Geiger
9802 E Sellarole

Tucson AZ 85730

Call Sign: KC7HNF
Scsott B Meder
1341 E Seneca St
Tucson AZ 85719

Call Sign: K7QPO
Lawrence W Lee
1525 E Seneca St
Tucson AZ 85719

Call Sign: KF7VDV
Benedict J Reynwar
1629 E Seneca St
Tucson AZ 85719

Call Sign: KF7IWB
Jefferson Park Elementary
ARC
1701 E Seneca St
Tucson AZ 85719

Call Sign: KE6RCR
Chia Han Hsieh
2809 E Seneca St
Tucson AZ 85716

Call Sign: KB7MFB
Reid H Kotwica
3230 E Seneca St
Tucson AZ 85716

Call Sign: W7JWF
Charles E Remus
4560 E Seneca St
Tucson AZ 85712

Call Sign: KD7WEM
John A Smith
4740 E Seneca St
Tucson AZ 85712

Call Sign: KF7DIL
Orson B Garnsey
7611 E Seneca St
Tucson AZ 85715

Call Sign: K7FDX

Orson B Garnsey
7611 E Seneca St
Tucson AZ 85715

Call Sign: KF7IGO
Ruth B Caldwell
8981 E Seneca St
Tucson AZ 85715

Call Sign: W7ZBS
Thomas R Custer
9080 E Seneca St
Tucson AZ 85715

Call Sign: KF7QKF
Donald R Roberts Jr
9081 E Seneca St
Tucson AZ 85715

Call Sign: KA7PAO
Willie King Jr
8548 E Shasta Dr
Tucson AZ 85730

Call Sign: N5RSQ
Michael W Jennings
8825 E Shenandoah Pl
Tucson AZ 85710

Call Sign: N7OFY
Allen A Bahr
8611 E Shiloh St
Tucson AZ 85710

Call Sign: N7THY
Guy B Potucek
8621 E Shiloh St
Tucson AZ 85710

Call Sign: N7GEG
Bernard J Winner
9902 E Shiloh St
Tucson AZ 85748

Call Sign: KE7WJC
Stephen A Ziel
9555 E Shiloh St Apt 6205
Tucson AZ 85748

Call Sign: K7RJR
John R Glenn III
6133 E Ship Rock Dr
Tucson AZ 857068948

Call Sign: K7SFG
Susan S Glenn
6133 E Ship Rock Dr
Tucson AZ 857068948

Call Sign: N7OJT
Wayne R Jolliffe
7500 E Shore Dr
Tucson AZ 85715

Call Sign: N2NB
Arthur M Blank
7535 E Shore Dr
Tucson AZ 85715

Call Sign: KK6PC
Craig A Siegel
9001 E Sierra St
Tucson AZ 85710

Call Sign: K7GI
Craig A Siegel
9001 E Sierra St
Tucson AZ 85710

Call Sign: W7NQ
Southern Arizona Dx Club
9001 E Sierra St
Tucson AZ 85710

Call Sign: KA7UML
Christan R Kemp
9042 E Sierra St
Tucson AZ 85710

Call Sign: KC7JWM
Karen D Walker
9736 E Sierra St
Tucson AZ 85748

Call Sign: KF7CNL
Marc A Ohden
2942 E Sierra Vista
Tucson AZ 85716

Call Sign: N7VGK
Elliott J Pritchard
864 E Silver St
Tucson AZ 85719

Call Sign: K7SEB
John P Diaz
1427 E Silver St
Tucson AZ 85719

Call Sign: KD7ZKI
Jon F Winkeller Jr
1720 E Silver St
Tucson AZ 85719

Call Sign: KD7GDA
Robert S Lonergan
2025 E Silver St
Tucson AZ 85719

Call Sign: W7HLD
Robert K Thurman
1008 E Simmons St
Tucson AZ 85719

Call Sign: NF7X
Nathan E Van Den Berg
10651 E Singing Canyon Dr
Tucson AZ 85747

Call Sign: KB0GRH
Diane M Hansey
2395 E Skipping Rock Way
Tucson AZ 85737

Call Sign: WA7IGV
Douglas B Gilliam Dds
4211 E Skyline Dr
Tucson AZ 85718

Call Sign: KG6JPW
Vicki L Guapo
4601 E Skyline Dr 107
Tucson AZ 857181655

Call Sign: KF7AS
Norman W Crane
12020 E Snyder Rd

Tucson AZ 85749

Call Sign: KF7QKI
Gerald W Meyer
7255 E Snyder Rd Unit 3105
Tucson AZ 85750

Call Sign: N7GWM
Gerald W Meyer
7255 E Snyder Rd Unit 3105
Tucson AZ 85750

Call Sign: KD7PNX
George W Wilson
8541 E Solar Pl
Tucson AZ 857509745

Call Sign: KB6QKE
John W Holmes
65755 E Solarwind Ct
Tucson AZ 85739

Call Sign: KE7OSA
Cynthia R Hernandez
11530 E Sonoran Moon Pl
Tucson AZ 85749

Call Sign: KF7ADQ
Russell T Tevis
12590 E Sonoran Ridge Dr
Tucson AZ 85749

Call Sign: KF7GYG
David R Perl
6991 E South Point Rd
Tucson AZ 85756

Call Sign: WD5GFY
Peter J Levine
5847 E South Wilshire
Tucson AZ 857114539

Call Sign: KE7VNP
Nathan J Seiter
9869 E Spanish Flower Ct
Tucson AZ 85748

Call Sign: KD7MOM
Kelly W Goudieloch

11455 E Speedway
Tucson AZ 85745

Call Sign: KE7VRJ
Scott R Mccown
12351 E Speedway
Tucson AZ 85748

Call Sign: KG7DX
Robert T Shaw
12851 E Speedway
Tucson AZ 85748

Call Sign: KE7PDX
Jonathan M Hanson
3400 E Speedway 118 138
Tucson AZ 85716

Call Sign: KE7PDY
Roseann Hanson
3400 E Speedway 118138
Tucson AZ 85716

Call Sign: KG7HL
John W Bash
7570 E Speedway 2
Tucson AZ 85710

Call Sign: W8GRI
James W Nichols
9350 E Speedway 21
Tucson AZ 857101838

Call Sign: WB4EAJ
William R Minor
7570 E Speedway 252
Tucson AZ 857108516

Call Sign: K9CPN
Albert J Cikas
7570 E Speedway 265
Tucson AZ 85710

Call Sign: KC7JB
Marvin B Mandell
7570 E Speedway 351
Tucson AZ 857108817

Call Sign: WA3YAI

David B Mc Clure
7570 E Speedway 413
Tucson AZ 85710

Call Sign: KB7VKD
Norman A Lawrence
7570 E Speedway 520
Tucson AZ 85710

Call Sign: W7EYN
George G Carlson
8080 E Speedway Apt 209
Tucson AZ 85710

Call Sign: KE4RYP
Andres H Martinez
1230 E Speedway Blvd
Tucson AZ 85721

Call Sign: KD7TXN
Michael S Bielas
6502 E Speedway Blvd
Tucson AZ 85710

Call Sign: KD7AQQ
Robert L Siegel
12575 E Speedway Blvd
Tucson AZ 85748

Call Sign: KB7USN
Robert E Greene
E Speedway Blvd
Tucson AZ 857108818

Call Sign: KD7ODO
John T Slattery
13141 E Speedway Blvd
Tucson AZ 85748

Call Sign: N0HPS
Steven C Gibb
8225 E Speedway Blvd 1106
Tucson AZ 85710

Call Sign: KB9ULW
Christopher A Maple
7401 E Speedway Blvd
11207
Tucson AZ 85710

Call Sign: K7EBW
David C Matteson
7570 E Speedway Blvd 128
Tucson AZ 85710

Call Sign: KE7ZPG
Steven R Blas
9000 E Speedway Blvd
15104
Tucson AZ 85710

Call Sign: KT4NA
Robert W Johnson
8151 E Speedway Blvd 249
Tucson AZ 85710

Call Sign: KB7WDL
Michael P Mitchell
8110 E Speedway Blvd 6369
Tucson AZ 857101780

Call Sign: KE7YAH
Donald W Peck
7424 E Speedway Blvd Apt
F90
Tucson AZ 85710

Call Sign: KD7NQ
David L Thompson
7570 E Speedway Blvd Sp
516
Tucson AZ 85710

Call Sign: KB7RFE
John W Martin
3400 E Speedway Blvd Ste
118
Tucson AZ 857163954

Call Sign: AB4OL
Craig S Bevan
3400 E Speedway Blvd Ste
118
Tucson AZ 857163960

Call Sign: W5VEM
Myrl L Coultas

7570 E Speedway Blvd
Unit229
Tucson AZ 857108815

Call Sign: N5NEQ
Ehud Gavron
4003 E Speedway Boulevard
Ste 119
Tucson AZ 85712

Call Sign: KC7LSG
Jeanne M Gonzalez
7424 E Speedway G110
Tucson AZ 85710

Call Sign: KB2W
Mike Izzo
8665 E Speedway No 1102
Tucson AZ 85710

Call Sign: W1OKB
Joseph C Nyman
9150 E Spire Ln
Tucson AZ 85715

Call Sign: KF7DSF
Star Stations ARC
2479 E Spring Pioneer Ln
Tucson AZ 85755

Call Sign: W0HF
Oro Valley ARC
2479 E Spring Pioneer Ln
Tucson AZ 85755

Call Sign: N7MCK
Catherine C Wasmann
1231 E Spring St
Tucson AZ 85719

Call Sign: N7USL
Douglas R Myrvold
1231 E Spring St
Tucson AZ 85719

Call Sign: KF7FIU
Joseph L Montani
1721 E Spring St
Tucson AZ 85719

Call Sign: W7DXW
Joseph L Montani
1721 E Spring St
Tucson AZ 85719

Call Sign: KF7GFF
Alexander Thome
1749 E Spring St
Tucson AZ 85719

Call Sign: KF7GFG
Katherine A Thome
1749 E Spring St
Tucson AZ 85719

Call Sign: N7SCI
Andrew H Rutter
2102 E Spring St
Tucson AZ 85719

Call Sign: K7EO
Paul S White Jr
7311 E Springcrest Dr
Tucson AZ 85715

Call Sign: KD7JUK
Stephen V Archibald
9231 E Springwater Ct
Tucson AZ 85749

Call Sign: W9OFQ
James E King
1779 E Starmist Pl
Tucson AZ 857373471

Call Sign: N7PRN
Donald C Adams II
10102 E Stella Rd
Tucson AZ 85730

Call Sign: KC5BGR
Robert L Cowan
7950 E Stella Rd Apt 13K
Tucson AZ 857301964

Call Sign: KD6AMB
Frank J Halicek
9110 E Sugar Sumac St

Tucson AZ 85747

Call Sign: K7VIP
William L Pilling
9181 E Sugar Sumac St
Tucson AZ 85747

Call Sign: KD7OLW
William L Pilling
9187 E Sugar Sumac St
Tucson AZ 85747

Call Sign: KE7NTL
Clde L Pretti
9320 E Summer Trl
Tucson AZ 85749

Call Sign: N7LDK
Judy E Matthews
9340 E Summer Trl
Tucson AZ 857478661

Call Sign: N7JUQ
Gary W Matthews
9340 E Summer Trl
Tucson AZ 857498661

Call Sign: N1DHS
Gary W Matthews
9340 E Summer Trl
Tucson AZ 857498661

Call Sign: N0JXB
David L Bunch
11630 E Summer Trl
Tucson AZ 85749

Call Sign: KE7FDO
Raul Dominguez
1900 E Summit St
Tucson AZ 85706

Call Sign: KF7GPR
Noemi G Rivera
2175 E Summit St 3
Tucson AZ 85706

Call Sign: KF7EFI
Miles A Linscott

3260 E Sun Cloud Pl
Tucson AZ 85718

Call Sign: N7HUL
William E Henry
5949 E Sun County Blvd
Tucson AZ 85712

Call Sign: N8NIE
George H Bliss
10661 E Sundance Cir
Tucson AZ 857499540

Call Sign: KC7SIR
Daniel J Mc Phedran
11220 E Sundance Dr
Tucson AZ 85749

Call Sign: KD7OXN
Linda L Mc Phedran
11220 E Sundance Dr
Tucson AZ 85749

Call Sign: KF7CEI
Brian H Hayes
7998 E Sundew Dr
Tucson AZ 85710

Call Sign: KF7FIW
Emmanuel Spiro
4500 E Sunrise Dr Apt P14
Tucson AZ 85718

Call Sign: N7UGI
Fernando R Lopez
4500 E Sunrise Dr D14
Tucson AZ 85718

Call Sign: KB7VMU
Diane M Flock
4500 E Sunrise Dr J15
Tucson AZ 85718

Call Sign: N7QBG
John R Fielder
4729 E Sunrise Dr Pmb 403
Tucson AZ 85718

Call Sign: N7SCK

Vivian L Fielder
4729 E Sunrise Dr Pmb 403
Tucson AZ 85718

Call Sign: KC7LAW
James J Hoiby
6890 E Sunrise Dr Ste 120
342
Tucson AZ 85750

Call Sign: KC7FXJ
Cheri Patch
4725 E Sunrise Dr Ste 211
Tucson AZ 85718

Call Sign: KC7GNP
Mark D Mc Fadden
10188 E Sunrise Meadow Pl
Tucson AZ 85747

Call Sign: KA8ILD
Richard D Walker
3644 E Sylvane
Tucson AZ 85713

Call Sign: KF7RLV
Sarah A Truebe
3113 E Table Mountain Rd
Tucson AZ 85718

Call Sign: KL2PS
Joseph D Sayles
6938 E Talon Dr Apt A
Tucson AZ 85708

Call Sign: W7KBV
Douglas A Beagles
7211 E Tamara Dr
Tucson AZ 85730

Call Sign: N7VOC
Pat Bertschi
8987 E Tanque Verde Box
291
Tucson AZ 85749

Call Sign: KD7NVL
Russell S Mayers

9121 E Tanque Verde Pmb
226
Tucson AZ 85749

Call Sign: KF7PV
James N Tyson Sr
11731 E Tanque Verde Rd
Tucson AZ 85749

Call Sign: W1JNT
James N Tyson Sr
11731 E Tanque Verde Rd
Tucson AZ 857499750

Call Sign: KE7PT
Martin B Rosenthal
7671 E Tanque Verde Rd 124
Tucson AZ 857153607

Call Sign: WD9DQH
Neil A Petersen
8987 E Tanque Verde Rd 309
323
Tucson AZ 85749

Call Sign: KE7NDK
Tim Jordan
7001 E Taos Pl
Tucson AZ 85715

Call Sign: AA4M
William H H Mullin III
6842 E Tawa St
Tucson AZ 857153345

Call Sign: AA7FV
Darrel T Emerson
3555 E Thimble Peak
Tucson AZ 85718

Call Sign: N7PTE
Christopher M Emerson
3555 E Thimble Peak Pl
Tucson AZ 85718

Call Sign: KB7OBA
Nicholas J Emerson
3555 E Thimble Peak Pl
Tucson AZ 85718

Call Sign: N7UGL
Pamela J Emerson
3555 E Thimble Peak Pl
Tucson AZ 85718

Call Sign: KC7NGL
Warren H Krause
10401 E Thunderbolt Dr
Tucson AZ 857483808

Call Sign: W8OIH
David L Casto
6047 E Timrod Pl
Tucson AZ 85711

Call Sign: KE7NDL
Tanya R Trubee
4403 E Timrod St
Tucson AZ 85711

Call Sign: W7EHL
Jack E Voorhies
4438 E Timrod St
Tucson AZ 85711

Call Sign: KB7RBT
Sharon L Voorhies
4438 E Timrod St
Tucson AZ 85711

Call Sign: KB7GTR
Kevin M Santos
6738 E Topke St
Tucson AZ 85715

Call Sign: W7FV
Norris I Sapp
6849 E Topke St
Tucson AZ 85715

Call Sign: WA7UTA
Joseph E Frazier
3247 E Towner Ave
Tucson AZ 85716

Call Sign: N7CUU
David L Knoper
2510 E Towner St

Tucson AZ 85716

Call Sign: KC7LIH
Lester D Mann
3125 E Towner St
Tucson AZ 857162220

Call Sign: W7VX
Charles E Mandt
7838 E Treetop Rd
Tucson AZ 85756

Call Sign: N7INN
George B Simons
11225 E Twin Hills Trl
Tucson AZ 85748

Call Sign: KE7RDE
Christopher J Wolff
130 E University 3
Tucson AZ 85705

Call Sign: N1SCL
Peter E Gamble
1303 E University Blvd
Tucson AZ 85719

Call Sign: W7ITQ
Robert L Morrison
307 E University Blvd
Tucson AZ 85705

Call Sign: KF7FTX
James D Howard II
1303 E University Blvd
20535
Tucson AZ 85719

Call Sign: N1JH
James D Howard II
1303 E University Blvd
20535
Tucson AZ 85719

Call Sign: KE7QOU
Aaron M Wilcox
1303 E University Blvd
20797
Tucson AZ 85719

Call Sign: KC7UMX
James E Myers
9335 E Vallarta Dr
Tucson AZ 85749

Call Sign: K7MMO
Michael M Oetting
2225 E Vera Cruz Vista
Tucson AZ 85713

Call Sign: KB0LAM
Michael M Oetting
2225 E Vera Cruz Vista
Tucson AZ 857137502

Call Sign: N4SGY
Denise K Jackman
6609 E Via Cedri
Tucson AZ 85750

Call Sign: N6DVK
David T Whittman
3481 E Via Colonia Del Sol
Tucson AZ 85718

Call Sign: KE7QQW
Vincent J Rizzi
8527 E Via Cortina De
Madera
Tucson AZ 85747

Call Sign: KE7QQX
Vincent J Rizzi Jr
8527 E Via Cortina De
Madera
Tucson AZ 85747

Call Sign: KE7QQV
Chirelle Weaver
8528 E Via Cortina De
Madera
Tucson AZ 85747

Call Sign: KE7KRI
Shawn P Degan
9846 E Via De Sisneroz
Tucson AZ 85747

Call Sign: N2FK
Steven F Adamson
10023 E Via Del Fandango
Tucson AZ 85747

Call Sign: KA1GUD
George M Brown
4041 E Via Del Vireo
Tucson AZ 85718

Call Sign: KE7BWQ
Gerald A King
1020 E Via Entrada
Tucson AZ 85718

Call Sign: AE7BT
Yongsup Park
1011 E Via Linterna
Tucson AZ 85718

Call Sign: W3KE
Yongsup Park
1011 E Via Linterna
Tucson AZ 85718

Call Sign: KE7PEB
Randall S Ortlinghaus
11331 E Via Madre
Tucson AZ 85749

Call Sign: K7RSO
Randall S Ortlinghaus
11331 E Via Madre
Tucson AZ 85749

Call Sign: K3KXR
Mark S Miner
3260 E Via Palos Verdes
Tucson AZ 857165854

Call Sign: N3BU
Mark S Miner
3260 E Via Palos Verdes
Tucson AZ 857165854

Call Sign: KC7AWJ
Daniel W Salvestrini
2555 E Via Sol Caliente
Tucson AZ 85706

Call Sign: N7ADS
Warren E Hender
9664 E Vicks Pl
Tucson AZ 85748

Call Sign: KC7DVL
Dennis E Regehr
8249 E Vicksburg St
Tucson AZ 85710

Call Sign: KF7EAH
Thomas E O'Neil
8831 E Vicksburg St
Tucson AZ 85710

Call Sign: W7DCM
David C Mosier
10230 E Vicksburg St
Tucson AZ 85748

Call Sign: KB7EEW
Linda L Libby
8221 E Victoria Dr
Tucson AZ 857303516

Call Sign: NU5G
James H Glenn
7275 E Vuelta Rancho
Mesquite
Tucson AZ 85715

Call Sign: KF7UTI
John M Che
4187 E Wading Pond Dr
Tucson AZ 85712

Call Sign: N7CC
Ian W Thomson
4831 E Wagon Train Rd
Tucson AZ 85737

Call Sign: WD7F
John P Slusser Sr
9411 E Walnut Tree Cir
Tucson AZ 857499267

Call Sign: KE7VKO
Niles S Stein II

9120 E Walnut Tree Dr
Tucson AZ 85749

Call Sign: KE7MMN
James S Keane
9160 E Walnut Tree Dr
Tucson AZ 85749

Call Sign: KD4ELT
Peter S Woodland
9200 E Walnut Tree Dr
Tucson AZ 85749

Call Sign: WB8SVK
Michael J Nofziger
9642 E Wasatch Pl
Tucson AZ 85749

Call Sign: KF7BRR
Christopher J Mcpherson
1410 E Water St
Tucson AZ 85719

Call Sign: W7QHD
Kurt D Cramer
2226 E Water St
Tucson AZ 85719

Call Sign: KA8UKB
Stephen T Portell
5023 E Water St
Tucson AZ 85717

Call Sign: NL7ES
Robert A Tapley
2323 E Water St Trlr 48
Tucson AZ 857193447

Call Sign: KF7NR
Edwin N Reiche
9417 E Watson Dr
Tucson AZ 85730

Call Sign: KF7PET
Malcolm C Hooe Sr
9454 E Watson Dr
Tucson AZ 85730

Call Sign: N7QPB

William V Sutherland
9464 E Watson Dr
Tucson AZ 85730

Call Sign: W0DVK
Melvin R Lehman
9762 E Watson Dr
Tucson AZ 85730

Call Sign: KD7HZT
Cyrus G Jones IV
2215 E Waverly St
Tucson AZ 85719

Call Sign: KA7YYD
Wesley E Morey Jr
2725 E Waverly St
Tucson AZ 857163080

Call Sign: KE7QIF
Moses P Milazzo
3243 E Waverly St
Tucson AZ 85716

Call Sign: KF7CUJ
Darin J Law
3343 E Waverly St
Tucson AZ 85716

Call Sign: KE7EKZ
Wanda J Wheelock
405 E Wetmore 117 202
Tucson AZ 85705

Call Sign: N6ESM
Francis W Chao
405 E Wetmore 117 484
Tucson AZ 857051792

Call Sign: KA7ZWD
Catherine D Hedrick
927 E Weymouth
Tucson AZ 85719

Call Sign: WA9IRH
John H Edris Jr
63425 E Whispering Tree Ln
Tucson AZ 85739

Call Sign: N7JZT
Michael J Raymond
5143 E Willard St
Tucson AZ 85712

Call Sign: KE7CYR
William A Lambert III
5400 E Williams Blvd Nr
5206
Tucson AZ 85711

Call Sign: KD7MON
Condie J Taylor
6117 E Window Ridge Ln
Tucson AZ 857069572

Call Sign: KC7LVL
Andy P Bates
621 E Windward Cir
Tucson AZ 85704

Call Sign: AG7H
Ronald W Bates
621 E Windward Cir
Tucson AZ 85704

Call Sign: WE7Z
Gary L Wood
7940 E Winnepeg Dr
Tucson AZ 85730

Call Sign: KD4KHZ
Donald J Lacey Jr
9114 E Wolfberry St
Tucson AZ 857475221

Call Sign: KD4QCZ
Nancy J Lacey
9114 E Wolfberry St
Tucson AZ 857475221

Call Sign: KO6EA
Loren L Dunham
5280 E Wolfer Dr
Tucson AZ 85739

Call Sign: KD7TXO
James C Walker
9959 E Wolford Pl

Tucson AZ 85749

Call Sign: KF7UNY
Scott W Logan
9968 E Wolford Pl
Tucson AZ 85749

Call Sign: KC7LIB
John M Kalmes
8360 E Wrightstown Rd
Tucson AZ 85715

Call Sign: KC7CJU
Lawrence F Caugh
9420 E Wrightstown Rd
Tucson AZ 85715

Call Sign: KC7RME
Richard J Wickizer
1920 E Wyoming St
Tucson AZ 85706

Call Sign: K0ACA
Wayne A Nelson
7301 Est Eli Dr
Tucson AZ 85710

Call Sign: W6GCO
Jeffrey E Baertsch
8480 Fernhill Dr
Tucson AZ 85715

Call Sign: K7CET
William F Mc Caughey
2549 Florence Dr
Tucson AZ 85716

Call Sign: N7KBU
Norman G Penwell
5444 Flying Cir W
Tucson AZ 85713

Call Sign: N7NRZ
William L Napier Jr
4202 Frankfort Ave
Tucson AZ 85706

Call Sign: WA0EJI
John M Marek

933 Garnette
Tucson AZ 85705

Call Sign: KB7IUF
Frank B Griffith Jr
5060 Golder Ranch Rd
Tucson AZ 85737

Call Sign: KE7HMV
Jesse Olvera
6450 Golf Links Rd
Tucson AZ 85730

Call Sign: WB7TLR
Willford F Watson
2888 Goret Rd
Tucson AZ 85745

Call Sign: WB8UBC
Charles J Harris
Hcr 3
Tucson AZ 85739

Call Sign: KB7GV
Ben Vallefuoco
1960 Hickory Hollow Ln
Tucson AZ 85704

Call Sign: KF7LNT
William A Madson
360 Hillcrest Pl
Tucson AZ 85704

Call Sign: N7KUA
Marc A Foggiano
2104 Horseshoe Trl
Tucson AZ 85745

Call Sign: KD7OIW
Peter R Petrotta
2300 Ina Rd Apt 8204
Tucson AZ 85741

Call Sign: K7NNY
Raymond S Chase Jr
2509 Indian Ridge Dr
Tucson AZ 857153311

Call Sign: K7KI

Bruce W Jorden Jr
6861 Kenanna Pl
Tucson AZ 85704

Call Sign: KA7BCR
Marjorie A Jorden
6861 Kenanna Pl
Tucson AZ 85704

Call Sign: KB7TRL
David W Eubank
1531 Kennington Ave
Tucson AZ 85746

Call Sign: W7AH
James C Wyant
1881 King St
Tucson AZ 85749

Call Sign: KJ7US
Preston J Taylor
4120 La Linda Rama
Tucson AZ 85718

Call Sign: KB7ZBK
Albert P Kinney
3126 Las Lomitas Rd
Tucson AZ 85741

Call Sign: WA7WFF
J Gordon Kirby
760 Las Lomitos Rd
Tucson AZ 857042706

Call Sign: K7ZAG
Jerome E Arnoldi
1133 Lehigh Dr
Tucson AZ 85710

Call Sign: N7HBB
Porter B Williamson
3900 Los Portales
Tucson AZ 85718

Call Sign: KF7PW
Charles R Lynde
457 Matterhorn
Tucson AZ 85704

Call Sign: W7BNZ
Walter A Bufe
741 McMillan Dr
Tucson AZ 85719

Call Sign: KB6CIP
Ardell G Rath
3701 Meadow Briar Dr
Tucson AZ 85741

Call Sign: K6ARF
Richard A Rath
3701 Meadow Briar Dr
Tucson AZ 85741

Call Sign: K2BPK
Dennis L Freeman
2220 Miraval Tercero
Tucson AZ 85718

Call Sign: N7CUA
Norris W Gilbert
3500 Montgomery St
Tucson AZ 85742

Call Sign: WW7Z
James J Torrey
1851 Moon Valley Pl
Tucson AZ 85745

Call Sign: KC7POI
Arlene G Norris
1525 Moonbeam Pl
Tucson AZ 85748

Call Sign: KB6LWW
Paul P Tretiakoff
1444 Moonflower Ln
Tucson AZ 85748

Call Sign: KC7NSL
Jack D Hysong
39116 Moonwood Dr
Tucson AZ 85739

Call Sign: KC7ODT
Nancy F Hysong
39116 Moonwood Dr
Tucson AZ 85739

Call Sign: KF7BMN
Southern Arizona Dx
Association
8925 Morningview Dr
Tucson AZ 85704

Call Sign: WS7DX
Southern Arizona Dx
Association
8925 Morningview Dr
Tucson AZ 85704

Call Sign: KB7KRO
John G James
661 Mtn Sunrise Pl
Tucson AZ 85704

Call Sign: KC7SQU
William D Wright
3215 Mustang Dr
Tucson AZ 85708

Call Sign: KD7HVG
Terri A Holcomb
717 N 10th Ave 3
Tucson AZ 85705

Call Sign: KD7YCO
Huilong H Huang
1319 N 1st Ave
Tucson AZ 85719

Call Sign: KC7DFE
Allan L Tigges
7845 N 1st Ave
Tucson AZ 857181065

Call Sign: N1IIB
Robert D Demers Jr
901 N 3rd Ave
Tucson AZ 85705

Call Sign: KC7WWN
Elise M Taylor
1930 N 49Er Dr
Tucson AZ 85749

Call Sign: KB7TEL

Ronald S Suddath
3801 N 4th Ave
Tucson AZ 85705

Call Sign: N7ZQL
Lee D Perin
3941 N 4th Ave 47
Tucson AZ 857053390

Call Sign: N5NCR
June R Raymond
835 N 6th Ave Apt 5
Tucson AZ 85705

Call Sign: N7SCD
Daniel A Mortlos Sr
1602 N 7th Ave
Tucson AZ 85705

Call Sign: KC7BTP
Mark S Bickerton
2410 N Aileen Ave
Tucson AZ 85715

Call Sign: WA2LTF
Michael R Miller
5411 N Airway Dr
Tucson AZ 85750

Call Sign: KC7THU
James C Ulmer II
810 N Alamo Ave
Tucson AZ 85711

Call Sign: KG7PZ
George G Caria
9444 N Albatross Dr
Tucson AZ 85742

Call Sign: N7OAW
Maria A Caria
9444 N Albatross Dr
Tucson AZ 85742

Call Sign: W7KVL
Milford J Borchert
4910 N Alicia Ave
Tucson AZ 85705

Call Sign: KF7RSP
Gary L Kirton
4942 N Alicia Ave
Tucson AZ 85705

Call Sign: KB7OGR
James E Gibson
6752 N Altos Primero
Tucson AZ 85718

Call Sign: KD7CRD
Jennifer J Johnson
3939 N Alvernon C
Tucson AZ 85718

Call Sign: KC7NPI
David F Foster
2767 N Alvernon Way
Tucson AZ 85712

Call Sign: KA7LBU
Ronald M Rife
2843 N Alvernon Way
Tucson AZ 85712

Call Sign: KF6TOK
Ralph Acosta Jr
2701 N Alvernon Way Apt 8
Tucson AZ 85712

Call Sign: KF7ERV
Christopher D Tarr
630 N Alvernon Way Ste 220
Tucson AZ 85711

Call Sign: N7EZ
Christopher D Tarr
630 N Alvernon Way Ste 220
Tucson AZ 85711

Call Sign: N4VPW
Louis L Hibbs
1170 N Amber Brooke Ave
Tucson AZ 85745

Call Sign: KF7IGS
David J Benitez
1601 N Andros Pl
Tucson AZ 85745

Call Sign: N7SQI
Paul A Suddath
5030 N Apache Hills Tr
Tucson AZ 85715

Call Sign: KC7TKM
Jeffrey P Brucker
1211 N Arbor Cir
Tucson AZ 85715

Call Sign: N7XJS
James P Wilding
2110 N Arbor Vista Cir
Tucson AZ 85749

Call Sign: N7XJT
Michael P Noonan
2110 N Arbor Vista Cir
Tucson AZ 85749

Call Sign: AE7QC
Christof Schmitt
1156 N Arcadia Ave
Tucson AZ 85712

Call Sign: W9AD
Arthur D Code
250 N Arcadia Ave 1024
Tucson AZ 85711

Call Sign: W7DCL
Walter R Parker
207 N Arcadia Blvd
Tucson AZ 85711

Call Sign: KE7BOI
Teri L Tracey
6954 N Asterion Ln
Tucson AZ 85741

Call Sign: K7TLT
Teri L Tracey
6954 N Asterion Ln
Tucson AZ 85741

Call Sign: KA7ZRD
Maria Ferrari
7996 N Atolia Dr

Tucson AZ 85743

Call Sign: NR7J
Roberto Ferrari
7996 N Atolia Dr
Tucson AZ 85743

Call Sign: KB7PMZ
Robert A Foote
7781 N Ave Cerlotta
Tucson AZ 85704

Call Sign: KD7MCW
Charles M Stanford
4664 N Ave De Franelah
Tucson AZ 857499510

Call Sign: N7MGD
Davis D Ewing
7870 N Avenida De Carlotta
Tucson AZ 85704

Call Sign: N7KUD
Ralph D Ewing
7870 N Avenida De Carlotta
Tucson AZ 85704

Call Sign: N7ZKZ
John H Perault
4632 N Avenida De Franelah
Tucson AZ 85749

Call Sign: K3TOU
Le Roy R Smith Jr
3631 N Avenida De La
Colina
Tucson AZ 857497506

Call Sign: N7GVU
Leonard H Youdelman
2587 N Avenida De La
Lantana
Tucson AZ 85749

Call Sign: AB7CG
Theodore A Geyler
4151 N Avenida De
Montezuma
Tucson AZ 857499176

Call Sign: KD7BIB
Paul B Cartter
16100 N Avenida Del
Canada
Tucson AZ 85739

Call Sign: KD7HVL
Frank S Zavada
16202 N Avenida Del Oro
Tucson AZ 85739

Call Sign: KE7DDT
Ruby I Belyeu
5143 N Avenida Primera
Tucson AZ 85704

Call Sign: W7LHU
Leonard E Herzmark
4631 N Avenida Ronca
Tucson AZ 85750

Call Sign: KF7MZY
David G Iadevaia
5700 N Avenida Silencioso
Tucson AZ 85750

Call Sign: KE7VAD
Montaque Brown
1050 N Avenida Venado
Tucson AZ 85748

Call Sign: KE7VAC
Barbara P Mccool
1050 N Avenida Venado
Tucson AZ 85748

Call Sign: KD7SPU
Linda A Catterson
16637 N Avenidade La
Canada
Tucson AZ 85739

Call Sign: N5XXM
Michael K Blackstock
5311 N Avra Rd Lot 2
Tucson AZ 85743

Call Sign: KE7BTE

Steve G Franks II
500 N Bahamas Dr
Tucson AZ 85710

Call Sign: K7CMS
William H Beatty
4721 N Bamboo Cir
Tucson AZ 85749

Call Sign: KB7WGF
Greg D Pallack
3532 N Banner Mine Dr
Tucson AZ 85745

Call Sign: K4HHX
C Vincent Baker
3760 N Banner Mine Dr
Tucson AZ 85745

Call Sign: KE7FEF
Robert B Harbour
4355 N Banyon Tree Dr
Tucson AZ 85749

Call Sign: KC0AYD
Eric K Davis
4525 N Banyon Tree Dr
Tucson AZ 85749

Call Sign: KE7SZW
Martha J Davis
4525 N Banyon Tree Dr
Tucson AZ 85749

Call Sign: KF7QQA
Joy L Florence
6351 N Barcelona Ct 817
Tucson AZ 85704

Call Sign: KD7QPA
William B Florence
6351 N Barcelona Ct 817
Tucson AZ 85704

Call Sign: KE6LKJ
C Beth Gould
2464 N Barnwall Ct
Tucson AZ 85749

Call Sign: KO7AA
Bear Canyon ARC
3391 N Bear Canyon Rd
Tucson AZ 85749

Call Sign: WB0O
William H Straw
3391 N Bear Canyon Rd
Tucson AZ 85749

Call Sign: KO7SS
William H Straw
3391 N Bear Canyon Rd
Tucson AZ 85749

Call Sign: KE7EDX
Jason R Mcneil
3825 N Bear Canyon Rd
Tucson AZ 85749

Call Sign: KE7VAA
Shirley A Requard
4251 N Bear Claw Way
Tucson AZ 85749

Call Sign: KD7CEC
James W Bolthouse
5991 N Belbrook
Tucson AZ 85741

Call Sign: KD7KHY
Donald R Harrison
5900 N Belbrook Dr
Tucson AZ 85741

Call Sign: AL7FA
Paul T Johnson
7640 N Bellwether Dr
Tucson AZ 85743

Call Sign: WW7J
James A Owen
1224 N Belvedere Ave
Tucson AZ 857124618

Call Sign: KC2AHT
Kristin P O Connor
626 N Belvedere Ave Apt 2
Tucson AZ 85711

Call Sign: KB7PZL
Steven J Brezovski Sr
600 N Benton Ave
Tucson AZ 85711

Call Sign: W7NOG
Jack E Bivin
4373 N Bidahochi Dr
Tucson AZ 85749

Call Sign: N8CRT
Edward F Augst Jr
13875 N Big Wash Overlook
Pl
Tucson AZ 85739

Call Sign: WB7CGQ
David R Hardman
9961 N Black Mesa Trl
Tucson AZ 857428854

Call Sign: WA7ZFT
Beauregard E Nelson
6955 N Bobcat Ridge Trl
Tucson AZ 85743

Call Sign: N7USQ
David K Carpenter
3281 N Bonanza
Tucson AZ 85749

Call Sign: KB7PNC
Maryann P Carpenter
3281 N Bonanza
Tucson AZ 85749

Call Sign: KD7OIV
Vernon B Watwood Jr
4922 N Bonita Ridge Ave
Tucson AZ 85750

Call Sign: N2KRW
Leonard J Rosenblum
5039 N Bonita Ridge Ave
Tucson AZ 85750

Call Sign: KD7TZW
Larry D Hawkins

8040 N Bounty Pl
Tucson AZ 85741

Call Sign: N7DDG
David C Burkert
4670 N Brightside Dr
Tucson AZ 85705

Call Sign: KC7VVC
Kristi K Mc Kinley
9030 N Brimstone Way
Tucson AZ 85742

Call Sign: KC7QYB
Michael R Mc Kinley
9030 N Brimstone Way
Tucson AZ 85742

Call Sign: KD7KRS
Patrick A Patton
4716 N Brookview Dr
Tucson AZ 85705

Call Sign: WB9ZMO
Michael L Banner
179 N Brown Ave
Tucson AZ 85710

Call Sign: KD7TMX
Clifford R Schneider
241 N Bull Run Dr
Tucson AZ 85748

Call Sign: AC7ZL
Hans P Friedrichs
8401 N Burke Dr
Tucson AZ 85742

Call Sign: WA7IIC
John R Smith Jr
3252 N Calle De Beso
Tucson AZ 85750

Call Sign: KG0RS
Michael A Pate
6679 N Calle De Calipso
Tucson AZ 857182090

Call Sign: NK7R

William L Faull
6450 N Calle De Estevan
Tucson AZ 85718

Call Sign: KF7JZA
James D Tompkins
6501 N Calle De Estevan
Tucson AZ 85718

Call Sign: KA7JCC
John C Carroll
5740 N Calle De La Reina
Tucson AZ 85718

Call Sign: KA7CAU
Daisy Dieguez
2704 N Calle De Romy
Tucson AZ 85712

Call Sign: AB7PC
Rodolfo Dieguez
2704 N Calle De Romy
Tucson AZ 85712

Call Sign: KA7ONQ
Rudolph Dieguez
2704 N Calle De Romy
Tucson AZ 85712

Call Sign: KC6WFP
Morris D Brown
1821 N Calle El Trigo
Tucson AZ 85749

Call Sign: WB7FBI
Michael G Magras
3875 N Calle Entrada
Tucson AZ 857499692

Call Sign: N7WEQ
Craig D Roberts
4822 N Calle Harmonia
Tucson AZ 85705

Call Sign: KD7SZ
Merrill E Dillon
5801 N Calle Kino
Tucson AZ 85704

Call Sign: KB3OXR
Jeffrey H Owen
5226 N Calle Ladero
Tucson AZ 85718

Call Sign: KC5FSA
Daniel W Manning
4671 N Calle Llanura
Tucson AZ 85745

Call Sign: AA6KI
Gerald D Palsson
4890 N Calle Llanura
Tucson AZ 857459313

Call Sign: KC7JWI
Jeffrey S Horowitz
6211 N Calle Minera
Tucson AZ 85718

Call Sign: KF7HLX
Joseph A Hamilton
2520 N Calle Noche
Tucson AZ 85749

Call Sign: KE7VTV
Darcy W Johnson
5060 N Calle Penascoso
Tucson AZ 85745

Call Sign: AC7QZ
Jay A Shumway
1849 N Calle Serena
Tucson AZ 85712

Call Sign: W6VVB
James A Rose
7433 N Calle Sin Desengano
Tucson AZ 857181203

Call Sign: KD7SPW
Leonard A Hoffman
7500 N Calle Sin Envidia
Tucson AZ 85718

Call Sign: N7BD
Ralph P Horian
7500 N Calle Sin Envidia
15102

Tucson AZ 85718

Call Sign: N9LMP
James E Babeckis
8571 N Calle Tioga
Tucson AZ 85704

Call Sign: W0KZD
Joshua Premack
4061 N Calle Vista Ciudad
Tucson AZ 85750

Call Sign: KC7NPW
Gregory T Kotsovolos
4062 N Calle Vista Ciudad
Tucson AZ 85750

Call Sign: NH6NS
Raymond C Bertram
3451 N Calle Vistosa
Tucson AZ 85750

Call Sign: KG6FWD
Cory A Saulsberry
2509 N Cambell Ave 121
Tucson AZ 85719

Call Sign: KF7RKB
Linda A Henderson
3636 N Cambell Ave Apt
4220
Tucson AZ 85719

Call Sign: N7PVG
Ronald K Shaffer
4668 N Camino Aire Fresco
Tucson AZ 85705

Call Sign: KD7UIQ
Mark A Gordon
6301 N Camino Almonte
Tucson AZ 85718

Call Sign: AE7AM
Mark A Gordon
6301 N Camino Almonte
Tucson AZ 85718

Call Sign: K7YWY

W Clayton Tatom
6302 N Camino Almonte
Tucson AZ 857183705

Call Sign: WB6GCJ
Steve E Hunley
6160 N Camino Almonte Dr
Tucson AZ 85718

Call Sign: KD7DDW
Glenn W Hilde
2240 N Camino Altar
Tucson AZ 85743

Call Sign: KD7EMA
Sheldon G Hilde
2240 N Camino Altar
Tucson AZ 85743

Call Sign: KC7AHF
Albert L Price
5981 N Camino Arturo
Tucson AZ 85718

Call Sign: KC7AWI
Shawn B Jordan
6000 N Camino Arturo
Tucson AZ 85718

Call Sign: KA7CME
Scott W Carlson
6440 N Camino Arturo
Tucson AZ 85718

Call Sign: W4PHG
Elbert E Warren
4661 N Camino Campero
Tucson AZ 85715

Call Sign: KD7KNP
John C Carroll
4473 N Camino Cardenal
Tucson AZ 857186850

Call Sign: KA0KHO
Gregory S Porter
4500 N Camino Cardenal
Tucson AZ 85718

Call Sign: N7IFM
Christine S Willett
11031 N Camino Central
Tucson AZ 85742

Call Sign: KD7SNW
Matthew M Willett
11031 N Camino Central
Tucson AZ 85742

Call Sign: KE7PO
T Michael Willett
11031 N Camino Central
Tucson AZ 857429690

Call Sign: N7NBV
Kenneth W Boyd
855 N Camino Cordon
Tucson AZ 85748

Call Sign: N7OHT
Victoria A Boyd
855 N Camino Cordon
Tucson AZ 85748

Call Sign: KC7UAY
Barbara J Bornemann
4369 N Camino De Carrillo
Tucson AZ 85750

Call Sign: KC7SBA
Carol J Trible
2121 N Camino De La
Cienega
Tucson AZ 85715

Call Sign: KD7CQY
Ronald F Arrington
4900 N Camino De La
Codorniz
Tucson AZ 87545

Call Sign: KF7SI
Valdemar Rauch
5493 N Camino De La
Culebra
Tucson AZ 85750

Call Sign: KC5IPL

Frederick D Leonard
5091 N Camino De La
Cumbre
Tucson AZ 85750

Call Sign: KC7QMN
Gregory J Goodman
5660 N Camino De La Noche
Tucson AZ 85718

Call Sign: WA6SMY
Lori J Fitzsimmons
5791 N Camino De La
Sombra
Tucson AZ 85718

Call Sign: AE7G
Robert C Koerner
8910 N Camino De La Tierra
Tucson AZ 85741

Call Sign: W7ETA
Robert C Koerner
8910 N Camino De La Tierra
Tucson AZ 85742

Call Sign: KC8TH
Ryosuke Sato
8930 N Camino De La Tierra
Tucson AZ 85741

Call Sign: KB8VA
Christine S Snyder
8930 N Camino De La Tierra
Tucson AZ 85742

Call Sign: KF8N
William G Snyder
8930 N Camino De La Tierra
Tucson AZ 85742

Call Sign: KB8VA
Sumikos Memorial Club
8930 N Camino De La Tierra
Tucson AZ 85742

Call Sign: KF5QY
Richard F Fahlsing

7015 N Camino De Los
Caballos
Tucson AZ 85743

Call Sign: KC7QYC
Mark R Easton
4071 N Camino De Lupo
Tucson AZ 85718

Call Sign: N7SEP
Barry F Watson
7743 N Camino De
Maximillian
Tucson AZ 85704

Call Sign: WB6CWV
Carl G Foster
6215 N Camino De Michael
Tucson AZ 85718

Call Sign: K7RME
Thomas W Johnson
3815 N Camino De Oeste
Tucson AZ 85745

Call Sign: KD6BAK
Daniel R Gibb
10791 N Camino De Oeste
Tucson AZ 85742

Call Sign: KC6PAK
Pat B Gibb
10791 N Camino De Oeste
Tucson AZ 85742

Call Sign: KF7HYD
Guy O Hatfield
10880 N Camino De Oeste
Tucson AZ 85742

Call Sign: W2BRT
James T Hiers
9332 N Camino De Plaza
Tucson AZ 85742

Call Sign: KC7YDH
Mark A Scott
3435 N Camino De Vista
Tucson AZ 85745

Call Sign: KD7UUO
Craig G Howlett
3572 N Camino De Vista
Tucson AZ 857459798

Call Sign: W7UCX
Howard T Douglas
701 N Camino Del Codorniz
Tucson AZ 85748

Call Sign: K7SEC
Phyllis S Douglas
701 N Camino Del Codorniz
Tucson AZ 85748

Call Sign: KC7SUR
Henry L Jacobs
801 N Camino Del Codorniz
Tucson AZ 85748

Call Sign: KC0CQX
Erik S Pytlak
525 N Camino Del Norte
Tucson AZ 857165139

Call Sign: N7IRP
Christopher A Gall
4421 N Camino Del Santo
Tucson AZ 85718

Call Sign: AE6DO
Anthony R Mollner
9920 N Camino Del Sauce
Tucson AZ 85742

Call Sign: N7YVG
Thomas W Johnson
3815 N Camino Dr Oeste
Tucson AZ 85745

Call Sign: KA7GPT
Michael B Burdoo
2302 N Camino Emiliano
Tucson AZ 857451347

Call Sign: K7LSW
Mary Jane Nichols
5545 N Camino Escuela

Tucson AZ 85718

Call Sign: WB7OZU
Leslie J Johnson
5675 N Camino Esplendora
4223
Tucson AZ 857184585

Call Sign: KD6BQT
Stephan J Gates Phd
5803 N Camino Esplendora
Apt 21 Unit 204
Tucson AZ 85718

Call Sign: N7AIG
David B Mc Clain
4391 N Camino Ferreo
Tucson AZ 85750

Call Sign: KC6NZQ
Ariella C Mollen
3419 N Camino La Jicarrilla
Tucson AZ 85712

Call Sign: KB7KDX
Jamie P Turner
6441 N Camino Libby
Tucson AZ 85718

Call Sign: WB7UMC
Ulrich F Michael
6160 N Camino Miraval
Tucson AZ 85718

Call Sign: N7JJL
Brian G Goodman
3900 N Camino Ojo De Agua
Tucson AZ 85749

Call Sign: KC7QMR
Margaret M Goodman
3900 N Camino Ojo De Agua
Tucson AZ 85749

Call Sign: KN6BZ
William H Pansing
5781 N Camino Padre Isidoro
Tucson AZ 85718

Call Sign: KF7LON
Elizardo A Jacobs
431 N Camino Santiago
Tucson AZ 85745

Call Sign: KC7NYW
Peter R Sickler
837 N Camino Santiago
Tucson AZ 85745

Call Sign: KB7YHE
Scott A Foss
902 N Camino Santiago
Tucson AZ 85745

Call Sign: WA7LHG
John W Mc Lean
3537 N Camino Seco
Tucson AZ 85749

Call Sign: KF7EFH
Max A Weisel
3760 N Camino Sinuoso
Tucson AZ 85718

Call Sign: AB5XW
Chris M Cooper
3351 N Camino Suerte
Tucson AZ 85750

Call Sign: AA7ZJ
Thomas R Wolf
4800 N Camino Sumo
Tucson AZ 85718

Call Sign: W0LTL
Marlyn J Zonnefeld
2701 N Camino Valle Verde
Tucson AZ 85715

Call Sign: KE7IJQ
Carl Ostermann
6340 N Camino Verde Dr
Tucson AZ 857439699

Call Sign: K6IHN
John H Hebert
4390 N Camino Vinorama
Tucson AZ 85715

Call Sign: KD7BPW
A H M Asadul Huq
8930 N Caminode Latierra
Tucson AZ 85741

Call Sign: KD7PPW
Harriet A Harrell
2509 N Campbell Ave 229
Tucson AZ 857193362

Call Sign: KB7LVT
Chris M Lescoulie
2509 N Campbell Ave 324
Tucson AZ 85719

Call Sign: KD6YIN
Jonah L Fontenot
2509 N Campbell Ave 357
Tucson AZ 85719

Call Sign: KJ7QC
Frank M Hegewald
2509 N Campbell Ave 404
Tucson AZ 85719

Call Sign: WA7CW
Frank M Hegewald
2509 N Campbell Ave 404
Tucson AZ 85719

Call Sign: KE7HOV
Danny A King
3661 N Campbell Ave 440
Tucson AZ 85719

Call Sign: W2LEO
Michael Katz
3661 N Campbell Ave 582
Tucson AZ 85719

Call Sign: KD7PPV
Jay K Burton
2509 N Campbell Ave Nr
229
Tucson AZ 85719

Call Sign: AC7D
Willard L Haskell

3915 N Campbell Ave Sp
102
Tucson AZ 85719

Call Sign: KB9YPA
James R Knitter
2509 N Campbell Ave Ste 74
Tucson AZ 85719

Call Sign: AD8O
James R Knitter
2509 N Campbell Ave Ste 74
Tucson AZ 85719

Call Sign: KD7JBM
Marc E Audiss
2509 N Campbell Pmb71
Tucson AZ 85719

Call Sign: K8NSW
Thomas D Welch
11266 N Canada Creek Dr
Tucson AZ 85737

Call Sign: KE7RIE
Gordon L Washburn
8430 N Canal Ct
Tucson AZ 85742

Call Sign: KD7PZS
Nicholas R Deluca
6655 N Canyon Crest 19 101
Tucson AZ 85750

Call Sign: KA5FVE
Wayne L Guerrini
280 N Carapan 304
Tucson AZ 85745

Call Sign: KD7SIS
Catherine E Green
2945 N Cardell Cir
Tucson AZ 85712

Call Sign: KC7DFC
Gary L Taylor
532 N Caribe
Tucson AZ 85710

Call Sign: W2KUO
Milton I Goldberg
1027 N Caribe Ave
Tucson AZ 85710

Call Sign: KW7CD
Cornell Drentea
757 N Carribean Ave
Tucson AZ 85748

Call Sign: KE6FUL
Edward B Cleveland
14385 N Caryota Wy
Tucson AZ 85737

Call Sign: W6TDR
Cullen B Tendick
11753 N Cassiopeia Dr
Tucson AZ 85737

Call Sign: KB7CYP
Ronald L Graham
3030 N Castro Ave
Tucson AZ 85705

Call Sign: KA0PFK
David L Bjorgaard
2525 N Castro Ave 22
Tucson AZ 85705

Call Sign: KE7TF
Gary A Rose
7370 N Catalina Ridge Dr
Tucson AZ 857181369

Call Sign: KC7AC
Howard A Chorost
7057 N Cathedral Rock Pl
Tucson AZ 85718

Call Sign: KE7ESN
Bryan D Jarman
9245 N Centipede Ave
Tucson AZ 85742

Call Sign: KE7PEE
Bryan D Jarman
9245 N Centipede Ave
Tucson AZ 85742

Call Sign: KE7QIG
Jonathan C Jarman
9245 N Centipede Ave
Tucson AZ 85742

Call Sign: KE7PDZ
Thomas G Jarman
9245 N Centipede Ave
Tucson AZ 85742

Call Sign: KE7QIH
Wendie D Jarman
9245 N Centipede Ave
Tucson AZ 85742

Call Sign: WD9GIX
Wallace G Panzer
9312 N Centipede Ave
Tucson AZ 85742

Call Sign: N7IUA
James A Telewski
4540 N Cerritos Dr
Tucson AZ 857459554

Call Sign: KC7NBZ
Robert R Parra
4621 N Cerritos Dr
Tucson AZ 857459555

Call Sign: KB7NQM
William W Whatley
4020 N Cerro De Falcon
Tucson AZ 85718

Call Sign: WA7AQK
James R Morse
531 N Chantilly Dr
Tucson AZ 85711

Call Sign: AB7VM
Bayard C Auchincloss
6724 N Chapultapec Cir
Tucson AZ 85750

Call Sign: KE7LOU
Bethany L Hay
7290 N Cherokee Pony Trl

Tucson AZ 85743

Call Sign: WA6VEU
Scott K Gordon
5681 N Chiefton Trl
Tucson AZ 857501302

Call Sign: KC7ZAR
Deborah P Gordon
5681 N Chietan Trl
Tucson AZ 857501302

Call Sign: KG7VV
Hardy M Benson Jr
7119 N Chimney Rock Pl
Tucson AZ 85718

Call Sign: KC7OX
Harold E Robertson
14310 N Choctaw Dr
Tucson AZ 85737

Call Sign: WA3HRM
Robert W Freund
3555 N Christmas Pl
Tucson AZ 857161230

Call Sign: KE7ZGT
Jenna Kloosterman
922 N Chrysler Dr Apt 1
Tucson AZ 85716

Call Sign: KB7VKF
George J Birmingham
6611 N Cibola Ave
Tucson AZ 85718

Call Sign: WB2ZNJ
Stephen F Feingold
4526 N Circulo De Kaiots
Tucson AZ 85750

Call Sign: W7BGD
Nick J Mansour Jr
4100 N Circulo Manzanillo
Tucson AZ 85715

Call Sign: KD7WEL
Creston A King III

5160 N Circulo Sobrio
Tucson AZ 85718

Call Sign: N7BR
Creston A King III
5160 N Circulo Sobrio
Tucson AZ 85718

Call Sign: N6FBS
Ronald I Swor
13950 N Cirrus Hill Dr
Tucson AZ 85737

Call Sign: W0KNM
William T Burke
920 N Citadel
Tucson AZ 85748

Call Sign: KC7GKS
Leslie L Mc Courtney
14022 N Clarion Way
Tucson AZ 85737

Call Sign: WA9PUB
Gary A Flynn
9750 N Cliff View Pl
Tucson AZ 85704

Call Sign: KC4BPO
Jhamal D Johnson
7825 N Coltrane Ln
Tucson AZ 85743

Call Sign: N9KFI
Brett R Zamir
8020 N Coltrane Ln
Tucson AZ 85743

Call Sign: K7GDP
Gene D Prantner
7849 N Coltrane Ln
Tucson AZ 85743

Call Sign: KB7TRY
Robert C Angus
6640 N Columbus
Tucson AZ 85718

Call Sign: KB8SOO

Scott H Plum
16606 N Columbus Blvd
Tucson AZ 85739

Call Sign: KC7HHB
Leoncio F Martinez
3401 N Columbus Blvd 30 E
Tucson AZ 85712

Call Sign: N7MXO
Karl W Gross
12775 N Como Dr
Tucson AZ 85742

Call Sign: N7UNL
Heath N Evans
13365 N Como Dr
Tucson AZ 85742

Call Sign: KB7NOX
Kenneth R Peterson
3023 N Conestoga Ave
Tucson AZ 85749

Call Sign: WB2YZE
Wilbert J Taebel
348 N Constitution
Tucson AZ 85748

Call Sign: W2NSG
Wilbert J Taebel
348 N Constitution
Tucson AZ 85748

Call Sign: N9APR
Albert Zadravetz
861 N Constitution Dr
Tucson AZ 85748

Call Sign: WB7UMF
Kenneth L Hendrix
1021 N Constitution Dr
Tucson AZ 857481978

Call Sign: KE6GRZ
Robert S Scott Jr
11685 N Copper Creek Dr
Tucson AZ 85737

Call Sign: KB7PMX
Ulysses G Upshaw Jr
12487 N Copper Queen Way
Tucson AZ 85747

Call Sign: KF7KRW
Anthony E Smith
7901 N Cortaro Rd 17201
Tucson AZ 85743

Call Sign: KC7UDI
Douglas R Kasian
3061 N Corte Lindo Cielo
Tucson AZ 85745

Call Sign: KF7QQG
Yuri Talalaev
3125 N Corte Lindo Cielo
Tucson AZ 85745

Call Sign: AE7AY
Kerry M Kugler
3242 N Cottontail Cir
Tucson AZ 85749

Call Sign: KE7LOS
Cynthia K Mccauley
3750 N Country Club Rd
Unit 2
Tucson AZ 85716

Call Sign: WD6CUH
Leonard E Hall
3786 N Creek Side Pl
Tucson AZ 857502230

Call Sign: WB7WHO
Carter H Harrison Jr
2425 N Creek Vista Dr
Tucson AZ 85749

Call Sign: KB7UPK
Constance T Harrison
2425 N Creek Vista Dr
Tucson AZ 85749

Call Sign: KF7QFQ
Art T Just Sr
2449 N Creek Vista Dr

Tucson AZ 85749

Call Sign: KC7VEJ
Duane L Bowans
5547 N Crescent Ridge Dr
Tucson AZ 85718

Call Sign: KE7UUR
Simone Komm
3692 N Crest Ranch Dr
Tucson AZ 85719

Call Sign: KE7KRD
Lawrence P Bush
9161 N Crested Owl Pl
Tucson AZ 85742

Call Sign: WA6ZTF
Brooks W Rettig
9460 N Crestone Dr
Tucson AZ 857425104

Call Sign: K6GGS
Brooks W Rettig
9460 N Crestone Dr
Tucson AZ 857425104

Call Sign: WA6CPI
Thomas A Durosko
9575 N Crestone Dr
Tucson AZ 85742

Call Sign: W7CPI
Thomas A Durosko
9575 N Crestone Dr
Tucson AZ 85742

Call Sign: K6PIY
Robert B Campbell
3832 N Crestwood Pl
Tucson AZ 85750

Call Sign: W6IK
Robert B Campbell
3832 N Crestwood Pl
Tucson AZ 85750

Call Sign: KC7PJV
Robert H Graham

15631 N Daisy Pl
Tucson AZ 85739

Call Sign: WB7WOJ
William T Schuler
1161 N Darlene Dr
Tucson AZ 85762

Call Sign: KA7PKD
Lawrence D Andrews Sr
5041 N Davis Ave
Tucson AZ 85705

Call Sign: KF7SAO
Steven Hoell
1421 N Day Rd
Tucson AZ 85715

Call Sign: KF7QQE
James E Corbin
503 N Daystar Mountain Dr
Tucson AZ 85745

Call Sign: N7IAV
Jean H Lahargoue
1620 N Debra Sue Pl
Tucson AZ 85715

Call Sign: N0RGC
Michael R Garman
8513 N Deer Valley Dr
Tucson AZ 82742

Call Sign: K9EAZ
Kenneth A Bunzey
11910 N Deerclover Ln
Tucson AZ 85737

Call Sign: KE7OSU
Kevin H Prodromides
9331 N Denise Ann Pl
Tucson AZ 85742

Call Sign: KD7CQW
Jerry L Hoffman
2802 N Desert Ave
Tucson AZ 85712

Call Sign: KA7FRI

Edward B Thompson
3036 N Desert Dr
Tucson AZ 85712

Call Sign: KD7HZQ
James M Fish
2500 N Desert Links Dr Apt
11107
Tucson AZ 85715

Call Sign: KF7HLY
Lon D Farr
1404 N Desert Mallow Dr
Tucson AZ 85715

Call Sign: K7KZ
Gerald B Clark
9532 N Desert Mist Ln
Tucson AZ 857435165

Call Sign: N7AJX
Maxine H Clark
9532 N Desert Mist Ln
Tucson AZ 857435165

Call Sign: KD7IFA
Vicente Sanchez
6370 N Desert Willow Dr
Tucson AZ 85743

Call Sign: KF7LTX
Aaron L Cromer
1834 N Desmond Ln
Tucson AZ 85712

Call Sign: KC7GKL
Robert E Gardner
6215 N Diamond Hills Ln
Tucson AZ 85743

Call Sign: AD7DU
Robert E Gardner
6215 N Diamond Hills Ln
Tucson AZ 85743

Call Sign: KC7HBJ
Susanne C Gardner
6215 N Diamond Hills Ln
Tucson AZ 85743

Call Sign: N7SVT
Ronald P Porter
7380 N Dickinson
Tucson AZ 85741

Call Sign: KC7ETA
Emett S Brown
7601 N Dido Pl
Tucson AZ 857411901

Call Sign: KE7PML
Matthew C Knatz
542 N Dodge Blvd
Tucson AZ 85716

Call Sign: K6KFS
Richard Babow
2818 N Dodge Blvd
Tucson AZ 857162010

Call Sign: N7NYV
Mark C Young
2430 N Dodge Blvd B120
Tucson AZ 85716

Call Sign: KC7TKL
Jeffrey W Pierce
350 N Doeskin Pl
Tucson AZ 85748

Call Sign: KE7LOV
Frederic T Hill
6969 N Donatello Way
Tucson AZ 85741

Call Sign: K7OFA
Frederic T Hill
6969 N Donatello Way
Tucson AZ 85741

Call Sign: KE7ZZW
Richard J Paye
1324 N Dorado Blvd
Tucson AZ 85715

Call Sign: K2AKO
Richard J Paye
1324 N Dorado Blvd

Tucson AZ 85715

Call Sign: K2MBA
Richard E Goedel
2525 N Dos Hombres Rd
Tucson AZ 85715

Call Sign: KF7UBI
John D Stone
4241 N Drake
Tucson AZ 85749

Call Sign: KE7RIF
Jacob M Moeller
9296 N Eagle Dancer Dr
Tucson AZ 85742

Call Sign: KD7ISC
Kenneth R Moeller
9296 N Eagle Dancer Dr
Tucson AZ 85742

Call Sign: KE7BOK
Lawrence O Sawicki
9309 N Eagle Dancer Dr
Tucson AZ 85742

Call Sign: W8KEP
Edwin D Harvey
11514 N Eagle Peak Dr
Tucson AZ 85737

Call Sign: KC7LIG
Monte D Gillespie
11567 N Eagle Peak Dr
Tucson AZ 85737

Call Sign: N7PEB
Neil M Rouhier
2538 N Edith Blvd
Tucson AZ 85716

Call Sign: N7DOW
William T Selby
3721 N Edith Blvd
Tucson AZ 85718

Call Sign: WA0YSK
Terry L Million

3455 N Edith Blvd Sp A
Tucson AZ 85716

Call Sign: KG4GPN
Robert C Fleming
1150 N El Dorado Pl Unit
6250
Tucson AZ 85715

Call Sign: AE7BV
Robert C Fleming
1150 N El Dorado Pl Unit
6250
Tucson AZ 85715

Call Sign: K6HPX
Kenneth A Hirschberg
1985 N El Moraga
Tucson AZ 85745

Call Sign: KE7BGM
Katherine S Mcdonough
1985 N El Moraga Dr
Tucson AZ 85745

Call Sign: K7KWH
Kevin K Williamson
9931 N El Uno Minor
Tucson AZ 85743

Call Sign: W7XF
Kevin K Williamson
9931 N El Uno Minor
Tucson AZ 85743

Call Sign: KE7QIM
Stephen T Shaw
9513 N Elan Ln
Tucson AZ 85742

Call Sign: KE7VKE
Dennis G Cole
3029 N Elena Maria
Tucson AZ 85750

Call Sign: KD7PZP
Cynthia L Cusack
3090 N Elena Maria
Tucson AZ 85750

Call Sign: W7EPK
Lewis M Harris
7522 N Ellison Dr
Tucson AZ 85704

Call Sign: KE7CVD
Thomas W Buban
5209 N Emerald Ave
Tucson AZ 85704

Call Sign: W8TWB
Thomas W Buban
5209 N Emerald Ave
Tucson AZ 85704

Call Sign: KD7NBL
Elliot R Berry
5405 N Estelle Dr
Tucson AZ 85718

Call Sign: W7QFF
Audrey I Unruh
2934 N Estrella
Tucson AZ 85705

Call Sign: W7JHX
Jack U Harrison
980 N Evelyn
Tucson AZ 85710

Call Sign: W7EAH
John E Taylor
2449 N Fair Oaks Ave
Tucson AZ 85712

Call Sign: N6BMU
Dorothy H Wickersham
3115 N Fairview Ave 177
Tucson AZ 857053738

Call Sign: KB6MX
Elmer L Wickersham
3115 N Fairview Ave 177
Tucson AZ 857053738

Call Sign: KC7QYD
Albert Fink
4621 N Fairview Ave 35

Tucson AZ 85705

Call Sign: KC0FPK
Donald E Davis
3833 N Fairview Lot 123
Tucson AZ 857052658

Call Sign: KC0FPJ
Pauline H Davis
3833 N Fairview Lot 123
Tucson AZ 857052658

Call Sign: N7VCV
Wilfred W Olschewski
8225 N Fairway View Dr
Tucson AZ 85741

Call Sign: W3OWR
Robert L Fodness
8101 N Fairway View Dr
Tucson AZ 85742

Call Sign: N7VCU
Rita Olschewski
8225 N Fairwayview Dr
Tucson AZ 85741

Call Sign: KD7YCM
Richard L Ritter
1231 N Falcon Ridge Dr
Tucson AZ 85745

Call Sign: KD7JGP
Bradley N Ream
3147 N Fenimore
Tucson AZ 85749

Call Sign: AB7YK
Paul J Meier
14640 N Flagstone Dr
Tucson AZ 85755

Call Sign: WA7FDN
William L Gage Jr
5341 N Flint Ave
Tucson AZ 85704

Call Sign: W7FDN
William L Gage Jr

5341 N Flint Ave
Tucson AZ 85704

Call Sign: KE7CVF
James R Valiton
4233 N Flowing Wells 168
Tucson AZ 85705

Call Sign: W0NM
Leslie A Venne
4550 N Flowing Wells 217
Tucson AZ 85705

Call Sign: KB7JTX
Felix J Cormier
4550 N Flowing Wells 8
Tucson AZ 85705

Call Sign: N1BMM
Raymond J Malatesta
4550 N Flowing Wells Rd
223
Tucson AZ 85705

Call Sign: WB2OPV
Harry A Haymes
4550 N Flowing Wells Rd
234
Tucson AZ 85705

Call Sign: K7EMT
Jenise D Martin
3450 N Flowing Wells Rd Sp
135
Tucson AZ 85705

Call Sign: W0HAL
Hal E Ethridge
4550 N Flowing Wells Rd
Unit 200
Tucson AZ 85705

Call Sign: KF7CNH
Richard S Watson
4550 N Flowing Wells Rd
Unit 201
Tucson AZ 85705

Call Sign: KF7SEE

Thomas L Pofahl
4315 N Flowing Wells Rd
Unit 25
Tucson AZ 85705

Call Sign: W7ICV
Arnold E Nemmers
2726 N Fontana Ave
Tucson AZ 85705

Call Sign: KF7CEM
Tyler G Chapman
3038 N Fontana Ave
Tucson AZ 85705

Call Sign: K1TGC
Tyler G Chapman
3038 N Fontana Ave
Tucson AZ 85705

Call Sign: W7GVN
Roderick B Stalker
4801 N Fontana Ave
Tucson AZ 85704

Call Sign: KD7MST
John E Wright
16680 N Forecastle
Tucson AZ 85739

Call Sign: W5JEW
John E Wright
16680 N Forecastle
Tucson AZ 85739

Call Sign: N7OAB
John A Bartolucci
3621 N Forgeus
Tucson AZ 85716

Call Sign: KC7TZR
Uri Palmer Gai
3624 N Forgeus
Tucson AZ 85716

Call Sign: KG7SB
Ronald G Fielder
5202 N Fort Yuma Tr
Tucson AZ 85715

Call Sign: N7VMN
Mildred E Fielder
5202 N Fort Yuma Trl
Tucson AZ 85715

Call Sign: KC7HHH
Donald C Stevens
14109 N Forthcamp
Tucson AZ 85737

Call Sign: W2LFU
Richard B Vosk
5950 N Fountain Ave 6103
Tucson AZ 85704

Call Sign: N6IZY
Ted Miyatake
8711 N Frampton Pl
Tucson AZ 857424885

Call Sign: KB7INP
David L Perry
1780 N Frances Blvd
Tucson AZ 85712

Call Sign: KA7CUZ
Scott E Bulau
610 N Freeman Rd
Tucson AZ 85748

Call Sign: KE7HFA
Betty J Kelsey
3501 N Freeway Rd
Tucson AZ 87505

Call Sign: N7IQI
Gregory V Galmarini
7733 N Gatewood Pl
Tucson AZ 85741

Call Sign: KC7ZQJ
Robert V Donohue
6460 N Gemstone Rd
Tucson AZ 85743

Call Sign: K7RVD
Robert V Donohue
6460 N Gemstone Rd

Tucson AZ 85743

Call Sign: KC7UZU
Ben T Ijams
5970 N Genematas Ln
Tucson AZ 85704

Call Sign: KB7ZIE
David E Collazo
3320 N Geronimo Ave
Tucson AZ 85705

Call Sign: KE7KSC
John M Valencia
2419 N Geronimo Ave Unit
D
Tucson AZ 85705

Call Sign: KM6YE
Charley Akins
10840 N Gila Rd
Tucson AZ 85742

Call Sign: NC2A
Charley Akins
10840 N Gila Rd
Tucson AZ 85742

Call Sign: KF7RNN
Stephen A Turcotte
10945 N Gila Rd
Tucson AZ 85742

Call Sign: WA4SFK
Nordien C Jackson
9261 N Golden Finch Ave
Tucson AZ 857429489

Call Sign: N7YGX
Kelly J Hritz
8756 N Golden Moon Way
Tucson AZ 85743

Call Sign: N7KLF
Kelly J Hritz
8756 N Golden Moon Way
Tucson AZ 85743

Call Sign: KE6IIB

George R Splane III
1267 N Golden Palomino Pl
Tucson AZ 85715

Call Sign: KB7HSA
Kevin E Heide
255 N Granada 2042
Tucson AZ 85701

Call Sign: KF7JGI
Michael A Pabst
255 N Granada Ave Apt
2022
Tucson AZ 85701

Call Sign: K5EDS
Dorsey D Price
2460 N Grannen Rd
Tucson AZ 85745

Call Sign: W7EDS
Dorsey D Price
2460 N Grannen Rd
Tucson AZ 857458934

Call Sign: KD7FRR
Kathleen B Heath
2618 N Grannen Rd
Tucson AZ 85745

Call Sign: KD7AUU
James R Knowlton
2612 N Grannen Rd
Tucson AZ 85745

Call Sign: KD7BFE
Nancy K Stevens
2612 N Grannen Rd
Tucson AZ 85745

Call Sign: W3KTM
Michael Sedore
4140 N Gregorio Cir
Tucson AZ 857052210

Call Sign: N0BUM
Robert H Graham
4141 N Gregorio Cir
Tucson AZ 85705

Call Sign: KA6YCW
Wanda G Brown
4481 N Grizzly Springs Dr
Tucson AZ 85745

Call Sign: W7EXG
William F Davis
4494 N Grizzly Springs Dr
Tucson AZ 85745

Call Sign: KO6F
Gerald E Brown
4481 N Grizzy Springs Dr
Tucson AZ 85745

Call Sign: KE7WIM
Manuel Montano
3855 N Gunnison Dr
Tucson AZ 85749

Call Sign: KE7WKT
Manuel Montano
3855 N Gunnison Dr
Tucson AZ 85749

Call Sign: W2GMU
Carl Perko
4311 N Gunpoint Dr
Tucson AZ 85749

Call Sign: KC2BQT
Richard E Gallagher
7171 N Guthrie Rd
Tucson AZ 85743

Call Sign: K7MB
Kim R Merley
13262 N Hammerstone Ln
Tucson AZ 85755

Call Sign: W7UPF
Donald W Richards
231 N Harris Ave
Tucson AZ 85716

Call Sign: WA7WHP
Dale A Roose
3622 N Harrison Rd

Tucson AZ 85749

Call Sign: KD7KDT
Karen W Craig
550 N Harrison Rd 7202
Tucson AZ 85748

Call Sign: KB1EDU
Chad M Brunell
550 N Harrison Rd Apt 2102
Tucson AZ 85748

Call Sign: KF7DDF
Alan W Schmall
2100 N Hayden Ave
Tucson AZ 85715

Call Sign: KD7FRD
Gerald W Boles
7647 N Hemingway Pl
Tucson AZ 85743

Call Sign: KD7FRE
Laura J Boles
7647 N Hemingway Pl
Tucson AZ 85743

Call Sign: N7IVG
Allen L Peterson
9471 N Heron Pl
Tucson AZ 85742

Call Sign: KB7JQ
James E Watry
9951 N High Meadow Trl
Tucson AZ 85742

Call Sign: KE7OQS
Christie A Bane
380 N Highland Ave
Tucson AZ 85719

Call Sign: KC7PGM
Aaron T Shultz
610 N Highland Ave Apt 219
Tucson AZ 85719

Call Sign: KA7KLY
Charles A Boyd

3209 N Hill Farm Dr
Tucson AZ 85712

Call Sign: KB2BLY
Cosmo J Recuparo
8070 N Hobby Horse Ct
Tucson AZ 85741

Call Sign: KD7HRI
Tucson Repeater Association
8741 N Holly Brook
Tucson AZ 857429589

Call Sign: N7WNZ
James E Harriman
8750 N Holly Brook
Tucson AZ 85741

Call Sign: KD6XH
Clifford E Hauser
8741 N Holly Brook Ave
Tucson AZ 85742

Call Sign: K7TRA
Tucson Repeater Association
8741 N Hollybrook
Tucson AZ 85742

Call Sign: KA7GGG
Zelma L Richardson
2002 N Homer Ave
Tucson AZ 85712

Call Sign: KE7DX
Gary L Keck
3601 N Homestead Ave
Tucson AZ 85749

Call Sign: WA5VGT
Robert A Davis
4541 N Homestead Ave
Tucson AZ 857499355

Call Sign: KE7VKC
Colleen M Leon
3112 N Homestead Pl
Tucson AZ 85749

Call Sign: KD7J

Edward C Berkeley
3131 N Homestead Pl
Tucson AZ 85749

Call Sign: KD7AJN
Edward C Berkeley
3131 N Homestead Pl
Tucson AZ 857499353

Call Sign: KB0YYM
Christopher L Hopkins
1272 N Honeyrose Ave
Tucson AZ 85745

Call Sign: KF7DRU
David B Jaksha
1648 N Horseshoe Trl
Tucson AZ 85745

Call Sign: W5DXN
Clyde V Taylor
3849 N Houghton Rd
Tucson AZ 85749

Call Sign: KE7ULD
Michael A Mccambridge
1411 N Howard Blvd
Tucson AZ 85716

Call Sign: KE7AC
Robert W Longley
8570 N Hummer Dr
Tucson AZ 857421076

Call Sign: KE6EBE
Jamie R Jones
4241 N Idaho Ln
Tucson AZ 85705

Call Sign: KC7KKO
Annita D Harlan
2862 N Indian Ruins Rd
Tucson AZ 85715

Call Sign: KC7KKP
Thomas P Harlan
2862 N Indian Ruins Rd
Tucson AZ 85715

Call Sign: NG4O
Michael H Mount
5731 N Indian Tr
Tucson AZ 85715

Call Sign: W7AEE
Michael H Mount
5731 N Indian Tr
Tucson AZ 85750

Call Sign: KB7OUB
Keith E Wright
5601 N Indian Trl
Tucson AZ 85715

Call Sign: KF7NUB
David T Kerns
5701 N Indian Trl
Tucson AZ 85750

Call Sign: KE7OYL
Janice E Prew
1610 N Indigo Dr
Tucson AZ 85745

Call Sign: KE7OYQ
Mark T Collins
1610 N Indigo Dr
Tucson AZ 85745

Call Sign: KF7ECO
John R Wolfe
11488 N Ingot Loop
Tucson AZ 85737

Call Sign: K0SBV
Carl W Dabelstein
8008 N Iron Ridge Dr
Tucson AZ 85743

Call Sign: WA6PBD
John C Sweeney
2280 N Ironwood Crest Dr
Tucson AZ 857459173

Call Sign: KC7MCE
David E Ludwig Sr
2552 N Ironwood Ridge Dr
Tucson AZ 85745

Call Sign: KF7SYT
Philip J June
3046 N Jackson Ave
Tucson AZ 85719

Call Sign: K7EEK
Philip J June
3046 N Jackson Ave
Tucson AZ 85719

Call Sign: KA7CTO
Eric L Hegstrom
3330 N Jackson Ave
Tucson AZ 85719

Call Sign: N7LHU
Timothy J Millhouse
915 N Javalina Pl
Tucson AZ 857482084

Call Sign: N7ICJ
George E Monroe
352 N Jefferson
Tucson AZ 85711

Call Sign: KA7VRB
David C Siwarski
7612 N Jensen Dr
Tucson AZ 85741

Call Sign: N8CBB
Wilbur H Martyn Sr
201 N Jessica 411
Tucson AZ 85710

Call Sign: WA6DBU
Benjamin T Strotman
201 N Jessica 417
Tucson AZ 85710

Call Sign: AB7EA
Helmut K Silge
201 N Jessica Apt 426
Tucson AZ 85710

Call Sign: KA9JMC
Ruthanne Burt
101 N Jessica Av 123

Tucson AZ 857102165

Call Sign: KC0POB
Charles D Hahn III
101 N Jessica Ave 244
Tucson AZ 857102131

Call Sign: KJ7VT
Howard L Brownstein
9072 N Jessy Ln
Tucson AZ 857428641

Call Sign: N5MTN
William J Kelleman Jr
7651 N John Hancock Ave
Tucson AZ 85724

Call Sign: KC7TFC
Jill P Kelleman
7651 N John Hancock Ave
Tucson AZ 85741

Call Sign: KB7WQY
William J Kelleman Jr
7651 N John Hancock Ave
Tucson AZ 85741

Call Sign: KE5ACR
Gary L Coriell
9351 N June Bug Dr
Tucson AZ 85742

Call Sign: KB7RJQ
Brett A Watins
1901 N Justin Ln
Tucson AZ 85712

Call Sign: KG6WVV
Mark A Lawrence
393 N Keepsake Pl
Tucson AZ 85748

Call Sign: KF7JGG
Robert L Cole III
4726 N Keet Seel Trl
Tucson AZ 85749

Call Sign: KC7JWL
Nathan E Shechter

5021 N Kevy
Tucson AZ 85704

Call Sign: KC7PUD
Kathy C Shechter
5021 N Kevy Pl
Tucson AZ 85704

Call Sign: AD7DE
Yoshihisa Matsuda
5751 N Kolb Rd
Tucson AZ 85750

Call Sign: N2UQ
Yoshihisa Matsuda
5751 N Kolb Rd
Tucson AZ 85750

Call Sign: N5MHW
Vance A Smith
5800 N Kolb Rd 13270E
Tucson AZ 85750

Call Sign: KC7FYC
Edward A Ajhar II
4700 N Kolb Rd 14111
Tucson AZ 85715

Call Sign: N4YCK
Larry Campion
5800 N Kolb Rd 2112E
Tucson AZ 85715

Call Sign: KF7SNJ
Ryan C Lunkley
4700 N Kolb Rd 5214
Tucson AZ 85750

Call Sign: WA6NYI
Ryan C Lunkley
4700 N Kolb Rd 5214
Tucson AZ 85750

Call Sign: KC7RMA
Darren Mc Collum
4700 N Kolb Rd Apt 12108
Tucson AZ 85750

Call Sign: NU4J

George R Chance
5751 N Kolb Rd Apt 33102
Tucson AZ 85750

Call Sign: KG6ILA
R Pinkney Foster
5751 N Kolb Rd Unit 20102
Tucson AZ 857500880

Call Sign: K7ILA
R Pinkney Foster
5751 N Kolb Rd Unit 20102
Tucson AZ 857500880

Call Sign: WA7GKJ
Stephen L Marcus
9716 N Korte Ln
Tucson AZ 857046865

Call Sign: N7NMH
Robert L Alvies II II
6220 N Kriscott Ct
Tucson AZ 85737

Call Sign: N7TVK
Robert W Maurer
11579 N Kriscott Ct
Tucson AZ 85737

Call Sign: KA7EZG
Steve J Sedor Jr
6980 N La Canada Dr
Tucson AZ 85704

Call Sign: N7LWW
Peter G Decker
8860 N La Canada Dr
Tucson AZ 85737

Call Sign: KC7GPL
Janice R Rasmussen
7887 N La Cholla 1065
Tucson AZ 85741

Call Sign: KC7FCF
Perry A D Rasmussen
7887 N La Cholla 1065
Tucson AZ 85741

Call Sign: N7BTX
Patrick F Legg
5000 N La Cholla 87
Tucson AZ 85705

Call Sign: KN7B
Patrick M Berry
7632 N La Cholla Blvd
Tucson AZ 85741

Call Sign: WB2QFW
Roberto J Orfila
7887 N La Cholla Blvd 1140
Tucson AZ 857414318

Call Sign: KB7TKD
William F Reeves
4160 N La Linda Rama
Tucson AZ 85718

Call Sign: KB7ZXK
Sandy L Doumas
4320 N La Linda Rama
Tucson AZ 85718

Call Sign: KB7ZXJ
William M Doumas
4320 N La Linda Rama
Tucson AZ 85718

Call Sign: W5ZSF
Joseph D Schauer Sr
7235 N La Oesta
Tucson AZ 85704

Call Sign: KA7RTY
David G Custer
8525 N La Oesta
Tucson AZ 85704

Call Sign: KA7RTZ
Sharon L Custer
8525 N La Oesta
Tucson AZ 85704

Call Sign: KB7PXG
Cynthia A Bieger
2626 N La Verne
Tucson AZ 85712

Call Sign: WX5ET
Edward J Tschupp
7900 N Lacanada Dr Apt
2242
Tucson AZ 85704

Call Sign: W9KU
Warren L Schlaugat
7887 N Lacholla Blvd 1008
Tucson AZ 85741

Call Sign: KJ7YD
David A Anderson
14232 N Lago Del Oro
Tucson AZ 85737

Call Sign: N7LBZ
Loretta R Martin
4871 N Lak A Yucca Rd
Tucson AZ 85743

Call Sign: NJ7N
Arthur Blank
5055 N Lak A Yucca Rd
Tucson AZ 85743

Call Sign: WA7NB
Arthur M Blank
5055 N Lak A Yucca Rd
Tucson AZ 85743

Call Sign: KC7FJT
Fred C Larson
2410 N Lake Star Dr
Tucson AZ 84062

Call Sign: KF7UFC
John B Lay
10340 N Lambert Ct
Tucson AZ 85742

Call Sign: KE7QIB
William E Leeson
9380 N Langur Pl
Tucson AZ 85742

Call Sign: KC7EYV
Morovat Tayefeh

4215 N Larkspur Rd
Tucson AZ 85749

Call Sign: KC7POM
Oliver C Van Hoesen
4240 N Lason Ln
Tucson AZ 85749

Call Sign: KE7RID
James Deroussel
2858 N Laurel Ave
Tucson AZ 85712

Call Sign: N7ZQS
Wayne D Cummings
761 N Lazy J Way
Tucson AZ 857483833

Call Sign: W7CFI
Wayne D Cummings
761 N Lazy J Way
Tucson AZ 857483833

Call Sign: KB7AZ
Carl G Foster
6970 N Leonardo Da Vinci
Way
Tucson AZ 85704

Call Sign: KE7FSK
Paul M Richards
7352 N Leonardo Da Vinci
Way
Tucson AZ 85704

Call Sign: AK1A
Richard A Newell
3551 N Lilly Pond Pl
Tucson AZ 85712

Call Sign: KB0DUB
Kermit D Hammar
12830 N Lindberg Dr
Tucson AZ 85742

Call Sign: KF7RLU
Tammy Kastre
13000 N Lindbergh Dr
Tucson AZ 85755

Call Sign: KA1BYF
Stephanie A Consalvo
14499 N Line Post Ln
Tucson AZ 857376664

Call Sign: N7SQJ
Gregg P White
7780 N Little Owl Ln
Tucson AZ 85743

Call Sign: WA6RYD
Preston T Maddocks
14200 N Lobelia Way
Tucson AZ 85737

Call Sign: N7DYJ
Warren C Zellmer
14500 N Lone Wolf Ln
Tucson AZ 85737

Call Sign: WA7URD
Warren C Zellmer
14500 N Lone Wolf Ln
Tucson AZ 857379339

Call Sign: KD7JMG
Richard E Goedel
821 N Longfellow Ave
Tucson AZ 85711

Call Sign: K7NX
Lloyd R Johnson
2841 N Longhorn Dr
Tucson AZ 85749

Call Sign: N5BMX
Albert M Bisbee
3101 N Longhorn Dr
Tucson AZ 857498844

Call Sign: N5BMY
Jane C Craig
3101 N Longhorn Dr
Tucson AZ 857498844

Call Sign: AA9KJ
Frank Sperber
3053 N Longhorn Dr

Tucson AZ 85749

Call Sign: W5WZY
Julian G Blakely
2416 N Loretta Dr
Tucson AZ 85716

Call Sign: KE7VTM
Edward J Root Jr
1727 N Louis Ln
Tucson AZ 85712

Call Sign: W9QAE
Robert H Sarikas
5044 N Louis River Way
Tucson AZ 85718

Call Sign: KC5MOP
Jon L Shay
7682 N Lundberg
Tucson AZ 85741

Call Sign: KC7OKE
Stephanie S Linhart
7682 N Lundberg Dr
Tucson AZ 85741

Call Sign: WB7BAE
Harold R Carpenter
250 N Maguire 403
Tucson AZ 857102402

Call Sign: W7HOT
Wilson Martin
10 N Maguire Ave Apt 227
Tucson AZ 857102459

Call Sign: NQ7J
George M Collenberg
207 N Maguire Ave Unit 271
Tucson AZ 857109028

Call Sign: NX7Y
George M Collenberg
207 N Maguire Ave Unit 271
Tucson AZ 857109028

Call Sign: KR7H
George M Collenberg

207 N Maguire Ave Unit 271
Tucson AZ 857109028

Call Sign: KC7KO
Joseph Michaluk
8608 N Mahogany Rd
Tucson AZ 85704

Call Sign: WB7TXQ
Robert F Magee
3343 N Manor Dr
Tucson AZ 85715

Call Sign: KE7OYK
Thomas E Eberhard
9449 N Mantis Way
Tucson AZ 85742

Call Sign: KF7DRT
Marcus L Perry
5550 N Maria Dr
Tucson AZ 85704

Call Sign: KD7OVV
Sharon D Pascoe
7001 N Maria Pl
Tucson AZ 85704

Call Sign: N7WES
William A Safieh
1030 N Martin 1108
Tucson AZ 85719

Call Sign: WA1WYG
Michael Hurwitz
2607 N Martin Ave
Tucson AZ 85719

Call Sign: WL7BHR
David B Walk
7630 N Massingale Ct
Tucson AZ 85746

Call Sign: W7CPQ
Carol A Demic
4921 N Mathews
Tucson AZ 85705

Call Sign: KE7VTO

Gordon L Chapell
9860 N Meadow Flower Pl
Tucson AZ 85742

Call Sign: KA7RHD
Glenn E Feuerbacher Jr
4531 N Meadow Ln
Tucson AZ 85749

Call Sign: KA7RFC
Olin G Feuerbacher
4531 N Meadow Ln
Tucson AZ 85749

Call Sign: KG4IYS
Chester C Fennell Jr
3263 N Meadow Mine Pl
Tucson AZ 85745

Call Sign: N7RKO
Timothy C Biss
11525 N Meadow Sage Dr
Tucson AZ 85737

Call Sign: W7MNU
William J Rothlisberger
615 N Medford Dr
Tucson AZ 857102576

Call Sign: KF3AL
Frank L Lederman
7019 N Mercer Spring Pl
Tucson AZ 857181415

Call Sign: KK7XQ
Frank L Lederman
7019 N Mercer Spring Pl
Tucson AZ 857181415

Call Sign: KF7CNI
Georgette I Escobar
239 N Meyer
Tucson AZ 85705

Call Sign: KF7KQ
David M Sarvis
7401 N Michelle Pl
Tucson AZ 85704

Call Sign: N7HY
David M Sarvis
7401 N Michelle Pl
Tucson AZ 85704

Call Sign: W7YDW
Richard L Woods
921 N Miller Dr
Tucson AZ 85710

Call Sign: WB4RTP
Avery R Davis
969 N Miller Dr
Tucson AZ 857102653

Call Sign: KB7FVI
Duncan W Campbell
5725 N Mina Vista
Tucson AZ 85718

Call Sign: N7QVL
Michael N Griffith
5540 N Moccasin Trl
Tucson AZ 85750

Call Sign: KC7PGS
Lester L Hair Jr
5700 N Moccasin Trl
Tucson AZ 85750

Call Sign: KD6BA
Ted C Lane
5840 N Moccasin Trl
Tucson AZ 85750

Call Sign: AE7CN
Nathan S Moyer
8739 N Moison Dr
Tucson AZ 857424141

Call Sign: N7TID
Jeffrey L Yates
7300 N Mona Lisa 9256
Tucson AZ 85741

Call Sign: KG7BX
Edward R Janney
7425 N Mona Lisa Rd 161
Tucson AZ 85741

Call Sign: KB7VYA
Nancy J Bowman
7425 N Mona Lisa Rd 213
Tucson AZ 85741

Call Sign: NZ2Q
William J Foley
7374 N Mona Lisa Rd Apt
11202
Tucson AZ 85741

Call Sign: KF7UXZ
Christine J Stephenson
3349 N Montezuma Ave
Tucson AZ 85712

Call Sign: KF7UYA
Mary Santin
3349 N Montezuma Ave
Tucson AZ 85712

Call Sign: KD7ECL
Alvin R Balius
6741 N Montrose Dr
Tucson AZ 85741

Call Sign: KE7VPF
Kristian S Smith
8818 N Moonfire Dr
Tucson AZ 85743

Call Sign: KC7EDU
David Brandt Erichsen
5100 N Moonstone Dr
Tucson AZ 85715

Call Sign: KG4KUL
Jason M Myrand
6760 N Morning Glory Dr
Tucson AZ 85741

Call Sign: KE4UBO
Robert P Myrand
6760 N Morning Glory Dr
Tucson AZ 85741

Call Sign: W7KQ
Bernie J Sasek

8925 N Morning View Dr
Tucson AZ 85704

Call Sign: KA7JGY
Gregg J Sasek
8925 N Morningview Dr
Tucson AZ 85737

Call Sign: WA0NNC
Karen B Sasek
8925 N Morningview Dr
Tucson AZ 85737

Call Sign: W7QJK
Karen B Sasek
8925 N Morningview Dr
Tucson AZ 85737

Call Sign: W0YOY
Pusch Ridge ARC
8925 N Morningview Dr
Tucson AZ 85737

Call Sign: KA7ILH
Larry B Copas
2832 N Mountain Ave
Tucson AZ 85719

Call Sign: KF7NKQ
George Gottlinger
3885 N Mountain Cove Dr
Tucson AZ 85750

Call Sign: KC7TEW
Dianne M Turausky
3955 N Mt Pleasant Dr
Tucson AZ 85749

Call Sign: KC7TYW
Andrew J Turausky
3955 N Mt Pleasant Dr
Tucson AZ 85749

Call Sign: KD7ZND
Stanley J Kartchner
7441 N Mtn Shadows Dr
Tucson AZ 857181082

Call Sign: KJ2I

Stanley J Kartchner
7441 N Mtn Shadows Dr
Tucson AZ 857181082

Call Sign: KC7YDL
Barbara K Plum
5225 N Myakka
Tucson AZ 85705

Call Sign: KB8SYF
Gregory K Plum
5225 N Myakka Ave
Tucson AZ 85705

Call Sign: KB8SOP
Harold C Plum Jr
5225 N Myakka Ave
Tucson AZ 85705

Call Sign: KF7EAJ
Jody M Blaylock
8802 N Myrtle Pl
Tucson AZ 85704

Call Sign: N5HWU
Joel S Empie
8470 N National Dr
Tucson AZ 85742

Call Sign: W7MHZ
Paul G Hadley
8765 N New Moon Pl
Tucson AZ 85743

Call Sign: KC7BTO
Brian K Schunk
7780 N Nicole Pl
Tucson AZ 85741

Call Sign: K9TPD
Brian K Schunk
7780 N Nicole Pl
Tucson AZ 85741

Call Sign: KC7ZEY
Richard A L Heureux
10177 N Nine Iron Dr
Tucson AZ 85737

Call Sign: AA7Q
Owen W Seagondollar
2601 N Norris Ave
Tucson AZ 85719

Call Sign: KH7TP
Grady S Weyenberg
215 N Norton Ave
Tucson AZ 85719

Call Sign: KF7QKE
Stan Rubin
1807 N Norton Ave
Tucson AZ 85719

Call Sign: KC7QHQ
Brian G Wicker
6841 N Nova Pl
Tucson AZ 85741

Call Sign: KB6AAW
William H Glore
11620 N Oceanus Pl
Tucson AZ 857373416

Call Sign: N7FD
James L Cole
4268 N Ocotillo Canyon Dr
Tucson AZ 85750

Call Sign: KE7WIO
Bernard M Goldstein
4329 N Ocotillo Canyon Dr
Tucson AZ 85750

Call Sign: WA7ZZE
Charles F Penson
4310 N Old Ranch Rd
Tucson AZ 85743

Call Sign: AK7U
William L Graves
4439 N Old Romero Rd Lot
44
Tucson AZ 857052150

Call Sign: WA4SWS
David H Emme
4902 N Old West Rd

Tucson AZ 85743

Call Sign: K6HSG
John E Cox
5420 N Old West Rd
Tucson AZ 85743

Call Sign: N7KZW
Earl V Skeen
7120 N Omar Dr
Tucson AZ 85741

Call Sign: KB7IRC
Gretchen K Gottfried
8215 N Oracle 149
Tucson AZ 85704

Call Sign: K9VSU
Otto B Kreipke
2801 N Oracle Apt 137
Tucson AZ 85705

Call Sign: WA9JFC
Roy J Babin
15770 N Oracle Rd
Tucson AZ 85737

Call Sign: N7HHC
Michael A Blue
12995 N Oracle Rd 141 Pmb
148
Tucson AZ 85739

Call Sign: W3RXN
Lavern W Bloedow
2721 N Oracle Rd 16
Tucson AZ 857054315

Call Sign: KE7AZO
Francis R Hawk
15301 N Oracle Rd 16
Tucson AZ 85739

Call Sign: KE7VTJ
Edward L Neman
6200 N Oracle Rd 165
Tucson AZ 85704

Call Sign: KB8AQG

William D Hawley
N Oracle Rd 392
Tucson AZ 85704

Call Sign: K9UXA
James R Beardsley
15301 N Oracle Rd 64
Tucson AZ 85739

Call Sign: KE7VTS
Paul W Tanner
4045 N Oracle Rd Apt 127
Tucson AZ 85705

Call Sign: KE7RPW
Robert J Maudsley
10333 N Oracle Rd Apt
16203
Tucson AZ 85737

Call Sign: KE7VJM
Michael A Wifall
10333 N Oracle Rd Apt 2202
Tucson AZ 85737

Call Sign: KE7IEF
Ronald H Smith
4045 N Oracle Rd Apt 257
Tucson AZ 85705

Call Sign: KC6ASA
Kirk M Wines
8215 N Oracle Rd Apt 77
Tucson AZ 857046448

Call Sign: WH6DX
Robert C Webster
15770 N Oracle Rd D5
Tucson AZ 85739

Call Sign: KD7CYV
Richard M Mc Kay
7090 N Oracle Rd Ste 178
Pmb 171
Tucson AZ 857044383

Call Sign: KE4UQF
Richard L Collins

6336 N Oracle Rd Ste 326
Pmb 215
Tucson AZ 85704

Call Sign: K7GZB
Eugene A Berg
7090 N Oracle Ste 178
Tucson AZ 85704

Call Sign: KD7JLM
Jolene M Berg
7090 N Oracle Ste 178 Pmb
123
Tucson AZ 85704

Call Sign: KF7TKJ
Taylor Peterson
7090 N Orade Rd Ste 178
192
Tucson AZ 85706

Call Sign: KD7JUL
Michael W Jennings
2700 N Orchard 2
Tucson AZ 85712

Call Sign: KE7VJV
Peter C Sabin
3389 N Orchard Pl
Tucson AZ 85712

Call Sign: KC7HHC
James D Campbell
3922 N Palm Grove Dr
Tucson AZ 85705

Call Sign: WB9RKY
William J Malcolm
14700 N Palm Ridge Dr
Tucson AZ 85737

Call Sign: N7YMI
Deborah A Bartolucci
2407 N Palo Hacha Dr
Tucson AZ 85745

Call Sign: KB7BDT
Ian R Gordon
555 N Pantano Rd

Tucson AZ 85710

Call Sign: W7KLK
Richard M Schotland
3726 N Pantano Rd
Tucson AZ 85715

Call Sign: W4NZJ
Mary W Ahls
3830 N Pantano Rd
Tucson AZ 857502349

Call Sign: AB0KF
William D Ahls
3830 N Pantano Rd
Tucson AZ 857502349

Call Sign: N7DMA
Karl E Rifenbark
2172 N Pantano Rd 216
Tucson AZ 85715

Call Sign: KG7DH
William R Heiny
555 N Pantano Rd 251
Tucson AZ 85710

Call Sign: W2EMA
George E Robinson Sr
345 N Pantano Rd 327
Tucson AZ 85710

Call Sign: K3VYP
E Ned Mac Gregor
555 N Pantano Rd 625
Tucson AZ 85710

Call Sign: W9PQR
Roger R M Kidd
550 N Pantano Rd Apt 110
Tucson AZ 857102354

Call Sign: KK7QO
Robert L Baker
445 N Pantano Rd Apt 276
Tucson AZ 857102305

Call Sign: KD3IP
James M Darlack

600 N Pantano Rd Apt 904
Tucson AZ 85710

Call Sign: WA0LSO
Melville H Crandell
555 N Pantano Rd Unit 665
Tucson AZ 857102335

Call Sign: KD7RUW
Claire E Rogers
555 N Pantano Unit 359
Tucson AZ 85710

Call Sign: WB7OYS
James H Mitchell
6325 N Papaya Pl
Tucson AZ 85741

Call Sign: KC7FRZ
Jason E Otto
1614 N Park
Tucson AZ 85719

Call Sign: NG7K
Marlyne J Freedman
6141 N Pascola Cir
Tucson AZ 85718

Call Sign: W7AQQ
James Liebman
6177 N Pascola Cir
Tucson AZ 85718

Call Sign: N2IYZ
Murray Manson
6213 N Pascola Cir
Tucson AZ 857183557

Call Sign: KE7MRT
David F Cray
6591 N Paseo De Gabriel
Tucson AZ 85741

Call Sign: N2MMA
Amalia M Walther
4622 N Paseo Del Barranco
Tucson AZ 85745

Call Sign: W7AMW

Amalia M Walther
4622 N Paseo Del Barranco
Tucson AZ 85745

Call Sign: W7AI
Ronald H Walther
4622 N Paseo Del Barranco
Tucson AZ 85745

Call Sign: KE7ULB
David W Child
4221 N Paseo Del Campo
Tucson AZ 85745

Call Sign: KA7CJQ
Donald Traicoff Jr
7760 N Paseo Del Norte
Tucson AZ 85704

Call Sign: KC7BHZ
Louis D Heindel
7380 N Paseo Montalban
Tucson AZ 85704

Call Sign: W7BV
Robert S Mc Cuskey
5841 N Paseo Niquel
Tucson AZ 85718

Call Sign: N7IRB
Mark A Caminker
5752 N Paseo Otono
Tucson AZ 85750

Call Sign: KC7JWN
Ruth L West
4632 N Paseo Pitiquito
Tucson AZ 85715

Call Sign: KD7SIU
Robert M Sharp
4601 N Paseo Presidio
Tucson AZ 85750

Call Sign: K7RMS
Robert M Sharp
4601 N Paseo Presidio
Tucson AZ 85750

Call Sign: KF7OSQ
Thomas M Shoemaker
4832 N Paseo Presidio
Tucson AZ 85750

Call Sign: KD7ETS
Loretta A Pastore
5472 N Paseo Sonoyta
Tucson AZ 857501403

Call Sign: N7IQC
Ricky L Garrison
4735 N Paseo Tubutama
Tucson AZ 85750

Call Sign: KG6RCL
Victor S Barahona
7980 N Paul Revere Pl
Tucson AZ 85741

Call Sign: KA4LQI
George E Hentz
7450 N Pear Tree Rd
Tucson AZ 85743

Call Sign: KA7TAV
James T Parker
6170 N Peppertree Ln
Tucson AZ 85741

Call Sign: KE7ZPJ
Gene L Ackson
1042 N Perry Ave
Tucson AZ 85705

Call Sign: WB0UIP
Curt W Laumann
6131 N Piedra Seca
Tucson AZ 85718

Call Sign: N7WBS
Nancy N Gray
5800 N Pla Amanecer
Tucson AZ 85718

Call Sign: KC7CPC
Edward G Robinson
4930 N Placita Aguilera
Tucson AZ 85745

Call Sign: N7VMO
Joan D Scott
5800 N Placita Amanecer
Tucson AZ 85718

Call Sign: KO4W
Joell T Turner
3221 N Placita Brazos
Tucson AZ 857502840

Call Sign: KB7FUE
Claus H Claassen
1955 N Placita Cartamo
Tucson AZ 857499203

Call Sign: N0KWP
Frank M Brady Jr
5919 N Placita Chico
Tucson AZ 85704

Call Sign: WA1IZE
David S Powers
8142 N Placita Chula
Tucson AZ 85704

Call Sign: KG6KSX
Catherine P Dela Cruz
1731 N Placita De Laroca
Tucson AZ 85745

Call Sign: KF7EC
Ernest G Parks Jr
7700 N Placita De Posada
Tucson AZ 857042046

Call Sign: KE7AZN
Michael A Guzik
8642 N Placita Del Cardo
Tucson AZ 85704

Call Sign: KD7VGH
Jonathan D Saints
8683 N Placita Del Cardo
Tucson AZ 85704

Call Sign: KD7LFX
James T Hawthorne
5700 N Placita Del Trueno

Tucson AZ 85718

Call Sign: K7UFZ
James T Hawthorne
5700 N Placita Del Trueno
Tucson AZ 85718

Call Sign: WB0JLG
Gregory S Winters
5145 N Placita Diaz
Tucson AZ 85718

Call Sign: KC7OVJ
Eugene R Cochran III
5154 N Placita Diaz
Tucson AZ 85718

Call Sign: KD7RYA
Larry I Mann
3024 N Placita Fuente
Tucson AZ 85715

Call Sign: W0WVK
Clifton D Adams
5926 N Placita Ligera
Tucson AZ 85750

Call Sign: KE7VKR
Jeff C Guthrie
4860 N Placita Lirio
Tucson AZ 85749

Call Sign: KD7WCM
Richard E Giachetti
6821 N Placita Sierra
Tucson AZ 85718

Call Sign: AA7GX
Catherine A Crandall
116 N Players Club Dr
Tucson AZ 85745

Call Sign: N7NLN
George J Mortimer
116 N Players Club Dr
Tucson AZ 85745

Call Sign: KD7ZGH
Samuel G Duwe

911 N Plumer Ave
Tucson AZ 85719

Call Sign: WA7IQK
Wanda E Rees
7000 N Pomona
Tucson AZ 85704

Call Sign: KQ4UW
Jerome S Deutscher
6805 N Pomona Rd
Tucson AZ 85704

Call Sign: KE7KCV
Charles Branson
6589 N Positano Way
Tucson AZ 85741

Call Sign: KC0LL
David F Branson
6589 N Positano Way
Tucson AZ 85741

Call Sign: KE7JYW
Mary E Branson
6589 N Positano Way
Tucson AZ 85741

Call Sign: N0TOY
Mary E Branson
6589 N Positano Way
Tucson AZ 85741

Call Sign: KE7IBB
Armand C Sperduti
5030 N Post Trl
Tucson AZ 85750

Call Sign: KI7J
Armand C Sperduti
5030 N Post Trl
Tucson AZ 85750

Call Sign: KF7DRP
Bruce A Cowan
5210 N Post Trl
Tucson AZ 85750

Call Sign: KE6LGV

Warren L Donnelly
6843 N Prairie Dr
Tucson AZ 85743

Call Sign: KF6JKF
Barbara E Cook
5066 N Pueblo Villas Dr
Tucson AZ 857043716

Call Sign: NL7GZ
Helmut F Troutman
5112 N Pueblo Villas Dr
Tucson AZ 85704

Call Sign: KB6SYZ
Geoffrey S Smith
5284 N Pueblo Villas Dr
Tucson AZ 85704

Call Sign: KC7ANU
Thomas J Price
1452 N Purple Cactus Pl
Tucson AZ 85715

Call Sign: W6SYW
Merlyn J Breiland
7680 N Quail Ridge Dr
Tucson AZ 85743

Call Sign: W6UMV
Robert C Morgan
2490 N Quesnel Loop
Tucson AZ 85715

Call Sign: KB7GAH
Bennie L Sanders
4318 N Radin Ave
Tucson AZ 85705

Call Sign: AA7FN
Alex R Jacobs
2112 N Rainbow Vista Dr
Tucson AZ 85712

Call Sign: KF4Z
William J Gross
2117 N Ralph Av
Tucson AZ 85712

Call Sign: WA7HHL
William G Matlock
2811 N Ralph Ave
Tucson AZ 85712

Call Sign: KB7YJ
Richard M Siefken
13500 N Rancho Vistoso
Blvd
Tucson AZ 85755

Call Sign: KI1T
Scott D Blessley
12112 N Rancho Vistoso
Blvd 150 301
Tucson AZ 85755

Call Sign: KE7EMQ
Edmund V Marcinkowski
6740 N Rapallo Pl
Tucson AZ 85741

Call Sign: KB8SJV
Patrick L Rinckey
3663 N Raven Wash Dr
Tucson AZ 85745

Call Sign: WA6VZK
William H Blaine
3900 N Red Ruby Ln
Tucson AZ 857499713

Call Sign: KB7ZPY
Robert A Perry
2566 N Redington Pl
Tucson AZ 85749

Call Sign: K7NN
Donald E Birch
7725 N Redwing Cir
Tucson AZ 85741

Call Sign: KE7OFK
Grand Canyon Dx & Contest
Club
7725 N Redwing Cir
Tucson AZ 857411334

Call Sign: W3RI

Grand Canyon Dx & Contest
Club
7725 N Redwing Cir
Tucson AZ 857411334

Call Sign: N7SCN
Francis C Sherlock
7660 N Redwing Pl
Tucson AZ 85741

Call Sign: N7THX
Wes J Dison Jr
7670 N Redwing Pl
Tucson AZ 85741

Call Sign: KF7RNM
Bruce Lowenthal
13274 N Regulation Dr
Tucson AZ 85755

Call Sign: KD7JNL
Ronald P Legan Sr
2518 N Richey Blvd
Tucson AZ 857162513

Call Sign: W7RPL
Ronald P Legan Sr
2518 N Richey Blvd
Tucson AZ 857162513

Call Sign: WA4DIB
Wilfred F Declercq
3645 N Ridge Port Pl
Tucson AZ 857502233

Call Sign: KD7MOO
Michial J Mcclellan
5267 N Ridge Spring Pl
Tucson AZ 85749

Call Sign: KF7BLZ
George L Best
5387 N Ridge Spring Pl
Tucson AZ 85749

Call Sign: K7QG
George L Best
5387 N Ridge Spring Pl
Tucson AZ 85749

Call Sign: KC7WBB
John W Florko
4219 N Rillito Creek Pl
Tucson AZ 85719

Call Sign: N0UCV
Ronald A Fevig
4357 N Rio Cancion 356
Tucson AZ 85718

Call Sign: KC7UBB
Garth Jones
2910 N Rio Verde Dr
Tucson AZ 85715

Call Sign: KE7VKL
Donald B Westcott
3761 N River Hills Dr
Tucson AZ 85750

Call Sign: KC7ZMX
Andrew W Guerrero Jr
3201 N Riverbend Cir E
Tucson AZ 85750

Call Sign: KF7HYE
Paul J Lambert III
3242 N Riverbend Pl
Tucson AZ 85750

Call Sign: KD4NSX
Joshua D Mellberg
3546 N Riverhaven Dr
Tucson AZ 85712

Call Sign: KD7PHX
Jennifer A Claver
5505 N Roanoke
Tucson AZ 85704

Call Sign: N7JEN
Jennifer A Claver
5505 N Roanoke
Tucson AZ 85704

Call Sign: K6QYL
Richard P Belden
14541 N Rock Springs Ln

Tucson AZ 85737

Call Sign: N7ZQK
Robert J Schmulian
4415 N Rockcliff Rd
Tucson AZ 857509780

Call Sign: KE7OLM
Blake A Rafferty
8267 N Rocky Brook Dr
Tucson AZ 85743

Call Sign: KE7OLL
Gretchen E Rafferty
8367 N Rocky Brook Dr
Tucson AZ 85743

Call Sign: WB6IFG
Steven C Cook
1860 N Rolling Stone Dr
Tucson AZ 85745

Call Sign: WG7K
Steven C Cook
1860 N Rolling Stone Dr
Tucson AZ 857453556

Call Sign: N6VLJ
Bruce J Bradshaw
3000 N Romero
Tucson AZ 85754

Call Sign: N6VEZ
William R Davis
3740 N Romero
Tucson AZ 85705

Call Sign: W7EVC
Harold N Rice
4039 N Romero
Tucson AZ 85705

Call Sign: N7HLH
Eugene B Steele
3405 N Romero A8
Tucson AZ 85705

Call Sign: KA7PPG
William C Redden

3426 N Romero Rd 46
Tucson AZ 85705

Call Sign: KA7CYL
James T Clemons
3426 N Romero Rd 48
Tucson AZ 85705

Call Sign: WA7PTR
Daniel F Gallagher
3740 N Romero Rd 56
Tucson AZ 85705

Call Sign: WB6LCI
Charles R Delpino
4100 N Romero Rd 68
Tucson AZ 85705

Call Sign: W7LAC
Warne Jeffrey
3810 N Romero Rd Sp 81
Tucson AZ 85705

Call Sign: KJ7OR
Henry L Sautter
7948 N Rondure Loop
Tucson AZ 85743

Call Sign: WB7UJL
William T Davis
642 N Ruston Ave
Tucson AZ 85711

Call Sign: KB7EDT
Borje O Ekman
5051 N Sabino Canyon Rd
Tucson AZ 85715

Call Sign: KE7TRL
John Kiniston
5215 N Sabino Canyon Rd
Tucson AZ 85750

Call Sign: K2LAJ
Lorene A Jayson
5363 N Sabino Canyon Rd 4
Tucson AZ 85750

Call Sign: K7VAU

Gus N Toures
4880 N Sabino Canyon Rd
Apt 6127
Tucson AZ 857507008

Call Sign: WA6GVJ
Donald J Hopper
3612 N Sabino Creek Pl
Tucson AZ 85715

Call Sign: WB6HNY
William P Laney Jr
3664 N Sabino Creek Pl
Tucson AZ 85750

Call Sign: KE6LWG
Mark H Hunt
5051 N Sabino Cyn Rd Apt
2206
Tucson AZ 85750

Call Sign: KB2VZ
Theodore C Moeller
1151 N Saddlewood Ranch
Dr
Tucson AZ 85745

Call Sign: KC5SXI
Andrew P Douglas
11640 N Sage Brook Rd
Tucson AZ 85737

Call Sign: N7NYR
Lee Wilson
8381 N Sage Pl
Tucson AZ 857042260

Call Sign: AC7QP
Lee Wilson
8381 N Sage Pl
Tucson AZ 857042260

Call Sign: WI7L
Lee Wilson
8381 N Sage Pl
Tucson AZ 857042260

Call Sign: KA7LVX
Gilbert T Matsushino

348 N Sahuara Ave
Tucson AZ 85711

Call Sign: KB7VKQ
James T Matsushino
348 N Sahuara Ave
Tucson AZ 85711

Call Sign: KA7LVZ
Karen A Matsushino
348 N Sahuara Ave
Tucson AZ 85711

Call Sign: KE7BIK
Kimberly A Matsushino
348 N Sahuara Ave
Tucson AZ 85711

Call Sign: W7JJM
Tony A Felber
1631 N Sahuara Ave
Tucson AZ 85712

Call Sign: KA7TWA
Hartley E Newkirk
7240 N San Anna
Tucson AZ 85704

Call Sign: KA7PAP
Ronald W Hutchinson
7501 N San Anna
Tucson AZ 85704

Call Sign: KC7UZO
Joseph M Cunningham
11157 N Sand Pointe Dr
Tucson AZ 857377021

Call Sign: KE7MMO
Stephen R Minor
6626 N Sandario Rd
Tucson AZ 85743

Call Sign: N7INR
Helen I Umstott
7811 N Sandario Rd
Tucson AZ 85743

Call Sign: WA7OEP

John A Umstott
7811 N Sandario Rd
Tucson AZ 85743

Call Sign: KD7XP
George R James
6350 N Sanders Rd
Tucson AZ 85743

Call Sign: KE7QFC
Kelsey L Mcguffee
9742 N Sandy Valley Dr
Tucson AZ 85743

Call Sign: KB7RKG
Richard C Lansdowne
9034 N Sanguine Dr
Tucson AZ 85743

Call Sign: KB7AOJ
Charles D Faas
3532 N Santa Rita Ave
Tucson AZ 85719

Call Sign: N7PHD
Wit T Wisniewski
1402 N Sarnoff Dr
Tucson AZ 85715

Call Sign: KB7HAD
Ronald R Griffith
1502 N Sarnoff Dr
Tucson AZ 85715

Call Sign: KB7YRI
Wayne E Langstroth
510 N Schrader Ln
Tucson AZ 85748

Call Sign: KB7YGM
Suzanne E Forgach
510 N Schrader Ln
Tucson AZ 85748

Call Sign: N7IQT
Mike P Hanoka
5701 N Senita Way
Tucson AZ 85743

Call Sign: W6AXK
William U Benesh
2406 N Shade Tree Ln
Tucson AZ 857153741

Call Sign: KG6PEL
Gregory C Rogan
6541 N Shadow Bluff Dr
Tucson AZ 85704

Call Sign: KC7YDK
Betty M Patterson
8730 N Shadow Mountain Dr
Tucson AZ 85704

Call Sign: W9JIU
John L Patterson
8730 N Shadow Mountain Dr
Tucson AZ 85704

Call Sign: N7LUZ
Jason M Chilcote
8906 N Shadow Mountain Dr
Tucson AZ 85737

Call Sign: KD6CCR
Thomas A Hanks
8901 N Shadow Rock Dr
Tucson AZ 85743

Call Sign: WB6IUK
Jeffrey J Caldie
8920 N Shadow Rock Dr
Tucson AZ 85743

Call Sign: KJ7RM
Terence J Plaza
6769 N Shadow Run
Tucson AZ 85704

Call Sign: KB7TSA
Weldon L Borton
6509 N Shadow Run Dr
Tucson AZ 85704

Call Sign: KE7ECV
Dan W Ewer
1790 N Shambala Ln
Tucson AZ 85743

Call Sign: KC7HWP
Steven D Nuckolls
4842 N Shannon 8
Tucson AZ 85705

Call Sign: N7DD
Larry Pace
10901 N Shannon Rd
Tucson AZ 85742

Call Sign: KA7RUB
Patricia E Pace
10901 N Shannon Rd
Tucson AZ 857428760

Call Sign: N7USN
Kenneth S Nehring
5445 N Shannon Rd 90
Tucson AZ 85705

Call Sign: N8VOE
Garrett T Sos
4651 N Shinumo Dr
Tucson AZ 857499135

Call Sign: KD7KUW
Tommy G James
7434 N Shirley Ln
Tucson AZ 85741

Call Sign: N7MZI
Paul E De Loe
4312 N Sierra De Luna Pl
Tucson AZ 85749

Call Sign: KI7WV
Joseph M Miller
145 N Sierra Vista Dr
Tucson AZ 85719

Call Sign: KD7DOI
Timothy J Crist
11378 N Silver Pheasant
Loop
Tucson AZ 85737

Call Sign: KD7VGG
Jo A Leeming

2831 N Silver Spur Dr
Tucson AZ 85745

Call Sign: K2HLW
Michael N Leeming
2831 N Silver Spur Dr
Tucson AZ 85745

Call Sign: KB7YSY
James L Barbre
7850 N Silverbell Rd 114
308
Tucson AZ 85743

Call Sign: KK4XX
Richard S Friedman
7850 N Silverbell Rd Pmb
114 255
Tucson AZ 85743

Call Sign: KE7ULA
George C W Runger
6531 N Silversmith Pl
Tucson AZ 85750

Call Sign: ND8N
Paul W Winroth
8629 N Siriga Way
Tucson AZ 85742

Call Sign: KD7CE
Richard B Atchison
3200 N Six Bar Spur
Tucson AZ 85745

Call Sign: N7LYK
Edna R Hoffman
14350 N Sky Trl
Tucson AZ 85737

Call Sign: KD7SPX
Edna R Hoffman
14350 N Sky Trl
Tucson AZ 85737

Call Sign: N7LYJ
Leonard A Hoffman
14350 N Sky Trl
Tucson AZ 85737

Call Sign: N7WBV
Edgar G Kilby
6856 N Solaz Cuarto
Tucson AZ 85718

Call Sign: N7KSB
Lewis R Smith
4176 N Soldier Trl
Tucson AZ 857499715

Call Sign: W9FI
James C Wysocki
5010 N Soldier Trl
Tucson AZ 85749

Call Sign: KA7NBZ
David E Young
3725 N Soldiers Trl
Tucson AZ 85749

Call Sign: W7GLV
Paul J Shubitz
8309 N Solitude Way
Tucson AZ 85743

Call Sign: W6VBT
Robert M Jones
7754 N Sombereo Peak Dr
Tucson AZ 85743

Call Sign: KD7GFB
Charles L Collins Jr
9331 N Sombrero Canyon Dr
Tucson AZ 857435160

Call Sign: K7ORI
Charles L Collins Jr
9331 N Sombrero Canyon Dr
Tucson AZ 857435160

Call Sign: K7NC
Charles L Collins Jr
9331 N Sombrero Canyon Dr
Tucson AZ 857435160

Call Sign: AD7BQ
Charles L Collins Jr
9331 N Sombrero Canyon Dr

Tucson AZ 857437530

Call Sign: K7ADS
Robert C Jones
7754 N Sombrero Peak Dr
Tucson AZ 857436013

Call Sign: WA7ABG
Robert C Jones
7754 N Sombrero Peak Dr
Tucson AZ 85743

Call Sign: KC7GCW
John D Bender
2444 N Sonoita Pl
Tucson AZ 85712

Call Sign: W6YKH
Robert W Andersen
16090 N Sotol Ave
Tucson AZ 85739

Call Sign: N0LMC
Janet A Mutchler
16180 N Sotol Ave
Tucson AZ 85739

Call Sign: N0FVG
W Warren Gretz
16180 N Sotol Ave
Tucson AZ 85739

Call Sign: KI6ZF
Joan S Shipley
16231 N Sotol Ave
Tucson AZ 85739

Call Sign: KI6XA
Robert N Shipley
16231 N Sotol Ave
Tucson AZ 85739

Call Sign: KD7FMB
James A Parks
3026 N Sparkman Blvd
Tucson AZ 85716

Call Sign: W5NSA
Nicholas Sadza

5239 N Spring Pointe Pl
Tucson AZ 85749

Call Sign: KE7EUA
Bear Canyon ARC
5316 N Spring View Dr
Tucson AZ 85749

Call Sign: N7XSS
Bradley W Fisher
6832 N Spring Wagon Dr
Tucson AZ 857438671

Call Sign: W7HAV
Richard B Hage
6736 N Springwagon Dr
Tucson AZ 85743

Call Sign: KB7RPX
Daniel W Watters
5145 N Standing Rock Pl
Tucson AZ 85750

Call Sign: WB6IQV
Frederick Dahnke
3380 N Star Valley Ln
Tucson AZ 85745

Call Sign: N7SQR
Bill A Blair
15801 N Starboard Dr
Tucson AZ 85739

Call Sign: KC7OYO
John M James
8381 N Starfinder Pl
Tucson AZ 85704

Call Sign: KE7KCW
Kristopher D Branson
8773 N Stargrass
Tucson AZ 85742

Call Sign: KC7PUH
Donna M Bieg
3336 N Stewart Ave
Tucson AZ 85716

Call Sign: KC7QDX

Stuart F Baker
3336 N Stewart Ave
Tucson AZ 85716

Call Sign: KB7JXB
Mark A West
3985 N Stone Ave Apt 125
Tucson AZ 85705

Call Sign: W9KOY
Bruce E Smith
9514 N Stonebrook Dr
Tucson AZ 85743

Call Sign: KA9UWQ
Faith K Alster
5260 N Strada De Rubino
Tucson AZ 85750

Call Sign: KG6MR
Maryanna J Foster
9990 N Stratton Saddle Trl
Tucson AZ 857428610

Call Sign: W7KQS
George D Givens
4829 N Sucamore
Tucson AZ 85712

Call Sign: KF7NUC
Ernest D Fasse
851 N Sugar Maple Pl
Tucson AZ 85710

Call Sign: K7EDF
Ernest D Fasse
851 N Sugar Maple Pl
Tucson AZ 85710

Call Sign: KJ7GE
Margaret F Cummings
4435 N Summer Pl
Tucson AZ 85749

Call Sign: KF7EMI
Michael M Olsen
6473 N Sun Bluff Dr
Tucson AZ 85704

Call Sign: KD7WEK
Victor A Cordero
5431 N Sundance Pl
Tucson AZ 85718

Call Sign: N2MZ
William M Stanger
5550 N Sundown Dr
Tucson AZ 85718

Call Sign: KC7NYU
Elmer K Mc Lay
8680 N Sunnyvale Dr
Tucson AZ 85742

Call Sign: KB7LTM
Laura J Markiewicz
4933 N Sunrise Ave
Tucson AZ 85705

Call Sign: N0SI
Richard K Dowse
2610 N Sunrock Ln
Tucson AZ 85745

Call Sign: KF7EAM
Maryanne Mott
2989 N Sunrock Ln
Tucson AZ 85745

Call Sign: WB0OEW
Elwood C Downey
8274 N Sunset Ranch Loop
Tucson AZ 857438201

Call Sign: KD7EIR
James M Myers
1200 N Sunspot Pl
Tucson AZ 85715

Call Sign: KC7TEX
John M Jamieson
1301 N Sunspot Pl
Tucson AZ 85715

Call Sign: WO7Q
Charles R Smith
9295 N Surgarfoot Dr
Tucson AZ 85743

Call Sign: KC7ZPJ
Leo M Hartke
1949 N Swan 10
Tucson AZ 85712

Call Sign: KD7PNW
Charles C Cooper
2626 N Swan Rd
Tucson AZ 85712

Call Sign: WB8ZNM
Donn T Bennett
14590 N Swan Rd
Tucson AZ 85739

Call Sign: KB7SRI
Charles C Koerber
5441 N Swan Rd 715
Tucson AZ 85718

Call Sign: WB9JVM
John P Santucci Jr
5441 N Swan Rd Ste 217
Tucson AZ 85718

Call Sign: KI8KH
Eric A Griff
3214 N Sycamore
Tucson AZ 85712

Call Sign: KC7FZU
Robert P Gaston
11880 N Tami Pl
Tucson AZ 85737

Call Sign: KE7ERJ
Pima County Az 4-H
13305 N Teal Blue Tr
Tucson AZ 85741

Call Sign: W7AAA
Douglas M Duy
13305 N Teal Blue Trl
Tucson AZ 85742

Call Sign: N7TVL
Austin D Boosted
4917 N Territory Ave

Tucson AZ 85750

Call Sign: NB7R
James E Miller
4957 N Territory Ave
Tucson AZ 857505961

Call Sign: WP4XD
Daniel E George
4844 N Territory Loop
Tucson AZ 81575

Call Sign: N7IAI
Leland J Groves
624 N Texas Cir
Tucson AZ 85711

Call Sign: KA7KMX
Christopher J Marcott
6320 N Thyme Pl
Tucson AZ 85741

Call Sign: KD7MSM
Thomas A Demma
6330 N Thyme Pl
Tucson AZ 85741

Call Sign: W2FMT
John L Dickinson
2470 N Tierra Verde Pl
Tucson AZ 85749

Call Sign: W9CAL
Ralph L Smith
2740 N Tomahawk Trl
Tucson AZ 85749

Call Sign: KC7JDW
Richard J Balser
4149 N Tortolita Rd
Tucson AZ 85745

Call Sign: KC6WUQ
Ann Brown
5200 N Tortolita Rd
Tucson AZ 85745

Call Sign: W6CCS
Walter P Brown

5200 N Tortolita Rd
Tucson AZ 85745

Call Sign: AD3P
Robert W Crain
1165 N Tracy Ave
Tucson AZ 85715

Call Sign: KD7EHP
Daniel G Barker
2135 N Treat 9
Tucson AZ 85716

Call Sign: KC7SXD
Everett H Lindsay
2771 N Treat Ave
Tucson AZ 85716

Call Sign: KF7QKJ
Steven W Hutton
3138 N Treat Ave
Tucson AZ 85716

Call Sign: KO2B
Steven W Hutton
3138 N Treat Ave
Tucson AZ 85716

Call Sign: KF7QKJ
Steven W Hutton
3138 N Treat Ave
Tucson AZ 85716

Call Sign: K7EU
Steven W Hutton
3138 N Treat Ave
Tucson AZ 85716

Call Sign: KD7AGR
Jeffrey R Struthers II
8430 N Treece Way
Tucson AZ 85742

Call Sign: N9IUK
George P Devich
3742 N Tres Lomas Dr
Tucson AZ 85749

Call Sign: KE7JJU

June D Sherlock
3832 N Tres Lomas Pl
Tucson AZ 85749

Call Sign: K6ESS
Edward S Sherlock
3832 N Tres Lomas Pl
Tucson AZ 85749

Call Sign: N7DQP
Stanley M Davis
5728 N Trisha Ln
Tucson AZ 85741

Call Sign: N7DZM
Regina Davis
5782 N Trisha Ln
Tucson AZ 85741

Call Sign: KF7UZA
Akadech Somboonjettana
1126 N Tucson Blvd
Tucson AZ 85716

Call Sign: N9LWY
James G Saling
2875 N Tucson Blvd 15
Tucson AZ 85716

Call Sign: K8KBX
Paul D Pender
7911 N Tuscany Dr
Tucson AZ 85742

Call Sign: WB3LCH
Kenneth W Ganzhorn
4168 N Tuttle Ave
Tucson AZ 85705

Call Sign: KC7PUJ
David A Mc Cray
14585 N Twin Lakes Dr
Tucson AZ 85739

Call Sign: KD6RFJ
Michael D Zolna
8884 N Twin Peaks Brook Dr
Tucson AZ 85743

Call Sign: KC0QEL
Neil H Dolan
11272 N Twin Spur Ct
Tucson AZ 85737

Call Sign: KB7QWJ
John H Hiett
1042 N Tyndall
Tucson AZ 85719

Call Sign: KB7DBJ
Rafeek M Kottai
1011 N Tyndall 108
Tucson AZ 85719

Call Sign: AA8CM
Craig A Kulesa
2744 N Tyndall Ave
Tucson AZ 85719

Call Sign: KC7LVU
Byron R Paulley
5500 N Valley View 211
Tucson AZ 85718

Call Sign: N6QBO
Mary Gates
625 N Van Buren Av 311
Tucson AZ 857112437

Call Sign: K0ZGG
Paul D Hopple
625 N Van Buren Ave Apt 415
Tucson AZ 85711

Call Sign: N9ZXW
Dan E Cox
8936 N Velvet Mesquite Pl
Tucson AZ 85742

Call Sign: KB7HU
Allen Swartz
655 N Venice Ave
Tucson AZ 85711

Call Sign: KD7MCZ
Stephen C Judith
2344 N Venice Pl

Tucson AZ 85712

Call Sign: KF7NKM
Jeffrey A Gerwin
6451 N Ventana Canyon Dr
Tucson AZ 85750

Call Sign: KD7KVH
Justin L Brunker
4900 N Ventana Ridge Pl
Tucson AZ 85750

Call Sign: KD7ZIP
Jonathan L Klein
6209 N Ventana View Pl
Tucson AZ 85750

Call Sign: KD7JMF
Jonathan L Klein
6209 N Ventura View Pl
Tucson AZ 85750

Call Sign: W8LYT
Sigmund P Stone
4372 N Vereda Rosada
Tucson AZ 85715

Call Sign: N7FGX
Lorneen E Magiera
7110 N Via Assisi
Tucson AZ 85704

Call Sign: WB0EUK
Bret D Goodrich
5251 N Via Condesa
Tucson AZ 85718

Call Sign: WA1QMZ
Steven M Wood
6219 N Via De La Tortola
Tucson AZ 857183324

Call Sign: WA6UDK
Everett H Lowman Jr
3980 N Via Del Sol
Tucson AZ 85749

Call Sign: KE7VJX
John W Behrens

6111 N Via Del Tecaco
Tucson AZ 85718

Call Sign: K7JWB
John W Behrens
6111 N Via Del Tecaco
Tucson AZ 85718

Call Sign: KF7DDH
Martin B Rosenthal
6516 N Via Divina
Tucson AZ 85750

Call Sign: N8NJD
John M Forinash
5585 N Via Elena
Tucson AZ 85718

Call Sign: KB7CGB
Edgar A Wald
4819 N Via Entrada
Tucson AZ 85718

Call Sign: KD7WCN
Ryan A Mansager
4505 N Via Entrada 139
Tucson AZ 85718

Call Sign: KE7GHY
David H Olson
4537 N Via Entrada Apt 246
Tucson AZ 85718

Call Sign: WB7PVI
Linda A Buczynski
5409 N Via Frassino
Tucson AZ 85750

Call Sign: KC7HWR
Leonard Sparrold
5485 N Via Frassino
Tucson AZ 85715

Call Sign: KC7OVP
John D Mac Innes
5540 N Via Frassino
Tucson AZ 85715

Call Sign: N7TOA

David W Bowen
7769 N Via Laguna Niguel
Tucson AZ 85743

Call Sign: KE7MRS
David M Scholl
5700 N Via Lozana
Tucson AZ 85750

Call Sign: KE7BC
Robert S Gensler
4400 N Via Noriega
Tucson AZ 85749

Call Sign: KD6LEJ
James L Warner Jr
4661 N Via Noriega
Tucson AZ 85749

Call Sign: KB6WCR
Terri R Rubin
4121 N Via Nueva
Tucson AZ 857501837

Call Sign: KF7UUP
Caleb K Brewer
1033 N Via Primavera
Tucson AZ 85710

Call Sign: KF7QQF
John T Perchorowicz
5631 N Via Salerosa
Tucson AZ 85750

Call Sign: W8RMZ
Robert M Zollinger Jr
5296 N Via Sempreverde
Tucson AZ 85750

Call Sign: W7RMZ
Robert M Zollinger Jr
5296 N Via Sempreverde
Tucson AZ 85750

Call Sign: KA3HEC
Samuel A Schechter
5337 N Via Sempreverde
Tucson AZ 85715

Call Sign: KB7DZE
Robert L Acosta
4750 N Via Sonrisa
Tucson AZ 85718

Call Sign: WB2COV
Robert F Sussman
4140 N Via Tranquilo
Tucson AZ 85750

Call Sign: N6CTS
Marilyn Devore
5580 N Via Umbrosa
Tucson AZ 85750

Call Sign: KD6DJV
Charles A Puchon Jr
5711 N Via Umbrosa
Tucson AZ 85750

Call Sign: N2LSM
Eugene E Smith
5714 N Via Umbrosa
Tucson AZ 85750

Call Sign: WA7GMG
Barbara Kaller
5326 N Via Velazquez
Tucson AZ 85715

Call Sign: KE7HUL
Jerry E Brucksieker
3340 N Viewcrest Dr
Tucson AZ 85745

Call Sign: KD7IYM
Stan C Bodenheimer
6946 N Village View Dr
Tucson AZ 85741

Call Sign: KD7TXM
Brian W Duffy
3864 N Vines End Pl
Tucson AZ 85719

Call Sign: KE7BUG
Theresa L Ryan
3864 N Vines End Pl
Tucson AZ 85719

Call Sign: KD6ZTK
Stephen M Lubliner
4801 N Vista De Loma
Segunda
Tucson AZ 85749

Call Sign: AB7YW
Carl G Slutter
4801 N Vista De Loma
Segunda
Tucson AZ 85749

Call Sign: W3BM
Carl G Slutter
4801 N Vista De Loma
Segunda
Tucson AZ 85749

Call Sign: KB7WQW
John J Sopko
4920 N Vista Del Cerro
Ranch Rd
Tucson AZ 85745

Call Sign: KE7OYN
Dale H Crockett
6945 N Vista Pl
Tucson AZ 85704

Call Sign: KE7OYO
Karla G Crockett
6945 N Vista Pl
Tucson AZ 857044221

Call Sign: KA7ZPU
Wiley E Greene
7000 N Vista Pl
Tucson AZ 85704

Call Sign: K7ZIM
Kenneth W Cook
5905 N Vista Val Verde
Tucson AZ 85718

Call Sign: KD7V
David B Rosenthal
5755 N Vista Valverde
Tucson AZ 85740

Call Sign: KF7UNU
Loretta M Bogdanowicz
13414 N Vistoso Bluff Pl
Tucson AZ 85755

Call Sign: KD7BOW
Christopher D Scholl
6352 N Vuelta Tajo
Tucson AZ 857182238

Call Sign: KE7VKN
Leslie M Muir
2611 N Vuelta Vista Antigua
Tucson AZ 85715

Call Sign: N4PT
Arthur C Prewitt
6945 N Wade Rd
Tucson AZ 85743

Call Sign: KD6VPT
Darlene Y Johnston Ms
6940 N Wade Rd
Tucson AZ 85743

Call Sign: KC7HWO
Robert I Hofacker
7911 N Wade Springs Dr
Tucson AZ 85743

Call Sign: KA5JHW
Gerald D Cain Jr
2818 N Walnut
Tucson AZ 85712

Call Sign: KG8LI
Larry M Cooper
8748 N Walter Hagen Dr
Tucson AZ 85742

Call Sign: N7CCT
Loran D Webb
7334 N Wanda Vista Way
Tucson AZ 85704

Call Sign: KC7MLV
Jude A Trautlein
2764 N Warren Ave

Tucson AZ 85719

Call Sign: KC7LII
Mark S Axer
2764 N Warren Ave
Tucson AZ 85719

Call Sign: KF7VDQ
Stephen A Schuldenfrei
2040 N Water View Ct
Tucson AZ 85749

Call Sign: KE7RHZ
Merrill Jackson
9851 N Western Fork Trl
Tucson AZ 85742

Call Sign: KB7OGE
Charles H Roth Jr
8210 N Wheatfield Dr
Tucson AZ 85741

Call Sign: KE6GBQ
Karl P Kennedy
5506 N Whitethorn Pl
Tucson AZ 857042634

Call Sign: KB6RNM
Anna Lise L Pratt Ferguson
13347 N Wide View Dr
Tucson AZ 85737

Call Sign: WD6BBQ
George H Jacoby
3066 N Willow Creek Dr
Tucson AZ 85712

Call Sign: W0OQX
Willis B Evans
6321 N Willowbrook Dr
Tucson AZ 85704

Call Sign: K9YKN
Robert T Chapko
1701 N Wilmot 115
Tucson AZ 85712

Call Sign: W7EP
Robert W Howe

602 N Wilmot Rd
Tucson AZ 85711

Call Sign: K7GPJ
James G Small
4361 N Wilmot Rd
Tucson AZ 85750

Call Sign: KC7PJG
William C Clark
1517 N Wilmot Rd 171
Tucson AZ 85712

Call Sign: WA1BZQ
Bruce C Betterley
205 N Wilmot Rd 357
Tucson AZ 85711

Call Sign: KJ4CAV
William J Tarbush
1620 N Wilmot Rd Unit
H110
Tucson AZ 85712

Call Sign: KA2RKH
Myron J Holak
14731 N Windshade Dr
Tucson AZ 857378827

Call Sign: KD7UIY
Benjamin R Pearson
1301 N Winstel
Tucson AZ 85716

Call Sign: KC7NPS
Katrina Ziegweid
N Winstel Blvd
Tucson AZ 85716

Call Sign: KE7QIC
Richard J Price
4411 N Wolford Rd
Tucson AZ 85749

Call Sign: N5BPY
Paul H Oglesby
9955 N Woodstone Trl
Tucson AZ 85741

Call Sign: K7ZY
Dale W Welch
1500 N Yavapai St
Tucson AZ 85745

Call Sign: W7LZ
Roger R Root
7349 N Yucca Via
Tucson AZ 857046226

Call Sign: KB2BUC
Richard A Saggese Sr
7731 N Zarragoza Dr
Tucson AZ 85704

Call Sign: KZ7Q
Richard A Saggese Sr
7731 N Zarragoza Dr
Tucson AZ 85704

Call Sign: N7TVO
Terry S Reagan
7913 N Zarragoza Dr
Tucson AZ 85741

Call Sign: KD7ECQ
Christopher L Tuttle
6255 N Zorrela Segundo
Tucson AZ 857183041

Call Sign: KD7ECP
Mark G Tuttle
6255 N Zorrela Segundo
Tucson AZ 857183041

Call Sign: KD7LNN
Daniel G Tuttle
6522 N Zorrela Segundo
Tucson AZ 857183041

Call Sign: KA4RSF
Bruce L Button
3333 Noflowing Wells Rd
121
Tucson AZ 85705

Call Sign: K1KOM
Richard J Cormier
15301 Noracle Rd 18

Tucson AZ 85739

Call Sign: N7QVN
Michael E Owen
4525 Old Ranch Rd
Tucson AZ 85743

Call Sign: KD7WM
Donald F Coonan
8029 Old Tanque Verde Rd
Tucson AZ 85749

Call Sign: KC7CJT
Ernest M Mc Clintock
7267 Onda Cir
Tucson AZ 85715

Call Sign: WA6HDD
Arpad Balo
Oracle Rd 1104
Tucson AZ 85705

Call Sign: KF7CNO
Solomon N Bachman
444 Orange Grove Rd 418
Tucson AZ 85704

Call Sign: KD5CMH
Johnathan M Starrett
8959 Orchid Vine Dr
Tucson AZ 85747

Call Sign: KZ9M
Donald J Sobey
120 Oro Valley Dr
Tucson AZ 85737

Call Sign: KD7NXN
Morton L Caplan
2811 Owl Vista Pl
Tucson AZ 85742

Call Sign: AA9VQ
Jerry L Clayton
555 Pantano Rd Unit 615
Tucson AZ 85710

Call Sign: KC0QBN
Edwin G Williams

4240 Paseo De Los
Rancheros
Tucson AZ 85745

Call Sign: W7IJO
Stanley J Goldberg
5620 Paseo De Tampico
Tucson AZ 85715

Call Sign: KC7YDJ
Gerald C Blossom
4657 Paseo Don Carlos
Tucson AZ 85746

Call Sign: KD7OOC
Dorothy L Olsen
1570 Paseo Dorado
Tucson AZ 85715

Call Sign: KD7OOD
Richard M Olsen
1570 Paseo Dorado
Tucson AZ 85715

Call Sign: N0AGY
William T Reese
4355 Paseo Rancho
Tucson AZ 85745

Call Sign: K7HQT
Robert W Hanson
2 Paseo San Pedro
Tucson AZ 85710

Call Sign: KC7FRX
Camille R Hickey
6333 Peregrine Way
Tucson AZ 85745

Call Sign: AB7AA
William P Hickey Jr
6333 Peregrine Way
Tucson AZ 85745

Call Sign: KC7PPZ
Billie A Closs
Pinto Ln
Tucson AZ 85739

Call Sign: KE7WIU
Kay Cagle
201 Pinto Pl
Tucson AZ 85748

Call Sign: N7SQA
John Hertig
9401 Placita Cascada
Tucson AZ 85715

Call Sign: KE5LG
Paul W Bowden
5926 Placita De La Oleada
Tucson AZ 85750

Call Sign: W7LMB
Alfred Christofferson Jr
8701 Placita De Reynaga
Tucson AZ 85704

Call Sign: N7MHT
Laverne M Emmerich
4454 Placita Gacela
Tucson AZ 85718

Call Sign: KD7JUM
Mark E Ray
1309 Placita Hojalata
Tucson AZ 85745

Call Sign: KC7JDX
Dan L Johnston
10521 Placita Loma Verde
Tucson AZ 85748

Call Sign: W5RLH
Elmer D Richardson
10673 Placita Los Reyes
Tucson AZ 85748

Call Sign: KE6HPX
Alex Anita Y Curtis
7334 Placita Luz De La Luna
Tucson AZ 85715

Call Sign: KC7QYI
Gerry K Furst
11979 Raining Star Ln
Tucson AZ 85743

Call Sign: WA7SBD
Arthur S Kastrinos
8230 Rawhide Trl
Tucson AZ 85715

Call Sign: K7HJD
Darrell G Kupelian
5961 Rex Strav
Tucson AZ 85706

Call Sign: KD7OBI
Kathryn E Paul
817 Rincon Rising Rd
Tucson AZ 85748

Call Sign: KB7GAI
Walter J Wegrzyn
Rollercoaster Rd
Tucson AZ 85704

Call Sign: KB7HHJ
Grant M Oltmann
8617 Rosewood St
Tucson AZ 85710

Call Sign: KG7UF
James E Draper
14279 Rusty Gate Trl
Tucson AZ 85737

Call Sign: KD7RPP
Miguel A Enriquez
3500 S 12th Ave
Tucson AZ 85713

Call Sign: KF7JBD
Pueblo Magnet High School
ARC
3500 S 12th Ave
Tucson AZ 85713

Call Sign: KF7GFI
Michael A Cruz
4802 S 15th Ave
Tucson AZ 85714

Call Sign: KC7QMI
Leroy A Smith

4918 S 17th Ave
Tucson AZ 85706

Call Sign: KC7UOR
Rosie F Smith
4918 S 17th Ave
Tucson AZ 85706

Call Sign: KC7JFC
Antonio V Montijo
4130 S 2nd Ave
Tucson AZ 85714

Call Sign: KF7DDD
Jhovana G Peralta
4430 S 2nd Ave
Tucson AZ 85714

Call Sign: W7HNT
Kenneth E Lohner
128 S 5th Ave Apt 41
Tucson AZ 85701

Call Sign: KC7RXW
Southwest Blind Rehab
Center 124
3601 S 6th Ave Va Medical
Center
Tucson AZ 85723

Call Sign: KD7RH
Christopher G Hansen
3611 S 8th Ave
Tucson AZ 85713

Call Sign: KA7RMC
Jenna S Hansen
3611 S 8th Ave
Tucson AZ 85713

Call Sign: KC7KKV
Joseph Smith
3646 S 8th Ave
Tucson AZ 85713

Call Sign: WB7QES
Jesus M Cardenas
5246 S 9th Ave
Tucson AZ 85706

Call Sign: KC7OVE
Sean M Johnson
6466 S Acacia Desert Ave
Tucson AZ 85706

Call Sign: W7UKM
Eugene H Bruce
2012 S Aida Ave
Tucson AZ 85710

Call Sign: KB7HPW
Alfredo F Diaz
5509 S Alaska Dr
Tucson AZ 85706

Call Sign: W7FPX
James H Reynolds
5862 S Aldorn Dr
Tucson AZ 85706

Call Sign: WB7ORB
Timmy B Bacchus
5126 S Aleppo Dr
Tucson AZ 857061606

Call Sign: KB6HZJ
Barbara Morrell
11145 S Alyce Ave
Tucson AZ 857369700

Call Sign: N6MDG
Donald P Morrell
11145 S Alyce Ave
Tucson AZ 857369700

Call Sign: N7TVP
Daniel J Hawkes
11265 S Alyce Ave
Tucson AZ 85736

Call Sign: K0TW
Thomas J Workman
4759 S Apple Tree Ave
Tucson AZ 857304334

Call Sign: W6TBO
John E Fernley
6031 S Arrow

Tucson AZ 85746

Call Sign: K1MFS
Richard K Somes
37714 S Arroyo Way
Tucson AZ 85739

Call Sign: NV9H
Dennis G Atteberry
38028 S Arroyo Way
Tucson AZ 85739

Call Sign: KF7NAX
John P Mccartney
38183 S Arroyo Way
Tucson AZ 85739

Call Sign: N6MZZ
Gary W Wood
38273 S Arroyo Way
Tucson AZ 85739

Call Sign: KF7QKG
Donald R Roberts
1817 S Augusta Cir
Tucson AZ 85710

Call Sign: KF7DDL
Karl W Yoerns
3173 S Austin Point Dr
Tucson AZ 85730

Call Sign: KA7LDS
James J O Reilly
1308 S Ave Conalea
Tucson AZ 85748

Call Sign: KC7LVK
Matthew W Mc Closkey
8010 S Ave San Candido
Tucson AZ 85746

Call Sign: KI7ND
William D Lynch
8031 S Avenida Ana
Tucson AZ 85747

Call Sign: KF7UAS
Bernard J Palazzolo

7790 S Avenida Bonita
Tucson AZ 85747

Call Sign: WB7OBE
Harvey Tom Jr
7941 S Avenida Bonita
Tucson AZ 85747

Call Sign: W4PPA
Robert H Levasseur
1359 S Avenida Conalea
Tucson AZ 85748

Call Sign: K7OLH
Richard C Chatfield Jr
1359 S Avenida Conalea
Tucson AZ 85748

Call Sign: KA7WID
James W Zimmerman
501 S Avenida Del Rey
Tucson AZ 85748

Call Sign: WD6ATO
Gayle D Strand
4360 S Avenida Don Gerardo
Tucson AZ 85746

Call Sign: WA7PWO
Ralph Emerson
1932 S Avenida Guillermo
Tucson AZ 857106312

Call Sign: N7TVN
Larry K Barrett
2795 S Avenida Los Reyes
Tucson AZ 85730

Call Sign: KE7HPO
Rincon Qrp Contest Club
620 S Avenida Princesa
Tucson AZ 85748

Call Sign: W7RIN
Rincon Qrp Contest Club
620 S Avenida Princesa
Tucson AZ 85748

Call Sign: AC7A

Thomas E Kuehl
620 S Avenida Princesa
Tucson AZ 85748

Call Sign: KE7WIQ
Matthew W Mccloskey
8010 S Avenida San Candido
Tucson AZ 85746

Call Sign: KE7WST
Matthew W Mccloskey
8010 S Avenida San Candido
Tucson AZ 85746

Call Sign: AD7XN
Matthew W Mccloskey
8010 S Avenida San Candido
Tucson AZ 85746

Call Sign: KB6KWQ
William A Bigelow
1251 S Avenida Sirio
Tucson AZ 857105200

Call Sign: AC7LB
William A Bigelow
1251 S Avenida Sirio
Tucson AZ 857105200

Call Sign: WE7H
Edward P Hutchinson
1802 S Avenida Ursa
Tucson AZ 85710

Call Sign: KE5AAA
John Kamaras
7226 S Badger Canyon Dr
Tucson AZ 85706

Call Sign: KF7EME
Daniel E Tonkovich
3955 S Bantry Ln
Tucson AZ 85735

Call Sign: N0AGT
Jera L Miller
1600 S Barbados Pl
Tucson AZ 857487619

Call Sign: N7WBP
Steven M Pulis
4650 S Barrington Pl
Tucson AZ 85730

Call Sign: AE5DA
David A Paul
1050 S Bill Martin Dr 3 103
Tucson AZ 85745

Call Sign: K0VTE
Stanley R Breckner
5941 S Birchwood Dr
Tucson AZ 85746

Call Sign: W7LB
Larry W Brown
2721 S Black Moon
Tucson AZ 85730

Call Sign: KJ7PC
William R Ogroski
2642 S Blackmoon Dr
Tucson AZ 857301465

Call Sign: KC7LCB
Richard L Reed
2821 S Blackmoon Dr
Tucson AZ 85730

Call Sign: KC0EDT
Douglas J Sheets
7892 S Blue Creek Ave
Tucson AZ 85747

Call Sign: KD7JBL
Geraldine N Pond
3721 S Bobby Dr
Tucson AZ 85730

Call Sign: K9SIT
Geraldine N Pond
3721 S Bobby Dr
Tucson AZ 85730

Call Sign: KD7IEY
James A Pond
3721 S Bobby Dr
Tucson AZ 85730

Call Sign: KF7ATR
Brian L Kimberling
2532 S Bonanza Ave
Tucson AZ 85748

Call Sign: KE7WJA
Ernest S Strong Jr
1656 S Bronze Morn Pl
Tucson AZ 85748

Call Sign: N7KTF
Claude L Plymate
5150 S Bryce Ave
Tucson AZ 85746

Call Sign: N7KTG
Teresa A Bippert Plymate
5150 S Bryce Ave
Tucson AZ 85757

Call Sign: WB7SAL
Steven D Pierce
8477 S Burien Rd
Tucson AZ 85747

Call Sign: KC7POH
Donna J Mc Cabe
3590 S Burnett Pl
Tucson AZ 85730

Call Sign: KA7OQA
Truman S Rue
216 S Busch Pl
Tucson AZ 85710

Call Sign: W7ERT
Eugene F Ireland
221 S Busch Pl
Tucson AZ 85710

Call Sign: WA1KNX
Dean H Mc Gorrill
5445 S Butts Rd
Tucson AZ 85757

Call Sign: W7RJ
Russell P Jordan
5120 S Caballo Rd

Tucson AZ 85746

Call Sign: W7HQE
George M Janssen Sr
5250 S Caballo Rd
Tucson AZ 85706

Call Sign: KE7BTC
Neal G Scofield
5131 S Cactus Wren Ave
Tucson AZ 85746

Call Sign: N7YGU
William G Vigasin
3726 S Calexico Ave
Tucson AZ 85730

Call Sign: WA7QXK
Daniel P Kelly
1425 S Calle Anasazi
Tucson AZ 85735

Call Sign: KC7YDI
Dale D Aiuto
1730 S Calle Anasazi
Tucson AZ 85735

Call Sign: KC7CJR
Michael G Ellis
1940 S Calle Anasazi
Tucson AZ 85735

Call Sign: K9FTN
Gerald D Pine
325 S Calle De Madrid
Tucson AZ 85711

Call Sign: KC7MGT
Edward E Coleman
2201 S Calle Hohokam
Tucson AZ 85735

Call Sign: KD7VRG
Michael W Mcauley
2140 S Calle Mesa Del Oso
Tucson AZ 85748

Call Sign: KD7ZRE
Robert H Jenney

4821 S Calle Ole
Tucson AZ 857143111

Call Sign: N7KGE
Frank P Peluso
3700 S Calle Polar 58 3
Tucson AZ 85730

Call Sign: KB7GCM
Kellie D Slaugenhoupt
2631 S Calle Yucatan
Tucson AZ 85730

Call Sign: KC7SIM
Walter E Meserve
4807 S Camino De La Pena
Tucson AZ 85746

Call Sign: KD6OSI
Brent A Myers
5141 S Camino De Oeste
Tucson AZ 85746

Call Sign: WB6EGV
James A Ogilvie
7100 S Camino Del Garanon
Tucson AZ 85747

Call Sign: KD7WJG
Donald J Redmon
7261 S Camino Mirlo
Tucson AZ 85747

Call Sign: KD7CQS
James C Johnsen
7262 S Camino Mirlo
Tucson AZ 85747

Call Sign: KD7JCJ
James C Johnsen
7262 S Camino Mirlo
Tucson AZ 85747

Call Sign: KC7HWG
Juan M Salazar
7310 S Camino Mirlo
Tucson AZ 85747

Call Sign: KA8DGG

Marie C Geraci
7900 S Camino Mirlo
Tucson AZ 85747

Call Sign: WA8UTX
Daniel C Wolfe
7940 S Camino Mirlo
Tucson AZ 85747

Call Sign: KI6AR
Jack L Hilton
1350 S Camino Seco
Tucson AZ 857106259

Call Sign: K7TNE
Mildred A Stiles
2101 S Camino Seco
Tucson AZ 85710

Call Sign: W7HT
Merrill G Stiles
2101 S Camino Seco
Tucson AZ 857107908

Call Sign: KA2IIB
Margaret K Rubin
3411 S Camino Seco 259
Tucson AZ 85730

Call Sign: KB0QLW
Linda S James
3411 S Camino Seco 264
Tucson AZ 85730

Call Sign: WB8AHW
Earl K Cusac
3411 S Camino Seco 52
Tucson AZ 85730

Call Sign: AF7H
Ronald A Perkins
3411 S Camino Seco Lot 38
Tucson AZ 857302807

Call Sign: KB7NCI
Johnny A Collins Sr
5250 S Campbell 165
Tucson AZ 85706

Call Sign: KD7AUS
Dale A King
6280 S Campbell 6102
Tucson AZ 85706

Call Sign: KD7SHE
Brian E Jones
5058 S Campbell Ave
Tucson AZ 857061510

Call Sign: KE7UZZ
Joan H Meyer
1510 S Cape Verde Pl
Tucson AZ 85748

Call Sign: KE7UZY
Rodger T Meyer
1510 S Cape Verde Pl
Tucson AZ 85748

Call Sign: N7GUO
Wilfred L Price
1515 S Cape Verde Pl
Tucson AZ 857487618

Call Sign: N9AJT
James C Burt
1001 S Carnegie Dr
Tucson AZ 85710

Call Sign: KD7VCK
Richard L Visotcky
1720 S Carthage Pl
Tucson AZ 85748

Call Sign: KA8SNI
Stanley J Dodds
7801 S Castle Bay
Tucson AZ 85747

Call Sign: AA7QE
Ronnie C Brickey
7370 S Cateus Thorn Ln
Tucson AZ 85747

Call Sign: N7WBU
Larry A Stafford
3522 S Chesin Dr
Tucson AZ 857302319

Call Sign: KD7ODT
Renee M Brollini
720 S Chimney Canyon Dr
Tucson AZ 85748

Call Sign: KC7FP
David O Dumas Sr
797 S Ciudad Cir
Tucson AZ 857106636

Call Sign: N7DAY
Mary L Dumas
797 S Ciudad Cir
Tucson AZ 857106636

Call Sign: N7QDF
Edward S Richards
37883 S Cleek Dr
Tucson AZ 85739

Call Sign: KV4OA
Kvoa ARC
7588 S Climbing Ivy Dr
Tucson AZ 85757

Call Sign: K0DVH
Steven R Arens
7588 S Climbing Ivy Dr
Tucson AZ 85757

Call Sign: WB7UOF
Charles W Spears Jr
1902 S Cloverland
Tucson AZ 857116516

Call Sign: KA7CYD
Darlene L Osborne
1453 S Coati Dr
Tucson AZ 857131221

Call Sign: K7ZMA
Edgar M Osborne Jr
1453 S Coati Dr
Tucson AZ 857131221

Call Sign: WB0OQG
Harry A Smith
6250 S Commerce Ct 1214

Tucson AZ 85746

Call Sign: N0CXI
Ruth F Smith
6250 S Commerce Ct 1214
Tucson AZ 85746

Call Sign: K7KYW
Walter H Rieke
6250 S Commerce Ct Apt
3116
Tucson AZ 857466012

Call Sign: W0RSS
Robert E Olson
6250 S Commerce Ct Apt
3201
Tucson AZ 85746

Call Sign: WA7GSY
Ken A Crossman
37430 S Copper Ridge Ct
Tucson AZ 85739

Call Sign: KB7RVM
Edward J Linehan
3721 S Country Club Rd
Tucson AZ 85713

Call Sign: KD7MLB
Vernon L Tester
5645 S Country Club Rd
Tucson AZ 85706

Call Sign: KD7IFB
Scott A Starker
39022 S Cracked Corn Dr
Tucson AZ 85739

Call Sign: KB7SLI
David P Myers
752 S Craycroft
Tucson AZ 85711

Call Sign: KE7SGD
Richard E Ferguson
1258 S Craycroft Apt C201
Tucson AZ 85711

Call Sign: KE7ORT
Philip L Heppel-Kennard
5535 S Crimson Thorn Dr
Tucson AZ 85757

Call Sign: KE7SZT
Peter J Lippert
7633 S Cross Hill Dr
Tucson AZ 85747

Call Sign: KF7PSZ
Donald L Osborne
7851 S Danforth Ave
Tucson AZ 85747

Call Sign: WL7WM
Jennifer M Michael
7537 S Daystar Ct
Tucson AZ 85747

Call Sign: AL7BN
Sue S Michael
7537 S Daystar Ct
Tucson AZ 85747

Call Sign: NL7D
Timothy H Michael
7537 S Daystar Ct
Tucson AZ 85747

Call Sign: KD7PHY
James O Beaman
4795 S Deaver Rd
Tucson AZ 85735

Call Sign: W7ZNS
James O Beaman
4795 S Deaver Rd
Tucson AZ 85735

Call Sign: WA9RWO
Lawrence A Kaja
1809 S Deer Head Pl
Tucson AZ 85748

Call Sign: KO2D
Carol I Acheson
38583 S Desert Bluff Dr
Tucson AZ 85739

Call Sign: KJ2A
Laurence F Acheson
38583 S Desert Bluff Dr
Tucson AZ 85739

Call Sign: KC8ODN
Denise P Rowell
38761 S Desert Bluff Dr
Tucson AZ 85739

Call Sign: WD8PDM
Frank E Rowell
38761 S Desert Bluff Dr
Tucson AZ 85739

Call Sign: KC0WVY
Jon A Henke
3587 S Desert Cache Rd
Tucson AZ 857355177

Call Sign: KE7MCL
George S Hupp
3599 S Desert Motif Rd
Tucson AZ 85735

Call Sign: N8MIH
Gary E Veverka
1121 S Desert Senna Loop
Tucson AZ 85748

Call Sign: KD7AUK
Nicholas H Rice
1144 S Desert Senna Loop
Tucson AZ 857483565

Call Sign: WB7QBT
James R Percival
1832 S Desert Vista Dr
Tucson AZ 85748

Call Sign: KA7HIT
David C Salkeld
2141 S Diamond D Dr
Tucson AZ 85713

Call Sign: KB7VKJ
Arlen F Hansen
6349 S Dorado Cir

Tucson AZ 85746

Call Sign: W7SEX
Edward F Geiser
522 S Downing Ln
Tucson AZ 85711

Call Sign: K3PSY
Harry L Sands III
4005 S Draper Rd
Tucson AZ 85746

Call Sign: KA7OFX
Dale R Grunseth
8557 S Dubloon Way
Tucson AZ 85706

Call Sign: WB9DUP
David E Dzurick
7541 S Dunbar Ct
Tucson AZ 857475607

Call Sign: WA7GCF
Jack L Van Cleave
37990 S Eagle Dr
Tucson AZ 85737

Call Sign: KD5UXE
William A Carrier
6228 S Eagles Roost Dr
Tucson AZ 85757

Call Sign: KF7EAP
Katie A Marascio
185 S Eastern Dawn Ave
Tucson AZ 85748

Call Sign: KG5NG
Frederick J Mc Clung Jr
240 S Eastern Dawn Ave
Tucson AZ 85748

Call Sign: WB2BSJ
Cary M Fishman
485 S Edgeside Ave
Tucson AZ 85748

Call Sign: K7OMR
Raymond P Bass

1361 S Edlin Ave
Tucson AZ 85711

Call Sign: KC7WKU
Richard L Johnston
39085 S Elbow Bend Dr
Tucson AZ 85739

Call Sign: KB5AF
James F Park
37850 S Escocia Ln
Tucson AZ 85739

Call Sign: N7NLR
David L Meyer
6149 S Euclid Ave
Tucson AZ 85706

Call Sign: N7TVM
David A Lyons
101 S Evelyn Ave
Tucson AZ 85710

Call Sign: KD6CRL
John D Bruchey
8080 S Farmbelt Dr
Tucson AZ 85706

Call Sign: KG7KV
Christopher T Borden
1902 S Farwell Ave
Tucson AZ 85711

Call Sign: WA7AHF
John B Borden
1902 S Farwell Ave
Tucson AZ 85711

Call Sign: KA7PKG
Matthew J Lepree
4649 S Fenwick Dr
Tucson AZ 85730

Call Sign: K7PKG
Matthew J Lepree
4649 S Fenwick Dr
Tucson AZ 85730

Call Sign: KA7YTX

Merlin F Kostal
5221 S Fickett Ave
Tucson AZ 85746

Call Sign: N7FGY
Paul E Bean
4811 S Fickett Pl 2
Tucson AZ 85746

Call Sign: W7EQ
Gordon A Yarte
3722 S Fighting Falcon Dr
Tucson AZ 85730

Call Sign: KD7UUL
Soven M Wiley
7520 S Fitzwater Ave
Tucson AZ 85746

Call Sign: KC7KKX
Fred B Schmoldt
2040 S Flying Q Ln
Tucson AZ 85713

Call Sign: KC7KKY
Marge R Schmoldt
2040 S Flying Q Ln
Tucson AZ 85713

Call Sign: KD7JUO
Ana M Eubanks
5134 S Fox Trot Dr
Tucson AZ 85746

Call Sign: N7ZQZ
Timothy W Eubanks
5134 S Fox Trot Dr
Tucson AZ 85746

Call Sign: KE2HS
Peter G Wulfing
36935 S Foxglen Ln
Tucson AZ 85739

Call Sign: KA7ABK
Diana D Wood
4160 S Frank Dr
Tucson AZ 857358880

Call Sign: WB7ELZ
Donald C Thomas
4160 S Frank Dr
Tucson AZ 857358880

Call Sign: WB7WOD
Sandy L Thomas
4160 S Frank Dr
Tucson AZ 857358880

Call Sign: KD7OBC
Tammy F Dockery
2850 S Freeman
Tucson AZ 85730

Call Sign: KC9ORD
Michael R Casey
100 S Freeman Rd
Tucson AZ 85748

Call Sign: KE7VJI
Robert H Wakefield
1380 S Freeman Rd
Tucson AZ 85748

Call Sign: NC7Z
Robert H Wakefield
1380 S Freeman Rd
Tucson AZ 85748

Call Sign: KD7MDA
Charles R Dockery
2850 S Freeman Rd
Tucson AZ 85730

Call Sign: N7UQ
Charles R Dockery
2850 S Freeman Rd
Tucson AZ 85730

Call Sign: KK7DB
Joseph Pinter Jr
5153 S Fremont Ave
Tucson AZ 857061458

Call Sign: N1IDN
Michael A Dzicek
3560 S Frick Ave
Tucson AZ 85730

Call Sign: WA7VUZ
Dale Baker
721 S Front Royal Dr
Tucson AZ 85710

Call Sign: KA9YZA
Beverly M Synovetz
751 S Front Royal Dr
Tucson AZ 85710

Call Sign: KA9YZB
Harry Synovetz Jr
751 S Front Royal Dr
Tucson AZ 85710

Call Sign: KB2JQX
Donald G Silvernail
2880 S Full Moon Dr
Tucson AZ 85713

Call Sign: KA5APU
Robert L Allen
8280 S Fuller Rd
Tucson AZ 85736

Call Sign: AD7C
Arthur D Code
7703 S Galileo Ln
Tucson AZ 85747

Call Sign: W6JDA
Ivar Sanders
7774 S Galileo Ln
Tucson AZ 85747

Call Sign: KC0VVD
Margaret M Parker
7775 S Galileo Ln
Tucson AZ 85747

Call Sign: KC0VVC
Richard E Parker
7775 S Galileo Ln
Tucson AZ 857479605

Call Sign: KF7CNN
Harry K Bonfield Jr
1162 S Georgetown Dr

Tucson AZ 85710

Call Sign: WA6TEJ
Bruce D Smith
3456 S Giovanna Dr
Tucson AZ 85730

Call Sign: KC5JID
Harold W Westerman
3610 S Gold Flower Ave
Tucson AZ 857351492

Call Sign: KC7JWP
David N Williams
30 S Gold Mine Loop
Tucson AZ 857486792

Call Sign: KC7TYZ
Norman E Schaeffler
37353 S Golf Course Dr
Tucson AZ 857391152

Call Sign: KF7FTV
James Perez
38178 S Golf Course Dr
Tucson AZ 85739

Call Sign: KD7KRV
Kurt A Lovrien
475 S Gollob Rd
Tucson AZ 85710

Call Sign: KD7KRU
Kyle D Lovrien
475 S Gollob Rd
Tucson AZ 85710

Call Sign: KD7KRT
Ryan C Lovrien
475 S Gollob Rd
Tucson AZ 85710

Call Sign: KC7ALR
Paul L Hanson
3230 S Grady Ave
Tucson AZ 85730

Call Sign: WB0WTP
David L Hanson

3230 S Grady Ave
Tucson AZ 85730

Call Sign: KD7SDX
Charles E Roebuck
4751 S Green Olive Dr
Tucson AZ 85730

Call Sign: KF7GPV
Chris O Cline
7048 S Gull Ln
Tucson AZ 85756

Call Sign: WB7BB
Robert W Bean
4675 S Harrison 194
Tucson AZ 857304553

Call Sign: KD6LMA
Robert A Heath
409 S Harvard Ave
Tucson AZ 857104630

Call Sign: KC7FZT
Marlin J Gregor
7550 S Hatch St
Tucson AZ 85747

Call Sign: KC7GFA
Nathan J Hattala
6018 S Hawks Hollow Ct
Tucson AZ 85747

Call Sign: KC7ALQ
Josefina Ruiz
2080 S Hermosa Dr
Tucson AZ 85713

Call Sign: W7MVV
Raul Rouzaud
6132 S Hildreth
Tucson AZ 857465127

Call Sign: KF7ATN
Vance A Addabbo
5910 S Hillerman Dr
Tucson AZ 85746

Call Sign: KC7OPK

Lupita Hernandez
3995 S Hogan Dr
Tucson AZ 85735

Call Sign: KA7HXL
Stephen Ondrish
3351 S Irene Pl
Tucson AZ 857302226

Call Sign: N7KXB
James L Porta
402 S Jerrie Ave
Tucson AZ 857114243

Call Sign: KF7GPS
John R Frugoli
3470 S Jessica Ave
Tucson AZ 85730

Call Sign: KE7GLA
Damian M Lalonde
5520 S Joseph Ave
Tucson AZ 85757

Call Sign: KB7QWH
Marquita A Mc Crone
5676 S Joseph Ave
Tucson AZ 85746

Call Sign: KC7DVI
Kenneth W Nelson II
650 S Kellond Pl
Tucson AZ 85710

Call Sign: KA7RAI
Richard D Warren
749 S Kenyon Dr
Tucson AZ 85710

Call Sign: KA7RAJ
Robert J Warren
749 S Kenyon Dr
Tucson AZ 85710

Call Sign: KC7IC
Edward C Scott
2740 S Kinney Rd
Tucson AZ 85746

Call Sign: N7DST
James C Brown
3100 S Kinney Rd 189
Tucson AZ 85713

Call Sign: W3ESF
Edward C Chaput
3100 S Kinney Rd 277
Tucson AZ 857135505

Call Sign: AA7RR
Jacquelin M Segui
3100 S Kinney Rd 58
Tucson AZ 85713

Call Sign: AA7RQ
Richard S Segui
3100 S Kinney Rd 58
Tucson AZ 85713

Call Sign: KA6DXE
Ellen A Scott
3100 S Kinney Rd 67
Tucson AZ 85713

Call Sign: KC7BI
James H Scott
3100 S Kinney Rd 67
Tucson AZ 85713

Call Sign: KD1C
Richard H Hale
3100 S Kinney Rd Lot 275
Tucson AZ 85713

Call Sign: KB7OTO
Maurice H Martin
8701 S Kolb Rd
Tucson AZ 85706

Call Sign: KD7BTH
Peter L Rabin
8701 S Kolb Rd 11187
Tucson AZ 85706

Call Sign: KF7FKE
Patricia Farwell
8701 S Kolb Rd 12 183
Tucson AZ 85756

Call Sign: W7MVA
Patricia Farwell
8701 S Kolb Rd 12 183
Tucson AZ 85756

Call Sign: KB7NCO
Fred C Anderegg
8701 S Kolb Rd 18 264
Tucson AZ 85706

Call Sign: KF6FCU
Harold M Hagner
8401 S Kolb Rd 193
Tucson AZ 85706

Call Sign: KC7QML
Robert L Miller
8701 S Kolb Rd 2 198
Tucson AZ 85706

Call Sign: KC7AHD
Mark A Haycock
8401 S Kolb Rd 221
Tucson AZ 85706

Call Sign: N8PYG
James H Walters
8401 S Kolb Rd 272
Tucson AZ 85706

Call Sign: N7ZBG
Katherine M Filkins
1345 S Kolb Rd 321
Tucson AZ 85710

Call Sign: KB1GQ
James E Harrison
8401 S Kolb Rd 363
Tucson AZ 85706

Call Sign: N7CEH
James L Stosberg
8401 S Kolb Rd 429
Tucson AZ 85706

Call Sign: WD8JTA
Ronald J Barthlemess
8401 S Kolb Rd 554

Tucson AZ 85706

Call Sign: KA8MCA
Wilbur E Rose
8701 S Kolb Rd Lot 2 270
Tucson AZ 85706

Call Sign: KD7UJA
Alvin G Covell
8401 S Kolb Rd Nr 224
Tucson AZ 85706

Call Sign: KB7OUO
Robert B Alderson
8701 S Kolb Rd Sp 1 275
Tucson AZ 85706

Call Sign: KJ7NU
Roy E Vastine
8701 S Kolb Rd Sp 10 182
Tucson AZ 85706

Call Sign: KA6SET
Gordon K Hoopes
8701 S Kolb Rd Sp 14 187
Tucson AZ 85756

Call Sign: W0CXC
Mary Jo Overbeck
8701 S Kolb Rd Sp 18 277
Tucson AZ 85706

Call Sign: N0HLM
James P Hawkins
8701 S Kolb Rd Sp 4 218
Tucson AZ 85706

Call Sign: KB7MYD
Kenneth E Koelsch
8701 S Kolb Rd Sp 5 308
Tucson AZ 85706

Call Sign: KB4VAV
Allan E Prust
8701 S Kolb Rd Sp 7 274
Tucson AZ 857069607

Call Sign: W6CSZ
Trefry A Ross

8701 S Kolb Rd Sp 8 176
Tucson AZ 85706

Call Sign: WA0BCZ
Hendrik J Aarts
8701 S Kolb Rd Ste 18 197
Tucson AZ 85706

Call Sign: KC7UDM
Colin A Brittan
8701 S Kolb Rd Unit 1 291
Tucson AZ 857069607

Call Sign: KB7PNZ
Donald C Rapley
8701 S Kolb Site 2 253
Tucson AZ 85706

Call Sign: KB7OVP
Hazel K Rapley
8701 S Kolb Site 2 253
Tucson AZ 85706

Call Sign: W0JFI
Robert H Overbeck
8701 S Kolb Sp 18 277
Tucson AZ 85706

Call Sign: NQ5A
Nicholas M De Luca III
8701 S Kold Rd 16 205
Tucson AZ 85706

Call Sign: KC7DVG
Leonel F Peterson
1750 S La Cholla
Tucson AZ 85713

Call Sign: KA7WON
Louis C Faircloth
4740 S Lacholla
Tucson AZ 85746

Call Sign: KE7VKS
Glenn A Fleck
2491 S Lance Ave
Tucson AZ 85748

Call Sign: KD7AIN

Burton E Kline
2503 S Lance Ave
Tucson AZ 85748

Call Sign: KA7CVE
Merlin R Wyatt
870 S Langley Ave
Tucson AZ 857104851

Call Sign: WB7ODM
Paul W La Bin
7912 S Lennox Ln
Tucson AZ 85747

Call Sign: KI7PN
Donald G Baker Sr
5735 S Leslie Ave
Tucson AZ 85706

Call Sign: NO7P
Donald G Baker Sr
5735 S Leslie Ave
Tucson AZ 85706

Call Sign: WB7OIL
Steve R Trujillo Sr
5939 S Liberty Ave
Tucson AZ 85706

Call Sign: WA7BGX
Hal H Hostetler
1934 S Lillian Cir
Tucson AZ 85713

Call Sign: N7RMX
Wilbur M Bailey III
4024 S Lone Palm Dr
Tucson AZ 85730

Call Sign: AB6BI
W David Hamill Jr
932 S Lucinda Dr
Tucson AZ 85748

Call Sign: KK7MT
Roger L Waltz
8591 S Magellan Dr
Tucson AZ 857069025

Call Sign: K7AYL
Darlyne M Waltz
8591 S Magellan Dr
Tucson AZ 857569025

Call Sign: N3SHA
Robert J Shoup
8572 S Magellin Dr
Tucson AZ 85706

Call Sign: KD7OHB
Walter Y Fish
6154 S Mainside Dr
Tucson AZ 85746

Call Sign: KA7NSA
Russell H Farnlof
3225 S Manitoba
Tucson AZ 85730

Call Sign: KB7ISS
Leslie A Mason
1405 S Marc Dr
Tucson AZ 85711

Call Sign: KC7DPK
Esther A Lathrop
2017 S Marc Dr
Tucson AZ 85710

Call Sign: KC7ANS
Salah H Obeid
3015 S Marissa
Tucson AZ 85730

Call Sign: KC7KLO
Arthur F Turnbull
1285 S Marmot Dr
Tucson AZ 85713

Call Sign: KF7LRF
Barney S Smith
5745 S Marshall Pl
Tucson AZ 85757

Call Sign: WA1B
William K Woody
8570 S Marstellar Rd
Tucson AZ 857361968

Call Sign: KC7WII
Teresa L Rill
249 S Martin Ave
Tucson AZ 85719

Call Sign: KC0MSJ
Jacob E Orvin
3633 S Marvin Pl
Tucson AZ 85730

Call Sign: KF7GPQ
Aaron J Dettmer
7686 S Meadow Spring Way
Tucson AZ 85747

Call Sign: N7UAV
Aaron J Dettmer
7686 S Meadow Spring Way
Tucson AZ 85747

Call Sign: KD7NED
Steven A Justen
7728 S Meadow Spring Way
Tucson AZ 85747

Call Sign: WA6NQO
Stirling R Sanford
1521 S Melpomene Way
Tucson AZ 85748

Call Sign: KB7CQK
Curt N Blair
43 S Melrose Ave
Tucson AZ 85745

Call Sign: AB7XH
Delbert C Fausey
35991 S Mesa Ridge Dr
Tucson AZ 85739

Call Sign: KF7SNK
Tom D Wuelpern
871 S Meyer
Tucson AZ 85701

Call Sign: KE7OSB
Guy D Deluca
1508 S Miller Creek Pl

Tucson AZ 85748

Call Sign: KC7ZPG
Barry T Fraser
2403 S Mission Rd
Tucson AZ 85713

Call Sign: KC7ZPH
Judy A Fraser
2403 S Mission Rd
Tucson AZ 85713

Call Sign: KF7UAV
Richard L Vaughan
4555 S Mission Rd
Tucson AZ 85746

Call Sign: KC7ZPI
James S Griffith
8008 S Mission Rd
Tucson AZ 85746

Call Sign: KA7SLW
Loma K Griffith
8008 S Mission Rd
Tucson AZ 85746

Call Sign: KF7UAU
Gilbert Caffrey
S Mission Rd
Tucson AZ 85746

Call Sign: W0RQI
Everett F La Rue
4555 S Mission Rd 281
Tucson AZ 85746

Call Sign: W0DBO
Grant C Schafer
4555 S Mission Rd 294
Tucson AZ 85746

Call Sign: KE7ZPF
James F Bennett
4555 S Mission Rd 353
Tucson AZ 85746

Call Sign: KB7KPW
Betty N Blackstock

4555 S Mission Rd 38
Tucson AZ 857462314

Call Sign: KE7RPU
Angel J Martinez III
4555 S Mission Rd 438
Tucson AZ 85746

Call Sign: W7AJM
Angel J Martinez III
4555 S Mission Rd 438
Tucson AZ 85746

Call Sign: KF7ADP
Jamison A Martinez
4555 S Mission Rd 438
Tucson AZ 85746

Call Sign: N7SCL
Lucas P Hart Jr
4555 S Mission Rd 516
Tucson AZ 85714

Call Sign: KI6VN
Dennis G Rodd
4555 S Mission Rd 542
Tucson AZ 85746

Call Sign: KB7JMV
Daniel E Barnhardt
4555 S Mission Rd 661
Tucson AZ 85714

Call Sign: WA7ODG
Maurice S Warner
4555 S Mission Rd 739
Tucson AZ 857462301

Call Sign: KD0ZA
Robert A Young
4555 S Mission Rd 961
Tucson AZ 857462301

Call Sign: KK7WY
Robert A Young
4555 S Mission Rd 961
Tucson AZ 857462301

Call Sign: KC7FXG

June C Jacobson
4555 S Mission Rd Lot 582
Tucson AZ 85746

Call Sign: KF0GW
Dale F Nichols
4555 S Mission Rd Sp 319
Tucson AZ 85746

Call Sign: AB6PD
James D Heimbach
4555 S Mission Rd Sp 624 J
Tucson AZ 85746

Call Sign: N7ORE
Charles G Blackstock
4555 S Missoin Rd 38
Tucson AZ 857462314

Call Sign: KF7EZI
Joseph J Hirte
22 S Monitor Pl
Tucson AZ 85710

Call Sign: KO4RY
Eva M Dunlap
5616 S Monroe St
Tucson AZ 857462177

Call Sign: AC7EO
Eva M Dunlap
5616 S Monroe St
Tucson AZ 857462177

Call Sign: KB5LLW
Charles S Mccarty
5947 S Moon Desert Dr
Tucson AZ 85747

Call Sign: N5EWF
Jerry L Welch
1350 S Moonflower Ln
Tucson AZ 85748

Call Sign: N7TVQ
J C Ramsdell
4701 S Mountain Ave
Tucson AZ 85714

Call Sign: KD7SD
Eric C Gustafson
610 S Mountvale Dr
Tucson AZ 85710

Call Sign: KF7BUT
Eliyaho Senior
51 S Mustang Pl
Tucson AZ 85748

Call Sign: KF7CQX
Eliyaho Senior
51 S Mustang Pl
Tucson AZ 85748

Call Sign: KD7QIS
Christopher J Kemsley
8070 S New Abbey Dr
Tucson AZ 85747

Call Sign: KD6BTW
David H Kemsley
8070 S New Abbey Dr
Tucson AZ 85747

Call Sign: WB9TSU
Alan D Drexler
74 S Night Fall Ave
Tucson AZ 85748

Call Sign: N7FG
Francis E Wargocki
318 S Nightfall Ave
Tucson AZ 85748

Call Sign: KB7OBG
Clell D Perrin
10010 S Nogales Hwy 15
Tucson AZ 85706

Call Sign: W2DJD
Roger D Kring
11030 S Nogales Hwy Unit 3
Tucson AZ 857069301

Call Sign: W9BOE
Emil T De Boe
2102 S Norton Ave
Tucson AZ 857133015

Call Sign: KC7VXM
Andrew L Jarms
1820 S Oak Park Dr
Tucson AZ 85710

Call Sign: KI6DJE
Jerry W Wheat
36599 S Ocotillo Canyon Rd
Tucson AZ 857382287

Call Sign: KE7SGE
Anthony S Lintow
9945 S Old Nogales Hwy
Tucson AZ 85706

Call Sign: KC7TFB
James M Loughlin
3699 S Old Spanish Trl
Tucson AZ 85730

Call Sign: N7CL
Eric S Gustafson
6730 S Old Spanish Trl
Tucson AZ 85747

Call Sign: KA7ENY
Weldon H Irby
5411 S Oriole
Tucson AZ 85746

Call Sign: KC7ZZ
William G Adams
2109 S Palm Springs Dr
Tucson AZ 85710

Call Sign: WK7K
William G Adams
2109 S Palm Springs Dr
Tucson AZ 85710

Call Sign: KC7ZZ
William G Adams
2109 S Palm Springs Dr
Tucson AZ 85710

Call Sign: KA3UQK
Paul E Nitchman
1776 S Palo Verde 0 4

Tucson AZ 85713

Call Sign: K7ANU
Ralph G Roberts
2802 S Pantano Rd
Tucson AZ 857301198

Call Sign: KG6OOZ
Evelyn C Hager
1800 S Pantano Rd 3021
Tucson AZ 85710

Call Sign: N4CSF
Louis J Raymond
2121 S Pantano Rd 392
Tucson AZ 857106117

Call Sign: N0DYZ
Hugo P Marquart
2121 S Pantano Rd 836
Tucson AZ 85710

Call Sign: AA7CI
Arthur W Storm
2121 S Pantano Rd Sp 214
Tucson AZ 85710

Call Sign: KC7EDW
Julio A Makepeace
6001 S Park 32
Tucson AZ 85706

Call Sign: KE7RPX
Joseph A Yount
5255 S Park Ave 123
Tucson AZ 857062574

Call Sign: K7IT
Harvey W Lance
4405 S Perlita Rd
Tucson AZ 857305687

Call Sign: AC0AV
Luke R Haywas
8223 S Placita Bilbao
Tucson AZ 85747

Call Sign: WB2OJA
Leon Rubin

1660 S Placita Churella
Tucson AZ 857487714

Call Sign: KC7OVQ
James R Harriger
938 S Placita Conalea
Tucson AZ 85748

Call Sign: KC7ABO
James R Givens
3310 S Placita Costa Rica
Tucson AZ 85713

Call Sign: KA7HVV
James D Oakden
8208 S Placita Del Parque
Tucson AZ 85747

Call Sign: KD7VRI
Jennifer S Ashbeck
6961 S Placita Del Perone
Tucson AZ 85746

Call Sign: N0EMW
James B Fetzer
4681 S Placita Dos Pajaritos
Tucson AZ 85730

Call Sign: KF7ABL
Jammie E Tompkins
8193 S Placita Gijon
Tucson AZ 85747

Call Sign: KA9MUR
Richard T Lossau
7824 S Placita Senora Maria
Tucson AZ 85747

Call Sign: KA7TXH
Wilbur B Gavin
7520 S Placta De Pina
Tucson AZ 85747

Call Sign: KD7ISE
Patrick G Crandall
1938 S Plumer
Tucson AZ 85713

Call Sign: KE7BTB

Della M Crandall
1938 S Plumer Ave
Tucson AZ 85713

Call Sign: KA3JUX
Norris L Alford
3268 S Prism Sky Dr
Tucson AZ 857136835

Call Sign: N7QVJ
Les C Erdman
4040 S Pulpwood Pl
Tucson AZ 85730

Call Sign: KF7TKL
David R Maestas Jr
2358 S Quail Hollow Dr
Tucson AZ 85710

Call Sign: N7NBQ
Tim S Loomis
3120 S Quail Trl
Tucson AZ 85731

Call Sign: KF7VDS
William A Praust Sr
14240 S Renegade Ave
Tucson AZ 85736

Call Sign: K0YWF
Frederick S Pepek
37413 S Ridgeview Blvd
Tucson AZ 85739

Call Sign: K7QOK
Jose L Rivas
5560 S Robin Ave
Tucson AZ 85746

Call Sign: WB7TDA
Harold L Stott
36343 S Rock Crest Dr
Tucson AZ 85739

Call Sign: KF7UAX
Eric L Swanson
1040 S Rockcrest Ave
Tucson AZ 85748

Call Sign: KB7KSG
Mario T Sivilli
450 S Rosemont Ave
Tucson AZ 85711

Call Sign: KD7RSP
Leopoldo D Viromontez
502 S Rosemont Ave
Tucson AZ 85711

Call Sign: KD7CHW
Jack E Walton
911 S Roundtail Pl
Tucson AZ 85748

Call Sign: W9FCM
Francisco J Carlos
5333 S Royal Richmond Dr
Tucson AZ 85706

Call Sign: KE7ZGU
Larry W Housner
1432 S Salamander Pl
Tucson AZ 85713

Call Sign: KA7ZWE
Laurel R Peterson
1468 S Salamander Pl
Tucson AZ 85713

Call Sign: W5HOS
Robert C Henderlong
3551 S San Joaquin Rd Lot
50
Tucson AZ 85735

Call Sign: W7PKS
H Parks Squyres
38615 S Sand Crest Dr
Tucson AZ 85739

Call Sign: W0QIY
Harry D Hoffman
39075 S Sand Crest Dr
Tucson AZ 857391814

Call Sign: AB7JM
Ray G Saldana
4019 S Sandy Palm Dr

Tucson AZ 85730

Call Sign: KD7CTI
Thomas W Morin
3400 S Saquaro Shadows Dr
Tucson AZ 857305629

Call Sign: N7EJC
William J Dluehosh Jr
431 S Sarnoff Dr
Tucson AZ 85710

Call Sign: KB7SWN
James E Parrett Jr
917 S Sarnoff Dr
Tucson AZ 85710

Call Sign: N7XJH
Kenneth R Mc Caslin
940 S Sarnoff Dr
Tucson AZ 85710

Call Sign: KE7VTI
James R Herbin
3631 S Sarnoff Dr
Tucson AZ 85730

Call Sign: AD7XD
James R Herbin
3631 S Sarnoff Dr
Tucson AZ 85730

Call Sign: N7BXX
Gail E Peterson
3217 S Serena Cir
Tucson AZ 85730

Call Sign: KE7VJQ
Susan Peterson
3217 S Serena Cir
Tucson AZ 85730

Call Sign: K7SSP
Susan Peterson
3217 S Serena Cir
Tucson AZ 85730

Call Sign: KE7NGR
Sparc

3217 S Serena Cir
Tucson AZ 85730

Call Sign: KF7NR
Sparc
3217 S Serena Cir
Tucson AZ 85730

Call Sign: W6BPK
Francis E Adams
38958 S Serenity Ln
Tucson AZ 857392142

Call Sign: KB7RFH
Andrea S Mendola
1452 S Shannon
Tucson AZ 85713

Call Sign: WB7RZY
John M Mendola
1452 S Shannon
Tucson AZ 85713

Call Sign: N7BLC
Roy T Kawamoto
3201 S Sheila Ave
Tucson AZ 85735

Call Sign: WO7H
Robert A Jenkins
5361 S Sheridan Ave
Tucson AZ 85746

Call Sign: W1PHX
Robert A Jenkins
5361 S Sheridan Ave
Tucson AZ 85757

Call Sign: KC7WLO
Janelle C Wilt
3035 S Shiela Ave
Tucson AZ 85735

Call Sign: AF9W
Robert E Stephens
39841 S Shortcut Ave
Tucson AZ 85739

Call Sign: KE7VJY

Cheryl D Williams
11200 S Sierrita Mountain
285
Tucson AZ 85736

Call Sign: KE7VJZ
Walters J Williams
11200 S Sierrita Mountain
Rd 285
Tucson AZ 85736

Call Sign: AB7JO
Raymond E Lucas
11200 S Sierrita Mtn Rd
Tucson AZ 857361434

Call Sign: W7IHW
Joseph C Stoupa
1702 S Sleepy Hollow Ave
Tucson AZ 85710

Call Sign: AA7KD
Nicholas W Lalli
4031 S Snapdragon St
Tucson AZ 85730

Call Sign: N7ZQQ
Peter R Trowbridge
5885 S Sorrel Ln
Tucson AZ 85746

Call Sign: KB7TVM
Darren S Cummings
6030 S Sorrel Ln
Tucson AZ 85746

Call Sign: N7ITV
James T Mc Dorman
5826 S Southland Blvd
Tucson AZ 85706

Call Sign: N7WUH
James A Phillips Jr
5790 S Springbrook
Tucson AZ 85746

Call Sign: KC2FOK
Carson E Smith
1989 S St Michael Dr

Tucson AZ 85713

Call Sign: N7RMG
Carl R Sosna
6590 S Star Diamond Pl
Tucson AZ 85757

Call Sign: KE0TM
Harold C Bartels
38716 S Starwood Dr
Tucson AZ 85739

Call Sign: N7BZA
John E Bartels
38716 S Starwood Dr
Tucson AZ 85739

Call Sign: WB2PWB
Richard A Runyon
418 S Staunton Dr
Tucson AZ 85710

Call Sign: KD7CKZ
John Paul Kurimsky
441 S Staunton Dr
Tucson AZ 85710

Call Sign: KC7WLM
Lai T Kurimsky
441 S Staunton Dr
Tucson AZ 85710

Call Sign: KD7QK
Paul A Kurimsky
441 S Staunton Dr
Tucson AZ 85710

Call Sign: KB7IEP
Clide L Lanigan Sr
735 S Stone
Tucson AZ 85701

Call Sign: W7US
Willis G Allen
372 S Stoner Ave
Tucson AZ 85748

Call Sign: KC7POK
Betty L Alexander

425 S Stratford Dr
Tucson AZ 857165617

Call Sign: KE7PED
Jeffry D Scott
426 S Stratford Dr
Tucson AZ 85716

Call Sign: KF7UAT
Shawn L Hull
9211 S Summer Breeze Ln
Tucson AZ 85756

Call Sign: KC7IDP
Stephen G Powlesland
928 S Suncove Dr
Tucson AZ 857482118

Call Sign: KC5EOU
Charles B Halligan
1112 S Suncove Dr
Tucson AZ 85748

Call Sign: KA7HXR
Gary P Roberts
690 S Sunfield Canyan Dr
Tucson AZ 85748

Call Sign: WA7BOD
Ronald G Swann
5541 S Sunset Blvd
Tucson AZ 85746

Call Sign: KB7BSM
Sherry L Swann
5541 S Sunset Blvd
Tucson AZ 85746

Call Sign: KC7ZGN
Tucson Dx Club
5541 S Sunset Blvd
Tucson AZ 85746

Call Sign: KA7DAC
Sharon L Jensen
38305 S Sunset View Ln
Tucson AZ 857397041

Call Sign: KC7WV

Donald L Jensen
38305 S Sunset View Ln
Tucson AZ 857397041

Call Sign: N0GQA
Thomas E Nelson
4112 S Tarantula Hawk Pl
Tucson AZ 85735

Call Sign: KE6GXF
Kevin H Fitz Simmons
7944 S Teaberry Ave
Tucson AZ 857475152

Call Sign: AD7NE
Kevin H Fitz Simmons
7944 S Teaberry Ave
Tucson AZ 857475152

Call Sign: KF7H
Kevin H Fitz Simmons
7944 S Teaberry Ave
Tucson AZ 857475152

Call Sign: KE7IBE
Ralph F Sabelhaus
2040 S Tilting T Pl
Tucson AZ 85713

Call Sign: AD7JK
Ralph F Sabelhaus
2040 S Tilting T Pl
Tucson AZ 85713

Call Sign: KE7PMJ
Carol M Mauch
2022 S Tree Moss Ave
Tucson AZ 85710

Call Sign: WL7BTG
Teddy R Wintersteen
2121 S Triangle X Ln
Tucson AZ 85713

Call Sign: KD7ZRQ
Sabbar Shrine Radops
450 S Tuson Blvd
Tucson AZ 85716

Call Sign: K7OPX
Sabbar Shrine Radops
450 S Tuson Blvd
Tucson AZ 85716

Call Sign: KC7UDH
Christopher Thornhill
8561 S Van Burne
Tucson AZ 85706

Call Sign: KB7RBS
Brenda J Le Flohic
8161 S Vandemoer Ln
Tucson AZ 85706

Call Sign: KB7QWI
George Le Flohic
8161 S Vandemoer Ln
Tucson AZ 85706

Call Sign: KB7SVL
John L Le Flohic
8161 S Vandemoer Ln
Tucson AZ 85706

Call Sign: KB7JHH
Dianne D Larson
6961 S Vereda Sombria
Tucson AZ 85746

Call Sign: KB7JHJ
Tony R Larson
6961 S Vereda Sombria
Tucson AZ 85746

Call Sign: KE7VAE
Thomas E Taylor Jr
8294 S Via Del Palacio
Tucson AZ 85747

Call Sign: K7TET
Thomas E Taylor Jr
8294 S Via Del Palacio
Tucson AZ 85747

Call Sign: KA1YZJ
Marilyn K Ross
6525 S Via Diego De Rivera
Tucson AZ 85757

Call Sign: W1HJT
Robert S Ross
6525 S Via Diego De Rivera
Tucson AZ 85757

Call Sign: KC7HU
Robert G Tullis
6745 S Via Perico
Tucson AZ 85746

Call Sign: WB2OIZ
James E Woodward Jr
2421 S Walking H Pl
Tucson AZ 857136763

Call Sign: KG6QNS
Alexander L Vinson III
646 S Watering Hole Pl
Tucson AZ 85748

Call Sign: KE6VCT
Stephen P Cooper
5385 S Wembly Rd
Tucson AZ 857463933

Call Sign: WB2YZJ
George Kuchcik
3640 S White Gold Ave
Tucson AZ 85746

Call Sign: WA2YZN
Laurette Kuchcik
3640 S White Gold Ave
Tucson AZ 85746

Call Sign: KC7FNJ
Richard Reed
4331 S White Pine Ave
Tucson AZ 85730

Call Sign: KC7LCC
Gloria M Reed
4331 S White Pine Ave
Tucson AZ 85730

Call Sign: KF7EZK
Noel E Charles
4783 S Wild Rose Dr

Tucson AZ 85730

Call Sign: AI6F
Kent K Kasper
39393 S Winding Trl
Tucson AZ 85739

Call Sign: N7GH
Kent K Kasper
39393 S Winding Trl
Tucson AZ 85739

Call Sign: AI7Z
Kent K Kasper
39393 S Winding Trl
Tucson AZ 85739

Call Sign: W6ZN
Walter Henry Memorial
Group
39676 S Winding Trl Dr
Tucson AZ 85739

Call Sign: KC7UGM
T R Reynolds
2371 S Window Rock Pl
Tucson AZ 857106120

Call Sign: W1VOT
Bruce A Anderson
39127 S Windwood Dr
Tucson AZ 85739

Call Sign: N7ZQV
Charles W Sheffield
601 S Woodstock Dr
Tucson AZ 85710

Call Sign: KE7NGB
Russell J Werner
622 S Woodstock Dr
Tucson AZ 857106238

Call Sign: K7RJW
Russell J Werner
622 S Woodstock Dr
Tucson AZ 857106238

Call Sign: WA7ZXZ

Leonard Plotz
2210 S Zuni
Tucson AZ 85711

Call Sign: K6FI
Byron W Looney
7440 San Lorenzo Dr
Tucson AZ 85704

Call Sign: W7RJH
Ernest L Hoffman
6040 San Mateo
Tucson AZ 85715

Call Sign: KA7WFC
Billy B Smith
Sasabe Star Rt Box 97D
Tucson AZ 85736

Call Sign: WB7CWI
Anthony A Bartoszek
2312 Sausalito Trl
Tucson AZ 857374737

Call Sign: KA7MKO
Wayne H Culver
112 Sells Star Rt
Tucson AZ 85735

Call Sign: W7OG
Edward N Wise
6914 Sesame Ln
Tucson AZ 85704

Call Sign: K7VNO
Ralph L Wheaton
8751 Shenandoah Pl
Tucson AZ 85710

Call Sign: KA7YXZ
Vivian C Carter
8802 Shiloh Pl
Tucson AZ 85710

Call Sign: K7ZFC
William H Carter Sr
8802 Shiloh Pl
Tucson AZ 85710

Call Sign: K7DY
George H Darwin
6630 St Andrews Dr
Tucson AZ 85718

Call Sign: WA6SMF
Betty J Sackett
36626 Stoney Flower
Tucson AZ 85739

Call Sign: AI7N
William F Clarke
36791 Stoney Flower Dr
Tucson AZ 85739

Call Sign: KA9UWP
Caliste J Alster
5260 Strada De Rubino
Tucson AZ 857156042

Call Sign: W7IGU
Garth F Mason
10710 Stromboli
Tucson AZ 85704

Call Sign: KE7KRJ
Jeremy M Ramirez
6261 Struth Pl
Tucson AZ 85746

Call Sign: K7OS
Philip D Richardson
535 Suffolk Dr
Tucson AZ 85704

Call Sign: K7CAY
Catherine B Rodriguez
6890 Sunrise Dr 120
Tucson AZ 85750

Call Sign: KD7YHO
Catherine B Rodriguez
6890 Sunrise Dr 120
Tucson AZ 85750

Call Sign: KE7WIX
Debi T Mitchell
2240 Tanque Verde Cir
Tucson AZ 85749

Call Sign: KB7RVK
Maxwell Van Horne
8555 Tanque Verde Rd
Tucson AZ 857498917

Call Sign: KB7SNH
Alexander R Mason
6514 Tillman Cir
Tucson AZ 85708

Call Sign: AB7ZZ
Tetsuo Kai
2421 Tom Watson Dr
Tucson AZ 85741

Call Sign: N7FHS
Marsha S Cessor
5874 Tucson Est Pkwy
Tucson AZ 85713

Call Sign: WA7HEU
John Joachim
6060 Tucson Est Pkwy
Tucson AZ 85713

Call Sign: KA7BSU
Lee E Behner
5620 Vista Karina Mia
Tucson AZ 85704

Call Sign: KF7CNQ
Philip M Pierce
312 W 28th St
Tucson AZ 85713

Call Sign: KC7EDV
Mary D Castillo
1954 W 44th St
Tucson AZ 85713

Call Sign: KC7DVJ
Miramon P Castillo
1954 W 44th St
Tucson AZ 85713

Call Sign: N7FKW
Samuel L Petty
1831 W Ahmed

Tucson AZ 85704

Call Sign: N6MVA
Sander Herzfeld
2601 W Aiden St
Tucson AZ 85745

Call Sign: KF7IGT
Nicholas B Speaks
2613 W Aiden St
Tucson AZ 85745

Call Sign: K4GAX
Frank H Wakefield
1606 W Ajo Way
Tucson AZ 85713

Call Sign: N7SCO
Jean M Wakefield
1606 W Ajo Way
Tucson AZ 857136606

Call Sign: N5UVU
Emmett R Zeigel
1302 W Ajo Way 201
Tucson AZ 85713

Call Sign: W7IEX
Frank E Gibes
1402 W Ajo Way 307
Tucson AZ 85713

Call Sign: KC7JHW
Joe C Warnock
1655 W Ajo Way 363
Tucson AZ 85713

Call Sign: W7MCS
Bruno F Grossi Sr
1302 W Ajo Way Sp 74
Tucson AZ 85713

Call Sign: KF6LYX
Diann L Vis
1302 W Ajo Way Unit 191
Tucson AZ 857135719

Call Sign: KA7OMD
James M Muzrall

3015 W Alaska St
Tucson AZ 85746

Call Sign: WB7TVG
Casimer L Swieczkowski
2018 W Amy Dr
Tucson AZ 85705

Call Sign: N7NWT
Ralph Hamilton
W Anklam
Tucson AZ 85745

Call Sign: KD7LNM
James C Robicheaux
837 W Annandale
Tucson AZ 85737

Call Sign: WR0BX
James C Robicheaux
837 W Annandale
Tucson AZ 85737

Call Sign: N7FIC
Albert W Jackson
10909 W Anthony Dr
Tucson AZ 85743

Call Sign: KA7YGB
Janet W Jackson
10909 W Anthony Dr
Tucson AZ 85743

Call Sign: K7FCC
John C Henderson
11205 W Anthony Dr
Tucson AZ 85743

Call Sign: KF7WG
Dennis M Robbins
590 W Atua
Tucson AZ 85737

Call Sign: KG6CTK
Lynn S Dana Davis
16062 W Aubrey Ave
Tucson AZ 85736

Call Sign: KA4QXM

Robert L Brown
2972 W Ave Cresta
Tucson AZ 85745

Call Sign: N7ZQY
Manuel A Campbell
3284 W Avenida Cancion
Tucson AZ 85746

Call Sign: KC7DVO
Steven E Ahrens
4115 W Azalea St
Tucson AZ 85741

Call Sign: KF7RJY
Robert E Elliott II
3885 W Bar Ranch Dr
Tucson AZ 85745

Call Sign: W5TXE
David S Foss
5430 W Bar S St
Tucson AZ 85713

Call Sign: NQ7Z
Charles V Goodrich
5432 W Bar X
Tucson AZ 85713

Call Sign: KC7AQ
Doris K Rieke
5516 W Bar X
Tucson AZ 857136405

Call Sign: WB7FCF
Arthur B Disney Jr
4455 W Barque Dr
Tucson AZ 85741

Call Sign: N7BHN
Bryant C Mothershed
3060 W Bartlett Pl
Tucson AZ 85741

Call Sign: KZ7C
Bryant C Mothershed
3060 W Bartlett Pl
Tucson AZ 85741

Call Sign: KA7UFR
J T Mothershed
3060 W Bartlett Pl
Tucson AZ 85741

Call Sign: KE7EQD
Lee C Mothershed
3060 W Bartlett Pl
Tucson AZ 85741

Call Sign: KF7RSQ
Michelle L Mothershed
3060 W Bartlett Pl
Tucson AZ 85741

Call Sign: KF7DDE
Rachel L Mothershed
3060 W Bartlett Pl
Tucson AZ 85741

Call Sign: KD7WXT
John M Mothershed
3060 W Bartlett Pl
Tucson AZ 85741

Call Sign: AD7KT
James W Cooper
3214 W Bartlett Pl
Tucson AZ 85741

Call Sign: W4VYD
Nunzio P Addabbo
1508 W Bathurst Dr
Tucson AZ 85746

Call Sign: KC7GPG
Scott D Rowin
3812 W Bayleaf Dr
Tucson AZ 85741

Call Sign: W6IHN
Bruce M Newlan
1510 W Beech Way
Tucson AZ 85737

Call Sign: N5FNB
Ronnie C Smith
3650 W Bellewood Pl
Tucson AZ 857415406

Call Sign: AA3OF
Diane D Zimmerman
5287 W Belmont Rd
Tucson AZ 85743

Call Sign: KB3IWD
Robert Zimmerman
5287 W Belmont Rd
Tucson AZ 85743

Call Sign: KF7BRS
Steven W Shipley
6416 W Belmont Rd
Tucson AZ 85743

Call Sign: KC7OYP
Steve J Waldrip
12311 W Bernice Ln
Tucson AZ 85743

Call Sign: KD7UUN
Michael W Hodges
7449 W Beverly Dr
Tucson AZ 85710

Call Sign: W7NLU
Leo J Mallas
4152 W Bilby Rd
Tucson AZ 85746

Call Sign: N7ONS
Harold H Halgrimson
2821 W Bird Ave
Tucson AZ 85746

Call Sign: KC7WTX
Norma A Miller
6201 W Black Hawk Pl
Tucson AZ 85713

Call Sign: KK6BM
Ronald R Miller
6201 W Black Hawk Pl
Tucson AZ 85713

Call Sign: KA9MSK
Earl E Leibforth

8099 W Blowing
Tumbleweed Pl
Tucson AZ 85743

Call Sign: KC7EYU
Byron A Taradena
5087 W Bluejay St
Tucson AZ 85742

Call Sign: WB7C
Anthony M Vernon
5106 W Bluejay St
Tucson AZ 857429480

Call Sign: N3KYL
Sandra D Lueken
5174 W Bluejay St
Tucson AZ 85742

Call Sign: KB7AL
Otto T Gal
7797 W Bodie Rd
Tucson AZ 85743

Call Sign: AA7K
Charles R Camp
8950 W Bopp Rd
Tucson AZ 857359781

Call Sign: KC7MMC
Virgil L Galaway
8961 W Bopp Rd
Tucson AZ 85735

Call Sign: KB7VJX
Gerald F Miller
8965 W Bopp Rd
Tucson AZ 85746

Call Sign: WE7O
Lian I Nasution
9021 W Bopp Rd
Tucson AZ 857358726

Call Sign: KD7QON
Samuel B Thornton III
2431 W Bovino Way
Tucson AZ 85741

Call Sign: KF7UNV
Denise A Pharris
915 W Brave River Pl
Tucson AZ 85704

Call Sign: KC7DPN
Christine E Harms
2601 W Broadway 285
Tucson AZ 85745

Call Sign: KD0AKK
Nicholas W Dawson
2800 W Broadway Blvd Apt
216
Tucson AZ 85745

Call Sign: KD6KBO
Ruthann C Johnson
3003 W Broadway Blvd Sp
114
Tucson AZ 85745

Call Sign: KE7QIJ
Justin Wright
5682 W Cactus Garden Dr
Tucson AZ 85742

Call Sign: KA7KAL
John C Allen
811 W Calle Antonia
Tucson AZ 85706

Call Sign: KB7RJY
James C Fortenberry
911 W Calle Casquilla
Tucson AZ 85704

Call Sign: WB7NXB
Alfred J Sciuto
905 W Calle Catavinos
Tucson AZ 85704

Call Sign: KC7FXN
Jessie D Wright
3211 W Calle Cereza
Tucson AZ 85741

Call Sign: KC7LJK
Daniel A Lansberry

3330 W Calle Cereza
Tucson AZ 85741

Call Sign: K7KZB
Jack A Buchanan
1631 W Calle Concordia
Tucson AZ 85737

Call Sign: KD7ISD
Scott Parson
921 W Calle Dadivoso
Tucson AZ 85704

Call Sign: KC7SIO
Norman B Tarr
3231 W Calle De La Bajada
Tucson AZ 85746

Call Sign: N7OYF
John Schmelzkopf
2752 W Calle Del Huerto
Tucson AZ 85741

Call Sign: KV7F
John Schmelzkopf
2752 W Calle Del Huerto
Tucson AZ 85741

Call Sign: KC7CC
Thomas L Scott
2886 W Calle Del Huerto
Tucson AZ 85741

Call Sign: KC7DWB
Thomas V Dempewolf
2886 W Calle Del Huerto
Tucson AZ 85741

Call Sign: KD7LFZ
Terry L Brown
2003 W Calle Del Reposo
Tucson AZ 85745

Call Sign: KA8GVS
Stephan W Shemenski
2151 W Calle Fortunado
Tucson AZ 85705

Call Sign: AK8E

Stephan W Shemenski
2151 W Calle Fortunado
Tucson AZ 85705

Call Sign: KB9KL
Clyde C Lanphear
3201 W Calle Fresa
Tucson AZ 85741

Call Sign: KE7KSE
John-Mark Linnaus
1675 W Calle Guadala Jara
Tucson AZ 85713

Call Sign: N7FBX
Adolph C Ekvall
1401 W Calle Kino
Tucson AZ 85704

Call Sign: W7JGZ
Edward J Marston
1501 W Calle Kino
Tucson AZ 85704

Call Sign: WB6DAS
Michael K Brinks
3050 W Calle Lucinda
Tucson AZ 85741

Call Sign: KD7HVF
Danny Tavarez
131 W Calle Nueva Vida
Tucson AZ 85706

Call Sign: KN7F
John W Hennessy
2025 W Calle Pacifica
Tucson AZ 85745

Call Sign: KC6VXD
James M Chapman
2516 W Calle Padilla
Tucson AZ 85745

Call Sign: W7HSG
Ralph S Turk
5232 W Calle Paint
Tucson AZ 85741

Call Sign: KE7VTN
Susan G Merila
2650 W Calle Puebla
Tucson AZ 85745

Call Sign: WB0AGY
Pedro J Martinez Pedroza
3131 W Camino Alto
Tucson AZ 85741

Call Sign: W2GGL
Lowell E Norton
1930 W Camino Bajio
Tucson AZ 85737

Call Sign: KA8LGQ
Fred R Rentzel Jr
4800 W Camino De La
Amapola
Tucson AZ 85745

Call Sign: NN1B
Christopher L Abbott
2600 W Camino De La Joya
Tucson AZ 85742

Call Sign: KC7INN
Owen D Sullivan
470 W Camino De La Reina
Tucson AZ 85747

Call Sign: KO6CG
Glenn N Fisher
2739 W Camino De Las
Grutas
Tucson AZ 85742

Call Sign: KE7IUK
Maddalena Fiorillo
5318 W Camino Del Desierto
Tucson AZ 85745

Call Sign: KE7IUJ
Michael Addis
5318 W Camino Del Desierto
Tucson AZ 85745

Call Sign: W2HDT
Michael Addis

5318 W Camino Del Desierto
Tucson AZ 85745

Call Sign: KB7IS
John C Trickey
643 W Camino Del Oro
Tucson AZ 85704

Call Sign: N7BLJ
Jan C Rasmussen
2550 W Camino Del Venegas
Tucson AZ 85742

Call Sign: KB7IUB
Richard Sebastian
812 W Camino Desierto
Tucson AZ 85704

Call Sign: KB7SGK
Jon R Heintz
2801 W Camino Ebano
Tucson AZ 85742

Call Sign: W7RDH
Jon R Heintz
2801 W Camino Ebano
Tucson AZ 85742

Call Sign: KC6QIE
Raymond R Faller
2561 W Camino Llano
Tucson AZ 85742

Call Sign: KD7AQR
Randy M Schuler
2620 W Camino Llano
Tucson AZ 85742

Call Sign: KD7LNK
Tobin C Bennett Gold
4456 W Camino Nuestro
Tucson AZ 85745

Call Sign: N7DZ
William E Bennett
4456 W Camino Nuestro
Tucson AZ 857459391

Call Sign: NW6N

Robert S Wendling
4860 W Candleberry Way
Tucson AZ 85742

Call Sign: WB7TGL
Troy D Goertz
2956 W Capistrano
Tucson AZ 85746

Call Sign: KD7GHV
James L Welborn
2984 W Capistrano
Tucson AZ 85746

Call Sign: W0DCG
Loring K Jensen
1496 W Carmel Pointe Dr
Tucson AZ 857377090

Call Sign: KB7VKE
Jeffrey S Horton
2817 W Carnauba
Tucson AZ 85705

Call Sign: KE7OSR
Brian D Rasmussen
5523 W Carriage Dr
Tucson AZ 85742

Call Sign: W7ITU
John W Worman
2621 W Casas Cir
Tucson AZ 85742

Call Sign: W8LGV
Donald V Urbytes
2297 W Catalina View Dr
Tucson AZ 857424481

Call Sign: KE7EGR
Kevin B Jones
2761 W Cattail Pl
Tucson AZ 857451361

Call Sign: WJ1F
Edward J Sander Jr
6617 W Cedar Branch Way
Tucson AZ 85757

Call Sign: KF7SRC
Milton W Brown
2633 W Cezanne Cir
Tucson AZ 85741

Call Sign: KK1J
Jay S Salo
2635 W Cezanne Cir
Tucson AZ 85741

Call Sign: WD5BYZ
Albert A Rosen
1435 W Chapala Dr
Tucson AZ 857042036

Call Sign: N0SLC
Mark E Lindquist
1479 W Chapala Dr
Tucson AZ 85704

Call Sign: KE7KSD
Daniel Carrillo
1769 W Chardonnay
Tucson AZ 85746

Call Sign: KD7EIQ
Alexander E Unger
1620 W Chimayo Pl
Tucson AZ 85704

Call Sign: KF7SEC
Virginia E Unger
1620 W Chimayo Pl
Tucson AZ 85704

Call Sign: W7DVE
Virginia E Unger
1620 W Chimayo Pl
Tucson AZ 85704

Call Sign: W7GVB
Albert P Gibes
5372 W Circle Z St
Tucson AZ 85713

Call Sign: KC7CQY
David E Brown
5461 W Circle Z St
Tucson AZ 857134412

Call Sign: KD7ACE
Richard A Foland
5583 W Circle Z St
Tucson AZ 85713

Call Sign: KD7RCC
Jeffery A Reuter
3406 W Clarisse
Tucson AZ 85741

Call Sign: N7MXL
Kay A Manley
3424 W Clarisse
Tucson AZ 85741

Call Sign: N7CRR
Lyle S Manley
3424 W Clarisse
Tucson AZ 85741

Call Sign: AE7KR
Richard D Reavis
2811 W Clearview Dr
Tucson AZ 85745

Call Sign: KB4PRJ
Dale C Cohen
450 W Coal Dr 138
Tucson AZ 85704

Call Sign: N7WEU
Nicholas Silberschlag
1151 W Coblewood Way
Tucson AZ 85737

Call Sign: KB1UBI
Robert J Blazewicz
1190 W Coblewood Way
Tucson AZ 857376942

Call Sign: K7UMK
David B Lawrence
7531 W Colony Park Dr
Tucson AZ 85743

Call Sign: K7OXX
Thomas P Mc Williams
726 W Comobabi Dr

Tucson AZ 85704

Call Sign: K7OXW
Sadie M Mc Williams
726 W Comobabi Dr
Tucson AZ 857043202

Call Sign: KE7OSX
Richard K Purdy
4801 W Condor Dr
Tucson AZ 85742

Call Sign: KE7RHW
Adam T Wardell
4811 W Condor Dr
Tucson AZ 85742

Call Sign: KE7GP
Jon C Huish
4850 W Condor Dr
Tucson AZ 85742

Call Sign: KA0GKT
Stephen D Claasen
4987 W Condor Dr
Tucson AZ 85742

Call Sign: KD7CQX
Geoffrey T Cheshire
407 W Congress 501
Tucson AZ 85701

Call Sign: KD7KOZ
Carey A Bunker III
405 W Congress Ste 2300
Tucson AZ 85701

Call Sign: K7PQI
William W Chapman Jr
645 W Cool Dr
Tucson AZ 85704

Call Sign: KB7PUN
Jay F Huff
450 W Cool Dr Apt 249
Tucson AZ 85741

Call Sign: KB9EG
Ronald K Stephens

7588 W Copper Crest Pl
Tucson AZ 85743

Call Sign: W0LHV
Kenneth J Benner
7669 W Copper Crest Pl
Tucson AZ 857435302

Call Sign: KE7RIC
Donald K Shiflet
5638 W Copperhead Dr
Tucson AZ 85742

Call Sign: N7SQH
Tim J De Vinney
3181 W Coriander
Tucson AZ 85741

Call Sign: KC7QWA
Marion R Baptie
2900 W Coriander Dr
Tucson AZ 85741

Call Sign: KB7LMG
Janet L Nicks
3031 W Coriander Dr
Tucson AZ 85741

Call Sign: KF7AON
Rudy L Milchak
3042 W Coriander Dr
Tucson AZ 85741

Call Sign: KF7PSX
William J Scott
3402 W Cortaro Farms Rd
Tucson AZ 85742

Call Sign: KF7EMG
Matthew A Mader
3205 W Cortaro Farms Rd 83
Tucson AZ 85742

Call Sign: KF5MPU
James R Crocker
7991 W Cottonwood Wash
Way
Tucson AZ 85743

Call Sign: KD7JEF
Addison A Lake
8055 W Cottonwood Wash
Way
Tucson AZ 85743

Call Sign: KC7LSF
Gary G Switzer
2942 W Cranbrook St
Tucson AZ 85746

Call Sign: N6IOF
John P Thorne
4202 W Crestview Rd
Tucson AZ 857459033

Call Sign: WB7UMA
Mike D Lawrence
7552 W Crimson Sky Dr
Tucson AZ 857431484

Call Sign: KC7ZEZ
Thomas A Wotring
1230 W Crystal Palace Pl
Tucson AZ 85737

Call Sign: N7DZN
James L Steele
2942 W Curtis Rd
Tucson AZ 85705

Call Sign: N7KAW
Justin R Schwarze
2530 W Curtis Rd 2
Tucson AZ 85705

Call Sign: KD7OGU
Allen R Keil
1520 W Cypress St
Tucson AZ 85704

Call Sign: AD7DT
Allen R Keil
1520 W Cypress St
Tucson AZ 85704

Call Sign: KE7OLO
Daniel E Aguayo
3020 W Dakota St

Tucson AZ 85746

Call Sign: WQ7I
John P Kuvik
1300 W Dawn Dr
Tucson AZ 85704

Call Sign: KD7CSH
Eugene A Anderson
1828 W Dawn Dr
Tucson AZ 85704

Call Sign: KB7YYZ
Kevin A George
1892 W Dawn Dr
Tucson AZ 85704

Call Sign: KC7OVF
Michael G Morris
1640 W Deacon Dr
Tucson AZ 85746

Call Sign: KC4KOH
Kerry K Reynolds
238 W Delano
Tucson AZ 85705

Call Sign: N7HOR
C Tom Long
9055 W Delfina Dr
Tucson AZ 85735

Call Sign: KA7WLG
Margaret M Long
9055 W Delfina Dr
Tucson AZ 85735

Call Sign: N7OEM
Tucson ARA
9055 W Delfina Dr
Tucson AZ 857359386

Call Sign: KG6JVN
Debra D Celek
2640 W Derest Brook Ct
Tucson AZ 85742

Call Sign: KE7BTG
Austin D Stucky

3390 W Desert Bend Loop
Tucson AZ 85742

Call Sign: AB7Q
David D Stucky III
3390 W Desert Bend Loop
Tucson AZ 85742

Call Sign: WD7O
Stephen V Archibald
3078 W Desert Bird Ct
Tucson AZ 85745

Call Sign: KA6TDO
Bernard J Celek II
2640 W Desert Brook Ct
Tucson AZ 85742

Call Sign: KE1BF
Peter J Crook
2655 W Desert Brook Ct
Tucson AZ 85742

Call Sign: KD3FN
Hiram Lopez
2945 W Desert Glory Drv
Tucson AZ 85745

Call Sign: W1NRJ
William B Hindle
7730 W Desert Spirits Dr
Tucson AZ 85743

Call Sign: W7EA
William B Hindle
7730 W Desert Spirits Dr
Tucson AZ 85743

Call Sign: W7MBZ
William B Dorris Jr
5651 W Diamond K
Tucson AZ 85713

Call Sign: W7JIC
Orval V Nemitz
5401 W Diamond K St
Tucson AZ 85713

Call Sign: KB7BEA

Donald W Travis
2762 W Diamond St
Tucson AZ 85705

Call Sign: K7DWT
Donald W Travis
2762 W Diamond St
Tucson AZ 85705

Call Sign: KE7VKK
John K Comaduran
7213 W Dimming Star Dr
Tucson AZ 85743

Call Sign: WB7NVB
Richard A Champlin
2580 W Dolbrook Way
Tucson AZ 85741

Call Sign: KE7SHQ
Andres Virgen Rivera
1913 W Donny Brook Rd
Tucson AZ 85713

Call Sign: KE7AVY
Elida Godinez
6700 W Drexel Rd
Tucson AZ 85746

Call Sign: KE7AVX
Rogelio R Godinez
6700 W Drexel Rd
Tucson AZ 85746

Call Sign: WB7PZY
David M Harding
6825 W Drexel Rd
Tucson AZ 85757

Call Sign: KE7OON
Sw Tucson Cw ARC
9020 W Dudley
Tucson AZ 85733

Call Sign: N7VGI
Joan K Hall
9020 W Dudley
Tucson AZ 85735

Call Sign: WB7SKJ
Daniel J Hochuli
1071 W Eagle Landing Pl
Tucson AZ 85737

Call Sign: KE7QIK
Michael O Daley
5300 W Eaglestone Loop
Tucson AZ 85742

Call Sign: KF7CNP
Wesley S Shepherd
752 W Edgewater
Tucson AZ 85705

Call Sign: KD7VUF
Douglas A Mentzer
4870 W El Camino Del Cerro
Tucson AZ 85745

Call Sign: AA7DU
Lloyd J Perper
6700 W El Camino Del Cerro
Tucson AZ 85745

Call Sign: KE7QIN
Dustin D Lauth-Clements
7351 W El Camino Del Cerro
Tucson AZ 85705

Call Sign: KF7SAN
Kent M Margason
6440 W Elks Falls Way
Tucson AZ 85757

Call Sign: KC7MVX
Lisa A Dill
4410 W Elvado
Tucson AZ 85746

Call Sign: KF7SQY
Harold L Carey
5041 W Elvado Rd
Tucson AZ 85757

Call Sign: W4GC
Robert J Schwartz
6541 W Emjay Ave
Tucson AZ 857359284

Call Sign: KC7ZEX
Dena K L Heureux
2551 W Falbrook Way
Tucson AZ 85741

Call Sign: KB7YPP
Kevin W Kinkade
3524 W Falling Star Ln
Tucson AZ 85741

Call Sign: KC7LVO
Benjamin C Sautter
4261 W Firethorn St
Tucson AZ 85741

Call Sign: K9KED
Robert G Syphers Sr
643 W Florence St
Tucson AZ 857054224

Call Sign: KU4SH
Robert G Hall
255 W Flores 10
Tucson AZ 85705

Call Sign: W7VAX
Chester A Brown Sr
9165 W Floyd St
Tucson AZ 85746

Call Sign: KB7LPC
Lewis P Fetzer Jr
5561 W Flying Cir
Tucson AZ 85713

Call Sign: KE6KKL
Dennis A Lepak
4247 W Flying Diamond Dr
Tucson AZ 85742

Call Sign: KE6UTV
Paula M Lepak
4247 W Flying Diamond Dr
Tucson AZ 85742

Call Sign: KC7NPV
Kenneth L Reed
4700 W Flying Diamond Dr

Tucson AZ 85742

Call Sign: K7KLR
Kenneth L Reed
4700 W Flying Diamond Dr
Tucson AZ 85742

Call Sign: KW6RO
Stanley J Dusza
6069 W Flying M St
Tucson AZ 85713

Call Sign: WB7VVK
Eugene A Wright
6961 W Flying W
Tucson AZ 85746

Call Sign: N7AEU
Donald L Brumbaugh
3572 W Foxes Neadow Dr
Tucson AZ 85745

Call Sign: N7QHV
James G Walsh
143 W Franklin St
Tucson AZ 85701

Call Sign: KC7VVG
Aaron E Gillihan
2264 W Frostwood Ln
Tucson AZ 85745

Call Sign: KC7VVH
Jennifer B Gillihan
2264 W Frostwwod Ln
Tucson AZ 85745

Call Sign: N7DZS
Charles B Hellyer
2070 W Ft Lowell Rd
Tucson AZ 85705

Call Sign: KC2AGN
James M Titone
4035 W Gentle Pl
Tucson AZ 85741

Call Sign: N7SFS
Frank E Yourison

5700 W Gerhart Rd
Tucson AZ 85745

Call Sign: KB7YGL
Margaret P Forgach
5750 W Gerhart Rd
Tucson AZ 85745

Call Sign: KI6QE
David J Medley
731 W Giaconda Way
Tucson AZ 85704

Call Sign: KD7HVH
Christin E Grace
3040 W Glenn Pt Ln
Tucson AZ 85745

Call Sign: KC7TQC
Justin W Johnson
1064 W Goldbar
Tucson AZ 85737

Call Sign: KD6VQX
Carol A Benedict
4139 W Golder Star Pl
Tucson AZ 85745

Call Sign: WA6GJO
Nathan D Benedict Jr
4139 W Golder Star Pl
Tucson AZ 85745

Call Sign: KC7INL
Cynthia D Garcia
1651 W Grant
Tucson AZ 85705

Call Sign: KC7GNR
Ruben R Garcia
1850 W Grant 110
Tucson AZ 85745

Call Sign: W7WOY
Ronald H Miles
2114 W Grant Rd Pmb 44
Tucson AZ 85745

Call Sign: AA5TM

Ernest A Beason
1716 W Great Oak Dr
Tucson AZ 85746

Call Sign: KB7YWK
Vickie M Johnson
1715 W Green Leaf Dr
Tucson AZ 85746

Call Sign: KB9EY
N Alan Lojka
3051 W Green Ridge Dr
Tucson AZ 85741

Call Sign: WA6EAH
Marlin E Hayes
3468 W Green Ridge Dr
Tucson AZ 85741

Call Sign: KB7KZ
Allen J Pawlowski
3418 W Green Trees Dr
Tucson AZ 85741

Call Sign: WA7BUQ
William F Barker
1507 W Greenlee St
Tucson AZ 85705

Call Sign: KF7HYG
Paul M Bruner
8045 W Greensleeves Way
Tucson AZ 85743

Call Sign: N3AID
Kevin D Vinson
5231 W Grouse Way
Tucson AZ 85721

Call Sign: KA7LFX
Paul E Van Beverhoudt
5231 W Grouse Way
Tucson AZ 857429492

Call Sign: KB9SV
Terry E Hathaway
7780 W Gypsum St
Tucson AZ 85735

Call Sign: KD7RCA
Thomas W Mccormick
1016 W Hadley St
Tucson AZ 85705

Call Sign: KD7WXS
John B Bradfield
1955 W Hadley St
Tucson AZ 85705

Call Sign: KA2EYP
Kevin S Bonnot
6959 W Harcuvar Dr
Tucson AZ 85743

Call Sign: AE7CI
David A Paul
7024 W Harcuvar Dr
Tucson AZ 85743

Call Sign: KF7SED
Kerry A Paul
7024 W Harcuvar Dr
Tucson AZ 85743

Call Sign: W7KRY
Kerry A Paul
7024 W Harcuvar Dr
Tucson AZ 85743

Call Sign: KF4FDY
Sandra L Bickmore
4824 W Hardy Rd
Tucson AZ 86742

Call Sign: KA7BRL
Elizabeth M Layton
733 W Hatfield
Tucson AZ 85706

Call Sign: W7LHN
Kenneth R Morgan
733 W Hatfield St
Tucson AZ 85706

Call Sign: KG6GTJ
Roy S Cho
934 W Hawaii Dr
Tucson AZ 85706

Call Sign: KA7STZ
Charles D Schroer
2403 W Helton Ln
Tucson AZ 85713

Call Sign: KE7RHX
Jay S Hoobler
5293 W Hematite Pl
Tucson AZ 85742

Call Sign: KE7RHY
Zach T Hoobler
5293 W Hematite Pl
Tucson AZ 85742

Call Sign: KF7RKA
Lawrence J Keri
3040 W Hermans Rd Unit B
Tucson AZ 85746

Call Sign: KG7VH
Mark D Lockwood
4330 W Holladay St
Tucson AZ 85746

Call Sign: WA4SIJ
Kenneth E Teague
1305 W Hopbush Way
Tucson AZ 85704

Call Sign: K7VET
Ronald L Short
3651 W Horizon Hills Dr
Tucson AZ 85741

Call Sign: KE7OSS
Daniel M Laprevote
5001 W Hurston Dr
Tucson AZ 85742

Call Sign: KF7FIV
Michael Felong Jr
7690 W Illinois St
Tucson AZ 85735

Call Sign: KE7VJW
James C Christian
1932 W Imuris Pl

Tucson AZ 85704

Call Sign: KC7YSO
Jeffrey W Glenn
10950 W Ina
Tucson AZ 85743

Call Sign: KA7ZWG
Joseph Kissel
202 W Ina Rd
Tucson AZ 857046248

Call Sign: N7WET
Melvin A Witte Jr
11459 W Ina Rd
Tucson AZ 857439559

Call Sign: KA6AOK
Ocie Rowe
W Ina Rd
Tucson AZ 85743

Call Sign: KA6AOL
Shirley I Rowe
W Ina Rd
Tucson AZ 85743

Call Sign: KE7VPJ
Megan S Gardner
2600 W Ina Rd Apt 127
Tucson AZ 85741

Call Sign: KE7VPI
Timothy S Gardner
2600 W Ina Rd Apt 127
Tucson AZ 85741

Call Sign: KC4IJH
Michael B Birdwell
2600 W Ina Rd Apt 182
Tucson AZ 85741

Call Sign: KE7IVZ
Phil A Pier
7698 W Innutian Ct
Tucson AZ 85743

Call Sign: KB7NTG
Michael D Zimmerman

2624 W Ironcrest Dr
Tucson AZ 85745

Call Sign: W7DLA
Low Band Dx Club
4325 W Ironwood Hill Dr
Tucson AZ 85745

Call Sign: W7DD
Donald L Andersen
4325 W Ironwood Hill Dr
Tucson AZ 85745

Call Sign: K7RQI
Vera C Marshall
4325 W Ironwood Hill Dr
Tucson AZ 85745

Call Sign: AJ7A
Breakfast Club
4325 W Ironwood Hill Dr
Tucson AZ 85745

Call Sign: K1AC
Low Band Dx Club
4325 W Ironwood Hill Dr
Tucson AZ 85745

Call Sign: W6AA
Western Single Side Band
Assn Inc
4325 W Ironwood Hill Dr
Tucson AZ 85745

Call Sign: KE7LIA
Lev A Vsevolozhskiy
2786 W Ironwood Ridge Dr
Tucson AZ 85745

Call Sign: KD7LVK
Charles M Colahan
2001 W Irvington Pl
Tucson AZ 85746

Call Sign: WB7OBF
Silvio Passeggio
2415 W Irvington Pl
Tucson AZ 85714

Call Sign: KA7IZC
Janet I Passeggio
2415 W Irvington Pl
Tucson AZ 85746

Call Sign: W9SEK
Ronald M Vaceluke
4020 W Isis Dr
Tucson AZ 857411921

Call Sign: W7AMH
Harold R Mills
630 W Jacinto
Tucson AZ 85705

Call Sign: N7KU
Rillito River Contest Club
4860 W Jacob Rd
Tucson AZ 85745

Call Sign: NJ6D
Chuck F Claver
4860 W Jacob Rd
Tucson AZ 85745

Call Sign: KC7RCR
Leonard E Eislage
1957 W Jay Pl
Tucson AZ 85705

Call Sign: W6SCC
Guy B Coleman
4955 W Jojoba Dr
Tucson AZ 85745

Call Sign: WA6MTT
Tracy L Schulberg
4955 W Jojoba Dr
Tucson AZ 85745

Call Sign: N7UKT
Hank G Langlinais
4142 W Jupiter St
Tucson AZ 85741

Call Sign: KC7FMY
Randy D Ryan
1031 W Kelting Dr
Tucson AZ 85704

Call Sign: N7IXV
David L Bunch Jr
1512 W Kennington Ave
Tucson AZ 85746

Call Sign: WB7RQR
Anna May Brendel
1976 W Khaibar Pl
Tucson AZ 85704

Call Sign: ND7G
Roger A Wilson
1503 W Kilburn St
Tucson AZ 857059233

Call Sign: KC7WBA
Diane M Mc Donald
1351 W Kimberly St 192
Tucson AZ 85704

Call Sign: KF4NDQ
Edward S Sykes
5043 W Kingbird St
Tucson AZ 85742

Call Sign: KA5RSC
James D Reed
1600 W Kitty Hawk Way
Tucson AZ 85737

Call Sign: N7ZQM
Josephine B Sierra
11475 W Kushmaul Rd
Tucson AZ 85735

Call Sign: KD7HZS
Ronald L Short
2242 W Labriego Dr
Tucson AZ 85741

Call Sign: N7LBY
Lawrence S Martin
12100 W Lak A Yucca Pl
Tucson AZ 85743

Call Sign: KC7NYT
David P Shafer
1530 W Lama Dr

Tucson AZ 85746

Call Sign: WA4PYZ
David R Campbell
16462 W Larkdale St
Tucson AZ 85736

Call Sign: KC7GNN
Charles W Pyeatt
750 W Las Lomitas
Tucson AZ 85704

Call Sign: KB7RFI
Charles W Michels
4707 W Lazy C Dr
Tucson AZ 85745

Call Sign: KE7CQF
William R Wilson
2590 W Lazybrook Dr
Tucson AZ 85741

Call Sign: K7MGY
William R Wilson
2590 W Lazybrook Dr
Tucson AZ 85741

Call Sign: KC7JTG
Geoffrey W Lampard
2625 W Lazybrook Dr
Tucson AZ 85341

Call Sign: KF7UAY
Michael F Steber
7150 W Leaf Bed Ln
Tucson AZ 85743

Call Sign: KB7IZC
Paul L P Avellar
2710 W Leawood Dr
Tucson AZ 85745

Call Sign: KB7IZD
Rebecca J P Avellar
2710 W Leawood Dr
Tucson AZ 85745

Call Sign: KC7WTJ
Greg W Murray

3176 W Liberty Tree Ln
Tucson AZ 85741

Call Sign: KC7ZSZ
Lynn A Murray
3176 W Liberty Tree Ln
Tucson AZ 85741

Call Sign: N7UDO
Clinton B Majors
6642 W Lightning L
Tucson AZ 85746

Call Sign: KE7OLI
Vaughan J Thompson
620 W Limberlost 26
Tucson AZ 857051658

Call Sign: N7DZO
Albert W Mc Grew
801 W Limberlost Dr 38
Tucson AZ 85705

Call Sign: KF7NC
Sherman W Mc Daniel
3806 W Limequat Pl
Tucson AZ 85741

Call Sign: KD7WNG
Robert H Pulver
5550 W Linda Vista Blvd
Tucson AZ 85742

Call Sign: KB7UIX
James S Redding
3980 W Linda Vista Blvd
Apt 1201
Tucson AZ 85742

Call Sign: WB3BFO
June S Simpson
3980 W Linda Vista Blvd
Apt 8103
Tucson AZ 85742

Call Sign: WA3PSB
Ronald W Simpson
3980 W Linda Vista Blvd
Apt 8103

Tucson AZ 85742

Call Sign: KC7FFR
Elizabeth A Kanto
3355 W Lobo Rd
Tucson AZ 85742

Call Sign: N7VK
Veikko A Kanto
3355 W Lobo Rd
Tucson AZ 85742

Call Sign: KE7BIL
Joyce H Pedersen
924 W Los Alamos
Tucson AZ 85704

Call Sign: KC7ITF
Robert J Stickle
2491 W Los Alamos
Tucson AZ 85741

Call Sign: KD7NTB
Harold S Pedersen
924 W Los Alamos St
Tucson AZ 85704

Call Sign: KB7VKP
Nora G Griffin
7777 W Los Reales
Tucson AZ 85746

Call Sign: KC7PLT
Jason Douglas
4155 W Lum Wash Ct
Tucson AZ 85745

Call Sign: K1LNH
Ronald F O Loughlin
699 W Magee Dr Apt 15104
Tucson AZ 85704

Call Sign: W7KRE
Joe E Gonzales
2862 W Magee Rd
Tucson AZ 85704

Call Sign: N7LCU
Thomas L Colson Sr

14825 W Magee Rd
Tucson AZ 85743

Call Sign: KD7BGF
Chris M Norton
1970 W Magee Rd 12201
Tucson AZ 85704

Call Sign: N7FDS
Jeffrey A Bishop
1631 W Maplewood Dr
Tucson AZ 85746

Call Sign: N7JDG
Lance G Coenen
4101 W Mars
Tucson AZ 85741

Call Sign: KC7HGX
Penelope A Herring
10270 W Mars Rd
Tucson AZ 85743

Call Sign: W7HD
Ronny G Herring
10270 W Mars Rd
Tucson AZ 85743

Call Sign: KE7YAE
Robert P Fink
3842 W Mars St
Tucson AZ 85741

Call Sign: KC7ZON
Franklin C Beckman
4143 W Massingale Rd
Tucson AZ 85741

Call Sign: WA7OCT
Paul G Zetocha
4890 W Massingale Rd
Tucson AZ 85741

Call Sign: KF7SYU
Tim Brown
1220 W Maximilian Way
Tucson AZ 85704

Call Sign: KB6NED

David T Rath
3711 W Meadow Briar Dr
Tucson AZ 85741

Call Sign: WB7SRM
Robert H Desilets
317 W Medina Rd
Tucson AZ 857066664

Call Sign: W7GJR
Joseph Schadl
1802 W Merlin Rd
Tucson AZ 85713

Call Sign: KF7LEE
Darryl K Smith
2791 W Mesa Verde Pl
Tucson AZ 85742

Call Sign: KF7LEC
Jordan K Smith
2791 W Mesa Verde Pl
Tucson AZ 85742

Call Sign: KF7LED
Sandra B Smith
2791 W Mesa Verde Pl
Tucson AZ 85742

Call Sign: WN8T
Daniel L Kester Sr
7346 W Mesquite River Dr
Tucson AZ 85743

Call Sign: WR0NG
Paul S Hilde Sr
11931 W Mile Wide Rd
Tucson AZ 857439148

Call Sign: N5IOE
Edna M Blunck
10064 W Milky Way Dr
Tucson AZ 85735

Call Sign: N1CE
George C Blunck
10064 W Milky Way Dr
Tucson AZ 85735

Call Sign: WB7DGP
Orrin T Layton
711 W Milton Rd
Tucson AZ 85706

Call Sign: WB7DJT
Lois M Layton
711 W Milton Rd
Tucson AZ 85706

Call Sign: N7PAT
Bobbie Boone Stapleton
4190 W Milton Rd
Tucson AZ 85746

Call Sign: WB7OMM
Stephen C Parkman
4563 W Milton Rd
Tucson AZ 85746

Call Sign: N7UGE
Edward E Wilkes
1402 W Miracle Mi 2134
Tucson AZ 85705

Call Sign: KQ0L
Harry S Thomas
1067 W Miracle Mi 70
Tucson AZ 85705

Call Sign: KF7SRB
Paul E Kuhn
435 W Miracle Mile Apt C
Tucson AZ 85705

Call Sign: KE7CYS
Julian A Martinez
7473 W Mission View Pl
Tucson AZ 85743

Call Sign: NC9L
James A Jakubin
7479 W Mission View Pl
Tucson AZ 85743

Call Sign: KE7TI
James A Jakubin
7479 W Mission View Pl
Tucson AZ 85743

Call Sign: KF7HMA
Marcus E Nesbit
144 W Missouri St
Tucson AZ 85713

Call Sign: KC8DON
Joel M Fraser
1441 W Mohawk Dr
Tucson AZ 85705

Call Sign: W7BBM
John J Molloy
5625 W Molloy
Tucson AZ 85745

Call Sign: KF7DWI
Jjm Eme
5625 W Molloy Rd
Tucson AZ 85745

Call Sign: W7JM
Jjm Eme
5625 W Molloy Rd
Tucson AZ 85745

Call Sign: KB7ZTM
Jon D Parker
5461 W Montana St
Tucson AZ 85746

Call Sign: AA7ZT
Suzanne M Parker
5461 W Montana St
Tucson AZ 85746

Call Sign: N7YUD
Ted C Parker
5461 W Montana St
Tucson AZ 85746

Call Sign: KC7OKF
John F Gracie
5514 W Montana St
Tucson AZ 85757

Call Sign: KF7CEL
Brian D Oneil
5010 W Monte Carlo Dr

Tucson AZ 85745

Call Sign: KA7BWJ
Joseph V Myefski
1301 W Monte Vista
Tucson AZ 85705

Call Sign: AD7XE
Paul M Wright Jr
7918 W Moonfire Ct
Tucson AZ 85743

Call Sign: KE6HAP
Gilbert W Alexander
1546 W Moore Rd
Tucson AZ 857378889

Call Sign: K3YAZ
Franklin J Cathell
3756 W Morgan Rd
Tucson AZ 85745

Call Sign: KC9DLC
David E Lowe
7863 W Morning Light Way
Tucson AZ 85743

Call Sign: KC7KKQ
Earl L Woodall
147 W Mossman Rd
Tucson AZ 85706

Call Sign: W0VII
David A Beveridge
1807 W Mtn Laurel Dr
Tucson AZ 857377829

Call Sign: KF6UWZ
Richard L Holder
7918 W Mural Hill Dr
Tucson AZ 85743

Call Sign: N8CNI
John L Dum
1992 W Myrtlewood Ln
Tucson AZ 85704

Call Sign: KE7ZHG
Sinan A Turel

1920 W Nava Dr
Tucson AZ 85746

Call Sign: KD6RLG
Noel T Marbella
1944 W Nava Dr
Tucson AZ 85746

Call Sign: N4ABY
Roy A Tucker
5500 W Nebraska St
Tucson AZ 857469533

Call Sign: N7AVA
Jerome D Muller
1461 W Neosho Pl
Tucson AZ 85704

Call Sign: N7ZBC
Frederick J Pingal
3930 W New York
Tucson AZ 85745

Call Sign: KE7TRK
Roger Evenson
2294 W Noble Heights Dr
Tucson AZ 85742

Call Sign: KF7UNS
Richard D Munoz
6702 W Nueva Vista Dr
Tucson AZ 85743

Call Sign: KE7QQY
Sydney L Degon
1821 W Oakway Dr
Tucson AZ 857468143

Call Sign: KC7LVD
Jo Andrea Grimaldi
4301 W Oasis Dr
Tucson AZ 85742

Call Sign: N2DGI
Richard D Grimaldi
4301 W Oasis Dr
Tucson AZ 857429322

Call Sign: N7THO

James E Braman
4420 W Oasis Dr
Tucson AZ 85742

Call Sign: KC7INJ
Emeterio R Godoy
2830 W Old Ajo Hwy
Tucson AZ 85746

Call Sign: KC7INK
Theresa L Godoy
2830 W Old Ajo Hwy
Tucson AZ 85746

Call Sign: N2ZSM
Richard M Schufreider
2851 W Old Ajo Way 3
Tucson AZ 85746

Call Sign: KE7BOL
Philip E Kortesis
4352 W Olivette Mine Pl
Tucson AZ 85745

Call Sign: W7PEK
Philip E Kortesis
4352 W Olivette Mine Pl
Tucson AZ 85745

Call Sign: AC7OT
Robert B Gillette
1909 W Omar Dr
Tucson AZ 85704

Call Sign: KE7VKJ
Paul F Eyssautier
7250 W Opossum
Tucson AZ 85743

Call Sign: KC2FUE
Clarence Bullock
7166 W Oracle Ridge Trl
Tucson AZ 85743

Call Sign: K9NIU
Dennis R Tallent
951 W Orange Grove 24 202
Tucson AZ 85704

Call Sign: KC7BEQ
Steven B Regehr
11265 W Orange Grove Rd
Tucson AZ 85743

Call Sign: K9SYU
Jean M Brown
951 W Orange Grove Rd 7
101
Tucson AZ 857044007

Call Sign: KV7K
Gordon H Stark
951 W Orange Grove Rd
77102
Tucson AZ 85704

Call Sign: WD6DRC
John C Smith
2255 W Orange Grove Rd
Apt 14104
Tucson AZ 85741

Call Sign: N7UGQ
Walter W Mc Cullor
951 W Orange Grove Rd Apt
55 204
Tucson AZ 85704

Call Sign: KG0IU
William H Leyva
951 W Orange Grove Rd Apt
67204
Tucson AZ 85704

Call Sign: AA7VX
William D Martin Jr
4146 W Orangewood Dr
Tucson AZ 85741

Call Sign: KB4VYM
Clarke W Mc Cullough
3225 W Overton Rd
Tucson AZ 85742

Call Sign: W2TPE
Glenn A Hartmann
11981 W Pajaro Verde
Tucson AZ 85743

Call Sign: KB7FRW
Bradley T Frazier
670 W Panorama
Tucson AZ 85704

Call Sign: KF7IZJ
Jeffrey Thompson
1694 W Park Wood Ln
Tucson AZ 85746

Call Sign: KB7RFJ
Fred H George
1696 W Parkwood Ln
Tucson AZ 85746

Call Sign: WB7VFW
Arthur C Antrim
2761 W Partridge Rd
Tucson AZ 85746

Call Sign: KF7VDT
Arthur C Antrim
2761 W Partridge St
Tucson AZ 85746

Call Sign: WB6NVO
James L Skinner
2941 W Paseo Bonito
Tucson AZ 85746

Call Sign: K6BPT
James L Skinner
2941 W Paseo Bonito
Tucson AZ 85746

Call Sign: KC6BNE
Sandra J Skinner
2941 W Paseo Bonito
Tucson AZ 85746

Call Sign: WB6NVO
Sandra J Skinner
2941 W Paseo Bonito
Tucson AZ 85746

Call Sign: KB7ZVZ
Robert B Nyberg
1942 W Paseo Cuenca

Tucson AZ 85704

Call Sign: N7EVV
Robert L Cassel
4901 W Paseo De Las
Colinas
Tucson AZ 85745

Call Sign: KF6JTK
Paul C Brabec
5175 W Paseo Del Barranco
Tucson AZ 85745

Call Sign: KC7AIL
Blaine A Martyn Dow
2269 W Paseo Luna
Tucson AZ 85741

Call Sign: K6PC
Robert M Crotinger
621 W Paseo Norteno
Tucson AZ 857044640

Call Sign: KF7AMO
Richard K Siebert
720 W Paseo Norteno
Tucson AZ 85704

Call Sign: N7WB
John E Munger
731 W Paseo Norteno
Tucson AZ 85704

Call Sign: N7KGF
Patricia J Mobray
1886 W Paseo Reforma N
Tucson AZ 85705

Call Sign: N7PAC
Jace M Harvey
421 W Pelaar Dr
Tucson AZ 85705

Call Sign: N7IQV
John R Holden
1142 W Pelaar St
Tucson AZ 857052558

Call Sign: KE7LHZ

Hector A Mendoza
518 W Pennsylvania Dr
Tucson AZ 85714

Call Sign: KB7TEM
Diana L Smith
2949 W Pepper Dr
Tucson AZ 85741

Call Sign: KF7BLX
John B Springer
3430 W Pepperwood Loop
Tucson AZ 85742

Call Sign: KF7ADM
Colton L Noble
1652 W Picton Arcade St
Tucson AZ 85746

Call Sign: N7NTC
Louise Argall Olm
7841 W Pima Farms Rd
Tucson AZ 85743

Call Sign: N7NTB
Mark C Olm
7841 W Pima Farms Rd
Tucson AZ 85743

Call Sign: KF7GFJ
Stuart C Slonaker
3012 W Pl Bernardo
Tucson AZ 85745

Call Sign: W4CZO
Ronald Stewart
1127 W Placita Camilla
Tucson AZ 85704

Call Sign: KE7MML
Michael R Jarvis
2891 W Placita De Juan
Tucson AZ 85745

Call Sign: KF7BJA
Arnold M Jimenez
663 W Placita De La Poza
Tucson AZ 85704

Call Sign: KC7RCS
David M Dryden
5400 W Placita De La
Promesa
Tucson AZ 85745

Call Sign: KD4GTJ
Victoria A Yuki
6651 W Placita De Las Botas
Tucson AZ 85743

Call Sign: W5DOI
Burnill B Healan
622 W Placita De Las
Lomitas
Tucson AZ 85704

Call Sign: WB0LWH
Andrew R Lamb
4951 W Placita De Los
Vientos
Tucson AZ 85745

Call Sign: KC7POF
Mary K Lamb
4951 W Placita De Los
Vientos
Tucson AZ 85745

Call Sign: N4GRA
Mary K Lamb
4951 W Placita De Los
Vientos
Tucson AZ 85745

Call Sign: KC7SXA
Frank A Reiser
1740 W Placita De Santos
Tucson AZ 85704

Call Sign: KD7OGT
Maureen B Reiser
1740 W Placita De Santos
Tucson AZ 85704

Call Sign: KB7KKU
Basil B Brashear Jr
3044 W Placita Del Pasillo
Tucson AZ 85746

Call Sign: KB7LCT
Betty L Brashear
3044 W Placita Del Pasillo
Tucson AZ 85746

Call Sign: WA7SNT
Frederick W Tate
1302 W Placita Del Rey
Tucson AZ 857043614

Call Sign: K7NET
Edward S Sykes
5473 W Placita Del Risco
Tucson AZ 85745

Call Sign: N7WEP
Kenneth F Mroczek
5143 W Placita Dle Herrero
Tucson AZ 85745

Call Sign: K4CJO
James W Tyson
2709 W Placita Mesa Alta
Tucson AZ 85742

Call Sign: KC7POG
Gregory J Trainor
3048 W Placita Montessa
Tucson AZ 85741

Call Sign: N5LPO
Ronald S Price
4961 W Placitadel Quetzal
Tucson AZ 857459692

Call Sign: WB7OPU
Robert R Ruthkauskas
828 W President
Tucson AZ 85714

Call Sign: KD7BTS
Bailey S Swartz
1602 W Prince
Tucson AZ 85705

Call Sign: WB7CPH
Norman I Baaba
1811 W Prince Rd

Tucson AZ 85705

Call Sign: KC7JTK
Mark F Holmes
1135 W Prince Rd 105
Tucson AZ 857053161

Call Sign: KD7JBP
Walter D Clay
1007 W Prince Rd 29
Tucson AZ 85705

Call Sign: KD7OXP
Walter R Pickett
570 W Prince Rd Nr 33
Tucson AZ 85705

Call Sign: KB7IEV
Frances A Clay
1007 W Prince Rd Sp 29
Tucson AZ 85705

Call Sign: WA9QWX
Roderick R Kobesko
1007 W Prince Unit 23
Tucson AZ 85705

Call Sign: KI7HC
Thomas M Crawford
3963 W Prosperity Mine Pl
Tucson AZ 85745

Call Sign: KE7DON
Michael E Sagara
4020 W Pyracantha Cir
Tucson AZ 85741

Call Sign: KE6EFK
Roy Naylor
3328 W Quail Haven Cir
Tucson AZ 85745

Call Sign: KI4JSG
Daniel B King
6874 W Quailwood Way
Tucson AZ 85746

Call Sign: KC7DPL
Marc R Hebl

8398 W Quattlebaum
Tucson AZ 85735

Call Sign: K7TYZ
John L Mc Ginley
8469 W Quattlebaum Dr
Tucson AZ 857351481

Call Sign: K4TYZ
John L Mc Ginley
8469 W Quattlebaum Dr
Tucson AZ 857351481

Call Sign: N7TBY
Fred M Eakin
3554 W Raintree
Tucson AZ 85741

Call Sign: N7FXH
William G Pekelder
12341 W Ranchettes
Tucson AZ 85743

Call Sign: KD7LGA
Kathryn Krieski
12405 W Ranchettes Dr
Tucson AZ 85743

Call Sign: K7EWE
James T Wiggins
12405 W Ranchettes Dr
Tucson AZ 857439750

Call Sign: N7KB
Kenneth G Brown
12081 W Ranchito Verde
Tucson AZ 857438863

Call Sign: KD7CRE
Frank Reiser
2224 W Rapallo Way
Tucson AZ 85741

Call Sign: W7FOX
Christopher F Douglas
2611 W Rapallo Way
Tucson AZ 85741

Call Sign: KE7FDP

Hyrum D Johnson
5708 W Rattler St
Tucson AZ 85742

Call Sign: KC7UDL
John W Stokes
3820 W Red Wing St
Tucson AZ 85741

Call Sign: KF7JYY
John J Gorski
4628 W Red Wolf Dr
Tucson AZ 85742

Call Sign: AB7JI
Stephan Kraus
4750 W Red Wolf Dr
Tucson AZ 85742

Call Sign: N7AKC
David E Coccio
3730 W Redfield Ln
Tucson AZ 85742

Call Sign: KE7OSQ
Aaron D Murray
4601 W Redwolf Dr
Tucson AZ 85742

Call Sign: KC7FSA
Robert D Keller
227 W Rillito St
Tucson AZ 85705

Call Sign: KE7AZQ
Kandis D Kile
1861 W River Otter Dr
Tucson AZ 85704

Call Sign: N7YMJ
Gabriel G Gomez
818 W River Rd
Tucson AZ 85704

Call Sign: N7YMK
Nancy R Gomez
818 W River Rd
Tucson AZ 85704

Call Sign: KA9FKB
Earl J Byford
5516 W Rocking Cir
Tucson AZ 857136316

Call Sign: N7OCX
Keith W Palmer
4411 W Rockwood Dr
Tucson AZ 85741

Call Sign: KC7UOS
John H Lowery
4420 W Rockwood Dr
Tucson AZ 85741

Call Sign: WB9SCN
Cecil F Allain
775 W Roger Rd 156
Tucson AZ 857052673

Call Sign: AA9T
Willard M Walsh
775 W Roger Rd 63
Tucson AZ 85705

Call Sign: K7YAT
Ronald A Hayes
775 W Roger Rd Sp 85
Tucson AZ 857052652

Call Sign: WA2JWF
Maurice E Walker
1800 W Ronceval Pl
Tucson AZ 85704

Call Sign: WD6FIJ
Charles W Benda
6392 W Rosamond Way
Tucson AZ 85743

Call Sign: KC7EMF
Edwin J Rudloff
2966 W Royal Copeland Dr
Tucson AZ 85745

Call Sign: WI7X
Gerald A Hoffman
2001 W Rudasill 7203
Tucson AZ 85704

Call Sign: N7WS
Wesley D Stewart Jr
9550 W Rudasill Rd
Tucson AZ 85743

Call Sign: K7ASJ
Robert L Spencer
10560 W Rudasill Rd
Tucson AZ 85743

Call Sign: W7TX
Kenneth G Macleish
2001 W Rudasill Rd Apt
1603
Tucson AZ 85704

Call Sign: K7BW
Quentin W Kuether
2001 W Rudasill Rd Apt
7208
Tucson AZ 85704

Call Sign: WB4LDS
Walter R Carter
1809 W Rue Du Fleuve
Tucson AZ 85746

Call Sign: N7UGR
Benjamin Senitzky
618 W Rushwood Dr
Tucson AZ 85704

Call Sign: K7OLD
Norman D Martin
2305 W Ruthrauff L 21
Tucson AZ 857051985

Call Sign: WB7OWA
Raymond E Santerre
2305 W Ruthrauff Rd Sp B25
Tucson AZ 85705

Call Sign: WV5N
Ward Stephens
6180 W Saddle Horn Cir
Tucson AZ 85743

Call Sign: KB7BTS

Randy L Jenott
2681 W Saddleranch Pl
Tucson AZ 85745

Call Sign: WB7RWQ
Charles E Stringfellow
2801 W Sahara
Tucson AZ 85705

Call Sign: K7OBB
Dana D Evans
3590 W Sahuaro Divide
Tucson AZ 85742

Call Sign: N7ZAZ
Faber C Tunison
132 W Sahuaro St
Tucson AZ 85705

Call Sign: KD7JBN
O Donell Trumper
1540 W San Annetta Dr
Tucson AZ 857041973

Call Sign: KB8WKJ
Leslie J Parsons
2580 W San Juan Ter
Tucson AZ 857132587

Call Sign: WB7FEA
Eugene J Gross
1612 W San Lucas Dr
Tucson AZ 85704

Call Sign: AA7Z
Ronald F Moody
2231 W San Marcos Blvd
Tucson AZ 857132545

Call Sign: KF7ITG
James E Angleton
1145 W San Martin Dr
Tucson AZ 85704

Call Sign: W6JS
Edwin M Carter Sr
2725 W Sandbrook Ln
Tucson AZ 857415200

Call Sign: WF7SOL
Brian E Jones
8252 W Sapphire Moon Way
Tucson AZ 857435245

Call Sign: KD7GPJ
Sabra V Albritton
1752 W Sauvignon Dr
Tucson AZ 85746

Call Sign: N7GIC
Josh A Albritton
1752 W Sauvignon Dr
Tucson AZ 857463170

Call Sign: AB8BG
James J Mellberg
1236 W Schafer Dr
Tucson AZ 85705

Call Sign: KR4IB
Kerry D Mellberg
1236 W Schafer Dr
Tucson AZ 85705

Call Sign: KE6WAS
Stuart L Joines
1655 W Scots Pine St
Tucson AZ 85705

Call Sign: KD7KYZ
Jonathan T Matsushino
1057 W Sea Lion Dr
Tucson AZ 85704

Call Sign: KH6TX
Frank P Nollette
1631 W Seabrooke Dr
Tucson AZ 85705

Call Sign: KD7CGP
Gregory O Spence
1703 W Seabrooke Dr
Tucson AZ 85705

Call Sign: KE7RIB
Ashleigh D Mcintosh
2011 W Shalimar Way
Tucson AZ 85704

Call Sign: WA6ZDW
Lynn C Allaben
253 W Shenandoah St
Tucson AZ 85704

Call Sign: W0PGA
Raymond T O Donnell Jr
2874 W Sheryl Dr
Tucson AZ 85713

Call Sign: N7VMM
Adrian J Hritz
7775 W Shining Moon Way
Tucson AZ 85743

Call Sign: KD7CYX
Paul A Rapisarda
7775 W Shining Moon Way
Tucson AZ 85743

Call Sign: W5PAR
Paul A Rapisarda
7775 W Shining Moon Way
Tucson AZ 85743

Call Sign: KG7WO
Gary J Neilson
7552 W Siesta Rock Dr
Tucson AZ 85743

Call Sign: KC7ZMW
Frank J Moreno
931 W Simmons St
Tucson AZ 857052561

Call Sign: KB7WXI
David A Hamer
1925 W Sindle Pl
Tucson AZ 85746

Call Sign: KE7QVA
Glenn A Hamblin
9691 W Sky Blue Dr
Tucson AZ 85735

Call Sign: WB4DQT
Clement R Flis Jr
3042 W Sky Ranch Trl

Tucson AZ 85742

Call Sign: KC7FQH
John C Flynn
3544 W Sky Ridge Loop
Tucson AZ 85741

Call Sign: KD7ECO
John R Harkey
4800 W Snow Leopard Dr
Tucson AZ 85742

Call Sign: WB7TLS
Glenn Griffith
3810 W South Aire Pl
Tucson AZ 857411305

Call Sign: KE7NTM
Berkeley M Krueger
504 W Spearhead Rd
Tucson AZ 85737

Call Sign: KE7CYT
Kurt M Krueger
504 W Spearhead Rd
Tucson AZ 85737

Call Sign: KC7LIL
Alice R Riesgo
1455 W Speedway
Tucson AZ 85745

Call Sign: KD7FHA
Christopher P Bell
2162 W Speedway Blvd 7102
Tucson AZ 85745

Call Sign: KJ6CYQ
Alex M Byron
1505 W St Marys Rd 369
Tucson AZ 85745

Call Sign: KD7UIR
Richard V Edwards III
1001 W St Marys Rd 410
Tucson AZ 85745

Call Sign: KB7KRZ
Wendy L Beardsley

2930 W St Tropaz
Tucson AZ 85713

Call Sign: KB7KRY
Burt J Beardsley
2930 W St Tropaz
Tucson AZ 85713

Call Sign: WB7QJR
Molly T Mc Kinney
2931 W St Tropaz
Tucson AZ 85713

Call Sign: KD7VBV
Ralph F Siedel
2881 W St Tropaz Ave
Tucson AZ 85713

Call Sign: N7UKK
John H Clayton
4229 W Stagestop Ct
Tucson AZ 85741

Call Sign: KF7IMK
Charles J Martin Jr
2878 W Staring Pl
Tucson AZ 85741

Call Sign: W7TNS
Gerald P Winder
1488 W Stockwell Pl
Tucson AZ 85746

Call Sign: KB5YFP
Sherry M Stallings
102 W Suffolk Dr
Tucson AZ 857047141

Call Sign: KB7ZBJ
Gene D Prantner
7578 W Sugar Ranch Rd
Tucson AZ 85743

Call Sign: WB5UKB
Everett A Ammann Jr
7675 W Summer Sky
Tucson AZ 85743

Call Sign: W1HUE

Larry V East
7479 W Suncatcher Dr
Tucson AZ 85743

Call Sign: KK7EH
Michael M Garay
4885 W Sundance Way
Tucson AZ 85745

Call Sign: KC7GRP
Jeanne M Paquette
1600 W Sunkist Rd
Tucson AZ 85737

Call Sign: W7RAP
Richard A Paquette
1600 W Sunkist Rd
Tucson AZ 85755

Call Sign: N4CZE
Richard Horn
7272 W Sunset Mtn Dr
Tucson AZ 85743

Call Sign: KC5SBX
Nancy K Kinsman
2772 W Sunset Rd
Tucson AZ 85741

Call Sign: AD6T
Jefferson H Harman
6175 W Sunset Rd
Tucson AZ 85743

Call Sign: KE7OEF
Edward D Beggy
6202 W Sunset Rd
Tucson AZ 85743

Call Sign: K7EDB
Edward D Beggy
6202 W Sunset Rd
Tucson AZ 85743

Call Sign: KB7YCH
Neill S Prohaska
6250 W Sunset Rd
Tucson AZ 85743

Call Sign: KD7YCN
Adam Little
6320 W Sunset Rd
Tucson AZ 85743

Call Sign: KD7YDF
John K Little
6320 W Sunset Rd
Tucson AZ 85743

Call Sign: KB7TCQ
Noah D Goodman
3325 W Sweetwater Ave
Tucson AZ 85745

Call Sign: KB7TCR
Allan S Goodman
3325 W Sweetwater Dr
Tucson AZ 85745

Call Sign: KE7ACK
Steven D Elder
7713 W Taltson Dr
Tucson AZ 85743

Call Sign: W7CRZ
Richard L Martin
1124 W Ternero St
Tucson AZ 857042740

Call Sign: KB9LDF
Robert O Loving IV
7787 W Touchstone St
Tucson AZ 85735

Call Sign: ND7D
John J Rivera
6326 W Trails End Rd
Tucson AZ 857459636

Call Sign: KE7SZY
Joseph C Vinson
3141 W Treeline Dr
Tucson AZ 85741

Call Sign: KE7SZX
Willard H Mcdougal
3219 W Treeline Dr
Tucson AZ 85741

Call Sign: KC7JFB
Rick L Pintor
3599 W Trevor Dr
Tucson AZ 85741

Call Sign: KA2NWM
Robert E Bartnik
6172 W Tucson Est Pky
Tucson AZ 85713

Call Sign: K7RGV
Robert G Venekamp
5665 W Tumbling F St
Tucson AZ 85713

Call Sign: KE7QIA
Thomas E Maloy
3655 W Turkey Ln
Tucson AZ 85742

Call Sign: WA6KWX
Thomas E Maloy
3655 W Turkey Ln
Tucson AZ 85742

Call Sign: W7KMY
Robert E Cousy
5840 W Turkey Ln
Tucson AZ 85742

Call Sign: KB6OPN
Frank Adams
115 W University Blvd
Tucson AZ 85705

Call Sign: KE7EWF
Jesse W Halek
1645 W Valenca Nr 109
Tucson AZ 85746

Call Sign: KD7UUJ
Jon Zeluff
1645 W Valencia 109 175
Tucson AZ 85746

Call Sign: W7DSM
George P Duvall Jr
334 W Valencia Apt G3

Tucson AZ 85706

Call Sign: KF7ATT
James K Wood
1645 W Valencia Rd 109
Tucson AZ 85746

Call Sign: KD6TPI
Keith W Hensley
1645 W Valencia Rd 109
Tucson AZ 857466040

Call Sign: KF7ADL
Samuel Wood
1645 W Valencia Rd 109
Pmb 232
Tucson AZ 85746

Call Sign: W7LAW
John W Havens
1970 W Valencia Rd Apt 193
Tucson AZ 857466534

Call Sign: KA1WK
Richard D Furash
425 W Valoro Dr
Tucson AZ 85737

Call Sign: KA7BRH
Richard L Terrell
734 W Vanover
Tucson AZ 85705

Call Sign: NP2KL
Gale Foster-Strauss
8196 W Velvet Ant Pl
Tucson AZ 85735

Call Sign: NP2CT
Milburn A Strauss
W Velvet Ant Pl
Tucson AZ 85735

Call Sign: KC7ZTA
Fernando S Gonzales
2571 W Verda De Gente
Tucson AZ 85746

Call Sign: KC7ZYL

Valerie S Gonzales
2571 W Verda De Gente
Tucson AZ 85746

Call Sign: W7YRV
Roy W Callison
307 W Veterans Blvd
Tucson AZ 85713

Call Sign: KB7PMY
Ernie S Milam
2807 W Via Del Santo
Tucson AZ 85741

Call Sign: KB7FFC
Rudolph D Adair
2855 W Via Del Santo
Tucson AZ 85741

Call Sign: KC7SLF
Gary L Becker
8253 W Via Garcia Marquez
Tucson AZ 85757

Call Sign: KB8NRI
Robert C Armstrong II
2831 W Via Hacienda
Tucson AZ 857413424

Call Sign: WA8JQP
William L Richards
1885 W Via Mandarina
Tucson AZ 85737

Call Sign: WB7TLT
Eugene C Barker
2984 W Via Principia
Tucson AZ 85741

Call Sign: KE7WRK
Harry F Arnold
3122 W Via San Andrea 2
Tucson AZ 85746

Call Sign: W7IC
Christopher D Pendleton
6770 W Via Tres Casas
Tucson AZ 85743

Call Sign: N7CPY
James L Davis
2410 W Viadisilvio
Tucson AZ 857414205

Call Sign: KD7LOX
Kevin R Hunt
4871 W Vicuna Dr
Tucson AZ 85742

Call Sign: KC6QAC
Barbara A Brusasca
6534 W Vinca Rose Dr
Tucson AZ 85757

Call Sign: KB7MOV
Laszlo Fabian
2210 W Wagon Wheel Dr
Tucson AZ 85745

Call Sign: KE7KFQ
John E Dunn Jr
2740 W Wagon Wheels Dr
Tucson AZ 85745

Call Sign: AD7PO
John E Dunn Jr
2740 W Wagon Wheels Dr
Tucson AZ 85745

Call Sign: KA7AHK
Gerald W Abitz
2002 W Water
Tucson AZ 85705

Call Sign: KD7OXQ
Howard H Elliott
4840 W Waterbuck Dr
Tucson AZ 85742

Call Sign: KC7VVF
David J Hernandez Sr
830 W Wedwick
Tucson AZ 85706

Call Sign: W7XH
William W Braden
12955 W Well Pump Dr
Tucson AZ 85743

Call Sign: WB7ESQ
Elio Zambrano
2001 W Wetmore Rd
Tucson AZ 85705

Call Sign: KE7TRJ
Daniel H Raburn Sr
1513 W Wetmore Rd 2
Tucson AZ 85705

Call Sign: KB7TRV
Mark F Sothman
1043 W Wetmore Sp 12
Tucson AZ 85705

Call Sign: KE7MMM
Effie L Williams
1300 W Wheatridge Dr
Tucson AZ 85704

Call Sign: KE7OEA
Thao T Stapleton
1300 W Wheatridge Dr
Tucson AZ 85704

Call Sign: KE7ODZ
Vy T Stapleton
1300 W Wheatridge Dr
Tucson AZ 85704

Call Sign: N7OXL
David B Stapleton
1300 W Wheatrudge Dr
Tucson AZ 85704

Call Sign: KF7KET
Martin A Vanwinkle
261 W Wheelwright Pl
Tucson AZ 85755

Call Sign: KA7WLN
Robert L Case
3120 W Wildwood Dr
Tucson AZ 85741

Call Sign: KB7UDV
Jose M Urena
1022 W Wilkenson Dr

Tucson AZ 85737

Call Sign: KB7UDU
Lisa Jo Urena
1022 W Wilkenson Dr
Tucson AZ 85737

Call Sign: KD6RHA
Delbert L Smith
1320 W Yaqui Dr 132
Tucson AZ 85704

Call Sign: KC7ABP
Ryan I Kanto
2924 W Yorkshire St
Tucson AZ 85741

Call Sign: KA7PDG
Alonzo A Berry
7551 W Zorro Rd
Tucson AZ 85746

Call Sign: KA7TDK
Carol A Berry
7551 W Zorro Rd
Tucson AZ 85746

Call Sign: WB7WSJ
Wolfram Quast
2130 Wagon Wheels Dr
Tucson AZ 857451806

Call Sign: KA7RLD
Robert D Mc Cord II
8540 Wanda Rd
Tucson AZ 85704

Call Sign: KC7NL
Rosemary J Braden
12955 Well Pump Dr
Tucson AZ 85743

Call Sign: WB6IRR
Mary Ann E Cade
39676 Winding Trl Dr
Tucson AZ 857392386

Call Sign: KC7UY
Mary J Bates

621 Windward Cir
Tucson AZ 85704

Call Sign: K4BQL
William H Nunn
1020 Woodland Dr
Tucson AZ 85711

Call Sign: KC7AMS
Dean S Lasko
Tucson AZ 85703

Call Sign: KB7TLH
Gene M Mesher
Tucson AZ 85703

Call Sign: KA7NSG
Robert W Broomfield
Tucson AZ 85703

Call Sign: KB5DUA
Tom A Johnson
Tucson AZ 85708

Call Sign: N7XJM
Joseph C Mc Cabe
Tucson AZ 85717

Call Sign: KB7YNX
Sanford B Evans
Tucson AZ 85717

Call Sign: KB7YNW
Shirley J Foley
Tucson AZ 85717

Call Sign: N7SCJ
Dennis K Luttrell
Tucson AZ 85726

Call Sign: KB7SXU
Donald D Hooks
Tucson AZ 85726

Call Sign: KB7LMH
Kelli L Cornell
Tucson AZ 85726

Call Sign: N4GGT

Kristi A Cornell
Tucson AZ 85726

Call Sign: K4FJV
Robert J Klug
Tucson AZ 85726

Call Sign: NT7E
Stephanie Vermette
Tucson AZ 85728

Call Sign: KC7BHV
Douglas K Runyon
Tucson AZ 85731

Call Sign: N7XJO
Terry R Friedrichsen
Tucson AZ 85731

Call Sign: KA7ITU
Paul F Mc Ginley Jr
Tucson AZ 85732

Call Sign: WA2VNT
Jeffrey M Seligman
Tucson AZ 85733

Call Sign: W7QFG
Cecil C Harshman
Tucson AZ 85740

Call Sign: KB7BVC
Robert E Knowles Jackman
Tucson AZ 85740

Call Sign: N5WMU
Alberta S Karber
Tucson AZ 85751

Call Sign: KA7UYE
Angela C Crane
Tucson AZ 85751

Call Sign: N7LDJ
Stanley J Caldwell
Tucson AZ 85751

Call Sign: KB5SQQ
Jacqueline E Raetz

Tucson AZ 85754

Call Sign: NY5O
William G Raetz Jr
Tucson AZ 85754

Call Sign: KD6LBL
David C Cunningham
Tucson AZ 857266149

Call Sign: K7BAB
Barbara J Levow
Tucson AZ 85702

Call Sign: KE7VKG
John W Wall
Tucson AZ 85702

Call Sign: K9VVX
John W Wall
Tucson AZ 85702

Call Sign: KF7FTY
Michael S Reynolds
Tucson AZ 85702

Call Sign: KF7IZG
Davin M Seidler
Tucson AZ 85703

Call Sign: KD7FHI
Don G East
Tucson AZ 85703

Call Sign: KF7SDZ
Phoebe Robinson
Tucson AZ 85703

Call Sign: N1VYY
Timothy J Rollins
Tucson AZ 85715

Call Sign: KC7JDQ
Bryan N Cardwell
Tucson AZ 85715

Call Sign: KE7VTP
Richard E George Sr
Tucson AZ 85716

Call Sign: N7GUL
Alexander R Carlin
Tucson AZ 85717

Call Sign: KD7JNM
Dave Avila
Tucson AZ 85717

Call Sign: KF7EMF
Francis S Rafka
Tucson AZ 85717

Call Sign: KC7PUK
Henry S Knight
Tucson AZ 85717

Call Sign: KD7HZO
John P Cox
Tucson AZ 85717

Call Sign: KC7MXE
Lawrence R Beck
Tucson AZ 85717

Call Sign: N7EAB
William H Ganoe
Tucson AZ 85717

Call Sign: KB7GJR
Sean G Mc Lachlan
Tucson AZ 85720

Call Sign: KC7QZO
Gabor Bakos
Tucson AZ 85721

Call Sign: KE7OST
David Islas
Tucson AZ 85721

Call Sign: KW7F
Extreme Team Contest Club
Tucson AZ 85722

Call Sign: KD7KIA
George W Alford
Tucson AZ 85726

Call Sign: KE7NOZ
Gerald R Innis
Tucson AZ 85726

Call Sign: W7FBT
John P Cox
Tucson AZ 85726

Call Sign: K9ZBE
Robert J Richter
Tucson AZ 85726

Call Sign: KC7ESE
Shirley R Musgrave
Tucson AZ 85726

Call Sign: WA7LZC
Wayne D Anderson
Tucson AZ 85726

Call Sign: K7WDA
Wayne D Anderson
Tucson AZ 85726

Call Sign: KD7VGJ
Southern Arizona Spread
Spectrum Experimenters
Tucson AZ 85728

Call Sign: KR7ST
Southern Arizona Spread
Spectrum Experimenters
Tucson AZ 85728

Call Sign: KJ7IV
John W Vermette
Tucson AZ 85728

Call Sign: KF7AOL
Manuel A Mello Jr
Tucson AZ 85728

Call Sign: KF7AOM
Manuel A Mello
Tucson AZ 85728

Call Sign: KF7BMA
Torsten K Leibold
Tucson AZ 85728

Call Sign: AE7ON
Torsten K Leibold
Tucson AZ 85728

Call Sign: N7KLW
Chad R James
Tucson AZ 85731

Call Sign: KD4ZBP
Clifford P Haycock
Tucson AZ 85731

Call Sign: K8JNE
David M Horton
Tucson AZ 85731

Call Sign: KH6IT
Frank H Lindley II
Tucson AZ 85731

Call Sign: N7UGP
John J Auvenshine
Tucson AZ 85731

Call Sign: KD6VLN
Richard A Joyce
Tucson AZ 85731

Call Sign: KD7GHW
Rita C Schroeder
Tucson AZ 85731

Call Sign: KE7VJK
Scott A Morgan
Tucson AZ 85731

Call Sign: K1TON
Scott A Morgan
Tucson AZ 85731

Call Sign: W6USA
Scott A Morgan
Tucson AZ 85731

Call Sign: WB8JXE
Sherry L Horton
Tucson AZ 85731

Call Sign: KE4VRW
Virgina A Haycock
Tucson AZ 85731

Call Sign: KD7WZS
Southern Arizona Rescue
Association
Tucson AZ 85732

Call Sign: N7SAR
Southern Arizona Rescue
Association
Tucson AZ 85732

Call Sign: K7SPH
Gerard M Bunge
Tucson AZ 85732

Call Sign: N4LIB
Judith D Bolt
Tucson AZ 85732

Call Sign: K9LP
Lawrence E Phillips Sr
Tucson AZ 85732

Call Sign: KD7SWS
Richard R Hurst
Tucson AZ 85732

Call Sign: KC6GEL
Sandra L Fox
Tucson AZ 85732

Call Sign: KC6GQF
Thomas F Fox
Tucson AZ 85732

Call Sign: KE7KGN
Arthur J Paisley
Tucson AZ 85733

Call Sign: W6CSE
Arthur J Paisley
Tucson AZ 85733

Call Sign: KD7GHX
Dave R Henken
Tucson AZ 85733

Call Sign: KD7KIC
Henry D Schneiker
Tucson AZ 85733

Call Sign: K2VNT
Jeffrey M Seligman
Tucson AZ 85733

Call Sign: KC7QDY
Marsha A Callaway
Tucson AZ 85733

Call Sign: KF7RJB
Maximo A Oana Jr
Tucson AZ 85733

Call Sign: KF7QQI
Robert J Hunter
Tucson AZ 85733

Call Sign: KD7ILA
William T Baggesen
Tucson AZ 85733

Call Sign: KF5AOH
Gerald E Davis
Tucson AZ 85734

Call Sign: AC7OU
John C Johnson
Tucson AZ 85734

Call Sign: N5XJB
Kirc A Breden
Tucson AZ 85734

Call Sign: KD7OLY
Pedro B Hernandez
Tucson AZ 85734

Call Sign: KC7DUN
Stephen H Roodhuyzen
Tucson AZ 85734

Call Sign: KE7ZGV
Karen J Gawron
Tucson AZ 85737

Call Sign: KH6FQU
Opal Nash
Tucson AZ 85737

Call Sign: KE7OYR
Gregory A Spieth
Tucson AZ 85738

Call Sign: KC7YDF
James R Smith
Tucson AZ 85738

Call Sign: KC7EGX
Kenichi Matsumura
Tucson AZ 85738

Call Sign: KF7ITB
Rachel E Spieth
Tucson AZ 85738

Call Sign: K7RST
Radio Society Of Tucson
Tucson AZ 85738

Call Sign: KB7PUM
Christine Mc Garvey
Tucson AZ 85740

Call Sign: WA6UIA
Douglas L Goodman
Tucson AZ 85740

Call Sign: N9EFO
Dwayne J Koval
Tucson AZ 85740

Call Sign: KC7JWJ
James F Huebner
Tucson AZ 85740

Call Sign: N7CBM
Janet W Lawwill
Tucson AZ 85740

Call Sign: KF7UJD
William E Walters
Tucson AZ 85740

Call Sign: WA7IYG

Univ Of Arizona ARC
Tucson AZ 85740

Call Sign: KE7VJJ
Bailey Perkins
Tucson AZ 85751

Call Sign: KD7HVJ
Cecilia M Stanford
Tucson AZ 85751

Call Sign: KE7RPS
David E Martines
Tucson AZ 85751

Call Sign: KD7UIP
Julie C Arter
Tucson AZ 85751

Call Sign: K6NH
Louis M Franklin
Tucson AZ 85751

Call Sign: KA0ONJ
Marc D Cunningham
Tucson AZ 85751

Call Sign: KD6RFA
Patrick J Cleary
Tucson AZ 85751

Call Sign: WA2JRY
Ronald B Mac Kinnon
Tucson AZ 85751

Call Sign: KF7KYP
Akebono B Airth
Tucson AZ 85752

Call Sign: KD7FDZ
Karmin M Laramie Lynam
Tucson AZ 85752

Call Sign: K8LJK
Lora J Kravec
Tucson AZ 85752

Call Sign: KF7QQC
Phillip D Davis

Tucson AZ 85752

Call Sign: W7ZMB
Phillip D Davis
Tucson AZ 85752

Call Sign: KB0OHM
Robert E Delaney
Tucson AZ 85752

Call Sign: W8TK
Thomas F Kravec
Tucson AZ 85752

Call Sign: KF7LMW
Thomas J Voelkel
Tucson AZ 85752

Call Sign: KE7OSV
Terry L Deuel
Tucson AZ 85754

Call Sign: W1TLD
Terry L Deuel
Tucson AZ 85754

Call Sign: K7CXY
Carey A Bunker III
Tucson AZ 85754

Call Sign: KC7VMG
Cherris J Oakland
Tucson AZ 85754

Call Sign: AA7YY
Donald W Oakland
Tucson AZ 85754

Call Sign: KD7QQV
Jacqueline E Raetz
Tucson AZ 85754

Call Sign: KD7SNV
Pedro Herrera
Tucson AZ 85754

Call Sign: KE7VKA
Ronald E Trimble
Tucson AZ 85754

Call Sign: KH6RW
Steve K Post
Tucson AZ 85754

Call Sign: KE7VKB
Trina G Trimble
Tucson AZ 85754

Call Sign: AC7SF
William G Raetz Jr
Tucson AZ 85754

Call Sign: AK7Z
Cholla Amateur Remote Base
Assn
Tucson AZ 85754

Call Sign: KE7KSI
Bruce D Stewart
Tucson AZ 857021129

Call Sign: W6XL
Jerry A Miel
Tucson AZ 857030622

Call Sign: N7GUN
John F Farber
Tucson AZ 857031607

Call Sign: NA8U
Dennis G Jeffrey
Tucson AZ 857170292

Call Sign: KD7SPR
David C Cunningham
Tucson AZ 857266149

Call Sign: WA6LKK
William G Deininger
Tucson AZ 857266203

Call Sign: KE7NHQ
Samuel J Hopkins
Tucson AZ 857266237

Call Sign: KC7ESF
John R Musgrave
Tucson AZ 857266578

Call Sign: N7KXE
Barbara A Porta
Tucson AZ 857267554

Call Sign: KB7DV
Elizabeth H Haskell
Tucson AZ 857284235

Call Sign: KC7OVT
William G Richardson
Tucson AZ 857284911

Call Sign: WA3BWT
Lionel A Waxman
Tucson AZ 857285869

Call Sign: N7RKN
Robert W Schroeder
Tucson AZ 857317929

Call Sign: W7LM
James S Serilla
Tucson AZ 857318022

Call Sign: N7ZBA
Sharon L Auvenshine
Tucson AZ 857318076

Call Sign: KB7FSW
Pamela S Mendel
Tucson AZ 857318507

Call Sign: KA7FNQ
Stuart E Mendel
Tucson AZ 857318507

Call Sign: KU7C
Lawrence J Massey
Tucson AZ 857318564

Call Sign: N7GCK
Lisa M Massey
Tucson AZ 857318564

Call Sign: AA7QQ
George M Collenberg
Tucson AZ 857318565

Call Sign: WV7G
George M Collenberg
Tucson AZ 857318565

Call Sign: KD6VLP
Barbara I Joyce
Tucson AZ 857319168

Call Sign: WB7CJF
Simon J Rosenblatt
Tucson AZ 857322847

Call Sign: KC7JWE
Maria M Call
Tucson AZ 857323563

Call Sign: KD7UIZ
Donald W Ernle
Tucson AZ 857327315

Call Sign: KC7FAH
Danny Lee
Tucson AZ 857332091

Call Sign: KD7AJV
Keith M Kumm
Tucson AZ 857333848

Call Sign: W7GV
Old Pueblo Radio Club
Tucson AZ 857339477

Call Sign: W7SA
Catalina Radio Club
Tucson AZ 857341337

Call Sign: WA6DCR
Robert W De Bro
Tucson AZ 857342973

Call Sign: N7DGS
Stephen V Graham
Tucson AZ 857380796

Call Sign: N7AZT
Stephen V Graham
Tucson AZ 857380796

Call Sign: K7BVN

Richard L Nichol
Tucson AZ 857405202

Call Sign: K7ARZ
William H Mc Garvey
Tucson AZ 857405386

Call Sign: WA6RJG
Frank J Gaskell
Tucson AZ 857405726

Call Sign: KA7CAO
Benjamin H Lawwill
Tucson AZ 857406269

Call Sign: WB2BUD
Wilson Morrow
Tucson AZ 857407258

Call Sign: KD7JNN
John M Sepp
Tucson AZ 857510804

Call Sign: KC7GVE
Gerald T Arzdorf
Tucson AZ 857511446

Call Sign: KB4IIX
Don Copler
Tucson AZ 857511981

Call Sign: AC4IV
David D Pedigo
Tucson AZ 857511984

Call Sign: KC2FMH
Lawrence M Goodsite
Tucson AZ 857512262

Call Sign: KC7FMZ
David L Riegel
Tucson AZ 857512680

Call Sign: N7FC
Michael Atlas
Tucson AZ 857520436

Call Sign: K6QZL
Donald P Cox

Tucson AZ 857520535

Call Sign: K7KT
Ernest G Eiting
Tucson AZ 857520566

Call Sign: KA7ZUP
Gary D Morgan
Tucson AZ 857521222

Call Sign: N9TRP
Steve A Engelman
Tucson AZ 857529420

FCC Amateur Radio Licenses in Tumacacori

Call Sign: KD7PNV
Daniel D Day
Tumacacori AZ 85640

Call Sign: KB7SDV
Jeff T Axel
Tumacacori AZ 85640

Call Sign: WD4CLN
John T Hayes
Tumacacori AZ 85640

Call Sign: KD7RNL
Jennifer Tougas
Tumacacori AZ 856400032

FCC Amateur Radio Licenses in Tusayan

Call Sign: KC7REO
Rodney G Rollins
Tusayan AZ 86023

FCC Amateur Radio Licenses in Vail

Call Sign: KD6ISM
James B Gilbreath
13892 Calle Nobleza
Vail AZ 85641

Call Sign: KC8KBQ

Ernest W Kuehn
11335 Cienega Park Pl
Vail AZ 85641

Call Sign: W7KBU
David C Donath
9449 E Barrel Springs Pl
Vail AZ 85606

Call Sign: N7ZQT
Stanley E Lalli
13595 E Bright Sky Loop
Vail AZ 85641

Call Sign: KC7QYJ
Joseph J Beckman Jr
3389 E Calle Agassiz
Vail AZ 85641

Call Sign: KD7RI
Charles D Abernathy
2441 E Calle Bacardi
Vail AZ 85641

Call Sign: KE7FJA
Shirley S Matsuhashi
1322 E Camino Aurelia
Vail AZ 85641

Call Sign: WA2OXV
Richard Kentla
13815 E Camino Costa
Teguise
Vail AZ 85641

Call Sign: KE7VPG
Robert P Metzelaars
14092 E Camino Galante
Vail AZ 85641

Call Sign: W7BLK
Robert P Metzelaars
14092 E Camino Galante
Vail AZ 85641

Call Sign: KD7KNO
Marie K Blake
2972 E Cardenas Dr
Vail AZ 85641

Call Sign: KD7HVI
Phil N Blake
2972 E Cardenas Dr
Vail AZ 85641

Call Sign: KD6OSL
Robert B Nace
14675 E Colossal Cave Rd
Vail AZ 856410370

Call Sign: KC6NSM
Anita M Petersen
13406 E Dawn Dr
Vail AZ 85641

Call Sign: KC6NSL
Crystal M Petersen
13604 E Dawn Dr
Vail AZ 85641

Call Sign: N6XNI
Stephen C Petersen
13604 E Dawn Dr
Vail AZ 85641

Call Sign: KB0UYL
Travus J Knotts
489 E Drawdown Trl
Vail AZ 85641

Call Sign: KD7RJE
Rex E Cook
13740 E Greystokes Dr
Vail AZ 85641

Call Sign: W7FDF
Frederick D Fitts
13522 E Hampden Green
Way
Vail AZ 856416529

Call Sign: KD7CLY
Chris Wardle
12796 E Hannah Trl
Vail AZ 85641

Call Sign: K7WMA
David A Lambert

15500 E Hilton Ranch Rd
Vail AZ 85641

Call Sign: N7JXK
Benjamin R Meeks Jr
16150 E Hilton Ranch Rd
Vail AZ 85641

Call Sign: W7LSN
Wade M Poteet
20705 E Marsh Station Rd
Vail AZ 85641

Call Sign: KF7ECQ
David A Rich Sr
3310 E Mescalero Dr
Vail AZ 85641

Call Sign: KD7PHW
Mark A Carter
13189 E Mesquite Flat
Spring
Vail AZ 85641

Call Sign: KE7ULC
Ronald P Barton
14326 E Nature Creek Pl
Vail AZ 85641

Call Sign: N7DEL
Delancy R Scrivner
11606 E Old Vail Rd
Vail AZ 85747

Call Sign: WD2AEM
Norman W Cramer
13828 E Placita Asta
Vail AZ 85641

Call Sign: KF7UNT
Jeffrey B Lane
14006 E Placita Derro De
Cara
Vail AZ 85641

Call Sign: KD5EIB
Jerry T Simpson
13993 E Placita Ocho Puntas
Vail AZ 856411421

Call Sign: WJ7T
Jerry T Simpson
13993 E Placita Ocho Puntas
Vail AZ 856411421

Call Sign: KD5HNQ
Nancy E Simpson
13993 E Placita Ocho Puntas
Vail AZ 856411421

Call Sign: K5NCY
Nancy E Simpson
13993 E Placita Ocho Puntas
Vail AZ 856411421

Call Sign: KF7RMZ
Blaine B Miller
14391 E Ranch Creek
Vail AZ 85641

Call Sign: AC7HT
John J Burns
13837 E Red Hawk Sky Trl
Vail AZ 85641

Call Sign: KD7KBZ
Marianne W Burns
13837 E Red Hawk Sky Trl
Vail AZ 85641

Call Sign: KF7BLY
Michael L Johnson Jr
13371 E Rex Molly Rd
Vail AZ 85641

Call Sign: KA1FWW
David W Ribblett
14361 E Rincon Valley Dr
Vail AZ 856416002

Call Sign: KD7SKS
Terry E Moore
2502 E Roslyn Ln
Vail AZ 85641

Call Sign: KE7PEC
David M Frysinger
13702 E Shadow Pines Ln

Vail AZ 85641

Call Sign: K7DMF
David M Frysinger
13702 E Shadow Pines Ln
Vail AZ 85641

Call Sign: WB5OGY
John L Thompson
9091 E Sholefield Springs Pl
Vail AZ 85641

Call Sign: KC1UK
Michael D Ambrose
9360 E Sycamore Crossing Pl
Vail AZ 85641

Call Sign: N7BOB
Robert F Scrivner
3761 E Tapia Dr
Vail AZ 85641

Call Sign: KB7LDW
Paul R Jonsson
13775 E Via Valderrama
Vail AZ 85641

Call Sign: KE7VKM
Margo C Weaver
12710 E Wentworth Ct
Vail AZ 85641

Call Sign: KB7TRW
John P Milus
3000 E Wetstones Rd
Vail AZ 85641

Call Sign: W1KSZ
Richard W Solomon
3190 E Wetstones Rd
Vail AZ 85641

Call Sign: AC6HB
David A Ghost
14144 E Whispering Ocotillo
Pl
Vail AZ 85641

Call Sign: K1UUG

Enrico M Bernardi
13132 Emesquite Flat Spring
Dr
Vail AZ 85641

Call Sign: K7HHH
Stephen H Roodhuyzen
16152 Hilton Ranch Rd
Vail AZ 85641

Call Sign: KB7VJW
Viola F Brown
20165 Mesquite Mesa Pl
Vail AZ 85641

Call Sign: KE7PMI
Gary M Kartchner
81 N Atrisco Dr
Vail AZ 85641

Call Sign: K7LKA
William F Arthur
1980 N Calle Rincolado Unit
2
Vail AZ 856419328

Call Sign: KE7KSF
William D Cunningham
1251 N Calle Rinconado
Vail AZ 85641

Call Sign: KD4YME
Neil J Bungard
950 N Davidson Rd
Vail AZ 85641

Call Sign: AC7PP
Neil J Bungard
950 N Davidson Rd
Vail AZ 85641

Call Sign: KE7BTF
John F Flanagan Jr
1081 N Reta Dr
Vail AZ 85641

Call Sign: N6PAD
Jerry Pulley
1441 N Reta Dr

Vail AZ 85641

Call Sign: KA3MJR
Anthony L Galmarini
221 N Slate Dr
Vail AZ 85641

Call Sign: K7LHR
Don C Stiver
1175 N Solar Dr
Vail AZ 85641

Call Sign: KF7GPW
Patrice Stiver
1175 N Solar Dr
Vail AZ 85641

Call Sign: K6WSC
William S Clark Jr
222 N Suntan Dr
Vail AZ 856419444

Call Sign: K7JLS
John L Shomenta
291 N Vail View Rd
Vail AZ 85641

Call Sign: KA7WHV
Ronald R Madsen
1101 N Vail View Rd
Vail AZ 85641

Call Sign: AK7X
Gerald J Gonda
Ranch
Vail AZ 85641

Call Sign: N6NFY
Michael G Brollini
12250 S Agua Verde Rd
Vail AZ 85641

Call Sign: KD7CDG
David R Hatch
13655 S Bird Dog Ave 3
Vail AZ 85641

Call Sign: KR7DH
David R Hatch

13655 S Bird Dog Ave 3
Vail AZ 85641

Call Sign: KE7MU
Bradford D Bilbrey
15555 S Calle Rinconado
Vail AZ 85641

Call Sign: KC7DZH
Normand R Lamoureux
9907 S Camino De La
Calinda
Vail AZ 85641

Call Sign: KC7BHS
Kim R Wettering
11067 S Camino San
Clemente
Vail AZ 85641

Call Sign: WA7UBA
Brent J Harmer
11487 S Cienega Dam Pl
Vail AZ 85641

Call Sign: KD7YGH
Thomas H Spencer
18355 S Cmo Chuboso
Vail AZ 85641

Call Sign: W9MT
Anthony J Bogusz
10536 S Coyote Melon Loop
Vail AZ 856412593

Call Sign: KE7HEV
Kurt G Markkola
13778 S Galloping Dee Ct
Vail AZ 85641

Call Sign: KE7CKL
John R Cox
17178 S Golden Sunrise Pl
Vail AZ 85641

Call Sign: K7JCX
John R Cox
17178 S Golden Sunrise Pl
Vail AZ 85641

Call Sign: AC4YV
Michael P Kelly
17487 S Indigo Crest Pass
Vail AZ 85641

Call Sign: KA0HGP
Timothy L Skaja
8606 S Long Bar Ranch Pl
Vail AZ 85641

Call Sign: KF7BRP
Douglas S Kovach
17940 S Maria Elena Ave
Vail AZ 85641

Call Sign: KB7YPO
David E Brown
20165 S Mesquite Mesa Pl
Vail AZ 85641

Call Sign: N7YSV
Randal Q Thornley
10509 S Miramar Canyon
Pass
Vail AZ 85641

Call Sign: KF7AYA
Landon L Stewart
17197 S Painted Vistas Way
Vail AZ 85641

Call Sign: W7AQT
James W Mc Crady
8944 S Placita Rancho De La
Vista
Vail AZ 85641

Call Sign: KD7YOT
Leslie A Mason
12757 S Red Horizon Trl
Vail AZ 85641

Call Sign: K7XYL
Joanne W Pattin
12757 S Red Horizon Trl
Vail AZ 85641

Call Sign: KD7DCW

Andy Bullock
16614 S Saguaro View Ln
Vail AZ 85641

Call Sign: KD7AMO
Brian S Bullock
16614 S Saguaro View Ln
Vail AZ 85641

Call Sign: KD7AKC
Crystal L Bullock
16614 S Saguaro View Ln
Vail AZ 85641

Call Sign: KW4H
Steven P Reed
9676 S San Esteban Dr
Vail AZ 85641

Call Sign: AI7AZ
Steven P Reed
9676 S San Esteban Dr
Vail AZ 85641

Call Sign: WB6TPF
Dennis C Reagin
17161 S Scarlet Cliff Pl
Vail AZ 85641

Call Sign: N7DCR
Dennis C Reagin
17161 S Scarlet Cliff Pl
Vail AZ 85641

Call Sign: W7KB
Dennis C Reagin
17161 S Scarlet Cliff Pl
Vail AZ 85641

Call Sign: WA2LVY
Rafael A Ihly
17950 S Sonoita Hwy
Vail AZ 85641

Call Sign: K6BHN
James D Whitfield
S Sonoita Hwy
Vail AZ 856419151

Call Sign: N3SAD
Kathleen R Szakonyi
17830 S Sonoita Hwy
Vail AZ 85641

Call Sign: N7TWF
Todd A Bordeaux
9580 S Spider Rock Rd
Vail AZ 85641

Call Sign: KC5ZGG
Gregory A Peters
564 S Sterling Vistas Way
Vail AZ 85641

Call Sign: N1XZX
Stephanie M Myers
460 S Sweet Ridge Dr
Vail AZ 85641

Call Sign: W6PBP
Stephen B Spires
8595 S Triangle H Ranch Pl
Vail AZ 85641

Call Sign: KE5DON
Donald D Mclain
10799 S Van Trap Spring Dr
Vail AZ 85641

Call Sign: KE7CVA
Richard L Rutherford
18267 S Via Del Minero
Vail AZ 85641

Call Sign: KF7LTW
Kenneth G Albrecht
643 W Charles L McKay St
Vail AZ 85641

Call Sign: W7MD
Damon S Raphael Md
2151 W Desert Serenity Pl
Vail AZ 85641

Call Sign: KF7UAW
Christopher A Hecht
29 W Eric Dorman
Vail AZ 85641

Call Sign: N9XKM
Karla J Staller
556 W Willis Pl
Vail AZ 85641

Call Sign: KF7AW
Kristopher D Staller
556 W Willis Pl
Vail AZ 85641

Call Sign: N7FWB
Ronald L Eshelman
Vail AZ 85641

Call Sign: KC7BHQ
William M Thompson
Vail AZ 85641

Call Sign: KE7KRG
Eric E Johnson
Vail AZ 85641

Call Sign: KK5XY
John F Jordan
Vail AZ 85641

Call Sign: KA7LGF
John P Kramer
Vail AZ 85641

Call Sign: KF7FCQ
Joy E Barton
Vail AZ 85641

Call Sign: KD7ODV
Tammy A Kramer
Vail AZ 85641

Call Sign: KC7MTO
Carmen Jarvis
Vail AZ 85641

Call Sign: KB7ZZY
Jack L Jarvis
Vail AZ 85641

Call Sign: N7LZK
Arthur L Mc Mahon

Vail AZ 856410021

Call Sign: KD7JYZ
Gay A Nace
Vail AZ 856410370

Call Sign: W7GMK
Gary M Kabrick
Vail AZ 856410831

FCC Amateur Radio Licenses in Valley Farms

Call Sign: KD7SSP
Jeffrey R Carpenter
11926 McGee Rd
Valley Farms AZ 85191

Call Sign: KB7OCG
Richard T Carpenter
11926 McGee Rd
Valley Farms AZ 85191

Call Sign: N7UTT
Joy M Carpenter
11927 McGee Rd
Valley Farms AZ 85191

Call Sign: KB7PUC
Kenneth L Carpenter
11927 McGee Rd
Valley Farms AZ 85291

Call Sign: N8PGP
Carl L Braddock III
11981 McGee Rd
Valley Farms AZ 85291

Call Sign: KB7DX
Carl L Braddock III
11981 McGee Rd
Valley Farms AZ 85291

Call Sign: KF7RZH
Max Zelenka
Valley Farms AZ 85191

Call Sign: KE7YUA
Tyler J Carpenter

Valley Farms AZ 85291

Call Sign: N7ZBB
Dawn L Carpenter
Valley Farms AZ 85291

FCC Amateur Radio Licenses in Vernon

Call Sign: KE5PZ
James E Hagan
28 Apache CR 3161
Vernon AZ 85940

Call Sign: K1RQF
Marshall M Dow
1528 CR 3140
Vernon AZ 85940

Call Sign: KD6YDO
John H Sneddon
CR 3176
Vernon AZ 85940

Call Sign: KD7WNK
John H Sneddon
CR 3176
Vernon AZ 85940

Call Sign: KJ6FI
Dan A Bloomquist
75 Rd 3151 Vernon
Vernon AZ 85940

Call Sign: KC7YAX
Albert Manry
Vernon AZ 85940

Call Sign: KC7LVA
Frank A Prati
Vernon AZ 85940

Call Sign: KC0QDK
George W Faulks
Vernon AZ 85940

Call Sign: KE7NTH
George W Faulks
Vernon AZ 85940

Call Sign: KC7YAW
Wanda Manry
Vernon AZ 85940

Call Sign: KE7SCQ
Richard D Chentfant
Vernon AZ 88940

Call Sign: KC6EKS
Janice M Sneddon
Vernon AZ 859400011

Call Sign: WB6ZEJ
Richard C Sneddon
Vernon AZ 859400011

FCC Amateur Radio Licenses in Wenden

Call Sign: KC9KZ
William H Jones
69115 Lindsey Rd
Wenden AZ 853570217

Call Sign: N0HDV
Larry D Rice
Wenden AZ 85358

FCC Amateur Radio Licenses in Whetstone

Call Sign: KD7NEC
Clair W Iverson
2251 Sands Ranch Rd
Whetstone AZ 85616

FCC Amateur Radio Licenses in White Mountain Lake

Call Sign: KB7UMH
Betty Jarrell
1796 Allen Pl
White Mountain Lake AZ
859120947

Call Sign: KB7TQC
Ken Jarrell

1796 Allen Pl
White Mountain Lake AZ
859120947

Call Sign: W5LCF
Alex C Fabris Jr
White Mountain Lake AZ
859120681

Call Sign: KC7ZAD
Gilbert L Bemus
White Mountain Lake AZ
859120761

FCC Amateur Radio Licenses in Whiteriver

Call Sign: KF6JXO
Jay W Hays II
Whiteriver AZ 85941

Call Sign: KF7GJS
Johann C Ngo
Whiteriver AZ 859410020

FCC Amateur Radio Licenses in Why

Call Sign: KB7NTH
Joseph A Gross
110 Guinn Rd
Why AZ 85321

Call Sign: KD7BDE
Charles C Nissley
Why AZ 85321

Call Sign: KD7FJD
Eileen M Adams
Why AZ 85321

Call Sign: KD7FJC
Maxine Nissley
Why AZ 85321

Call Sign: W6JBD
James L Saxon
Why AZ 853217237

FCC Amateur Radio Licenses in Wilcox

Call Sign: KA7IOM
Helen M Hardy
Box 167
Willcox AZ 85643

Call Sign: KA7IIK
James L Amalong
Box 614
Willcox AZ 85643

Call Sign: WA7VVV
James R Sober Jr
Box 788A
Willcox AZ 85643

Call Sign: KA7ILO
Nancy R Sloan
Box 790
Willcox AZ 85643

Call Sign: KB7OV
Gordon M Sloan
Box 790
Willcox AZ 85643

Call Sign: KA7YZS
Charles J Wadsworth
Box 819B
Willcox AZ 85643

Call Sign: N7ILW
Diane W Madruga
Box 850A
Willcox AZ 85643

Call Sign: K7TES
Edward A Kimmick
Box 996
Willcox AZ 85643

Call Sign: W7ILI
Richard W Riggs
8243 E Mogul Rd
Willcox AZ 85643

Call Sign: W7JPY

Charles F Compton
6540 Jeffords Trl
Willcox AZ 85643

Call Sign: N7EFH
Francis L Harmon
524 Maley
Willcox AZ 85643

Call Sign: N7EJN
Fred M Buck
360 N Cochise Ave
Willcox AZ 85643

Call Sign: KD7JTY
Amanda D Johnson
805 N Douglas Ave
Willcox AZ 85643

Call Sign: AC7BP
Glenwood T Jennings
3799 N Ingram Rd
Willcox AZ 85643

Call Sign: N0ONI
Luverne G Elliott
504 N Lapaz St
Willcox AZ 85644

Call Sign: KB7PZD
Ann M Franklin
911 N Prescott Ave
Willcox AZ 85643

Call Sign: N7DZH
Richard K Franklin
911 N Prescott Ave
Willcox AZ 85643

Call Sign: KD7JIL
Timothy Sowards
911 N Prescott Ave
Willcox AZ 85643

Call Sign: WA7ZXB
Nancy S Sober
1685 N Taylor Rd
Willcox AZ 85643

Call Sign: KC7RIJ
Dawn C Placencia
405 S Arizona Ave
Willcox AZ 85643

Call Sign: KC7RII
Michael Placencia
405 S Arizona Ave
Willcox AZ 85643

Call Sign: KD7BHJ
Charles B Smith
10151 S Calle Contento
Willcox AZ 85643

Call Sign: WW0X
James W Kessel
6650 S Covered Wagon Rd
Willcox AZ 85643

Call Sign: KF7PDV
Kurt Edelman
6659 S Covered Wagon Rd
Willcox AZ 85643

Call Sign: KB6TAL
James F Walden
780 S Vista Ave
Willcox AZ 85643

Call Sign: KD7BOV
David N Walters
9250 W Airport Rd
Willcox AZ 85643

Call Sign: KD7JFE
David N Walters
9250 W Airport Rd
Willcox AZ 85643

Call Sign: KB6KYW
Jerry R Walpert
Willcox AZ 85644

Call Sign: N7FGZ
Matthew S Ajeman
Willcox AZ 856439723

Call Sign: KB7VAL
Albert F Dunaway
Box 55
Williams AZ 860469802

Call Sign: KD7QCS
Air Museum ARC
Box 55
Williams AZ 860469802

Call Sign: AI7MU
Air Museum ARC
Box 55
Williams AZ 860469802

Call Sign: W7OCL
Jonathan R Barrett
2892 Castle Pines
Williams AZ 86046

Call Sign: N7OCL
Teresa A Barrett
2892 Castle Pines
Williams AZ 86046

Call Sign: N7UKH
Edward A Coffin
616 E Fulton Ave
Williams AZ 86046

Call Sign: N7AD
Albert F Dunaway
3940 E Greeley Dr
Williams AZ 86046

Call Sign: K6SPL
Charles F De Witt Jr
202 E Sherman
Williams AZ 86046

Call Sign: WA6NWE
James V Rominger
1502 E Tangerine St
Williams AZ 86046

Call Sign: KG7PM

Paul A Lawler
896 Liane St
Williams AZ 86046

Call Sign: KB7TEI
La Rita L Merryman
8075 N Cassity Trl
Williams AZ 86046

Call Sign: WA8UQD
Martin T Merryman
8075 N Cassity Trl
Williams AZ 86046

Call Sign: AC7PK
Martin T Merryman
8075 N Cassity Trl
Williams AZ 86046

Call Sign: W7BUZ
Martin T Merryman
8075 N Cassity Trl
Williams AZ 86046

Call Sign: KC7BPJ
Lynn K Caldwell
410 N Cedar
Williams AZ 86046

Call Sign: KC7ZNT
Judy A Shimel
6362 N Santa Fe
Williams AZ 86046

Call Sign: KB7BOJ
Robert R Shimel
6362 N Santa Fe
Williams AZ 86046

Call Sign: KD7XO
Frank J Berberich
7751 Robin Hood Rd
Williams AZ 86046

Call Sign: K7RU
Reiner P M Uebel
311 S 1st St
Williams AZ 86046

Call Sign: KB7LAD
Noel A Riner
228 S 2nd St
Williams AZ 860460085

Call Sign: KB9VGR
Jeremiah L Sheward
111 S 3rd St Apt 7
Williams AZ 86046

Call Sign: KE7IOU
David E Garlock
202 S 5th St
Williams AZ 86046

Call Sign: N7HYR
Sheila L Kennedy
208 S 5th St
Williams AZ 86046

Call Sign: KA7RLI
Nancy S Sereno
621 S Friar Tuck Trl
Williams AZ 86046

Call Sign: N5DFV
Elvin A Williams
762 S Torrey Pine Dr
Williams AZ 86046

Call Sign: KF7PLJ
Anthony J Morris
641 S Walnut Rd
Williams AZ 86046

Call Sign: KF7PLM
Susan E Morris
641 S Walnut Rd
Williams AZ 86046

Call Sign: KF7NPU
Thomas D Morris
641 S Walnut Rd
Williams AZ 86046

Call Sign: WB7WAR
James M Hansen
1125 Stockmens Rd
Williams AZ 86046

Call Sign: KF7IAH
Mary F Hansen
1125 Stockmens Rd
Williams AZ 86046

Call Sign: WB7WAS
Sue A Hansen
1125 Stockmens Rd
Williams AZ 86046

Call Sign: KD5TSU
Norma J Williams
762 Torrey Pines Dr
Williams AZ 86046

Call Sign: KC7NVR
Kevin S Mc Grath
101 W Farview Ave
Williams AZ 86046

Call Sign: KB7PWZ
Ian S James
341 W Grant Ave
Williams AZ 86046

Call Sign: WA6ZZL
William M Kahn
1686 W Maverick Ln
Williams AZ 86046

Call Sign: KD7KLG
Christopher C Becker
1020 W Mcpherson
Williams AZ 86046

Call Sign: N7JG
Jimmie F Glasscock
711 W Oak
Williams AZ 86046

Call Sign: WB6RLG
Larry G Addison
Williams AZ 86046

Call Sign: KA5WPX
Rick D Caylor
Williams AZ 86046

Call Sign: N7YIP
Thomas R Adams
Williams AZ 86046

Call Sign: KD7AEN
Barbara A Adams
Williams AZ 86046

Call Sign: KB5KBQ
Elisa C Wilson
Williams AZ 86046

Call Sign: KD5QEM
Geoffrey Wallis
Williams AZ 86046

Call Sign: N5MYI
James L Wilson
Williams AZ 86046

Call Sign: KF7PLL
Peggy S Starnes
Williams AZ 86046

Call Sign: KD7EZT
Renee W Coffman
Williams AZ 86046

Call Sign: KC7ILT
George R Lockhart
Williams AZ 86046

Call Sign: KI6KEX
Tim A Starnes
Williams AZ 860460417

Call Sign: AD7PA
Tim A Starnes
Williams AZ 860460417

Call Sign: KG6OFB
Mark A Cole
Williams AZ 860460744

FCC Amateur Radio Licenses in Window Rock

Call Sign: KB7LQB
Arlene Garfield

Window Rock AZ 86515

Call Sign: N7JVO
Bruce W Begay
Window Rock AZ 86515

Call Sign: KB7PEJ
Christopher B Larsen
Window Rock AZ 86515

Call Sign: KB7QZP
Dicky Bain
Window Rock AZ 86515

Call Sign: N7ZJB
Judy Rae Kimbrough
Window Rock AZ 86515

Call Sign: KB7IOU
Sadie Yazzie
Window Rock AZ 86515

Call Sign: N7ZJC
Val G Kimbrough
Window Rock AZ 86515

Call Sign: KB7LTC
Dallas O John
Window Rock AZ 86515

Call Sign: KE7KUI
Cj Woodie
Window Rock AZ 86515

Call Sign: N7HRB
Herbert Goodluck
Window Rock AZ 86515

Call Sign: N7HG
Herbert Goodluck
Window Rock AZ 86515

Call Sign: KC7KYM
Irvin J Williams
Window Rock AZ 86515

Call Sign: KD7YCF
Larry L Towne
Window Rock AZ 86515

Call Sign: KE7NGL
Melvin Young
Window Rock AZ 86515

FCC Amateur Radio Licenses in Winkelman

Call Sign: AA7GR
Michael R Peed
Winkelman AZ 85292

FCC Amateur Radio Licenses in Winslow

Call Sign: N7SQT
Clyde J Oplinger
Box 100
Winslow AZ 86047

Call Sign: KB7UMG
Jeffery M Pectol
Box 101
Winslow AZ 86047

Call Sign: KB7UMK
Linda A Pectol
Box 101
Winslow AZ 86047

Call Sign: KB7VVV
Willard J Pectol
Box 101
Winslow AZ 86047

Call Sign: KE7JXU
Charles B Nelson
133 Cochise Dr
Winslow AZ 86047

Call Sign: N7PQF
Henri W Lyet Jr
Desert Hills Dr
Winslow AZ 86047

Call Sign: K0ZSG
Richard J Mc Glinn
101 E Cherry St
Winslow AZ 860473844

Call Sign: KC7IFW
Kenneth E Conatser
1333 E Oak St
Winslow AZ 86047

Call Sign: KC7LUY
Shane D Thomas
2042 Easy St
Winslow AZ 86047

Call Sign: N7JWM
Janet M Fish
2117 Easy St
Winslow AZ 86047

Call Sign: KC7JOE
William F Fish Jr
2117 Easy St
Winslow AZ 86047

Call Sign: N7JWN
William F Fish Sr
2117 Easy St
Winslow AZ 86047

Call Sign: KB7PXX
Jerry W Kincaid
873 French Rd
Winslow AZ 86047

Call Sign: N7RQP
Michael T Haggard
943 Jolly Rd
Winslow AZ 860470218

Call Sign: N7WQS
Sandra J Haggard
943 Jolly Rd
Winslow AZ 860470218

Call Sign: KD7UVU
Donna M Duran
121 Kell Pl
Winslow AZ 86047

Call Sign: KD7UVT
Michael J Duran
121 Kell Pl

Winslow AZ 86047

Call Sign: KC7CPE
Jerry S Jue
614 Kingsley Ave
Winslow AZ 86047

Call Sign: KK7JU
Jackie W Betts
1901 Mountain Dr
Winslow AZ 86047

Call Sign: KB7TQB
Lisa M Mc Hugh
2300 Mountain Dr
Winslow AZ 86047

Call Sign: KC7FYM
George T Kalisz
2300 Mt Ararat Rd
Winslow AZ 86047

Call Sign: AC7YF
George T Kalisz
2300 Mt Ararat Rd
Winslow AZ 86047

Call Sign: KF7FWJ
James E Deck
412 N Kinsley Ave
Winslow AZ 86047

Call Sign: KN7MCQ
Nanette M Mc Hugh
501 N Winslow Ave
Winslow AZ 86047

Call Sign: KG7NZ
Francis J Mc Hugh
501 N Winslow Ave
Winslow AZ 860473545

Call Sign: KF7MCQ
Francis J Mc Hugh
501 N Winslow Ave
Winslow AZ 860473545

Call Sign: N6UWE
Nanette M Mc Hugh

501 N Winslow Ave
Winslow AZ 860473545

Call Sign: KB7PWW
G Douglas Hanley
16 Papago Blvd
Winslow AZ 86047

Call Sign: KK7TF
John L Scott
148 Papago Blvd
Winslow AZ 86047

Call Sign: KD7SIL
Michael R Cunningham
200 Papago Blvd
Winslow AZ 86047

Call Sign: KA2OAR
Patricia A Snyder
236 Papago Blvd
Winslow AZ 86047

Call Sign: KB7UQM
Andrew N Oplinger
1027 S Desert Dr
Winslow AZ 86047

Call Sign: N7QQQ
Daniel E Oplinger
1027 S Desert Dr
Winslow AZ 86047

Call Sign: N7RDI
Rose L Oplinger
1027 S Desert Dr
Winslow AZ 86047

Call Sign: KB7KMF
Sterling C West Jr
613 Taylor
Winslow AZ 86047

Call Sign: W3KIP
Kip H Cooley
2125 W 3rd St 10
Winslow AZ 86047

Call Sign: KF7QQK

Kip H Cooley
2125 W 3rd St 10
Winslow AZ 86047

Call Sign: K3EXE
Kip H Cooley
2125 W 3rd St 10
Winslow AZ 86047

Call Sign: KD7ZLO
Patrick D Fast
W 4th St
Winslow AZ 86047

Call Sign: KC7NZG
Kevin P Notz
950 W Aspinwall
Winslow AZ 86047

Call Sign: KD7SOW
Mark C Mileham
201 W Gilmore St
Winslow AZ 86047

Call Sign: KC7JAE
Chuck E Eavenson
644 W Hillview
Winslow AZ 86047

Call Sign: N7RDZ
Donald E Siegmund
1006 W Hillview
Winslow AZ 86047

Call Sign: KD7TYS
John C Paulsell
108 W Hillview St
Winslow AZ 86047

Call Sign: W7NLR
Roy A Kenna
332 W Maple
Winslow AZ 86047

Call Sign: KD7ZYG
William I Evans
408 W Maple St
Winslow AZ 86047

Call Sign: KC7SBE
Aaron J Rubi
606 W Oak St
Winslow AZ 86047

Call Sign: KB7PWV
Darlene K Oplinger Mack
Winslow AZ 86047

Call Sign: KB7UQN
Rebecca L Oplinger
Winslow AZ 86047

Call Sign: N7QQO
Richard L Mack Jr
Winslow AZ 86047

Call Sign: KF7HPP
Cydnie M Martin
Winslow AZ 86047

Call Sign: N7SQV
Danny K Wyrick
Winslow AZ 86047

Call Sign: KB7TOX
Earl E Lucas
Winslow AZ 86047

Call Sign: AD7EO
Earl E Lucas
Winslow AZ 86047

Call Sign: KC7JVF
Janet L Wyrick
Winslow AZ 86047

Call Sign: N7TWU
John H Stephenson
Winslow AZ 86047

Call Sign: KF7HIA
Lance L Mileham
Winslow AZ 86047

Call Sign: KD7ONR
Nelson Lewis Jr
Winslow AZ 86047

Call Sign: KF7HHZ
Steven M Harvey
Winslow AZ 86047

FCC Amateur Radio Licenses in Woodruff

Call Sign: KD7IOH
Mathan T Tenney
6453 Country Rd
Woodruff AZ 85942

Call Sign: K0DER
Augusto Falco Jr
6457 Hummingbird Ln
Woodruff AZ 85942

Call Sign: KB7TQD
Augusto Falco Jr
Woodruff AZ 85942

Call Sign: KA7YYW
Edmond A Marvin
Woodruff AZ 85942

FCC Amateur Radio Licenses in Young

Call Sign: KE7SBK
Anglela Rodriguez
133 E Hilltop Rd
Young AZ 85554

Call Sign: N0GVT
Richard L Rudeen
350 Rolling Hills Rd
Young AZ 85554

Call Sign: KC7KGF
Robert L Benne
963 Walnut Creek Rd
Young AZ 85554

Call Sign: KA7JJQ
Carol L Clark
Young AZ 85554

Call Sign: KA7JJP
Kenneth L Clark

Young AZ 85554

Call Sign: K7GCC
Vivian I Teel
Young AZ 85554

Call Sign: W7GCC
Walter I Teel
Young AZ 85554

Call Sign: KA7YXO
Denzil B Clark
Young AZ 85554

Call Sign: KC7IAW
Duane A Gagnon
Young AZ 85554

Call Sign: KC7ILW
Gene M Charpentier
Young AZ 85554

Call Sign: KF7UNN
Bill Tilton
Young AZ 85554

Call Sign: KC7GZZ
Candace M Wisdom
Young AZ 85554

Call Sign: KD7SYI
Charlie Wolfe
Young AZ 85554

Call Sign: N7SFD
Daniel A Munn
Young AZ 85554

Call Sign: KB7YQS
Eddie E Wisdom
Young AZ 85554

Call Sign: KA7CQT
Geraldine G Ewing
Young AZ 85554

Call Sign: WB7TPK
Keith E Ewing
Young AZ 85554

Call Sign: KA7BTK
Patricia G Meredith
Young AZ 85554

Call Sign: AA7US
Ted O Meredith Sr
Young AZ 855540193